Cryptography
A Primer

Cryptography
A Primer

ALAN G. KONHEIM
Mathematical Sciences Department
IBM Thomas J. Watson Research Center

A Wiley-Interscience Publication

JOHN WILEY & SONS

New York • Chichester • Brisbane • Toronto • Singapore

Published by John Wiley & Sons, Inc.

Library of Congress Cataloging in Publication Data:

Konheim, Alan G 1934–
Cryptography, a primer.

Includes index.
1. Cryptography. 2. Computers—Access control.
3. Telecommunication—Security measures. I. Title.

Z103.K66 001.54′36 80-24978
ISBN 0-471-08132-9

Printed in the United States of America

10 9 8 7 6 5 4 3

To my wife
Carol

Preface

This book was conceived in the Spring of 1978 when Professor Jack Schwartz of New York University asked me to offer a one-semester course in cryptographic methods at the Courant Institute. Some ten years earlier, IBM Research had begun to study the role of cryptography in the protection of computer data. Initiating a research program in cryptography presents special problems above those met in starting any new technical effort. There is not an extensive literature in cryptography, and few experts are willing or able to provide guidance. We were fortunate at IBM Research to be initiated into the mysteries of cryptography by my colleague Horst Feistel, who had spent many years working on cryptographic design. Our primary efforts were directed at learning the principles of cryptanalysis. Although cryptanalysis does not involve "new" mathematics *per se*, it requires the skilled application of ideas from many diverse fields of mathematics and, above all, perseverance. In some sense, cryptanalysis is the penultimate branch of applied mathematics—after all the theorems have been proved, the proof of the pudding is the ability to find the solution. This is an introductory book and does not attempt to cover all of the various methods of encipherment. In particular, tranposition systems are not covered (with the exception of one problem in Chapter 2). The book is divided into two parts: the first covers the foundations of cryptography, while the second part is concerned with its applications.

A word about the problems in this book: Cryptanalysis, like other parts of mathematics, requires practice and experimentation. I have included a relatively small number of problems that ask the student to decipher the text. I urge the instructor to generate other examples along the lines of those included.

ACKNOWLEDGMENTS

I have benefited greatly from students in my classes at NYU and the Technion. My colleagues Roy Adler, Don Coppersmith, Edna Grossman, and Bryant Tuckerman have been of great help to me. Sigmund Handelman, Robert McNeill, Alan Jones (of IBM Endicott), and Jim White (of IBM Charlotte) aided in preparing the data for the dust cover. I want to thank my friends Allen J. Rose of the Scientific Time Sharing Corporation for reading an early version of the book and Lester Rosenbaum for his perceptive comments at the Okemo Mountain ski lodge. I am grateful to John Blancuzzi and Ron Salvatore of the operations staff of the IBM Research Center Computing Center for their assistance on many weekends. Finally, my gratitude to Horst Feistel, who started IBM thinking about cryptography in the first place.

ALAN G. KONHEIM

Yorktown Heights, New York
January 1981

Contents

Cryptography

A Primer

PART ONE

FOUNDATIONS OF CRYPTOGRAPHY

CHAPTER I

Introduction

"Yet it may be roundly asserted that human ingenuity cannot concoct a cipher which human ingenuity cannot resolve," from The Gold Bug by Edgar Allan Poe

"It Ain't Necessarily So," from Porgy and Bess by George and Ira Gershwin

Cryptography, from the Greek *kryptos* meaning *hidden* and *graphein* meaning *to write,* is the art and science of making communications unintelligible to all except the intended recipient(s). The origins of secret writing can be traced back nearly four millenia to the hieroglyphic writing system of the Egyptians. *The Codebreakers* [KA] is a history of cryptography from the earliest attempts at concealment through the Second World War.

Until recently, the use of cryptographic methods to secure communications has been the sole province of governments, zealously guarded over and directed by their national cryptologic services. When the private sector has felt the need for such protection, it has been forced to improvise on its own. A few cryptographic devices are available for nongovernmental applications, including modern day versions of the M209 or *Hagelin machine* shown in Fig. 1.1.1.

Under provisions of Public Law 89-306 and Executive Order 11717, the Secretary of Commerce was authorized to establish uniform Federal Automatic Data Processing Standards. Solicitations for computer data encryption algorithms were published by the National Bureau of Standards in the *Federal Register* issues of May 15, 1973 and August 27, 1974.

Specifications for the Data Encryption Standard

The Data Encryption Standard (DES) shall consist of the following Data Encryption Algorithm implemented in a special purpose electronic device. This device shall be designed in such a way that it may be embedded in a computer system or network and provide cryptographic protection to binary coded data. The method of implementation, the control of the cryptographic device and the interface of the device to its associated equipment will depend upon the application and environment. The device shall be designed and implemented in such a way that it may be tested and validated as accurately performing the transformations specified in the following algorithm. Certification of compliance with this standard is the responsibility of the designer and manufacturer of the device.

Figure 1.1.1. The M209 (Hagelin Machine).

An algorithm submitted by the International Business Machines Corporation was found to meet the primary technical requirements for a Data Encryption Standard. The DES algorithm was published for comment in the *Federal Register,* March 17, 1975 [DES].

1.1 THE PROBLEM

The digital computer is both a scientific tool—extending the range of practical numerical computations—and a major component in business systems. Information processing systems collect, store, process, and interpret data in a wide range of financial, commercial, geopolitical, and social areas. Many current business enterprises are feasible only as a result of the economies attributable to information processing.

Currently, information processing systems play several roles in business operations:

- Analysis of data: accounting services, billing, market forecasting.
- Maintenance of files, such as design data, sales information, customer lists; in the insurance, banking, and the health care industries; in consumer credit organizations; in federal and state agencies.
- Managing transactions, such as travel reservations and savings bank transactions.
- As a component in communication systems, for example, the Bell System's ESS.

In the next decade, applications will include (1) automated trading of stocks, bonds, and commodities; (2) expanded use of point-of-sale transactions; (3) electronic mail and facsimile. These applications are examples of *transaction systems,* which electronically manage the exchange of goods or services and may operate without requiring either voice or physical contact of the participants.

Information processing has accentuated an existing problem, one with wide-ranging economic and social implications for society—the problem of data security. Communications and stored information have always been vulnerable to various attacks. Wiretapping of telephone conversations and digital data transmitted on microwave links is possible today without actual physical intrusion. In fact, the suspicion that the Soviet Union routinely monitors economic activity by probing microwave transmissions for key words or phrases has lead to the routing of certain traffic between Washington and New York by underground cables. Mail can be opened and telegrams can be monitored for key words or phrases. The theft and resale of credit cards has become an increasingly profitable criminal activity; business systems which identify a customer by a credit card and password are open to various types of attacks.

The corollary issue of *privacy,* the concern that information contained in medical, employment, credit, or criminal records might be released without adequate safeguards, has made the security of computer systems a concern of the United States Congress and the designers and users of computing systems. Information processing has only changed the nature and degree of the problem; along with the capability to access information centrally stored in a data base is the risk that the information may be improperly obtained or changed. Information processing systems require "locks" to guard the contents of files and procedures to minimize the value of wiretapping.

Some processing system resources can be protected by controlling physical access; for example, tapes may snuggle safely in the tape library guarded by the librarian. However, restricting access to their contents when mounted in the system is another matter. The components of a computing system are often physically dispersed, and monitoring physical access provides protection against only a limited class of threats. Moreover, the economic advantages of information processing are derived from the sharing of resources: storage devices (disks, drums), arithmetic units, and communications subsystems. The operating system is designed to partition the resources temporally, enforcing disjointness between the programs and data of different users. However, no operating system today can guarantee that the information of one user is beyond the grasp of another. By and large, today's systems do not monitor user activity at a fine enough level to detect attempted or unintended file access.

Time-sharing systems using the public telephone network with data transmitted over common or value-added carriers, microwave, and satellite links are vulnerable to wiretapping. Dial-up users are often physically remote from the computer center and may be able to peruse any stored information. Finally *privileged status,* which does not limit the access to any part of a system, is routinely granted certain classes of users. At least two types of threats exist: (1) *passive,* that is, the release of information; and (2) *active,* that is, the alteration (addition to/deletion from/modification of) data communications and files.

Cryptography appears to provide the only practical method of protecting data. While it does not guarantee absolute security, encipherment of data in storage and during transmission often make it more costly and risky to penetrate systems.

1.2 NOMENCLATURE

Cryptography attempts to protect information by altering its form, making it unreadable to all but the authorized parties. Encipherment is a transformation process; the original text, called *plaintext* or *cleartext,* is replaced by text called *ciphertext.* Text is formed by the concatenation of symbols or *letters* from an *alphabet.* A typical alphabet may consist of lower and upper case letters,

```
abcdefghijklmnopqrstuvwxyzABCDEFGHIJKLMNOPQRSTUVWXYZ
```

augmented by numerals,

```
0123456789
```

punctuation and blank space,

```
' " , . : ; ?
```

and special symbols,

```
+ − × ÷ / -
```

Thus

```
Yet it may be roundly asserted that human ingenuity cannot
concoct a cipher which human ingenuity cannot resolve,
Edgar Allan Poe.
```

is an example of plaintext written in this alphabet. The corresponding ciphertext,

```
Ekz oz sge hk xuatjre gyykxzkj zngz nasgt omktaoze igttuz
iutiuiz g iovnkx cnoin nasgt otmktaoze igttuz xkyurbk,
Kjmgx Grrkt Vuk.
```

is obtained from the plaintext by (1) retaining blank spaces and punctuation, and (2) replacing each letter (in its case) by the letter that stands six places to the right in the alphabet.

A cryptographic system is a family $\boldsymbol{T}$ of transformations on plaintext. The members of the family are indexed or labeled by a parameter k called the *key*. The *key space* $\boldsymbol{K}$ is the set of possible values for the key. Typically, the key is a sequence of letters from an alphabet and the associated transformation T_k is an algorithm determined by k. The effectiveness of encipherment to secure information depends upon keeping the key secret. In the military and diplomatic applications of cryptography, a secure path is established for distributing the keys to users. The terms *key distribution* and *key management* refer to procedures in an information processing system that generate and distribute keys to the users.

1.3 THE GROUND RULES OF CRYPTANALYSIS

One of the problems to be examined in this book is the effectiveness of encipherment. Does ciphertext really hide the information? Is there some way in which the process can be reversed and the plaintext recovered without knowledge of the key? If so, can we quantify how much effort as measured by computational time and/or cost is required in this process?

Cryptography is a contest between two adversaries: (1) the designer of the system specifying the family of transformations, and (2) the *opponent* attempting to recover the plaintext and/or key and thus defeat the effect of encipherment. The process by which an opponent attempts to recover plaintext and/or key from ciphertext is called *cryptanalysis*. The ground rules of this struggle between the designer and opponent were formulated in the nineteenth century by Kerckhoffs* in his book *La Cryptographie militare:*

- *K1.* The system should be, if not theoretically unbreakable, unbreakable in practice.
- *K2.* Compromise of the system should not inconvenience the correspondents.
- *K3.* The method for choosing the particular member (key) of the cryptographic system to be used should be easy to memorize and change.
- *K4.* Ciphertext should be transmittable by telegraph.
- *K5.* The apparatus should be portable.
- *K6.* Use of the system should not require a long list of rules or mental strain.

Discussion

Cryptographic methods have always been heavily influenced by the current technology. Cryptography has survived by adapting as the technology changed. Kerckhoffs' criteria were formulated in an era of low-speed communication typified by telegraphy.

K1. Some encipherment schemes are asserted to be "unbreakable," meaning that no cryptanalytic technique *exists* to recover the plaintext and/or key from

* Jean-Guillaume-Hubert-Victor-François-Alexandre-Auguste-Kerckhoffs von Niuewenhof born 1835 at Nuth, Holland, Professor of German at the Ecole des Etudes Commerciales and Ecole Arago, Paris,

the ciphertext. Unbreakable cryptographic systems exist, though their applicability in an information processing environment is somewhat in question. The relevant notion in cryptography today is that of the *work function,* the complexity of the recovery process as measured by computation time and/or cost. The larger the work function, the more secure the system. The minimal work function requirement of a cryptographic system depends upon the intended application; secrecy may be necessary only for a short interval of time or the work function may be too large compared to the gain to be achieved by a decipherment. An order "to attack" needs to be kept secret only until the battle has started; on the other hand, a file of design data or marketing projections may require protection for several years. Cryptographic systems that have a finite key space $\boldsymbol{K}$ may always be cryptanalyzed by *key trial,* the testing of all keys until recognizable plaintext is obtained. A cryptographic system with a finite key space may still be *effectively* unbreakable if the time and computation required for key trial makes it impractical to carry out exhaustive key search. Being effectively unbreakable is a technology dependent assertion; for example, many of the monalphabetic substitution systems to be described in Chapter 3, which may have served their purpose in the nineteenth century, are no longer acceptable ways of hiding information due to the introduction of digital processing in this century.

K2. Any encipherment system will consist of two types of information; *public* and *private.* By public information we mean the family of rules or algorithms by which information is enciphered. If a cryptographic system is realized in hardware, the specifications will be published, service manuals will be available, and an opponent may be able to purchase a commercially available system. The same considerations apply in a software implementation; the code cannot be kept secret indefinitely. By *compromise of the system,* Kerckhoffs meant the knowledge of the public information. The private information, presumptively unavailable to the opponent, is the key used to encipher plaintext, the parameters which select one from many possible enciphering transformations. Thus any security achieved by the substitution systems to be studied in Chapters 3–5 is not derived from the opponent's ignorance as to what family of substitutions has been used (the *public information*), but rather from lack of knowledge as to which specific transformation in the family has been used to encipher the text (the *private information*).

K3. It is not uncommon for users to choose names `ALAN G. KONHEIM` or phrases `NOW IS THE TIME` . . . to serve as keys in order to make memorization easy. In many business applications of cryptography, the key will be magnetically recorded on a credit card, but in others the user will be required to memorize the key or part of it. The requirement for a short memorizable key remains an important human factors design consideration.

K4. The fourth requirement reflects the dominant technology of the nineteenth century; we interpret it to mean that the text may be represented in a format suitable for transmission and recording. We will exclude the methods of *steganography,* which hide the very existence of a message on a microdot or with invisible ink.

K5. The portability of equipment is less of an issue in information processing applications.

K6. The ease of use, cost of encipherment, and its impact on the performance of a system (generally in terms of speed) are important issues. The cost of providing data protection must ultimately be passed on to the user, so that there must be a clear need for encipherment and even more important, an assessment of whether or not a particular cryptographic system meets its objectives.

1.4 SIDE INFORMATION

The following puzzle appeared on a place mat at an otherwise undistinguished Chinese restaurant in Virginia:

Unravel each of the following letter transpositions.

DFOR KIBUC TECRELOHV DONSHU

KADCRAP GEDOD LADCLIAC NOCILLN

It is not very difficult to identify the words,* but the puzzle can certainly be solved well before the dumplings arrive, if we use the clue provided:

The words correspond to names of automobiles.

This is an example of *side information,* and it makes this puzzle nearly trivial. Side information refers also to ancillary information and capabilities available to an opponent. In a recent case involving the improper transfer of funds from a bank in California, the alleged opponent was a consultant who obtained (side) information allowing him to circumvent the controls of the system. What capabilities do we assume available to an opponent? The opponent may be a member of a computing community and have access to some system resources; a systems operator may be in a position to access all data files. The opponent may be familiar with the operational procedures of a transaction system and attempt to bypass the controls of the system.

When evaluating the effectiveness of a cryptographic system, we shall assume that one of the following holds:

1. Ciphertext only: the opponent has access to only ciphertext.
2. Corresponding plaintext and ciphertext: the opponent has access to some corresponding plaintext and ciphertext.
3. Chosen plaintext: the opponent can obtain the encipherment of plaintext selected by the opponent.

The effectiveness of a cryptographic system in protecting information depends in part upon the side information we assume available to the opponent. While wire-tapping reveals *only ciphertext,* an opponent might obtain from an accomplice carelessly discarded corresponding plaintext. Some encipherment systems will provide no security under (2) or (3) above.

---

* FORD BUICK CHEVROLET HUDSON
PACKARD DODGE CADILLAC LINCOLN

Side information also includes the context of the data being transmitted or filed. The subject matter of the plaintext being sought provides valuable information for the cryptanalytic process. For example, the entries in a file of sales data may be organized in a special way: the name and address of the customer in one segment, the sales order in a second segment, and the delivery date in a third segment. We must assume that the organization of the data is known by the opponent. Words like `plan, delivery, date` which might appear many times in an operating plan of a corporation can be made the basis of a cryptanalytic attack.

1.5 THE TOOLS OF CRYPTANALYSIS

Cryptanalysis was largely an art until the twentieth century. When the importance of military and diplomatic intelligence to the conduct of foreign policy became evident, the basic concepts of cryptanalysis were developed as a branch of applied mathematics. Cryptanalysis uses the tools of (1) probability theory and statistics, (2) linear algebra, (3) abstract algebra (group theory), and (4) complexity theory.

In Chapter 2, we set the stage for cryptanalysis, formulating the basic statistical models for plaintext. In Chapters 3–5, we examine the cryptanalysis of specific monalphabetic and polyalphabetic substitution systems. The Data Encryption Standard is discussed in Chapter 6. Finally in Chapters 7–10, we consider the application of cryptographic methods to information processing systems, that is, key management and the exciting current research on public key systems. The mathematical methods used in this book rely heavily on probability theory. We review the basic concepts of probability theory used in this book in Appendix P.

CHAPTER II

Secrecy Systems

2.1 INTRODUCTION

The communication and encipherment of information are processes that have common features. In the former, a noisy transmission channel, for example, radio, satellite, or telephone, *unintentionally* introduces distortion during transmission:

noisy transmission channel

transmitted message → *received message*

so that the received and transmitted messages are generally different. The *receiver's* task is to recover the transmitted message from the received message and a probabilistic description of the noisy transmission channel.

In the encipherment process the objects corresponding to the transmitted and received messages are referred to as *plaintext* and *ciphertext,* respectively. Ciphertext is the result of a now *intentional* distortion of the plaintext by a cryptographic transformation introduced in order to hide the information in the plaintext:

cryptographic transformation

plaintext → *ciphertext*

The role of the receiver is played by an opponent, whose goal is to recover the plaintext from the ciphertext and a partial specification of the encipherment process.

In 1948 Claude Shannon's fundamental paper on the mathematical theory of communication was published, giving birth to *information theory.* In a second paper in 1949 [SHA], Shannon pointed out the common features of communication and encipherment of information. In this chapter, we introduce the language and notation of encipherment and develop the main ideas in Shannon's theory of secrecy systems.

2.2 ALPHABETS

Encipherment transforms plaintext to ciphertext in order to hide the information in the plaintext. Both plaintext and ciphertext are composed of *letters* from a finite set of symbols called an *alphabet.* Examples of alphabets are:

- *Upper case letters*

ABCDEFGHIJKLMNOPQRSTUVWXYZ

- *Upper case letters and numerals*

ABCDEFGHIJKLMNOPQRSTUVWXYZ0123456789

- *Upper and lower case letters and numerals*

ABCDEFGHIJKLMNOPQRSTUVWXYZabcdefghijklmnopqrstuvwxyz
0123456789

- *Upper and lower case letters, numerals, blank space, and punctuation*

ABCDEFGHIJKLMNOPQRSTUVWXYZabcdefghijklmnopqrstuvwxyz
0123456789 .,;:"?'

- The 256 *binary sequences of length 8 (bytes)*

00000000 00000001 ... 11111110 11111111

- *Words* from some edition of *Webster's New Collegiate Dictionary*

A AARDVARK . . . ZYMURGY

We generate new alphabets by concatenating the letters of an alphabet $\boldsymbol{A} = \{a_0, a_1, \ldots, a_{m-1}\}$; the alphabet $\boldsymbol{A}^2$ containing the m^2 *2-grams* or *di-grams,*

$$a_0a_0 \; a_0a_1 \ldots a_{m-1}a_{m-1}$$

and the alphabet $\boldsymbol{A}^3$ containing the m^3 *3-grams* or *tri-grams,*

$$a_0a_0a_0 \; a_0a_0a_1 \ldots a_{m-1}a_{m-1}a_{m-1}$$

More generally, by concatenating n letters $a_{i_0}a_{i_1} \ldots a_{i_{n-1}}$ we obtain the alphabet $\boldsymbol{A}^n$ containing the m^n *n-grams*. Thus the alphabet

$$\boldsymbol{A} = \{\texttt{ABCDEFGHIJKLMNOPQRSTUVWXYZ}\}$$

generates by the concatenation operation the alphabet of 676 2-grams,

AA AB AC . . . XZ YZ ZZ

and the alphabet of 17,576 3-grams,

AAA AAB AAC . . . XZZ YZZ ZZZ

A word like AARDVARK admits several descriptions; it is an 8-gram composed of letters from the alphabet $\boldsymbol{A} = \{\texttt{A B . . . Z}\}$,

/A/A/R/D/V/A/R/K/

- a 4-gram composed of letters from the alphabet $\boldsymbol{A}^2$,

/AA/RD/VA/RK/

- a 2-gram composed of letters from the alphabet A^4,

/AARD/VARK/

- a 1-gram composed of letters from the alphabet of words from *Webster's New Collegiate Dictionary,*

/AARDVARK/

where a slash (/) has been used to mark the boundaries between letters.

It is helpful to replace the letters of an alphabet by integers 0, 1, 2, . . . , to make algebraic manipulation easier. A natural correspondence between

$$A = \{\text{ABCDEFGHIJKLMNOPQRSTUVWXYZ}\}$$

and the integers $\mathbf{Z}_{26} = \{0, 1, \ldots, 25\}$ is given in Table 2.2.1:

TABLE 2.2.1
$\mathbf{Z}_{26} \leftarrow \rightarrow$ {ABCDEFGHIJKLMNOPQRSTUVWXYZ}

A	←→	0	J	←→	9	S	←→	18
B	←→	1	K	←→	10	T	←→	19
C	←→	2	L	←→	11	U	←→	20
D	←→	3	M	←→	12	V	←→	21
E	←→	4	N	←→	13	W	←→	22
F	←→	5	O	←→	14	X	←→	23
G	←→	6	P	←→	15	Y	←→	24
H	←→	7	Q	←→	16	Z	←→	25
I	←→	8	R	←→	17			

We will use the alphabet $\mathbf{Z}_m = \{0, 1, \ldots, m - 1\}$ containing m "letters" in our development of cryptography. Replacing the letters of a conventional alphabet by numbers brings the main ideas more sharply into focus and allows the formulation of concepts that are largely independent of the alphabet. On the other hand, recognizing word fragments in text written with a numerical alphabet is difficult. Therefore, we will carry out a dual development, formulating concepts in terms of the alphabet $\mathbf{Z}_m$, while presenting illustrative material using the alphabet

$$A = \{\text{ABCDEFGHIJKLMNOPQRSTUVWXYZ}\}$$

Definition 2.2.1 *Text with letters from the alphabet* $\mathbf{Z}_m$ is an n-gram

$$\text{text} : \mathbf{x} = (x_0, x_1, \ldots, x_{n-1}) \qquad x_i \in \mathbf{Z}_m^* \qquad 0 \le i < n$$

for some integer n = 1, 2, ... We write $\mathbf{Z}_{m,n}$ for the set of n-grams formed from letters in $\mathbf{Z}_m$.

* $x_i \in \mathbf{Z}_m$ is read: *x_i is an element of the set* $\mathbf{Z}_m$.

Examples of alphabets and corresponding text are given in Table 2.2.2. We will impose no restrictions upon which letters may be juxtaposed in plaintext. Thus . . . QVK . . . is permitted as a possible fragment of plaintext, even though it would not be considered conventional English text. The characteristics of a language will be modeled probabilistically.

TABLE 2.2.2
Examples of Text

Alphabet	Text
A B . . . Z	/T/H/I/S/I/S/T/E/X/T/
AA AB . . . ZZ	/TH/IS/IS/TE/XT/
A B . . . Z a b . . . z	/T/h/i/s/i/s/t/e/x/t/
A B . . . Z a b . . . z 0 . . . 9 , . ' " : ; ?	/T/h/i/s/ /i/s/ /t/e/x/t/
words from some edition of Webster's New Collegiate Dictionary	/This/is/text/

2.3 THE PLAINTEXT SOURCE

Encipherment is a process applied to text in some language, examples of which include (1) English language text, (2) computer programs, and (3) data communications; for example, in an airline reservation or electronic funds transfer system. The rules of a language define which n-grams are admissible. Thus

- In English: the letter Q is invariably followed by the letter U.
- In assembly language: instruction numbers normally appear in columns 73–80.
- In Fortran: instructions normally start in column 7.
- In the language of an *airline reservation system:* the date and flight number might appear in predetermined segments of the message.

A language is defined by specifying the set of admissible n-grams for every value of n. Unlike programming languages, most natural languages do not admit a concise enough description for purposes of analysis. We will represent a language within a probabilistic framework. A (finite) *plaintext source* $\boldsymbol{S}$ *for text from* $\boldsymbol{Z_m}$ is a stochastic process, a finite or infinite sequence of random variables:

$$X_0, X_1, \ldots, X_{n-1}, \ldots \qquad (\text{resp. } X_0, X_1, \ldots, X_{N-1})$$

A source models the generation of plaintext by a chance experiment, whose outcome is the sequence of letters $X_0, X_1, \ldots X_{n-1}, \ldots$ A source $\boldsymbol{S}$ is defined by specifying the probability $\Pr_{PLAIN}\{X_j = x_0, X_{j+1} = x_1, \ldots, X_{j+n-1} = x_{n-1}\}$ of each of the events

$$\{X_j = x_0, X_{j+1} = x_1, \ldots, X_{j+n-1} = x_{n-1}\}$$

for every n-gram $\mathbf{x} = (x_0, x_1, \ldots, x_{n-1})$, $j = 0, 1, \ldots$ and $n = 1, 2, \ldots$ We will write $Pr_{PLAIN}\{(x_0,x_1, \ldots, x_{n-1})\}$ to denote the probability of the event

$$\{X_0 = x_0, X_1 = x_1, \ldots, X_{n-1} = x_{n-1}\}$$

The n-gram probabilities $Pr_{PLAIN}\{(x_0,x_1, \ldots, x_{n-1})\}$ are required to satisfy three conditions:

$$Pr_{PLAIN}\{(x_0, x_1, \ldots, x_{n-1})\} \geq 0$$

$$(2.3.1) \qquad 1 = \sum_{(x_0,x_1,\ldots,x_{n-1})} Pr_{PLAIN}\{(x_0, x_1, \ldots, x_{n-1})\}$$

$$Pr_{PLAIN}\{(x_0, x_1, \ldots, x_{n-1})\} = \sum_{\{x_n,\ldots,x_{s-1}\}} Pr_{PLAIN}\{(x_0, x_1, \ldots, x_{s-1})\} \quad \text{if } s > n$$

Equation (2.3.1) is a version of *Kolmogorov's consistency condition.* It connects the probability assigned by the source of the set of s-grams with a given *n-gram prefix* $(x_0, x_1, \ldots, x_{n-1})$,

$$\sum_{\{x_n,\ldots,x_{s-1}\}} Pr_{PLAIN}\{(x_0,x_1, \ldots, x_{s-1})\}$$

to the probability assigned by the source to the prefix $Pr_{PLAIN}\{(x_0,x_1, \ldots, x_{n-1})\}$. Thus the probability $Pr_{PLAIN}\{$`HELP`$\}$ of the 4-gram `HELP` is equal to the sum of the probabilities assigned to the set of 26^3 7-grams `HELP***`, which have the prefix `HELP`.

A stochastic process provides a mathematical model for the generation of plaintext and is only an approximation of the language. A probabilistic model avoids the necessity of specifying the set of admissible n-grams. For this approach to be of value, the model must embody the principal characteristics of the language, while being simple enough to permit numerical calculations. In principle, models can be defined that reflect the structure of a language to any desired degree of accuracy. The price is usually a highly detailed mathematical description which often limits the usefulness of the model. Here are several examples of plaintext sources to be used in this book.

Definition 2.3.1 A plaintext source $\boldsymbol{S}$ generates *1-grams by independent and identical trials* if

$$(2.3.2) \qquad Pr_{PLAIN}\{(x_0, x_1, \ldots, x_{n-1})\} = p(x_0)p(x_1) \ldots p(x_{n-1})$$

for each integer n, $n = 1, 2, \ldots$ and n-gram $(x_0, x_1, \ldots, x_{n-1})$. The 1-gram or letter probabilities $\{p(t) : 0 \leq t < m\}$ satisfy

$$p(t) \geq 0 \qquad 0 \leq t < m$$

$$(2.3.3) \qquad 1 = \sum_{0 \leq t < m} p(t)$$

Equation (2.3.3) implies that for $n \geq 2$,

$$p(t_0)p(t_1) \ldots p(t_{n-2}) = \sum_{t_{n-1}} p(t_0)p(t_1) \ldots p(t_{n-1})$$

or equivalently,

$$\Pr_{PLAIN}\{(x_0, x_1, \ldots, x_{n-2})\} = \sum_{x_{n-1}} \Pr_{PLAIN}\{(x_0, x_1, \ldots, x_{n-1})\}$$

which implies that the Kolmogorov consistency condition is satisfied. Thus Eq. (2.3.2) defines a source ***S***.

Example 2.3.1 *Plaintext one-grams generated by independent trials.* For the alphabet {A B . . . Z} the letter probabilities p(A), p(B), . . . , p(Z) are listed in Table 2.3.1.

The source ***S*** in Example 2.3.1 assigns to the 4-grams SEND and SEDN and the 2-gram QU the probabilities

$$\Pr_{PLAIN}\{\texttt{SEND}\} = p(\texttt{S}) \times p(\texttt{E}) \times p(\texttt{N}) \times p(\texttt{D})$$
$$= 0.0607 \times 0.1304 \times 0.0707 \times 0.0378 \approx 2.119 \times 10^{-5}$$
$$\Pr_{PLAIN}\{\texttt{SEDN}\} = p(\texttt{S}) \times p(\texttt{E}) \times p(\texttt{D}) \times p(\texttt{N})$$
$$= 0.0607 \times 0.1304 \times 0.0378 \times 0.0707 \approx 2.119 \times 10^{-5}$$
$$\Pr_{PLAIN}\{\texttt{QU}\} = p(\texttt{Q}) \times p(\texttt{U}) = 0.0012 \times 0.0249 \approx 2.988 \times 10^{-5}$$

$\Pr_{PLAIN}\{\texttt{SEND}\}$ and $\Pr_{PLAIN}\{\texttt{QU}\}$ are the frequencies of occurrence of SEND and QU in "typical" samples of plaintext 4-grams and 2-grams, respectively. The law of large numbers implies that in text generated by the source described in Example 2.3.1 there will be approximately

- 21 occurrences each of SEND and SEDN in a sample of 10^6 4-grams
- 25 occurrences of a 4-gram QU ** beginning with the letters QU in a sample of 10^6 4-grams

TABLE 2.3.1
One-Gram Probability Distribution

Letter	p	Letter	p	Letter	p
A	0.0856	J	0.0013	S	0.0607
B	0.0139	K	0.0042	T	0.1045
C	0.0279	L	0.0339	U	0.0249
D	0.0378	M	0.0249	V	0.0092
E	0.1304	N	0.0707	W	0.0149
F	0.0289	O	0.0797	X	0.0017
G	0.0199	P	0.0199	Y	0.0199
H	0.0528	Q	0.0012	Z	0.0008
I	0.0627	R	0.0677		

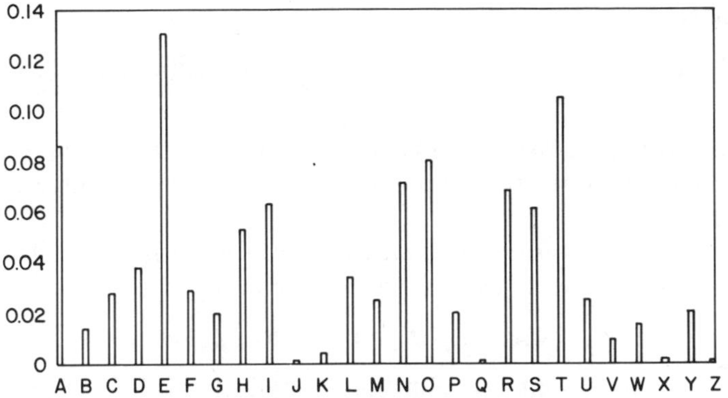

Figure 2.3.2. One-gram probability distribution.

The letter probabilities are shown graphically in Fig. 2.3.2. The important characteristic of this distribution is the alternation of peaks and valleys—the division of the letters into subsets of high, medium, low, and very low frequency of usage:

- AET high
- ONIRSH medium
- DLFCMUGPYWBV low
- JKXQZ very low

The assignment of a probability $Pr_{PLAIN}\{\mathbf{x}\}$ to the n-gram **x** by Eq. (2.3.2) fails to reflect the characteristics of English language text in at least two respects: (1) the nonzero probability assigned by Eq. (2.3.2) to the 2-grams of the form Q * with * ≠ U, and (2) the equal probability assigned by Eq. (2.3.2) to n-grams composed of the same letters, like **SEND** and **SEDN**. On the contrary, the interletter dependence in standard English text (1) permits **EQ** but not **QE** to appear within an n-gram, and (2) suggests that the 4-grams **SEND** and **SEDN** ought to be assigned different probabilities. Some interletter dependence is present in the following two plaintext sources.

Definition 2.3.2 A plaintext source *S* generates *2-grams of* Z_m *by independent and identical trials* if

(2.3.4) $$Pr_{PLAIN}\{(x_0, x_1, \ldots, x_{2n-1})\} = p(x_0,x_1)p(x_2,x_3) \ldots p(x_{2n-2},x_{2n-1})$$

for every integer n = 1, 2, . . . and 2n-gram $(x_0, x_1, \ldots, x_{2n-1})$, where the *2-gram probabilities* $\{p(t,s) : 0 \le t,s < m\}$ satisfy two conditions:

(2.3.5) $$p(t,s) \ge 0 \qquad 0 \le t,s < m$$
$$1 = \sum_{0 \le t,s < m} p(t,s)$$

Equation (2.3.5) shows that

$$p(t_0,t_1)p(t_2,t_3) \ldots p(t_{2n-4},t_{2n-3}) = \sum_{(t_{2n-2},t_{2n-1})} p(t_0,t_1)p(t_2,t_3) \ldots p(t_{2n-2},t_{2n-1})$$

or equivalently,

$$\text{(2.3.6)} \quad \Pr_{PLAIN}\{(x_0, x_1, \ldots, x_{2n-3})\} = \sum_{(x_{2n-2}, x_{2n-1})} \Pr_{PLAIN}\{(x_0, x_1, \ldots, x_{2n-1})\}$$

Equation (2.3.6) implies that the assignment of probabilities by Eq. (2.3.4) satisfies the Kolmogorov consistency condition and thus defines a source.

Example 2.3.2 *Two-grams generated by independent trials.* In Table 2.3.3, the number of occurrences of each of the 676 2-grams

$$\begin{matrix} N(A,A) & N(A,B) & \ldots & N(A,Z) \\ N(B,A) & N(B,B) & \ldots & N(B,Z) \\ \cdot & \cdot & \ldots & \cdot \\ \cdot & \cdot & \ldots & \cdot \\ \cdot & \cdot & \ldots & \cdot \\ N(Z,A) & N(Z,B) & \ldots & N(Z,Z) \end{matrix}$$

obtained from a sample of 67,320 2-grams is tabulated. The 2-gram probabilities $\{p(A,A), p(A,B), \ldots, p(Z,Z)\}$ are the *frequencies of occurrence* of the 2-grams from Table 2.3.3:

$$p(A,A) = N(A,A)/67{,}320$$
$$p(A,B) = N(A,B)/67{,}320$$
$$\ldots$$
$$\ldots$$
$$\ldots$$
$$p(Z,Z) = N(Z,Z)/67{,}320$$

There are tabulated in Table 2.3.4. The probabilities assigned by the plaintext source of Example 2.2 to **SEND** and **SEDN**, and **QE** are

$$\Pr_{PLAIN}\{SEND\} = p(S,E) \times p(N,D) = 0.0088 \times 0.0113 \approx 0.9991 \times 10^{-4}$$

$$\Pr_{PLAIN}\{SEDN\} = p(S,E) \times p(D,N) = 0.0088 \times 0.0001 \approx 0.88 \times 10^{-6}$$

$$\Pr_{PLAIN}\{QE\} = p(Q,E) = 0$$

Thus **QE** is ruled out as a possible 2-gram, and **SEDN** is assigned a much lower probability than **SEND**, more in accordance with the characteristics of English. A sample of text can be used in another way to define a plaintext source.

Definition 2.3.3 A plaintext source S generates *1-grams of* Z_m *by a Markov chain with transition matrix* P:

$$P = (p(s/t)) \qquad 0 \le t, s < m$$

TABLE 2.3.3

Count of 2-Grams

	A	B	C	D	E	F	G	H	I	J	K	L	M	N	O	P	Q	R	S	T	U	V	W	X	Y	Z
A	7	125	251	304	13	65	151	13	311	13	67	681	182	1216	5	144	0	764	648	1019	89	137	37	17	202	15
B	114	7	2	1	394	0	0	0	74	7	0	152	6	0	118	0	0	81	28	6	89	2	0	0	143	0
C	319	0	52	1	453	0	0	339	202	0	86	98	4	3	606	0	1	113	23	237	92	0	0	0	25	0
D	158	3	4	33	572	1	20	1	273	5	0	19	27	8	111	0	1	49	75	2	91	15	6	0	40	0
E	492	27	323	890	326	106	93	16	118	4	27	340	253	1029	30	143	25	1436	917	301	36	160	153	113	90	3
F	98	0	0	0	150	108	0	0	188	0	0	35	1	1	326	0	0	142	3	58	54	0	0	0	5	0
G	122	0	0	2	271	0	20	145	95	0	0	23	3	51	129	0	0	150	29	28	58	0	0	0	6	0
H	646	2	5	3	2053	0	0	2	426	0	0	6	6	14	287	0	0	56	10	85	31	0	4	0	15	0
I	236	51	476	285	271	80	174	1	10	0	31	352	184	1550	554	62	5	212	741	704	7	155	0	14	1	49
J	18	0	0	0	26	0	0	0	5	0	0	0	0	0	45	0	0	1	0	0	48	0	0	0	0	0
K	14	1	0	1	187	1	0	7	56	0	4	7	1	20	7	0	0	3	39	1	1	0	0	0	4	0
L	359	5	6	197	513	28	29	0	407	0	21	378	22	1	208	11	0	9	104	68	72	15	3	0	219	0
M	351	65	5	0	573	2	0	0	259	0	0	2	126	8	240	139	0	5	47	1	65	1	0	0	37	0
N	249	2	281	761	549	46	630	6	301	4	30	33	47	88	239	2	3	5	340	743	56	31	8	1	71	2
O	48	57	91	130	21	731	46	14	52	8	44	234	397	1232	125	164	0	861	201	223	533	188	194	7	23	2
P	241	0	1	0	310	0	0	42	75	0	0	144	13	1	268	103	0	409	32	51	81	0	0	0	3	0
Q	0	0	0	0	0	0	0	0	0	0	0	0	0	0	0	0	0	0	0	0	73	0	0	0	0	0
R	470	15	79	129	1280	14	80	8	541	0	94	75	139	149	510	25	0	97	300	273	88	65	8	1	140	0
S	200	4	94	9	595	8	0	186	390	0	30	48	37	7	234	128	3	9	277	823	192	0	13	0	27	0
T	381	2	22	1	872	4	1	2161	865	0	0	62	27	9	756	2	0	295	257	131	120	3	54	0	125	3
U	72	87	103	51	91	11	80	2	54	0	3	230	69	318	4	81	0	306	256	263	6	3	0	2	3	1
V	65	0	0	2	522	0	0	0	223	0	0	0	1	0	46	0	0	0	2	0	1	1	0	0	5	0
W	282	1	0	4	239	0	0	175	259	0	0	5	0	44	159	0	0	13	45	2	0	0	0	0	3	0
X	9	0	15	0	17	0	0	1	15	0	0	0	1	0	1	47	0	0	0	23	0	0	0	5	0	0
Y	17	1	3	2	84	0	0	0	20	0	1	5	11	5	64	9	0	9	44	5	4	0	3	0	2	1
Z	18	0	0	0	36	0	0	0	17	0	0	1	0	0	4	0	0	0	0	0	1	0	0	0	0	2

Table 2.3.4
Two-Gram Probability Distribution

	A	B	C	D	E	F	G	H	I	J	K	L	M
A	0.0001	0.0019	0.0037	0.0045	0.0002	0.0010	0.0022	0.0002	0.0046	0.0002	0.0010	0.0101	0.0027
B	0.0017	0.0001	0.0000	0.0000	0.0059	0.0000	0.0000	0.0000	0.0011	0.0001	0.0000	0.0023	0.0001
C	0.0047	0.0000	0.0008	0.0000	0.0067	0.0000	0.0000	0.0050	0.0030	0.0000	0.0013	0.0015	0.0001
D	0.0023	0.0000	0.0001	0.0005	0.0085	0.0000	0.0003	0.0000	0.0041	0.0001	0.0000	0.0003	0.0004
E	0.0073	0.0004	0.0048	0.0132	0.0048	0.0016	0.0014	0.0002	0.0018	0.0001	0.0004	0.0051	0.0038
F	0.0015	0.0000	0.0000	0.0000	0.0022	0.0016	0.0000	0.0000	0.0028	0.0000	0.0000	0.0005	0.0000
G	0.0018	0.0000	0.0000	0.0000	0.0040	0.0000	0.0003	0.0022	0.0014	0.0000	0.0000	0.0003	0.0000
H	0.0096	0.0000	0.0001	0.0000	0.0305	0.0000	0.0000	0.0000	0.0063	0.0000	0.0000	0.0001	0.0001
I	0.0035	0.0008	0.0071	0.0042	0.0040	0.0012	0.0026	0.0000	0.0001	0.0000	0.0005	0.0052	0.0027
J	0.0003	0.0000	0.0000	0.0000	0.0004	0.0000	0.0000	0.0000	0.0001	0.0000	0.0000	0.0000	0.0000
K	0.0002	0.0000	0.0000	0.0000	0.0028	0.0000	0.0000	0.0001	0.0008	0.0000	0.0001	0.0001	0.0000
L	0.0053	0.0001	0.0001	0.0029	0.0076	0.0004	0.0004	0.0000	0.0060	0.0000	0.0003	0.0056	0.0003
M	0.0052	0.0010	0.0001	0.0000	0.0085	0.0000	0.0000	0.0000	0.0038	0.0000	0.0000	0.0000	0.0019
N	0.0037	0.0000	0.0042	0.0113	0.0082	0.0007	0.0094	0.0001	0.0045	0.0001	0.0004	0.0005	0.0007
O	0.0007	0.0008	0.0014	0.0019	0.0003	0.0109	0.0007	0.0002	0.0008	0.0001	0.0007	0.0035	0.0059
P	0.0036	0.0000	0.0000	0.0000	0.0046	0.0000	0.0000	0.0006	0.0011	0.0000	0.0000	0.0021	0.0002
Q	0.0000	0.0000	0.0000	0.0000	0.0000	0.0000	0.0000	0.0000	0.0000	0.0000	0.0000	0.0000	0.0000
R	0.0070	0.0002	0.0012	0.0019	0.0190	0.0002	0.0012	0.0001	0.0080	0.0000	0.0014	0.0011	0.0021
S	0.0030	0.0001	0.0014	0.0001	0.0088	0.0001	0.0000	0.0028	0.0058	0.0000	0.0004	0.0007	0.0005
T	0.0057	0.0000	0.0003	0.0000	0.0130	0.0001	0.0000	0.0321	0.0128	0.0000	0.0000	0.0009	0.0004
U	0.0011	0.0013	0.0015	0.0008	0.0014	0.0002	0.0012	0.0000	0.0008	0.0000	0.0000	0.0034	0.0010
V	0.0010	0.0000	0.0000	0.0000	0.0078	0.0000	0.0000	0.0000	0.0033	0.0000	0.0000	0.0000	0.0000
W	0.0042	0.0000	0.0000	0.0001	0.0036	0.0000	0.0000	0.0026	0.0038	0.0000	0.0000	0.0001	0.0000
X	0.0001	0.0000	0.0002	0.0000	0.0003	0.0000	0.0000	0.0000	0.0002	0.0000	0.0000	0.0000	0.0000
Y	0.0003	0.0000	0.0000	0.0000	0.0012	0.0000	0.0000	0.0000	0.0003	0.0000	0.0000	0.0001	0.0002
Z	0.0003	0.0000	0.0000	0.0000	0.0005	0.0000	0.0000	0.0000	0.0003	0.0000	0.0000	0.0000	0.0000

	N	O	P	Q	R	S	T	U	V	W	X	Y	Z
A	0.0181	0.0001	0.0021	0.0000	0.0113	0.0096	0.0151	0.0013	0.0020	0.0005	0.0003	0.0030	0.0002
B	0.0000	0.0018	0.0000	0.0000	0.0012	0.0004	0.0001	0.0013	0.0000	0.0000	0.0000	0.0021	0.0000
C	0.0000	0.0090	0.0000	0.0000	0.0017	0.0003	0.0035	0.0014	0.0000	0.0000	0.0000	0.0004	0.0000
D	0.0001	0.0016	0.0000	0.0000	0.0007	0.0011	0.0000	0.0014	0.0002	0.0001	0.0000	0.0006	0.0000
E	0.0153	0.0004	0.0021	0.0004	0.0213	0.0136	0.0045	0.0005	0.0024	0.0023	0.0017	0.0013	0.0000
F	0.0000	0.0048	0.0000	0.0000	0.0021	0.0000	0.0009	0.0008	0.0000	0.0000	0.0000	0.0001	0.0000
G	0.0008	0.0019	0.0000	0.0000	0.0022	0.0004	0.0004	0.0009	0.0000	0.0000	0.0000	0.0001	0.0000
H	0.0002	0.0043	0.0000	0.0000	0.0008	0.0001	0.0013	0.0005	0.0000	0.0001	0.0000	0.0002	0.0000
I	0.0230	0.0082	0.0009	0.0001	0.0031	0.0110	0.0105	0.0001	0.0023	0.0000	0.0002	0.0000	0.0007
J	0.0000	0.0007	0.0000	0.0000	0.0000	0.0000	0.0000	0.0007	0.0000	0.0000	0.0000	0.0000	0.0000
K	0.0003	0.0001	0.0000	0.0000	0.0000	0.0006	0.0000	0.0000	0.0000	0.0000	0.0000	0.0001	0.0000
L	0.0000	0.0031	0.0002	0.0000	0.0001	0.0015	0.0010	0.0011	0.0002	0.0000	0.0000	0.0033	0.0000
M	0.0001	0.0036	0.0021	0.0000	0.0001	0.0007	0.0000	0.0010	0.0000	0.0000	0.0000	0.0005	0.0000
N	0.0013	0.0036	0.0000	0.0000	0.0001	0.0051	0.0110	0.0008	0.0005	0.0001	0.0000	0.0011	0.0000
O	0.0183	0.0019	0.0024	0.0000	0.0128	0.0030	0.0033	0.0079	0.0028	0.0029	0.0001	0.0003	0.0000
P	0.0000	0.0040	0.0015	0.0000	0.0061	0.0005	0.0008	0.0012	0.0000	0.0000	0.0000	0.0000	0.0000
Q	0.0000	0.0000	0.0000	0.0000	0.0000	0.0000	0.0000	0.0011	0.0000	0.0000	0.0000	0.0000	0.0000
R	0.0022	0.0076	0.0004	0.0000	0.0014	0.0045	0.0041	0.0013	0.0010	0.0001	0.0000	0.0021	0.0000
S	0.0001	0.0035	0.0019	0.0000	0.0001	0.0041	0.0122	0.0029	0.0000	0.0002	0.0000	0.0004	0.0000
T	0.0001	0.0112	0.0000	0.0000	0.0044	0.0038	0.0019	0.0018	0.0000	0.0008	0.0000	0.0019	0.0000
U	0.0047	0.0001	0.0012	0.0000	0.0045	0.0038	0.0039	0.0001	0.0000	0.0000	0.0000	0.0000	0.0000
V	0.0000	0.0007	0.0000	0.0000	0.0000	0.0000	0.0000	0.0000	0.0000	0.0000	0.0000	0.0001	0.0000
W	0.0007	0.0024	0.0000	0.0000	0.0002	0.0007	0.0000	0.0000	0.0000	0.0000	0.0000	0.0000	0.0000
X	0.0000	0.0000	0.0007	0.0000	0.0000	0.0000	0.0003	0.0000	0.0000	0.0000	0.0001	0.0000	0.0000
Y	0.0001	0.0010	0.0001	0.0000	0.0001	0.0007	0.0001	0.0001	0.0000	0.0000	0.0000	0.0000	0.0000
Z	0.0000	0.0001	0.0000	0.0000	0.0000	0.0000	0.0000	0.0000	0.0000	0.0000	0.0000	0.0000	0.0000

and *equilibrium distribution*

$$\pi = (\pi(0), \pi(1), \ldots, \pi(m-1))$$

if

$$\text{(2.3.7)} \quad \Pr_{PLAIN}\{(x_0, x_1, \ldots, x_{n-1})\} = \pi(x_0)p(x_1/x_0)p(x_2/x_1) \ldots p(x_{n-1}/x_{n-2})$$

for each integer n, n = 1, 2, ... and n-gram $(x_0, x_1, \ldots, x_{n-1})$. The *transition probabilities* $\{p(s/t) : 0 \leq t,s < m\}$ and the equilibrium distribution π satisfy the conditions

$$p(s/t) \geq 0 \qquad 0 \leq t,s < m$$

$$1 = \sum_{0 \leq s < m} p(s/t) \qquad 0 \leq t < m$$

$$\text{(2.3.8)} \qquad \pi(t) \geq 0 \qquad 0 \leq t < m$$

$$1 = \sum_{0 \leq t < m} \pi(t)$$

$$\text{(2.3.9)} \qquad \pi(s) = \sum_{0 \leq t < m} \pi(t)p(s/t) \qquad 0 \leq s < m$$

Equation (2.3.8) shows that

$$\pi(t_0)p(t_1/t_0)p(t_2/t_1) \ldots p(t_{n-2}/t_{n-3})$$
$$= \sum_{0 \leq t_{n-1} < m} \pi(t_0)p(t_1/t_0)p(t_2/t_1) \ldots p(t_{n-1}/t_{n-2})$$

or equivalently,

$$\text{(2.3.10)} \quad \Pr_{PLAIN}\{(x_0, x_1, \ldots, x_{n-2})\} = \sum_{x_{n-1}} \Pr_{PLAIN}\{(x_0, x_1, \ldots, x_{n-1})\}$$

Equation (2.3.10) implies that the Kolmogorov consistency condition holds, and therefore Eq. (2.3.7) defines a source.

Equation (2.3.9) yields the relationship

$$\pi(t_1)p(t_2/t_1)p(t_3/t_2) \ldots p(t_{n-1}/t_{n-2})$$
$$= \sum_{0 \leq t_0 < m} \pi(t_0)p(t_1/t_0)p(t_2/t_1) \ldots p(t_{n-1}/t_{n-2})$$

or equivalently,

$$\text{(2.3.11)} \quad \Pr_{PLAIN}\{(x_1, x_2, \ldots, x_{n-2})\} = \sum_{x_0} \Pr_{PLAIN}\{(x_0, x_1, \ldots, x_{n-1})\}$$

The left-hand side of Eq. (2.3.11) is the probability that the source will generate text satisfying

$$\{X_0 = x_1, X_1 = x_2, \ldots, X_{n-2} = x_{n-1}\}$$

while the right-hand side is the probability that the source will generate text satisfying

$$\{X_1 = x_1, X_2 = x_2, \ldots, X_{n-1} = x_{n-1}\}$$

Equation (2.3.11) is a special case of the more general relationship

$$\text{(2.3.12)} \quad Pr_{PLAIN}\{X_j = x_0, X_{j+1} = x_1, \ldots, X_{j+n-1} = x_{n-1}\}$$
$$= Pr_{PLAIN}\{X_0 = x_0, X_1 = x_1, \ldots, X_{n-1} = x_{n-1}\}$$

which holds for every nonnegative integer j. The special case of Eq. (2.3.12) with $n = 1$ states that the marginal distribution of letters (1-grams)

$$Pr_{PLAIN}\{X_j = t\} = p(t)$$

is the same for every position j in the plaintext.

A Markov process is an example of a stochastic process with *intersymbol dependence* or *memory;* the value of the letter X_i is dependent on the value of the previous X_{i-1}; the dependency on consecutive trials is expressed by the transition probability $p(x_i/x_{i-1})$. The equilibrium distribution π is the solution of the linear system of equations

$$\pi(0) = \pi(0)p(0/0) + \pi(1)P(0/1) + \ldots + \pi(m-1)p(0/m-1)$$
$$\pi(1) = \pi(0)p(1/0) + \pi(1)p(1/1) + \ldots + \pi(m-1)p(1/m-1)$$
$$\ldots$$
$$\ldots$$
$$\pi(m-1) = \pi(0)p(m-1/0) + \pi(1)p(m-1/1) + \ldots$$
$$+ \pi(m-1)p(m-1/m-1)$$

which may be compactly written in matrix notation as

$$\pi = \pi P$$

where $\pi = (\pi(0), \pi(1), \ldots, \pi(m-1))$.

Example 2.3.3 *Plaintext generated by a Markov chain on one-grams.* The sample values in Table 2.3.4 are used to construct a *transition matrix* P.

$$P = \begin{vmatrix} p(\texttt{A}/\texttt{A}) & p(\texttt{B}/\texttt{Z}) & \ldots & p(\texttt{Z}/\texttt{A}) \\ p(\texttt{A}/\texttt{B}) & p(\texttt{B}/\texttt{B}) & \ldots & p(\texttt{Z}/\texttt{B}) \\ \cdot & \cdot & \ldots & \cdot \\ \cdot & \cdot & \ldots & \cdot \\ \cdot & \cdot & \ldots & \cdot \\ p(\texttt{A}/\texttt{Z}) & p(\texttt{B}/\texttt{Z}) & \ldots & p(\texttt{Z}/\texttt{Z}) \end{vmatrix}$$

The transition probabilities are defined as the ratios

$$p(\mathtt{A}/\mathtt{A}) = N(\mathtt{A}/\mathtt{A})/N(\mathtt{A}) \quad p(\mathtt{B}/\mathtt{A}) = N(\mathtt{A}/\mathtt{B})/N(\mathtt{A}) \quad \ldots \quad p(\mathtt{Z}/\mathtt{A}) = N(\mathtt{A}/\mathtt{Z})/N(\mathtt{A})$$

$$p(\mathtt{A}/\mathtt{B}) = N(\mathtt{B},\mathtt{A})/N(\mathtt{B}) \quad p(\mathtt{B}/\mathtt{B}) = N(\mathtt{B},\mathtt{B})/N(\mathtt{B}) \quad \ldots \quad p(\mathtt{Z}/\mathtt{B}) = N(\mathtt{B},\mathtt{Z})/N(\mathtt{B})$$

$$\ldots$$

$$\ldots$$

$$\ldots$$

$$p(\mathtt{A}/\mathtt{Z}) = N(\mathtt{Z}/\mathtt{A})/N(\mathtt{Z}) \quad p(\mathtt{B}/\mathtt{Z}) = N(\mathtt{Z},\mathtt{B})/N(\mathtt{Z}) \quad \ldots \quad p(\mathtt{Z}/\mathtt{Z}) = N(\mathtt{Z},\mathtt{Z})/N(\mathtt{Z})$$

where

$$N(\mathtt{A}) = N(\mathtt{A},\mathtt{A}) + N(\mathtt{A},\mathtt{B}) + \ldots + N(\mathtt{A},\mathtt{Z})$$

$$N(\mathtt{B}) = N(\mathtt{B},\mathtt{A}) + N(\mathtt{B},\mathtt{B}) + \ldots + N(\mathtt{B},\mathtt{Z})$$

$$\ldots$$

$$\ldots$$

$$\ldots$$

$$N(\mathtt{Z}) = N(\mathtt{Z},\mathtt{A}) + N(\mathtt{Z},\mathtt{B}) + \ldots + N(\mathtt{Z},\mathtt{Z})$$

The transition matrix P obtained from the sample data is displayed in Table 2.3.5. The transition probability $p(\mathtt{E}/\mathtt{A}) = N(\mathtt{A},\mathtt{E})/N(\mathtt{A})$ is the probability of the event $\{X_i = \mathtt{E}\}$ *conditioned by* or *given* the event $\{X_{i-1} = \mathtt{A}\}$; $p(\mathtt{E}/\mathtt{A})$ is the ratio of the number of times the 2-gram **AE** appears in the sample ($N_{AE} = 13$) to the total number of 2-grams in the sample that begin with the letter A ($N_A = 6476$). The equilbrium distribution $\{\pi(t) : 0 \leq t < m\}$ for Example 2.3.3 is given in Table 2.3.6

Example 2.3.3 assigns to SEND, SEDN, and QE the probabilities

$$\Pr_{PLAIN}\{\mathtt{SEND}\} = \pi(\mathtt{S}) \times p(\mathtt{E}/\mathtt{S}) \times p(\mathtt{N}/\mathtt{E}) \times p(\mathtt{D}/\mathtt{N})$$

$$= 0.0715 \times 0.1795 \times 0.1381 \times 0.1681 \approx 2.978 \times 10^{-4}$$

$$\Pr_{PLAIN}\{\mathtt{SEDN}\} = \pi(\mathtt{S}) \times p(\mathtt{E}/\mathtt{S}) \times p(\mathtt{D}/\mathtt{E}) \times p(\mathtt{N}/\mathtt{D})$$

$$= 0.0715 \times 0.1795 \times 0.1194 \times 0.0053 \approx 8.1218 \times 10^{-6}$$

$$\Pr_{PLAIN}\{\mathtt{QU}\} = \pi(\mathtt{Q}) \times p(\mathtt{U}/\mathtt{Q}) = 0.0007 \times 1.000 \approx 7 \times 10^{-4}$$

Models can be introduced with more extensive interletter dependence. Start by counting the number of occurrences of each of the 26^k k-grams in some sample of text; then

TABLE 2.3.5

Transition Probabilities P = (p(j/i))

	A	B	C	D	E	F	G	H	I	J	K	L	M
A	0.0011	0.0193	0.0388	0.0469	0.0020	0.0100	0.0233	0.0020	0.0480	0.0020	0.0103	0.1052	0.0281
B	0.0931	0.0057	0.0016	0.0008	0.3219	0.0000	0.0000	0.0000	0.0605	0.0057	0.0000	0.1242	0.0049
C	0.1202	0.0000	0.0196	0.0004	0.1707	0.0000	0.0000	0.1277	0.0761	0.0000	0.0324	0.0369	0.0015
D	0.1044	0.0020	0.0026	0.0218	0.3778	0.0007	0.0132	0.0007	0.1803	0.0033	0.0000	0.0125	0.0178
E	0.0660	0.0036	0.0433	0.1194	0.0438	0.0142	0.0125	0.0021	0.0158	0.0005	0.0036	0.0456	0.0340
F	0.0838	0.0000	0.0000	0.0000	0.1283	0.0924	0.0000	0.0000	0.1608	0.0000	0.0000	0.0299	0.0009
G	0.1078	0.0000	0.0000	0.0018	0.2394	0.0000	0.0177	0.1281	0.0839	0.0000	0.0000	0.0203	0.0027
H	0.1769	0.0005	0.0014	0.0008	0.5623	0.0000	0.0000	0.0005	0.1167	0.0000	0.0000	0.0016	0.0016
I	0.0380	0.0082	0.0767	0.0459	0.0437	0.0129	0.0280	0.0002	0.0016	0.0000	0.0050	0.0567	0.0297
J	0.1259	0.0000	0.0000	0.0000	0.1818	0.0000	0.0000	0.0000	0.0350	0.0000	0.0000	0.0000	0.0000
K	0.0395	0.0028	0.0000	0.0028	0.5282	0.0028	0.0000	0.0198	0.1582	0.0000	0.0113	0.0198	0.0028
L	0.1342	0.0019	0.0022	0.0736	0.1918	0.0105	0.0108	0.0000	0.1521	0.0000	0.0079	0.1413	0.0082
M	0.1822	0.0337	0.0026	0.0000	0.2975	0.0010	0.0000	0.0000	0.1345	0.0000	0.0000	0.0010	0.0654
N	0.0550	0.0004	0.0621	0.1681	0.1212	0.0102	0.1391	0.0013	0.0665	0.0009	0.0066	0.0073	0.0104
O	0.0085	0.0101	0.0162	0.0231	0.0037	0.1299	0.0082	0.0025	0.0092	0.0014	0.0078	0.0416	0.0706
P	0.1359	0.0000	0.0006	0.0000	0.1747	0.0000	0.0000	0.0237	0.0423	0.0000	0.0000	0.0812	0.0073
Q	0.0000	0.0000	0.0000	0.0000	0.0000	0.0000	0.0000	0.0000	0.0000	0.0000	0.0000	0.0000	0.0000
R	0.1026	0.0033	0.0172	0.0282	0.2795	0.0031	0.0175	0.0017	0.1181	0.0000	0.0205	0.0164	0.0303
S	0.0604	0.0012	0.0284	0.0027	0.1795	0.0024	0.0000	0.0561	0.1177	0.0000	0.0091	0.0145	0.0112
T	0.0619	0.0003	0.0036	0.0002	0.1417	0.0007	0.0002	0.3512	0.1406	0.0000	0.0000	0.0101	0.0044
U	0.0344	0.0415	0.0491	0.0243	0.0434	0.0052	0.0382	0.0010	0.0258	0.0000	0.0014	0.1097	0.0329
V	0.0749	0.0000	0.0000	0.0023	0.6014	0.0000	0.0000	0.0000	0.2569	0.0000	0.0000	0.0000	0.0012
W	0.2291	0.0008	0.0000	0.0032	0.1942	0.0000	0.0000	0.1422	0.2104	0.0000	0.0000	0.0041	0.0000
X	0.0672	0.0000	0.1119	0.0000	0.1269	0.0000	0.0000	0.0075	0.1119	0.0000	0.0000	0.0000	0.0075
Y	0.0586	0.0034	0.0103	0.0069	0.2897	0.0000	0.0000	0.0000	0.0690	0.0000	0.0034	0.0172	0.0379
Z	0.2278	0.0000	0.0000	0.0000	0.4557	0.0000	0.0000	0.0000	0.2152	0.0000	0.0000	0.0127	0.0000

	N	O	P	Q	R	S	T	U	V	W	X	Y	Z
A	0.1878	0.0008	0.0222	0.0000	0.1180	0.1001	0.1574	0.0137	0.0212	0.0057	0.0026	0.0312	0.0023
B	0.0000	0.0964	0.0000	0.0000	0.0662	0.0229	0.0049	0.0727	0.0016	0.0000	0.0000	0.1168	0.0000
C	0.0011	0.2283	0.0000	0.0004	0.0426	0.0087	0.0893	0.0347	0.0000	0.0000	0.0000	0.0094	0.0000
D	0.0053	0.0733	0.0000	0.0007	0.0324	0.0495	0.0013	0.0601	0.0099	0.0040	0.0000	0.0264	0.0000
E	0.1381	0.0040	0.0192	0.0034	0.1927	0.1231	0.0404	0.0048	0.0215	0.0205	0.0152	0.0121	0.0004
F	0.0009	0.2789	0.0000	0.0000	0.1215	0.0026	0.0496	0.0462	0.0000	0.0000	0.0000	0.0043	0.0000
G	0.0451	0.1140	0.0000	0.0000	0.1325	0.0256	0.0247	0.0512	0.0000	0.0000	0.0000	0.0053	0.0000
H	0.0038	0.0786	0.0000	0.0000	0.0153	0.0027	0.0233	0.0085	0.0000	0.0011	0.0000	0.0041	0.0000
I	0.2498	0.0893	0.0100	0.0008	0.0342	0.1194	0.1135	0.0011	0.0250	0.0000	0.0023	0.0002	0.0079
J	0.0000	0.3147	0.0000	0.0000	0.0070	0.0000	0.0000	0.3357	0.0000	0.0000	0.0000	0.0000	0.0000
K	0.0565	0.0198	0.0000	0.0000	0.0085	0.1102	0.0028	0.0028	0.0000	0.0000	0.0000	0.0113	0.0000
L	0.0004	0.0778	0.0041	0.0000	0.0034	0.0389	0.0254	0.0269	0.0056	0.0011	0.0000	0.0819	0.0000
M	0.0042	0.1246	0.0722	0.0000	0.0026	0.0244	0.0005	0.0337	0.0005	0.0000	0.0000	0.0192	0.0000
N	0.0194	0.0528	0.0004	0.0007	0.0011	0.0751	0.1641	0.0124	0.0068	0.0018	0.0002	0.0157	0.0004
O	0.2190	0.0222	0.0292	0.0000	0.1530	0.0357	0.0396	0.0947	0.0334	0.0345	0.0012	0.0041	0.0004
P	0.0006	0.1511	0.0581	0.0000	0.2306	0.0180	0.0287	0.0457	0.0000	0.0000	0.0000	0.0017	0.0000
Q	0.0000	0.0000	0.0000	0.0000	0.0000	0.0000	0.0000	1.0000	0.0000	0.0000	0.0000	0.0000	0.0000
R	0.0325	0.1114	0.0055	0.0000	0.0212	0.0655	0.0596	0.0192	0.0142	0.0017	0.0002	0.0306	0.0000
S	0.0021	0.0706	0.0386	0.0009	0.0027	0.0836	0.2483	0.0579	0.0000	0.0039	0.0000	0.0081	0.0000
T	0.0015	0.1229	0.0003	0.0000	0.0479	0.0418	0.0213	0.0195	0.0005	0.0088	0.0000	0.0203	0.0005
U	0.1517	0.0019	0.0386	0.0000	0.1460	0.1221	0.1255	0.0029	0.0014	0.0000	0.0010	0.0014	0.0005
V	0.0000	0.0530	0.0000	0.0000	0.0000	0.0023	0.0000	0.0012	0.0012	0.0000	0.0000	0.0058	0.0000
W	0.0357	0.1292	0.0000	0.0000	0.0106	0.0366	0.0016	0.0000	0.0000	0.0000	0.0000	0.0024	0.0000
X	0.0000	0.0075	0.3507	0.0000	0.0000	0.0000	0.1716	0.0000	0.0000	0.0000	0.0373	0.0000	0.0000
Y	0.0172	0.2207	0.0310	0.0000	0.0310	0.1517	0.0172	0.0138	0.0000	0.0103	0.0000	0.0069	0.0034
Z	0.0000	0.0506	0.0000	0.0000	0.0000	0.0000	0.0000	0.0127	0.0000	0.0000	0.0000	0.0000	0.0253

TABLE 2.3.6
Equilibrium Distribution π for the Markov Chain of *Example 2.3.3*

Letter	π	Letter	π	Letter	π
A	0.0723	J	0.0006	S	0.0715
B	0.0060	K	0.0064	T	0.0773
C	0.0282	L	0.0396	U	0.0272
D	0.0483	M	0.0236	V	0.0117
E	0.1566	N	0.0814	W	0.0078
F	0.0167	O	0.0716	X	0.0030
G	0.0216	P	0.0161	Y	0.0168
H	0.0402	Q	0.0007	Z	0.0010
I	0.0787	R	0.0751		

- Generalize Example 2.3.2 by hypothesizing that k-grams are generated by independent and identical repeated trials.
- Generalize Example 2.3.3 by hypothesizing that X_i is dependent on the previous k − 1 letters generated by the source $(X_{i-1}, X_{i-2}, \ldots, X_{i-k+1})$.

The sample of text provides the numerical parameters, that is, the k-gram and transition probabilities, to define the source ***S***. As k and the size of the sample increases, the model reflects more of the characteristics of the language. Since we must build a catalogue counting the number of occurrences of each of the 26^k k-grams, the practical range for k is limited.

Each of the preceding plaintext sources is *stationary;* the probability that the n-gram $(x_0, x_1, \ldots, x_{n-1})$ will occur in the text starting with the jth letter

$$\Pr_{PLAIN}\{X_j = x_0, X_{j+1} = x_1, \ldots, X_{j+n} = x_{n-1}\}$$

does not depend on j. Stationarity is inappropriate in some applications.

Example 2.3.4 A message in an electronic funds transfer system might contain the following: sending and receiving bank identification, sending and receiving account numbers, date, and transaction amount, as indicated in Fig. 2.3.7. Suppose plaintext is written in the letters in an alphabet $\boldsymbol{Z}_{12}$, the ten numerals, period, and blank space. The message originating at *bank 117* to *bank 184* requesting that $1000.00 be transferred from *account 86341* to *account 88753* might be written as the string of 44 characters,

```
--- 117--- 184-8634 1-88753 1003 1979----- 1000.00)
```

Sending Bank	*Receiving Bank*	*Sending Account*	*Receiving Account*	*Date*	*Transfer Amount*
6 letters	6 letters	6 letters	6 letters	8 letters	12 letters

Figure 2.3.7. Format of an electronic funds transfer message.

where we have used – to indicate a blank space. The finite plaintext source $\boldsymbol{S}$ generates 44-grams $\mathbf{x} = (x_0, x_1, \ldots, x_{43})$ with $x_i \in \boldsymbol{Z}_{12}$ in which

Segment	Length	Contents
$(x_0, x_1, \ldots, x_5)$	6 letters	Sending Bank Identification
$(x_6, x_7, \ldots, x_{11})$	6 letters	Receiving Bank Identification
$(x_{12}, x_{13}, \ldots, x_{17})$	6 letters	Sending Account Number
$(x_{18}, x_{19}, \ldots, x_{23})$	6 letters	Receiving Account Number
$(x_{24}, x_{25}, \ldots, x_{31})$	8 letters	Date
$(x_{32}, x_{33}, \ldots, x_{43})$	12 letters	Transfer Amount

The letters that can appear in a particular segment of plaintext are dependent on the location of the segment in the plaintext; for example,

2-Gram	Representing	Number of Possible 2-Gram Values
(x_{24}, x_{25})	month	12
(x_{26}, x_{27})	day	30

A model of the generation of this type of plaintext should reflect the fact that the marginal distributions $\Pr_{PLAIN}\{X_{24} = x_{24}, X_{25} = x_{25}\}$ and $\Pr_{PLAIN}\{X_{26} = x_{26}, X_{27} = x_{27}\}$ are different. The plaintext sources described in Definitions 2.3.1–3 can be generalized to produce sources which exhibit nonstationarity.

Definition 2.3.4 The (finite) plaintext source $\boldsymbol{S}$

$$X_0, X_1, \ldots, X_{n-1}, \ldots \qquad (\text{resp. } X_0, X_1, \ldots, X_{N-1})$$

generates *1-grams by independent trials* if

$$\Pr_{PLAIN}\{(x_0, x_1, \ldots, x_{n-1})\} = p_0(x_0)p_1(x_1) \ldots p_{n-1}(x_{n-1})$$

where $\{p_j(t) : 0 \leq t < m\}$ is a probability distribution on the letters of $\boldsymbol{Z}_m$ for each j

$$p_j(t) \geq 0 \qquad 0 \leq t < m$$

$$1 = \sum_{0 \leq t < m} p_j(t) \qquad 0 \leq j < \infty \qquad (0 \leq j < N)$$

Definition 2.3.5 The (finite) plaintext source $\boldsymbol{S}$

$$X_0, X_1, \ldots, X_{n-1}, \ldots \qquad (\text{resp. } X_0, X_1, \ldots, X_{2N-1})$$

generates *2-grams by independent trials* if

$$\Pr_{PLAIN}\{(x_0, x_1, \ldots, x_{2n-1})\} = p_0(x_0,x_1)p_1(x_2,x_3) \ldots p_{n-1}(x_{2n-2},x_{2n-1})$$

where $\{p_j(t,s) : 0 \le t,s < m\}$ is a probability distribution of the letters of $\boldsymbol{Z}_{m,2}$ for each j

$$p_j(t,s) \ge 0 \qquad 0 < t,s < m$$

$$1 = \sum_{0 \le t,s < m} p_j(t,s) \qquad 0 \le j < \infty \qquad (0 \le j < N)$$

Definition 2.3.6 The (finite) plaintext source $\boldsymbol{S}$

$$X_0, X_1, \ldots, X_{n-1}, \ldots \qquad (\text{resp. } X_0, X_1, \ldots, X_{2N-1})$$

generates *1-grams by a Markov chain* if

$$Pr_{PLAIN}\{(x_0, x_1, \ldots, x_{n-1})\} = \pi(x_0)p_0(x_1/x_0)p_1(x_2/x_1) \ldots p_{n-2}(x_{n-1}/x_{n-2})$$

where $\{\pi(t) : 0 \le t < m\}$ is the probability distribution of initial letters and $P_j = (p_j(s/t))$ is a transition matrix for each value of j

$$\pi(t) \ge 0 \qquad 0 \le t < m$$

$$1 = \sum_{0 \le t < m} \pi(t)$$

$$p_j(s/t) \ge 0 \qquad 0 \le t,s < m$$

$$1 = \sum_{0 \le s < m} p_j(s/t) \qquad 0 \le t < m \qquad 0 \le j < \infty \qquad (0 \le j < N)$$

In Example 2.3.4 we might model for the generation of plaintext using Definition 2.3.4, and define

$$p_{12}(t,s) = \begin{cases} 1/12 & \text{if } (t,s) \in \{(0,1), (0,2), \ldots, (1,1), (1,2)\} \\ 0 & \text{otherwise} \end{cases}$$

$$p_{13}(t,s) = \begin{cases} 1/31 & \text{if } (t,s) \in \{(0,1), (0.2), \ldots, (3,1)\} \\ 0 & \text{otherwise} \end{cases}$$

$$p_{14}(t,s) = \begin{cases} 1 & \text{if } (t,s) = (1,9) \\ 0 & \text{otherwise} \end{cases}$$

$$p_{15}(t,s) = \begin{cases} 1 & \text{if } (t,s) = (8,0) \\ 0 & \text{otherwise} \end{cases}$$

Now that we have provided a mathematical framework to describe text, we must specify how plaintext is altered by encipherment.

2.4 CRYPTOGRAPHIC SYSTEMS

Definition 2.4.1 A *cryptographic transformation* T is a sequence of transformations $T = \{T^{(n)} : 1 \le n < \infty\}$

$$T^{(n)} : \boldsymbol{Z}_{m,n} \to \boldsymbol{Z}_{m,n} \qquad (2.4.1)$$

$T^{(n)}$ specifies how each plaintext n-gram $\mathbf{x} \in \boldsymbol{Z}_{m,n}$ is replaced by a ciphertext n-gram $T(\mathbf{x}) = \mathbf{y} \in \boldsymbol{Z}_{m,n}$. For each n, the mapping in Eq. (2.4.1) is required to be a one-to-one transformation* on $\boldsymbol{Z}_{m,n}$ in order that the plaintext can be unambiguously recovered from the ciphertext.

We do not require in Definition 2.4.1 any relationship between the encipherment of s-grams and n-grams for $s \neq n$. For example, $T^{(4)}($`SEND`$)$ and $T^{(8)}($`SENDHELP`$)$ need not bear any special relationship to one another.

Definition 2.4.2 A *cryptographic system* $\boldsymbol{T}$ is a family of cryptographic transformations

$$\boldsymbol{T} = \{T_k : k \in \boldsymbol{K}\}$$

indexed or labeled by a parameter k called the *key*. The set of key values is the *key space* $\boldsymbol{K}$. We do not insist the distinct keys $k_1 \neq k_2$ yield distinct cryptographic transformations $T_{k_1} \neq T_{k_2}$.

Remarks

Definition 2.4.1 involves four important elements:

- Plaintext and ciphertext are written using the same alphabet.
- Encipherment is defined for *every* plaintext n-gram and $n = 1, 2, \ldots$.
- Each plaintext n-gram is enciphered into precisely one ciphertext.
- The length of text is not altered by encipherment.

There is no necessity for imposing any of these conditions in the definition of a cryptographic transformation:

- Different alphabets can be used for plaintext and ciphertext.
- Encipherment need not be defined for *all* plaintext n-grams.
- More than one ciphertext could be associated with each plaintext.
- The length of text could change under encipherment.

The requirements imposed in Definition 2.4.1 are natural in the application of cryptography to information processing systems. For in this environment

- Plaintext and ciphertext are both written using the same alphabet $\{0,1\}$.
- Any n-gram might represent plaintext, so that $T(\mathbf{x})$ must be defined for *all* plaintext.

*A transformation F from a set A to a set B

$$F : A \rightarrow B$$

associates with each α in A (called the *domain* of F) an element $F(\alpha)$ in B. The set of image elements $F(A) = \{F(\alpha) : \alpha \in B\}$ is called the *range* of F. F is said to be a *one-to-one* transformation on A, if for each $\beta \in F(A)$, there is exactly one α in A with $F(\alpha) = \beta$.

- If encipherment T is not singled-valued, that is, if plaintext can be replaced by several different ciphertexts called *homophones,* or if the length of text changes under encipherment, then necessarily some plaintext must be expanded in length.

Expansion of text under encipherment in an information processing system can be the source of difficulty, as the following points illustrate.

1. A useful option in file security is the ability to overwrite plaintext with the ciphertext. If the lengths of texts can change in an unpredictable manner, then a programmer must estimate the expansion factor and allocate sufficient storage for the larger of the two texts. A change in the length of text under encipherment would unnecessarily complicate the computing environment by requiring changes in data set attributes, in application-program array sizes, and string lengths.

2. In some applications, only selected fields of the records of a file are to be enciphered. For example, a file of medical records might organize the data in various *fields:*

Patient	Symptoms	Diagnosis	Treatment	Condition
16 bytes	64 bytes	64 bytes	64 bytes	64 bytes

Often there are reasons for sharing information in files with other organizations in order to extract statistical information; for example, the efficacy of a particular drug, or the recovery rate after a certain type of surgical procedure. Can the files be shared while respecting the privacy of the patient? If the first 16 byte field of each record is enciphered, the file can be disseminated without compromising privacy. The ciphertext of the field *Patient* serves as a label identifying records. If encipherment is allowed to lengthen the text, the records must be reformatted.

3. Expansion of the length of text by encipherment when securing telecommunication lines reduces the effective rate at which data is transmitted, thereby increasing the cost.

A cryptographic system $\boldsymbol{T} = \{T_k : k \in \boldsymbol{K}\}$ can be depicted as a sequence of *oriented bipartite graphs* $\{G_n(\boldsymbol{T}) : n = 1, 2, \ldots\}$, as shown in Fig. 2.4.1.

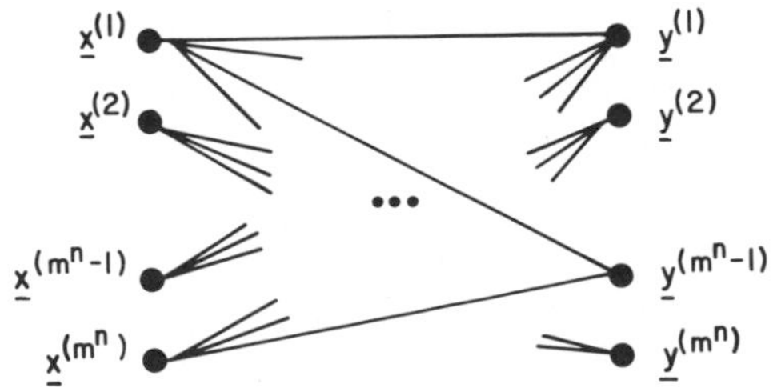

Figure 2.4.1. Encipherment graph G_n (T).

A *oriented graph* G = (E,V) is a collection of *vertices* v ∈ V and *edges* e ∈ E. Edges are ordered pairs of vertices e = (v_1, v_2) (v_1, v_2 ∈ V). We say that the edge e joins the vertex v_1 to the vertex v_2. An *oriented bipartite graph* is a graph in which the vertices are divided into two disjoint sets L and R; edges join only vertex pairs (v,v′) with v ∈ L and v′ ∈ R.

The $2m^n$ *vertices* of the graph $G_n(T)$ correspond to the m^n plaintext and m^n ciphertext n-grams. An *edge* labeled by the key k joins the (plaintext) vertex $x^{(i)}$ to the ciphertext vertex $y^{(j)} = T_k(x^{(i)})$. Observe that each key k will appear as a label on m^n edges.

Example 2.4.1 The Vigenère Substitution System. The substitutions $\{T_k : 0 \le k < 26\}$ on the letters of {AB . . . z} are defined in the *Vigenère table* (Table 2.4.2). The row

A̲ B̲ C̲ D̲ E̲ F̲ G̲ H̲ I̲ J̲ K̲ L̲ M̲ N̲ O̲ P̲ Q̲ R̲ S̲ T̲ U̲ V̲ W̲ X̲ Y̲ Z̲

9   J K L M N O P Q R S T U V W X Y Z A B C D E F G H I

specifies T_9, which makes the substitutions

A → J   B → K   ...   Z → I

TABLE 2.4.2

Vigenère Table

Key	A̲	B	C̲	D̲	E̲	F̲	G̲	H̲	I	J̲	K̲	L̲	M̲	N̲	O̲	P̲	Q̲	R̲	S̲	T̲	U̲	V̲	W̲	X̲	Y̲	Z̲
0	A	B	C	D	E	F	G	H	I	J	K	L	M	N	O	P	Q	R	S	T	U	V	W	X	Y	Z
1	B	C	D	E	F	G	H	I	J	K	L	M	N	O	P	Q	R	S	T	U	V	W	X	Y	Z	A
2	C	D	E	F	G	H	I	J	K	L	M	N	O	P	Q	R	S	T	U	V	W	X	Y	Z	A	B
3	D	E	F	G	H	I	J	K	L	M	N	O	P	Q	R	S	T	U	V	W	X	Y	Z	A	B	C
4	E	F	G	H	I	J	K	L	M	N	O	P	Q	R	S	T	U	V	W	X	Y	Z	A	B	C	D
5	F	G	H	I	J	K	L	M	N	O	P	Q	R	S	T	U	V	W	X	Y	Z	A	B	C	D	E
6	G	H	I	J	K	L	M	N	O	P	Q	R	S	T	U	V	W	X	Y	Z	A	B	C	D	E	F
7	H	I	J	K	L	M	N	O	P	Q	R	S	T	U	V	W	X	Y	Z	A	B	C	D	E	F	G
8	I	J	K	L	M	N	O	P	Q	R	S	T	U	V	W	X	Y	Z	A	B	C	D	E	F	G	H
9	J	K	L	M	N	O	P	Q	R	S	T	U	V	W	X	Y	Z	A	B	C	D	E	F	G	H	I
10	K	L	M	N	O	P	Q	R	S	T	U	V	W	X	Y	Z	A	B	C	D	E	F	G	H	I	J
11	L	M	N	O	P	Q	R	S	T	U	V	W	X	Y	Z	A	B	C	D	E	F	G	H	I	J	K
12	M	N	O	P	Q	R	S	T	U	V	W	X	Y	Z	A	B	C	D	E	F	G	H	I	J	K	L
13	N	O	P	Q	R	S	T	U	V	W	X	Y	Z	A	B	C	D	E	F	G	H	I	J	K	L	M
14	O	P	Q	R	S	T	U	V	W	X	Y	Z	A	B	C	D	E	F	G	H	I	J	K	L	M	N
15	P	Q	R	S	T	U	V	W	X	Y	Z	A	B	C	D	E	F	G	H	I	J	K	L	M	N	O
16	Q	R	S	T	U	V	W	X	Y	Z	A	B	C	D	E	F	G	H	I	J	K	L	M	N	O	P
17	R	S	T	U	V	W	X	Y	Z	A	B	C	D	E	F	G	H	I	J	K	L	M	N	O	P	Q
18	S	T	U	V	W	X	Y	Z	A	B	C	D	E	F	G	H	I	J	K	L	M	N	O	P	Q	R
19	T	U	V	W	X	Y	Z	A	B	C	D	E	F	G	H	I	J	K	L	M	N	O	P	Q	R	S
20	U	V	W	X	Y	Z	A	B	C	D	E	F	G	H	I	J	K	L	M	N	O	P	Q	R	S	T
21	V	W	X	Y	Z	A	B	C	D	E	F	G	H	I	J	K	L	M	N	O	P	Q	R	S	T	U
22	W	X	Y	Z	A	B	C	D	E	F	G	H	I	J	K	L	M	N	O	P	Q	R	S	T	U	V
23	X	Y	Z	A	B	C	D	E	F	G	H	I	J	K	L	M	N	O	P	Q	R	S	T	U	V	W
24	Y	Z	A	B	C	D	E	F	G	H	I	J	K	L	M	N	O	P	Q	R	S	T	U	V	W	X
25	Z	A	B	C	D	E	F	G	H	I	J	K	L	M	N	O	P	Q	R	S	T	U	V	W	X	Y

The key space $\boldsymbol{K} = \boldsymbol{Z}_{26}$ contains 26 elements. The cryptographic transformation T_k is *letter-by letter* substitution:

$$T_k : \mathbf{x} = (x_0, x_1, \ldots, x_{n-1}) \rightarrow \mathbf{y} = (y_0, y_1, \ldots, y_{n-1})$$

$$y_i = T_k(x_i) \qquad 0 \leq i < n$$

Thus, T_4(HELP) = LIPT and T_6(HELP) = NKRV.

2.5 CRYPTANALYSIS BY THE BAYESIAN OPPONENT

Let $\boldsymbol{T} = \{T_k : k \in \boldsymbol{K}\}$ be a cryptographic system. Users agree upon a key, thereby selecting a particular transformation from the family $\boldsymbol{T}$. We assume that an opponent observes ciphertext **y** enciphered by some transformation in $\boldsymbol{T}$. The system $\boldsymbol{T}$ is known to the opponent, meaning a description of the key space $\boldsymbol{K}$ and the manner by which a key k in $\boldsymbol{K}$ determines T_k, but not the particular key selected by the users. The Bayesian formulation of cryptanalysis represents the opponent's knowledge of the key by a probability distribution on keys; $Pr_{KEY}\{k\}$ is the opponent's *a priori* estimate of the probability that users select the key k. We assume that the generation of plaintext and the selection of a key are independent statistical processes. The relationship of the opponent to the cryptographic system is shown in Fig. 2.5.1. The opponent's problem is to estimate the plaintext and/or key based on the information provided by

- Ciphertext **y**.
- Knowledge of the family of cryptographic transformations $\{T_k : K \in \boldsymbol{K}\}$.
- The probability distribution on plaintext Pr_{PLAIN}.
- The probability distribution on keys Pr_{KEY}.

Encipherment transforms a plaintext-key pair $(\mathbf{x},k)$ into ciphertext $\mathbf{y} = T_k(\mathbf{x})$. The *a priori* probability distributions Pr_{PLAIN} and Pr_{KEY} induce the following joint and conditional distributions:

$Pr_{PLAIN,KEY}\{\mathbf{x},k\}$	*joint distribution of plaintext* **x** *and key k*
$Pr_{PLAIN,CIPHER}\{\mathbf{x},\mathbf{y}\}$	*joint distribution of plaintext* **x** *and ciphertext* **y**
$Pr_{CIPHER,KEY}\{\mathbf{y},k\}$	*joint distribution of ciphertext* **y** *and key k*

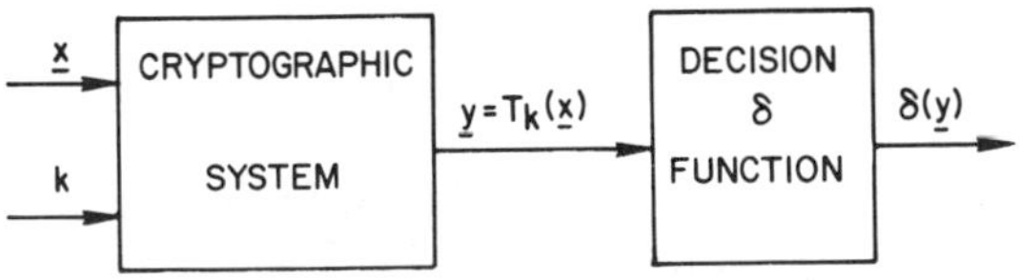

Figure 2.5.1. The Bayesian formulation of cryptanalysis.

$Pr_{CIPHER}\{\mathbf{y}\}$	*marginal distribution of ciphertext y*
$Pr_{PLAIN/CIPHER}\{\mathbf{x}/\mathbf{y}\}$	*conditional distribution of plaintext **x** given ciphertext y*
$Pr_{KEY/CIPHER}\{k/\mathbf{y}\}$	*conditional distribution of key k given ciphertext y*

which are defined by

$$Pr_{PLAIN,KEY}\{\mathbf{x},k\} = Pr_{PLAIN}\{\mathbf{x}\}Pr_{KEY}\{k\}$$

$$Pr_{PLAIN,CIPHER}\{\mathbf{x},\mathbf{y}\} = \sum_{\{k:T_k(\mathbf{x})=\mathbf{y}\}} Pr_{PLAIN}\{\mathbf{x}\}Pr_{KEY}\{k\}$$

$$Pr_{CIPHER,KEY}\{\mathbf{y},k\} = \sum_{\{\mathbf{x}:T_k(\mathbf{x})=\mathbf{y}\}} Pr_{PLAIN}\{\mathbf{x}\}Pr_{KEY}\{k\}$$

$$Pr_{CIPHER}\{\mathbf{y}\} = \sum_{\{(\mathbf{x},k):T_k(\mathbf{x})=\mathbf{y}\}} Pr_{PLAIN}\{\mathbf{x}\}Pr_{KEY}\{k\}$$

$$Pr_{PLAIN/CIPHER}\{\mathbf{x}/\mathbf{y}\} = Pr_{PLAIN,CIPHER}\{\mathbf{x},\mathbf{y}\}/Pr_{CIPHER}\{\mathbf{y}\}$$

$$Pr_{KEY/CIPHER}\{k/\mathbf{y}\} = Pr_{CIPHER,KEY}\{\mathbf{y},k\}/Pr_{CIPHER}\{\mathbf{y}\}$$

The conditional distributions are defined *only* when $Pr_{CIPHER}\{\mathbf{y}\} > 0$.

The probability distributions Pr_{PLAIN} and Pr_{KEY} and the intercepted ciphertext $\mathbf{y} = T_k(\mathbf{x})$ constitute the total information upon which the opponent will base the estimation of the plaintext **x** and key k. The action taken by an opponent is represented in Fig. 2.5.1 by the decision function δ, which makes the decision

"ciphertext **y** originated from the encipherment of plaintext $\delta(\mathbf{y})$"

Definition 2.5.1 A *deterministic decision function* $\delta = \{\delta^{(n)}\}$ is a sequence of transformations

$$\delta^{(n)} : \boldsymbol{Z}_{m,n} \to \boldsymbol{Z}_{m,n} \qquad n = 1,2, \ldots$$

$$\delta^{(n)} : \mathbf{y} \to \delta^{(n)}(\mathbf{y})$$

We let Δ_D denote the family of deterministic decision functions.

Note that the opponent's decision $\delta(\mathbf{y})$ is the same for *all* pairs $(\mathbf{x},k)$ which satisfy $T_k(\mathbf{x}) = \mathbf{y}$. Therefore a decision function δ will produce an incorrect estimate of the plaintext for the opponent for all pairs $(\mathbf{x},k)$ that satisfy $\delta(T_k(\mathbf{x})) \neq \mathbf{x}$. To compare decision functions, we introduce a *loss function* L_δ defined by

$$L_\delta(\mathbf{x},\mathbf{y}) = \begin{cases} 1 & \text{if } \delta(\mathbf{y}) \neq \mathbf{x} \\ 0 & \text{if } \delta(\mathbf{y}) = \mathbf{x} \end{cases}$$

$L_\delta(\mathbf{x},T_k(\mathbf{x}))$ assigns the loss of zero to a correct decision and the loss of one to an incorrect decision. The *average loss of the deterministic decision function δ on n-grams* is the expectation of the random variable $L_\delta(\mathbf{X},\mathbf{Y})$ with respect to the joint probability distribution $Pr_{PLAIN,CIPHER}$ on the set of n-grams pairs $(\mathbf{X},\mathbf{Y})$

$$l_{n,\delta} \equiv E\{L_{\delta(n)}\} = \sum_{\{x,y \in Z_{m,n}\}} Pr_{PLAIN,CIPHER}\{x,y\}\ L_\delta(x,y)$$

The *average loss of the function* δ is the sequence of values

$$l_\delta = \{l_{n,\delta} : n = 1,2, \ldots\}.$$

The (deterministic) *Bayesian strategy* is to use a function δ in Δ_D that mimimizes the loss $l_{\delta,n}$ for every n, $1 \leq n < \infty$.

Definition 2.5.2 A deterministic decision function δ^* is *optimal* if

$$l_{n,\delta^*} \leq l_{n,\delta} \qquad \text{for all } \delta \in \Delta_D \quad \text{and } n = 1,2, \ldots$$

A special class of deterministic decision functions are easy to describe.

Definition 2.5.3 A deterministic decision function δ_B is *Bayesian* if

$$Pr_{PLAIN/CIPHER}\{\delta_B(y)/y\} = \max_x P_{PLAIN/CIPHER}\{x/y\}$$

$$\delta_B(y) = x \text{ only if } Pr_{PLAIN/CIPHER}\{x/y\} = \max_v Pr_{PLAIN/CIPHER}\{v/y\}.$$

The decision function δ_B is defined for ciphertext y that satisfies $Pr_{CIPHER}\{y\} > 0$.

Note that there may be more than one plaintext (n-gram) x that maximizes the a posteriori conditional probabiility $Pr_{PLAIN/CIPHER}\{x/y\}$ and hence possibly more than one Bayesian decision function δ_B. The optimal decision functions in Δ_D are easy to describe.

Theorem 2.5.4 A deterministic decision function δ is optimal if and only if it is Bayesian.

Proof. The expected loss of δ on n-grams is

$$l_{n,\delta} = \sum_{\{y \in Z_{m,n}\}} Pr_{CIPHER}\{y\} \sum_{\{x \in Z_{m,n}\}} Pr_{PLAIN/CIPHER}\{x/y\}\ L_\delta(x,y)$$

$$= \sum_{\{y \in Z_{m,n}\}} Pr_{CIPHER}\{y\}\ (1 - Pr_{PLAIN/CIPHER}\{\delta^{(n)}(y)/y\})$$

$l_{n,\delta}$ will be a minimum if and only if $\delta^{(n)}(y)$ makes

$$\sigma^{(n)}(y) = Pr_{PLAIN/CIPHER}\{\delta^{(n)}(y)/y\}$$

a maximum for each n-gram y (of positive probability $Pr_{CIPHER}\{y\}$). Thus $l_{n,\delta}$ will be a minimum if and only if $\delta^{(n)}(y)$ satisfies

$$Pr_{PLAIN/CIPHER}\{\delta^{(n)}(y)/y\} = \max_{\{x \in Z_{m,n}\}} Pr_{PLAIN/CIPHER}\{x/y\}$$

proving that the Bayesian decision functions δ_B are optimal in the class of deterministic decision functions. Moreover, every Bayesian decision function has the same expected cost l_δ. ◀

A more general class of decision functions, called *stochastic decision functions* may be introduced.

Definition 2.5.5 A *stochastic decision function* δ is the sequence of m^n by m^n matrices

$$\delta = \{\delta^{(n)} = (\delta^{(n)}(\mathbf{y},\mathbf{x})), \mathbf{x},\mathbf{y} \in \boldsymbol{Z}_{\mathbf{m,n}} : n = 1,2, \ldots\}$$

The entries of $\delta^{(n)}(\mathbf{y}, \mathbf{x})$ are nonnegative real numbers; the sum of the entries in $\delta^{(n)}$ along every row $\mathbf{y}$ is equal to one.

$$\delta^{(n)}(\mathbf{y},\mathbf{x}) \geq 0$$

$$1 = \sum_{\mathbf{x}} \delta^{(n)}(\mathbf{y},\mathbf{x}) \qquad \text{for all } \mathbf{y} \in \boldsymbol{Z}_{\mathbf{m,n}}$$

Δ_S denotes the family of stochastic decision functions.

Having intercepted the ciphertext n-gram $\mathbf{y}$, the decision of the opponent is determined as the result of a chance experiment whose outcome is the plaintext n-gram $\mathbf{x}$ with probability $\delta^{(n)}(\mathbf{y},\mathbf{x})$. A deterministic decision function δ is a special case of a stochastic decision function $\delta^{(n)}(\mathbf{y},\mathbf{x})$, in which the entry in row $\mathbf{y}$ and column $\mathbf{x} = \delta^{(n)}(\mathbf{y})$ is equal to one, and all remaining entries are equal to zero.

An r by s matrix $S = (s_{i,j})$ is called a *stochastic matrix* if

$$s_{i,j} \geq 0 \qquad 0 \leq i < r,\ 0 \leq j < s$$

$$1 = \sum_{0 \leq j < s} s_{i,j} \qquad 0 \leq i < r$$

A stochastic matrix P in which every row contains a single entry equal to one is called a *permutation matrix*. Every stochastic matrix S may be expressed as a *convex combination* of a finite number of permutation matrices.

$$S = \sum_i \lambda_i P_i$$

$$\lambda_i \geq 0 \qquad 1 = \sum_i \lambda_i$$

For example, the 2 by 2 stochastic matrix

$$S = \begin{vmatrix} \frac{1}{2} & \frac{1}{2} \\ \frac{1}{2} & \frac{1}{2} \end{vmatrix}$$

is the convex combination

$$S = (\tfrac{1}{2})P_1 + (\tfrac{1}{2})P_2$$

with

$$P_1 = \begin{vmatrix} 1 & 0 \\ 0 & 1 \end{vmatrix} \qquad P_2 = \begin{vmatrix} 0 & 1 \\ 1 & 0 \end{vmatrix}$$

A stochastic decision function δ is a convex combination of deterministic decision functions in the sense that

$$\delta^{(n)}(\mathbf{y},\mathbf{x}) = \sum_i \lambda_{i,n}\delta_i^{(n)}(\mathbf{y},\mathbf{x}) \qquad n = 1,2,\ldots$$

(2.5.1)
$$\lambda_{i,n} \geq 0 \qquad \sum_i \lambda_{i,n} = 1$$

The decision made by the opponent using the function $\delta^{(n)}$ in Eq. (2.5.1) is a two-step process:

Step 1 Perform a chance experiment; the outcome is $\delta_i^{(n)}$ with probability $\lambda_{i,n}$.

Step 2 Make the decision associated with the deterministic function $\delta_i^{(n)}$.

Do stochastic decision functions improve the ability of the Bayesian opponent to make better estimates of the unknown plaintext? The answer is no.

The *average loss of the stochastic decision function* δ *on n-grams* is the expectation

$$\begin{aligned} l_{n,\delta} &= \sum_{\{\mathbf{y}\in Z_{m,n}\}} \Pr_{CIPHER}\{\mathbf{y}\} \sum_{\{\mathbf{x},\mathbf{v}\in Z_{m,n},\mathbf{x}\neq\mathbf{v}\}} \Pr_{PLAIN/CIPHER}\{\mathbf{x}/\mathbf{y}\}\, \delta^{(n)}(\mathbf{y},\mathbf{v}) \\ &= \sum_{\{\mathbf{y}\in Z_{m,n}\}} \Pr_{CIPHER}\{\mathbf{y}\}\,(1 - \sum_{\{\mathbf{x}\in Z_{m,n}\}} \Pr_{PLAIN/CIPHER}\{\mathbf{x}/\mathbf{y}\}\, \delta^{(n)}(\mathbf{y},\mathbf{x})) \end{aligned}$$

$l_{n,\delta}$ will be a minimum if and only if $\delta^{(n)}(\mathbf{y},\mathbf{x})$ minimizes

$$(1 - \sum_{\{\mathbf{x}\in Z_{m,n}\}} \Pr_{PLAIN/CIPHER}\{\mathbf{x}/\mathbf{y}\}\, \delta^{(n)}(\mathbf{y},\mathbf{x}))$$

for each n-gram $\mathbf{y}$ with $\Pr_{CIPHER}\{\mathbf{y}\} > 0$. Equivalently, δ is optimal if and only if $\delta^{(n)}(\mathbf{y},\mathbf{x})$ maximizes

$$\sigma^{(n)}(\mathbf{y}) = \sum_{\{\mathbf{x}\in Z_{m,n}\}} \Pr_{PLAIN/CIPHER}\{\mathbf{x}/\mathbf{y}\}\, \delta^{(n)}(\mathbf{y},\mathbf{x})$$

for every n-gram $\mathbf{y}$ with $\Pr_{CIPHER}\{\mathbf{y}\} > 0$ and $n = 1, 2, \ldots$. Finally, $\sigma^{(n)}(\mathbf{y})$ is maximized if and only if $\delta^{(n)}(\mathbf{y},\mathbf{x}) = 0$ whenever

$$\Pr_{PLAIN/CIPHER}\{\mathbf{x}/\mathbf{y}\} < \max_{\{\mathbf{v}\in Z_{m,n}\}} \Pr_{PLAIN/CIPHER}\{\mathbf{v}/\mathbf{y}\}$$

Thus we have proved the following theorem.

Theorem 2.5.6 A stochastic decision function δ is optimal if and only if

$$\delta^{(n)}(\mathbf{y},\mathbf{x}) > 0 \text{ implies } \Pr_{PLAIN/CIPHER}\{\mathbf{x}/\mathbf{y}\} = \max_{\{\mathbf{v}\in Z_{m,n}\}} \Pr_{PLAIN/CIPHER}\{\mathbf{v}/\mathbf{y}\}$$

for all pairs of n-grams $(\mathbf{x},\mathbf{y})$ and every $n = 1, 2, \ldots$.

If there is more than one plaintext $\mathbf{x}$ that maximizes $\Pr_{PLAIN/CIPHER}\{\mathbf{x}/\mathbf{y}\}$ for some $\mathbf{y}$, or equivalently, if more than one deterministic Bayesian decision function δ_B

exists, the probabilities $\{\lambda_{i,n}\}$ in Eq. (2.5.1) can be assigned in any way by the opponent to the family of deterministic Bayesian decisions $\{\delta_i^{(n)}\}$ generating the optimal stochastic decision functions. Every optimal stochastic decision function has the same average loss.

Example 2.5.2 Assume that each of the 26 keys in the Vigenère substitution system of Example 2.4.1 are assigned equal probabilitity, $\Pr_{KEY}\{k\} = 1/26$. We encipher SENDHELP with T_7, obtaining

$$\texttt{ZLUKOLSW} = T_7(\texttt{SENDHELP})$$

In Table 2.5.2 we list the conditional probability

$$\Pr_{PLAIN/CIPHER}\{\mathbf{x}/\texttt{ZLUKOLSW}\}$$

for all plaintext n-grams for which $\Pr_{PLAIN/CIPHER}\{\mathbf{x}/\texttt{ZLUKOLSW}\} > 0$. To compute $\Pr_{PLAIN/CIPHER}\{\mathbf{x}/\texttt{ZLUKOLSW}\}$ replace the letters of ZLUKOLSW and SENDHELP by their numerical representations using the correspondence in Table 2.2.1:

$$\texttt{ZLUKOLSW} \rightarrow (25, 11, 20, 10, 14, 11, 18, 22) = (y_0, y_1, \ldots, y_7)$$

$$\texttt{SENDHELP} \rightarrow (18, 4, 13, 3, 7, 4, 11, 15)$$

$$(25, 11, 20, 10, 14, 11, 18, 22) = T_7(18, 4, 13, 3, 7, 4, 11, 15)$$

$$= (18, 4, 13, 3, 7, 4, 11, 15) + 7 \text{ (modulo 26)}$$

The only plaintext 8-grams that can be enciphered into ZLUKOLSW are

$$\mathbf{y} - k = (y_0 - k, y_1 - k, \ldots, y_7 - k) \text{ (modulo 26)}$$

where k is allowed to assume any of the values in $\boldsymbol{Z}_{26}$.

Thus

$$\Pr_{PLAIN,CIPHER}\{\mathbf{x},\mathbf{y}\} = \begin{cases} (1/26)\Pr_{PLAIN}\{\mathbf{y} - k\} & \text{if } \mathbf{x} = \mathbf{y} - k \text{ for some } k \in \boldsymbol{Z}_{26} \\ 0 & \text{otherwise} \end{cases}$$

and

$$\Pr_{CIPHER}\{\mathbf{y}\} = \sum_{0 \le i < 26} \Pr_{PLAIN,CIPHER}\{\mathbf{y} - i, \mathbf{y}\} = \sum_{0 \le i < 26} (1/26)\Pr_{PLAIN}\{\mathbf{y} - i\}$$

yielding

$$\Pr_{PLAIN/CIPHER}\{\mathbf{y} - k/\mathbf{y}\} = \Pr_{PLAIN}\{\mathbf{y} - k\} \Big/ \sum_{0 \le i < 26} \Pr_{PLAIN}\{\mathbf{y} - i\}$$

In each of the three examples,

$$\Pr_{PLAIN/CIPHER}\{\mathbf{x}/\texttt{ZLUKOLSW}\}$$

is maximized by a single 8-gram $\mathbf{x}$, and δ_B yields the decisions

TABLE 2.5.2
Conditional Probability of Plaintext, Given Ciphertext `ZLUKOLSW`

k	x	*Example 2.3.1*	*Example 2.3.2*	*Example 2.3.3*
0	ZLUKOLSW	0.00002353	0.00000089	0.00000309
1	YKTJNKRV	0.00000736	0.00000000	0.00000000
2	XJSIMJQU	0.00000003	0.00000000	0.00000000
3	WIRHLIPT	0.05269719	0.00418837	0.00033815
4	VHQGKHOS	0.00004373	0.00000000	0.00000000
5	UGPFJGNR	0.00012522	0.00000000	0.00000000
6	TFOEIFMQ	0.00601645	0.00000000	0.00000000
7	SENDHELP	0.35013155	**0.99580491**	**0.99965766**
8	RDMCGDKO	0.00158882	0.00000088	0.00000000
9	QCLBFCJN	0.00000412	0.00000000	0.00000000
10	PBKAEBIM	0.00100489	0.00000000	0.00000000
11	OAJZDAHL	0.00013951	0.00000000	0.00000000
12	NZIYCZGK	0.00000043	0.00000000	0.00000000
13	MYHXBYFJ	0.00000164	0.00000000	0.00000000
14	LXGWAXEI	0.00007197	0.00000000	0.00000000
15	KWFVZWDH	0.00000134	0.00000000	0.00000000
16	JVEUYVCG	0.00001388	0.00000000	0.00000000
17	IUDTXUBF	0.00037299	0.00000000	0.00000000
18	HTCSWTAE	**0.58014350**	0.00000495	0.00000111
19	GSBRVSZD	0.00006560	0.00000000	0.00000000
20	FRAQURYC	0.00066643	0.00000000	0.00000000
21	EQZPTQXB	0.00000002	0.00000000	0.00000000
22	DPYOSPWA	0.00658287	0.00000000	0.00000000
23	COXNROVZ	0.00003584	0.00000000	0.00000000
24	BNWMQNUY	0.00005462	0.00000000	0.00000000
25	AMVLPMTX	0.00020646	0.00000000	0.00000000

Example	δ_B(`ZLUKOLSW`)	**k**
2.3.1	HTCSWTAE	18
2.3.2	SENDHELP	7
2.3.3	SENDHELP	7

If the opponent models the generation of plaintext as in Example 2.3.1, the Bayesian decision makes an incorrect decision. The source of the error is the simplicity of the model of Definition 2.3.1, which ignores the interletter dependence in the English language text and the small amount of intercepted ciphertext. Thus `HTCSWTAE`, which contains more high frequency letters (`A`, `E`, `S`, `T`) than does `SENDHELP`, is accorded a higher conditional probability of occurrence.

If a Bayesian rule δ_B is applied to a longer segment of ciphertext, say the 12-gram `ZLUKOLSWZVVU` = T_7(`SENDHELPSOON`), then δ_B(`ZLUKOLSWZVVU`) = `SENDHELPSOON` for each of the plaintext sources (Examples 2.3.1–3) as shown in Table 2.5.3.

TABLE 2.5.3

Conditional Probability of Plaintext, Given Ciphertext ZLUKOLSWZVVU

k	x	*Example 2.3.1*	*Example 2.3.2*	*Example 2.3.3*
0	ZLUKOLSWZVVU	0.00000000	0.00000000	0.00000000
1	YKTJNKRVYUUT	0.00000086	0.00000000	0.00000000
2	XJSIMJQUXTTS	0.00000000	0.00000000	0.00000000
3	WIRHLIPTWSSR	0.01786092	0.00000591	0.00000398
4	VHQGKHOSVRRQ	0.00000020	0.00000000	0.00000000
5	UGPFJGNRUQQP	0.00000001	0.00000000	0.00000000
6	TFOEIFMQTPPO	0.00180525	0.00000000	0.00000000
7	SENDHELPSOON	**0.86667452**	**0.99999407**	**0.99999602**
8	RDMCGDKORNNM	0.00121590	0.00000002	0.00000000
9	QCLBFCJNQMML	0.00000001	0.00000000	0.00000000
10	PBKAEBIMPLLK	0.00000871	0.00000000	0.00000000
11	OAJZDAHLOKKJ	0.00000002	0.00000000	0.00000000
12	NZIYCZGKNJJI	0.00000000	0.00000000	0.00000000
13	MYHXBYFJMIIH	0.00000077	0.00000000	0.00000000
14	LXGWAXEILHHG	0.00001228	0.00000000	0.00000000
15	KWFVZWDHKGGF	0.00000001	0.00000000	0.00000000
16	JVEUYVCGJFFE	0.00000018	0.00000000	0.00000000
16	IUDTXUBFIEED	0.00136843	0.00000000	0.00000000
17	HTCSWTAEHDDC	0.11101794	0.00000000	0.00000000
18	GSBRVSZDGCCB	0.00000129	0.00000000	0.00000000
19	FRAQURYCFBBA	0.00002909	0.00000000	0.00000000
20	EQZPTQXBEAAZ	0.00000000	0.00000000	0.00000000
21	DPYOSPWADZZY	0.00000026	0.00000000	0.00000000
23	COXNROVZCYYX	0.00000006	0.00000000	0.00000000
24	BNWMQNUYBXXW	0.00000000	0.00000000	0.00000000
25	AMVLPMTXAWWV	0.00000328	0.00000000	0.00000000

2.6 THE BAYESIAN DECISION AS $n \to \infty$

The previous example suggests an obvious conjecture: *a Bayesian decision function will recover the plaintext provided the decision is based upon a large enough sample of ciphertext.* In this section, we shall show that this is true at least if (1) plaintext is generated according to Definition 2.3.1, and (2) encipherment is by the Vigenère system (Example 2.4.1). We begin by calculating the conditional probability $\Pr_{PLAIN/CIPHER}\{\mathbf{x}/\mathbf{y}\}$. Associate with the n-gram $\mathbf{z} = (z_0, z_1, \ldots, z_{n-1})$ (in the alphabet Z_m) the vector $N(\mathbf{z})$ of *letter counts,*

$$N(\mathbf{z}) = (N_0(\mathbf{z}), N_1(\mathbf{z}), \ldots, N_{m-1}(\mathbf{z}))$$

where

$N_0(\mathbf{z})$	the number of times the letter 0 occurs in $\mathbf{z}$
$N_1(\mathbf{z})$	the number of times the letter 1 occurs in $\mathbf{z}$
	. . .
$N_{m-1}(\mathbf{z})$	the number of times the letter $m-1$ occurs in $\mathbf{z}$

We can express $N_i(\mathbf{X})$ by means of the formula

$$N_t(\mathbf{X}) = \sum_{0 \le i < n} \chi_t(X_i)$$

where the *indicator* function χ_t is defined by

$$\chi_t(X_i) = \begin{cases} 1 & \text{if } X_i = t \\ 0 & \text{if } X_i \neq t \end{cases}$$

Since the random variables $X_0, X_1, \ldots, X_{n-1}$ are independent and identically distributed, the same is true of the random variables

$$\chi_t(X_0), \chi_t(X_1), \ldots, \chi_t(X_{n-1})$$

for each *fixed* t, $0 \le t < m$. The n random variables $\{\chi_t(X_i) : 0 \le i < n\}$ take the values 0 or 1 with probabilities

$$\Pr\{\chi_t(X_i) = k\} = \begin{cases} p(t) & \text{if } k = 1 \\ 1 - p(t) & \text{if } k = 0 \end{cases}$$

$\{\chi_t(X_i) : 0 \le i < n\}$ is therefore an example of a *Bernoulli sequence,* so that

$$N_t(\mathbf{X}) = N_t(X_0, X_1, \ldots, X_{n-1}) = \sum_{0 \le i < n} \chi_t(X_i)$$

has the *binomial distribution* $B(n,p(t))$,

$$\Pr\{N_t(\mathbf{X}) = k\} = C(n,k)(p(t))^k(1 - p(t))^{n-k} \qquad 0 \le k \le n$$

with expectation and variance

$$E\{N_t(\mathbf{X})\} = np(t) \qquad \mathrm{Var}\{N_t(\mathbf{X})\} = np(t)(1 - p(t))$$

The generating function of $N_t(\mathbf{X})$ is the polynomial in z defined by

$$\begin{aligned} E\{z^{N_t(\mathbf{X})}\} &= \sum_{0 \le k < n} \Pr\{N_t(\mathbf{X}) = k\}z^k \\ &= \sum_{0 \le k < n} C(n,k)(p(t))^k(1 - p(t))^{n-k}z^k \\ &= (1 - p(t) + p(t)z)^n \end{aligned}$$

While the $\{X_i : 0 \le i < n\}$ are independent, the $\{N_t(\mathbf{X}) : 0 \le t < m\}$ are not. The $\{N_t(\mathbf{x})\}$ are dependent because they satisfy the relationship

$$n = N_0(\mathbf{X}) + N_1(\mathbf{X}) + \ldots + N_{m-1}(\mathbf{X})$$

The random variables $\{N_t(\mathbf{X}) : 0 \le t < m\}$ have the *multinomial distribution*

$$\begin{aligned} &\Pr\{N_0(\mathbf{X}) = k_0, N_1(\mathbf{X}) = k_1, \ldots, N_{m-1}(\mathbf{X}) = k_{m-1}\} \\ &\quad = C(n,k_0,k_1, \ldots, k_{m-1})\, (p(0))^{k_0}(p(1))^{k_1} \ldots (p(m - 1))^{k_{m-1}} \end{aligned}$$

as their joint distribution, where the integers $k_0, k_1, \ldots, k_{m-1}$ satisfy

$$0 \le k_j \le n \qquad 0 \le j < m \qquad n = k_0 + k_1 + \ldots + k_{m-1}$$

and $C(n, k_0, k_1, \ldots, k_{m-1})$ is the *multinomial coefficient*

$$C(n, k_0, k_1, \ldots, k_{m-1}) = n!/k_0!k_1!\cdots k_{m-1}!$$

The joint generating function of the m-dimensional random variable $(N_0(\mathbf{X}), N_1(\mathbf{X}), \ldots, N_{m-1}(\mathbf{X}))$ is the polynomial in the m variables $z_0, z_1, \ldots, z_{m-1}$ defined by

$$E\{z_0^{N_0(\mathbf{X})} z_1^{N_1(\mathbf{X})} \ldots z_{m-1}^{N_{m-1}(\mathbf{X})}\}$$

$$= \sum_{\{k_0, k_1, \ldots, k_{m-1}\}} \Pr\{N_0(\mathbf{X}) = k_0, N_1(\mathbf{X}) = k_1, \ldots, N_{m-1}(\mathbf{X}) = k_{m-1}\} z_0^{k_0} z_1^{k_1} \ldots z_{m-1}^{k_{m-1}}$$

$$= \sum_{\{k_0, k_1, \ldots, k_{m-1}\}} C(n, k_0, k_1, \ldots, k_{m-1})(z_0 p(0))^{k_0}(z_1 p(1))^{k_1} \ldots (z_{m-1} p(m-1))^{k_{m-1}}$$

$$= (p(0)z_0 + p(1)z_1 + \ldots + p(m-1)z_{m-1})^n$$

Now it remains to repeat this analysis for the ciphertext $(Y_0, Y_1, \ldots, Y_{n-1})$. The relationship between plaintext $(X_0, X_1, \ldots, X_{n-1})$ and ciphertext $(Y_0, Y_1, \ldots, Y_{n-1})$ is

$$(Y_0, Y_1, \ldots, Y_{n-1}) = (X_0, X_1, \ldots, X_{n-1}) + k \text{ (modulo m)}$$

where k is the key and the addition above is component-by-component addition modulo m — $Y_i = k + X_i$ (modulo m). The relationship

$$\mathbf{Y} = \mathbf{X} + k \text{ (modulo m)}$$

implies $N(\mathbf{Y}) = N^{(k)}(\mathbf{X})$, where $N^{(k)}(\mathbf{X})$ is the *right cyclic rotation* of $N(\mathbf{X})$ by k places

$$N^{(k)}(\mathbf{X}) = (N_{0-k}(\mathbf{X}), N_{1-k}(\mathbf{X}), \ldots, N_{m-1-k}(\mathbf{X}))$$

It follows that $N_i(\mathbf{Y})$ has the same probability distribution as $N_{i-k}(\mathbf{X})$ for *some* value of k and we have therefore proved the following theorem.

Theorem 2.6.1 If (1) the source is as in Definition 2.3.1, and (2) encipherment is as in Example 2.4.1,

$$\mathbf{Y} = T_k(\mathbf{X})$$

Then:

- For each t, $0 \le t < m$, the number of occurrences $N_t(\mathbf{X})$ of t in an n-gram sample of plaintext $\mathbf{X}$ has the binomial distribution $B(n,p(t))$.
- For each t, $0 \le t < m$, the number of occurrences $N_t(\mathbf{Y})$ of t in an n-gram of ciphertext $\mathbf{Y} = T_k(\mathbf{X})$ has the binomial distribution $B(n,p(t-k))$.

Now we are prepared to study the Bayesian decision function δ_B. If $\mathbf{z} = (z_0, z_1, \ldots, z_{n-1})$ is an n-gram, let

$$p[N^{(k)}(\mathbf{z})] = (p(0))^{N_{0-k}(\mathbf{z})}(p(1))^{N_{1-k}(\mathbf{z})} \dots (p(m-1))^{N_{m-1-k}(\mathbf{z})}$$
$$= Pr_{PLAIN}\{(X_0, X_1, \dots, X_{n-1}) = (z_0, z_1, \dots, z_{n-1}) - k \text{ (modulo m)}\}$$

The conditional probability $Pr_{PLAIN}\{\mathbf{x}/\mathbf{y}\}$ is positive if and only if $\mathbf{y} = \mathbf{x} + k = T_k(\mathbf{x})$ for some k, $0 \leq k < m$, so that

$$Pr_{PLAIN,CIPHER}\{\mathbf{x},\mathbf{y}\} = \begin{cases} p[N^{(-j)}(\mathbf{y})]\,Pr_{KEY}\{j\} & \text{if } \mathbf{x} = \mathbf{y} - j \text{ (modulo m) for some } j,\ 0 \leq j < m \\ 0 & \text{otherwise} \end{cases}$$

and

$$Pr_{CIPHER}\{\mathbf{y}\} = \sum_{0 \leq i < m} p[N^{(-i)}(\mathbf{y})]\,Pr_{KEY}\{i\}$$

yielding

$$(2.6.1) \qquad Pr_{PLAIN/CIPHER}\{\mathbf{x}/\mathbf{y}\} = p[N^{(-j)}(\mathbf{y})]\,Pr_{KEY}\{j\} \Big/ \sum_{0 \leq i < m} p[N^{(-i)}(\mathbf{y})]\,Pr_{KEY}\{i\}$$

if $\mathbf{x} = \mathbf{y} - j$ (modulo m) for some j, $0 \leq j < m$ and 0 otherwise.

Only the numerator of Eq. (2.6.1) depends upon j, and thus the conditional probability $Pr_{PLAIN/CIPHER}\{\mathbf{y} - j/\mathbf{y}\}$ is maximized by values of j, which make

$$p[N^{(-j)}(\mathbf{y})]\,Pr_{KEY}\{j\} = (p(-j))^{N_0(\mathbf{y})}(p(1-j))^{N_1(\mathbf{y})} \dots (p(m-1-j))^{N_{m-1}(\mathbf{y})}Pr_{KEY}\{j\}$$

a maximum. Finally, $p[N^{(-j)}\mathbf{y})]\,Pr_{KEY}\{j\}$ is a maximum for values of j that minimize

$$(2.6.2) \qquad -(1/n) \log p[N^{(-j)}(\mathbf{y})]\,Pr_{KEY}\{j\}$$
$$= -(1/n) \log Pr_{KEY}\{j\} - \sum_{0 \leq i < m} (N_i(\mathbf{y})/n) \log p(i-j)$$

with respect to j. As $n \to \infty$, $(1/n) \log Pr_{KEY}\{j\} \to 0$, while the (strong) law of large numbers states that the ratio $N_i(\mathbf{Y})/n$ will have a limiting value as $n \to \infty$. Thus $(1/n) \log p[N^{(-j)}(\mathbf{Y})]\,Pr_{KEY}\{j\}$ has the limiting value as $n \to \infty$:

$$\text{limit}_{n\to\infty} - (1/n) \log p[N^{(-j)}(\mathbf{Y})]\,Pr_{KEY}\{j\} = - \sum_{0 \leq i < m} E\{\chi_i(Y_0)\} \log p(i-j)$$

with probability one. If $\mathbf{Y} = \mathbf{X} + k$ (modulo m),

$$\text{limit}_{n\to\infty} - (1/n) \log p[N^{(-j)}(\mathbf{Y})]\,Pr_{KEY}\{j\}$$
$$= - \sum_{0 \leq i < m} E\{\chi_i(X_0 + k)\} \log p(i-j) = - \sum_{0 \leq i < m} p(i-k) \log p(i-j)$$
$$= - \sum_{0 \leq i < m} p(i) \log p(i + k - j)$$

with probability one.

We will prove in Theorem 2.8.3 that

$$-\sum_{0<i<m} p(i) \log p(t+i) > -\sum_{0\leq i<m} p(i) \log p(i)$$

for all $t \neq 0$, provided that the probability distribution satisfies the condition

$$\bigstar\ p(t+i) = p(i) \quad \text{for every } i,\ 0 \leq i < m \quad \text{if and only if } t = 0$$

If condition ★ fails to hold, say if

$$p(i+s) = p(i) \qquad 0 \leq i < m$$

for some $s \neq 0$, then we are unable to distinguish statistically in Example 2.3.1 between plaintext and the encipherment of plaintext by T_{-s} since the joint distributions of

$$(N_0(\mathbf{X}), N_1(\mathbf{X}), \ldots, N_{m-1}(\mathbf{X}))$$
$$(N_0(T_{-s}(\mathbf{X})), N_1(T_{-s}(\mathbf{X})), \ldots, N_{m-1}(T_{-s}(\mathbf{X})))$$

are the same. We note that condition ★ holds when there exists a unique index i, for which

$$p(i) = \max_{0\leq j<m} p(j)$$

Table 2.3.1 shows that a unique maximizing probability ($p(4) = p(\text{E})$) exists for the source in Example 2.3.1. We have thus proved the following theorem.

Theorem 2.6.2 If (1) plaintext is generated as in Definition 2.3.1, (2) encipherment is as in Example 2.4.1 (3) condition ★ holds, and (4) $\mathbf{Y} = \mathbf{X} + k$ (modulo m), then $Pr_{PLAIN/CIPHER}\{\mathbf{X} + k - j/\mathbf{X} + k\}$ is maximized by $j = k$ as $n \to \infty$ with probability 1. In other words, the Bayesian opponent will be successful in recovering the plaintext as $n \to \infty$ with probability approaching one.

One final observation: the conditional probability of key given ciphertext $Pr_{KEY/CIPHER}\{j/\mathbf{y}\}$ is also given by Eq. (2.6.1), that is,

$$Pr_{KEY/CIPHER}\{j/\mathbf{y}\} = p[N^{(-j)}(\mathbf{y})]\, Pr_{KEY}\{j\} \Big/ \sum_{0\leq i<n} p[N^{(-i)}(\mathbf{y})]\, Pr_{KEY}\{i\}$$

so that the Bayesian opponent can also recover the key by maximizing the conditional probability $Pr_{KEY/CIPHER}\{j/(Y_0, Y_1, \ldots, Y_{n-1})\}$ with respect to j.

2.7 PERFECT SECRECY

The information available to an opponent about plaintext **x** is provided by the probability distribution Pr_{PLAIN}. Suppose the opponent wants to estimate what plaintext will be transmitted *before* observing the actual transmitted ciphertext? If an n-gram is to be transmitted, what is the best Bayesian estimate *before* intercepting ciphertext? The best a priori estimate is any n-gram that maximizes the probability $Pr_{PLAIN}\{(x_0, x_1, \ldots, x_{n-1})\}$. If the source is that described in Example 2.3.1–3 and n = 2, the a priori Bayesian estimates are

Example 2.3.1	Example 2.3.2	Example 2.3.3
EE	TH	TH

After intercepting ciphertext, the opponent's estimate can be revised, making use of the information contained in the intercepted ciphertext, as described in Sec. 2.6. Is it possible that ciphertext **y** could fail to provide additional information? If the a posteriori probability distribution $Pr_{PLAIN/CIPHER}\{\mathbf{x}/\mathbf{y}\}$ (*after the interception of ciphertext* **y**) is identical to the a priori probability distribution $Pr_{PLAIN}\{\mathbf{x}\}$ *(before the interception of ciphertext)*,

$$Pr_{PLAIN/CIPHER}\{\mathbf{x}/\mathbf{y}\} = Pr_{PLAIN}\{\mathbf{x}\} \text{ for all } \mathbf{y} \text{ with } Pr_{CIPHER}\{\mathbf{y}\} > 0$$

then knowledge of ciphertext does not improve the opponent's a priori estimate of which plaintext **x** was transmitted. In this case, the cryptographic system ***T*** was said by Shannon to have *perfect secrecy*. Since

$$Pr_{PLAIN/CIPHER}\{\mathbf{x}/\mathbf{y}\}Pr_{CIPHER}\{\mathbf{y}\} = Pr_{CIPHER/PLAIN}\{\mathbf{y}/\mathbf{x}\}Pr_{PLAIN}\{\mathbf{x}\}$$

whenever

$$Pr_{PLAIN}\{\mathbf{x}\} > 0 \quad Pr_{CIPHER}\{\mathbf{y}\} > 0$$

we see that perfect secrecy is also equivalent to the following condition:

(2.7.1) $$Pr_{CIPHER/PLAIN}\{\mathbf{y}/\mathbf{x}\} = Pr_{CIPHER}\{\mathbf{y}\} \text{ for all } \mathbf{x} \text{ with } Pr_{PLAIN}\{\mathbf{x}\} > 0$$

We will give an example of a system with perfect secrecy in Section 4.1.

Theorem 2.7.1 In order that Eq. (2.7.1) hold for all n-grams **x** and **y** for which $Pr_{PLAIN}\{\mathbf{x}\} > 0$ and $Pr_{CIPHER}\{\mathbf{y}\} > 0$, it is necessary that there be at least as many keys in ***K*** as there are n-grams of plaintext **x** of positive probability.

Proof. Introduce the notation

$$\mathbf{Z}_{m,n,+,PLAIN} \qquad \mathbf{Z}_{m,n,+,CIPHER}$$

for the sets of plaintext and ciphertext n-grams of positive probability, respectively. Thus

(2.7.2) $$Pr_{PLAIN/CIPHER}\{\mathbf{x}/\mathbf{y}\} = Pr_{PLAIN}\{\mathbf{x}\}$$

for all $\mathbf{x} \in \mathbf{Z}_{m,n+,PLAIN}$ and $\mathbf{y} \in \mathbf{Z}_{m,n,+,CIPHER}$ is equivalent to

$$Pr_{CIPHER/PLAIN}\{\mathbf{y}/\mathbf{x}\} = Pr_{CIPHER}\{\mathbf{y}\}$$

for all $\mathbf{x} \in \mathbf{Z}_{m,n,+,PLAIN}$ and $\mathbf{y} \in \mathbf{Z}_{m,n,+,CIPHER}$. Theorem 2.7.1 follows from two observations.

1. Each key k in the key space $\boldsymbol{K}$ gives a one-to-one correspondence between *all* of the plaintext n-grams in $\boldsymbol{Z}_{m,n,+,PLAIN}$ and *some* of the ciphertext n-grams $\mathbf{y}$ in $\boldsymbol{Z}_{m,n,+,CIPHER}$. Thus there must be at least as many ciphertext n-grams in $\boldsymbol{Z}_{m,n,+,CIPHER}$ as there are plaintext n-grams in $\boldsymbol{Z}_{m,n,+,PLAIN}$.

2. For any fixed ciphertext n-gram $\mathbf{y} \in \boldsymbol{Z}_{m,n,+,CIPHER}$, there must be at least one edge (and corresponding key) from each plaintext n-gram in $\boldsymbol{Z}_{m,n,+,PLAIN}$ to $\mathbf{y}$; for if there is no edge (and hence no key) joining (enciphering) $\mathbf{x}$ to $\mathbf{y}$, we would have

$$\Pr_{PLAIN/CIPHER}\{\mathbf{x}/\mathbf{y}\} = 0 < \Pr_{PLAIN}\{\mathbf{x}\}$$

which contradicts Eq. (2.7.2). The edges joining a fixed plaintext n-gram $\mathbf{x}$ to the set of ciphertext n-grams in $\boldsymbol{Z}_{m,n,+,CIPHER}$ correspond to different keys. Thus the size of the key space $\boldsymbol{K}$ is at least as great as the size of the set of ciphertext n-grams of positive probability, and hence by (1) above is at least as great as the size of the set of plaintext n-grams of positive probability. ◀

2.8 ENTROPY

Theorem 2.6.2 shows that the conditional probabilities

$$\Pr_{PLAIN/CIPHER}\{(x_0, x_1, \ldots, x_{n-1})/(Y_0, Y_1, \ldots, Y_{n-1})\}$$

$$\Pr_{KEY/CIPHER}\{j/(Y_0, Y_1, \ldots, Y_{n-1})\}$$

$$(Y_0, Y_1, \ldots, Y_{n-1}) = K + (X_0, X_1, \ldots, X_{n-1}) \text{ (modulo m)}$$

will be maximized by $(x_0, x_1, \ldots, x_{n-1}) = (X_0, X_1, \ldots, X_{n-1})$ and $j = K$ for some plaintext sources and encipherment systems. If these conditional probabilities varied monotonically with n, then increasing the amount of the ciphertext would improve the estimate of correct key. Unfortunately, the variation with n is not monotonic, as shown in Table 2.8.1.

TABLE 2.8.1
Variation of $\Pr_{PLAIN/CIPHER}\{(x_0, x_1, \ldots, x_{n-1})/(y_0, y_1, \ldots, y_{n-1})\}$ with n

n	*Example 2.3.1*	*Example 2.3.2*	*Example 2.3.3*
1	0.0607		0.0609
2	0.1989	0.2269	0.2259
3	0.3881		0.6219
4	0.2729	0.9097	0.9576
5	0.3173		0.9158
6	0.6330	0.9499	0.9748
7	0.6295		0.9941
8	0.3501	0.9257	0.9876
9	0.3956		0.9791
10	0.5791	0.9971	0.9971
11	0.7378		0.9887
12	0.8667	0.9998	0.9991

$$\text{MYHXBYFJMIIH} = T_{20}(\text{SENDHELPSOON})$$

$$(x_0, x_1, \ldots, x_{11}) = \text{SENDHELPSOON}$$

$$(y_0, y_1, \ldots, y_{11}) = \text{MYHXBFFJMIIH}$$

$$\mathbf{Pr}_{\mathbf{PLAIN/CIPHER}}\{(x_0, \ldots, x_{n-1})/(y_0, \ldots, y_{n-1})\}$$

The *equivocation of plaintext given ciphertext* to be defined shortly is a weighted average of the conditional probabilities $\Pr_{\text{PLAIN/CIPHER}}\{\mathbf{x}/\mathbf{y}\}$. It exhibits the desired monotonic variation with n. The word equivocation, suggesting indeterminacy, is a synonym for entropy, a concept that originated in thermodynamics but has found wide applicability in mathematics. The *entropy of a probability distribution* $\mathbf{p}$

$$\mathbf{p} = (p(0), p(1), \ldots, p(m-1))$$

$$p(t) \geq 0 \quad 0 \leq t < m$$

$$1 = p(0) + p(1) + \ldots + p(m-1)$$

is the number $H(\mathbf{p})$ defined by

$$H(\mathbf{p}) = -\sum_{1 \leq t < m} p(t) \log p(t) \tag{2.8.1}$$

Remarks

1. If $p(t) = 0$, the indeterminate form $0 \log 0$ is evaluated as 0.
2. The choice of the base for the logarithm in Eq. (2.8.1) is a matter of taste; different bases only change $H(\mathbf{p})$ by a multiplicative constant. We follow the convention in information theory and use logarithms to the base 2.

Although entropy has been defined as a number $H(\mathbf{p})$ associated with a probability distribution $\mathbf{p}$, we also speak of the *entropy of random variables,* meaning by this the following:

1. If X is a random variable with probability distribution

$$p_X(t) = \Pr\{X = t\} \qquad 0 \leq t < m$$

the *entropy of X* is the entropy of the probability distribution of X

$$H(X) = -\sum_{0 \leq t < m} p_X(t) \log p_X(t)$$

2. If $X_0, X_1, \ldots, X_{n-1}$ are random variables with joint distribution

$$p_{X_0, X_1, \ldots, X_{n-1}}(t_0, t_1, \ldots, t_{n-1}) = \Pr\{X_0 = t_0, X_1 = t_1, \ldots, X_{n-1} = t_{n-1}\}$$

the entropy of the (vector-valued) random variable $(X_0, X_1, \ldots, X_{n-1})$ is

$$H(X_0, X_1, \ldots, X_{n-1}) =$$

$$-\sum_{\{t_0, t_1, \ldots, t_{n-1}\}} p_{X_0, X_1, \ldots, X_{n-1}}(t_0, t_1, \ldots, t_{n-1}) \log p_{X_0, X_1, \ldots, X_{n-1}}(t_0, t_1, \ldots, t_{n-1})$$

3. The *conditional entropy of X given Y = j* is the entropy of the conditional distribution of X given Y = j:

$$p_{X/Y}(s/j) = \Pr\{X = s/Y = j\}$$

$$H(X/Y = j) = -\sum_{0 \le s < m} p_{X/Y}(s/j) \log p_{X/Y}(s/j)$$

4. The *entropy of X given Y* is defined by

$$H(X/Y) = \sum_{0 \le t < m} p_{X,Y}(s, t) \log p_{X/Y}(s/t)$$

where $p_{X,Y}(s, t) = \Pr\{X = s, Y = t\}$. Since $p_{X,Y}(s, t) = p_{X/Y}(s/t)p_Y(t)$ with

$$p_Y(t) = \Pr\{Y = t\} = \sum_{s} p_{X,Y}(s, t)$$

we have

$$H(X/Y) = \sum_{t} H(X/Y = t)p_Y(t)$$

The basic entropy relationships are given by the following theorem.

Theorem 2.8.1

(2.8.2) $$H(X, Y) = H(Y) + H(X/Y)$$

(2.8.3) $$H(X, Y) = H(X) + H(Y/X)$$

Proof. Equation (2.8.2) follows directly from the formula for conditional probability

(2.8.4) $$p_{X,Y}(s, t) = p_Y(t)p_{X/Y}(s/t)$$

First, take the negative logarithm of the relation in Eq. (2.8.4):

$$-\log p_{X,Y}(s, t) = -\log p_Y(t) - \log p_{X/Y}(s/t)$$

Multiply by $p_{X,Y}(s, t)$:

(2.8.5) $$-p_{X,Y}(s, t) \log p_{X,Y}(s, t)$$
$$= -p_{X,Y}(s, t) \log p_Y(t) - p_{X,Y}(s, t) \log p_{X/Y}(s/t)$$

Then sum over all possible values of s and t:

1. The left-hand-side in Eq. (2.8.5) is H(X, Y).
2. The first term on the right-hand side in Eq. (2.8.5) is

$$-\sum_{s,t} p_{X,Y}(s, t) \log p_Y(t) = -\sum_{t} p_Y(t) \log p_Y(t) = H(Y)$$

3. The second term on the right-hand side in Eq. (2.8.5) is

$$-\sum_{s,t} p_X(s)p_{X/Y}(s/t) \log p_{X/Y}(s/t) = -\sum_{t} p_Y(t)p_{X/Y}(s/t) \log p_{X/Y}(s/t)$$

$$= H(X/Y)$$

which proves Eq. (2.8.2). Equation (2.8.3) follows immediately by interchanging the roles of X and Y. ◀

Remark

The equation $H(X,Y) = H(X) + H(Y/X)$ is but one member of a family of entropy relationships. Note that the definition of $H(X)$ is independent of the dimension of a random variable; that is, $H(X)$ is defined in the same way if

- X is a random variable taking the values $\boldsymbol{Z}_m$.
- X is a vector-valued random variable $(X_0, X_1, \ldots, X_{n-1})$ each of whose components $X_0, X_1, \ldots, X_{n-1}$ take values in $\boldsymbol{Z}_m$.

In the first instance, $H(X)$ is the sum of the products $-p_X(t) \log p_X(t)$ over the possible values that X can assume, while in the second instance, $H(X_0, X_1, \ldots, X_{n-1})$ is the sum of the products $-p_{X_0,X_1,\ldots,X_{n-1}}(t_0, t_1, \ldots, t_{n-1}) \log p_{X_0,X_1,\ldots,X_{n-1}}(t_0, t_1, \ldots, t_{n-1})$ over the possible values $(t_0, t_1, \ldots, t_{n-1})$ that $(X_0, X_1, \ldots, X_{n-1})$ can assume. One generalization of Eq. (2.8.2) is obtained by replacing X and Y by multidimensional random variables $(X_0, X_1, \ldots, X_{s-1})$ and $(Y_0, Y_1, \ldots, Y_{t-1})$, obtaining

$$H(X_0, X_1, \ldots, X_{s-1}, Y_0, \ldots, Y_{t-1})$$
$$= H(Y_0, Y_1, \ldots, Y_{t-1}) + H(X_0, X_1, \ldots, X_{t-1}/Y_0, Y_1, \ldots, Y_{s-1})$$

We can also generalize Eq. (2.8.2) by conditioning the random variables X and Y by a third random variable Z, obtaining

$$H(X,Y/Z) = H(Y/Z) + H(X/Y,Z)$$

Finally, we may combine these generalizations to obtain

$$H(X_0, X_1, \ldots, X_{s-1}, Y_0, \ldots, Y_{t-1}/Z_0, Z_1, \ldots, Z_{u-1})$$
$$= H(Y_0, Y_1, \ldots, Y_{t-1}/Z_0, Z_1, \ldots, Z_{u-1})$$
$$+ H(X_0, X_1, \ldots, X_{t-1}/Y_0, Y_1, \ldots, Y_{s-1}, Z_0, Z_1, \ldots, Z_{u-1})$$

Now that we have defined entropy, it is natural to examine the value $H(\mathbf{p})$ assigned to a probability distribution $\mathbf{p}$. The basic result is surprisingly simple.

Theorem 2.8.2 *For all probability m-vectors* $\mathbf{p} = (p(0), p(1), \ldots, p(m-1))$

$$0 \leq H(\mathbf{p}) \leq \log m$$

The maximum value of $H(\mathbf{p})$ is $\log m$, and it is achieved if and only if $p(t) = 1/m$ for $0 \leq t < m$.

Proof. The proof is by induction on m; if m = 2,

$$H(p, 1 - p) = -[p \log p + (1 - p) \log (1 - p)] \tag{2.8.6}$$

with p(0) = p and p(1) = 1 − p. Differentiating the right-hand side of Eq. (2.8.6) to determine the stationary points of H(p, 1 − p), we obtain

$$(d/dp)H(p, 1 - p) = \log (1 - p) - \log p$$

The derivative of H(p, 1 − p) is equal to zero if and only if p = 1/2. Since

$$(d^2/dp^2)H(p, 1 - p) = 1/p(p - 1) < 0 \quad \text{for} \quad 0 < p < 1$$

and

$$H(0, 1) = H(1, 0) = 0$$

we conclude that p = 1/2 is the unique point at which H(p, 1 − p) attains its maximum value and H(1/2, 1/2) = log 2. This proves Theorem 2.8.2 when m = 2.

Assume now by induction that we have proved Theorem 2.8.2 for probability (m − 1)-vectors; that is,

$$\max_{\{p(0),p(1), \ldots ,p(m-2)\}} H(p(0), p(1), \ldots , p(m - 2)) = \log m - 1$$

To find the maximum,

$$\max_{\{p(0),p(1), \ldots ,p(m-1)\}} H(p(0), p(1), \ldots , p(m - 1))$$

for probability m-vectors, we may assume that p(m − 1) < 1. If, on the contrary, p(m − 1) = 1, then H(**p**) = 0, which is certainly not a maximum. We first maximize H(p(0), p(1), . . . , p(m − 1)) when **p** satisfies the conditions

$$q(t) = p(t)/(1 - p(m - 1)) \qquad 0 \leq t < m - 1 \tag{2.8.7}$$

where **q** = (q(0), q(1), . . . , q(m − 2)) is a probability (m − 1)-vector.

The maximum of H(**p**) subject to the conditions in Eq. (2.8.7),

$$H^{(*)}(\mathbf{q}) = \max_{\{\mathbf{p}:p(t)=(1-p(m-1))q(t),0 \leq t<m-1\}} H(\mathbf{p})$$

is a maximum over a one-dimensional set; fixing a value for p(m − 1) determines the values of p(t) for $0 \leq t < m - 1$ by means of Eq. (2.8.7).

If **p** and **q** are related by Eq. (2.8.7), then

$$H(\mathbf{p}) = (1 - p(m - 1))H(\mathbf{q}) - [1 - p(m - 1)] \log [1 - p(m - 1)] - p(m - 1) \log p(m - 1)$$

To maximize H(**p**) subject to the conditions of Eq. (2.8.7), we compute the partial derivative of H(**p**) with respect to p(m − 1), obtaining

$$(\partial/\partial p(m - 1))H(\mathbf{p}) = \log [1 - p(m - 1)]/p(m - 1) - H(\mathbf{q})$$

This derivative is zero only when p(m − 1) = p* with

$$p^* = 1/[1 + \exp H(\mathbf{q})]$$

Since the second derivative of H(**p**) is negative, we see that the maximum of H(p(0), p(1), . . . , p(m − 1)) subject to the conditions of Eq. (2.8.7) is

$$H^{(*)}(\mathbf{q}) = \log(1 + \exp H(\mathbf{q}))$$

By the induction hypothesis, $H(\mathbf{q}) \leq \log(m - 1)$, so that

$$H(\mathbf{p}) \leq H^{(*)}(\mathbf{q}) \leq \log m$$

whenever **p** satisfies the condition of Eq. (2.8.7). Since this upper bound is independent of the probability (m − 1)-vector **q**, it is also a bound for H(**p**).

The induction hypothesis also implies that H(**q**) [and consequently H(**p**)] attains its maximum only when

$$q(t) = p(t)/(1 - p(m - 1)) = 1/(m - 1) \qquad 0 \leq t < m$$

Thus $p(t) = 1/m$ for $0 \leq t < m$ is the unique probability distribution that maximizes H(**p**). ◀

In addition to the entropy relations typified by Eq. (2.8.2), the entropy of random variables satisfies a variety of inequalities that are consequences of the *convexity* of the logarithm function,

$$\text{(2.8.8)} \qquad \log(px + (1 - p)y) \geq p \log x + (1 - p) \log y$$

$$0 < x \leq y < \infty, 0 \leq p \leq 1$$

with strict inequality unless p = 0 or 1 or if x = y. Geometrically, the inequality (2.8.8) states that the curve y = log x is above the straight line joining the point (x, log x) to (y, log y), as shown in Fig. 2.8.2.

To prove the inequality (2.8.8), we let

$$f(u) = \log(px + (1 - p)u) - p \log x - (1 - p) \log u \qquad 0 < x \leq u < \infty$$

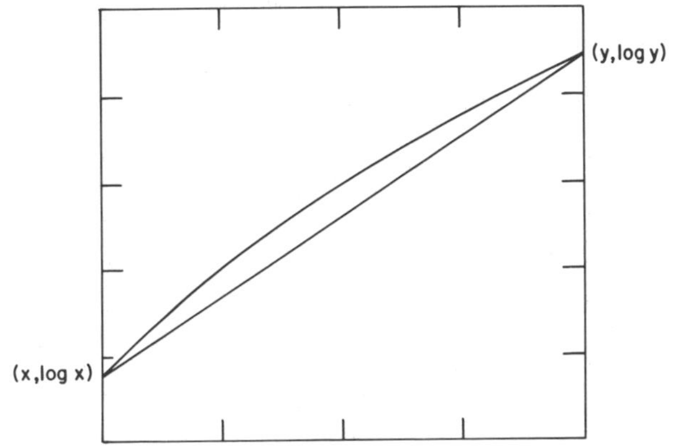

Figure 2.8.2. Convexity of the logarithm function.

Then $f(x) = 0$ and

$$(d/du)f(u) = p(1 - p)(u - x)/u[px + (1 - p)u] \geq 0$$

so that

$$0 \leq \int_x^y (d/du)f(u)\, du = f(y)$$

The inequality is strict unless $(d/du)f(u)$ is identically zero on the interval $x \leq u \leq y$. Inequality (2.8.8) is a special case of the more general inequality

$$\log\left[\sum_{0\leq t<m} p(t)x(t)\right] \geq \sum_{0\leq t<m} p(t)\log x(t) \tag{2.8.9}$$

$$p(t) \geq 0 \qquad 0 \leq t < m \qquad 1 = \sum_{0\leq t<m} p(t)$$

$$x(t) > 0 \qquad 0 \leq t < m$$

Exponentiating both sides of inequality (2.8.9), we obtain the classical inequality of the arithmetic and geometric means of the numbers $\{x(t) : 0 \leq t < m\}$

$$\text{(arithmetic mean)} \sum_{0\leq t<m} p(t)x(t) \geq \prod_{0\leq t<m} (x(t))^{p(t)} \text{(geometric mean)}$$

Convexity yields the following basic inequality for entropy.

Theorem 2.8.3 If $\mathbf{p} = (p(0), p(1), \ldots, p(m - 1))$ and $\mathbf{q} = (q(0), q(1), \ldots, q(m - 1))$ are probability m-vectors,

$$-\sum_{0\leq t<m} p(t)\log p(t) \leq -\sum_{0\leq t<m} p(t)\log q(t) \tag{2.8.10}$$

with equality if and only if $p(t) = q(t)$ for $0 \leq t < m$.

Proof. We may assume without loss of generality that $p(t) > 0$ for $0 \leq t < m$. Then setting $x(t) = q(t)/p(t)$ in inequality (2.8.9), we obtain the inequality (2.8.10). ◀

An immediate corollary of Theorem 2.8.2 is the following theorem.

Theorem 2.8.4

$$H(X/Y) \leq H(X) \tag{2.8.11}$$

$$H(X,Y) \leq H(X) + H(Y) \tag{2.8.12}$$

with equality in both cases if and only if the random variables are independent.

Proof.

$$H(X) + H(Y) = -\sum_t p_X(t)\log p_X(t) - \sum_s p_Y(s)\log p_Y(s)$$

$$= -\sum_{t,s} p_{X,Y}(t,s)\log p_X(t)p_Y(s)$$

since

$$p_X(t) = \sum_s p_{X,Y}(t,s) \qquad p_Y(s) = \sum_t p_{X,Y}(t,s)$$

Applying Theorem 2.8.2, we obtain

$$\begin{aligned} H(X) + H(Y) &= - \sum_{t,s} p_{X,Y}(t,s) \log p_X(t)p_Y(s) \\ &\geq - \sum_{t,s} p_{X,Y}(t,s) \log p_{X,Y}(t,s) = H(X,Y) \end{aligned}$$

with equality if and only if

$$p_{X,Y}(t,s) = p_X(t)p_Y(s)$$

which is equivalent to independence. ◀

Just as the relation $H(X,Y) = H(Y) + H(X/Y)$ admitted several generalizations, $H(X/Y) \leq H(X)$ and $H(X,Y) \leq H(X) + H(Y)$ are examples of a family of entropy inequalities. We state only two generalizations:

(2.8.13) $$H(X/Y,Z) \leq H(X/Z)$$

(2.8.14) $$H(X,Y/Z) \leq H(X/Z) + H(Y/Z)$$

2.9 THE PLAINTEXT SOURCE ENTROPY

Example 2.9.1 *Plaintext one-grams generated by independent and identical trials.* The plaintext n-gram

$$X_0, X_1, \ldots, X_{n-1}$$

consists of independent and identically distributed random variables

$$\Pr\{X_i = t\} = p(t) \quad 0 \leq i < n, 0 \leq t < m$$

According to Theorem 2.8.4,

$$H(X_0, X_1, \ldots, X_{n-1}) = nH(X_0) = -n \sum_t p(t) \log p(t)$$

Using the numerical values in Example 2.3.1 we find

$$H(X_0, X_1, \ldots, X_{n-1}) = H(X_0) + H(X_1) + \ldots + H(X_{n-1}) \approx 4.1291n$$

Example 2.9.2 *Plaintext generated by a Markov chain.* The plaintext n-gram

$$x_0, x_1, \ldots, x_{n-1}$$

is assigned the probability

$$\Pr_{PLAIN}\{(x_0, x_1, \ldots, x_{n-1})\} = \pi(x_0)p(x_1/x_0)p(x_2/x_1) \ldots p(x_{n-1}/x_{n-2})$$

where $P = (p(s/t))$ is the transition matrix, and $\pi = (\pi(0), \pi(1), \ldots, \pi(m-1))$ is the equilibrium distribution. Let

$$H_n = H(X_0, X_1, \ldots, X_{n-1})$$
$$= - \sum_{\{x_0, x_1, \ldots, x_{n-1}\}} Pr_{PLAIN}\{(x_0, x_1, \ldots, x_{n-1})\} \log Pr_{PLAIN}\{(x_0, x_1, \ldots, x_{n-1})\}$$

and

$$H_\infty = - \sum_{t,s} \pi(t) p(s/t) \log p(s/t)$$

Theorem 2.9.5

$$H_n = H_1 + (n-1)H_\infty \tag{2.9.1}$$

Proof. Write

$$\beta_1 + \beta_2 = \pi(x_0)p(x_1/x_0) \ldots p(x_{n-1}/x_{n-2}) \log \pi(x_0)p(x_1/x_0) \ldots p(x_{n-1}/x_{n-2})$$

where

$$\beta_1 = \pi(x_0)p(x_1/x_0) \ldots p(x_{n-1}/x_{n-2}) \log \pi(x_0)p(x_1/x_0) \ldots p(x_{n-2}/x_{n-3})$$

and

$$\beta_2 = \pi(x_0)p(x_1/x_0) \ldots p(x_{n-1}/x_{n-2}) \log p(x_{n-1}/x_{n-2})$$

First, sum β_1 over the possible values of x_{n-1}:

$$\sum_{x_{n-1}} \beta_1 = \sum_{x_{n-1}} \pi(x_0)p(x_1/x_0) \ldots p(x_{n-1}/x_{n-2}) \log \pi(x_0)p(x_1/x_0) \ldots p(x_{n-2}/x_{n-3})$$
$$= \pi(x_0)p(x_1/x_0) \ldots p(x_{n-2}/x_{n-3}) \log \pi(x_0)p(x_1/x_0) \ldots p(x_{n-2}/x_{n-3})$$

and then in succession over all $(n-1)$-grams $(x_0, x_1, \ldots, x_{n-2})$, obtaining

$$\sum_{\{x_0, x_1, \ldots, x_{n-2}\}} \sum_{x_{n-1}} \beta_1$$
$$= \sum_{x_0, \ldots, x_{n-1}\}} \pi(x_0)p(x_1/x_0) \ldots p(x_{n-1}/x_{n-2}) \log \pi(x_0)p(x_1/x_0) \ldots p(x_{n-2}/x_{n-3})$$
$$= H_{n-1}$$

For the second term β_2, we use the relationship $\pi P = \pi$, which implies that

$$\sum_{x_s} \pi(x_s)p(x_{s+1}/x_s) \ldots p(x_{n-2}/x_{n-1}) \log p(x_{n-2}/x_{n-1})$$
$$= \pi(x_{s+1})p(x_{s+2}/x_{s+1}) \ldots p(x_{n-2}/x_{n-1}) \log p(x_{n-2}/x_{n-1})$$

for $0 \leq s < n-2$, so that by induction,

$$\sum_{\{x_0, x_1, \ldots, x_{n-1}\}} \beta_2 = H_\infty$$

Combining these results, we obtain

$$H_n = H_{n-1} + H_\infty \qquad n > 1$$

which is equivalent to Eq. (2.9.1). ◀

The ratio H_n/n is the *average entropy per letter* of the plaintext source with limiting value H_∞ as $n \to \infty$. For the alphabet {AB ... Z} and the transition matrix P in Table 2.3.6, we find the values

$$H_1 \approx 4.0657$$
$$H_\infty \approx 3.3354$$

which provides the values for H_n and H_n/n given in Table 2.9.1.

TABLE 2.9.1
Entropy and Average Entropy/Letter in
Example 2.3.3

n	$\mathbf{H_n}$	$\mathbf{H_n/n}$
1	4.0657	4.0657
2	7.4011	3.7006
3	10.7365	3.5788
4	14.0719	3.5180
5	17.4073	3.4815
∞	∞	3.3354

2.10 THE VARIATION OF EQUIVOCATION WITH THE LENGTH OF INTERCEPTED CIPHERTEXT

Let $\boldsymbol{S}$ be a plaintext source,

$$X_0, X_1, \ldots, X_{n-1}, \ldots$$

$\boldsymbol{T} = \{T_k : k \in \boldsymbol{K}\}$ a cryptographic system, and K a random variable (independent of $\boldsymbol{S}$) with values in the key space $\boldsymbol{K}$. We write

$$(Y_0, \ldots, Y_{n-1}) = T_K(X_0, \ldots, X_{n-1})$$

to denote the encipherment of the plaintext n-gram $\mathbf{X} = (X_0, X_1, \ldots, X_{n-1})$ by the key K.

Definition 2.10.1 The *equivocation of key given ciphertext (of length n)* is the conditional entropy

$$H(K/Y_0, \ldots, Y_{n-1})$$

The *equivocation of plaintext given ciphertext (of length n)* is the conditional entropy

$$H(X_0, \ldots, X_{n-1}/Y_0, \ldots, Y_{n-1})$$

Since it is possible that more than one key will satisfy

$$(Y_0, \ldots, Y_{n-1}) = T_k(X_0, \ldots, X_{n-1})$$

the equivocation of the key given the ciphertext is always at least as large as the equivocation of the plaintext given the ciphertext. We give the following theorem.

Theorem 2.10.1

$$(2.10.1) \qquad H(X_0, \ldots, X_{n-1}/Y_0, \ldots, Y_{n-1}) \leq H(K/Y_0, \ldots, Y_{n-1})$$

Proof. We start with Eq. (2.8.2), $H(U,V/W) = H(U/W) + H(V/U,W)$; since entropy is nonnegative, we have

$$H(U/W) \leq H(U,V/W)$$

Setting

$$U = (X_0, X_1, \ldots, X_{n-1}) \qquad V = K \qquad W = (Y_0, Y_1, \ldots, Y_{n-1})$$

we obtain

$$(2.10.2) \qquad H(X_0, X_1, \ldots, X_{n-1}/Y_0, Y_1, \ldots, Y_{n-1})$$
$$\leq H(X_0, X_1, \ldots, X_{n-1}, K/Y_0, Y_1, \ldots, Y_{n-1})$$

Next, we use the same relationship $H(U,V/W) = H(U/W) + H(V/U,W)$, this time setting

$$U = K \qquad V = (X_0, X_1, \ldots, X_{n-1}) \qquad W = (Y_0, Y_1, \ldots, Y_{n-1})$$

to obtain

$$(2.10.3) \qquad H(X_0, X_1, \ldots, X_{n-1}, K/Y_0, Y_1, \ldots, Y_{n-1})$$
$$= H(K/Y_0, Y_1, \ldots, Y_{n-1}) + H(X_0, X_1, \ldots, X_{n-1}/K, Y_0, Y_1, \ldots, Y_{n-1})$$
$$= H(K/Y_0, Y_1, \ldots, Y_{n-1})$$

since the key K and ciphertext $(Y_0, Y_1, \ldots, Y_{n-1})$ together uniquely determine the plaintext, implying that

$$H(X_0, X_1, \ldots, X_{n-1}/K, Y_0, Y_1, \ldots, Y_{n-1}) = 0$$

Combining eqs. (2.10.2–3) completes the proof. ◀

Theorem 2.10.2 The equivocation of the plaintext s-gram $(X_0, X_1, \ldots, X_{s-1})$, given the ciphertext n-gram $(Y_0, Y_1, \ldots, Y_{n-1})$,

$$H(X_0, \ldots, X_{s-1}/Y_0, \ldots, Y_{n-1})$$

is a nonincreasing function of n for fixed s;

$$H(X_0, \ldots, X_{s-1}/Y_0, \ldots, Y_{N-1}) \le H(X_0, \ldots, X_{s-1}/Y_0, \ldots, Y_{n-1}) \qquad N \ge n$$

The equivocation of key K, given ciphertext $(Y_0, \ldots, Y_{n-1})$,

$$H(K/Y_0, \ldots, Y_{n-1})$$

is a nonincreasing function of n;

$$H(K/Y_0, \ldots, Y_{N-1}) \le H(K/Y_0, \ldots, Y_{n-1}) \qquad N \ge n$$

Proof. Both results are derived from the same entropy inequality $H(U/V,W) \le H(U/V)$. First, we set

$$U = (X_0, X_1, \ldots, X_{s-1}) \quad V = (Y_0, Y_1, \ldots, Y_{n-1})$$
$$W = (Y_n, Y_{n+1}, \ldots, Y_{N-1})$$

and obtain

$$H(X_0, X_1, \ldots, X_{s-1}/Y_0, Y_1, \ldots, Y_{N-1}) \le H(X_0, X_1, \ldots, X_{s-1}/Y_0, Y_1, \ldots, Y_{n-1}) \quad N > n$$

Next, we replace U above by K and obtain

$$H(K/Y_0, Y_1, \ldots, Y_{N-1}) \le H(K/Y_0, Y_1, \ldots, Y_{n-1})$$ ◀

2.11 RANDOM CRYPTOGRAPHIC SYSTEMS

Even for simple models of plaintext and cryptographic systems, the numerical calculation of equivocation can be made only for small values of n, due to the exponential growth of the number of n-grams with n. To obtain results for large n, Shannon used the technique of "randomization," which was employed with such success in his 1948 paper to prove the coding theorem of information theory. In randomization, the single cryptographic system $\boldsymbol{T}$ is replaced by an *ensemble* of systems $\{\boldsymbol{T}^{(i)}\}$ with a probability distribution. Expectations are calculated with respect to the ensemble. If the expected value relative to the ensemble of some variable satisfies some condition ★, then we deduce that at least one of the cryptographic systems in the ensemble satisfies condition ★, and most of the systems in the ensemble come close in some sense to satisfying condition ★. The technical advantage in randomization is the ability to evaluate an expectation that is difficult to calculate for individual members of the ensemble.

We make the following assumptions about the plaintext source and key space.

- There are N_K keys in the key space $\boldsymbol{K}$ each of probability $1/N_K$
- The set of n-grams $\boldsymbol{Z}_{m,n}$ is partitioned into two subsets $\boldsymbol{Z}_{m,n,H}$ and $\boldsymbol{Z}_{m,n,L}$

- n-Grams in $Z_{m,n,H}$ are each of probability $(1 - \epsilon)/|Z_{m,n,H}|$, where $|Z_{m,n,H}|$ is equal to the number of n-grams in $Z_{m,n,H}$
- The n-grams in $Z_{m,n,L}$ are of negligible total probability ϵ

$Z_{26,n}$ contains $26^n = 2^{4.7004n}$ n-grams. Let $R_n = \log_2 |Z_{m,n,H}|$.

For ϵ close to 0, the entropy $H(X_0, X_1, \ldots, X_{n-1})$ of the first n letters of plaintext is approximately R_n, and R_n/n is the approximate rate (in bits per letter) at which the source S outputs letters. The *redundancy* of the source S is the difference $D_n = 4.7000n - R_n$, and D_n/n is the *average redundancy per plaintext letter.* In Table 2.11.1, we tabulate the entropy and redundancy for the sources of Examples 2.3.1 and 2.3.3.

Now we introduce randomization: consider a chance experiment with sample space $\Omega' = \{\omega'\}$ and probability distribution Pr′. Let T be a random variable defined on Ω', whose value $T(\omega')$ at the sample point ω' is a cryptographic system in the sense of Definition 2.4.1:

$$T : \omega' \rightarrow T(\omega') = \{T_k(\omega') : k \in K\}$$

The *ensemble* of random cryptographic systems is the collection of cryptographic systems

$$T(\omega') = \{T_k(\omega') : k \in K\}$$

where ω' serves as a label identifying the members of the ensemble and varies over the sample space Ω'. We use a prime (′) to distinguish the sample space Ω', which labels the *random cryptographic systems* from the sample space Ω, which describes the generation of *plaintext and key*. We now assume that the chance mechanism that generates the ensemble of cryptographic systems

$$T(\omega') \qquad \omega' \in \Omega'$$

TABLE 2.11.1
Source Entropy and Redundancy for *Examples 2.3.1 and 2.3.3*

	Example 2.3.1		***Example 2.3.3***	
n	H_n	D_n	H_n	D_n
1	4.1291	0.5714	4.0657	0.6347
2	8.2581	1.1428	7.4011	1.9998
3	12.3872	1.7142	10.7365	3.3648
4	16.5162	2.2855	14.0719	4.7298
5	20.6453	2.8569	17.4073	6.0949
6	24.7743	3.4283	20.7427	7.4599
7	28.9034	3.9997	24.0781	8.8250
8	33.0324	4.5711	27.4135	10.1900
9	37.1615	5.1425	30.7489	11.5551

satisfies the following condition ★; if

$$E_k(\mathbf{y}) = \{\omega' \in \Omega' : T_k(\omega')^{-1}(\mathbf{y}) \in \boldsymbol{Z}_{m,n,H}\} \tag{2.11.1}$$

where k is a key and **y** is a ciphertext n-gram, then

- $Pr'\{E_k(\mathbf{y})\} = 2^{-D_n}$
- If $(k,\mathbf{y}) \neq (j,\mathbf{z})$, then

$$Pr'\{E_k(\mathbf{y}) \cap E_j(\mathbf{z})\} = Pr'\{E_k(\mathbf{y})\}Pr'\{E_j(\mathbf{z})\}$$

In Sec. 2.4 we saw that a cryptographic system could be represented by a sequence of bipartite graphs. Each member of the ensemble

$$\{\boldsymbol{T}(\omega') : \omega' \in \Omega'\}$$

corresponds to a sequence of graphs. Condition ★ states that the subset $E_k(\mathbf{y})$ of the sample space Ω', consisting of systems in which the edge labeled by the key k links a plaintext n-gram in $\boldsymbol{Z}_{m,n,H}$ to the ciphertext n-gram vertex **y**, is assigned Pr′-probability 2^{-D_n}. A typical graph $G_n(\boldsymbol{T}(\omega'))$ is shown in Fig. 2.11.2. The sample point ω' belongs to the set $E_k(\mathbf{y})$ but *not* to the set $E_j(\mathbf{y})$.

We begin by calculating the *ensemble average equivocation of key given ciphertext*. In what follows, we use the subscript ω' to indicate that the computation is being made with respect to the cryptographic system $\boldsymbol{T}(\omega')$. Thus

$$Pr_{\omega',CIPHER,KEY}\{\mathbf{y},k\}$$

$$Pr_{\omega',KEY/CIPHER}\{k/\mathbf{y}\}$$

$$Pr_{\omega',CIPHER}\{\mathbf{y}\}$$

means that we calculate the probability Pr (on the sample space Ω) of ciphertext and key $(\mathbf{y},k)$ for the system $\boldsymbol{T}(\omega')$. Since

- $Pr_{KEY}\{k\} = 1/N_K$, and
- $Pr_{PLAIN}\{\mathbf{x}\} = 2^{-R_n}$ for $\mathbf{x} \in \boldsymbol{Z}_{m,n,H}$

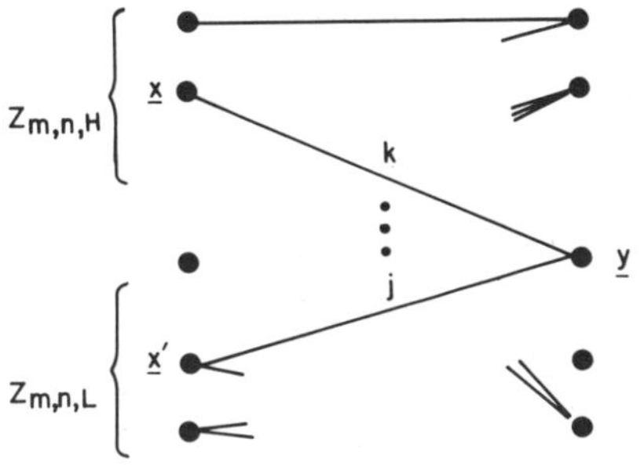

Figure 2.11.2. The graph of T(ω′).

we obtain*

$$\text{(2.11.2)} \quad Pr_{\omega',\text{CIPHER,KEY}}\{\mathbf{y},k\} = \begin{cases} 2^{-R_n}/N_K & \text{if } T_{k,i}^{-1}(\mathbf{y}) \in \boldsymbol{Z}_{m,n,H} \\ 0 & \text{if } T_{k,i}^{-1}(\mathbf{y}) \in \boldsymbol{Z}_{m,n,L} \end{cases}$$

Equation (2.11.2) yields

$$\text{(2.11.3)} \qquad Pr_{\omega',\text{CIPHER}}\{\mathbf{y}\} = 2^{-R_n}\Xi_{n,i}(\mathbf{y})/N_K$$

where $\Xi_{n,\omega'}(\mathbf{y})$ is equal to the number of keys for which $T_k(\omega')^{-1}(\mathbf{y})$ belongs to $\boldsymbol{Z}_{m,n,H}$. From Eqs. (2.11.2–3), it follows that

$$Pr_{\omega',\text{KEY/CIPHER}}\{k/\mathbf{y}\} = \begin{cases} 1/\Xi_{n,\omega'}(\mathbf{y}) & \text{if } T_k(\omega')^{-1}(\mathbf{y}) \in \boldsymbol{Z}_{m,n,H} \\ 0 & \text{if } T_k(\omega')^{-1}(\mathbf{y}) \in \boldsymbol{Z}_{m,n,L} \end{cases}$$

The conditional equivocation of key given ciphertext $H_{\omega'}(K/(Y_0, \ldots, Y_{n-1}))$, calculated for the cryptographic system $\boldsymbol{T}(\omega')$, is

$$\begin{aligned} H_{\omega'}(K/Y_0, \ldots, Y_{n-1}) &= -\sum_{\mathbf{y},k} Pr_{\text{CIPHER,KEY}}\{\mathbf{y},k\} \log Pr_{\text{KEY/CIPHER}}\{k/\mathbf{y}\} \\ \text{(2.11.4)} \qquad &= \sum_{\mathbf{y}} (2^{-R_n}/N_K)\,|\{k : T_k^{-1}(\mathbf{y}) \in \boldsymbol{Z}_{m,n,H}\}| \log \Xi_{n,\omega'}(\mathbf{y}) \\ &= \sum_{\mathbf{y}} (2^{-R_n}\Xi_{n,\omega'}(\mathbf{y})/N_K) \log \Xi_{n,\omega'}(\mathbf{y}) \end{aligned}$$

It remains to compute the *ensemble average* of $H_{\omega'}(K/Y_0, \ldots, Y_{n-1})$, the expectation of the random variable $H_{\omega'}(K/Y_0, \ldots, Y_{n-1})$ on the sample space Ω':

$$H^*(K/Y_0, Y_1, \ldots, Y_{n-1}) \equiv E'\{H_{\omega'}(K/Y_0, \ldots, Y_{n-1})\}$$

where

$$E'\{H_{\omega'}(K/Y_0, \ldots, Y_{n-1})\} = \sum_{\{\omega' \in \Omega'\}} Pr'\{\omega'\}H_{\omega'}(K/Y_0, \ldots, Y_{n-1})$$

Condition ★ implies that the random variable $\Xi_{n,\omega'}(\mathbf{y})$ has the binomial distribution $B(N_K, 2^{-D_n})$:

$$Pr\{\Xi_{n,\omega'}(\mathbf{y}) = m\} = C(N_K,m)2^{-D_n m}(1 - 2^{-D_n})^{N_K-m} \qquad 0 \leq m \leq N_K$$

independent of $\mathbf{y}$. Equation (2.11.4) thus yields the following theorem.

---

*In order to simplify the the calculations, we have assumed $Pr_{\text{PLAIN}}\{\boldsymbol{Z}_{m,n,L}\} = \epsilon = 0$. A trivial modification, replacing $Pr_{\omega',\text{CIPHER,KEY}}\{k,\mathbf{y}\}$ in Eq. (2.11.2) by

$$Pr_{\omega',\text{CIPHER,KEY}}\{k,\mathbf{y}\} = \begin{cases} (1-\epsilon)2^{-R_n}/N_K & \text{if } T_k(\omega')^{-1}(\mathbf{y}) \in \boldsymbol{Z}_{m,n,H} \\ \epsilon & \text{if } T_k(\omega')^{-1}(\mathbf{y}) \in \boldsymbol{Z}_{m,n,L} \end{cases}$$

with ϵ small does not substantially change the argument given above.

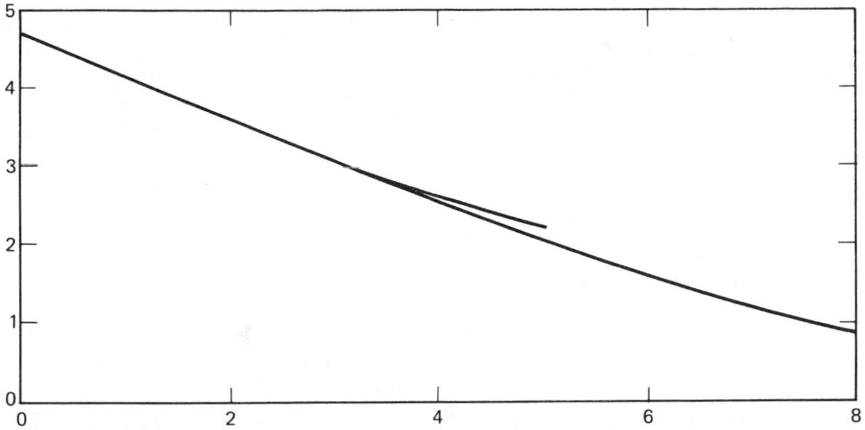

Figure 2.11.3. $H(K/Y_0, \ldots, Y_{n-1})$; n = 0(1)(4); *Example 2.3.1* ● Exact ▶ Eq. (2.11.5).

Theorem 2.11.1 The ensemble average equivocation of key given ciphertext is

$$(2.11.5) \quad H^*(K/Y_0, \ldots, Y_{n-1}) = 2^{D_n}/N_K \sum_{1 \le m \le N_K} C(N_K,m)2^{-D_n m}(1 - 2^{-D_n})^{N_K - m} m \log m$$

In Figs. 2.11.3 and 2.11.4, we compare the variation of equivocation *of key given ciphertext* with the length n of ciphertext in Examples 2.3.1 and 2.3.3 with the result obtained by randomization [Eq. (2.11.5)].

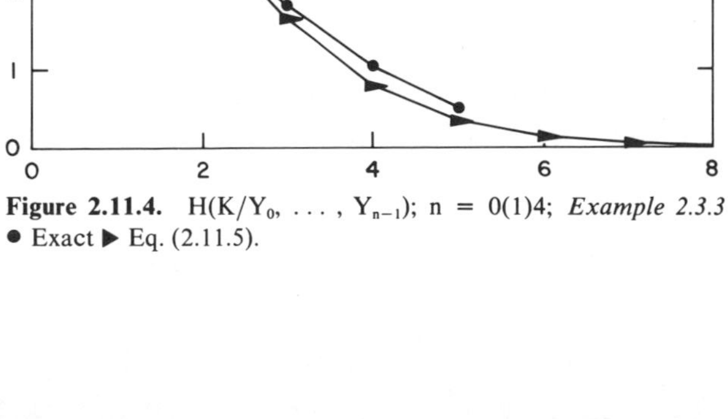

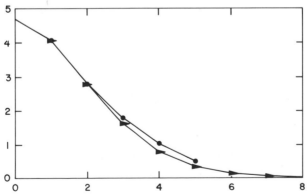

Figure 2.11.4. $H(K/Y_0, \ldots, Y_{n-1})$; n = 0(1)4; *Example 2.3.3* ● Exact ▶ Eq. (2.11.5).

To examine the variation of $H^*(\boldsymbol{K}/Y_0, \ldots, Y_{n-1})$ defined in Eq. (2.11.5) with n, we need to examine three intervals:

$$\text{Interval I: } E\{\Xi_{n,\omega'}(\mathbf{y})\} = N_K 2^{-D_n} \gg 1$$

$$\text{Interval II: } E\{\Xi_{n,\omega'}(\mathbf{y})\} = N_K 2^{-D_n} \approx 1$$

$$\text{Interval III: } E\{\Xi_{n,\omega'}(\mathbf{y})\} = N_K 2^{-D_n} \ll 1$$

For the sources in Examples 2.3.1 and 2.3.3, the intervals of values of n can be determined from the values in Table 2.11.5.

TABLE 2.11.5
Variation of $2^{-D_n N_K}$ with n

	Example 2.3.1	***Example 2.3.3***
n	$\mathbf{2^{-D_n}N_K}$	$\mathbf{2^{-D_n}N_K}$
1	17.4972	16.7457
2	11.7751	6.5011
3	7.9243	2.5239
4	5.3328	0.9798
5	3.5888	0.3804
6	2.4152	0.1477
7	1.6253	0.0573
8	1.0938	0.0223
9	0.7361	0.0086
10	0.4954	0.0034
11	0.3334	0.0013
12	0.2243	0.0005
13	0.1510	0.0002
14	0.1016	0.0001
15	0.0684	0.0000

Case 1 $2^{-D_n}N_K \gg 1$

The mth term in the binomial distribution,

$$C(N_K,m)2^{-D_n m}(1 - 2^{-D_n})^{N_K-m} \qquad 0 \leq m \leq N_K$$

attains its maximum value on an interval centered about the expectation $2^{-D_n}N_K$. When $2^{-D_n}N_K \gg 1$, the function log m varies slowly when m is near $2^{-D_n}N_K$ (its derivative decreases as 1/m). We approximate Eq. (2.11.5) by replacing log m by log 2^{-D} N_K, obtaining

$$\text{On Interval I: } H^*(\boldsymbol{K}/Y_0, Y_1, \ldots, Y_{n-1}) \approx \log N_K - D_n$$

For values of n in the first interval, the *ensemble average equivocation of key given ciphertext* is decreased by D_n. If $D_n = \alpha n$ (as in Example 2.3.1) or $D_n = \alpha n + \beta$ (as in Example 2.3.3), the *average equivocation of key given ciphertext* decreases linearly with n.

Case 2 $2^{-D_n}N_K \approx 1$

If N_K is large, and 2^{-D_n} is small, but their product is close to unity, the Poisson approximation to the binomial distribution is applicable. Accordingly,

$$C(N_K,m)2^{-D_n m}(1 - 2^{-D_n})^{N_K - m} \approx e^{-\lambda}\lambda^m/m$$

with $\lambda = 2^{-D_n}N_K$. On the second interval, the ensemble average equivocation of key given ciphertext is approximately given by the series

$$\text{On Interval II: } H^*(\boldsymbol{K}/Y_0, Y_1, \ldots, Y_{n-1}) \approx e^{-\lambda} \sum_{2 \le m < \infty} \lambda^m/m \log (m + 1)$$

Case 3 $2^{-D_n}N_K \ll 1$

Only the term $m = 2$ in Eq. (2.11.5) makes a significant contribution to $H^*(\boldsymbol{K}/Y_0, Y_1, \ldots, Y_{n-1})$. On the final interval, we therefore approximate the ensemble average equivocation of key given ciphertext by

$$\text{On Interval III: } H^*(\boldsymbol{K}/Y_0, Y_1, \ldots, Y_{n-1}) \approx 2^{-D_n}K \log 2$$

Thus $H^*(\boldsymbol{K}/Y_0, Y_1, \ldots, Y_{n-1})$ decreases linearly with D_n, and after a transition interval, exponentially with D_n.

2.12 THE UNICITY DISTANCE

How much ciphertext do we have to intercept to uniquely determine the key? If $\mathbf{p}$ is a probability distribution $\mathbf{p} = (p(0), p(1), \ldots, p(m - 1))$, and $H(\mathbf{p}) < \epsilon$, then $-p(i) \log p(i) < \epsilon$ for every i, $0 \le i < m$. Since the continuous function $-x \log x$ vanishes on the closed interval [0,1] only when $x = 0$ or $x = 1$, we conclude that

$$H(\mathbf{p}) \text{ is small if and only if } p(i) \text{ is either close to 0 or 1 for each i}$$

For a random cryptographic system, $H(\boldsymbol{K}/Y_0, \ldots, Y_{n-1}) \to 0$ as $n \to \infty$.

Definition 2.12.1 The *unicity distance* for a cryptographic system is the smallest value of n for which $H(\boldsymbol{K}) \le D_n$.

Remarks
For an ensemble of random cryptographic systems,

$$H(\boldsymbol{K}/Y_0, \ldots, Y_{n-1}) \approx H(\boldsymbol{K}) - D_n = \log N_k - D_n$$

for small values of n. When D_n increases linearly with n, the curve $H(\boldsymbol{K}) - D_n$ is essentially tangent to $H(\boldsymbol{K}/Y_0, \ldots, Y_{n-1})$ and intercepts the y-axis at n equal to the unicity distance. The unicity distance measures the average amount of ciphertext needed to uniquely fix the value of the key.

$\{T_k : k \in \boldsymbol{K}\}$: ***Example 2.4.1***

	Example 2.3.1	***Example 2.3.3***
unicity distance	9	5
average redundancy/letter	0.5714	1.3650

The average redundancy per letter for these sources is small compared to the accepted redundancy value of 3.2 bits/letter in English. This empirical value for the redundancy is obtained by sampling text, determining the frequency distribution for n-grams, and computing the source entropy $H(X_0, X_1, \ldots, X_{n-1})$ for each n, n = 1, 2,. . . . The value 3.2 is the limiting value,

$$\text{limit}_{n\to\infty} H(X_0, X_1, \ldots, X_{n-1})/n$$

PROBLEMS

2.1 Compute the source entropy, redudancy and unicity distance for the plaintext source $\boldsymbol{S}$ of Example 2.3.2.

2.2 Prove that the conclusion of Theorem 2.6.2 holds for the plaintext sources in Example 2.3.3.

2.3 Let

$$(Y_0, Y_1, \ldots, Y_{n-1}) = T_K(X_0, X_1, \ldots, X_{n-1})$$

with $\boldsymbol{T} = \{T_k : k \in \boldsymbol{Z}_m\}$, the Vigenère substitution system (Example 2.4.1). What can you say about the output ciphertext source if the plaintext source $\boldsymbol{S}$ satisfies Definition 2.3.1; are the $\{Y_i\}$ independent? What is their (joint) distribution?

2.4 **Continuation.** What can you say if the plaintext source satisfies Definition 2.3.3?

2.5 If $P = (p(t/s))$ is a transition matrix and π a probability distribution for the letters of a Markov source as in Definition 2.3.3, define

$$p^{(1)}(t/s) = p(t/s)$$

$$p^{(n)}(t/s) = \sum_{0 \le u < m} p^{(n-1)}(t/u)p(u/s) \qquad 2 \le n < \infty$$

Prove that $P^{(n)} = (p^{(n)}(t/s))$ is a transition matrix. What is the significance of $\pi(t)p^{(n)}(s/t)$?

2.6 Let r be an integer (at least two) and $\mathrm{SYM}(\boldsymbol{Z}_r)$ denote the set of all permutations of $\boldsymbol{Z}_r$. Define the transposition system

$$\mathrm{TRAN}_r = \{T_\pi : \pi \in \mathrm{SYM}(\boldsymbol{Z}_r)\}$$

by

$$T_\pi^{(nr)} : \mathbf{x} = (x_0, x_1, \ldots, x_{nr-1}) \rightarrow \mathbf{y} = (y_0, y_1, \ldots, y_{rn-1})$$

$$y_{i+sr} = x_{\pi(i)+sr} \quad 0 \leq i < r, 0 \leq s < n$$

Thus $T_\pi^{(nr)}$ transposes the letters in an nr-gram within each r-block according to π. Can you prove a generalization of Theorem 2.6.2 for the transposition system with a Markov source?

2.7 For a general plaintext source,

$$X_0, X_1, \ldots, X_{n-1}, \ldots$$

$$X_n \in \boldsymbol{Z}_m \quad (0 \leq n < \infty)$$

define

$$R_n = H(X_0, X_1, \ldots, X_{n-1}),$$

$$D_n = n \log_2 m - R_n$$

Prove

$$H(\boldsymbol{K}/Y_0, Y_1, \ldots, Y_{n-1}) \geq H(\boldsymbol{K}) - D_n$$

CHAPTER III

Monalphabetic Substitution

3.1 PERMUTATIONS OF n-GRAMS

A *permutation* of the integers (0, 1, . . . , N − 1) is a rearrangement or reordering σ of (0, 1, . . . , N − 1). We will use the notation

$$\sigma = (\sigma(0), \sigma(1), \ldots, \sigma(N-1))$$

to indicate that the integer i has been moved *from* position i *to* position $\sigma(i)$ for $0 \leq i < N$. The number of permutations of (0, 1, . . . , N − 1) is $N! = N(N-1)\ldots 2 . 1$. σ induces a one-to-one mapping of any set $S = \{s_0, s_1, \ldots, s_{N-1}\}$ of N elements *onto** itself:

$$\sigma : S \rightarrow S$$

$$\sigma : s_i \rightarrow S_{\sigma(i)} \qquad 0 \leq i < N$$

We will use the same symbol and say that σ is *a permutation of (the elements of)* S. Conversely, a one-to-one mapping of S onto S corresponds to a permutation of the integers (0, 1 2, . . . , N − 1).

A cryptographic transformation T for the alphabet $\boldsymbol{Z}_{\mathbf{m}}$ is a sequence of one-to-one mappings $T = \{T^{(n)} : 1 \leq n < \infty\}$:

$$T^{(n)} : \boldsymbol{Z}_{\mathbf{m,n}} \rightarrow \boldsymbol{Z}_{\mathbf{m,n}} \qquad 1 \leq n < \infty$$

Each $T^{(n)}$ is thus a permutation of the set of n-grams $\boldsymbol{Z}_{\mathbf{m,n}}$. Since $T^{(i)}$ and $T^{(j)}$ with $i \neq j$ may be specified independently, the number of cryptographic transformations on plaintext of length n is $(m^n)!$, a number that increases very rapidly with m and n; with m = 26 and n = 2, there are already approximately 10^{1623} different cryptographic transformations. While this shows that potentially there exist a very

*A mapping σ of a set A *into* a set B is a function with *domain* A taking values in the set B,

$$\sigma : A \rightarrow B$$

which maps the point α in A to the point $\sigma(\alpha)$ in B. The *range* of σ is the set of image points $\sigma(A) = \{\sigma(\alpha) : \alpha \in A\}$ under σ. The mapping σ is *onto* B, and we write $\sigma(A) = B$ if every point β in B is the *image* of at least one point α in A; the equation $\sigma(\alpha) = \beta$ has *at least* one solution α in A for each β in B. The mapping σ is *one-to-one* onto its range $\sigma(A)$, if for every point β in $\sigma(A)$, there is *exactly one* solution α in A of the equation $\sigma(\alpha) = \beta$.

large number of mappings of plaintext to ciphertext this enumeration is largely illusory. Any practical implementation of a cryptographic system requires that the transformations $\{T_k : k \in \boldsymbol{K}\}$ be defined by *algorithms* depending upon a relatively small number of parameters (the key). In this chapter, we begin the study of a class of such algorithmically defined systems. They are constructed from *letter substitutions,* which serve as basic building blocks in many cryptographic systems.

3.2 LETTER SUBSTITUTIONS

Definition 3.2.1 A *substitution* on the alphabet $\boldsymbol{Z}_m$ is a one-to-one mapping π from $\boldsymbol{Z}_m$ onto $\boldsymbol{Z}_m$:

$$\pi : \boldsymbol{Z}_m \rightarrow \boldsymbol{Z}_m$$

$$\pi : t \rightarrow \pi(t)$$

which replaces the plaintext letter t by the ciphertext letter $\pi(t)$. The set of all substitutions on $\boldsymbol{Z}_m$ is called the *symmetric group of* $\boldsymbol{Z}_m$ and will be denoted by $\text{SYM}(\boldsymbol{Z}_m)$.

Lemma 3.2.2 $\text{SYM}(\boldsymbol{Z}_m)$ enjoys the following properties.

1. *Closure:* The *product* of substitutions $\pi_1\pi_2$ is a substitution

$$\pi : \boldsymbol{Z}_m \xrightarrow{\pi_2} \boldsymbol{Z}_m \xrightarrow{\pi_1} \boldsymbol{Z}_m$$

$$\pi : t \rightarrow \pi_1(\pi_2(t))$$

2. *Associativity:* Both ways of parenthesizing the product $\pi_1\pi_2\pi_3$

$$\pi_1(\pi_2\pi_3) = (\pi_1\pi_2)\pi_3$$

   yield the same result.
3. *Identity:* The substitution ι defined by

$$\iota(t) = t \qquad 0 \leq t < m$$

   is the unique *identity element* of $\text{SYM}(\boldsymbol{Z}_m)$ under multiplication

$$\iota\pi = \pi\iota \qquad \text{for all } \pi \in \text{SYM}(\boldsymbol{Z}_m)$$

4. *Inverse:* For every substitution π, there is a uniquely determined *inverse substitution* denoted by π^{-1}, which satisfies

$$\pi\pi^{-1} = \pi^{-1} = \iota$$

The four properties (1) the product of substitutions is a substitution, (2) multiplication is associative, (3) the existence of an identity, and (4) the existence of an inverse are the axioms of a *group* [WA]. The number of substitutions in the symmetric group of $\boldsymbol{Z}_m$ called the *order* of SYM($\boldsymbol{Z}_m$) is

$$m! = m(m - 1) \dots 2 \,.\, 1$$

3.3 SUBSTITUTION SYSTEMS

Definition 3.3.1 A *substitution key* k for $\boldsymbol{Z}_m$ is a sequence of elements of the symmetric group of $\boldsymbol{Z}_m$:

$$k = (\pi_0, \pi_1, \dots, \pi_{n-1}, \dots) \qquad \pi_n \in \mathrm{SYM}(\boldsymbol{Z}_m) \qquad 0 \leq n < \infty$$

The *substitution defined by the key* k is the cryptographic transformation T_k, which enciphers the plaintext n-gram $(x_0, x_1, \dots, x_{n-1})$ into the ciphertext n-gram $(y_0, y_1, \dots, y_{n-1})$, where

$$y_i = \pi_i(x_i) \qquad 0 \leq i < n$$

for every n, n = 1, 2,. . . . T_k is called a *monalphabetic substitution* if π_i is the same for every i, i = 0, 1, . . . ; otherwise, T_k is called a *polyalphabetic substitution.*

Remarks
The essential characteristics of the substitution T_k, which is depicted in Fig. 3.3.1, are:

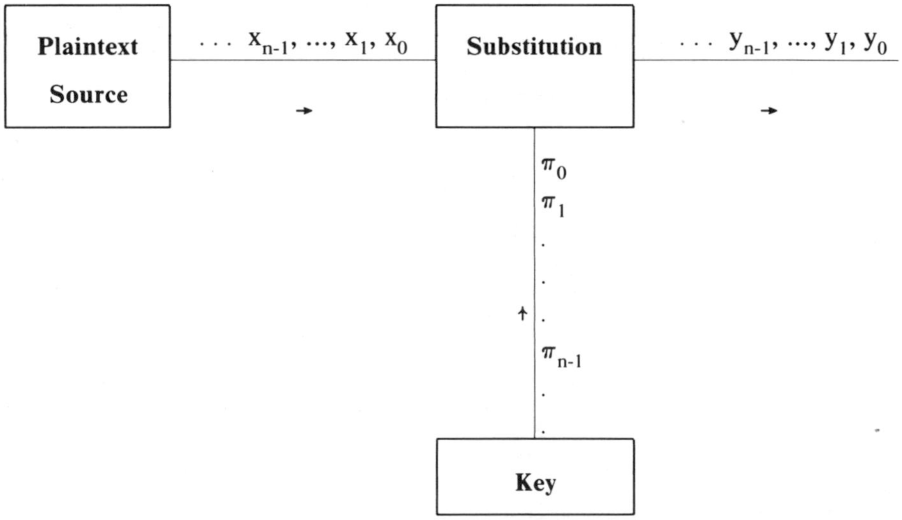

Figure 3.3.1. The Substitution T_k.

- The plaintext is enciphered letter-by-letter. The encipherment of the n-gram $(x_0, x_1, \ldots, x_{n-1})$ and its s-gram prefix $(x_0, x_1, \ldots, x_{s-1})$ are related by

$$T_k(x_0, x_1, \ldots, x_{n-1}) = (y_0, y_1, \ldots, y_{n-1})$$

$$(y_0, y_1, \ldots, y_{s-1}) = T_k(x_0, x_1, \ldots, x_{s-1})$$

- The ith ciphertext letter y_i is a function of only the ith component of the key π_i and the ith plaintext letter x_i.

3.4 EXAMPLES OF PLAINTEXT

In Chapters 3–5 we will study the cryptanalysis of several substitution systems. To illustrate encipherment and to provide examples to test various techniques of cryptanalysis, we need examples of plaintext. We will use the following three examples of plaintext in this book:

Many organizations rely on computers and data communications to keep their operations running smoothly, by making information more accessible to more people within the organization. But as it becomes more accessible, information requires more protection than you may now have.

You can now protect information stored on your premises by physical measures that limit access to authorized people. Similarly, IBM hardware and software products have features that can be used to identify and check the authorization of people trying to gain access to a system and its information.

Now, there is a way to protect information even further. The IBM cryptographic Subsystem can extend data control and protection to the data communications terminals and links that speed information from one location to another. It uses a sophisticated algorithm (a strict set of rules) to encrypt or scramble data before it is stored or transmitted to another location and decrypt it when needed for processing. It employs encryption techniques that can reduce information exposures within your communications network, as well as provide a system base for the development of encryption programs.

The IBM cryptographic Subsystem is a versatile tool for controlling and protecting information through encryption. By a combination of programming and SNA terminal hardware features, it can encrypt and decrypt information automatically and without intervention by the terminal user or application.

Using an algorithm and a key which individualizes the algorithm, the Subsystem encrypts application information before it is sent from a terminal or computer location and enters your data communications network. At the receiving terminal or computer location, the same key is used to decrypt the information after it leaves the network. In addition to the algorithm, the IBM Subsystem provides key generation, key management, verification and operational features that enhance the basic cryptographic security of the Subsystem.

Figure 3.4.1. *PLAIN(1)*. Reprinted by permission from G520-3233-0 IBM Cryptographic Subsystem. © 1978 by International Business Machines Corporation.

The issue of performance evaluation and prediction has concerned users throughout the history of computer evolution. In fact, as in any other technological development, the issue is most acute when the technology is young; the persistent pursuit of products with improved cost-performance characteristics then constantly leads to designs with untried uncertain features.

From the initial conception of a system's architectural design to its daily operation after installation. In the early planning phase of a new computer system product, the manufacturer must usually make two types of prediction. The first type is to forecast the nature of applications and the levels of "system wordloads" of these applications. Here the term workload means, informally, the amount of service requirements placed on the system. We shall elaborate more on workload characterization in section 1.4. The second type of prediction is concerned with the choice between architectural design alternatives, based on hardware and software technologies that will be available in the development period of the planned system. Here the criterion of selection is what we call "cost-performance tradeoff". The accuracy of such prediction rests to a considerable extent on our capability of mapping the performance characteristics of the system components into the overall system-level performance characteristics. Such translation procedures are by no means straightforward or well established.

Once the architectural decisions have been made and the system design and implementation started, the scope of performance prediction and evaluation becomes more specific. What is the best choice of machine organization? What is the operating system to support and what are the functions it should provide? The interactions among the operating system components - algorithms for job scheduling, processor scheduling, and storage management - must be understood, and their effects on the performance must be predicted. The techniques used for performance evaluation and prediction during the design and implementation phases range from simple hand calculation to quite elaborate simulation. Comparing the predicted performance with the actual achieved performance often reveals major defects in the design or errors in the system programming. It is now a widely accepted belief that the performance prediction and evaluation process should be an integral part of the development efforts throughout the design and implementation activities.

Hishahi Kobayashi, "Modelling And Analysis: An Introduction To Performance Evaluation Methodology
© 1978, Addison-Wesley Publishing Company, Inc.

Figure 3.4.2. *PLAIN(2).* Hisashi Kobayashi, *Modelling and Analysis: An Introduction To Performance Evaluation Methodology,* © 1978, Addison-Wesley Publishing Company, Inc.

These examples of plaintext are written using an alphabet containing upper and lower case letters, punctuation, blank space and numerals. We will rewrite the plaintext, translating it to the alphabet containing only upper case letters {`AB . . . Z`}. We must decide how to translate numerals, blank space and punctuation; there are several options available to us:

- Express numbers in words: `TWENTYTWO` for `22`.
- Delete or express punctuation in words: `PERIOD` for `.`.
- Retain blank spaces, introduce an additional symbol for the blank space or *block* the plaintext into b letter *blocks.*

Typically, 18% of text will be the blank space, so that retaining blank spaces or equivalently introducing an additional letter to represent the blank space sup-

Different people have different objectives in their quest for fitness. To an athlete, it's seconds shaved off a mile, or that extra burst of speed in the last minute of the game. To a lawyer, it's alertness after hours of hard bargainning. To a housewife, a dress two sizes smaller, or maybe just the sense of abundant well-being, the positive outlook and regained youthfulness that comes from really being "fit".

No matter what your particular exercise aim may be, the most important thing is to achieve it safely. After all, you want to gain your health, not lose it. That's why a thorough physical examination should be the very first step on your road to fitness.

Emphasizing the importance of such an exmaination is the following tragic incident. On July 23, 1968, a leading West Coast newspaper exploded a banner headline: TWO MORE JOGGERS! Other newspapers across the country picked up the story. Occurring shortly after a wave of enthusiasm had made jogging something of a nationwide sport, the tragedy suddenly focused national concern on the problem of safety in exercise.

My phone range almost constantly. Physicians and law people alike were anxiously asking under what conditions exercise might be dangerous, and prominent doctors were wondering out loud in newspapers and magazines whether perhaps the idea of exercise had been oversold to the public.

In response to this widespread concern, I decided to investigate more closely the case of the two joggers who had suffered fatal heart attacks during the exercise. Both, it turned out had severe heart disease, and one of them had been told by a prominent West Coast physician that he should under no circumstances engage in vigorous exercise. Yet, contrary to medical advice, the man starting jogging at a strenuous rate, mistakening believing that this would help him overcome his heart condition more quickly. Instead, jogging at a hard pace strained his weak heart beyond its limits.

The one good thing growing out of this tragedy was the realization on the part of physicians that anyone entering an exercise or physical conditioning program should have a medical check up before starting. So before you embark on any exercise program, get your doctor's approval.

Figure 3.4.3. *PLAIN(3).* From *The New Aerobics,* by Kenneth H. Cooper, M.D. Copyright 1970 by Kenneth H. Cooper. Reprinted by permission of the publisher, M. Evans and Company, Inc., New York, N.Y.

plies too much information to a cryptanalyst. Words like A, I, IF, OF, THE, AN, IN, TO, and BE occur so often in plaintext that word boundaries usually make the problem of cryptanalysis trivial. We will normally format plaintext into 5 letter blocks. Numbers will be expressed in words and punctuation deleted in both *PLAIN(1)* and *PLAIN(3);* in *PLAIN(2)* we will express both numbers and punctuation in words. The formatted plaintext is shown in Figs. 3.4.4–6.

3.5 CAESAR SUBSTITUTION

The subset $\boldsymbol{C}_m = \{C_k : 0 \leq k < m\}$ of the symmetric group SYM($\boldsymbol{Z}_m$), containing the m substitutions,

$$C_k : j \rightarrow (j + k) \text{ (modulo m)} \qquad 0 \leq k < m$$

```
MANYO RGANI ZATIO NSREL YONCO MPUTE RSAND DATAC OMMUN ICATI ONSTO KEEPT
HEIRO PERAT IONSR UNNIN GSMOO THLYB YMAKI NGINF ORMAT IONMO REACC ESSIB
LETOM OREPE OPLEW ITHIN THEOR GANIZ ATION BUTAS ITBEC OMESM OREAC CESSI
BLEIN FORMA TIONR EQUIR ESMOR EPROT ECTIO NTHAN YOUMA YNOWH AVEYO UCANN
OWPRO TECTI NFORM ATION STORE DONYO URPRE MISES BYPHS YICAL MEASU RESTH
ATLIM ITACC ESSTO AUTHO RIZED PEOPL ESIMI LARLY IBMHA RDWAR EANDS OFTWA
REPRO DUCTS HAVEF EATUR ESTHA NCANB EUSED TOIDE NTIFY ANDCH ECKTH EAUTH
ORIZA TIONO FPEOP LETRY INGTO GAINA CCESS TOASY STEMA NDITS INFOR MATIO
NNOWT HEREI SAWAY TOPOR TECTI NFORM ATION EVENF URTHE RTHEI BMCRY PTOGR
APHIC SUBSY STEMC ANEXT ENDDA TACON TROLA NDPRO TECTI ONTOT HEDAT ACOMM
UNICA TIONS TERMI NALSA NDLIN KSTHA TSPEE DINFO RMATI ONFRO MONEL OCATI
ONTOA NOTHE RITUS ESASO PHIST ICATE DALGO RITHM ASTRI CTSET OFRUL ESTOE
NCRYP TORSC RAMBL EDATA BEFOR EITIS STORE DORTR ANSMI TTEDT OANOT HERLO
CATIO NANDD ECRYP TITWH ENNEE DEDFO RPROC ESSIN GITEM PLOYS ENCRY PTION
TECHN IQUES THANC ANRED UCEIN FORMA TIONE XPOSU RESWI THINY OURCO MMUNI
CATIO NSNET WORKA SWELL ASPRO VIDEA SYSTE MBASE FORTH EDEVE LOPME NTOFE
NCRYP TIONP ROGRA MSTHE IBMCR YPTOG RAPHI CSUBS YSTEM ISAVE RSATI LETOO
LFORC ONTRO LLING ANDPR OTECT INGIN FORMA TIONT HROUG HENCR YPTIO NBYAC
OMBIN ATION OFPRO GRAMM INGAN DSNAT ERMIN ALHAR DWARE FEATU RESIT CANEN
CRYPT ANDDE CRYPT INFOR MATIO NAUTO MATIC ALLYA NDWIT HOUTI NTERV ENTIO
NBYTH ETERM INALU SEROR APPLI CATIO NUSIN GANAL GORIT HMAND AKEYW HICHI
NDIVI DUALI ZESTH EALGO RITHM THESU BSYST EMENC RYPTS APPLI CATIO NINFO
RMATI ONBEF OREIT ISSEN TFROM ATERM INALO RCOMP UTERL OCATI ONAND ENTER
SYOUR DATAC OMMUN ICATI ONSNE TWORK ATTHE RECEI VINGT ERMIN ALORC OMPUT
ERLOC ATION THESA MEKEY ISUSE DTODE CRYPT THEIN FORMA TIONA FTERI TLEAV
ESTHE NETWO RKINA DDITI ONTOT HEALG ORITH MTHEI BMSUB SYSTE MPROV IDESK
EYGEN ERATI ONKEY MANAG EMENT VERIF ICATI ONAND OPERA TIONA LFEAT UREST
HATEN HANCE THEBA SICCR YPTOG RAPHI CSECU RITYO FTHES UBSYS TEM
```

Figure 3.4.4. Formatted *PLAIN(1)*.

is the group of *Casear substitutions*. Multiplication is commutative, $C_kC_j = C_jC_k = C_{j+k}$, C_0 is the identity substitution, and the inverse of C_k is $C_k^{-1} = C_{m-k}$ for $0 < k < m$. The family of Caesar substitutions is named for Julius Gaius Caesar, Emperor of Rome, who it is claimed wrote to Marcus Tullius Cicero around 50 B.C.E. using C_3.

A substitution is defined in a *substitution table* listing the corresponding plain-text-ciphertext letter pairs. The substitution table for C_3 is shown in Table 3.5.1.*

TABLE 3.5.1
C_3 Substitution Table; m = 26

A	→	d	J	→	m	S	→	v
B	→	e	K	→	n	T	→	w
C	→	f	L	→	o	U	→	x
D	→	g	M	→	p	V	→	y
E	→	h	N	→	q	W	→	z
F	→	i	O	→	r	X	→	a
G	→	j	P	→	s	Y	→	b
H	→	k	Q	→	t	Z	→	c
I	→	l	R	→	u			

*To better distinguish plaintext from ciphertext, for example, when we have a partial decipherment of ciphertext and are searching for recognizable word fragments, we will write ciphertext using lower case letters.

```
THEIS SUEOF PERFO RMANC EEVAL UATIO NANDP REDIC TIONH ASCON CERNE DUSER
STHRO UGHOU TTHEH ISTOR YOFCO MPUTE REVOL UTION PERIO DINFA CTCOM MAASI
NANYO THERT ECHNO LOGIC ALDEV ELOPM ENTCO MMATH EISSU EISMO STACU TEWHE
NTHET ECHNO LOGYI SYOUN GTHEP ERSIS TENTP URSUI TOFPR ODUCT SWITH IMPRO
VEDCO STHYP HENPE RFORM ANCEC HARAC TERIS TICST HENCO NSTAN TLYLE ADSTO
DESIG NSWIT HUNTR IEDAN DUNCE RTAIN FEATU RESPE RIODF ROMTH EINIT IALCO
NCEPT IONOF ASYST EMSAR CHITE CTURA LDESI GNTOI TSDAI LYOPE RATIO NAFTE
RINST ALLAT IONPE RIODI NTHEE ARLYP LANNI NGPHA SEOFA NEWCO MPUTE RSYST
EMPRO DUCTC OMMAT HEMAN UFACT URERM USTUS UALLY MAKET WOTYP ESOFP REDIC
TIONP ERIOD THEFI RSTTY PEIST OFORE CASTT HENAT UREOF APPLI CATIO NSAND
THELE VELSO FSYST EMWOR KLOAD SOFTH ESEAP PLICA TIONS PERIO DHERE THETE
RMWOR KLOAD MEANS COMMA INFOR MALLY COMMA THEAM OUNTO FSERV ICERE QUIRE
MENTS PLACE DONTH ESYST EMPER IODWE SHALL ELABO RATEM OREON WORKL OADCH
ARACT ERIZA TIONI NSECT IONON EPOIN TFOUR PERIO DTHES ECOND TYPEO FPRED
ICTIO NISCO NCERN EDWIT HTHEC HOICE BETWE ENARC HITEC TURAL DESIG NALTE
RNATI VESCO MMABA SEDON HARDW AREAN DSOFT WARET ECHNO LOGIE STHAT WILLB
EAVAI LABLE INTHE DEVEL OPMEN TPERI ODOFT HEPLA NNEDS YSTEM PERIO DHERE
THECR ITERI ONOFS ELECT IONIS WHATW ECALL COSTH YPHEN PERFO RMANC ETRAD
EOFFP ERIOD THEAC CURAC YOFSU CHPRE DICTI ONRES TSTOA CONSI DERAB LEEXT
ENTON OURCA PABIL ITYOF MAPPI NGTHE PERFO RMANC ECHAR ACTER ISTIC SOFTH
ESYST EMCOM PONEN TSINT OTHEO VERAL LSYST EMHYP HENLE VELPE RFORM ANCEC
HARAC TERIS TICSP ERIOD SUCHT RANSL ATION PROCE DURES AREBY NOMEA NSSTR
AIGHT FORWA RDORW ELLES TABLI SHEDP ERIOD ONCET HEARC HITEC TURAL DECIS
IONSH AVEBE ENMAD EANDT HESYS TEMDE SIGNA NDIMP LEMEN TATIO NSTAR TEDCO
MMATH ESCOP EOFPE RFORM ANCEP REDIC TIONA NDEVA LUATI ONBEC OMESM ORESP
ECIFI CPERI ODWHA TISTH EBEST CHOIC EOFMA CHINE ORGAN IZATI ONQUE STION
WHATI STHEO PERAT INGSY STEMT OSUPP ORTAN DWHAT ARETH EFUNC TIONS ITSHO
ULDPR OVIDE QUEST IONTH EINTE RACTI ONSAM ONGTH EOPER ATING SYSTE MCOMP
ONENT SHYPH ENALG ORITH MSFOR JOBSC HEDUL INGCO MMAPR OCESS ORSCH EDULI
NGCOM MAAND STORA GEMAN AGEME NTHYP HENMU STBEU NDERS TOODC OMMAA NDTHE
IREFF ECTSO NTHEP ERFOR MANCE MUSTB EPRED ICTED PERIO DTHET ECHNI QUESU
SEDFO RPERF ORMAN CEEVA LUATI ONAND PREDI CTION DURIN GTHED ESIGN ANDIM
PLEME NTATI ONPHA SESRA NGEFR OMSIM PLEHA NDCAL CULAT IONTO QUITE ELABO
RATES IMULA TIONP ERIOD COMPA RINGT HEPRE DICTE DPERF ORMAN CEWIT HTHEA
CTUAL ACHIE VEDPE RFORM ANCEO FTENR EVEAL SMAJO RDEFE CTSIN THEDE SIGNO
RERRO RSINT HESYS TEMPR OGRAM MINGP ERIOD ITISN OWAWI DELYA CCEPT EDBEL
IEFTH ATTHE PERFO RMANC EPRED ICTIO NANDE VALUA TIONP ROCES SSHOU LDBEA
NINTE GRALP ARTOF THEDE VELOP MENTE FFORT STHRO UGHOU TPERI OD
```

Figure 3.4.5. Formatted *PLAIN(2)*.

The arrow (→) indicates that the plaintext letter (on the left) is enciphered by C_3 into the ciphertext letter (on the right). A second tabular representation for C_3 is

```
A B C D E F G H I J K L M N O P Q R S T U V W X Y Z
↓ ↓ ↓ ↓ ↓ ↓ ↓ ↓ ↓ ↓ ↓ ↓ ↓ ↓ ↓ ↓ ↓ ↓ ↓ ↓ ↓ ↓ ↓ ↓ ↓ ↓
d e f g h i j k l m n o p q r s t u v w x y z a b c
```

in which the plaintext-ciphertext letter-pairs are written vertically.

Definition 3.5.1 The *Caesar system* is the monalphabetic substitution that enciphers the plaintext n-gram $(x_0, x_1, \ldots, x_{n-1})$ into the ciphertext n-gram $(y_0, y_1, \ldots, y_{n-1})$ according to the rule

$$y_i = C_k(x_i) \qquad 0 \leq i < n$$

SENDM OREMO NEY is C_3-enciphered to vhqgp ruhpr qhb.

```
DIFFE RENTP EOPLE HAVED IFFER ENTOB JECTI VESIN THEIR QUEST FORFI TNESS
TOANA THLET EITSS ECOND SSHAV EDOFF AMILE ORTHA TEXTR ABURS TOFSP EEDIN
THELA STMIN UTEOF THEGA METOA LAWYE RITSA LTERN ESSAF TERHO URSOF HARDB
ARGAI NINGT OAHOU SEWIF EADRE SSTWO SIZES SMALL ERORM AYBEJ USTTH ESENS
EOFAB UNDAN TWELL BEING THEPO SITIV EOUTL OOKAN DREGA INEDY OUTHF ULNES
STHAT COMES FROMR EALLY BEING FITIM PORTA NTTHI NGIST OACHI EVEIT SAFEL
YAFTE RALLY OUWAN TTOGA INYOU RHEAL THNOT LOSEI TTHAT SWHYA THORO UGHPH
YSICA LEXAM INATI ONSHO ULDBE THEVE RYFIR STSTE PONYO URROA DTOFI TNESS
EMPHA SIZIN GTHEI MPORT ANCEO FSUCH ANEXA MINAT IONIS THEFO LLOWI NGTRA
GICIN CIDEN TONJU LYTWE NTYTH IRDNI NETEE NHUND REDAN DSIXT YEIGH TALEA
DINGW ESTCO ASTNE WSPAP EREXP LODED ABANN ERHEA DLINE TWOMO REJOG GERSD
IEOTH ERNEW SPAPE RSACR OSSTH ECOUN TRYPI CKEDU PTHES TORYO CCURR INGSH
ORTLY AFTER AWAVE OFENT HUSIA MHASM ADEJO GGING SOMET HINGO FANAT IONWI
SESPO RTTHE TRAGE DYSUD DENLY FOCUS EDNAT IONAL CONCE RNONT HEPRO BLEMO
FSAFE TYINE XERCI SEMYP HONER ANGAL MOSTC ONSTA NTLYP HYSIC IANSA NDLAY
PEOPL EALIK EWERE ANXIO USLYA SKING UNDER WHATC ONDIT IONSE XERCI SEMIG
HTBED ANGER OUSAN DPROM INENT DOCTO RSWER EWOND ERING OUTLO UDINN EWSPA
PERSA NDMAG AZINE SWHET HERPE RHAPS THEID EAOFE XERCI SEHAD BEENO VERSO
LDTOT HEPUB LICIN RESPO NSETO THISW IDESP READC ONCER NIDEC IDEDT OINVE
STIGA TEMOR ECLOS ELYTH ECASE OFTHE TWOJO GGERS WHOHA DSUFF EREDF ATALH
EARTA TTACK SDURI NGTHE EXERC ISEBO THITT URNED OUTHA DSEVE REHEA RTDIS
EASEA NDONE OFTHE MHADB EENTO LDBYA PROMI NENTW ESTCO ASTPH YSICI ANTHA
THESH OULDU NDERN OCIRC UMSTA NCESE NGAGE INVIG OROUS EXERC ISEYE TCONT
RARYT OMEDI CALAD VICET HEMAN START EDJOG GINGA TASTR ENUOU SRATE MISTA
KENIN GBELI EVING THATT HISWO ULDHE LPHIM OVERC OMEHI SHEAR TCOND ITION
MOREQ UICKL YINST EADJO GGING ATAHA RDPAC ESTRA INEDH ISWEA KHEAR TBEYO
NDITS LIMIT STHEO NEGOO DTHIN GGROW INGOU TOFTH ISTRA GEDYW ASTHE REALI
ZATIO NTHAT ANYON EENTE RINGA NEXER CISEP ROGRA MSHOU LDHAV EAMED ICALC
HECKU PBEFO RESTA RTING SOBEF OREYO UEMBA RKONA NYMED ICALE XERCI SEPRO
GRAMG ETYOU RDOCT ORSAP PROVA L
```

Figure 3.4.6. Formatted *PLAIN(3)*.

3.6 ANALYSIS OF CAESAR SUBSTITUTION—I

If an opponent has obtained either (1) *corresponding plaintext and ciphertext,* or (2) *ciphertext of opponent-chosen plaintext,* the recovery of key and plaintext is immediate. We shall assume that *only ciphertext* is available to the opponent. *CIPHER(1.1)* shown in Fig. 3.6.1 is a Caesar encipherment of *PLAIN(1).*

It is clear that Caesar substitution is a weak method of encipherment, since the only information denied the opponent is knowing which of the 26 elements of the key space serves as the key. We can recover the *PLAIN(1)* and the key k from *CIPHER(1.1)* by *key trial,* deciphering *CIPHER(1.1)* with each key until recognizable plaintext is obtained. For example, when we decipher the first 40 letters of *CIPHER(1.1)* with each of the 26 keys, we obtain the information in Table 3.6.2. Only k = 7 provides recognizable plaintext. The success of the key trial depends upon two factors:

- The existence of a relatively small key space, making exhaustive testing of the keys feasible, and
- The unlikelihood that two keys produce recognizable plaintext upon decipherment

The second factor is connected to the unicity distance of the cryptographic system, that is, the average number of letters of ciphertext needed to uniquely determine

```
thufv ynhup ghapv uzyls fvujv twbal yzhuk khahj vttbu pjhap vuzav rllwa
olpyv wlyha pvuzy buupu nztvv aosfi fthrp unpum vytha pvutv ylhjj lzzpi
slavt vylwl vwsld paopu aolvy nhupg hapvu ibahz pailj vtlzt vylhj jlzzp
islpu mvyth apvuy lxbpy lztvy lwyva ljapv uaohu fvbth fuvdo hclfv bjhuu
vdwyv aljap umvyt hapvu zavyl kvufv bywyl tpzlz ifwoz fpjhs tlhzb ylzao
haspt pahjj lzzav hbaov ypglk wlvws lzptp shysf pitoh ykdhy lhukz vmadh
ylwyv kbjaz ohclm lhaby lzaoh ujhui lbzlk avpkl uapmf hukjo ljrao lhbao
vypgh apvuv mwlvw slayf punav nhpuh jjlzz avhzf zalth ukpaz pumvy thapv
uuvda olylp zhdhf avwvy aljap umvyt hapvu lclum byaol yaolp itjyf wavny
hwopj zbizf zaltj hulea lukkh ahjvu ayvsh ukwyv aljap vuava olkha hjvtt
bupjh apvuz alytp uhszh ukspu rzaoh azwll kpumv ythap vumyv tvuls vjhap
vuavh uvaol ypabz lzhzv wopza pjhal khsnv ypaot hzayp jazla vmybs lzavl
ujyfw avyzj yhtis lkhah ilmvy lpapz zavyl kvyay huztp aalka vhuva olysv
jhapv uhukk ljyfw apado luull klkmv ywyvj lzzpu npalt wsvfz lujyf wapvu
aljou pxblz aohuj huylk bjlpu mvyth apvul ewvzb ylzdp aopuf vbyjv ttbup
jhapv uzula dvyrh zdlss hzwyv cpklh zfzal tihzl mvyao lklcl svwtl uavml
ujyfw apvuw yvnyh tzaol pitjy fwavn yhwop jzbiz fzalt pzhcl yzhap slavv
smvyj vuayv sspun hukwy valja punpu mvyth apvua oyvbn olujy fwapv uifhj
vtipu hapvu vmwyv nyhtt punhu kzuha lytpu hsohy kdhyl mlhab ylzpa jhulu
jyfwa hukkl jyfwa pumvy thapv uhbav thapj hssfh ukdpa ovbap ualyc luapv
uifao lalyt puhsb zlyvy hwwsp jhapv ubzpu nhuhs nvypa othuk hrlfd opjop
ukpcp kbhsp glzao lhsnv ypaot aolzb izfza ltluj yfwaz hwwsp jhapv upumv
ythap vuilm vylpa pzzlu amyvt halyt puhsv yjvtw balys vjhap vuhuk lualy
zfvby khahj vttbu pjhap vuzul advyr haaol yljlp cpuna lytpu hsvyj vtwba
lysvj hapvu aolzh tlrlf pzbzl kavkl jyfwa aolpu mvyth apvuh malyp aslhc
lzaol uladv yrpuh kkpap vuava olhsn vypao taolp itzbi zfzal twyvc pklzr
lfnlu lyhap vurlf thuhn ltlua clypm pjhap vuhuk vwlyh apvuh smlha bylza
ohalu ohujl aolih zpjjy fwavn yhwop jzljb ypafv maolz bizfz alt
```

Figure 3.6.1. *CIPHER(1.1)*: Caesar encipherment of *PLAIN(1)*.

TABLE 3.6.2
Trial Decipherment of *CIPHER(1.1)*

Key	Trial Decipherment						
0	THUFV	YNHUP	GHAPV	UZYLS	FVUJV	TWABL	YZHUK	KHAHJ
1	SGTEU	XMGTO	FGZOU	TYXKR	EUTIU	SVAZK	XYGTJ	JGZGI
2	RFSDT	WLFSN	EFYNT	SXWJQ	DTSHT	RUZYJ	WXFSI	IFYFH
3	QERCS	VKERM	DEXMS	RWVIP	CSRGS	QTYXI	VWERH	HEXEG
4	PDQBR	UJDQL	CDWLR	QVUHO	BRQFR	PSXWH	UVDQG	GDWDF
5	OCPAQ	TICPK	BCVKQ	PUTGN	AQPEQ	ORWVG	TUCPF	FCVCE
6	NBOZP	SHBOJ	ABUJP	OTSFM	ZPODP	NQVUF	STBOE	EBUBD
7	MANYO	RGANI	ZATIO	NSREL	YONCO	MPUTE	RSAND	DATAC
8	LZMXN	QFZMH	YZSHN	MRQDK	XNMBN	LOTSD	QRZMC	CZSZB
9	KYLWM	PEYLG	XYRGM	LQPCJ	WMLAM	KNSRC	PQYLB	BYRYA
10	JXKVL	ODXKF	WXQFL	KPOBI	VLKZL	JMRQB	OPXKA	AXQXZ
11	IWJUK	NCWJE	VWPEK	JONAH	UKJYK	ILQPA	NOWJZ	ZWPWY
12	HVITJ	MBVID	UVODJ	INMZG	TJIXJ	HKPOZ	MNVIY	YVOVX
13	GUHSI	LAUHC	TUNCI	HMLYF	SIHWI	GJONY	LMUHX	XUNUW
14	FTGRH	KZTGB	STMBH	GLKXE	RHGVH	FINMX	KLTGW	WTMTV
15	ESFQG	JYSFA	RSLAG	FKJWD	QGFUG	EHMLW	JKSFV	VSLSU
16	DREPF	IXREZ	QRKZF	EJIVC	PFETF	DGLKV	IJREU	URKRT
17	CQDOE	HWQDY	PQJYE	DIHUB	OEDSE	CFKJU	HIQDT	TQJQS
18	BPCND	GVPCX	OPIXD	CHGTA	NDCRD	BEJIT	GHPCS	SPIPR
19	AOBMC	FUOBW	NOHWC	BGFSZ	MCBQC	ADIHS	FGOBR	ROHOQ
20	ZNALB	ETNAV	MNGVB	AFERY	LBAPB	ZCHGR	EFNAQ	QNGNP
21	YMZKA	DSMZU	LMFUA	ZEDQX	KAZOA	YBGFQ	DEMZP	PMFMO
22	XLYJZ	CRLYT	KLETZ	YDCPW	JZYNZ	XAFEP	CDLYO	OLELN
23	WKXIY	BQKXS	JKDSY	XCBOV	IYXMY	WZEDO	BCKXN	NKDKM
24	VJWHX	APJWR	IJCRX	WBANU	HXWLX	VYDCN	ABJWM	MJCJL
25	UIVGW	ZOIVQ	HIBQW	VAZMT	GWVKW	UXCBM	ZAIVL	LIBIK

	Table 2.3.1	*PLAIN(1)*	*PLAIN(2)*	*PLAIN(3)*	*CIPHER(1.1)*
Letter	**Probability**	**Frequency**	**Frequency**	**Frequency**	**Frequency**
A	0.0856	0.0843	0.0739	0.0815	0.1052
B	0.0139	0.0143	0.0079	0.0119	0.0251
C	0.0279	0.0424	0.0506	0.0300	0.0072
D	0.0378	0.0269	0.0387	0.0402	0.0096
E	0.1304	0.0992	0.1285	0.1274	0.0012
F	0.0289	0.0185	0.0242	0.0215	0.0263
G	0.0199	0.0143	0.0132	0.0300	0.0030
H	0.0528	0.0329	0.0453	0.0487	0.0843
I	0.0627	0.0825	0.0695	0.0708	0.0143
J	0.0013	0.0000	0.0009	0.0045	0.0424
K	0.0042	0.0066	0.0018	0.0057	0.0269
L	0.0339	0.0257	0.0326	0.0317	0.0992
M	0.0249	0.0412	0.0370	0.0215	0.0185
N	0.0707	0.0819	0.0687	0.0725	0.0143
O	0.0797	0.0926	0.0858	0.0787	0.0329
P	0.0199	0.0293	0.0392	0.0221	0.0825
Q	0.0012	0.0012	0.0022	0.0011	0.0000
R	0.0677	0.0723	0.0682	0.0612	0.0066
S	0.0607	0.0562	0.0599	0.0668	0.0257
T	0.1045	0.1052	0.0920	0.0900	0.0412
U	0.0249	0.0251	0.0255	0.0266	0.0819
V	0.0092	0.0072	0.0084	0.0091	0.0926
W	0.0149	0.0096	0.0106	0.0159	0.0293
X	0.0017	0.0012	0.0004	0.0074	0.0012
Y	0.0199	0.0263	0.0141	0.0210	0.0723
Z	0.0008	0.0030	0.0009	0.0023	0.0562

Figure 3.6.3. Comparison of the frequency of occurrence of letters in *PLAIN(1–3)*, *CIPHER(1.1)* with the probability distribution in Table 2.3.1.

the key. We computed in Sec. 2.12 that 9 letters would be enough *if* Caesar substitution exhibited the characteristics of a random cryptographic system, so that 40 letters is probably sufficient.

The characteristic frequencies with which letters (and n-grams) occur in plaintext may be made the basis of a variety of powerful methods of cryptanalysis. In Fig. 3.6.3, we list

- The frequency of occurrence of letters in *PLAIN(1–3)* and *CIPHER(1.1)*.
- The probability distribution of one-grams from Table 2.3.1.

Note the deviations of the letter frequencies from the probabilities for the letters in *PLAIN(1–3)*; the frequency of `T` is larger than that of `E` in *PLAIN(1)*, contrary to the ordering in Table 2.3.1. In Figs. 3.6.4–6, we compare the probability distribution from in Fig. 2.3.1 and the letter frequencies in *PLAIN(1–3)*. If

$$N(PLAIN(1)) = (N_0(PLAIN(1)), N_1(PLAIN(1)), \ldots, N_{25}(PLAIN(1)))$$

$$N(CIPHER(1.1))$$

$$= (N_0(CIPHER(1.1)), N_1(CIPHER(1.1)), \ldots, N_{25}(CIPHER(1.1)))$$

denote the vectors of *letter counts* in *PLAIN(1)* and *CIPHER(1.1)*

$N_t(PLAIN(1))$: the number of times the letter t appears in *PLAIN(1)*

$N_t(CIPHER(1.1))$: the number of times the letter t appears in *CIPHER(1.1)*

then $\mathbf{N}(PLAIN(1))$ and $\mathbf{N}(CIPHER(1.1))$ are related by

(3.6.1) $$\mathbf{N}^{(7)}(PLAIN(1)) = \mathbf{N}(CIPHER(1.1))$$

where $\mathbf{N}^{(k)}(PLAIN(1))$ denotes the *right cyclic rotation* of the vector $\mathbf{N}(PLAIN(1))$ by k places,

(3.6.2) $$\mathbf{N}^{(k)}(PLAIN(1)) = (N_{0-k}(PLAIN(1)), N_{1-k}(PLAIN(1)), \ldots, N_{m-1-k}(PLAIN(1)))$$

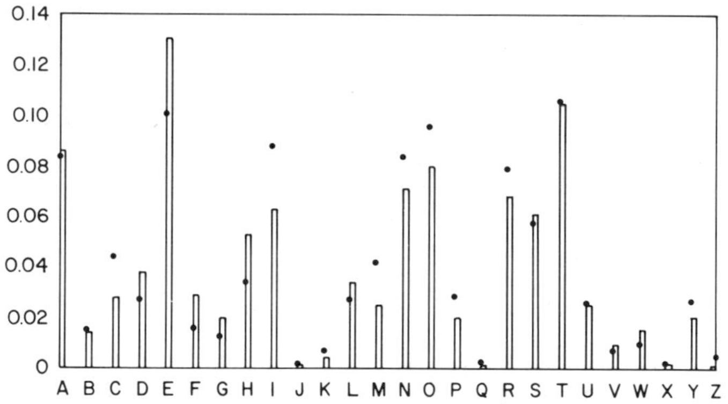

Figure 3.6.4. Comparison of the frequency of occurrence of letters in *PLAIN(1)* with the probability distribution in Table 2.3.1.

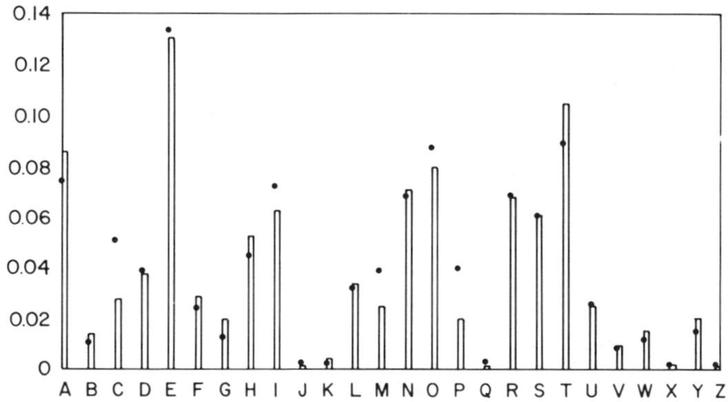

Figure 3.6.5. Comparison of the frequency of occurrence of letters in *PLAIN(2)* with the probability distribution in Table 2.3.1.

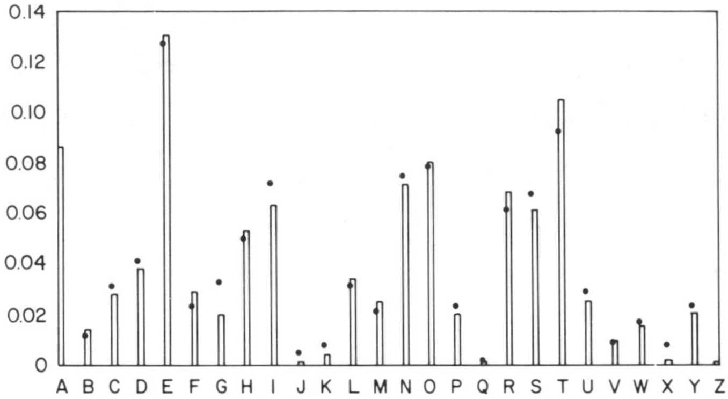

Figure 3.6.6. Comparison of the frequency of occurrence of letters in *PLAIN(3)* with the probability distribution in Table 2.3.1.

In Eq. (3.6.2), as elsewhere in this chapter, arithmetic operations, addition, subtraction, and multiplication, on indices and text are carried out modulo m. To decipher *CIPHER(1.1)*, we will compare the left cyclic shift of the vector of letter counts $\mathbf{N}(CIPHER(1.1))^{(-k)}$ for each k, $0 \leq k < m$, with the probability vector

$$\mathbf{p} = (p(0), p(1), \ldots, p(m-1))$$

derived from Table 2.3.1. The values of k for which $\mathbf{N}^{(-k)}(CIPHER(1.1))$ is closest to $\mathbf{p}$, in a sense to be defined, are the probable choices for the key ?

$$CIPHER(1.1) = C_?(PLAIN(1))$$

Comparing the observed frequencies to a standard probability distribution in order to determine the key is an example of a process that we shall use throughout this book. We pause in the analysis and make a short digression to formulate the ideas underlying what we refer to as the operational procedure.

3.7 THE OPERATIONAL PROCEDURE

We use the term *operational procedure* to describe the cryptanalytic process in which we

(1) Postulate that plaintext is generated by some plaintext source ***S***.
(2) Analyze the ciphertext and methods of recovering the key and/or plaintext using the model provided by ***S***, and
(3) Apply the results developed in (1) and (2) to the actual ciphertext.

The success of this operational procedure depends upon how accurately the model represents actual plaintext. We will show that even crude models of English language plaintext are sufficient to carry out the cryptanalysis of a variety of substitution systems.

The simplest model of plaintext generation is based on the probability of occurrence of letters in text $\{p(t) : 0 \le t < m\}$; it postulates that plaintext is generated by independent and identically distributed trials. The n-gram of plaintext $(x_0, x_1, \ldots, x_{n-1})$ is assigned the probability

$$\Pr_{PLAIN}\{X_0 = x_0, X_1 = x_1, \ldots, X_{n-1} = x_{n-1}\} = p(x_0)p(x_1)\ldots p(x_{n-1}) \tag{3.7.1}$$

Each of the random variables $X_0, X_1, \ldots, X_{n-1}$ takes values in the alphabet $\boldsymbol{Z_m}$ with marginal distribution

$$\Pr_{PLAIN}\{X_i = t\} = p(t) \qquad 0 \le t < m$$

As we have already noted in Chapter 2, this model only approximates English language plaintext. For example, Eq. (3.7.1) assigns the probability $0.00552 \approx 0.1045 \times 0.0528$ to the 2-gram **TH**, while **TH** is actually observed in plaintext with a frequency of approximately 0.0321 (Table 2.3.5).

The number of occurrences of the letter t in an n-gram of plaintext $X_0, X_1, \ldots, X_{n-1}$ will be denoted by $N_t(\mathbf{X})$. The random variable $N_t(\mathbf{X})$ is the sum of the indicator functions

$$N_t(\mathbf{X}) = \sum_{0 \le i < n} \chi_t(X_i)$$

$$\chi_t(X_i) = \begin{cases} 1 & \text{if } X_i = t \\ 0 & \text{if } X_i \ne t \end{cases}$$

Since the random variables $X_0, X_1, \ldots, X_{n-1}$ are independent and identically distributed,

$$\Pr_{PLAIN}\{X_i = t\} = p(t) \qquad 0 \le i < n, 0 \le t < m$$

the random variables $\chi_t(X_0), \chi_t(X_1), \ldots, \chi_t(X_{n-1})$ for each t, $0 \le t < m$, are also independent and identically distributed. This sequence of random variables takes the values 0 and 1 with probabilities

$$\Pr_{PLAIN}\{\chi_t(X_i) = k\} = \begin{cases} p(t) & \text{if } k = 1 \\ 1 - p(t) & \text{if } k = 0 \end{cases}$$

Therefore, the random variables $\chi_t(X_0), \chi_t(X_1), \ldots \chi_t(X_{n-1})$ constitute a *Bernoulli sequence,* and their sum $N_t(\mathbf{X})$ has the *binomial distribution*

$$\Pr\{N_t(\mathbf{X}) = k\} = C(n,k)p(t))^k(1 - p(t))^{n-k} \qquad 0 \le k \le n \qquad 0 \le t < m$$

where C(n,k) is the *binomial coefficient*

$$C(n,k) = n!/k!(n - k)! \qquad 0 \le k \le n$$

The *expectation* and *variance* of $N_t(\mathbf{X})$ are

$$E\{N_t(\mathbf{X})\} = np(t) \qquad Var\{N_t(\mathbf{X})\} = np(t)(1 - p(t)).$$

The central limit theorem provides a measure of the difference between $N_t(\mathbf{X})$ and its expectation $E\{N_t(\mathbf{X})\}$. The random variable

$$[N_t(\mathbf{X}) - n\mu(t)]/\sigma(t)\sqrt{n}$$

obtained by subtracting the mean $n\mu(t)$ from $N_t(\mathbf{X})$ *(centering)* and dividing by the standard deviation $\sigma(t)\sqrt{n}$ *(scaling)*, where $\mu(t)$ and $\sigma(t)$ are given by

$$\mu(t) = p(t) \quad \sigma(t) = [p(t)(1 - p(t))]^{0.5}$$

has the normal distribution as $n \rightarrow \infty$. For sufficiently large n we expect that

$$\Pr\{-3\sigma(t)\sqrt{n} \leq [N_t(\mathbf{X}) - n\mu(t)] \leq 3\sigma(t)\sqrt{n}\} \approx 0.9973 \tag{3.7.2}$$

According to Eq. (3.7.2), the value taken by the random variable $N_t(\mathbf{X})$ will belong to the *3σ-confidence interval*

$$[-3\sigma(t)\sqrt{n} + n\mu(t), n\mu(t) + 3\sigma(t)\sqrt{n}]$$

with probability 0.9973 as n increases to ∞. In Table 3.7.1, we list (1) the number of occurrences $N_t(\mathbf{X})$ of each letter in *PLAIN(1–3)*, and (2) the lower and upper limits $\lambda(t) = np(t) - 3p(t)\sigma(t)\sqrt{n}$ and $\rho(t) = np(t) + 3p(t)\sigma(t)\sqrt{n}$ of the 3σ-confidence interval.

The frequencies of occurrence of several of the letters in *PLAIN(1)*, `C E H I`

TABLE 3.7.1
The Number of Occurrences of Each Letter in *PLAIN(1–3)* and Their Respective 3σ-Confidence Intervals

	PLAIN(1)			***PLAIN(2)***			***PLAIN(3)***		
Letter	**λ(t)**	**N_t(X)**	**ρ(t)**	**λ(t)**	**N_t(X)**	**ρ(t)**	**λ(t)**	**N_t(X)**	**ρ(t)**
A	108.92	141	177.59	154.53	168	234.55	115.94	144	186.49
B	8.93	24	37.71	14.90	18	48.43	9.84	21	39.40
C	26.44	71	66.84	39.80	115	86.88	28.48	53	69.99
D	39.89	45	86.71	58.68	88	113.24	42.76	71	90.87
E	176.88	166	259.53	248.18	292	344.49	187.88	225	272.80
F	27.76	31	68.85	41.66	55	89.55	29.88	38	72.10
G	16.17	24	50.46	25.27	30	65.22	17.55	53	52.78
H	60.85	55	115.72	87.92	103	151.86	65.00	86	121.38
I	75.19	138	134.69	107.84	158	177.19	80.21	125	141.34
J	−2.25	0	6.58	−2.20	2	8.08	−2.25	8	6.82
K	−0.92	11	14.91	.27	4	18.73	−0.75	10	15.52
L	34.44	43	78.83	51.05	74	102.77	36.98	56	82.58
M	22.53	69	60.76	34.27	84	78.83	24.32	38	63.60
N	86.82	137	149.72	123.96	156	197.26	92.53	128	157.15
O	100.03	155	166.48	142.25	195	219.69	106.53	139	174.80
P	16.17	49	50.46	25.27	89	65.22	17.55	39	52.78
Q	−2.24	2	6.24	−2.23	5	7.65	−2.25	2	6.47
R	82.44	121	144.10	117.90	155	189.75	87.89	108	151.24
S	72.30	94	130.92	103.84	136	172.14	77.15	118	137.37
T	137.36	176	212.44	193.77	209	281.27	146.05	159	223.20
U	22.53	42	60.76	34.27	58	78.83	24.32	47	63.60
V	3.63	12	27.01	7.19	19	34.43	4.17	16	28.19
W	10.10	16	39.87	16.59	24	51.28	11.08	28	41.67
X	−2.21	2	7.88	−2.03	1	9.72	−2.19	13	8.17
Y	16.17	44	50.46	25.27	32	65.22	17.55	37	52.78
Z	−2.11	5	4.68	−2.22	2	5.70	−2.14	4	4.84

`M Z`, lie outside of their respective 3σ-confidence intervals. These discrepancies are consequences of the subject matter of *PLAIN(1)*, the large number of times the words `information`, `cryptography`, `cryptographic`, and `organization` appear. More refined statistical methods for testing if the values in Table 3.7.1 are *consistent* with the sources defined in Chapter 2 are available, but wc will not go into this matter.

3.8 ANALYSIS OF CAESAR SUBSTITUTION—II

To cryptanalyze *CIPHER(1.1)*, we begin by tabulating the frequency of occurrence of each letter in the *CIPHER(1.1)* and the probability distribution from Table 2.3.1. They are arranged in decreasing order in Table 3.8.1.

We cannot simply match ciphertext and plaintext letters in decreasing order of occurrence,

```
E T A O N R I
↓ ↓ ↓ ↓ ↓ ↓ ↓
a l v h p u y
```

since the frequency of letters in plaintext will vary from the typical profile in Table 2.3.1. Divergence of the frequency of occurrence of individual letters from the probabilities in Table 2.3.1 is typical and due to the subject matter of the plaintext. What we can expect in "real" plaintext is rough agreement; although it might occur that neither `E` or `T` is the most frequent letter in some specific example of plaintext, it would be most unusual for the letter `W`, say, to have the highest frequency of occurrence. And if this is the case, it is only a reflection on our choice of model, which may have to be adjusted to special circumstances. The relationships between the components of the *entire* vector **N**(*CIPHER(1.1)*) will enable us to identify the key.

TABLE 3.8.1
Comparison of the Frequency of Occurrence of the Letters in *CIPHER(1.1)* with the Probability Distribution from Table 2.3.1

CIPHER(1.1)		***Table 2.3.1***		***CIPHER(1.1)***		***Table 2.3.1***	
Letter	**Frequency**	**Letter**	**Probability**	**Letter**	**Frequency**	**Letter**	**Probability**
a	0.1052	E	0.1304	f	0.0263	M	0.0249
l	0.0992	T	0.1045	s	0.0257	U	0.0249
v	0.0926	A	0.0856	b	0.0251	G	0.0199
h	0.0843	O	0.0797	m	0.0185	P	0.0199
p	0.0825	N	0.0707	i	0.0143	Y	0.0199
u	0.0819	R	0.0677	n	0.0143	W	0.0149
y	0.0723	I	0.0627	d	0.0096	B	0.0139
z	0.0562	S	0.0607	c	0.0072	V	0.0092
j	0.0424	H	0.0528	r	0.0066	K	0.0042
t	0.0412	D	0.0378	g	0.0030	X	0.0017
o	0.0329	L	0.0339	e	0.0012	J	0.0013
w	0.0293	F	0.0289	x	0.0012	Q	0.0012

To cryptanalyze *CIPHER(1.1)* we will first match the set $HIGH_{PLAIN(1)}$ of plaintext letters having the highest probability of occurrence {`E T A O N R I S H`} with the set $HIGH_{CIPHER(1.1)}$ of ciphertext letters {`a l v h p u y z`} having the highest frequency of occurrence in *CIPHER(1.1)*. Matching assumes that there is a partial correspondence between these two sets of letters, although perhaps not in the given order. Replacing the alphabetic letters by their corresponding numerical values, we have

$$\mathrm{HIGH}_{\mathrm{PLAIN(1)}} = \{4, 19, 0, 14, 13, 17, 8, 18, 7\}$$

$$\mathrm{HIGH}_{\mathrm{CIPHER(1.1)}} = \{0, 11, 21, 7, 15, 20, 24, 25, 9\}$$

Since the relationship between the plaintext and ciphertext is

$$\text{ciphertext} = (\text{plaintext} + 7) \pmod{26}$$

the number of letters common to both ($HIGH_{CIPHER(1.1)}$ − j) and $HIGH_{PLAIN(1)}$ should be large when j = 7. If every letter in $HIGH_{CIPHER(1.1)}$ corresponds to some letter in $HIGH_{PLAIN(1)}$, then the number of letters in the intersection

$$\mathrm{INT}(j) = |(\mathrm{HIGH}_{\mathrm{CIPHER(1.1)}} - j) \cap \mathrm{HIGH}_{\mathrm{PLAIN(1)}}|$$

is equal to $|HIGH_{CIPHER(1.1)}|$ when j = 7, and is likely to be smaller for $j \neq 7$. When INT(j) = s, there are s pairs of letters (x_i, y_i) $(0 \leq i < s)$ with $x_i \in HIGH_{PLAIN(1)}$ and $y_i \in HIGH_{CIPHER(1.1)}$ that satisfy $y_i = x_i + j$ $(0 \leq i < s)$. The most likely estimates for the key are those values of j that maximize INT(j) (listed in Table 3.8.3) *or* N(j), the number of times j is represented as a difference y − x (modulo 26) with $x \in HIGH_{PLAIN(1)}$ and $y \in HIGH_{CIPHER(1.1)}$ (Table 3.8.2).

TABLE 3.8.2
Count of Differences
$HIGH_{CIPHER(1.1)} - HIGH_{PLAIN(1)}$

j:	0	1	2	3	4	5	6	7	8	9	10	11	12	13	14	15	16	17	18	19	20	21	22	23	24	25
	↓	↓	↓	↓	↓	↓	↓	↓	↓	↓	↓	↓	↓	↓	↓	↓	↓	↓	↓	↓	↓	↓	↓	↓	↓	↓
N(j):	2	3	4	4	2	2	3	8	4	2	1	4	3	3	2	2	4	4	4	3	4	3	3	2	3	2

The value j = 7 that maximizes INT(j) and N(j) must be checked by a partial decipherment of *CIPHER(1.1)*. If there are only a small number of values of j for which INT(j) or N(j) is large, the problem reduces to distinguishing between these values by trial decipherment. Matching the ciphertext letters of highest frequency with the plaintext letters of highest probability is an example of a test that reduces the effective size of the key space to be searched; for Caesar substitution, the key space is small to begin with, so that little is achieved by a reduction, but we will study systems later on in which a single test drastically reduces the likely choices of the key.

An alternate method of cryptanalysis uses *correlation*. Normalize the vector

TABLE 3.8.3
$\text{INT}(j) = |((HIGH_{CIPHER(1.1)} - j) \cap HIGH_{PLAIN(1)}|$

j	INT(j)	j	INT(j)
0	2	13	3
1	3	14	2
2	4	15	2
3	4	16	4
4	2	17	4
5	2	18	4
6	3	19	3
7	**8**	20	4
8	4	21	3
9	2	22	3
10	1	23	2
11	4	24	3
12	3	25	2

N(*CIPHER(1.1)*) of letter counts by dividing its components by n, the number of letters in the ciphertext, and denote the resulting vector by **F**(*CIPHER(1.1)*)

$$\mathbf{F}(CIPHER(1.1)) = (F_0(CIPHER(1.1), F_1(CIPHER(1.1), \ldots, F_{25}(CIPHER(1.1)))$$

$$F_t(CIPHER(1.1)) = N_t(CIPHER(1.1))/n \qquad 0 \leq t < 26$$

The relationship $\mathbf{N}(CIPHER(1.1)) = \mathbf{N}^{(7)}(PLAIN(1))$ suggests that the vector $\mathbf{F}^{(-k)}(CIPHER(1.1))$ will be close in some sense to the probability vector **p** derived from Table 2.3.1,

$$\mathbf{p} = (p(0), p(1), \ldots, p(25))$$

when k = 7. The *correlation* between the vectors $\mathbf{F}^{(-j)}(CIPHER(1.1))$ and **p** is defined by

$$\rho[j : \mathbf{F}(CIPHER(1.1)), \mathbf{p}] = \sum_{0 \leq t < 26} F_t(CIPHER(1.1))p(t - j)$$

We use the operational procedure to show that maximizing the correlation ρ_j between **F**(*CIPHER(1.1)*) and **p** provides a good estimate for the key. If plaintext $\mathbf{X} = (X_0, X_1, \ldots, X_{n-1})$ has been enciphered by a Caesar substitution into ciphertext $\mathbf{Y} = (Y_0, Y_1, \ldots, Y_{n-1})$,

$$Y_i = C_k(X_i) \qquad 0 \leq i < n$$

the vectors of letter counts in the plaintext **X** and ciphertext **Y**

$$\mathbf{N}(\mathbf{Y}) = (N_0(\mathbf{Y}), N_1(\mathbf{Y}), \ldots, N_{m-1}(\mathbf{Y}))$$

$$\mathbf{N}(\mathbf{X}) = (N_0(\mathbf{X}), N_1(\mathbf{X}), \ldots, N_{m-1}(\mathbf{X}))$$

are related by $\mathbf{N}(\mathbf{Y}) = (N_{0-k}(\mathbf{X}), N_{1-k}(\mathbf{X}), \ldots, N_{m-1-k}(\mathbf{X})$. According to the law of large numbers,

$$\text{limit}_{n\to\infty} N_t(\mathbf{X})/n = p(t) \qquad 0 \le t < m$$

For any two positive numbers $\epsilon > 0$ and $\delta > 0$, there exists an integer M (depending on ϵ, δ, and t), such that

$$\Pr\{|N_t(\mathbf{X})/n - p(t)| \le \epsilon\} \ge 1 - \delta \tag{3.8.1}$$

The probability that the frequency of occurrences $N_t(\mathbf{X})/n$ of the letter t is closer than ϵ to its expected value p(t) is at least $1 - \delta$ when the size n of the plaintext sample **X** is at least M. While the probability in Eq. (3.8.1) pertains to the number of occurrences of just the letter t, a simple probabilistic argument implies the stronger condition; there exists an integer M′ for which *all* of the differences

$$|N_t(\mathbf{X})/n - p(t)| \qquad 0 \le t < m$$

are simultaneously smaller than ϵ in a sample of size n with probability at least $1 - \delta$; that is,

$$\Pr\{\max_t |N_t(\mathbf{X})/n - p(t)| > \epsilon\} < \delta \tag{3.8.2}$$

for all integers $n \ge M'$. A crude relationship involving ϵ, δ, and M can be obtained from Chebychev's inequality,

$$\Pr\{|X - E\{X\}| > \alpha\} \le \text{Var}\{X\}/\alpha^2$$

which yields

$$\Pr\{|N_t(\mathbf{X})/n - p(t)| \le \epsilon\} \ge 1 - p(t)(1 - p(t))/n\epsilon^2$$

Any integer $M' > np(t)(1 - p(t))/\delta\epsilon^2$ will serve in Eq. (3.8.2).

Inequality (3.8.2) means that the distance between the vectors **F**(**X**) and **p** is small with probability close to one as $n \to \infty$. The *distance* between the vectors **F**(**X**) and **p** referred to here is distance in the *maximum norm*

$$\|\mathbf{F}(\mathbf{X}) - \mathbf{p}\|_\infty = \max_t |N_t(\mathbf{X})/n - p(t)|$$

Since $\mathbf{F}(\mathbf{Y}) = \mathbf{F}^{(-k)}(\mathbf{X})$, we may deduce that

$$\|\mathbf{F}^{(-j)}(\mathbf{Y}) - \mathbf{p}\|_\infty = \max_t |N_t(\mathbf{X})/n - p(t)|$$

is minimized when $j = k$ as $n \to \infty$ with probability 1. The relationship between the correlation coefficient and distance in the maximum norm $\|\mathbf{F}^{(-j)}(\mathbf{Y}) - \mathbf{p}\|_\infty$ is standard linear algebra.

The *Euclidean distance* between the two n-dimensional vectors

$$\mathbf{a} = (a_0, a_1, \ldots, a_{n-1})$$

$$\mathbf{b} = (b_0, b_1, \ldots, b_{n-1})$$

is

$$\|\mathbf{a} - \mathbf{b}\|_2 = \left(\sum_{0 \le i < n} (a_i - b_i)^2 \right)^{1/2}$$

The distance between vectors as measured by the Euclidean and maximum norms are comparable; that is, there exist constants C_1 and C_2 (depending only on the dimension n) such that

$$C_1\|\mathbf{a} - \mathbf{b}\|_2 \le \|\mathbf{a} - \mathbf{b}\|_\infty \le C_2\|\mathbf{a} - \mathbf{b}\|_2$$

for arbitrary n-dimensional vectors **a** and **b**. If the Euclidean distance between vectors **a** and **b** is "small," the distance in the maximum norm is also "small," and conversely. Thus we expect

$$\|\mathbf{F}^{(-j)}(\mathbf{Y}) - \mathbf{p}\|_2$$

to be minimized by $j = k$ as $n \to \infty$. Finally, we use the n-dimensional version of the law of cosines

$$\|\mathbf{a} - \mathbf{b}\|_2 = (\|\mathbf{a}\|_2^2 + \|\mathbf{b}\|_2^2 - 2(\mathbf{a},\mathbf{b}))^{1/2}$$

where $\|\mathbf{a}\|_2^2$ and $\|\mathbf{b}\|_2^2$ are the squares of the Euclidean distances of **a** and **b** from the vector $\mathbf{0} = (0, 0, \ldots, 0)$,

$$\|\mathbf{a}\|_2^2 = \sum_{0 \le i < n} a_i^2 \qquad \|\mathbf{b}\|_2 = \sum_{0 \le i < n} b_i^2$$

and $(\mathbf{a},\mathbf{b})$ is the *inner product* defined by

$$(\mathbf{a},\mathbf{b}) = \sum_{0 \le i < n} a_i b_i$$

If $\mathbf{a} = \mathbf{F}^{(-j)}(\mathbf{Y})$ and $\mathbf{b} = \mathbf{p}$, then (1) the square of the Euclidean norm of $\mathbf{F}^{(-j)}(\mathbf{Y})$ has the same value for each j, $0 \le j < m$, and (2) the inner product $(\mathbf{F}^{(-j)}(\mathbf{Y}),\mathbf{p})$ is the correlation

$$\rho[j : \mathbf{F}(\mathbf{Y}),\mathbf{p}] = \sum_{0 \le t < m} F_t(\mathbf{Y})p(t - j)$$

Therefore, minimizing the Euclidean distance between $\mathbf{F}^{(-j)}(\mathbf{Y})$ and **p** over values of j, $0 \le j < m$, is the same as maximizing $\rho[j : \mathbf{F}(\mathbf{Y}),\mathbf{p}]$. In Table 3.8.4, the tabulation of the correlation coefficient for $0 \le j < 26$ for $\mathbf{Y} =$ *CIPHER(1.1)* shows that $\rho[j : \mathbf{F}(\mathbf{Y}),\mathbf{p}]$ is maximized when $j = 7$.

3.9 MIXED STANDARD ALPHABETS

Caesar encipherment is particularly simple to cryptanalyze because the identification of a *single* plaintext-ciphertext letter-pair correspondence reveals the entire substitution. One method of improving the strength of Caesar encipherment is to replace the *standard alphabet table* or *Vigenère table* of Figure 2.4.2 by a *mixed alphabet table* as in Fig. 3.9.1. To obtain a mixed alphabet table, we begin by selecting a *key word* or *phrase*. Starting with the key word ATOMIC, the letters

TABLE 3.8.4
Correlation Between F*(CIPHER(1.1))* and p

j	ρ[j:F(*CIPHER(1.1)*),p]	j	ρ[j:F(*CIPHER(1.1)*),p]
0	0.0366	13	0.0369
1	0.0382	14	0.0369
2	0.0378	15	0.0352
3	0.0424	16	0.0374
4	0.0324	17	0.0394
5	0.0353	18	0.0437
6	0.0386	19	0.0387
7	***0.0666***	20	0.0445
8	0.0400	21	0.0390
9	0.0330	22	0.0460
10	0.0286	23	0.0344
11	0.0425	24	0.0340
12	0.0340	25	0.0277

k_2	A	B	C	D	E	F	G	H	I	J	K	L	M	N	O	P	Q	R	S	T	U	V	W	X	Y	Z
0	A	T	O	M	I	C	B	D	E	F	G	H	J	K	L	N	P	Q	R	S	U	V	W	X	Y	Z
1	T	O	M	I	C	B	D	E	F	G	H	J	K	L	N	P	Q	R	S	U	V	W	X	Y	Z	A
2	O	M	I	C	B	D	E	F	G	H	J	K	L	N	P	Q	R	S	U	V	W	X	Y	Z	A	T
3	M	I	C	B	D	E	F	G	H	J	K	L	N	P	Q	R	S	U	V	W	X	Y	Z	A	T	O
4	I	C	B	D	E	F	G	H	J	K	L	N	P	Q	R	S	U	V	W	X	Y	Z	A	T	O	M
5	C	B	D	E	F	G	H	J	K	L	N	P	Q	R	S	U	V	W	X	Y	Z	A	T	O	M	I
6	B	D	E	F	G	H	J	K	L	N	P	Q	R	S	U	V	W	X	Y	Z	A	T	O	M	I	C
7	D	E	F	G	H	J	K	L	N	P	Q	R	S	U	V	W	X	Y	Z	A	T	O	M	I	C	B
8	E	F	G	H	J	K	L	N	P	Q	R	S	U	V	W	X	Y	Z	A	T	O	M	I	C	B	D
9	F	G	H	J	K	L	N	P	Q	R	S	U	V	W	X	Y	Z	A	T	O	M	I	C	B	D	E
10	G	H	J	K	L	N	P	Q	R	S	U	V	W	X	Y	Z	A	T	O	M	I	C	B	D	E	F
11	H	J	K	L	N	P	Q	R	S	U	V	W	X	Y	Z	A	T	O	M	I	C	B	D	E	F	G
12	J	K	L	N	P	Q	R	S	U	V	W	X	Y	Z	A	T	O	M	I	C	B	D	E	F	G	H
13	K	L	N	P	Q	R	S	U	V	W	X	Y	Z	A	T	O	M	I	C	B	D	E	F	G	H	J
14	L	N	P	Q	R	S	U	V	W	X	Y	Z	A	T	O	M	I	C	B	D	E	F	G	H	J	K
15	N	P	Q	R	S	U	V	W	X	Y	Z	A	T	O	M	I	C	B	D	E	F	G	H	J	K	L
16	P	Q	R	S	U	V	W	X	Y	Z	A	T	O	M	I	C	B	D	E	F	G	H	J	K	L	N
17	Q	R	S	U	V	W	X	Y	Z	A	T	O	M	I	C	B	D	E	F	G	H	J	K	L	N	P
18	R	S	U	V	W	X	Y	Z	A	T	O	M	I	C	B	D	E	F	G	H	J	K	L	N	P	Q
19	S	U	V	W	X	Y	Z	A	T	O	M	I	C	B	D	E	F	G	H	J	K	L	N	P	Q	R
20	U	V	W	X	Y	Z	A	T	O	M	I	C	B	D	E	F	G	H	J	K	L	N	P	Q	R	S
21	V	W	X	Y	Z	A	T	O	M	I	C	B	D	E	F	G	H	J	K	L	N	P	Q	R	S	U
22	W	X	Y	Z	A	T	O	M	I	C	B	D	E	F	G	H	J	K	L	N	P	Q	R	S	U	V
23	X	Y	Z	A	T	O	M	I	C	B	D	E	F	G	H	J	K	L	N	P	Q	R	S	U	V	W
24	Y	Z	A	T	O	M	I	C	B	D	E	F	G	H	J	K	L	N	P	Q	R	S	U	V	W	X
25	Z	A	T	O	M	I	C	B	D	E	F	G	H	J	K	L	N	P	Q	R	S	U	V	W	X	Y

Figure 3.9.1. Mixed Vigenere Table : k_1 = ATOMIC.

of the alphabet {AB . . . Z} are then ordered by writing the letters of the key word ATOMIC (repetitions, if any, deleted) in the first row followed by the remaining letters in the alphabet

BDEFGHJKLNPQRSUVWXYZ

yielding

A T O M I C B D E F G H J K L N P Q R S U V W X Y Z

The remaining 25 rows of the *mixed Vigenère table* are generated by successive left cyclic rotations of this permutation of the alphabet.

By *word* or *phrase* we do not necessarily mean only a word or phrase in some natural language; when building the table in Fig. 3.9.1 we may start with *any* permutation of the letters {A B . . . Z} in the first row and obtain the remaining rows by cyclic rotation. There are m! different mixed Vigenère tables for the alphabet Z_m; for m = 26 there are 26! ≈ 4×10^{26} different tables.

The *mixed Caesar substitution MC* = $\{MC_{k_1,k_2} : 0 \le k_2 < m\}$ employs the two-part key $k = (k_1, k_2)$ in which (1) k_1 is the first row in the mixed Vigenère table; k_1 = ATOMIC means that the remaining alphabet letters are written in the normal order, and (2) k_2 selects the row in the table. The transformation $MC_{\text{ATOMIC},7}$ makes the letter substitutions

$$MC_{\text{ATOMIC},7}(\text{A}) = \text{D} \quad MC_{\text{ATOMIC},7}(\text{B}) = \text{E} \quad \ldots \quad MC_{\text{ATOMIC},7}(\text{Z}) = \text{B}$$

The identification of the single mixed Caesar substitution pair A → d does not reveal the plaintext-to-ciphertext correspondences for the remaining letters.

We encounter in the mixed Caesar substitution *equivalent keys:* keys (k_1, k_2) and (k_1', k_2'), which produce the same substitution. If the key word k_1 is rotated cyclically (to the left) s places $k_1 \to k_1'$, then (k_1,k_2) and $(k_1', k_2 + s)$ generate the same substitution. For example, k = (ATOMIC,2) and k′ = (OMICBD . . . ZAT,0) are equivalent keys. Cryptanalysis can only recover the k_1 up to an arbitrary cyclic rotation. The number of nonequivalent keys k_1 is 25! ≈ 8×10^{24}. The encipherment *CIPHER(1.2)* of *PLAIN(1)* by this table is shown in Fig. 3.9.2.

In Tables 3.9.3 and 3.9.4 we list

- The frequency of occurrence (in decreasing order) of the 1-grams in *CIPHER(1.2)* and the probabilities from Table 2.3.1.
- The 20 2-grams having the largest number of occurrences in *CIPHER(1.2)* and their *reversals* and the corresponding data for plaintext from Table 2.3.3.

We begin by searching for the ciphertext 2-gram in *CIPHER(1.2)*, which is the encipherment of plaintext TH, assuming that the plaintext T has been enciphered into one of the letters a h v d from Table 3.9.3. The likely choices for the ciphertext of TH from Table 3.9.4 are

an (2.4:1) al (∞:1) ah (3.2:1)

`av`	(2.6:1)	`hz`	(2.3:1)	`hy`	(0.96:1)
`vu`	(5.9:1)	`da`	(5.9:1)	`du`	(1.8:1)

The figures in parentheses are the ratios of the frequency of occurrence of the ciphertext 2-gram to the frequency of its reversal. We observe that the reversal `HT` of `TH` occurs far less frequently than `TH` (in the ratio 25:1). Only `al`, `vu` and `da` among these 2-grams is consistent with this description.

If plaintext `TH` → `al` or `vu` or `da`, the ciphertext letter corresponding to `E` is likely to be one of the remaining high frequency ciphertext letters `a h v d`. We decide among the possibilities for the ciphertext of `TH` by the following observation:

- `ER` and its reversal `RE` appear in Table 3.9.4.
- `HE` but not its reversal `EH` appear in Table 3.9.4.

If `TH` → `al`, there exists a ciphertext 2-gram (y_0, y_1) with the following characteristics:

- (y_0,y_1) and (y_1,y_0) have approximately the same number of occurrences in *CIPHER(1.2)* and both appear in Table 3.9.4.
- (`l`, y_0) but not (y_0, `l`) *or* (`l`, y_1) but not (y_1, `l`) appear in Table 3.9.4.

```
sducv ykdun bdanv uzyhr cvufv swtah yzdug gdadf vsstu nfdan vuzav qhhwa
lhnyv whyda nvuzy tuunu kzsvv alrce csdqn uknuj vysda nvusv yhdff hzzne
rhavs vyhwh vwrhm nalnu alhvy kdunb danvu etadz naehf vshzs vyhdf fhzzn
erhnu jvysd anvuy hxtny hzsvy hwyva hfanv ualdu cvtsd cuvml dohcv tfduu
vmwyv ahfan ujvys danvu zavyh gvucv tywyh snzhz ecwlz cnfdr shdzt yhzal
darns nadff hzzav dtalv ynbhg whvwr hznsn rdyrc nesld ygmdy hdugz vjamd
yhwyv gtfaz ldohj hdaty hzald ufdue htzhg avngh uanjc dugfl hfqal hdtal
vynbd anvuv jwhvw rhayc nukav kdnud ffhzz avdzc zahsd ugnaz nujvy sdanv
uuvma lhyhn zdmdc avwvy ahfan ujvys danvu hohuj tyalh yalhn esfyc wavky
dwlnf ztezc zahsf duhia huggd adfvu ayvrd ugwyv ahfan vuava lhgda dfvss
tunfd anvuz ahysn udrzd ugrnu qzald azwhh gnujv ysdan vujyv svuhr vfdan
vuavd uvalh ynatz hzdzv wlnza nfdah gdrkv ynals dzayn fazha vjytr hzavh
ufycw avyzf ydser hgdad ehjvy hnanz zavyh gvyay duzsn aahga vduva lhyrv
fdanv udugg hfycw anaml huuhh ghgjv ywyvf hzznu knahs wrvcz hufyc wanvu
ahflu nxthz alduf duyhg tfhnu jvysd anvuh iwvzt yhzmn alnuc vtyfv sstun
fdanv uzuha mvyqd zmhrr dzwyv onghd zczah sedzh jvyal hghoh rvwsh uavjh
ufycw anvuw yvkyd szalh nesfy cwavk ydwln fztez czahs nzdoh yzdan rhavv
rjvyf vuayv rrnuk dugwy vahfa nuknu jvysd anvua lyvtk lhufy cwanv uecdf
vsenu danvu vjwyv kydss nukdu gzuda hysnu drldy gmdyh jhdat yhzna fduhu
fycwa duggh fycwa nujvy sdanv udtav sdanf drrcd ugmna lvtan uahyo huanv
uecal hahys nudrt zhyvy dwwrn fdanv utznu kdudr kvyna lsdug dqhcm lnfln
ugnon gtdrn bhzal hdrkv ynals alhzt ezcza hshuf ycwaz dwwrn fdanv unujv
ysdan vuehj vyhna nzzhu ajyvs dahys nudrv yfvsw tahyr vfdan vudug huahy
zcvty gdadf vsstu nfdan vuzuh amvyq daalh yhfhn onuka hysnu drvyf vswta
hyrvf danvu alhzd shqhc nztzh gavgh fycwa alhnu jvysd anvud jahyn arhdo
hzalh uhamv yqnud ggnan vuava lhdrk vynal salhn eszte zczah swyvo nghzq
hckhu hydan vuqhc sdudk hshua ohynj nfdan vudug vwhyd anvud rjhda tyhza
ldahu ldufh alhed znffy cwavk ydwln fzhft ynacv jalhz tezcz ahs
```

Figure 3.9.2. *CIPHER(1.2)* : $MC_{ATOMIC,7}$ encipherment of *PLAIN(1)*.

TABLE 3.9.3

Comparison of the Frequency of Occurrence of Letters in *CIPHER(1.2)* with the Probability Distribution in Table 2.3.1

CIPHER(1.2)				Table 2.3.3			
Letter	**Frequency**	**Letter**	**Frequency**	**Letter**	**Probability**	**Letter**	**Probability**
a	0.1052	c	0.0263	E	0.1304	M	0.0249
h	0.0992	r	0.0257	U	0.0249	T	0.1045
v	0.0926	t	0.0251	G	0.0199	A	0.0856
d	0.0843	j	0.0185	P	0.0199	O	0.0797
n	0.0825	e	0.0143	Y	0.0199	N	0.0707
u	0.0819	k	0.0143	W	0.0149	R	0.0677
y	0.0723	m	0.0096	B	0.0139	I	0.0627
z	0.0562	o	0.0072	V	0.0092	S	0.0607
f	0.0424	q	0.0066	K	0.0042	H	0.0528
s	0.0412	b	0.0030	X	0.0017	D	0.0378
l	0.0329	i	0.0012	J	0.0013	L	0.0339
w	0.0293	x	0.0012	Q	0.0012	F	0.0289
g	0.0269	p	0.0000	Z	0.0008	C	0.0279

If TH → vu, there exists a ciphertext 2-gram (y_0, y_1) with the following characteristics:

- (y_0, y_1) and (y_1, y_0) have approximately the same number of occurrences in *CIPHER(1.2)* and both appear in Table 3.9.4.
- (u, y_0) but not (y_0, u) *or* (u, y_1) but not (y_1, u) appear in Table 3.9.4.

TABLE 3.9.4

Number of Occurrences of 2-Grams in Table 2.3.3 and *CIPHER(1.2)*

Table 2.3.3				*CIPHER(1.2)*			
TH	2161	HT	85	an	48	na	20
HE	2053	EH	16	da	46	ad	8
IN	1550	NI	301	vu	41	uv	7
ER	1436	RE	1280	al	39	la	0
RE	1280	ER	1436	vy	39	vy	17
ON	1232	NO	239	nv	36	vn	1
AN	1216	NA	249	nu	33	un	9
EN	1029	NE	549	du	31	ud	17
AT	1019	TA	381	ah	29	ha	9
ES	917	SE	595	lh	25	hl	0
ED	890	DE	572	za	24	az	5
TE	872	ET	301	av	23	va	9
TI	865	IT	704	hz	23	zh	10
OR	861	RO	510	yh	23	hy	22
ST	823	TS	257	hy	22	yh	23
AR	764	RA	470	na	20	an	48
ND	761	DN	8	sd	20	ds	4
TO	756	OT	223	fd	19	df	9
NT	743	TN	9	hu	18	uh	10
IS	741	SI	390	ua	17	au	0

If **TH** → **da**, there exists a ciphertext 2-gram (y_0, y_1) with the following characteristics:

- (y_0, y_1) and (y_1, y_0) have approximately the same number of occurrences in *CIPHER(1.2)* and both appear in Table 3.9.4.
- (a, y_0) but not (y_0, a) *or* (a, y_1) but not (y_1, a) appear in Table 3.9.4.

Examination of Table 3.9.4 shows

- If **TH** → **al**, the correspondences **HE** → **lh** and **ER** → **hy** are likely.
- If **TH** → **vu**, the correspondences **HE** → **ua** and **ER** → **an** are likely.
- If **TH** → **da**, **HE** → **al**, there is no letter * such that both l* and its reversal *l appear in Table 3.9.4.

Thus only **TH** → **al**, **HE** → **lh**, **ER** → **hy** *or* **TH** → **vu**, **HE** → **ua**, **ER** → **an** remain as likely solutions. To eliminate one of the two, we attempt to identify the ciphertext corresponding to **N**. We observe that the four plaintext 2-grams, **IN**, **ON**, **AN**, **EN**, occur frequently in plaintext, and we will search for a ciphertext letter * with the property that

- * Is the final letter of four 2-grams in Table 3.9.4.
- * Appears in Table 3.9.3 among the high frequency plaintext letters.
- The ciphertext of **E** appears paired with * in Table 3.9.4.

Only u meets this description, so that **TH** → **al**, **HE** → **lh**, **ER** → **hy** and {**IN**, **ON**, **AN**, **EN**} → {**vu**, **nu**, **du**, **hu**} in some order. Since **E** → **h**, we will next test the six ways of making a correspondence between **I O A** and **v n d** by deciphering a fragment of the ciphertext using the partial specification of the substitution table already determined.

Case 1:

A	B	C	D	E	F	G	H	I	J	K	L	M	N	O	P	Q	R	S	T	U	V	W	X	Y	Z
↓	↓	↓	↓	↓	↓	↓	↓	↓	↓	↓	↓	↓	↓	↓	↓	↓	↓	↓	↓	↓	↓	↓	↓	↓	↓
n	?	?	?	h	?	?	l	d	?	?	?	?	u	v	?	?	?	?	a	?	?	?	?	?	?

```
sINcO ykINA bITAO NzyEr cONfO swtTE yzINg gITIf OsstN AfITA ONzTO qEEwT
HEAyO wEyIT AONzy tNNAN kzsOO THrce csIqA NkANj OysIT AONsO yEIff EzzAe
rETOs OyEwE OwrEm ATHAN THEOy kINAb ITAON etTIz ATeEf OsEzs OyEIf fEzzA
erEAN jOysI TAONy ExtAy EzsOy EwyOT EfTAO NTHIN cOtsI cNOmH IoEcO tfINN
OmwyO TEfTA NjOys ITAON zTOyE gONcO tywyE sAzEz ecwHz cAfIr sEIzt yEzTH
ITrAs ATIff EzzTO ItTHO yAbEg wEOwr EzAsA rIyrc AesHI ygmIy EINgz OjTmI
yEwyO gtfTz HIoEj EITty EzTHI NfINe EtzEg TOAgE NTAjc INgfH EfqTH EItTH
OyAbI TAONO jwEOw rETyc ANkTO kIANI ffEzz TOIzc zTEsI NgATz ANjOy sITAO
```

Case 2:

A	B	C	D	E	F	G	H	I	J	K	L	M	N	O	P	Q	R	S	T	U	V	W	X	Y	Z
↓	↓	↓	↓	↓	↓	↓	↓	↓	↓	↓	↓	↓	↓	↓	↓	↓	↓	↓	↓	↓	↓	↓	↓	↓	↓
v	?	?	?	h	?	?	l	d	?	?	?	?	u	n	?	?	?	?	a	?	?	?	?	?	?

```
sINcA ykINO bITOA NzyEr cANfA swtTE yzINg gITIf AsstN OfITO ANzTA qEEwT
HEOyA wEyIT OANzy tNNON kzsAA THrce csIqO NkONj AysIT OANsA yEIff EzzOe
rETAs AyEwE AwrEm OTHON THEAy kINOb ITOAN etTIz OTeEf AsEzs AyEIf fEzzO
erEON jAysI TOANy ExtOy EzsAy EwyAT EfTOA NTHIN cAtsI cNAmH IoEcA tfINN
AmwyA TEfTO NjAys ITOAN zTAyE gANcA tywyE sOzEz ecwHz cOfIr sEIzt yEzTH
ITrOs OTIff EzzTA ItTHA yObEg wEAwr EzOsO rIyrc OesHI ygmIy EINgz AjTmI
yEwyA gtfTz HIoEj EITty EzTHI NfINe EtzEg TAOgE NTOjc INgfH EfqTH EItTH
AyObI TOANA jwEAw rETyc ONkTA kIONI ffEzz TAIzc zTEsI NgOTz ONjAy sITOA
```

Case 3:	A	B	C	D	E	F	G	H	I	J	K	L	M	N	O	P	Q	R	S	T	U	V	W	X	Y	Z
	↓	↓	↓	↓	↓	↓	↓	↓	↓	↓	↓	↓	↓	↓	↓	↓	↓	↓	↓	↓	↓	↓	↓	↓	↓	↓
	n	?	?	?	h	?	?	l	v	?	?	?	?	u	d	?	?	?	?	a	?	?	?	?	?	?

```
sONcI ykONA bOTAI NzyEr cINfI swtTE yzONg gOTOf IsstN AfOTA INzTI qEEwT
HEAyI wEyOT AINzy tNNAN kzsII THrce csOqA NkANj IysOT AINsI yEOff EzzAe
rETIs IyEwE IwrEm ATHAN THEIy kONAb OTAIN etTOz ATeEf IsEzs IyEOf fEzzA
erEAN jIysO TAINy ExtAy EzsIy EwyIT EfTAI NTHON cItsO cNImH OoEcI tfONN
ImwyI TEfTA NjIys OTAIN zTIyE gINcI tywyE sAzEz ecwHz cAfOr sEOzt yEzTH
OTrAs ATOff EzzTI OtTHI yAbEg wEIwr EzAsA rOyrc AesHO ygmOy EONgz IjTmO
yEwyI gtfTz HOoEj EOTty EzTHO NfONe EtzEg TIAgE NTAjc ONgfH EfqTH EOtTH
IyAbO TAINI jwEIw rETyc ANkTI kOANO ffEzz TIOzc zTEsO NgATz ANjIy sOTAI
```

Case 4:	A	B	C	D	E	F	G	H	I	J	K	L	M	N	O	P	Q	R	S	T	U	V	W	X	Y	Z
	↓	↓	↓	↓	↓	↓	↓	↓	↓	↓	↓	↓	↓	↓	↓	↓	↓	↓	↓	↓	↓	↓	↓	↓	↓	↓
	d	?	?	?	h	?	?	l	v	?	?	?	?	u	n	?	?	?	?	a	?	?	?	?	?	?

```
sANcI ykANO bATOI NzyEr cINfI swtTE yzANg gATAf IsstN OfATO INzTI qEEwT
HEOyI wEyAT OINzy tNNON kzsII THrce csAqO NkONj IysAT OINsI yEAff EzzOe
rETIs IyEwE IwrEm OTHON THEIy kANOb ATOIN etTAz OTeEf IsEzs IyEAf fEzzO
erEON jIysA TOINy ExtOy EzsIy EwyIT EfTOI NTHAN cItsA cNImH AoEcI tfANN
ImwyI TEfTO NjIys ATOIN zTIyE gINcI tywyE sOzEz ecwHz cOfAr sEAzt yEzTH
ATrOs OTAff EzzTI AtTHI yObEg wEIwr EzOsO rAyrc OesHA ygmAy EANgz IjTmA
yEwyI gtfTz HAoEj EATty EzTHA NfANe EtzEg TIOgE NTOjc ANgfH EfqTH EAtTH
IyObA TOINI jwEIw rETyc ONkTI kAONA ffEzz TIAzc zTEsA NgOTz ONjIy sATOI
```

Case 5:	A	B	C	D	E	F	G	H	I	J	K	L	M	N	O	P	Q	R	S	T	U	V	W	X	Y	Z
	↓	↓	↓	↓	↓	↓	↓	↓	↓	↓	↓	↓	↓	↓	↓	↓	↓	↓	↓	↓	↓	↓	↓	↓	↓	↓
	v	?	?	?	h	?	?	l	n	?	?	?	?	u	d	?	?	?	?	a	?	?	?	?	?	?

```
sONcA ykONI bOTIA NzyEr cANfA swtTE yzONg gOTOf AsstN IfOTI ANzTA qEEwT
HEIyA wEyOT IANzy tNNIN kzsAA THrce csOqI NkINj AysOT IANsA yEOff EzzIe
rETAs AyEwE AwrEm ITHIN THEAy kONIb OTIAN etTOz ITeEf AsEzs AyEOf fEzzI
erEIN jAysO TIANy ExtIy EzsAy EwyAT EfTIA NTHON cAtsO cNAmH OoEcA tfONN
AmwyA TEfTI NjAys OTIAN zTAyE gANcA tywyE sIzEz ecwHz cIfOr sEOzt yEzTH
OTrIs ITOff EzzTA OtTHA yIbEg wEAwr EzIsI rOyrc IesHO ygmOy EONgz AjTmO
yEwyA gtfTz HOoEj EOTty EzTHO NfONe EtzEg TAIgE NTIjc ONgfH EfqTH EOtTH
AyIbO TIANA jwEAw rETyc INkTA kOINO ffEzz TAOzc zTEsO NgITz INjAy sOTIA
```

Case 6:	A	B	C	D	E	F	G	H	I	J	K	L	M	N	O	P	Q	R	S	T	U	V	W	X	Y	Z
	↓	↓	↓	↓	↓	↓	↓	↓	↓	↓	↓	↓	↓	↓	↓	↓	↓	↓	↓	↓	↓	↓	↓	↓	↓	↓
	d	?	?	?	h	?	?	l	n	?	?	?	?	u	v	?	?	?	?	a	?	?	?	?	?	?

```
sANcO RkANI bATIO NzREr cONfO swtTE RzANg gATAf OsstN IfATI ONzTO qEEwT
HEIRO wERAT IONzR tNNIN kzsOO THrce csAqI NkINj ORsAT IONsO REAff EzzIe
rETOs OREwE OwrEm ITHIN THEOR kANIb ATION etTAz ITeEf OsEzs OREAf fEzzI
erEIN jORsA TIONR ExtIR EzsOR EwROT EfTIO NTHAN cOtsA cNOmH AoEcO tfANN
OmwRO TEfTI NjORs ATION zTORE gONcO tRwRE sIzEz ecwHz cIfAr sEAzt REzTH
ATrIs ITAff EzzTO AtTHO RIbEg wEOwr EzIsI rARrc IesHA RgmAR EANgz OjTmA
REwRO gtfTz HAoEj EATtR EzTHA NfANe EtzEg TOIgE NTIjc ANgfH EfqTH EAtTH
ORIbA TIONO jwEOw rETRc INkTO kAINA ffEzz TOAzc zTEsA NgITz INjOR sATIO
```

Finally, we search for word fragments in the partially deciphered ciphertext; only in Case 6 do we recognize words or word fragments for example, **ORk-ANIbTION** which we can guess to be **ORGANIZATION**. Changing `k` to `G` and `b` to `Z`, we obtain

```
sANcO RGANI ZATIO NzREr cONfO swtTE RzANg gATAf OsstN IfATI ONzTO qEEwT
HEIRO wERAT IONzR tNNIN GzsOO THrce csAqI NGINj ORsAT IONsO REAff EzzIe
rETOs OREwE OwrEm ITHIN THEOR GANIZ ATION etTAz ITeEf OsEzs OREAf fEzzI
erEIN jORsA TIONR ExtIR EzsOR EwROT EfTIO NTHAN cOtsA cNOmH AoEcO tfANN
OmwRO TEfTI NjORs ATION zTORE gONcO tRwRE sIzEz ecwHz cIfAr sEAzt REzTH
ATrIs ITAff EzzTO AtTHO RIZEg wEOwr EzIsI rARrc IesHA RgmAR EANgz OjTmA
REwRO gtfTz HAoEj EATtR EzTHA NfANe EtzEg TOIgE NTIjc ANgfH EfqTH EAtTH
ORIZA TIONO jwEOw rETRc INGTO GAINA ffEzz TOAzc zTEsA NgITz INjOR sATIO
```

We can now guess that **INjORsATION** is **INFORMATION** and change `j` to `F` and `s` to `M`, obtaining

```
MANcO RGANI ZATIO NzREr cONfO MwtTE RzANg gATAf OMMtN IfATI ONzTO qEEwT
HEIRO wERAT IONzR tNNIN GzMOO THrce cMAqI NGINF ORMAT IONMO REAff EzzIe
rETOM OREwE OwrEm ITHIN THEOR GANIZ ATION etTAz ITeEf OMEzM OREAf fEzzI
erEIN FORMA TIONR ExtIR EzMOR EwROT EfTIO NTHAN cOtMA cNOmH AoEcO tfANN
OmwRO TEfTI NFORM ATION zTORE gONcO tRwRE MIzEz ecwHz cIfAr MEAzt REzTH
ATrIM ITAff EzzTO AtTHO RIZEg wEOwr EzIMI rARrc IeMHA RgmAR EANgz OFTmA
REwRO gtfTz HAoEF EATtR EzTHA NfANe EtzEg TOIgE NTIFc ANgfH EfqTH EAtTH
ORIZA TIONO FwEOw rETRc INGTO GAINA ffEzz TOAzc zTEMA NgITz INFOR MATIO
```

We will not pursue the matter further, leaving the details to the reader.

3.10 AFFINE CAESAR SUBSTITUTION

Caesar encipherment used the additive structure of the set of integers $\boldsymbol{Z}_m$. We may also multiply the letters in $\boldsymbol{Z}_m$ modulo m and obtain a substitution system which we will refer to as *affine Caesar substitution.* Define the transformation

$$T_{a,b} : \boldsymbol{Z}_m \rightarrow \boldsymbol{Z}_m$$

$$T_{a,b} : t \rightarrow T_{a,b}(t) = at + b \text{ (modulo m)}$$

$T_{a,b}$ is not a one-to-one mapping on $\boldsymbol{Z}_m$ for all choices of a and b. For example, if m = 26, a = 2, and b = 3, then

$$T_{2,3}(0) = T_{2,3}(13) = 3$$

The transformations $\{T_{a,b}\}$, which are substitutions, are specified by the next elementary result from number theory.

Lemma 3.10.1 $T_{a,b}$ is a one-to-one mapping on $\boldsymbol{Z}_m$ if and only if the *greatest common divisor* of a and m denoted by gcd{a,m} is equal to 1. If gcd{a,m} = 1, a and m are said to be *relatively prime.*

Proof. $T_{a,b}(t) = T_{a,b}(s)$ $(0 \leq s \leq t < m)$ if and only if m divides $a(t - s)$. If gcd{a,m} = 1, then $T_{a,b}(t) = T_{a,b}(s)$ $(0 \leq s \leq t < m)$ if and only if t = s. If gcd{a,m} = k > 1, then $T_{a,b}(s) = T_{a,b}(t)$ if $t = s + m/k \neq s$. ◀

The twelve affine Caesar substitutions for {A B . . . Z} are shown in Table 3.10.1.

TABLE 3.10.1

$T_{a,b}$: Affine Caesar Substitutions for {A B . . . Z}

a	A	B	C	D	E	F	G	H	I	J	K	L	M	N	O	P	Q	R	S	T	U	V	W	X	Y	Z
1	A	B	C	D	E	F	G	H	I	J	K	L	M	N	O	P	Q	R	S	T	U	V	W	X	Y	Z
3	A	D	G	J	M	P	S	V	Y	B	E	H	K	N	Q	T	W	Z	C	F	I	L	O	R	U	X
5	A	F	K	P	U	Z	E	J	O	T	Y	D	I	N	S	X	C	H	M	R	W	B	G	L	Q	V
7	A	H	O	V	C	J	Q	X	E	L	S	Z	G	N	U	B	I	P	W	D	K	R	Y	F	M	T
9	A	J	S	B	K	T	C	L	U	D	M	V	E	N	W	F	O	X	G	P	Y	H	Q	Z	I	R
11	A	L	W	H	S	D	O	Z	K	V	G	R	C	N	Y	J	U	F	Q	B	M	X	I	T	E	P
15	A	P	E	T	I	X	M	B	Q	F	U	J	Y	N	C	R	G	V	K	Z	O	D	S	H	W	L
17	A	R	I	Z	Q	H	Y	P	G	X	O	F	W	N	E	V	M	D	U	L	C	T	K	B	S	J
19	A	T	M	F	Y	R	K	D	W	P	I	B	U	N	G	Z	S	L	E	X	Q	J	C	V	O	H
21	A	V	Q	L	G	B	W	R	M	H	C	X	S	N	I	D	Y	T	O	J	E	Z	U	P	K	F
23	A	X	U	R	O	L	I	F	C	Z	W	T	Q	N	K	H	E	B	Y	V	S	P	M	J	G	D
25	A	Z	Y	X	W	V	U	T	S	R	Q	P	O	N	M	L	K	J	I	H	G	F	E	D	C	B

3.11 GENERAL MONALPHABETIC SUBSTITUTION

Up to this point, we have allowed only special letter substitutions to define a substitution system. Now we assume that any element of the symmetric group SYM($\boldsymbol{Z}_m$) can be used as a key. While there were only 26 additive and 12 × 26 multiplicative Caesar substitutions for the alphabet {A B . . . Z}, there are $26! \approx 4 \times 10^{26}$ different monalphabetic substitutions on $\boldsymbol{Z}_{26}$. Key trial is no longer a viable method for finding the key. Still, as we shall show, a monalphabetic substitution offers little in the way of secrecy.

Figure 3.11.1 shows *CIPHER(2.1)*, the encipherment of *PLAIN(2)* under a randomly selected element of the symmetric group of $\boldsymbol{Z}_{26}$. We list in Table 3.11.2 the frequency of occurrence of ciphertext letters in *CIPHER(2.1)*.

The subject matter of *PLAIN(2)* provides *side information,* which will enable us to recover the substitution producing *CIPHER(2.1)*. *PLAIN(2)* describes some aspects of *the performance evaluation of computer systems,* and it is likely that the words

PERFORMANCE EVALUATION SYSTEM

```
etrbp pvrfu drluf lnwxm rrowc vwebf xwxkd lrkbm ebfxt wpmfx mrlxr kvprl
petlf vytfv eetrt bpefl sfumf ndver lrofc vebfx drlbf kbxuw memfn nwwpb
xwxsf etrle rmtxf cfybm wckro rcfdn rxemf nnwet rbppv rbpnf pewmv eratr
xetre rmtxf cfysb psfvx yetrd rlpbp erxed vlpvb efudl fkvme pabet bndlf
orkmf petsd trxdr lufln wxmrm twlwm erlbp ebmpe trxmf xpewx ecscr wkpef
krpby xpabe tvxel brkwx kvxmr lewbx urwev lrpdr lbfku lfnet rbxbe bwcmf
xmrde bfxfu wpspe rnpwl mtber mevlw ckrpb yxefb epkwb csfdr lwebf xwuer
lbxpe wccwe bfxdr lbfkb xetrr wlcsd cwxxb xydtw prfuw xramf ndver lpspe
rndlf kvmem fnnwe trnwx vuwme vlrln vpevp vwccs nwhre afesd rpfud lrkbm
ebfxd rlbfk etrub lpees drbpe fuflr mwpee trxwe vlrfu wddcb mwebf xpwxk
etrcr orcpf upspe rnafl hcfwk pfuet rprwd dcbmw ebfxp drlbf ktrlr etrer
lnafl hcfwk nrwxp mfnnw bxufl nwccs mfnnw etrwn fvxef uprlo bmrlr jvblr
nrxep dcwmr kfxet rpspe rndrl bfkar ptwcc rcwgf lwern flrfx aflhc fwkmt
wlwme rlbiw ebfxb xprme bfxfx rdfbx eufvl drlbf ketrp rmfxk esdrf udlrk
bmebf xbpmf xmrlx rkabe tetrm tfbmr grear rxwlm tberm evlwc krpby xwcer
lxweb orpmf nnwgw prkfx twlka wlrwx kpfue awlre rmtxf cfybr petwe abccg
rwowb cwgcr bxetr krorc fdnrx edrlb fkfue trdcw xxrkp spern drlbf ktrlr
etrml berlb fxfup rcrme bfxbp atwea rmwcc mfpet sdtrx drluf lnwxm relwk
rfuud rlbfk etrwm mvlwm sfupv mtdlr kbmeb fxlrp epefw mfxpb krlwg crrqe
rxefx fvlmw dwgbc besfu nwddb xyetr drluf lnwxm rmtwl wmerl bpebm pfuet
rpspe rnmfn dfxrx epbxe fetrf orlwc cpspe rntsd trxcr orcdr lufln wxmrm
twlwm erlbp ebmpd rlbfk pvmte lwxpc webfx dlfmr kvlrp wlrgs xfnrw xppel
wbyte uflaw lkfla rccrp ewgcb ptrkd rlbfk fxmre trwlm tberm evlwc krmbp
bfxpt worgr rxnwk rwxke trpsp ernkr pbyxw xkbnd crnrx ewebf xpewl erkmf
nnwet rpmfd rfudr lufln wxmrd lrkbm ebfxw xkrow cvweb fxgrm fnrpn flrpd
rmbub mdrlb fkatw ebpet rgrpe mtfbm rfunw mtbxr flywx biweb fxjvr pebfx
atweb petrf drlwe bxyps perne fpvdd flewx katwe wlret ruvxm ebfxp beptf
vckdl fobkr jvrpe bfxet rbxer lwmeb fxpwn fxyet rfdrl webxy psper nmfnd
fxrxe ptsdt rxwcy flbet npufl zfgpm trkvc bxymf nnwdl fmrpp flpmt rkvcb
xymfn nwwxk peflw yrnwx wyrnr xetsd trxnv pegrv xkrlp effkm fnnww xketr
blruu rmepf xetrd riful nwxmr nvpeg rdlrk bmerk drlbf ketre rmtxb jvrpv
prkuf ldrlu flnwx mrrow cvweb fxwxk dlrkb mebfx kvlbx yetrk rpbyx wxkbn
dcrnr xeweb fxdtw prplw xyrul fnpbn dcrtw xkmwc mvcwe bfxef jvber rcwgf
lwerp bnvcw ebfxd rlbfk mfndw lbxye trdlr kbmer kdrlu flnwx mrabe tetrw
mevwc wmtbr orkdr lufln wxmrf uerxl rorwc pnwzf lkrur mepbx etrkr pbyxf
lrllf lpbxe trpsp erndl fylwn nbxyd rlbfk bebpx fawab krcsw mmrde rkgrc
bruet weetr drluf lnwxm rdlrk bmebf xwxkr owcvw ebfxd lfmrp pptfv ckgrw
xbxer ylwcd wlefu etrkr orcfd nrxer uufle petlf vytfv edrlb fk
```

Figure 3.11.1. *CIPHER(2.1)* : monalphabetic encipherment of *PLAIN(2)*.

TABLE 3.11.2
Frequency of Occurrences of Letters in *CIPHER(2.1)*

Letter	Frequency	Letter	Frequency	Letter	Frequency
r	0.1285	t	0.0453	a	0.0106
e	0.0920	d	0.0392	o	0.0084
f	0.0858	k	0.0387	g	0.0079
w	0.0739	n	0.0370	j	0.0022
b	0.0695	c	0.0326	h	0.0018
x	0.0687	v	0.0255	i	0.0009
l	0.0682	u	0.0242	z	0.0009
p	0.0599	s	0.0141	q	0.0004
m	0.0506	y	0.0132		

will appear several times in the plaintext. We will search *CIPHER(2.1)* for the ciphertext corresponding to these words. To find the ciphertext of PERFORMANCE in *CIPHER(2.1)* we search for a ciphertext 11-gram

$$(y_0, y_1, \ldots, y_{10})$$

containing nine different letters with $y_1 = y_{10}$ and $y_2 = y_5$.

We list in Tables 3.11.3–5 the results of the search of *CIPHER(2.1)* for the

TABLE 3.11.3
Results of the Search for the Word PERFORMANCE in *CIPHER(2.1)*

Ciphertext	**Count**	**Ciphertext**	**Count**
drluflnwxmr	11	mebfxbpatwe	1

TABLE 3.11.4
Results of the Search for the Word EVALUATION in *CIPHER(2.1)*

Ciphertext	**Count**	**Ciphertext**	**Count**	**Ciphertext**	**Count**
drluflnwxm	11	rbpnfpewmv	1	perndrlbfk	2
rowcvwebfx	4	pabetbndlf	1	mebfxbpatw	1
rkbmebfxtw	1	wcmfxmrdeb	1	xpewlerkmf	1
lsfumfndve	1	tbermevlwc	3	wlretruvxm	1
rlbfkbxuwm	1	bfxpwxketr	1	eptsdtrxwc	1
lfnpbndcrt	1	kgrcbruetw	1		

TABLE 3.11.5
Results of the Search for the Word SYSTEM in *CIPHER(2.1)*

Ciphertext	**Count**	**Ciphertext**	**Count**	**Ciphertext**	**Count**
xwxkdl	2	rorcpf	1	xwxkbn	2
trtbpe	1	rerlna	1	rnrxew	2
rlrofc	1	rlrjvb	1	ewebfx	2
xwxsfe	1	rnrxep	1	xwxkro	2
fcfybm	1	crcwgf	1	bubmdr	1
rorcfd	3	xbxprm	1	rgrpem	1
rermtx	3	rprmfx	1	xrxept	1
fcfysb	1	wgwprk	1	wxwyrn	1
rdrlpb	1	fcfybr	1	rnrxet	1
pbperx	1	fkfuet	1	pvprku	1
mrmtwl	3	fxfupr	1	rkrpby	2
wlwmer	4	rcrmeb	1	prplwx	1
cscrwk	1	epefwm	1	tetrwm	1
bebwcm	1	fxfvlm	1	wcwmtb	1
fxfuwp	1	wdwgbc	1	rorwcp	1
pspern	11	bcbesf	1	rurmep	1
xbxydt	1	rdrluf	3	lflpbx	1
lrlnvp	1	xrxepb	1	bebpxf	1
fuflrm	1	fkfxmr	1	awabkr	1
xbxery	1	epetlf	1		

words **PERFORMANCE**, **EVALUATION**, and **SYSTEM**, listing the number of times each ciphertext fragment appears in *CIPHER(2.1)*.

Assuming that **PERFORMANCE** appears several times in *PLAIN(2)*, there are two possible corresponding ciphertext 22-grams.

π : PERFORMANCE → drluclnwxmr
π' : PERFORMANCE → mebfxbpatwe

and these yield the following partial specifications of the ciphertext alphabet:

π

A	B	C	D	E	F	G	H	I	J	K	L	M	N	O	P	Q	R	S	T	U	V	W	X	Y	Z
↓	↓	↓	↓	↓	↓	↓	↓	↓	↓	↓	↓	↓	↓	↓	↓	↓	↓	↓	↓	↓	↓	↓	↓	↓	↓
w	?	m	?	r	?	?	?	?	?	?	?	n	x	f	d	?	l	?	?	?	?	?	?	?	?

π'

A	B	C	D	E	F	G	H	I	J	K	L	M	N	O	P	Q	R	S	T	U	V	W	X	Y	Z
↓	↓	↓	↓	↓	↓	↓	↓	↓	↓	↓	↓	↓	↓	↓	↓	↓	↓	↓	↓	↓	↓	↓	↓	↓	↓
a	?	w	?	e	f	?	?	?	?	?	?	p	t	x	m	?	b	?	?	?	?	?	?	?	?

Under π, the only ciphertext 10-gram that can be the encipherment of **EVALUATION** is **rowcvwebfx**, since **E** → **r** and **N** → **x**, while under π', none of the ciphertext 10-grams can correspond to **EVALUATION**. Thus we reject π' and assume

π

A	B	C	D	E	F	G	H	I	J	K	L	M	N	O	P	Q	R	S	T	U	V	W	X	Y	Z
↓	↓	↓	↓	↓	↓	↓	↓	↓	↓	↓	↓	↓	↓	↓	↓	↓	↓	↓	↓	↓	↓	↓	↓	↓	↓
w	?	m	?	r	u	?	?	b	?	?	c	n	x	f	d	?	l	?	e	v	o	?	?	?	?

is a correct partial specification of the unknown substitution.

From the list of possible ciphertext 5-grams for **SYSTEM**, the only ciphertext consistent with π is **pspern**, which enables us to augment the partial specification of π,

π

A	B	C	D	E	F	G	H	I	J	K	L	M	N	O	P	Q	R	S	T	U	V	W	X	Y	Z
↓	↓	↓	↓	↓	↓	↓	↓	↓	↓	↓	↓	↓	↓	↓	↓	↓	↓	↓	↓	↓	↓	↓	↓	↓	↓
w	?	m	?	r	u	?	?	b	?	?	c	n	x	f	d	?	l	p	e	v	o	?	?	s	?

Replacing the ciphertext letters in *CIPHER(2.1)* identified above by their plaintext correspondents, the following partially deciphered fragment of plaintext is obtained

```
TtEIS SUEOF PERFO RMANC EEVAL UATIO NANkP REkIC TIONt ASCON CERNE kUSER
STtRO UYtOU TTtEt ISTOR YOFCO MPUTE REVOL UTION PERIO kINFA CTCOM MAASI
NANYO TtERT ECtNO LOyIC ALkEV ELOPM ENTCO MMATt EISSU EISMO STACU TEAtE
NTtET ECtNO LOyYI SYOUN yTtEP ERSIS TENTP URSUI TOFPR OkUCT SaITt IMPRO
```

Further entries in π can be gleaned from this partial decipherment

- TtEIS SUEOF is certainly THE ISSUE OF, yielding H → t.
- TIONH ASCON CERNE kUSER is certainly TION HAS CONCERNED USER yielding D → k.

We will not proceed any further, leaving the details to the reader.

3.12 TWO-GRAM SUBSTITUTIONS: PLAYFAIR ENCIPHERMENT

To try to defeat cryptanalysis based upon the frequency of occurrence of letters of 1-grams, we can encipher n-grams with $n > 1$, since the probability distribution of n-grams discriminates between the n-grams far less than the probability distribution of 1-grams discriminates between letters. In this section, we study the *Playfair 2-gram substitution* named after the first Baron Playfair of St. Andrews [KA]. The historical Playfair substitution does not satisfy our definition of a substitution system in three respects:

- Playfair encipherment is defined for the alphabet {ABC . . . HIK . . . Z} in which J and I are regarded as the same letter.
- There is a slight increase in the length of the ciphertext because a *null letter* (usually Q) is *sometimes* inserted between repeated letters in plaintext, as in the word BETTER.
- Plaintext containing an odd number of letters after the insertion of nulls to split double letters) is augmented by a null on the right.

A *Playfair square* for AB . . . Z based on the key word (or phrase) PICKLE is shown in Fig. 3.12.1. The letters of the key word (repetitions, if any, deleted) are entered by rows, followed by the remaining letters of the alphabet in their usual order.

Let $\Gamma = (\gamma_{i,j})$ $(0 \leq i, j \leq 5)$ denote the 5 by 5 matrix obtained by replacing the letters in Fig. 3.12.1 by their numerical values from Table 2.2.1. We will refer to the *row* and *column coordinates* of a letter in the Playfair square Γ; thus

P has coordinates (0,0) (row 0, column 0)

I has coordinates (0,1) (row 0, column 1)

E has coordinates (1,0) (row 1, column 0)

P	I	C	K	L
E	A	B	D	F
G	H	M	N	O
Q	R	S	T	U
V	W	X	Y	Z

Figure 3.12.1. Playfair square derived from the key word PICKLE.

The Playfair encipherment of the plaintext 2-gram (x,x′) by Γ will be denoted by $P_\Gamma(x,x') = (y,y')$.

Definition 3.12.1 The rules for Playfair encipherment are as follows.

(P1) If the letters of the plaintext 2-gram (x,x′) are in the *same row* but *different columns* of Γ, that is,

$$(x,x') = (\gamma_{i,s}, \gamma_{i,t}) \qquad (s \neq t)$$

then (x,x′) is $\mathbf{P}_\Gamma$-enciphered into the ciphertext 2-gram (y,y′) composed of the letters in the *same row* and in the *right-adjacent column* of the respective letters of (x,x′):

$$P_\Gamma(x, x') = (y, y') = (\gamma_{i,s+1}, \gamma_{i,t+1})$$

Column 0 in Γ stands to the right of column 4 in Γ. Thus

AD → bf US → qt

(P2) If the letters of the plaintext 2-gram (x, x′) are in the *same column* but in *different rows* of Γ, that is,

$$(x, x') = (\gamma_{i,s}, \gamma_{j,s}) \; (i \neq j)$$

then (x, x′) is P_Γ-enciphered into the ciphertext 2-gram (y, y′) composed of the letters in the *same column* and *row directly below* the respective letters of (x, x′):

$$P_\Gamma(x, x') = (y, y') = (\gamma_{i+1,s}, \gamma_{j+1,s})$$

Row 0 in Γ is immediately below row 4. Thus

RI → wa BX → mc

(P3) If the letters of the plaintext 2-gram (x, x′) are in *different rows* and *different columns* of Γ, that is,

$$(x, x') = (\gamma_{i,j}, \gamma_{s,t}) \qquad (i \neq s, j \neq t)$$

then (x, x′) is P_Γ-enciphered into the ciphertext 2-gram (y, y′) composed of the letters which are in the *same row* and at *opposite corners* of the rectangle determined by the coordinates (i,j) (i,t) (s,t) (s,j)

$$\begin{array}{ccc} \gamma_{i,j} \bullet & \qquad\qquad & \bullet\, \gamma_{i,t} \\ \gamma_{s,j} \bullet & & \bullet\, \gamma_{s,t} \end{array}$$

$$P_\Gamma(x, x') = (y, y') = (\gamma_{i,t}, \gamma_{s,j})$$

Thus

AN → dh GA → he

(P4) The length of the plaintext is increased by the insertion of *nulls* (some

letter from {AB ... HIK ... Z}, usually Q) whenever a 2-gram with repeated letter is to be enciphered. Thus the plaintext which begins with

THEISSUEOFPERFORMANCE . . .

is first divided into 2-grams,

TH EI SS UE OF PE RF OR MA NC E* . . .

and a Q is inserted to split the double S.

TH EI SQ SU EO FP ER FO RM AN CE . . .

Note that not all repeated letters require insertions of a null.

```
rn ap tr tq fg el aq ou sh dh pb gp fi rf rk go dh ek qa ak ks lh om br lm
mk aq gd ft qb st rn uh qo mg qu rn ag cr un tw uo lm gc qu aq gp uf qu lh
gk aq lh ak od bi sk gn hb br kh dh zn rn aq qd im og fu hp ib kf gp fp gl
gb ty lm gs hb rn ap tr tq ap xs mu rd ls qd ir dg rn dq bp mo uf gh wk tx
uz oh rn ge aq rc tu dg qk qs tq kr uo iq nf sl ut ia rn ch iq gz af lm tu
nw ig dg eg ua hu hb mk bp rh wh ks aq cr rk bx rn dg lm mt rd ty kz pf bf
tu nf bq ph mt ia rn to us pa fb tn to pb su ha od ab uq qa qc aq lh fe uh
ns ga kh kr ah pk go pb kq lh og eb tx tu bg rb si ra qd ks qs fi fa rc ho
un kr tb ha kz gl aq dr lh hd du aq kh tu fi if rk go eg wa nf kh rn gv ab
ui vk if gt hk oh ig br fg eb gd xi gn lq qd st xt qd gc uh ft ks lm gs hb
rn bg dh zo bi uq qa sh qt uq tq fi kz hb pd ry nu vk bq uo iq af ck rk go
eg wa nf rn ae aw tu yk eg cr un ou qa ib tu rn dg dr qs fg eb ev ip ck dr
lh mt dh ny ga pf pg cu uo tx tu bg zh ti fu bf um du ga qb ei ip ck dr lh
mt eg wa nf ga qa rn dq aq hx hu lp hf bn ab mt lm gs hb kh ou sh fi kz lm
gs hb rn ab ng to un bu aq wp pb qa rq aw bg dg ut ip bi af go rn bq xt qd
gc aq lh ay bq rh pu pf if fm wh qd ng qa go zh ti fu bf im hw bi qd wa wf
rk go kh qb ks lh og gd lg kh ud uz qi aq lh ny ga qb lm tn yk eg uo iq af
ck rk go cr lm mk aq gd ay kr nr ga im hl pb da ry gv dg hw im kr bp uq wh
kf bq ph hd ku aq hd rk pg xb gn hb db qb fn om hw ay hw ab tn um du ih qa
qd im og fu hp bq rn dr ia pu cf ab we cp bd pf kh rn af gp fp gl gb ty eg
wa nf uo rn ge if gt gd bt xt qd gc aq lh an aq dq ga is kr aq lh og bu fp
bp rk go cr ir dr va ib pu pk mu rn vk ga gk aq ou sh dh pb us bf fg eu el
aq lh ny ga bi ls wh kx uo tq im iq af ck rk go qa tu tu hf lm mt ka aq bd
pf bv qd ty go uz si ei bd cp kr zn bo ei ic oh rn ge aq ou sh dh pb im hw
bi qd wa tu ck um du ga tx tu bg lm gc go dg ut kh un rn fg pg wh pu cu xt
qd nm vk ga ok gp fp eg ua hu hb mk bp rh wh ks aq cr rk bx eg wa nf tq im
us dh uc dr lh gk uh pb ft qa rb qa dx og gb dh tr tu wh ph nr ou wi hw fn
wi fp pf tu bd pc rm af eg wa nf go pb rn ab si ra qd ks qs fi fa kc rc go
rm ew ad gv dg hb fa dh ny ga tx tu bg fa rc ho dh ak gc pf gb ty dr lh mt
rd su af lm gs hb rn bq lm eg uo eg ua hu hb mk ge qa ak ks lh hd tn gp fi
rf rk go da lm gb xs hu bq eg kc al ki aq lh ay rh rk tu ga da tu im hl pb
uo hb im kh fg qh dh lw dr lh gt qf tu lh hy rh rk tu ga gl aq dr kh mq xt
qd ns mu ql lg su dh ay rh rd qa rn ae to ks lh mt kr rm uz kf iq gz ka gv
qf tu lh ty ga kh qd wh ks lh mt bh go nq ga gl aq dr kh mq xt qd sb gn lg
gd ty rm vk ga hd po hu kr mn ub hu lh mx im af zf kh mp gn hb iq ml bq um
st im af zf kh mp gn hb dh bt un wh qg hb hd qg gb ty nw ig dg os tu da to
fa st un nf lm gs hb dh ny ga aw ae ea ks um ty ga eg ua hu hb mk bg qt sd
ge qa ak ks af eg wa nf rn dq bp mo pr qf tq qb fe hu eg ua hu hb mk gv gp
fi rf rk go dh ek qa ak ks lh tn qs kh nq ga fa rc ho dh ak gc pf gb ty dr
lh gk rh qb ts dh qg au gn rc gc pf rh tn ib pk zf dr lh ty gu rl qd fp bd
hu dr bq ch zf dr lh gk aq lh bk gn ie wa oh rn ge qa ak ks af eg ua hu hb
mk av kr nr ga bi uq fi bi ra gp af eg ua hu hb mk fg du dg qa pg fi xs ha
hu fa ea ks rc ty ga fa rc ho hu aq uh st kh rn bq xt qd gc uh hq bh hc oh
eg wa nf kr cr og ih ia fa kz bi pb kq af da pc ae rn dr rn ge aq ou sh dh
pb iq af ck rk go dh fa we fz dr lh gk uh pb tr tr rm uz kf da dh kh qd hq
fi ie su uo rn af gp fp gl gb ty ae ou su tu rw uz hm uz qk aq lh et
```

Figure 3.12.2. *CIPHER(2.2)* : playfair encipherment of *PLAIN(2)*.

(P5) If the plaintext, after step *(P4)*, contains an odd number of letters, a null is adjoined (on the right).

Enciphering *PLAIN(2)* with the Playfair square of Fig. 3.12.1, we obtain *CIPHER(2.2)* shown in Fig. 3.12.2 (departing from our usual format).

Playfair encipherment admits a potentially large set of keys, since any 5 by 5 square can serve as the key Γ. The use of a *key word* is a convenient device to facilitate memorization. Not all of the 25! Playfair squares yield distinct transformations; Γ and Γ' are equivalent if Γ' may be obtained by cyclic rotation of the rows and columns of Γ. Thus

H	M	N	O	G
R	S	T	U	Q
W	X	Y	Z	V
I	C	K	L	P
A	B	D	F	E

obtained by rotating the rows in Fig. 3.12.1 up by two and the columns to the left by one yields the same Playfair substitution as in Fig. 3.12.1.

Even though the key space is too large for key trial, Playfair encipherment is *not* a strong form of encipherment; its weakness is a consequence of the structural constraints imposed by the rules in Definition 3.12.1. The principal properties of Playfair encipherment, which indicate the type of constraints, are given next.

Theorem 3.12.2

(i) If $\Gamma[s,t]$ denotes the *cyclic rotation* of Γ, that is,

$$\Gamma[s,t] = \begin{vmatrix} \gamma_{s,t} & \gamma_{s,t+1} & \cdots & \gamma_{s,t+4} \\ \gamma_{s+1,t} & \gamma_{s+1,t+1} & \cdots & \gamma_{s+1,t+4} \\ \cdot & \cdot & \cdots & \cdot \\ \cdot & \cdot & \cdots & \cdot \\ \cdot & \cdot & \cdots & \cdot \\ \gamma_{s+4,t} & \gamma_{s+4,t+1} & \cdots & \gamma_{s+4,t+4} \end{vmatrix}$$

then $P_{\Gamma[s,t]}(x, x') = P_\Gamma(x, x')$. Thus Γ may be determined only up to an arbitrary cyclic rotation of columns and rows.

(ii) If $P_\Gamma(x, x') = (y, y')$, then $x \neq y$ and $x' \neq y'$.

(iii) $P_\Gamma(x, x') = (y, y')$ *implies* $P_\Gamma(x', x) = (y', y)$. (x', x) is the *reversal* of (x, x').

(iv) $P_\Gamma(x, x') = (y, y')$ *implies* $P_\Gamma(y, y') = (x, x')$ whenever $(x, x') = (\gamma_{i,j}, \gamma_{s,t})$ with $i \neq s$ and $j \neq t$. The pair of equations

$$P_\Gamma(x, x') = (y, y') \qquad P_\Gamma(y, y') = (x, x')$$

are called *reciprocal*.

(v) If the 2-gram (x, x′) with $x = \gamma_{i,j}$ is P_Γ-enciphered into the 2-gram (y, y′), that is,

$$P_\Gamma(x, x') = (y, y')$$

then the ciphertext equivalent y of x can have one of five possible values:

- One of the four entries in the ith row of Γ other than $\gamma_{i,j}$, or
- The entry in row i and column j + 1 in Γ directly below $\gamma_{i,j}$.

We denote the set of *ciphertext equivalents* of $\gamma_{i,j}$ by $E_{\gamma_{i,j}}$.

(vi) If the 2-gram (x, x′) with $x' = \gamma_{i,j}$ is P_Γ-enciphered into the 2-gram (y, y′), that is,

$$P_\Gamma(x, x') = (y, y')$$

then the ciphertext equivalent y′ of x′ can have one of five possible values:

- One of the four entries in the ith row of Γ other than $\gamma_{i,j}$, or
- The entry in row i and column j + 1 in Γ directly below $\gamma_{i,j}$.

We denote the set of *ciphertext equivalents* of $\gamma_{i,j}$ by $E_{\gamma_{i,j}}$.

(vii) If x and y are distinct plaintext letters, the numbers of letters that are ciphertext equivalents of both x and y is either 0, 1, or 3, More precisely,

$$|E_x \cap E_y| = \begin{cases} 1 & \text{if the rows in } \Gamma \text{ containing x and y are adjacent and the columns in } \Gamma \text{ containing x and y are different.} \\ 3 & \text{if x and y are in the same row of } \Gamma \\ 0 & \text{otherwise} \end{cases}$$

where $|E_x|$ denotes the number of elements in the set E_x.

(viii) If the letters x and y are each ciphertext equivalents of one another, that is,

$$x \in E_y \qquad y \in E_x$$

and x and y are in the same row of Γ.

(ix) If the letter x is an equivalent of both the letters y and z, that is,

$$x \in E_y \qquad x \in E_z$$

then one of the following relationships* exists:

---

*We will use the following notation:

- $z \downarrow x$ indicates that z is in the same column and in the row above x.
- $z \rightarrow x$ indicates that x is in the right-adjacent column and the same row of z.
- z - x if z and x are in the same row (although perhaps not in adjacent columns).

- x and y are in the same row of Γ; x and z are in the same column of Γ with z above x; z ↓ x - y *or*
- x and z are in the same row of Γ; x and y are in the same column of Γ with y above x; y ↓ x - z *or*
- x, y, and z are in the same row of Γ; x - y - z

(*x*) If the 2-gram (x, x′) is P_Γ-enciphered into the 2-gram (x″, x), that is,

$$P_\Gamma(x, x') = (x'', x)$$

then one of the following two relationships exists:

- x, x′, and x″ are in the same column and adjacent rows of Γ; x′ ↓ x ↓ x″
- x, x′, and x″ are in the same row and adjacent columns of Γ; x′ → x → x″

(xi) If the 2-gram (x, x′) is P_Γ-enciphered into the 2-gram (x′, x″), that is,

$$P_\Gamma(x, x') = (x', x'')$$

then one of the following two relationships exists:

- x, x′, and x″ are in the same column and adjacent rows of Γ; x ↓ x′ ↓ x″
- x, x′, and x″ are in the same row and adjacent columns of Γ; x → x′ → x″.

Proof.

Property (vii): If letters x and y have common ciphertext equivalents, then either x and y must be in the same row, in which case the three remaining row elements are the common ciphertext equivalents of x and y, so that $|E_x \cap E_y| = 3$, *or* x and y are in adjacent rows but different columns, y → z, x ↓ z, and $|E_x \cap E_y| = 1$.

Property (viii): If x is a ciphertext equivalent of y, then either

◆ x - y   or   ▲ y ↓ x

In the second case, we conclude that $y \notin E_x$, which contradicts the hypothesis.

Property (ix): If x is a ciphertext equivalent of both y and z, then

◆ x - y   or   ▲ y ↓ x

and

★ x - z   or   ▶ z ↓ x

Only the relationship ▲ - ▶ leads to a contradiction, so that either z ↓ x - y, y ↓ x - z, or x - y - z.

Property (x): If $P_\Gamma(x, x') = (x'', x)$, x″ is a ciphertext equivalent of x, so that

◆ x - x″   or   ▲ x ↓ x″

and x is a ciphertext equivalent of x′, so that

★ x′ - x or ▶ x′ ↓ x

Two of the four possible relationships, ◆ - ▶ and ▲ - ★, lead to contradictions. Thus either x′ ↓ x ↓ x″ or x′ - x - x″, which with P_Γ(x, x′) = (x″, x), implies x′ → x → x″.

Property (xi): If P_Γ(x, x′), = (x′, x″), x′ is a ciphertext equivalent of x so that

◆ x - x′ or ▲ x ↓ x′

and x″ is a ciphertext equivalent of x′ so that

★ x′ - x″ or ▶ x′ ↓ x″

Two of the four possible relationships, ◆ - ▶ and ▲ - ★, lead to contradictions. Thus either x ↓ x′ ↓ x″ or x - x′ - x″, which with P_Γ(x, x′) = (x′, x″) implies x → x′ → x″. ◀

3.13 CRYPTANALYSIS OF *CIPHER(2.2)*

The cryptanalysis of *CIPHER(2.2)* is based upon an examination of the 2-gram frequencies and the constraints described in Theorem 3.12.2. We give the analysis in a sequence of steps.

Step 1 The plaintext 2-gram that normally occurs with the highest frequency is `TH`. Table 3.13.1 lists the count of occurrences of plaintext and ciphertext 2-grams and their reversals for the most frequently occurring 2-grams in *CIPHER(2.2)* and Table 2.3.3. The ciphertext 2-grams with the largest count in *CIPHER(2.2)* are `rn`, `aq` and `lh`. Plaintext `*H` cannot be Playfair enciphered to ciphertext `lh` for any choice of letter `*`. Next, the ciphertext `aq` and its reversal `qa` occur with comparable frequency, as is the case with the probability of the plaintext 2-grams `ER` and `RE`, but not with `TH` and `HT`, suggesting that we make the plaintext-to-ciphertext correspondences `TH` → `rn` and `ER` → `aq`.

Step 2 Table 3.13.2 lists for each letter the right and left plaintext contact letters and the number of times they follow and precede from Table 2.3.3. The entries $\texttt{N}_{1216}$ and $\texttt{H}_{646}$ for the letter `A` mean the plaintext `A` was followed 1216 times by plaintext `N` and was preceded 646 times by plaintext `H` in the sample count (Table 2.3.3) of 2-grams. `E` is the most frequent right contact plaintext letter of `H`. In Table 3.13.3, the counts of the ciphertext 2-grams that follow `rn` in *CIPHER(2.2)* are given. The right contact letters of ciphertext `n` weighted by the number of times they appear in Table 3.13.3 are

`a`(10) `d`(7) `g`(6) `b`(4) `f`(1) `t`(1) `u`(1) `v`(1)

TABLE 3.13.1
Table of 2-Grams (and Their Reversals) Having the Highest Number of Occurrences in *CIPHER(2.2)* and Table 2.3.3

Plaintext				Ciphertext			
2-Gram	**Count**	**Reversal**	**Count**	**2-Gram**	**Count**	**Reversal**	**Count**
TH	2161	HT	85	rn	32	nr	3
HE	2053	EH	16	aq	31	qa	17
IN	1550	NI	301	lh	31	hl	2
ER	1436	RE	1280	ga	22	ag	1
RE	1280	ER	1436	tu	22	ut	3
ON	1232	NO	239	dh	21	hd	6
AN	1216	NA	249	hb	21	bh	2
EN	1029	NE	549	qd	20	dq	4
AT	1019	TA	381	eg	19	ge	7
ES	917	SE	595	go	18	og	7
ED	890	DE	572	kh	18	hk	1
TE	872	ET	301	dr	17	rd	4
TI	865	IT	704	aq	17	aq	31
OR	861	RO	510	af	16	fa	10
ST	823	TS	257	lm	16	ml	1
AR	764	RA	470	hu	15	uh	7
ND	761	DN	8	ks	15	sk	1
TO	756	OT	223	rk	15	kr	11
NT	743	TN	9	pb	13	bp	6
IS	741	SI	390	ty	13	yt	0
OF	731	FO	326	im	12	mi	0
IT	704	TI	865	bq	11	qb	7
AL	681	LA	359	dg	11	gd	6
AS	648	SA	200	fi	11	if	4
HA	646	AH	13	kr	11	rk	15

This suggests that we assume a, d, g, and b are ciphertext equivalents of E.

Step 3 *PLAIN(2)* describes some aspects of *the performance evaluation of computer systems* and PERFORMANCE, EVALUATION, PREDICTION, SYSTEM, OPERATING and COMPUTER should appear several times. We begin by searching for PERFORMANCE using the correspondence ER → aq. The search for probable words in Playfair ciphertext is more complicated than in the case of monalphabetic 1-gram substitutions (Sec. 3.11); there may be more than one Playfair encipherment of PERFORMANCE, depending upon (1) how PERFORMANCE is divided into 2-grams,

PE RF OR MA NC E* *P ER FO RM AN CE

and (2) which plaintext letters * follow E or precede P. We will search for *P ER FO RM AN CE, since we have assumed ER → aq. The results of the search are given in Table 3.13.4. **aqoushdhpb

TABLE 3.13.2

Number of Occurrences of Right and Left Plaintext Contact Letters Derived from Table 2.3.3

Left Contact Letters					**Letter**	**Right Contact Letters**				
L_{359}	T_{381}	R_{470}	E_{492}	H_{646}	A	N_{1216}	T_{1019}	R_{764}	L_{681}	S_{648}
I_{51}	O_{57}	M_{65}	U_{87}	A_{125}	B	E_{394}	L_{152}	Y_{143}	O_{118}	A_{114}
U_{103}	A_{251}	N_{281}	E_{323}	I_{476}	C	O_{606}	E_{453}	H_{339}	A_{319}	T_{237}
L_{197}	I_{285}	A_{304}	N_{761}	E_{890}	D	E_{572}	I_{273}	A_{158}	O_{111}	U_{91}
M_{573}	S_{595}	T_{872}	R_{1280}	H_{2053}	E	R_{1436}	N_{1029}	S_{917}	D_{890}	A_{492}
A_{65}	I_{80}	E_{106}	F_{108}	O_{731}	F	O_{326}	I_{188}	E_{150}	R_{142}	F_{108}
R_{80}	E_{93}	A_{151}	I_{174}	N_{630}	G	E_{271}	R_{150}	H_{145}	O_{129}	A_{122}
G_{145}	W_{175}	S_{186}	C_{339}	T_{2161}	H	E_{2053}	A_{646}	I_{426}	O_{287}	T_{85}
S_{390}	L_{407}	H_{426}	R_{541}	T_{865}	I	N_{1550}	S_{741}	T_{704}	O_{554}	C_{476}
E_{4}	D_{5}	B_{7}	O_{8}	A_{13}	J	U_{48}	O_{45}	E_{26}	A_{18}	I_{5}
I_{31}	O_{44}	A_{67}	C_{86}	R_{94}	K	E_{187}	I_{56}	S_{39}	N_{20}	A_{14}
O_{234}	E_{340}	I_{352}	L_{378}	A_{681}	L	E_{513}	I_{407}	L_{378}	A_{359}	Y_{219}
R_{139}	A_{182}	I_{184}	E_{253}	O_{397}	M	E_{573}	A_{351}	I_{259}	O_{240}	P_{139}
U_{318}	E_{1029}	A_{1216}	O_{1232}	I_{1550}	N	D_{761}	T_{743}	G_{630}	E_{549}	S_{340}
F_{326}	R_{510}	I_{554}	C_{606}	T_{756}	O	N_{1232}	R_{861}	F_{731}	U_{533}	M_{397}
S_{128}	M_{139}	E_{143}	A_{144}	O_{164}	P	R_{409}	E_{310}	O_{268}	A_{241}	L_{144}
C_{1}	S_{3}	N_{3}	I_{5}	E_{25}	Q	U_{73}	A_{0}	B_{0}	C_{0}	D_{0}
U_{306}	P_{409}	A_{764}	O_{861}	E_{1436}	R	E_{1280}	I_{541}	O_{510}	A_{470}	S_{300}
R_{300}	N_{340}	A_{648}	I_{741}	E_{917}	S	T_{823}	E_{595}	I_{390}	S_{277}	O_{234}
E_{301}	I_{704}	N_{743}	S_{823}	A_{1019}	T	H_{2161}	E_{872}	I_{865}	O_{756}	A_{381}
D_{91}	C_{92}	T_{120}	S_{192}	O_{533}	U	N_{318}	R_{306}	T_{263}	S_{256}	L_{230}
R_{65}	A_{137}	I_{155}	E_{160}	O_{188}	V	E_{522}	I_{223}	A_{65}	O_{46}	Y_{5}
S_{13}	A_{37}	T_{54}	E_{153}	O_{194}	W	A_{282}	I_{259}	E_{239}	H_{175}	O_{159}
X_{5}	O_{7}	I_{14}	A_{17}	E_{113}	X	P_{47}	T_{23}	E_{17}	C_{15}	I_{15}
T_{125}	R_{140}	B_{143}	A_{202}	L_{219}	Y	E_{84}	O_{64}	S_{44}	I_{20}	A_{17}
N_{2}	T_{3}	E_{3}	A_{15}	I_{49}	Z	E_{36}	A_{18}	I_{17}	O_{4}	Z_{2}

TABLE 3.13.3

Two-Grams in *CIPHER(2.2)* which Follow rn

	Count		**Count**
rnge	5	rndq	3
rnbq	3	rnap	2
rndg	2	rnae	2
rnab	2	rndr	2
rnaf	2	rnuh	1
rnag	1	rnaq	1
rnch	1	rnto	1
rngv	1	rnbg	1
rnvk	1	rnfg	1

TABLE 3.13.4
Results of the Search for *P ER FO RM AN CE in *CIPHER(2.2)*

12-Gram	Count	12-Gram	Count
kaaqbdpfbvqd	1	gcaqlhaybqrh	1
ksaqcrrkbxeg	1	kiaqlhayrhrk	1
ksaqcrrkbxrn	1	gkaqlhbkgnie	1
anaqdqgaiskr	1	qcaqlhfeuhns	1
glaqdrkhmqxt	2	elaqlhnygabi	1
glaqdrlhhddu	1	qiaqlhnygaqb	1
mkaqgdaykrnr	1	kraqlhogbufp	1
mkaqgdftqbst	1	elaqoushdhpb	1
quaqgpufqulh	1	gkaqoushdhpb	1
kuaqhdrkpgxb	1	geaqoushdhpb	2
dqaqhxhulphf	1	rnaqqdimogfu	1
duaqkhtufiif	1	geaqrctudgqk	1
gkaqlhakodbi	1	huaquhstkhrn	1
gcaqlhanaqdq	1	buaqwppbqarq	1

appears four times in Table 3.13.4, more often than any other 10-gram. We will assume the correspondence

*P ER FO RM AN CE → ** aq ou sh dh pb

noting that it is consistent with our assumption that b is a ciphertext equivalent of E. This provides additional ciphertext equivalents, which we summarize in Table 3.13.5. Now we use the structural constraints

TABLE 3.13.5
Ciphertext Equivalents : *Steps 1–3*

Letter	Equivalents	Letter	Equivalents	Letter	Equivalents
A	d	B		C	p
D		E	a d b g	F	o
G		H	n	I	
K		L		M	h
N	h	O	u	P	e k l
Q		R	q s	S	
T	r	U		V	
W		X		Y	
Z					

of Playfair encipherment to deduce the arrangement of the letters in the Playfair square.

Step 4 L – K – P ↓E

Proof. A, D, B, G are ciphertext equivalents of E, and E, K, L are equivalents of P. IF E – P, then either E – K – P or E – L – P, which gives more than five letters in the row containing E.

Step 5 A – D – B – E ↓G *or* A – D – G – E ↓B

Proof. D is an equivalent of E and A and A and D are equivalents of E.

Step 6 N – H

Proof. N is a ciphertext equivalent of H and H is a ciphertext equivalent of N.

Step 7 The word PERFORMANCE can also occur in *CIPHER(2.2)* with an alignment that results in it being divided into the 2-grams

PE RF OR MA NC E*

We will use a heuristic to search for the encipherment of PE RF OR MA NC E*. If $(x_0, x_1, \ldots, x_{n-1})$ is a plaintext n-gram, and Δ_{x_i} is the set of ciphertext equivalents of x_i already identified, let

$$\mu = \mu(y_0,y_1, \ldots, y_{n-1} \mid \Delta_{x_0},\Delta_{x_1}, \ldots,\Delta_{x_{n-1}})$$

$$= \chi_{\Delta_{x_0}}(y_0) + \chi_{\Delta_{x_1}}(y_1) + \ldots + \chi_{\Delta_{x_{n-1}}}(y_{n-1})$$

where $\chi_{\Delta_{x_i}}$ is the indicator function of the set Δ_{x_i}. μ counts the number of letters in the (ciphertext) n-gram $(y_0, y_1, \ldots, y_{n-1})$ that satisfy the conditions $y_i \in \Delta_{x_i}$. We will call $\mu(y_0,y_1, \ldots, y_{n-1} \mid \Delta_{x_0},\Delta_{x_1}, \ldots,\Delta_{x_{n-1}})$ the *matching value* of $(y_0,y_1, \ldots, y_{n-1})$ relative to the sets of equivalents $(\Delta_{x_0},\Delta_{x_1}, \ldots,\Delta_{x_{n-1}})$. The larger the matching value, the more likely that $(y_0,y_1, \ldots,y_{n-1})$ is the ciphertext of $(x_0,x_1, \ldots,x_{n-1})$. The results of matching with a matching value of at least 3 are shown in Table 3.13.6.

The 11-gram eguahuhbmk* with * either a, b, f, or g appears seven times in Table 3.13.6 with $\mu = 4$. There are only three other 11-grams (each with $\mu = 3$) that are repeated. We will assume that eguahuhbmk* corresponds to various encipherments of PE RF OR MA NC E*. This yields additional corresponding plaintext-ciphertext 2-grams

TH → rn	ER → aq	FO → ou
RM → sh	AN → dh	CE → pb
PE → eg	RF → ua	OR → hu
MA → hb	NC → mk	

and the additional ciphertext letter equivalents shown in Table 3.13.7.

TABLE 3.13.6
Results of the Search for PE RF OR MA NC E* in *CIPHER(2.2)* with a Matching Value of at Least 3

11-Gram	μ	11-Gram	μ	11-Gram	μ
absiraqdksq	3	gaeguahuhbm	4	pbqarqawbgd	4
adgvdghbfad	3	gafarchodha	3	pbsuhaodabu	3
afeguahuhbm	3	gafarchohua	4	pgcuuotxtub	3
afeguahuhbm	3	gagkaqoushd	3	pgfixshahuf	4
aflmgshbrnb	3	gaqbeiipckd	3	qaakkslhhdt	3
akkslhhdtng	3	gdbtxtqdgca	3	qaakkslhomb	3
aqdrlhhddua	3	hdkuaqhdrkp	4	qagozhtifub	3
bdpfbvqdtyg	3	hueguahuhbm	3	qaqcaqlhfeu	3
bgdgutipbia	3	iesuuornafg	3	qarndqaqhxh	3
bgfarchodha	3	kfbqphhdkua	4	qdfpbdhudrb	3
bgqtsdgeqaa	3	khmpgnhbdhb	3	qdgcaqlhana	3
bhgonqgagla	3	khmqxtqdsbg	3	qdgcaqlhayb	3
dadhkhqdhqf	3	khqbkslhogg	4	qdgcuhhqbhh	3
dalmgbxshub	3	khqdhqfiies	3	qdimogfuhpi	3
dbqbfnomhwa	4	khrnafgpfpg	3	qdimogfuhpb	4
dgeguahuhbm	4	khrnbqxtqdg	3	qdstxtqdgcu	3
dgqkqstqkru	3	krbpuqwhkfb	4	qdwhkslhmtb	3
eaksumtygae	3	krmnubhulhm	3	raqdksqsfif	3
egcrunouqai	3	krrmuzkfiqg	3	raqdksqsfif	3
eguahuhbmkb	4	kruoiqnfslu	3	rbqadxoggbd	3
eguahuhbmkb	4	kslmgshbrnb	4	rbsiraqdksq	3
eguahuhbmkg	4	kxuotqimiqa	4	rhqbtsdhqga	3
eguahuhbmkb	4	kzlmgshbrna	4	rlqdfpbdhud	4
eguahuhbmkg	4	lggdtyrmvkg	3	rndqaqhxhul	3
eguahuhbmka	4	lgkhuduzqia	4	rntouspafbt	3
eguahuhbmkf	3	lgsudhayrhr	3	shqtuqtqfik	3
eguoeguahuh	4	lhgkaqlhbkg	3	tqimusdhucd	3
eguoiqafckr	4	lhtnqskhnqg	3	tygouzsieib	3
egwanfkhrng	3	lmgbxshubqe	3	tygurlqdfpb	3
egwanfrnaea	3	lmmkaqgdayk	3	tylmgshbrna	3
egwanfrndqb	3	lmmkaqgdftq	3	uhqomgqurna	3
egwanfuorng	3	lqqdstxtqdg	3	uoeguahuhbm	3
euelaqlhnyg	3	lsqdirdgrnd	3	uzqiaqlhnyg	3
faeaksrctyg	3	mtkaaqbdpfb	3	uzsieibdcpk	3
fastunnflmg	4	murdlsqdird	3	wanftqimusd	3
fgelaqoushd	3	ngtounbuaqw	3	whqghbhdqgg	4
fpeguahuhbm	3	odabuqqaqca	4	xtqdgcuhhqb	3
gabiuqfibir	3	odbiskgnhbb	3		

Step 8 P – L – K E – A – B – D – E – F and P ↓E ↓G.
Proof. *Steps 4, 5,* and the correspondence PE → eg.

Step 9 M – N – N – O.
Proof. H is a ciphertext equivalent of M, N, and O, and M is a ciphertext equivalent of N.

Step 10 F ↓O ↓U and G – H – M – N – O.
Proof. *Steps 8, 9,* and the correspondence FO → ou.

TABLE 3.13.7
Ciphertext Equivalents : *Steps 1–7*

Letter	Equivalents	Letter	Equivalents	Letter	Equivalents
A	d b	B		C	p k
D		E	a d b g f	F	o a
G		H	n	I	
K		L		M	h
N	h m	O	u h	P	e k l
Q		R	q s u	S	
T	r	U		V	
W		X		Y	
Z					

Step 11 Q – U – R.
Proof. Since U is a ciphertext equivalent of R and O ↓U, it follows that U – R. Next, ER → aq and E and R are not in the same row in Γ, which implies Q – R.

Steps 1–11 show that

E – D – A – B – F

G – H – M – N – O

are full rows.

Step 12 Q – R – S – T – U is a full row, H ↓R and M ↓S.
Proof. RM → sh and R is not in the same row as S in Γ.

Step 13 P – C – K – L and C ↓B.
Proof. CE → pb and C and E are neither in the same row nor column in Γ.

Step 14 A ↓H and G ↓Q.
Proof. ER → aq and E and R are neither in the same row nor column in Γ.

Step 15 D ↓N.
Proof. AN → dh and A and N are neither in the same row nor column in Γ.

Step 16 B ↓M.

Proof. MA → hb and M and A are neither in the same row nor column in Γ.

Step 17 N ↓T.

Proof. TH → rn and T and H are neither in the same row nor column in Γ.

Step 18 K ↓D.

Proof. NC → mk and N and C are neither in the same row nor column in Γ.

Steps 1–18 yield the ciphertext equivalents shown in Table 3.13.8, which partially determines the Playfair square shown in Table 3.13.9. The relative position of L in the row P – C – K – L is yet to be determined and consequently we have omitted L in Table 3.13.9.

Step 19 A search of *CIPHER(2.2)* for the ciphertext of

EV AL UA TI ON

using the information provided in Tables 3.13.8–9, yields three occurrences of

gp fi rf rk go

with a matching value of 7.

TABLE 3.13.8
Ciphertext Equivalents: *Steps 1–18*

Letter	Equivalents	Letter	Equivalents	Letter	Equivalents
A	d b e f h	B	e a d f m	C	p k l b
D	e a b f n	E	a d b g f	F	o a e b d
G	q h m n o	H	n g m o r	I	
K	p c k d	L	p c k	M	g h n o s
N	h m g h t	O	u h g m n	P	e k l c
Q	r s t u	R	q s u t	S	q r t u
T	r q s u	U	q r s t	V	
W		X		Y	
Z					

TABLE 3.13.9
Partial Determination of the Playfair Square: *Steps 1–18*

```
P -     - C - K
↓         ↓
E - A - B - D - F
↓   ↓   ↓   ↓   ↓
G - H - M - N - O
↓   ↓   ↓   ↓   ↓
Q - R - S - T - U
```

Step 20 P ↓E ↓G ↓Q ↓V.
Proof. EV → gp

Step 21 I ↓A ↓H ↓H ↓R and K ↓D ↓N ↓T.
Proof. TI → rk.

Step 22 L ↓F ↓O ↓U.
Proof. AL → fi.

Step 23 N → O → G.
Proof. ON → go.

We have now filled in 21 of the 25 entries in the Playfair square, where the arrows to the right of the column L F O U indicate that this column is to the left of the column P E G Q V (Table 3.13.10). We now make a partial decipherment of a fragment of the ciphertext to determine the missing horizontal connections in Table 3.13.10.

TABLE 3.13.10
Partial Determination of the Playfair Square: *Steps 1–23*

```
P - I - C - K → L →
↓   ↓   ↓   ↓   ↓
E - A - B - C → F →
↓   ↓   ↓   ↓   ↓
G - H - M - N → O →
↓   ↓   ↓   ↓   ↓
Q - R - S - T → U →
↓
V
```

TABLE 3.13.11
Partial Decipherment of *CIPHER(2.2)* Based on Table 3.13.10

```
TH EI tr tq EO FP ER FO RM AN CE EV AL UA TI ON AN DP RE DI CT IO om AS CO
NC ER NE DU SE st TH RO UG mg UT TH EH IS TO tw OF CO MP UT ER EV OL UT IO
NP ER IO DI NF AC TC gn MA AS IN AN zn TH ER TE CH NO LO GI CA LD EV EL OP
```

Step 24 H → M → N.
Proof. The fragment

DP RE DI CT IO om AS CO NC ER NE DU

is most likely the plaintext

D PREDICTION HAS CONCERNED U.

Step 25 R ↓ W and T ↓ Y.
Proof. The fragment EHISTOtw is most likely the plaintext EHISTORY.

Step 26 U ↓ Z.
Proof. The fragment

IN AN zn TH ER

is most likely the plaintext

IN ANY OTHER.

Thus we arrive at the Playfair square given in Table 3.13.12.

TABLE 3.13.12
Determination of the Playfair Square : *Steps 1–26*

```
P → I → C → K → L
↓   ↓   ↓   ↓   ↓
E → A → B → C → F
↓   ↓   ↓   ↓   ↓
G → H → M → N → O
↓   ↓   ↓   ↓   ↓
Q → R → S → T → U
↓   ↓   ↓   ↓   ↓
V → W → X → Y → Z
```

3.14 N-GRAM SUBSTITUTION: LINEAR ALGEBRA OVER Z_m

An algebraic theory that generalizes the affine Caesar substitution

$$T_{a,b} : \boldsymbol{Z}_m \rightarrow \boldsymbol{Z}_m$$

$$T_{a,b} : t \rightarrow at + b \text{ (modulo m)}$$

to define the substitution of n-grams was formulated by Lester Hill [HIL 1,2]. The set of integers $\boldsymbol{Z}_m$ with the operations of addition, subtraction, and multiplication modulo m is an example of a ring. A *ring* R is an algebraic system in which the operations of addition, subtraction, and multiplication on pairs of elements can be defined and which enjoys the properties:

- The elements of R form a commutative group under addition. The identify element under addition is denoted by 0 and the inverse of a is $-a$

  $$\alpha + \beta = \beta + \alpha \qquad \alpha + 0 = 0 + \alpha = \alpha$$

  $$\alpha + -\alpha = -\alpha + \alpha = 0$$

- Multiplication and addition satisfy the associative and distributive laws

  $$\alpha(\beta\gamma) = (\alpha\beta)\gamma \text{ (modulo m)} \qquad \textit{associative law}$$

  $$\alpha(\beta+\gamma) = \alpha\beta + \alpha\gamma \text{ (modulo m)}$$

  $$(\alpha+\beta)\gamma = \alpha\beta + \alpha\gamma \text{ (modulo m)} \qquad \textit{distributive laws}$$

Division in a ring arises when we want to solve the linear equation

$$\alpha x = \beta \text{ (modulo m)} \tag{3.14.1}$$

for x given α and β in R. The formal solution of Eq. (3.14.1) is

$$x = \alpha^{-1}\beta \text{ (modulo m)}$$

provided that the inverse α^{-1} of α under multiplication exists. The multiplicative inverse of a ring element α may not always exist; for example, when m = 26, the product $2 \times 13 = 0$ in $\boldsymbol{Z}_{26}$ without either the elements 2 or 13 being the zero element, which implies that 2^{-1} and 13^{-1} cannot exist. Thus there may not be solutions of the equations 2x = b or 13x = b. For example, the equation 2x = 5 has no solutions in $\boldsymbol{Z}_{26}$, while the equation 2x = 6 has two solutions (x = 3 and x = 16). When m is a prime p, the inverse of every nonzero element t of $\boldsymbol{Z}_p$ exists, since

$$t \text{ (modulo m)}, 2t \text{ (modulo m)}, 3t \text{ (modulo m)}, \ldots, (p - 1)t \text{ (modulo m)}$$

are distinct if $1 \le t < p$; if, on the contrary, there exist α and β

$$\alpha t = \beta t \text{ (modulo m)} \qquad 0 < \alpha \le \beta < p$$

then $(\beta - \alpha)t = 0$ (modulo m), which means that p must divide either t or $(\beta - \alpha)$, which implies $\alpha = \beta$. Thus there exists some value of t such that

$$\alpha t = 1 \text{ (modulo m)}$$

which means that $\alpha = t^{-1}$.

$\boldsymbol{Z}_p$ is an example of an algebraic system called a *field*. In a field we can always solve the linear equation

$$\alpha x = \beta \text{ (modulo m)}$$

for x, given α and β, and provided $\alpha \neq 0$. The nonzero elements of $\boldsymbol{Z}_p$ form a group under multiplication.

The set of all n-tuples $\mathbf{x} = (x_0, x_1, \ldots, x_{n-1})$ with components in the ring $\boldsymbol{Z}_m$ is an example of an algebraic system called a *vector space of dimension n over a ring;* each n-tuple $\mathbf{x}$ is called a *vector.* We continue to use the notation $\boldsymbol{Z}_{m,n}$ to denote the vector space of dimension n over the ring $\boldsymbol{Z}_m$.

We may define the addition and subtraction of vectors in the vector space $\boldsymbol{Z}_{m,n}$,

$$(x_0, x_1, \ldots, x_{n-1}) + (y_0, y_1, \ldots, y_{n-1})$$
$$= (x_0 + y_0, x_1 + y_1, \ldots, x_{n-1} + y_{n-1}) \text{ (modulo m)}$$

$$(x_0, x_1, \ldots, x_{n-1}) - (y_0, y_1, \ldots, y_{n-1})$$
$$= (x_0 - y_0, x_1 - y_1, \ldots, x_{n-1} - y_{n-1}) \text{ (modulo m)}$$

and scalar multiplication of a vector by an element of the ring $\boldsymbol{Z}_m$,

$$t(x_0, x_1, \ldots, x_{n-1}) = (tx_0, tx_1, \ldots, tx_{n-1}) \text{ (modulo m)}$$

Addition and scalar multiplication are commutative, associative, and distributive operations:

$$\mathbf{x} + \mathbf{y} = \mathbf{y} + \mathbf{x} \text{ (modulo m)} \qquad \textit{commutativity}$$

$$(\mathbf{x} + \mathbf{y}) + \mathbf{z} = \mathbf{x} + (\mathbf{y} + \mathbf{z}) \text{ (modulo m)} \qquad \textit{associativity}$$

$$(t + s)\mathbf{x} = t\mathbf{x} + s\mathbf{x} \text{ (modulo m)} \qquad t(\mathbf{x} + \mathbf{y}) = t\mathbf{x} + t\mathbf{y} \text{ (modulo m)}$$

distributivity

$\mathbf{x}$ is a *linear combination of the vectors* $\{x^{(i)} : 0 \leq i < L\}$ if

$$\mathbf{x} = t_0\mathbf{x}^{(0)} + t_1\mathbf{x}^{(1)} + \ldots + t_{L-1}\mathbf{x}^{(L-1)} \text{ (modulo m)}$$

A *linear transformation* T from the vector space $\boldsymbol{Z}_{m,n}$ into $\boldsymbol{Z}_{m,n}$ is a mapping

$$T : \boldsymbol{Z}_{m,n} \rightarrow \boldsymbol{Z}_{m,n}$$

$$T : \mathbf{x} \rightarrow \mathbf{y} = T(\mathbf{x})$$

which satisfies the *linearity condition*

$$T(t\mathbf{x} + s\mathbf{y}) = tT(\mathbf{x}) + sT(\mathbf{y}) \text{ (modulo m)}$$

for all s,t in $\boldsymbol{Z}_m$ and $\mathbf{x}, \mathbf{y}$ in $\boldsymbol{Z}_{m,n}$. The linear transformation T may be represented by an n by n matrix with entries $\{\gamma_{i,j}\}$ in $\boldsymbol{Z}_{m,n}$:

$$(3.14.2) \qquad T = \begin{vmatrix} \gamma_{0,0} & \gamma_{0,1} & \cdots & \gamma_{0,n-1} \\ \gamma_{1,0} & \gamma_{1,1} & \cdots & \gamma_{1,n-1} \\ \cdot & \cdot & \cdots & \cdot \\ \cdot & \cdot & \cdots & \cdot \\ \cdot & \cdot & \cdots & \cdot \\ \gamma_{n-1,0} & \gamma_{n-1,1} & \cdots & \gamma_{n-1,n-1} \end{vmatrix}$$

$$y_i = \sum_{0 \le j < n} \gamma_{i,j} x_j \pmod{m} \qquad 0 \le i < n$$

The n vectors

$$\mathbf{u}^{(i)} = (\underbrace{0, 0, \ldots, 0}_{i-1 \text{ zeros}}, 1, \underbrace{0, 0, \ldots, 0}_{n-i \text{ zeros}}) \qquad 0 \le i < n$$

are called the *unit vectors* of $\boldsymbol{Z}_{m,n}$. The *image* of the unit vector $\mathbf{u}^{(i)}$ under T is the ith column of the matrix in Eq. (3.14.2):

$$T(\mathbf{u}^{(i)}) = (\gamma_{0,i}, \gamma_{1,i}, \ldots, \gamma_{n-1,i})$$

so that the images $T(\mathbf{u}^{(i)})$ of $\mathbf{u}^{(i)}$ for $0 \le i < n$ reveal the entries of T.

A set of vectors $\{\mathbf{x}^{(i)} : 0 \le i < L\}$ in $\boldsymbol{Z}_{m,n}$ are called *linearly independent* (*over* $\boldsymbol{Z}_m$) if the only solution $(t_0, t_1, \ldots, t_{L-1})$ of the equation

$$\mathbf{0} = t_0\mathbf{x}^{(0)} + t_1\mathbf{x}^{(1)} + \ldots + t_{L-1}\mathbf{x}^{(L-1)} \pmod{m}$$

is the *trivial solution,* the solution in which all the scalars $\{t_i\}$ are zero:

$$0 = t_0 = t_1 = \ldots = t_{L-1}$$

$\mathbf{0}$ denotes the *null vector* in $\boldsymbol{Z}_{m,n}$, all of whose components are zero.

The opposite of linear independence is linear dependence; a set of vectors $\{\mathbf{x}^{(i)} : 0 \le i < L\}$ in $\boldsymbol{Z}_{m,n}$ are *linearly dependent* (*over* $\boldsymbol{Z}_m$) if there exists a non-trivial solution $(t_0, t_1, \ldots, t_{L-1})$ of the equation

$$\mathbf{0} = t_0\mathbf{x}^{(0)} + t_1\mathbf{x}^{(1)} + \ldots + t_{L-1}\mathbf{x}^{(L-1)} \pmod{m}$$

For example:

- The unit vectors in $\boldsymbol{Z}_{m,n}$ are linearly independent over $\boldsymbol{Z}_{m,n}$.
- The three vectors

  $$(0, 1, 7) \qquad (1, 4, 0) \qquad (0, 0, 11)$$

  are linearly independent over $\boldsymbol{Z}_{26,3}$.
- The three vectors

  $$(0, 1, 7) \qquad (1, 4, 0) \qquad (0, 0, 2)$$

  are linearly dependent over $\boldsymbol{Z}_{26,3}$ with $t_0 = t_1 = 0$ and $t_2 = 13$.

The set of vectors $\{\mathbf{x}^{(i)} : 0 \le i < L\}$ in $\boldsymbol{Z}_{m,n}$ *spans* $\boldsymbol{Z}_{m,n}$, if every vector $\mathbf{x}$ in $\boldsymbol{Z}_{m,n}$ can be written as a linear combination of the $\{\mathbf{x}^{(i)} : 0 \le i < L\}$

$$\mathbf{x} = t_0\mathbf{x}^{(0)} + t_1\mathbf{x}^{(1)} + \ldots + t_{L-1}\mathbf{x}^{(l-1)} \pmod{m}$$

A *basis* for $\boldsymbol{Z}_{m,n}$ is a set of vectors $\{\mathbf{x}^{(i)} : 0 \le i < L\}$, which are linearly independent over and span $\boldsymbol{Z}_{m,n}$.

The basic relationships between independence are given in the following theorem.

Theorem 3.14.1

(i) Every basis for $Z_{m,n}$ contains n vectors.
(ii) Every set of n vectors that are linearly independent over $Z_{m,n}$ is a basis.
(iii) Every set of $L > n$ vectors in $Z_{m,n}$ are linearly dependent over $Z_{m,n}$.
(iv) If T is the linear transformation corresponding to the matrix in Eq. (3.14.2),

$$T : Z_{m,n} \rightarrow Z_{m,n}$$

- The images $\{T(\mathbf{x}^{(i)}) : 0 \leq i < L\}$ of any set of $L > n$ vectors $\{\mathbf{x}^{(i)} : 0 \leq i < L\}$ in $Z_{m,n}$ are linearly dependent over $Z_{m,n}$.
- If the vectors $\{\mathbf{x}^{(i)} : 0 \leq i < n\}$ are linearly independent over $Z_{m,n}$ then their images $\{T(\mathbf{x}^{(i)}) : 0 \leq i < n\}$ under T are linearly independent over $Z_{m,n}$ if and only if the *determinant** of T, denoted by det(T), is not divisible by modulo p for any prime p that divides m. In this case, T is called an *invertible* or *non singular* linear transformation with inverse transformation T^{-1}

$$T^{-1} : Z_{m,n} \rightarrow Z_{m,n}$$

$$TT^{-1} = T^{-1}T = I$$

where I is the identity matrix. Moreover, T^{-1} is a linear transformation.

(v) If $\{\mathbf{x}^{(i)} : 0 \leq i < n\}$ and $\{\mathbf{x}^{(i)\prime} : 0 \leq i < n\}$ are two bases for $Z_{m,n}$, there exists a nonsingular linear transformation T such that

$$T : \mathbf{x}^{(i)} \rightarrow \mathbf{x}^{(i)\prime} \quad 0 \leq i < n$$

For example, when m = 26 and

$$T = \begin{vmatrix} 17 & 17 & 5 \\ 21 & 18 & 21 \\ 2 & 2 & 19 \end{vmatrix}$$

then

$$\det(T) = -939 = 1 \text{ (modulo 2)}$$

$$\det(T) = -939 = 10 \text{ (modulo 13)}$$

so that T^{-1} exists. It is simple to check that

$$T^{-1} = \begin{vmatrix} 4 & 9 & 15 \\ 15 & 17 & 6 \\ 24 & 0 & 17 \end{vmatrix}$$

*The determinant of a matrix T over $Z_{m,n}$ is defined in the usual way as the sum over all permutations $\{\pi\}$ of $(0, 1, \ldots, n-1)$ of the products

$$\pm \gamma_{0,\pi_0}\gamma_{1,\pi_1} \cdots \gamma_{n-1,\pi_{n-1}} \text{ (modulo m)}$$

satisfies

$$TT^{-1} = T^{-1}T = I = \begin{vmatrix} 1 & 0 & 0 \\ 0 & 1 & 0 \\ 0 & 0 & 1 \end{vmatrix}$$

The images of $\{\mathbf{u}^{(i)} : 0 \leq i < 3\}$ are

$$T(\mathbf{u}^{(0)}) = (17, 21, 2)$$

$$T(\mathbf{u}^{(1)}) = (17, 18, 2)$$

$$T(\mathbf{u}^{(2)}) = (5, 21, 19)$$

which can be shown to be a basis for $Z_{26,3}$.

3.15 N-GRAM SUBSTITUTION: HILL ENCIPHERMENT

Let T be the linear transformation on $Z_{26,3}$ with matrix

(3.15.1) $$T = \begin{vmatrix} 17 & 17 & 5 \\ 21 & 18 & 21 \\ 2 & 2 & 19 \end{vmatrix}$$

We use T to define a 3-gram substitution for the alphabet {A B . . . Z}; first divide each plaintext n-gram into 3-grams, when n is a multiple of 3. Thus the 12-gram PAYMOREMONEY is divided into the four 3-grams,

PAYMOREMONEY ←→ PAY MOR EMO NEY

Each of the 3-grams is then assigned its numerical representation from Table 2.2.1:

PAY ←→ 15 0 24 MOR ←→ 12 14 17

EMO ←→ 4 12 14 NEY ←→ 13 4 27

The *Hill*$_3$ *encipherment* of the 12-gram PAYMOREMONEY by the linear transformation T is lnshdlewmtrw, since

T(15, 0, 24) = (11, 13, 18) ←→ lns

T(12, 14, 17) = (7, 3, 11) ←→ hdl

T(4, 12, 14) = (4, 22, 12) ←→ ewm

T(13, 4, 24) = (19, 17, 22) ←→ trw

The Hill$_3$ encipherment of *PLAIN(3)* by T in Eq. (3.15.1) is shown in Fig. 3.15.1 (departing from our usual format). The Hill substitution system will be analyzed when the *opponent* has obtained either (1) the encipherment of *chosen plaintext,* or (2) sufficient *corresponding plaintext and ciphertext.*

```
ean eod upf dfs uzy qqx duk its gad uwh xrm swl yeo hip dnj ias etn gdb edp wgw
pbo ewx oni ppq rja qys ydk jky yed kvd kuu nzk xox fkk tmr nws oop xiq fdk smj
uly rla vdg gsl tzb uly gog tsa fqw wqm aqv xll iwf pvm tpb iwf png pny wxy hqh
hqs tbd xia pbo png qcu hey gvr wgw nxk vhh wgw zpz ckp pue xlp jqq wbt rza pum
tzb nws mpg elo ytf vbg caj cov mgi swl qca iho sgw tir oku nso jji wzd muz pvm
ojz vuy uwy itf hjl tdj cil jhl tus zpw gor ywz feb xia rhx oyo plc xfu fvw ast
rln iwf inx sgo xhf ove mii xlc opz tdj nsn sjp sak izz gal nlf jtt acb kaa tsv
aic lnf rec ptb zqi dwg png juv kbx daw ukv vuc wet dys xlc mrh tth ocf edp wgw
jrf bfs dgk caj txs jki oxu pdc xiq tfv hgy jho tmq jfi fpu uly oqn pja xia odu
oao dcc zuu qzs gxi owp nbn uif cyp axc uqf tnd eap wlm myt hjm cdu aqi ava vre
smj cic pii qwg spk bjb pqc ecl sbg eqt rsc uty mvu czh nso nxk hdl fug qgw mqx
ooe uly kzg bjb pqc xfs dss fjr pbi trd eni lhg thh oxp rza wuz gsk rfd wul bzz
ylh xns mlu jnk nuo fak hip kcu fzb cee tie fve rxp kqc dvd isr bpf naa jfi lfo
www gor feb idf skk dpg qrz gdj rem waw cvb zqi ric fpg pdc ibo hip sjx yxf ewm
bnu oep llz lka zpi sam wld loa qgv btn mye lbw yih ejx uqr tvo ciq zoe clf vhk
dfs uzy tcs kqe ngo ypv gii pou sos xia ept zus gal zvt wit xrf vxn dqc uey gcy
fqt pio fxk dpa hbx bov ocw quv cty lcw dzu ngo bzh wyz xia xnn fto smj jbk pyo
sqx hbx vte tbt nso nlf kbx qdp crt hyi uly zuu dtt lka zpi tzv exz tnd rcq pny
viz ydr huc kxu brh fbu mit brp ydr gsc zuu wrz frn zvt fdx imv mci eqt dnk aho
tes pfj ewm ddc vdc lgs uly uei tzb uly nxk fve vjf nlf teq pbg its iyv ykh ohz
xzt csj vzy xzj tks caj zru ycn asy zgq orw sro kzg zhy afa ndo qmj ziu udf rna
cum dtv qqv tzb uly lom kjg upf yjd jly qfs ptb upf mce lbw lvh ajg ksm tzd afa
uly bse wfp ept gnd aec hhc hnf xqm eyq lrm ccq unm jhz ssu lka zpi asg lag irz
kmt vwo bxl owu uib jds kbx mog yih udf ipd giy xia lem mlh zky ssu ucf aac fsw
rjp xia kml xfh xia afa feb gsc jbr ins jyd ucu qmj uaa tos dqw udf zvt wit xrf
hdl yme myc lzo yih frn fve rxp pfj pwo zyn cqc mlh tbd yzr gsc oiq flw tsn aek
abc isx qgk wet xtc hds xlj orw pnw nfm xia xnn cdj hti odu dbz cqo ojz ngo tcs
aov xrf afa ywz jpl tnd iwf xia hgy ycn asy sjx jfz iwc png nqf nuo qow ppi pgi
pbi nbh gqb bii fsw cjq xfq pgc smx aek aqq yon fhj dko bxl owu ggz dqc uey qfs
bqu oci vho ujb dbd tqo snd ikt
```

Figure 3.15.1. *CIPHER(3.1)* : Hill_3 encipherment of *PLAIN(3)*.

3.16 CRYPTANALYSIS OF HILL ENCIPHERMENT WITH CHOSEN PLAINTEXT

The images $\{T(\mathbf{u}^{(i)}) : 0 \leq i < n\}$ of the unit vectors $\{\mathbf{u}^{(i)} : 0 \leq i < n\}$ of $\boldsymbol{Z}_{\mathbf{m,n}}$ under a linear transformation T reveal the columns of the matrix corresponding to T. Thus the ciphertext of the n chosen plaintext n-grams

$$(\mathtt{B}, \mathtt{A}, \mathtt{A}, \ldots, \mathtt{A}, \mathtt{A}) \longleftrightarrow \mathbf{u}^{(0)}$$

$$(\mathtt{A}, \mathtt{B}, \mathtt{A}, \ldots, \mathtt{A}, \mathtt{A}) \longleftrightarrow \mathbf{u}^{(1)}$$

$$(\mathtt{A}, \mathtt{A}, \mathtt{A}, \ldots, \mathtt{A}, \mathtt{B}) \longleftrightarrow \mathbf{u}^{(n-1)}$$

reveals the columns of T.

3.17 CRYPTANALYSIS OF HILL SUBSTITUTION WITH CORRESPONDING PLAINTEXT AND CIPHERTEXT

The cryptanalysis of Hill substitution with corresponding plaintext and ciphertext is only slightly more complicated. Suppose that

$$T : \mathbf{x}^{(i)} = (x_{ni}, x_{ni+1}, \ldots, x_{ni+n-1}) \rightarrow \mathbf{y}^{(i)} = (y_{ni}, y_{ni+1}, \ldots, y_{ni+n-1}) \quad 0 \leq i < L$$

We shall assume that we have a sufficient number of corresponding pairs $\{(\mathbf{x}^{(i)}, \mathbf{y}^{(i)}) : 0 \leq i < L\}$; by sufficient we mean that the set of vectors $\{\mathbf{x}^{(i)} : 0 \leq i < L\}$ (or equivalently the set of vectors $\{\mathbf{y}^{(i)} : 0 \leq i < L\}$) span $\boldsymbol{Z}_{\mathbf{m,n}}$.

The method of solution uses *Gaussian elimination,* a procedure in which we successively perform the operations of (1) multiplying a vector by a scalar and (2) adding vectors, in order to express the unit vectors as linear combinations of the $\{\mathbf{x}^{(j)}\}$ or the $\{\mathbf{y}^{(j)}\}$:

$$\mathbf{u}^{(i)} = \sum_{0 \le j < L} \alpha_{i,j}\mathbf{x}^{(j)} \text{ (modulo m)} \qquad 0 \le i < n$$

$$\mathbf{u}^{(i)} = \sum_{0 \le j < L} \beta_{i,j}\mathbf{y}^{(j)} \text{ (modulo m)} \qquad 0 \le i < n$$

If we perform Gaussian elimination on the plaintext $\{\mathbf{x}^{(j)}\}$,

$$T(\mathbf{u}^{(i)}) = \sum_{0 \le j < L} \alpha_{i,j}T(\mathbf{x}^{(j)}) = \sum_{0 \le j < L} \alpha_{i,j}\mathbf{y}^{(j)} \text{ (modulo m)} = i^{th}\text{-column of } T$$

we obtain the entries in T, while if we perform Gaussian elimination on the ciphertext $\{\mathbf{y}^{(j)}\}$,

$$T^{-1}(\mathbf{u}^{(i)}) = \sum_{0 \le j < L} \beta_{i,j}T^{-1}(\mathbf{y}^{(j)}) = \sum_{0 \le j < L} \beta_{i,j}\mathbf{x}^{(j)} \text{ (modulo m)} = i^{th}\text{-column of } T^{-1}$$

we obtain the entries in T^{-1}.

In cryptanalyzing *CIPHER(3.1)*, we shall assume that we have the corresponding plaintext and ciphertext

```
DIF FER ENT PEO PLE HAV EDI FFE REN TOB JEC TIV →
                    ean eod upf dfs uzy qqx duk its gad uwh xrm swl
```

We will carry out Gaussian elimination on the plaintext (on the left) and on the ciphertext (on the right) obtaining with this process both T and T^{-1}.

Step 1 Represent both plaintext and ciphertext as 12 by 3 arrays. | Represent both plaintext and ciphertext as 12 by 3 arrays.

Plaintext			Ciphertext			Ciphertext			Plaintext		
3	8	5	4	0	13	4	0	13	3	8	5
5	4	17	4	14	3	4	14	3	5	4	17
4	13	19	20	15	5	20	15	5	4	13	19
15	4	14	3	5	18	3	5	18	15	4	14
15	11	4	20	25	24	20	25	24	15	11	4
7	0	21	16	16	23	16	16	23	7	0	21
4	3	8	3	20	10	3	20	10	4	3	8
5	5	4	8	19	18	8	19	18	5	5	4
17	4	13	6	0	3	6	0	3	17	4	13
19	14	1	20	22	7	20	22	7	19	14	1
9	4	2	23	17	12	23	17	12	9	4	2
19	8	21	18	22	11	18	22	11	19	8	21

Step 2 Multiply row 1 by 9 and subtract a suitable multiple of it from all remaining rows in order to make all but one entry in column 1 equal to 0.

Plaintext			Ciphertext		
1	20	19	10	0	13
0	8	0	6	14	16
0	11	21	6	15	5
0	16	15	9	5	5
0	23	5	0	25	11
0	16	18	24	16	10
0	1	10	15	20	10
0	9	13	10	19	5
0	2	2	18	0	16
0	24	4	12	22	20
0	6	13	11	17	25
0	18	24	10	22	24

Multiply row 4 by 9 and subtract a suitable multiple of it from all remaining rows in order to make all but one entry in column 1 equal to 0.

Ciphertext			Plaintext		
0	2	15	9	20	21
0	16	5	11	16	7
0	25	15	8	21	21
1	19	6	5	10	22
0	9	8	19	19	6
0	24	5	5	22	7
0	15	18	15	25	20
0	23	22	17	3	10
0	16	19	13	22	11
0	6	17	23	22	3
0	22	4	24	8	16
0	18	7	7	10	15

Step 3 Multiply row 3 by 19 and subtract a suitable multiple from all remaining rows in order to make all but one entry in column 2 equal to 0.

Plaintext			Ciphertext		
1	0	21	18	20	11
0	0	6	4	22	10
0	1	9	10	25	17
0	0	1	5	21	19
0	0	6	4	22	10
0	0	4	20	6	24
0	0	1	5	21	19
0	0	10	24	2	8
0	0	10	24	2	8
0	0	22	6	20	2
0	0	11	3	23	1
0	0	18	12	14	4

Multiply row 3 by 25 and subtract a suitable multiple from all remaining rows in order to make all but one entry in column 2 equal to 0.

Ciphertext			Plaintext		
0	0	19	25	10	11
0	0	11	9	14	5
0	1	11	18	5	5
1	0	5	1	19	5
0	0	13	13	0	13
0	0	1	15	6	17
0	0	9	5	2	23
0	0	3	19	18	25
0	0	25	11	20	9
0	0	3	19	18	25
0	0	22	18	2	10
0	0	17	21	24	3

Step 4 Multiply row 4 by 1 and subtract a suitable multiple from all remaining rows in order to make all but one entry in column 3 equal to 0.

Plaintext			Ciphertext		
1	0	0	17	21	2
0	0	0	0	0	0

Multiply row 1 by 11 and subtract a suitable multiple from all remaining rows in order to make all but one entry in column 3 equal to 0.

Ciphertext			Plaintext		
0	0	1	15	6	17
0	0	0	0	0	0

Plaintext			Ciphertext		
0	1	0	17	18	2
0	0	1	5	21	19
0	0	0	0	0	0
0	0	0	0	0	0
0	0	0	0	0	0
0	0	0	0	0	0
0	0	0	0	0	0
0	0	0	0	0	0
0	0	0	0	0	0
0	0	0	0	0	0

Ciphertext			Plaintext		
0	1	0	9	17	0
1	0	0	4	15	24
0	0	0	0	0	0
0	0	0	0	0	0
0	0	0	0	0	0
0	0	0	0	0	0
0	0	0	0	0	0
0	0	0	0	0	0
0	0	0	0	0	0
0	0	0	0	0	0

The matrix T and its inverse T^{-1} are

$$T = \begin{vmatrix} 17 & 17 & 5 \\ 21 & 18 & 21 \\ 2 & 2 & 19 \end{vmatrix}$$

$$T^{-1} = \begin{vmatrix} 4 & 9 & 15 \\ 15 & 17 & 6 \\ 24 & 0 & 17 \end{vmatrix}$$

How realistic is it to assume that an opponent has some corresponding plaintext and ciphertext? In many instances, the plaintext will contain fragments known to an opponent; for example, a letter may begin `Dear Sir:` or some of the opponent's data may be part of the enciphered plaintext.

How much corresponding plaintext and ciphertext is "sufficient"? We can give a crude estimate as follows: suppose

$$T : \boldsymbol{Z}_{m,n} \to \boldsymbol{Z}_{m,n}$$

$$T : \mathbf{x}^{(i)} \to \mathbf{y}^{(i)} \quad 0 \le i < I$$

and $\{\mathbf{x}^{(i)} : 0 \le i < I\}$ span an s-dimensional subspace $\boldsymbol{U}$ of $\boldsymbol{Z}_{m,n}$. By this we mean that there are s vectors in $\{\mathbf{x}^{(i)} : 0 \le i < I\}$ that are linearly independent over $\boldsymbol{Z}_m$, *and* every subset of more than s of these vectors are linearly dependent over $\boldsymbol{Z}_m$. If a chance experiment is performed with outcome **X**, what is the probability that $\mathbf{X} \notin \boldsymbol{U}$, so that $\{\mathbf{x}_i : 0 \le i < I\} \cup \{\mathbf{X}\}$ is s + 1-dimensional? If the probability distribution on n-grams were the uniform distribution

$$\Pr_{PLAIN}\{\mathbf{X} = \mathbf{x}\} = m^{-n} \qquad \mathbf{x} \in \boldsymbol{Z}_{m,n}$$

then the event $\mathbf{X} \in \boldsymbol{U}$ has probability m^{s-n}. Now consider the experiment in which we repeatedly (and independently) choose plaintext $\mathbf{X}^{(0)}, \mathbf{X}^{(1)}, \ldots$, stopping after r trials if

$$\mathbf{X}^{(i)} \in \boldsymbol{U} \qquad 0 \le i < r - 1 \qquad \mathbf{X}^{(r-1)} \notin \boldsymbol{U}$$

The number of trials needed to achieve the *success* $\mathbf{X}^{(r-1)} \notin \boldsymbol{U}$ is a random variable $R_{n,m,s}$ which has the geometric distribution

$$\Pr_{PLAIN}\{R_{n,m,s} = r\} = (\rho_{n,m,s})^{r-1}(1 - \rho_{n,m,s})$$

where $\rho_{n,m,s} = m^{s-n}$. The expectation of $R_{n,m,s}$ is thus

$$E\{R_{n,m,s}\} = 1/[1 - m^{s-n}]$$

If we start with one plaintext-ciphertext pair $(\mathbf{x}^{(0)}, \mathbf{y}^{(0)})$ (with $\mathbf{x}^{(0)} \neq \mathbf{0}$) and sample plaintext from $\boldsymbol{Z}_{m,n}$, the *waiting time* until we have n vectors that are linearly independent over $\boldsymbol{Z}_m$—the number of *additional* pairs of corresponding plaintext and ciphertext n-grams needed to assure the recovery of T or T^{-1} by Gaussian elimination—is given by the sum

$$W_{n,m} = \sum_{1 \leq s < n} R_{n,m,s}$$

which has expectation

$$E\{W_{n,m}\} = \sum_{1 \leq s < n} 1/[1 - m^{-s}]$$

Of course the assumption that the plaintext n-grams are sampled according to a uniform distribution over $\boldsymbol{Z}_{m,n}$ is incorrect, and so the values of $E\{W_{n,m}\}$ tabulated in Table 3.17.1 are only approximations to the true values.

TABLE 3.17.1
$E\{W_{n,m}\}$

n	$E\{W_{n,m}\}$	n	$E\{W_{n,m}\}$
2	1.0400	7	6.0415
3	2.0415	8	7.0415
4	3.0415	9	8.0415
5	4.0415	10	9.0415
6	5.0415	11	10.0415

PROBLEMS

3.1 *CIPHER(P3.1)*, given in Fig. P3.1 and consisting of 1209 letters, is the result of the Caesar encipherment C_k of *PLAIN(P3.1)*. Find k. In Table P3.2, we list the frequency of occurrence of each of the ciphertext letters in *CIPHER(P3.1)*.

3.2 The weakness of Caesar substitution was due in part to a small key space. We can enlarge the key space by enciphering n-grams. The key space is $\boldsymbol{Z}_{m,n}$. For $(u_0, u_1, \ldots, u_{n-1})$ in $\boldsymbol{Z}_{m,n}$, we will write $r = \|(u_0, u_1, \ldots, u_{n-1})\|$ if

$$r = \sum_{0 \leq s < n} u_s m^{n-1-s}$$

so that $(u_0, u_1, \ldots, u_{n-1})$ is the base m representation of the integer r. We encipher the plaintext n-gram $(x_0, x_1, \ldots, x_{n-1})$ into the ciphertext n-gram $(y_0, y_1, \ldots, y_{n-1})$:

$$(x_0, x_1, \ldots, x_{n-1}) \rightarrow (y_0, y_1, \ldots, y_{n-1})$$

```
espzm úpnet gpzqa pcqzc xlynp pglwf letzy mjdtx fwlet zytdl whljd ezdlg
pnzde dlyoe txpty nzxal ctdzy htese fytyr ldjde pxtye spqtp woesp cpqzc
pespp iapyd pdqzc dstqe tyres ppglw fletz yaczn pofcp qczxe spcpl wzmup
neezl ylmde clnew pgpwl cpzqt xazce lynpe spdpp iapyd pdopa pyozy espop
rcppz qlmde clnet zyzco peltw zqesp xzopw hstns lqqpn edxzo pwacp alcle
tzyet xpdtx fwlet zyetx plyod ezclr popxl yotql xzopw nzyel tydxz cpope
ltwdz qespz mupne estdc pdfwe dtylw lcrpc yfxmp czqpi epyez cxzcp opdnc
taetz ydele pxpye dlwlc rpcyf xmpcz qtyaf eolel lwlcr pcyfx mpczq eclyd
tetzy etxpn lwnfw letzy dezmp pipnp fepod awtee tyrfa zqdtx fwlet zypgp
yeddt xfwle tzyzg pcspl olyop iepyd tzypi epydt zyzqe spxzo pwwty raczn
pddmf epgpy tqhpe cjezd szcep yespx zopww tyras ldpmj opgpw zatyr xzopw
wtyre zzwdl dhpot oespz espca ztyed lcpwp qelyo hplcp qzcnp oezqt yolyl
nnpae lmwpn zxact xtdpm pehpp yopel twzqx zopwo pgpwz axpye lyodt xfwle
tzyet xplyo espbf lwtej zqesp lydhp cdhph lyeez rpeqc zxdtx fwlet zycpd
fwedy pgpce spwpd dopel twpox zopwd lcpzq epyop dtcpo pgpyt qnzxa wpidj
depxd zqnzx afepc ypehz cvdlc ptygp detrl epodz epzcj lyoxp cepya czazd
poesp dtxfw letzy zqlxz opwht esehz otqqp cpyew pgpwd zqope ltwty epcpd
etyrn zxazy pyedq zcxty delyn pespm zeewp ypnvd zqesp djdep xxljm pcpac
pdpye potyg pcjqt ypope ltwsz hpgpc opelt wdesp ylctd plees ptyep cqlnp
zqehz otqqp cpyew jopel twpox zopwd tqxzo pwtyd ecfne tzydl cpzqo tqqpc
pyeop eltw
```

Figure P3.1. *CIPHER(P3.1)* : Caesar encipherment of *PLAIN(P3.1)*.

TABLE P3.2

The Frequency of Occurrence of Letters in *CIPHER(P3.1)*

Letter	Frequency	Letter	Frequency	Letter	Frequency
a	0.0215	b	0.0008	c	0.0562
d	0.0620	e	0.1042	f	0.0199
g	0.0132	h	0.0124	i	0.0058
j	0.0099	k	0.0000	l	0.0670
m	0.0132	n	0.0240	o	0.0447
p	0.1547	q	0.0364	r	0.0124
s	0.0265	t	0.0720	u	0.0025
v	0.0017	w	0.0471	x	0.0389
y	0.0720	z	0.0811		

where

$$X = \|(x_0, x_1, \ldots, x_{n-1})\|$$

$$Y = \|(y_0, y_1, \ldots, y_{n-1})\|$$

$$K = \|(k_0, k_1, \ldots, k_{n-1})\|$$

and $Y = X + K$ (modulo m^n). To encipher plaintext, divide it into n-grams,

$$\mathbf{x}^{(i)} = (x_{i,0}, x_{i,1}, \ldots, x_{i,n-1}) \quad 0 \le i < N$$

and encipher each individually as above. For example, if $n = 3$, $m = 26$, and $k = 1877$, then the plaintext

SEND MONEY

is divided into the 3-grams

$$\texttt{SEN DMO NEY} \longleftrightarrow (18,4,13)\ (3,12,14)\ (13,4,24)$$

The key 1877 represented by the triple (2,20,5) (base 26) is added to the plaintext

$$\begin{array}{lrrr} \texttt{SEN DMO NEY} \longleftrightarrow & 18\ \ 4\ 13 & 3\ 12\ 14 & 13\ \ 4\ 24 \\ & +\ 2\ 20\ \ 5 & 2\ 20\ \ 5 & 2\ 20\ \ 5 \\ \hline \texttt{uys ggj pzd} \longleftrightarrow & 20\ 24\ 18 & 6\ \ 6\ \ 9 & 15\ 25\ \ 3 \end{array}$$

This addition of triples is also described as *component-wise addition modulo 26 with carry*. Discuss the cryptanalysis of this system.

3.3 *CIPHER(P3.2)*, shown in Fig. P3.3, is the result of a multiplicative Caesar substitution $T_{a,b}$. The frequencies of letters in *CIPHER(P3.2)* are listed in Table P3.4. Determine a and b.

3.4 Suppose T(x) is a polynomial of degree n,

$$T(x) = a_n x^n + a_{n-1} x^{n-1} + \ldots + a_0$$

with coefficients in $\boldsymbol{Z}_m$. T(x) defines a mapping of $\boldsymbol{Z}_m$ into $\boldsymbol{Z}_m$ by the rule

```
kerqy tueri xehiy ratgd qyrsy kfohg taerz zehes ykkor isehi
yrahy wggfh bgity fgteh iyrat orrir uakyy hbdql qkewi ruirn
ytkeh iyrky tgess gaail dghyk ytgfg yfdgc ihbir hbgyt uerix
gakyt gftyh gshiy rhber qyoke qrycb evgqy oserr ycfty hgshi
rnytk ehiyr ahytg zyrqy otftg kiaga lqfba qised kgeao tgahb
ehdik ihess gaahy eohby tixgz fgyfd gaiki detdq ilkbe tzcet
gerza ynhce tgfty zosha bevgn gehot gahbe rserl goagz hyizg
rhinq erzsb gswhb geohb ytixe hiyry nfgyf dghtq iruhy ueire
ssgaa hyeaq ahgke rziha irnyt kehiy rrych bgtgi aeceq hyfyt
hgshi rnytk ehiyr gvgrn othbg thbgi lkstq fhyut efbis aolaq
ahgks ergjh grzze hesyr htyde rzfty hgshi yrhyh bgzeh esykk
orise hiyra hgtki redae rzdir wahbe hafgg zirny tkehi yrnty
kyrgd ysehi yrhye ryhbg tihoa gaeay fbiah isehg zeduy tihbk
eahti shagh yntod gahyg rstqf hytas tekld gzehe lgnyt gihia
ahytg zytht eraki hhgzh yeryh bgtdy sehiy rerzz gstqf hihcb
grrgg zgzny tftys gaair uihgk fdyqa grstq fhiyr hgsbr imoga
hbers ertgz osgir nytke hiyrg jfyao tgaci hbirq yotsy kkori
sehiy rargh cytwe acgdd eafty vizge aqahg kleag nythb gzgvg
dyfkg rhyng rstqf hiyrf tyute kahbg ilkst qfhyu tefbi saola
qahgk iaevg taehi dghyy dnyts yrhty ddiru erzft yhgsh iruir
nytke hiyrh btyou bgrst qfhiy rlqes yklir ehiyr ynfty utekk
iruer zareh gtkir edbet zcetg ngeho tgaih sergr stqfh erzzg
stqfh irnyt kehiy reohy kehis eddqe rzcih byohi rhgtv grhiy
rlqhb ghgtk iredo agtyt effdi sehiy roair uered uytih bkerz
ewgqc bisbi rzivi zoedi xgahb geduy tihbk hbgao laqah gkgrs
tqfha effdi sehiy rirny tkehi yrlgn ytgih iaagr hntyk ehgtk
iredy tsykf ohgtd ysehi yrerz grhgt aqyot zehes ykkor isehi
yrarg hcytw ehhbg tgsgi viruh gtkir edyts ykfoh gtdys ehiyr
hbgae kgwgq iaoag zhyzg stqfh hbgir nytke hiyre nhgti hdgev
```

Figure P3.3. *CIPHER(P3.2)* : Caesar encipherment of *PLAIN(P3.2)*.

TABLE P3.4
The Frequency of Occurrence of Letters in *CIPHER(P3.2)*

Letter	Frequency	Letter	Frequency	Letter	Frequency
a	0.0627	b	0.0367	c	0.0107
d	0.0287	e	0.0940	f	0.0327
g	0.1107	h	0.1173	i	0.0920
j	0.0013	k	0.0460	l	0.0160
m	0.0013	n	0.0207	o	0.0280
p	0.0000	q	0.0293	r	0.0913
s	0.0473	t	0.0807	u	0.0160
v	0.0080	w	0.0073	x	0.0033
y	0.1033	z	0.0300		

$$T(t) : t \rightarrow T(t) \text{ (modulo m)}$$

When T(t) is one-to-one mapping on Z_m, it may be used as a letter substitution by defining the ciphertext of letter t to be T(t). For n = 2, find all polynominal substitutions. Is there an analog of matching?

3.5 *CIPHER(P3.3)*, given in Fig. P3.6, is the result of an encipherment by a

```
caney foank pabky nqfsr eynwy cjmbs fqanh habaw yccmn kwabk
ynqby gssjb zskfy jsfab kynqf mnnkn oqcyy bzrel ecagk noknd
yfcab kyncy fsaww sqqkl rsbyc yfsjs yjrsi kbzkn bzsyf oankp
abkyn lmbaq kblsw ycsqc yfsaw wsqqk lrskn dyfca bkynf sumkf
sqcyf sjfyb swbky nbzan eymca enyiz axsey mwann yijfy bswbk
ndyfc abkyn qbyfs hyney mfjfs ckqsq lejzq ekwar csaqm fsqbz
abrkc kbaww sqqby ambzy fkpsh jsyjr sqkck rafre klcza fhiaf
sanhq ydbia fsjfy hmwbq zaxsd sabmf sqbza nwanl smqsh bykhs
nbkde anhwz swgbz sambz yfkpa bkyny djsyj rsbfe knoby oakna
wwsqq byaqe qbsca nhkbq kndyf cabky nnyib zsfsk qaiae byjyf
bswbk ndyfc abkyn sxsnd mfbzs fbzsk lcwfe jbyof ajzkw qmlqe
qbscw anstb snhha bawyn bfyra nhjfy bswbk ynbyb zshab awycc
mnkwa bkynq bsfck narqa nhrkn gqbza bqjss hkndy fcabk yndfy
cynsr ywabk ynbya nybzs fkbmq sqaqy jzkqb kwabs haroy fkbzc
aqbfk wbqsb ydfmr sqbys nwfej byfqw faclr shaba lsdyf skbkq
qbyfs hyfbf anqck bbshb yanyb zsfry wabky nanhh swfej bkbiz
snnss hshdy fjfyw sqqkn okbsc jryeq snwfe jbkyn bswzn kumsq
bzanw anfsh mwskn dyfca bkyns tjyqm fsqik bzkne ymfwy ccmnk
wabky nqnsb iyfga qisrr aqjfy xkhsa qeqbs claqs dyfbz shsxs
ryjcs nbyds nwfej bkynj fyofa cqbzs klcwf ejbyo fajzk wqmlq
eqbsc kqaxs fqabk rsbyy rdyfw ynbfy rrkno anhjf ybswb knokn
dyfca bkynb zfymo zsnwf ejbky nleaw yclkn abkyn ydjfy ofacc
knoan hqnab sfckn arzaf hiafs dsabm fsqkb wansn wfejb anhhs
wfejb kndyf cabky namby cabkw arrea nhikb zymbk nbsfx snbky
nlebz sbsfc knarm qsfyf ajjrk wabky nmqkn oanar oyfkb zcanh
agsei zkwzk nhkxk hmark psqbz saroy fkbzc bzsqm lqeqb scsnw
fejbq ajjrk wabky nkndy fcabk ynlsd yfskb kqqsn bdfyc absfc
knary fwycj mbsfr ywabk ynanh snbsf qeymf habaw yccmn kwabk
ynqns biyfg abbzs fswsk xknob sfckn aryfw ycjmb sfryw abkyn
bzsqa csgse kqmqs hbyhs wfejb bzskn dyfca bkyna dbsfk brsax
```

Figure P3.6. *CIPHER(P3.3)* : encipherment of *PLAIN(P3.3)* by a polynomial substitution of degree 2.

TABLE P3.5
The Frequency of Occurrence of Letters in *CIPHER(P3.3)*

Letter	Frequency	Letter	Frequency	Letter	Frequency
a	0.0847	b	0.1040	c	0.0420
d	0.0187	e	0.0253	f	0.0740
g	0.0053	h	0.0273	i	0.0100
j	0.0300	k	0.0827	l	0.0133
m	0.0253	n	0.0833	o	0.0133
p	0.0033	Q	0.0553	r	0.0273
s	0.0953	t	0.0013	u	0.0013
v	0.0000	w	0.0433	x	0.0067
y	0.0960	z	0.0307		

polynomial of degree two. The frequency of occurrence of letters is given in Table P3.5. Find the coefficients of the polynomial.

3.6 *CIPHER(P3.4)*, given in Fig. P3.7, is the monalphabetic encipherment by a substitution from the symmetric group SYM(Z_{26}) of *PLAIN(P3.4)*, which describes some aspects of **BUSINESS INVESTMENTS**. A search

```
bxetr dlrob fvpmt wderl partw orkrw ceabe tetrf drlwe bfxwc
wpdrm epfuw gvpbx rppet rwxwc spbpf ulrpv cepwx ketrd lfzrm
ebfxf ufdrl webxy mfxkb ebfxp bxgfe tmwpr partw kefwp pvnre
tweet rkrmb pbfxp efbxo rpewx kefub xwxmr etrpr fdrlw ebfxp
twkgr rxnwk rbxwx wddlf dlbwe ruwpt bfxef drlnb edlfu bewgc
rfdrl webfx efewh rdcwm rbxet bpmtw derla rptwc cmfxm rxelw
erfxe trwxw csebm wcerm txbjv rpatb mtwlr vprke fpvdd flegv
pbxrp pbxor penrx ekrmb pbfxp arptw ccwpp vnret weetr lrrqb
pepbx wmfnd wxset rmwdw gbcbe seffd rlwer xrauw mbcbe brpwx
kfetr lbxor penrx epwxk etwee trxrm rppwl smwdb ewcmw xgrdl
fobkr kefub xwxmr etrbx orpen rxepv xkrll robra etrdl fmrpp
fubxo rpenr xebxc wxkdl fkvme borrj vbdnr xegvb ckbxy paflh
bxymw dbewc lwanw erlbw ckrdf pbepw xkfet rlwpp repuf luvev
lrrmf xfnbm ywbxb pdwle bmvcw lcskb uubmv cewxk wmwvp ruflm
wlruv cwxwc spbpk rmbpb fxpbx etbpw lrwvp vwccs mfnnb ewgvp
bxrpp rxerl dlbpr uflwm fxpbk rlwgc rebnr drlbf kefwx wmebo
bescb xrfug vpbxr ppfly rfylw dtbml rybfx wpfxr fuetr etlrr
gwpbm wlrwp fukrm bpbfx nwhbx ybxor penrx efdrl webfx pwxku
bxwxm bxyet rbxor penrx edlfm rpptw petrc fxyrp eebnr tflbi
fxwxk lrpep nfpet rwobc sfxmw lruvc uflmw pepwx kkrew bcrkw
ppvnd ebfxp wgfve etrcb hrcsu vevlr mfxkb ebfxp atbmt abccd
lfobk retrr mfxfn bmywb xefzv pebus etrmf xernd cwerk fvecw
sfuuv xkpgr uflra relvx efpdr mbubm mfxmr depwx ketru lwnra
flhuf lwxwc spbpb eptfv ckgrr ndtwp birke twebx etbpg ffhar
wlrlr obrab xyetr mwdbe wcbxo rpenr xedlf gcrnw dwlef umwdb
ewcgv kyreb xybxw xwllf aprxp retrm lbebm wcewp hfunw xwyrn
rxebp efrpe wgcbp tetry rxrlw cfgzr mebor pwxkp drmbu bmyfw
cpfue trrxe rldlb prfxe trgwp bpfue trprw xketr hxfax pelrx
yetpw xkcbn beweb fxpbx wknbx bpelw ebore wcrxe nwxdf arler
mtxbm wchxf atfan wlhre pewxk bxyub xwxmb xydfp pbgbc bebrp
wxkpf fxnwx wyrnr xenvp eufln vcwer wddlf dlbwe rpewe rybrp
```

Figure P3.7. *CIPHER(P3.4)* : monalphabetic substitution of *PLAIN(P3.4)*.

of *CIPHER(P3.4)* for the probable words BUSINESS, CAPITAL, and INVESTMENT yields the results given in Tables P3.8 and P3.9. Find the substitution *PLAIN(P3.4)* → *CIPHER(P3.4)*.

3.7 *CIPHER(P3.5)*, given in Fig. P3.10, is the result of a monalphabetic substitution applied to *PLAIN(P3.5)*, text that describes some aspects of *one* of the following sports: TENNIS, SOCCER, or FOOTBALL. The 1-gram frequencies in *CIPHER(P3.5)* are given in Table P3.11. The search for the probable words TENNIS, SOCCER, FOOTBALL, and PRACTICE in *CIPHER(P3.5)* yields the results given in Tables P3.12–14. Determine the monalphabetic substitution.

3.8 *CIPHER(P3.6)*, given in Fig. P3.15, is the Playfair encipherment of *PLAIN(P3.6)*, plaintext that deals with some aspects of FINANCIAL PLANNING. In the Table P3.16, the 2-grams in *CIPHER(P3.6)* and Fig. 2.3.3 of highest frequency of occurrence are compared. Begin the analysis assuming that TH → hy. Table P3.17 gives the right contact letters in *CIPHER(P3.6)* of hy. Determine the Playfair encipherment matrix, first answering the following questions.

1. What conclusions can be drawn from TH → hy?

TABLE P3.8

Results of the Search for the Words BUSINESS and INVESTMENT in *CIPHER(P3.4)*

BUSINESS		INVESTMENT	
Ciphertext	**Count**	**Ciphertext**	**Count**
gvpbxrpp	4	bxorpenrxe	7

TABLE P3.9

Results of the Search for the Word CAPITAL in *CIPHER(P3.4)*

Ciphertext	Count	Ciphertext	Count	Ciphertext	Count
erlpart	1	drlwerx	1	gwpbmwl	1
artwork	1	rxepwxk	1	penrxef	1
rpvcepw	1	pwlsmwd	1	penrxed	2
bxymfxk	1	mwdbewc	4	tflbifx	1
twkefwp	1	trbxorp	2	pebuset	1
pewxkef	1	rxepvxk	1	gruflra	1
bweruwp	1	braetrd	1	relvxef	1
rbxetbp	1	penrxeb	1	dbewcbx	1
etbpmtw	1	xkdlfkv	1	rpwxkpd	1
werfxet	1	nbmywbx	2	yfwcpfu	1
orpenrx	7	uflwmfx	1	orewcrx	1
penrxek	1	crebnrd	1	rxenwxd	1
nrxekrm	1	obescbx	1	rmtxbmw	1
rpwxkpf	1	xenvpeu	1		

```
armwc cfvly wnruf fegwc cwxkb usfvm wxxfe hbmhs fvmwx xfegr
mfnrw uffeg wccrl busfv crwlx efhbm habet rbetr luffe sfvab
ccgrw xbxub xberc snflr owcvw gcrdc wsrle twxbu sfvhb mhabe
tfxrw xkvpr etrfe trlnr lrcse fpewx kfxet rlrwl rfumf vlprk
buurl rxepe scrpf uhbmh bxywg wccwx kwpcb ytelr wkzvp enrxe
fuerm txbjv rbpxr rkrku flwgw cclvx xbxyw awsul fnetr hbmhr
lflmf nbxyu lfnet rcrue fllby tebus fvwlr bxsfv lerrx psfvm
wxxfe srerq drmee frqrl envmt dfarl gveet rlrwl rmrle wbxuv
xkwnr xewcd lbxmb dcrpb xhbmh bxyhr rdsfv lrsrf xetrg wccrx
pvlre twesf vwlrg wcwxm rkdfp bebfx etrxf xhbmh bxyuf femfl
lrmec sufcc faetl fvyta betet rhbmh bxycr ywbnu flwmm vlwms
lwetr letwx dfarl crevp cffhn flrmc fprcs weetr owlbf vpnre
tfkpf uhbmh bxywu ffegw ccwxk arptw cckbp mforl etrbn dflew
xmrfu etrpr ubord lbxmb dcrph bmhbx yabet etrbx perde tbpbp
dlfgw gcset rnfpe mfnnf xawsf uhbmh bxywx kbpow cvwgc ratrx
dwppb xywxk ptffe bxyat retrl ptfle cfxyc faflt byt
```

Figure P3.10. *CIPHER(P3.5)* : monalphabetic substitution of *PLAIN(P3.5)*.

TABLE P3.11

The Frequency of Occurrence of Letters in *CIPHER(P3.5)*

Letter	Frequency	Letter	Frequency	Letter	Frequency
a	0.0189	b	0.0744	c	0.0555
d	0.0177	e	0.0820	f	0.0933
g	0.0177	h	0.0303	i	0.0000
j	0.0013	k	0.0189	l	0.0618
m	0.0429	n	0.0214	o	0.0063
p	0.0366	q	0.0025	r	0.1097
s	0.0277	t	0.0492	u	0.0328
v	0.0328	w	0.0706	x	0.0719
y	0.0227	z	0.0013		

TABLE P3.12

Results of the Search for the Words `TENNIS` or `SOCCER` in *CIPHER(P3.5)*

Word	Count	Word	Count
mwccfv	1	lerrxp	1
ruffeg	1	gveetr	1
mwxxfe	3	yhrrds	1
wuffeg	2	gwccrx	1
gwccrl	1	yuffem	1
luffes	1	pcffhn	1
abccgr	1	sweetr	1
kbuurl	1	twcckb	1
gwcclv	1	dwppbx	1
efllby	1	ptffeb	1

TABLE P3.13

Results of the Search for the Word **PRACTICE** in *CIPHER(P3.5)*

Word	Count	Word	Count
xfehbmhs	1	crpbxhbm	1
xefhbmha	1	vlretwes	1
lrowcvwg	1	hbxycryw	1
sfvhbmha	1	dfarlcre	1
etfxrwxk	1	retfkpfu	1
kvpretrf	1	bxperdet	1
rcsefpew	1	mhbxywxk	1
wlrfumfv	1	bpowcvwg	1
ewbxuvxk	1	wgcratrx	1

TABLE P3.14

Results of the Search for the Word **FOOTBALL** in *CIPHER(P3.5)*

Word	Count
uffegwcc	3

```
pb hy im hl wf va qd uy mw lh pz my fu ly fy ez np hy hy fm mi ud we pu df
do mi yx mp of an pl hi ms mz ym bu df dm lp vo hl or ez od rb hy im us kf
yx fp up ov mi ud we gr aq rb ew fp rp pb ap hy db ml pz my by vm do or tm
hy yv hy ly ky lp fp rp vm pb tf mz bu yz vo pb bu yk hy lm fm mi ud we pu
mr by yi ih oy yl pb bu bo sn pq nl yv fi do ne pu vm mi hs ew sn vo ew bc
ef pq lh yv fp hw mv cf im fd yk pb hy lp yg bo hm nz lm uy ks kd pu yk hw
ud hm pu hy fy ub ed we db ez ky ug kp hf pz ne yg du fh ml yz pm no qp hz
an pl hi ms pl uw lm ht ih zy ky lp fp rp ti mr df fd ms or tm hy yv hy lh
km kt lp zm pb bd po ob hb hy ky bo bc ke ew eh ps pq lh yv ih it of bk ek
we lm bu as hy lh pb tf mz tm hw od rb hy yv hy ih ky lm od hd db wp vy kd
bu yi sn vu lb ly vm ik ub gb mh ym pb tf mz tm hw or rb lh hl wf it hy im
us yk ms mp ik uw lm ht ih we ri bu bs us ar yx fw km km nf qo ih wy nf sl
pb rq vp gl pb ck bo ew df ud tp yv lh fb sl im pm ew od rb mv ym ud ms ml
zm ov ul hv nh km ky pu po kb uc pb lp ob hz kb rf du ed bl ko ik ag ez bu
yb db ro fi su db hl oa fd ub ed pl zl ky lp fp rp pb hy lp du fy ro af ks
ed aq os pe vy an pl hi ms ml hw lh sn lp fi su bd pu pl yl ud di mh ep im
lh fp yz vf ub yx fw ew de pb fm ia ro pb lm mp hr fm rh bo ne dg kh fp ub
mp hi vo hy mh uh km iy do kb du fy mp la ky lp fp hp cf pb nk uw lm ht ih
vm mi ud we pu od rb ik ub gb pb hx ym pb tf mz tm hw sn qa lm mr do hy fe
pu hk mz we tm um nl vs ub rb hl mz mo pm hy fy wf ed pu db hl oa ei su db
mz od rb yl vy ke ly do or oq we pu od ap hv hy fe kl fe ae hv nh ky pu bl
we pu pz ne yg np ks is us wf yl hy km ky pu po kb uc pb vm fn mz ki eh ym
aq hw mt si yv ly va ze ba vo oa rb pd fi su it mh hn hw pm mi bk ik kx aq
gb im zm bu yz ym lu yo it su li su bu df dm lp ew mr va sl yi mt mn do lw
ly hy yv pb hy lp ap qf ti du lh ft kf np gr hy ky bo ew df pb tf mz tm hw
sn pa ef oy ob hz vo db wp vy id ra hk we gr pb bu du us zp ih ml hy ky nl
we db ez do fq eo bu cu mt ih we mz mf mz bc ek mr hy kh ih lh df pa kf yx
fw lm bu lz mi bk ik kc vf sz vo hy km ih hm ns nl ml pu hy iy do lp vo hy
lm fy rb hy fl up nb mz hl gr hy od rb ek pe vy we pu pl ub ys pb lp zh yv
fw mh df ih ht bu qp ti hz ky ug kb df ig pv um tp du lf zm vy rb pb uk pb
bu bk gr qp ms pl ip ek we lm bu lz ps pu oy ub hk tm hw oh mz ov hs rf yv
```

Figure P3.15. *CIPHER(P3.6)* : playfair encipherment of *PLAIN(P3.6)*.

TABLE P3.16
Comparison of Number of Occurrences of 2-Grams (and their Reversals) in *CIPHER(P3.6)* with those in Figure 2.3.3.

Figure 2.3.3				***CIPHER(P3.7)***			
2-Gram	**Count**	**Reversal**	**Count**	**2-Gram**	**Count**	**Reversal**	**Count**
TH	2161	HT	85	hy	33	yh	0
HE	2053	EH	16	pb	25	bp	0
IN	1550	NI	301	pu	17	up	2
ER	1436	RE	1280	bu	16	ub	9
RE	1280	ER	1436	we	15	ew	9
ON	1232	NO	239	lm	14	ml	6
AN	1216	NA	249	lp	14	pl	8
EN	1029	NE	549	mz	14	zm	4
AT	1019	TA	381	ky	13	yk	4
ES	917	SE	595	ih	12	hi	4
ED	890	DE	572	rb	12	br	0
TE	872	ET	301	yv	12	vy	7
TI	865	IT	704	lh	11	hl	7
OR	861	RO	510	hw	10	wh	0
ST	823	TS	257	db	9	bd	2
AR	764	RA	470	df	9	fd	3
ND	761	DN	8	do	9	od	8
TO	756	OT	223	ew	9	we	15
NT	743	TN	9	fp	9	pf	0
IS	741	SI	390	ub	9	bu	16
OF	731	FO	326	mi	8	im	7
IT	704	TI	865	od	8	do	9
AL	681	LA	359	pl	8	lp	14
AS	648	SA	200	tm	8	mt	3
HA	646	AH	13	ud	8	du	7

TABLE P3.17
Ciphertext Letters Which Follow the 2-Gram **hy**

Letter	Count	Letter	Count
l	8	h	1
f	6	d	1
k	6	m	1
i	5	o	1
y	4		

2. Prove that y $\notin E_E$ if

$$\{\mathtt{l, k, i, f}\} \subseteq E_E$$

is assumed.

3. y $\in E_*$ for what letter *?
4. Assuming that the ciphertext of **EN** and **ES** appears in the list of the first 12 ciphertext 2-grams of highest frequency of occurrence

```
pb pu bu we lm lp
mz ky ih rb yv lh
```

what are the obvious choices for *?

EN → *   ES → *

5. *PLAIN(P3.6)* describes some aspects of financial planning, so that the words INVESTMENT, BUSINESS, FINANCE, FINANCING, FINANCIAL, and OPERATIONAL are likely to appear in the plaintext. The results of the search for these words are given in Tables P3.18–21. Starting with the results of the search for INVESTMENT, find the Playfair enciphering matrix.

3.9 What substitution system results when we Playfair encipher plaintext written in the alphabet {A B . . . Z} using a 26 by 1 Playfair "square"?

3.10 Discuss the cryptanalysis of ciphertext resulting when we Playfair encipher plaintext written in the alphabet {A B . . . Z} using a 13 by 2 Playfair "square"?

3.11 *CIPHER(P3.7)*, given in Fig. P3.22, is the result of $Hill_3$ encipherment. Determine the 3 by 3 matrix T which has $Hill_3$-enciphered *PLAIN(P3.5)* using the information that T has enciphered the plaintext

NOW IST HET IME FOR ALL GOO DWO MEN TOC OME
TOT HEA IDO FTH EIR COU NTR

TABLE P3.18

Results of the Search for *I NV ES TM EN T* in *CIPHER(P3.6)*

Word	Count	Word	Count
himsmzymbudf	1	nkuwlmhtihvm	1
rpvmpbtfmzbu	1	udwepuodrbik	1
fdykpbhylpyg	1	hxympbtfmztm	1
pluwlmhtihzy	1	hyfepuhkmzwe	1
lmhtihzykylp	1	vsubrbhlmzmo	1
tmhyyvhylhkm	1	sudbmzodrbyl	1
kmktlpzmpbbd	1	nhkypublwepu	1
pspqlhyvihit	1	hyyvpbhylpap	1
bkekwelmbuas	1	ewdfpbtfmztm	1
hylhpbtfmztm	1	rahkwegrpbbu	1
hwodrbhyyvhy	1	mlhykynlwedb	1
rbhyyvhyihky	1	cumtihwemzmf	1
yvhyihkylmod	1	ihwemzmfmzbc	1
mhympbtfmztm	1	vohylmfyrbhy	1
ikuwlmhtihwe	1	yspblpzhyvfw	1
htihweribubs	1	mhdfihhtbuqp	1
fprppbhylpdu	1	vyrbpbukpbbu	1
mlhwlhsnlpfi	1	ipekwelmbulz	1

TABLE P3.19
Results of the Search for `*B US IN ES S*` in *CIPHER(P3.6)*

Word	Count	Word	Count
miudwepudf	1	iaropblmmp	1
hylykylpfp	1	mplakylpfp	1
pbtfmzbuyz	1	miudwepuod	1
yzvopbbuyk	1	puhkmzwetm	1
miudwepumr	1	oroqwepuod	1
oyylpbbubo	1	hvnhkypubl	1
efpqlhyvfp	1	publwepupz	1
ihzykylpfp	1	hykmkypupo	1
pspqlhyvih	1	lyhyyvpbhy	1
pqlhyvihit	1	wegrpbbudu	1
bkekwelmbu	1	cumtihwemz	1
ekwelmbuas	1	mtihwemzmf	1
ashylhpbtf	1	hykhihlhdf	1
yvhyihkylm	1	yxfwlmbulz	1
hyihkylmod	1	pevywepupl	1
hworrblhhl	1	ubyspblpzh	1
lmhtihweri	1	zmvyrbpbuk	1
udtpyvlhfb	1	pbukpbbubk	1
nhkmkypupo	1	ipekwelmbu	1
kbucpblpob	1	ekwelmbulz	1
plzlkylpfp	1	pqnlyvlmvy	1

into the ciphertext

```
xze rhx wut wam smx inx uwu bze zzt zra uwy
                         gkl flw xwc bwz dnj imw fkx
```

yielding the following table of corresponding plaintext and ciphertext 3-grams:

Plaintext	Ciphertext	Plaintext	Ciphertext
(13, 14, 22)	(23, 25, 4)	(8, 18, 19)	(17, 7, 23)
(7, 4, 19)	(22, 20, 19)	(8, 12, 4)	(22, 0, 12)
(5, 14, 17)	(18, 12, 23)	(0, 11, 11)	(8, 13, 23)
(6, 14, 14)	(20, 22, 20)	(3, 22, 14)	(1, 25, 4)
(12, 4, 13)	(25, 25, 19)	(19, 14, 2)	(25, 17, 0)
(14, 12, 4)	(20, 22, 24)	(19, 14, 19)	(6, 10, 11)
(7, 4, 0)	(5, 11, 22)	(8, 3, 14)	(23, 22, 2)
(5, 19, 7)	(1, 22, 25)	(4, 8, 17)	(3, 13, 9)
(2, 14, 20)	(8, 12, 22)	(13, 19, 17)	(5, 10, 23)

TABLE P3.20
Results of the Search for `*F IN AN CE **/*F IN AN CI AL` in *CIPHER(P3.6)*

Word	Count	Word	Count
kmkypupokb	2	ropblmmphr	1
udwepudfdo	1	lakylpfphp	1
lykylpfprp	1	udwepuodrb	1
tfmzbuyzvo	1	hkmzwetmum	1
vopbbuykhy	1	oqwepuodap	1
udwepumrby	1	nhkypublwe	1
ylpbbubosn	1	blwepupzne	1
pqlhyvfphw	1	hyyvpbhylp	1
zykylpfprp	1	grpbbuduus	1
pqlhyvihit	1	mtihwemzmf	1
lhyvihitof	1	ihwemzmfmz	1
ekwelmbuas	1	khihlhdfpa	1
welmbuashy	1	fwlmbulzmi	1
hylhpbtfmz	1	vywepuplub	1
hyihkylmod	1	yspblpzhyv	1
ihkylmodhd	1	vyrbpbukpb	1
orrblhhlwf	1	ukpbbubkgr	1
htihweribu	1	ekwelmbulz	1
tpyvlhfbsl	1	welmbulzps	1
ucpblpobhz	1	nlyvlmvyhm	1
zlkylpfprp	1		

3.12 Probable Words. A *partition* of $\{0, 1, \ldots, n-1\}$ (into s sets) is a family of subsets of $\{0, 1, \ldots, n-1\}$ that satisfies the conditions

- The sets $\{\xi_i\}$ are disjoint

$$\xi_i \cap \xi_j = \phi \qquad 0 \leq i, j < s \qquad i \neq j$$

- The union of the sets $\{\xi_i\}$ is $\{0, 1, \ldots, n-1\}$

$$\bigcup_{0 \leq i < s} \xi_i = \{0, 1, \ldots, n-1\}$$

The family of partitions of $\{0, 1, \ldots, n-1\}$ into s sets is denoted by $\Xi_s = \Xi_s[\{0, 1, \ldots, n-1\}]$. We call the plaintext n-gram $\mathbf{x} = (x_0, x_1, \ldots, x_{n-1})$ a $\{\xi_i\}$-*word* if

$$x_i = x_j \textit{ if and only if } i,j \in \xi_k$$

for *some* k, $0 \leq k < s$. Thus

PERFORMANCE

TABLE P3.21
Results of the Search for OP ER AT IO N*/OP ER AT IO NA L* in *CIPHER(P3.6)*

Word	Count	Word	Count
kmkypupokbuc	2	ropblmmphrfm	1
udwepudfdomi	1	lakylpfphpcf	1
lykylpfprpvm	1	udwepuodrbik	1
tfmzbuyzvopb	1	hkmzwetmumnl	1
vopbbuykhylm	1	oqwepuodaphv	1
udwepumrbyyi	1	nhkypublwepu	1
ylpbbubosnpq	1	blwepupzneyg	1
pqlhyvfphwmv	1	hyyvpbhylpap	1
zykylpfprpti	1	grpbbuduuszp	1
pqlhyvihitof	1	mtihwemzmfmz	1
lhyvihitofbk	1	ihwemzmfmzbc	1
ekwelmbuashy	1	khihlhdfpakf	1
welmbuashylh	1	fwlmbulzmibk	1
hylhpbtfmztm	1	vywepuplubys	1
hyihkylmodhd	1	yspblpzhyvfw	1
ihkylmodhddb	1	vyrbpbukpbbu	1
orrblhhlwfit	1	ukpbbubkgrqp	1
htihweribubs	1	ekwelmbulzps	1
tpyvlhfbslim	1	welmbulzpspu	1
ucpblpobhzkb	1	nlyvlmvyhmnk	1
zlkylpfprppb	1		

is a $\{\xi_i\}$-word with

$$\xi_0 = \{0\} \qquad \xi_1 = \{1,10\} \qquad \xi_2 = \{2,5\}$$

$$\xi_3 = \{3\} \qquad \xi_4 = \{4\} \qquad \xi_5 = \{6\}$$

$$\xi_6 = \{7\} \qquad \xi_7 = \{8\} \qquad \xi_8 = \{9\}$$

If

$$a_i = |\xi_i| \qquad 0 \le i < s$$

we denote by $q(a_0, a_1, \ldots, a_{s-1})$ the sum

$$\sum_{i_0, i_1, \ldots, i_{s-1}}{}' (p(i_0))^{a_0}(p(i_1))^{a_1} \ldots (p(i_{s-1}))^{a_{s-1}}$$

where the prime indicates summation over distinct indices $i_0, i_1, \ldots, i_{s-1}$. Thus $q(a_0, a_1, \ldots, a_{s-1})$ is the probability that an n-gram will have identical letters in the coordinates that belong to the same set ξ_i for each i, $0 \le i < s$, in the partition, and different letters in coordinates that belong to different sets of the partition. Prove that $q(a_0, a_1, \ldots, a_{s-1})$ satisfies the recurrence formula

```
ean eod upf dfs uzy qqx duk its gad uwh xrm swl yeo hip dnj ias etn gdb
edp wgw pbo ewx oni ppq rja qys ydk jky yed kvd kuu nzk xox fkk tmr nws
oop xiq fdk smj uly rla vdg gsl tzb uly gog tsa fqw wqm aqv xll iwf pvm
tpb iwf png pny wxy hqh hqs tbd xia pbo png qcu hey gvr wgw nxk vhh wgw
zpz ckp pue xlp jqq wbt rza pum tzb nws mpg elo ytf vbg caj cov mgi swl
qca iho sgw tir oku nso jji wzd muz pvm ojz vuy uwy itf hjl tdj cil jhl
tus zpw gor ywz feb xia rhx oyo plc xfu fvw ast rln iwf inx sgo xhf ove
mii xlc opz tdj nsn sjp sak izz gal nlf jtt acb kaa tsv aic lnf rec ptb
zqi dwg png juv kbx daw ukv vuc wet dys xlc mrh tth ocf edp wgw jrf bfs
dgk caj txs jki oxu pdc xiq tfv hgy jho tmq jfi fpu uly oqn pja xia odu
oao dcc zuu qzs gxi owp nbn uif cyp axc uqf tnd eap wlm myt hjm cdu aqi
ava vre smj cic pii qwg spk bjb pqc ecl sbg eqt rsc uty mvu czh nso nxk
hdl fug qgw mqx ooe uly kzg bjb pqc xfs dss fjr pbi trd eni lhg thh oxp
rza wuz gsk rfd wul bzz ylh xns mlu jnk nuo fak hip kcu fzb cee tie fve
rxp kqc dvd isr bpf naa jfi lfo www gor feb idf skk dpg qrz gdj rem waw
cvb zqi ric fpg pdc ibo hip sjx yxf ewm bnu oep llz lka zpi sam wld loa
qgv btn mye lbw yih ejx uqr tvo ciq zoe clf vhk dfs uzy tcs kqe ngo ypv
gii pou sos xia ept zus gal zvt wit xrf vxn dqc uey gcy fqt pio fxk dpa
hbx bov ocw quv cty lcw dzu ngo bzh wyz xia xnn fto smj jbk pyo sqx hbx
vte tbt nso nlf kbx qdp crt hyi uly zuu dtt lka zpi tzv exz tnd rcq pny
viz ydr huc kxu brh fbu mit brp ydr gsc zuu wrz frn zvt fdx imv mci eqt
dnk aho tes pfj ewm ddc vdc lgs uly uei tzb uly nxk fve vjf nlf teq pbg
its iyv ykh ohz xzt csj vzy xzj tks caj zru ycn asy zgq orw sro kzg zhy
afa ndo qmj ziu udf rna cum dtv qqv tzb uly lom kjg upf yjd jly qfs ptb
upf mce lbw lvh ajg ksm tzd afa uly bse wfp ept gnd aec hhc hnf xqm eyq
lrm ccq unm jhz ssu lka zpi asg lag irz kmt vwo bxl owu uib jds kbx mog
yih udf ipd giy xia lem mlh zky ssu ucf aac fsw rjp xia kml xfh xia afa
feb gsc jbr ins jyd ucu qmj uaa tos dqw udf zvt wit xrf hdl yme myc lzo
yih frn fve rxp pfj pwo zyn cqc mlh tbd yzr gsc oiq flw tsn aek abc isx
qgk wet xtc hds xlj orw pnw nfm xia xnn cdj hti odu dbz cqo ojz ngo tcs
```

Figure P3.22. *CIPHER(P3.7)* : playfair encipherment of *PLAIN(P3.7)*.

$$q(a_0, a_1, \ldots, a_{s-1}) = \begin{cases} s_{a_0} & \text{if } s = 1 \\ s_{a_{s-1}} q(a_0, a_1, \ldots, a_{s-2}) & \\ \quad - \sum_{0 \le r < s-1} q(a_0, \ldots, a_{r-1}, a_{r-1} + a_{s-1}, a_{r+1}, \ldots, a_{s-2}) & \text{if } s > 1 \end{cases}$$

where

$$s_j = \sum_{0 \le t < m} (p(t))^j \qquad 0 \le j < \infty$$

3.13 Continuation. Prove the formula

$$q(a_0, a_1, \ldots, a_{s-1}) = \sum_{\Xi} \sum_{0 \le i < s-1} (-1)^{|\xi|-1}(|\xi_i| - 1)!\, s[\xi_i]$$

the sum above being over all partitions Ξ of $\{0, 1, \ldots, s - 1\}$ and

$$s[\xi_i] = s_{a_{i,0}+\cdots}$$

the sum above over the terms $a_{i,0}$ in ξ_i.

3.14 Continuation. For the partition corresponding to the word PERFORMANCE, evaluate $q(a_0, a_1, \ldots, a_{s-1})$ when the probabilities are those given in Table 2.3.1.

3.15 **Matching.** Suppose $\{\Delta_{i_j} : 0 \leq j < n\}$ are sets of ciphertext equivalents for the letters in the Playfair encipherment of the n-gram

$$\mathbf{x} = (x_0, x_{n-1}, \ldots, x_{n-1})$$

For the plaintext source in Example 2.3.1, find a formula for the expectation of the number of matches in the ciphertext.

3.16 A *transposition system* on r-grams is a family of coordinate permutations $\boldsymbol{K}$ (a subset of $\boldsymbol{Z}_r$), which enciphers the plaintext r-gram $\mathbf{x} = (x_0, x_1, \ldots, x_{r-1})$ by the rule

$$T_\tau : \mathbf{x} = (x_0, x_1, \ldots, x_{r-1}) \rightarrow \mathbf{y}$$

$$= (y_0, y_1, \ldots, y_{r-1}) = (x_{\tau(0)}, x_{\tau(1)}, \ldots, x_{\tau(r-1)})$$

Extend T_τ to plaintext n-grams with $n = tr$ in the obvious way. How can the information contained in Tables 2.3.1 and 2.3.5 be used to test for transposition encipherment?

3.17 Develop an alternate method of extending T_τ to plaintext n-grams for arbitrary $n \geq r$.

3.18 Let plaintext be enciphered by a transposition system $\boldsymbol{K}$ as in Problem 3.16, with $n = tr$ and r known. For $0 \leq i < j < r$ and $s,t \in \boldsymbol{Z}_m$, let $N_{i,j,s,t}(\mathbf{y})$ denote the number of letter pairs (y_u, y_v) in the ciphertext

$$\mathbf{y} = (y_0, y_1, \ldots, y_{tr-1})$$

with

$$u = i \text{ (modulo r)} \quad v = j \text{ (modulo r)} \quad y_u = s \quad y_v = t$$

How can the array $\{N_{i,j,s,t} : 0 \leq i < j < r,\ s,t \in \boldsymbol{Z}_m$ be used to recover τ?

CHAPTER IV

Polyalphabetic Systems

4.1 THE ONE-TIME SYSTEM

A *polyalphabetic substitution* is defined by a key $\pi = (\pi_0, \pi_1, \ldots)$ containing at least two distinct substitutions. We start this chapter with a discussion of the *non plus ultra* of polyalphabetic substitutions systems.

Let $\{K_i : 0 \leq i < n\}$ be independent and identically distributed random variables taking values in and uniformly distributed on the set $\boldsymbol{Z_m}$.

$$Pr_{KEY}\{K_0, K_1, \ldots, K_{n-1}) = (k_0, k_1, \ldots, k_{n-1})\} = (1/m)^n$$

The *one-time system* enciphers the plaintext

$$\mathbf{X} = (X_0, X_1, \ldots, X_{n-1})$$

into the ciphertext

$$\mathbf{Y} = (Y_0, Y_1, \ldots, Y_{n-1})$$

by Caesar substitution,

$$Y_i = C_{K_i}(x_i) = (K_i + X_i) \text{ (modulo m)} \qquad 0 \leq i < n \tag{4.1.1}$$

The terms *one-time tape* or *one-time pad* are also used to describe this substitution system. The key space $\boldsymbol{K}$ of this one-time system is the range the vector $(K_0, K_1, \ldots, K_{n-1})$ and contains m^n points. The important observation about the one-time system is given by the following theorem.

Theorem 4.1.1 For *any* source $\boldsymbol{S}$, the random variables $Y_0, Y_1, \ldots, Y_{n-1}$ defined by Eq. (4.1.1) are independent and identically distributed; each Y_i has the uniform distribution on $\boldsymbol{Z_m}$,

$$Pr_{CIPHER}\{(Y_0, Y_1, \ldots, Y_{n-1}) = \mathbf{y}\} = (1/m)^n \tag{4.1.2}$$

for all $(y_0, y_1, \ldots, y_{n-1})$ in $\boldsymbol{Z_{m,n}}$.

Proof. The statements

- X_i and Y_i uniquely determine the key K_i

$$Y_i - X_i = K_i \text{ (modulo m)}$$

- $K_0, K_1, \ldots, K_{n-1}$ are independent and uniformly distributed random variables on $\boldsymbol{Z}_m$
- $(K_0, K_1, \ldots, K_{n-1})$ and $(X_0, X_1, \ldots, X_{n-1})$ are independent

imply that the joint distribution of plaintext and ciphertext is

(4.1.3) $\quad \Pr_{PLAIN,CIPHER}\{\mathbf{X} = \mathbf{x} \text{ and } \mathbf{Y} = \mathbf{y}\} = m^{-n}\Pr_{PLAIN}\{\mathbf{X} = \mathbf{x}\}$

The sum of the right-hand side of Eq. (4.1.3) over all n-grams $(x_0, x_1, \ldots, x_{n-1})$ gives Eq. (4.1.2) and proves that the $\{Y_i\}$ are independent.

Equation (4.1.3) also implies that

$$\Pr_{PLAIN/CIPHER}\{\mathbf{X} = \mathbf{x}/\mathbf{Y} = \mathbf{y}\} = \Pr_{PLAIN}\{\mathbf{X} = \mathbf{x}\}$$

which means that the one-time system has perfect secrecy for plaintext of length n.

The two random vectors

$$(K_0, K_1, \ldots, K_{n-1})$$

$$(Y_0, Y_1, \ldots, Y_{n-1})$$

are *equivalent,* meaning they share the same joint distribution given by Eq. (4.1.2). These sequences are examples of (discrete) *white noise.* The invention of the *one-time system* is usually attributed to Joseph O. Mauborgne of the U.S. Army Signal Corps. *One-time* refers to the use of each component K_i of the key to encipher only a *single* plaintext letter.

The plaintext cannot be recovered from the ciphertext without the key. For example, the plaintext

SENDM OREMO NEY ←→ 18 4 13 3 12 14 17 4 12 14 13 4 24

is enciphered by the key stream

9 0 1 7 23 15 21 14 11 11 2 8 9

into the ciphertext `beokj dmsxz pmh`:

SENDM OREMO NEY	←→	18	4	13	3	12	14	17	4	12	14	13	4	24
	+	9	0	1	7	23	15	21	14	11	11	2	8	9
`beokj dmsxz pmh`	←→	1	4	14	10	9	3	12	18	23	25	15	12	7

When we decipher the ciphertext `beokj dmsxz pmh` with the 26^{13} key 13-grams, we find the 26^{13} 13-element possible alphabetic fragments. Most will not be readable English language fragments, but some will. The three examples of plaintext,

GIVEM OREMO NEY ←→ 6 8 21 14 12 14 17 4 12 14 13 4 24

LOANM OREMO NEY ←→ 11 14 0 13 12 14 17 4 12 14 13 4 24

SENDM OREMO NEY ←→ 18 4 13 3 12 14 17 4 12 14 13 4 24

yield the same ciphertext `beokj dmsxz pmh` when they are enciphered with the keys:

21 22 19 22 23	15 21 14 11 11	2 8 9
16 16 14 23 23	15 21 14 11 11	2 8 9
9 0 1 7 23	15 21 14 11 11	2 8 9

GIVEN OREMO NEY ←→	6 8 21 14 12	14 17 4 12 14	13 4 24
	+ 21 22 19 22 23	15 21 14 11 11	2 8 9
beokj dmsxz pmh ←→	1 4 14 10 9	3 12 18 23 25	15 12 7
LOANM OREMO NEY ←→	11 14 0 13 12	14 17 4 12 14	13 4 24
	+ 16 16 14 23 23	15 21 14 11 11	2 8 9
beokj dmsxz pmh ←→	1 4 14 10 9	3 12 18 23 25	15 12 7
SENDM OREMO NEY ←→	18 4 13 3 12	14 17 4 12 14	13 4 24
	+ 9 0 1 7 23	15 21 14 11 11	2 8 9
beokj dmsxz pmh ←→	1 4 14 10 9	3 12 18 23 25	15 12 7

There is no basis for deciding which of the three examples of plaintext corresponds to the ciphertext `beokj dmsxz pmh` *from the ciphertext alone*. Adding white noise to the plaintext has submerged the statistical characteristics of the underlying source language. The one-time-system is theoretically *unbreakable*, contrary to Poe's admonition, because the ciphertext contains insufficient information to recover the plaintext. Why then is the one-time system not a satisfactory solution for applications to information processing security? The one-time system is limited by practical considerations; we require an independently chosen key value for each letter of plaintext to be enciphered. While this requirement may not be too burdensome in some applications—for example, in the Moscow-New York hot line—it is too severe a requirement in an information processing system in which we may need to encipher many millions of characters.

What happens when we relax the requirement of one key value per plaintext letter?

4.2 VIGENÈRE ENCIPHERMENT

Start with a finite sequence of key values

$$\mathbf{k} = (k_0, k_1, \ldots, k_{r-1})$$

called the *user key* and extend **k** to an infinite sequence by periodicity to obtain the *working key*,

$$\mathbf{k} = (k_0, k_1, \ldots)$$

$$k_j = k_{(j \text{ modulo } r)} \qquad 0 \leq j < \infty$$

For example with r = 8 and user key 15 8 2 10 11 4 18, the working key is the periodic sequence

15 8 2 10 11 4 18 15 8 2 10 11 4 18 15 8 2 10 11 4 18 . . .

Definition 4.2.1 *Vigenère substitution* $VIG_{\mathbf{k}}$ is defined by

$$VIG_{\mathbf{k}} : (x_0, x_1, \ldots, x_{n-1}) \to (y_0, y_1, \ldots, y_{n-1})$$

$$= (x_0 + k_0, x_1 + k_1, \ldots, x_{n-1} + k_{n-1}) \text{ (modulo m)}$$

Thus (1) the plaintext $\mathbf{X}$ is divided into r *plainsubtexts,*

$$\mathbf{X}_i = (x_i, x_{i+r}, \ldots, x_{i+r(n_i-1)}) \qquad 0 \leq i < r$$

and (2) the ith plainsubtext $\mathbf{X}_i$ is enciphered by the Caesar substitution C_{k_i},

$$(x_i, x_{i+r}, \ldots, x_{i+r(n_i-1)}) \to (y_i, y_{i+r}, \ldots, y_{i+r(n_i-1)})$$

The special case m = 2 of the Vigenère system is the *Vernam system,* invented in 1917 by Gilbert S. Vernam of the American Telephone and Telegraph Company. The Vernam key $\mathbf{k} = (k_0, k_1, \ldots, k_{r-1})$ was recorded on a paper tape. Each plaintext letter in the alphababet {A B . . . Z} (augmented by several additional characters) was first coded into a 5-bit letter $(b_0, b_1, \ldots, b_4) \in \boldsymbol{Z}_{2,5}$, using the *Baudot code* shown in Table 4.2.1.

The key was added (modulo 2) to the Baudot-plaintext. Figure 4.2.2 shows an early A. T. & T. teletypewriter with Vernam tape reader and enciphering equipment used by the U.S. Army Signal Corps.

A frequent and cryptographically unsound practice is to use some word or phrase as a key in order that $\mathbf{k} = (k_0, k_1, \ldots, k_{r-1})$ is easy to commit to memory.

TABLE 4.2.1
Baudot Code

A	11000	B	10011	C	01110	D	10010
E	10000	F	10110	G	01011	H	00101
I	01100	J	11010	K	11110	L	01001
M	00111	N	00110	O	00011	P	01101
Q	11101	R	01010	S	10100	T	00001
U	11100	V	01111	W	11001	X	10111
Y	10101	Z	10001	α	01000	β	00010
γ	11111	δ	11011	ε	00100	η	00000

α : *paragraph break*
β : *carriage return*
γ : *shift from numbers to letters*
δ : *shift from letters to numbers*
ε : *idle*
η : *blank space*

(a)

Figure 4.2.2. Vernam tape reader. Courtesy of Bell Telephone Laboratories.

For example, the Vigenère system enciphers *PLAIN(1)* to *CIPHER(1.3)* shown in Fig. 4.2.3 with the user key

$$\texttt{PICKLES} \leftarrow\rightarrow 15\ 8\ 2\ 10\ 11\ 4\ 18$$

The key space $\boldsymbol{K}$ for the Vigenère system is the set of all r-grams $\boldsymbol{Z}_{m,r}$ for every r, $1 \leq r < \infty$. We will assume that r *and* $k_0, k_1, \ldots, k_{r-1}$ are both unknown by the opponent.

4.3 ANALYSIS OF THE VIGENÈRE SYSTEM IF THE PERIOD r IS KNOWN

We begin our assessment of the Vigenère system assuming that the length r of the user key $\mathbf{k} = (k_0, k_1, \ldots, k_{r-1})$ is known by the opponent. The cryptanalysis of $VIG_\mathbf{k}$-enciphered plaintext then reduces to the cryptanalysis of r separately enciphered plaintexts.

To recover *PLAIN(1)* we divide $\mathbf{y}$ = *CIPHER(1.3)* into subtexts

$$\mathbf{y}_i = (y_i, y_{i+7}, \ldots, y_{i+238}) \qquad 0 \leq i < 7$$

placing every seventh letter into a subtext. The number of occurrences of each letter in each subtext arranged in decreasing order are listed in Table 4.3.1.

```
bipiz vypvk jlxad vubpp qdvey xtmim tclrv sivkn sebcp snelx
wpces ctmrd siagw rocel xwpcc yfcqp qdqgd bjvjf qbims ykacn
qbxel xwpwz vwpke odwaq tgdzq ggmro ztdte kdsmf ipgyc kscqb
kemgc jwdlw aijgm zqwhu qbpeu rmuct fdtqp pzvep bkyyv wfckb
pwedz gzcsl tkvsz rlwip izyep gpyhl skmay fgscv qgavg imedt
rxdzo kemgc avyci vdvay fvhgm osdik qgrrd carin wpekj zgcel
sitkw txsrk gcdxg pcvrz vaomf zpsha musxm dpzni tfewi tnhej
tipnd sxiec bptjd lwmew zpdgp peljz gcels ckcxm imhmf dzmvt
vvsqc scler pgcip gkfxz dzkjl xadvq paige tgdcc acovy reaci
empwk iwccj wltuc xomlh qppzv epbky yrglb jocia hiykj xgewt
dpglx vhycq siqqx pzwcn wbelw gbjot ferza zesyg irrtg kjjui
dxwbk cxpbl tvfnl xsrwp dcsdp vfzcs ltkvs zrldb jooel pkqwx
yfxkc dtsfh bgbxm fptuk yhdxv mcels iarop hacnq bxelx wppcs
edvgv zgsiq qxess cwvrp vaicu odekd xjsdx arivo oedvw tsele
pavbt glhmv yqvma mudzi frzaz esjhk tkxfd tlcdl fwuwt otxah
avyci vdzvb lrkbq vdphl dipye lwgtq mlxad vcxoh wrzaz emllp
gxyiw smfpz vhgwe odwac okdpq hawac prugg rdtsf imery mijmu
dsefr ipbph mrmkx qsjbi vszrw mxqcf vwhek dsmfn wwbns ebcps
nelxw pcyil lwtul wottn kdtjd dknpe knavo xfshm hycxz tlgfp
pgeug xesxt vebjt lxwpz csygi ocelw xjomc chiwi bltzx kuemw
qhbgw twskm tclxa amvyz pxdze yyxjd tnsyk sclrb zxwrb kxrmf
uwtwl xadvv rcsmv pgxnv qebky yfqpk qwmmf pbkyy sxezq qceeb
qpqlr vhvcd pvexv cvsej secbp jwpbw bpwai kcxpr uggrd lrvsm
ebjtl xvhyc qsiqq xlyld ucdtg satak yhoxb jyfxa cbgbg ifiqq
xmclw mvocq acine dijdz czapa rivsz rmhqp qlrsa oqbtx zbipn
lowne jsnla clkft hmptk jpwlw mcvrs jxbjw elwhc dcjwl tugxn
vqebu katdx kcdts fxvhy cqsiq qxmix dzgse mkhmp dqvgb ivocq
aciny cggbx wdpvd dkcdt sfpvf oyxwg aayfv vpbcm zqejv kmlxa
dvuxp xodzm kexzt zgmpm nxvid pvexv cvzvu duree ijawe kemgc
bjode etsgi twmhm fdzhw rzaze xztqp pzvep bkyye ximts epwpd
gcelw cmvgz vcxvc nomlx wpdzx ztinq zvaip odsia quuem wqhbg
wavgk qfodo wnogx pvsiq qxviq bipkr ietvv fpvau qekem gcipn
ztwgi vszrs angke yjtav rlxwc pcxni lwmdk dmurz azesy girrt
gktkw btxqd nvrpw mqaac eie
```

Figure 4.2.3. *CIPHER(1.3)* : Vigenère encipherment of *PLAIN(1)*.

Each of the subtexts may be cryptanalyzed individually by several of the methods discussed in Chapter 3. Here is a variant on matching.

The plaintext and ciphertext letters of highest frequency of occurrence in Subtext 0 are

$$\mathrm{HIGH}_{PLAIN(1)} = \{\mathtt{E\ T\ A\ O\ N\ R\ I\ S\ H}\} \leftarrow\rightarrow \{4\ 19\ 0\ 14\ 13\ 17\ 8\ 18\ 7\}$$

$$\mathrm{HIGH}_{CIPHER(1.3)} = \{\mathtt{d\ c\ i\ t\ x\ p\ h\ r\ g}\} \leftarrow\rightarrow \{3\ 2\ 8\ 19\ 23\ 15\ 7\ 17\ 6\}$$

Assume that the ciphertext corresponding to the plaintext letters `E T A O` appear in the set {`d c t i x p h r g`}. It follows that each of the following four sets,

$$\{3\ 2\ 8\ 19\ 23\ 15\ 7\ 17\ 6\} - 4 = \{25\ 24\ 4\ 15\ 19\ 11\ 3\ 13\ 2\}$$

$$\{3\ 2\ 8\ 19\ 23\ 15\ 7\ 17\ 6\} - 19 = \{10\ 9\ 15\ 0\ 4\ 22\ 14\ 24\ 13\}$$

TABLE 4.3.1
Number of Occurrences of Letters in Each Subtext of *CIPHER(1.3)*

Subtext 0		**Subtext 1**		**Subtext 2**		**Subtext 3**		**Subtext 4**		**Subtext 5**		**Subtext 6**	
d	27	m	27	g	26	d	28	p	32	v	26	a	29
c	23	v	26	p	26	y	24	e	28	x	26	l	27
i	21	i	25	v	26	b	21	z	28	s	23	w	24
t	21	w	21	c	21	x	20	c	22	e	19	s	21
x	21	b	20	k	18	c	17	l	19	i	19	e	18
p	20	z	18	q	17	o	17	t	19	m	18	g	15
h	17	q	16	e	12	s	17	d	15	w	16	f	14
r	14	k	15	u	12	k	16	y	14	r	14	j	11
g	13	t	9	a	11	r	10	n	8	l	11	d	9
b	12	a	8	r	11	z	10	x	8	q	10	k	9
a	8	u	7	t	10	w	9	f	6	g	9	m	9
e	6	c	6	j	9	m	8	j	6	t	9	q	9
j	5	l	6	f	8	n	7	m	6	f	8	z	8
w	5	p	6	n	7	p	7	s	6	h	8	v	7
n	4	e	5	w	7	i	5	a	5	c	5	x	7
q	4	n	5	o	5	q	5	o	5	p	5	h	5
s	4	g	4	h	4	v	5	q	4	y	5	u	5
k	3	j	4	m	3	e	4	r	4	k	3	y	4
l	3	o	4	d	2	f	3	h	2	o	2	c	3
u	3	d	3	i	2	j	3	g	1	b	1	o	3
v	2	x	3	b	1	g	2	v	1	j	1	i	1
f	1	s	1	y	1	u	1	b	0	z	1	n	1
m	1	f	0	l	0	a	0	i	0	a	0	b	0
o	1	h	0	s	0	h	0	k	0	d	0	p	0
y	0	r	0	x	0	l	0	u	0	n	0	r	0
z	0	y	0	z	0	t	0	w	0	u	0	t	0

$$\{3\ 2\ 8\ 19\ 23\ 15\ 7\ 17\ 6\} - 0 = \{3\ 2\ 8\ 19\ 23\ 15\ 7\ 17\ 6\}$$

$$\{3\ 2\ 8\ 19\ 23\ 15\ 7\ 17\ 6\} - 14 = \{15\ 14\ 20\ 5\ 9\ 1\ 19\ 3\ 18\}$$

contains the key k_0 for which:

$$\textit{ciphersubtext 0} = (\textit{plainsubtext 0} + k_0) \text{ (modulo 26)}$$

The only value common to the four sets is $k_0 = 15$, corresponding to the letter `P`. We repeat this procedure to recover k_j for $1 \leq j < 7$.

4.4 GENERALIZED VIGENÈRE ENCIPHERMENT

There is no need to define the Vigenère system using only Caesar substitutions. Let Ξ be a subset of the symmetric group SYM($\boldsymbol{Z}_m$).

Definition 4.4.1 An *r-polyalphabetic encipherment key* is an r-tuple

$$\pi = (\pi_0, \pi_1, \ldots, \pi_{r-1})$$

with elements in Ξ.

Generalized Vigenère encipherment enciphers the plaintext $\mathbf{x} = (x_0, x_1, \ldots, x_{n-1})$ into the ciphertext $\mathbf{y} = (y_0, y_1, \ldots, y_{n-1})$ with the key $\pi = (\pi_0, \pi_1, \ldots, \pi_{r-1})$ by the rule

$$\mathrm{VIG}_\pi : \mathbf{x} = (x_0, x_1, \ldots, x_{n-1}) \rightarrow y = (y_0, y_1, \ldots, y_{n-1})$$
$$= (\pi_0(x_0), \pi_1(x_1), \ldots, \pi_{n-1}(x_{n-1}))$$

where we use the convention $\pi_i = \pi_{(i \text{ modulo } r)}$. The opponent's problem is (1) to discover the *period* r of the polyalphabetic substitution,* and (2) to recover the r substitutions $(\pi_0, \pi_1, \ldots, \pi_{r-1})$.

When sufficient corresponding plaintext and ciphertext is available to the opponent, the problem of recovery of the key is straightforward. We shall assume therefore that *only ciphertext* is available and begin by trying to determine if

$$\mathbf{y} = (y_0, y_1, \ldots, y_{n-1})$$

is the result of monalphabetic ($r = 1$) or polyalphabetic ($r > 1$) substitution.

Suppose plaintext

$$(X_0, X_1, \ldots, X_{n-1})$$

consisting of independent and identically distributed random variables in $\boldsymbol{Z}_m$ is enciphered by a Vigenère substitution with user key $(\Pi_0, \Pi_1, \ldots, \Pi_{r-1})$. We assume that

- The $(\Pi_0, \Pi_1, \ldots, \Pi_{r-1})$ are independent and identically distributed random variables with values in Ξ and distribution,

$$\Pr_{KEY}\{\Pi = \pi\} = q(\pi)$$

- $(\Pi_0, \Pi_1, \ldots, \Pi_{r-1})$ and $(X_0, X_1, \ldots, X_{n-1})$ are independent

In our discussion of generalized Vigenère systems, we will use three examples of key selection.

Examples of Key Selection

(KS1)	$\Xi = \mathrm{SYM}(\boldsymbol{Z}_m)$	$q(\pi) = 1/m!$
(KS2)	$\Xi = \boldsymbol{C}_m$: Caesar substitutions	$q(\pi) = 1/m$
(KS3)	$\Xi = \boldsymbol{C}_m$: Caesar substitutions	$\{q(\pi)\}$ from Table 2.3.1.

*If the user key $\pi = (\pi_0, \pi_1, \ldots, \pi_{r-1})$ is periodic with period s ($r = st$)

$$\pi_i = \pi_{i+s} \qquad 0 \le i < r - s$$

the Vigenère substitutions $\mathrm{VIG}_{(\pi_0, \pi_1, \ldots, \pi_{r-1})}$ and $\mathrm{VIG}_{(\pi_0, \pi_1, \ldots, \pi_{s-1})}$ are the same. We can therefore only determine the period of the working key. We may assume without loss of generality that π is not periodic.

In (KS1), the opponent must search for the key in a key space containing $(m!)^r$ equally probable r-tuples $(\pi_0, \pi_1, \ldots, \pi_{r-1})$. In (KS2), the opponent's key space contains only m^r equally probable r-tuples $(C_{k_0}, C_{k_1}, \ldots, C_{k_{r-1}})$. The key spaces (KS2) and (KS3) are the same but the a priori probability in KS3 that the substitution $(C_{k_0}, C_{k_1}, \ldots, C_{k_{r-1}})$ is chosen is $p(k_0)p(k_1) \ldots p(k_{r-1})$, where $\{p(t) : 0 \le t < m\}$ is the probability distribution from Table 2.3.1 on the letters of the alphabet $\boldsymbol{Z}_m$.

The opponent is assumed to know (1) the set Ξ from which the substitutions are selected, and (2) the probabilities $\{q(\pi) : \pi \in \Xi\}$ with which the keys are chosen, but *not* the actual value of the key $\pi = (\pi_0, \pi_1, \ldots, \pi_{r-1})$ *or* the value of r.

4.5 THE PHI TEST

The number $\phi(\mathbf{y})$, read the *phi-value* of (the ciphertext) **y**, is defined by

$$\phi(\mathbf{y}) = \sum_{0 \le t < m} N_t(\mathbf{y})(N_t(\mathbf{y}) - 1)$$

where $N_t(\mathbf{y})$ is the number of times the letter t in $\boldsymbol{Z}_m$ appears in the ciphertext $\mathbf{y} = (y_0, y_1, \ldots, y_{n-1})$. To decide if $\mathbf{y} = (y_0, y_1, \ldots, y_{n-1})$ is the result of a monalphabetic or polyalphabetic substitution, $\phi(\mathbf{y})$ is compared to *reference values* that are defined by considering the effects of monalphabetic and polyalphabetic substitution,

$$\mathbf{X} = (X_0, X_1, \ldots, X_{n-1}) \to \mathbf{Y} = (Y_0, Y_1, \ldots, Y_{n-1})$$

$$(Y_0, Y_1, \ldots, Y_{n-1}) = (\Pi_0(Y_0), \Pi_1(Y_1), \ldots, \Pi_{n-1}(Y_{n-1}))$$

on a plaintext n-gram $\mathbf{X} = (X_0, X_1, \ldots, X_{n-1})$, whose components are independent and identically distributed random variables with values in $\boldsymbol{Z}_m$:

$$Pr_{PLAIN}\{(X_0, X_1, \ldots, X_{n-1}) = (x_0, x_1, \ldots, x_{n-1})\} = p(x_0)p(x_1) \ldots p(x_{n-1})$$

The rth reference value $E\{\Phi(\mathbf{Y})\}$ is the expectation of the random variable $\Phi(\mathbf{Y})$

$$\Phi(\mathbf{Y}) = \sum_{0 \le t < m} N_t(\mathbf{Y})(N_t(\mathbf{Y}) - 1)$$

when the length of the user key is equal to r and the substitutions $(\Pi_0, \Pi_1, \ldots, \Pi_{r-1})$ are chosen independently and according to one of the key selection examples. Why does $E\{\Phi(\mathbf{Y})\}$ discriminate between monalphabetic and polyalphabetic substitution?

The law of large numbers predicts that the vector of letter frequencies in ciphertext

$$(N_0(\mathbf{Y})/n, N_1(\mathbf{Y})/n, \ldots, N_{m-1}(\mathbf{Y})/n)$$

which results from the monalphabetic substitution

$$\Pi = \Pi_0 = \ldots = \Pi_{r-1} = \pi$$

should be close to the vector

$$(p(\pi^{-1}(0)),\ p(\pi^{-1}(1)),\ \ldots,\ p(\pi^{-1}(m-1)))$$

We will show in Sec. 4.6 that the expectation of the random variable $\Phi(\mathbf{Y})$ in each of the examples of key selection for monalphabetic substitution is $n(n-1)s_2$, where

$$s_2 = \sum_{0 \le t < m} p^2(t)$$

If **Y** should result from a polyalphabetic substitution, the plaintext is divided into r plainsubtexts,

$$\mathbf{X}_i = (X_i, X_{i+r}, \ldots, X_{i+r(n_i-1)}) \qquad 0 \le i < r$$

$$n_{r-1} \le \ldots \le n_1 \le n_0$$

$$n_0 - n_{r-1} \le 1$$

and each plainsubtext is monalphabetically enciphered:

$$\Pi_i : \mathbf{X}_i \to \mathbf{Y}_i = (Y_i, Y_{i+r}, \ldots, Y_{i+r(n_i-1)})$$

$$= (\Pi_i(X_i), \Pi_i(X_{i+r}), \ldots, \Pi_i(X_{i+r(n_i-1)}))$$

The number $N_t(\mathbf{Y})$ of occurrences of the letter t in polyalphabetically enciphered **Y** is the sum

$$N_t(\mathbf{Y}) = \sum_{0 \le i < r} N_t(\mathbf{Y}_i)$$

The frequency of occurrence $N_t(\mathbf{Y})/n$ of the letter t in **Y**

$$\frac{N_t(\mathbf{Y})}{n} = \sum_{0 \le i < r} \frac{n_i}{n} \frac{N_t(\mathbf{Y}_i)}{n_i}$$

is an average of the frequencies $N_t(\mathbf{Y}_i)/n_i$ of the letter t in each ciphersubtext $\mathbf{Y}_i$ weighted according to the relative size n_i/n of $\mathbf{Y}_i$ in **Y.** The law of large numbers implies that the vector

$$(N_0(\mathbf{Y}_i)/n_i,\ N_1(\mathbf{Y}_i)/n_i,\ \ldots,\ N_{m-1}(\mathbf{Y}_i)/n_i)$$

will be close to the probability distribution

$$\text{(4.5.1)} \qquad \mathbf{p}_{\pi_i} = (p(\pi_i^{-1}(0)),\ p(\pi_i^{-1}(1)),\ \ldots,\ p(\pi_i^{-1}(m-1))$$

as the sample size $n \to \infty$. Thus the law of large numbers implies that

$$(N_0(\mathbf{Y})/n,\ N_1(\mathbf{Y})/n,\ \ldots,\ N_{m-1}(\mathbf{Y})/n)$$

will be a *mixture* of the probability distributions in Eq. (4.5.1). Mixing, like averaging, tends to smooth out or uniformize the letter frequency distribution in the ciphertext. In Table 4.5.1 we show the cumulative effect of a particular type

TABLE 4.5.1
Effect of Polyalphabetic Encipherment on 1-Gram Probabilities

Letter	$C_{[0\text{-}0]}$	$C_{[0\text{-}1]}$	$C_{[0\text{-}2]}$	$C_{[0\text{-}3]}$	$C_{[0\text{-}4]}$	$C_{[0\text{-}5]}$	$C_{[0\text{-}6]}$	$C_{[0\text{-}7]}$	$C_{[0\text{-}8]}$	$C_{[0\text{-}9]}$
A	0.0856	0.0432	0.0354	0.0270	0.0246	0.0220	0.0224	0.0327	0.0358	0.0390
B	0.0139	0.0498	0.0334	0.0301	0.0244	0.0228	0.0209	0.0214	0.0306	0.0336
C	0.0279	0.0209	0.0425	0.0321	0.0296	0.0250	0.0235	0.0217	0.0221	0.0303
D	0.0378	0.0329	0.0266	0.0413	0.0332	0.0310	0.0268	0.0253	0.0235	0.0237
E	0.1304	0.0841	0.0654	0.0525	0.0591	0.0494	0.0452	0.0398	0.0370	0.0342
F	0.0289	0.0797	0.0657	0.0563	0.0478	0.0541	0.0465	0.0432	0.0386	0.0362
G	0.0199	0.0244	0.0597	0.0543	0.0490	0.0431	0.0492	0.0432	0.0406	0.0367
H	0.0528	0.0363	0.0339	0.0580	0.0540	0.0496	0.0445	0.0497	0.0442	0.0418
I	0.0627	0.0577	0.0451	0.0411	0.0589	0.0554	0.0515	0.0468	0.0511	0.0461
J	0.0013	0.0320	0.0389	0.0342	0.0331	0.0493	0.0477	0.0452	0.0417	0.0461
K	0.0042	0.0027	0.0227	0.0302	0.0282	0.0283	0.0429	0.0423	0.0407	0.0380
L	0.0339	0.0190	0.0131	0.0255	0.0310	0.0291	0.0291	0.0418	0.0413	0.0400
M	0.0249	0.0294	0.0210	0.0161	0.0254	0.0300	0.0285	0.0286	0.0399	0.0397
N	0.0707	0.0478	0.0431	0.0334	0.0270	0.0329	0.0358	0.0338	0.0332	0.0430
O	0.0797	0.0752	0.0584	0.0523	0.0427	0.0358	0.0396	0.0413	0.0389	0.0379
P	0.0199	0.0498	0.0568	0.0488	0.0458	0.0389	0.0335	0.0372	0.0389	0.0370
Q	0.0012	0.0106	0.0336	0.0429	0.0393	0.0384	0.0335	0.0295	0.0332	0.0351
R	0.0677	0.0344	0.0296	0.0421	0.0478	0.0440	0.0426	0.0378	0.0337	0.0366
S	0.0607	0.0642	0.0432	0.0374	0.0458	0.0500	0.0464	0.0448	0.0403	0.0364
T	0.1045	0.0826	0.0777	0.0585	0.0508	0.0556	0.0578	0.0537	0.0515	0.0467
U	0.0249	0.0647	0.0634	0.0645	0.0518	0.0465	0.0512	0.0537	0.0505	0.0488
V	0.0092	0.0170	0.0462	0.0498	0.0534	0.0447	0.0412	0.0460	0.0487	0.0463
W	0.0149	0.0120	0.0163	0.0384	0.0429	0.0470	0.0405	0.0379	0.0425	0.0453
X	0.0017	0.0083	0.0086	0.0127	0.0310	0.0360	0.0405	0.0356	0.0339	0.0384
Y	0.0199	0.0108	0.0122	0.0114	0.0141	0.0292	0.0337	0.0379	0.0339	0.0325
Z	0.0008	0.0103	0.0075	0.0093	0.0093	0.0119	0.0251	0.0296	0.0338	0.0306

of polyalphabetic substitution. In column r we list the 1-gram probabilities for the letters of **Y** that result if plaintext

$$(X_0, X_1, \ldots, X_{n-1})$$

is divided into r plainsubtexts (of length approximately n/r), which are monalphabetically enciphered by the Caesar substitutions $C_0, C_1, \ldots, C_{r-1}$.

The probability distribution of the 1-grams shown in Table 4.5.1 is the mixture

$$(n_0/n)\mathbf{p}^{(0)} + (n_1/n)\mathbf{p}^{(1)} + \ldots + (n_{r-1}/n)\mathbf{p}^{(r-1)}$$

If general monalphabetic substitutions $\pi_0, \pi_1, \ldots, \pi_{r-1}$ are used in place of the Caesar substitutions $C_0, C_1, \ldots, C_{r-1}$, the probability distribution of the occurrence of letters in the ciphertext is a mixture of the form

$$(n_0/n)\mathbf{p}_{\pi_0} + (n_1/n)\mathbf{p}_{\pi_1} + \ldots + (n_{r-1}/n)\mathbf{p}_{\pi_{r-1}}$$

As n and r increase, the mixture approaches the uniform distribution on $\boldsymbol{Z}_{\mathbf{m}}$

$$\mathrm{Pr}_{\mathrm{CIPHER}}\{Y_i = t\} = 1/m$$

When m = 26, the difference $E\{\Phi(\mathbf{Y})\} - 1/26 \approx 0.03028n(n - 1)$ provides the margin that enables one to discriminate between monalphabetic and polyalphabetic substitution.

4.6 THE PHI REFERENCE VALUE FOR MONALPHABETIC SUBSTITUTION

We assume that plaintext $(X_0, X_1, \ldots, X_{n-1})$ is generated by independent and identically distributed trials with

$$\Pr_{PLAIN}\{X_i = t\} = p(t) \qquad 0 \leq t < m, 0 \leq i < n$$

and monalphabetically enciphered

$$\Pi : (X_0, X_1, \ldots, X_{n-1}) \rightarrow (Y_0, Y_1, \ldots, Y_{n-1})$$

by a substitution Π in Ξ chosen according to the probabilities $\{q(\pi) : \pi \in \Xi\}$. The distribution of Y_i conditioned by $\{\Pi = \pi\}$ is

$$(4.6.1) \qquad \Pr_{CIPHER/KEY}\{Y_i = t/\Pi = \pi\} = p_\pi(t) \qquad 0 \leq t < m, 0 \leq i < n$$

where $p_\pi(t) = p(\pi^{-1}(t))$. The (unconditional) distribution of Y_i is

$$(4.6.2) \qquad \Pr_{CIPHER}\{Y_i = t\} = \sum_{\pi \in \Xi} q(\pi)p_\pi(t)$$

To derive Eq. (4.6.1) and (4.6.2), observe that if the substitution $\Pi = \pi$ enciphers the plaintext, the event $\{Y_i = t\}$ can occur if and only if the event $\{X_i = \pi^{-1}(t)\}$ occurs. This latter event has probability of occurrence $p(\pi^{-1}(t)) = p_\pi(t)$. The unconditional probability in Eq. (4.6.2) is obtained from Eq. (4.6.1) by averaging $p_\pi(t)$ over the substitutions π in Ξ with respect to the probability distribution $\{q(\pi) : \pi \in \Xi\}$.

Let $N_t(\mathbf{Y})$ denote the number of times t occurs in the sequence $\{Y_i : 0 \leq i < n\}$. $N_t(\mathbf{Y})$ is the sum of *indicator functions,*

$$N_t(\mathbf{Y}) = \sum_{0 \leq i < n} \chi_t(Y_i)$$

Since the random variables $\{Y_i : 0 \leq i < n\}$ are independent, the (0,1)-valued random variables $\{\chi_t(Y_i) : 0 \leq i < n\}$ are also independent. Thus the random variable $N_t(\mathbf{Y})$ conditioned by $\{\Pi = \pi\}$ is the sum of n independent and identically distributed (0,1)-valued random variables and has the *binomial distribution* $B(n,p_\pi(t))$:

$$\Pr_{CIPHER/KEY}\{N_t(\mathbf{Y}) = k/\Pi = \pi\} = C(n,k)(p_\pi(t))^k(1 - p_\pi(t))^{n-k}$$

$$0 \leq k \leq n$$

The random variables $\{N_t(\mathbf{Y}) : 0 \leq t < m\}$ conditioned by the event $\{\Pi = \pi\}$ are not independent, since they are constrained by the relationship

$$n = N_0(\mathbf{Y}) + N_1(\mathbf{Y}) + \ldots + N_{m-1}(\mathbf{Y})$$

The joint distribution of the vector random variable

$$(N_0(\mathbf{Y}), N_1(\mathbf{Y}), \ldots, N_{m-1}(\mathbf{Y}))$$

conditioned by the event $\{\Pi = \pi\}$ is the *multinomial distribution*

$$\Pr_{\text{CIPHER/KEY}}\{N_t(\mathbf{Y}) = k_t, 0 \le t < m/\Pi = \pi\}$$
$$= C(n,k_0,k_1,\ldots,k_{m-1}) \prod_{0\le t<m} (p_\pi(t))^{k_t}$$

$$0 \le k_t < m \qquad (0 \le t < m) \qquad k_0 + k_1 + \ldots + k_{m-1} = n$$

The marginal joint distribution of $N_t(\mathbf{Y})$ and $N_s(\mathbf{Y})$ conditioned by the event $\{\Pi = \pi\}$,

$$\Pr_{\text{CIPHER/KEY}}\{N_t(\mathbf{Y}) = k_t, N_s(\mathbf{Y}) = k_s/\Pi = \pi\}$$
$$0 \le k_t < n, \qquad 0 \le k_s < n, \qquad 0 \le k_t + k_s < n$$

is found by summing

$$\Pr_{\text{CIPHER/KEY}}\{N_u(\mathbf{Y}) = k_u, 0 \le u < m/\Pi = \pi\}$$

over all $(m - 2)$-grams

$$(k_0, k_1, \ldots, k_{t-1}, k_{t+1}, \ldots, k_{s-1}, k_{s+1}, \ldots, k_{m-1})$$
$$0 \le k_u < n \quad 0 \le u < m, u \ne t,s \quad n - k_t - k_s = \sum_{\{0\le u<m, u\ne t,s\}} k_u$$

We obtain

$$\Pr_{\text{CIPHER/KEY}}\{N_t(\mathbf{Y}) = k_t, N_s(\mathbf{Y}) = k_s/\Pi = \pi\}$$
$$= C(n,k_t,k_s)(p_\pi(t))^{k_t}(p_\pi(s))^{k_s}(1 - p_\pi(t) - p_\pi(s))^{n-k_t-k_s}$$

whenever (k_t, k_s) satisfies

$$0 \le k_t < n \quad 0 \le k_s < n \quad 0 \le k_t + k_s < n$$

The mean and variance of $N_t(\mathbf{Y})$ and the mixed moments of $N_t(\mathbf{Y})$ and $N_s(\mathbf{Y})$ conditioned by the event $\{\Pi = \pi\}$ are the derivatives of the conditional joint generating function

$$E\{z^{N_t(\mathbf{Y})}w^{N_s(\mathbf{Y})}/\Pi = \pi\} = \sum_{\{0\le j,k\le n, j+k=n\}} \Pr\{N_t(\mathbf{Y}) = j, N_s(\mathbf{Y}) = k\}z^j w^k$$
$$= (p_\pi(t)z + p_\pi(s)w + 1 - p_\pi(t) - p_\pi(s))^n$$

evaluated at the point $z = w = 1$. The conditional generating function is found by multiplying

$$\Pr_{\text{CIPHER/KEY}}\{N_t(\mathbf{Y}) = k_t, N_s(\mathbf{Y}) = k_s/\Pi = \pi\}$$

by $z^{k_t}w^{k_s}$ and summing over all pairs (k_t, k_s), where

$$0 \le k_t < n \quad 0 \le k_s < n \quad 0 \le k_t + k_s < n$$

The *mixed moment of order (i,j),*

$$E\{(N_t(\mathbf{Y}))^i(N_s(\mathbf{Y}))^j\}$$

is the mixed partial derivative

$$(\partial/\partial z)^i\,(\partial/\partial w)^j\,E\{z^{N_t(\mathbf{Y})}w^{N_s(\mathbf{Y})}/\Pi = \pi\}$$

evaluated at the point $z = w = 1$. The derivatives may be expressed in terms of the Stirling numbers $S(i,u)$, $S(j,v)$ and the moments $E\{(N_t(\mathbf{Y}))^u(N_s(\mathbf{Y}))^v\}$ with $0 \le u < i$ and $0 \le v < j$:

(4.6.3)
$$(\partial/\partial z)^i\,(\partial/\partial w)^j\,E\{z^{N_t(\mathbf{Y})}w^{N_s(\mathbf{Y})}/\Pi = \pi\}_{|w=z=1}$$
$$= \sum_{0\le u<i}\sum_{0\le v<j}(-1)^{i-u+j-v}\,S(i,u)S(j,v)E\{N_t^u(\mathbf{Y})N_s^v(\mathbf{Y})\}$$

The *Stirling number of the first kind* $S(i,u)$ [KN] is defined by

$$x(x-1)(x-2)\ldots(x-i+1) = \sum_{0\le u<i}(-1)^{i-u}S(i,u)x^u$$

From Eq. (4.6.3) we find the expressions

$$E\{N_t(\mathbf{Y})/\Pi = \pi\} = np_\pi(t)$$

$$\mathrm{Var}\{N_t(\mathbf{Y})/\Pi = \pi\} = np_\pi(t)[1 - p_\pi(t)]$$

$$E\{N_t(\mathbf{Y})(N_t(\mathbf{Y}) - 1)/\Pi = \pi\} = n(n-1)p_\pi^2(t) \quad 0 \le t < m$$

$$E\{N_t(\mathbf{Y})N_s(\mathbf{Y})/\Pi = \pi\} = n(n-1)p_\pi(t)p_\pi(s) \quad 0 \le s,t < m,\ s \ne t$$

$$E\{N_t(\mathbf{Y})(N_t(\mathbf{Y}) - 1)N_s(\mathbf{Y})(N_s(\mathbf{Y}) - 1)/\Pi = \pi\}$$
$$= n(n-1)(n-2)(n-3)p_\pi^2(t)p_\pi^2(s)$$

$$0 \le t,s < m,\ t \ne s$$

$$E\{[N_t(\mathbf{Y})(N_t(\mathbf{Y}) - 1)]^2/\Pi = \pi\} = n(n-1)(n-2)(n-3)p_\pi^4(t)$$
$$+ 4n(n-1)(n-2)p_\pi^3(t)^3 + 2n(n-1)p_\pi^2(t)$$

which give the following theorem.

Theorem 4.6.1 The expectation, second moment, and variance of $\Phi(\mathbf{Y})$ are given by

$$E\{\Phi(\mathbf{Y})\} = \sum_{0\le t<m} E\{N_t(\mathbf{Y})(N_t(\mathbf{Y}) - 1)\} = n(n-1)s_2$$

$$E\{\Phi^2(\mathbf{Y})\} = \sum_{0\le t<m} E\{N_t(\mathbf{Y})(N_t(\mathbf{Y}) - 1)^2\}$$

$$+ \sum_{\{0\le s,t<m,s\ne t\}} E\{N_t(\mathbf{Y})(N_t(\mathbf{Y}) - 1)N_s(\mathbf{Y})(N_s(\mathbf{Y}) - 1)\}$$

$$= n(n-1)(n-2)(n-3)s_4 + 4n(n-1)(n-2)s_3 + 2n(n-1)s_2$$
$$+ n(n-1)(n-2)(n-3)[s_2^2 - s_4]$$
$$\mathrm{Var}\{\Phi(\mathbf{Y})\} = = 4n^3[s_3 - s_2^2] + 2n^2[5s_2^2 + s_2 - 6s_3]$$
$$+ 2n[4s_3 - s_2 - 3s_2^2]$$

where

$$n^{(k)} = \sum_{0 \le i < r} n_i^k$$

Since

$$s_2 = \sum_{0 \le t < m} p^2(t) = (1/m) + \sum (p(t) - 1/m)^2$$

we see that

$$s_2 \geq 1/m$$

with equality if and only if $p(t) = 1/m$ for *all* t, $0 \le t < m$.

Several special cases are worth pointing out:

- If plaintext $\mathbf{U} = (U_0, U_1, \ldots, U_{n-1})$ is uniformly distributed on $\boldsymbol{Z}_{m,n}$,

$$\Pr_{PLAIN}\{(U_0, U_1, \ldots, U_{n-1}) = (u_0, u_1, \ldots, u_{n-1})\} = m^{-n}$$

- we have

$$E\{\Phi(\mathbf{U})\} = n(n-1)/m$$
$$\sigma^2\{\Phi(\mathbf{U})\} = \mathrm{Var}\{\Phi(\mathbf{U})\} = 2n(n-1)(1-1/m)/m$$

- If plaintext $\mathbf{X}$ is generated by independent and identically distributed trials with probabilities $\{p(t) : 0 \le t < m\}$ from Table 2.3.1, then

$$E\{\Phi(\mathbf{X})\} \cong 0.06875n(n-1)$$
$$\sigma^2\{\Phi(\mathbf{X})\} = \mathrm{Var}\{\Phi(\mathbf{X})\} \cong 0.004999n^3 + 0.11305n^2 - 0.11805n$$

Since *CIPHER(1.3)* is the result of a polyalphabetic encipherment of *PLAIN(1)*, the values of $\{N_t(\mathbf{Y})\}$ from Table 4.3.1 give

$$n = 1673 \qquad \phi[\mathit{CIPHER(1.3)}] = 116646$$

For monalphabetically enciphered plaintext of length $n = 1673$,

$$E\{\Phi(\mathbf{X})\} \cong 192307.8 \qquad \sigma\{\Phi(\mathbf{X})\} \cong 4870.68$$
$$E\{\Phi(\mathbf{U})\} \cong 107586.8 \qquad \sigma\{\Phi(\mathbf{U})\} \cong 454.86$$

so that $\phi[\mathit{CIPHER(1.3)}]$ is more than three standard deviations away from the monalphabetic value $E\{\Phi(\mathbf{X})\}$.

4.7 THE PHI REFERENCE VALUE FOR POLYALPHABETIC SUBSTITUTION

Now we repeat the calculation made in Sec. 4.6, this time for polyalphabetic substitution. Divide the plaintext $\mathbf{X} = (X_0, X_1, \ldots, X_{n-1})$ into r plainsubtexts:

$$\mathbf{X}_i = (X_i, X_{i+r}, \ldots, X_{i+r(n_i-1)})$$

The ith plainsubtext $\mathbf{X}_i$ is monalphabetically enciphered by Π_i chosen from the set of substitutions Ξ according to the probability distribution $\{q(\pi) : \pi \in \Xi\}$, resulting in the ciphersubtexts

$$\mathbf{Y}_i = (Y_i, Y_{i+r}, \ldots, Y_{i+r(n_i-1)}) = (\Pi_i(X_i), \Pi_i(X_{i+r}), \ldots, \Pi_i(X_{i+r(n_i-1)})$$

The opponent intercepts the interleaved r subtexts

$$(Y_0, Y_1, \ldots, Y_{n-1})$$

and is assumed to know the set Ξ, from which the key $(\Pi_0, \Pi_1, \ldots, \Pi_{r-1})$ has been selected, and the a priori probabilities $\{q(\pi) : \pi \in \Xi\}$ of choosing $\Pi = \pi$, but *not* the value of r.

The distribution of Y_{i+jr} conditioned by the event $\{\Pi_i = \pi_i\}$ is

$$\Pr_{CIPHER/KEY}\{Y_{i+jr} = t/\Pi_i = \pi_i\} = p_{\pi_i}(t)$$

$$0 \le t < m \qquad 0 \le j < n_i$$

The unconditional distribution is

$$(4.7.1) \qquad \Pr_{CIPHER}\{Y_{i+jr} = t\} = \sum_{\pi \in \Xi} p_{\pi_i}(t)q(\pi_i) \qquad 0 \le t < m, \quad 0 \le j < n_i$$

It will be convenient to introduce a notation for the sum in Eq. (4.7.1) and similar sums that will arise shortly. Define

$$(4.7.2) \qquad p[\mathbf{t}] = p[t_0,t_1, \ldots, t_{n-1}] = \sum_{\pi \in \Xi} q(\pi) \prod_{0 \le s < n} p_\pi(t_s)$$

allowing repetitions in the indices $(t_0,t_1, \ldots, t_{n-1})$. The function $p[\mathbf{t}]$ defined in Eq. (4.7.2) on the set of all n-grams $\boldsymbol{Z}_{m,n}$,

$$\{p[\mathbf{t}] = p[t_0,t_1, \ldots, t_{n-1}] : t_j \in \boldsymbol{Z}_m, 0 \le j < n\}$$

is a probability distribution on $\boldsymbol{Z}_{m,n}$ with the following interpretation: $p[\mathbf{t}] = p[t_0,t_1, \ldots, t_{n-1}]$ is the probability that plaintext $(X_0, X_1, \ldots, X_{n-1})$, consisting of independent and identically distributed random variables

$$\Pr_{PLAIN}\{X_i = t\} = p(t)$$

and enciphered by a single substitution Π chosen from Ξ with the distribution $\{q(\pi) : \pi \in \Xi\}$, yields the ciphertext $(Y_0, Y_1, \ldots, Y_{n-1}) = (t_0,t_1, \ldots, t_{n-1})$.

For the three models of key selection, we find

$$p[t] = \begin{cases} 1/m & \text{in KS1} \\ 1/m & \text{in KS2} \\ \sum_{0 \le s < m} p(s)p(t-s) & \text{in KS3} \end{cases}$$

$$p[t_0,t_1] = \begin{cases} [1 - s_2]/m(m-1) & \text{in KS1 if } t_0 \ne t_1 \\ s_2/m & \text{in KS1 if } t_0 = t_1 \\ (1/m) \sum_{0 \le s < m} p(t_0 - s)p(t_1 - s) & \text{in KS2} \\ \sum_{0 \le s < m} p(s)p(t_0 - s)p(t_1 - s) & \text{in KS3} \end{cases}$$

Note that

$$s_k = \sum_{0 \le t < m} p^k(t) = \sum_{0 \le t < m} p[\underbrace{t,t,\ldots,t}_{\text{k copies}}]$$

The (unconditional) distribution of Y_{i+jr} is

$$Pr_{CIPHER}\{Y_{i+jr} = t\} = p[t] \qquad 0 \le t < m \qquad 0 \le j < n_i$$

More generally, the unconditional joint distribution of $(Y_{i+rj_0}, Y_{i+rj_1}, \ldots, Y_{i+rj_{u-1}})$ is

$$Pr_{CIPHER}\{Y_{i+rj_s} = t_s, 0 \le s < u\} = p[t_0,t_1, \ldots ,t_{u-1}]$$

Without the value of r, an opponent only observes the sum

$$N_t(\mathbf{Y}) = N_t(\mathbf{Y}_0) + N_t(\mathbf{Y}_1) + \ldots + N_t(\mathbf{Y}_{m-1})$$

and not the individual terms $\{N_t(\mathbf{Y}_i)\}$. $\Phi(\mathbf{Y})$ is the sum

$$\begin{aligned} \Phi(\mathbf{Y}) &= \sum_{0 \le t < m} N_t(\mathbf{Y})(N_t(\mathbf{Y}) - 1) \\ &= \sum_{0 \le t < m} \left(\sum_{0 \le i < r} N_t(\mathbf{Y}_i) \right) \left(\sum_{0 \le i < r} N_t(\mathbf{Y}_i) - 1 \right) \\ &= \sum_{0 \le i < r} \sum_{0 \le t < m} N_t(\mathbf{Y}_i)(N_t(\mathbf{Y}_i) - 1) + \sum_{0 \le t < m} \sum_{\{(i,j):0 \le i,j < r, i \ne j\}} N_t(\mathbf{Y}_i)N_t(\mathbf{Y}_j) \end{aligned}$$

The joint generating function of $N_t(\mathbf{Y}_i)$ conditioned by the event $\{\Pi_i = \pi_i\}$ is

$$E\{z^{N_t(\mathbf{Y}_i)}/\Pi_i = \pi_i\} = [p_{\pi_i}(t)z + (1 - p_{\pi_i}(t))]^{n_i} \tag{4.7.3}$$

From Eq. (4.7.3) and the independence of $N_t(\mathbf{Y}_i)$ and $N_t(\mathbf{Y}_j)$ $(i \ne j)$, we obtain the moments by differentiation,

$$E\{N_t(\mathbf{Y}_i)/\Pi_i = \pi_i\} = n_i p_{\pi_i}(t) \qquad 0 \le i < r \qquad 0 \le t < m$$

$$E\{N_t(\mathbf{Y}_i)(N_t(\mathbf{Y}_i) - 1)/\Pi_i = \pi_i\} = n_i(n_i - 1)p^2_{\pi_i}(t)$$

$$0 \le t < m, 0 \le i < r$$

$$E\{N_t(\mathbf{Y}_i)N_t(\mathbf{Y}_j)/\Pi_k = \pi_k, k = i,j\} = n_i n_j p_{\pi_i}(t)p_{\pi_j}(t)$$

$$0 \le i,j < r, i \ne j, 0 \le t < m$$

yielding the expectations

(4.74) $$E\{N_t(\mathbf{Y}_i)\} = n_i p[t] \qquad 0 \le i < r \; 0 \le t < m$$

(4.7.5) $$E\{N_t(\mathbf{Y}_i)(N_t(\mathbf{Y}_i) - 1)\} = n_i(n_i - 1)p[t,t]$$

$$0 \le i < r \qquad 0 \le t < m$$

(4.76) $$E\{N_t(\mathbf{Y}_i)N_t(\mathbf{Y}_j)\} = n_i n_j p^2[t] \qquad 0 \le i,j < r, i \ne j \qquad 0 \le t < m$$

Combining Eq. (4.7.4–6) we obtain the following theorem.

Theorem 4.7.1

$$E\{\Phi(\mathbf{Y})\} = s_2[n^{(2)} - n^{(1)}] + \left(\sum_{0\le t<m} p^2[t]\right)[(n^{(1)})^2 - n^{(2)}]$$

where

$$n^{(k)} = \sum_{0\le i<r} n_i^k \qquad 0 \le k < \infty$$

The computation of the variance of $\Phi(\mathbf{Y})$ is much more tedious; the details are given in Appendix V. The imposing result is given as follows.

Theorem 4.7.2

$$\mathrm{Var}\{\Phi(\mathbf{Y})\} =$$

$$4n^{(3)}[s_3 - s_2^2] + 2n^{(2)}[5s_2^2+s_2-6s_3 +2n^{(1)}[4s_3 - s_2 - 3s_2^2]$$

$$+ \left(\sum_{0\le t<m} p^2[t]\right)^2 [-4(n^{(1)})^2n^{(2)}+8n^{(1)}n^{(3)}- 6n^{(4)} + 2(n^{(2)})^2]$$

$$+ \left(\sum_{\{(s,t):0\le s,t<m\}} p[t,s]p[t]p[s]\right)$$

$$\times 4[2n^{(4)}+(n^{(1)})^2n^{(2)}-(n^{(2)})^2-2n^{(1)}n^{(3)}+3n^{(1)}n^{(2)} - (n^{(1)})^3 - 2n^{(3)}]$$

$$+ \left(\sum_{0\le t<m} p^3[t]\right) 4[(n^{(1)})^3+2n^{(3)}-3n^{(1)}n^{(2)}]$$

$$+ \left(\sum_{\{(s,t):0\le s,t<m\}} p^2[t,s]\right) 2[(n^{(2)})^2-n^{(4)}- 2n^{(1)}n^{(2)} + 2n^{(3)} - n^{(2)} + (n^{(1)})^2]$$

$$+ \left(\sum_{0\le t<m} p^2[t]\right) 2[(n^{(1)})^2-n^{(2)}]$$

$$+ \left(2s_2 \sum_{0 \leq t < m} p^2[t] - 3 \sum_{0 \leq t < m} p[t,t]p^2[t] \right) 4[-n^{(1)}n^{(2)} + n^{(3)} + (n^{(1)})^2 - n^{(2)}]$$

CIPHER(1.1) and *CIPHER(1.2)* are monalphabetically enciphered, while *CIPHER(1.3)* results from polyalphabetic encipherment. The observed values $\phi(y)$ are

$\phi(\mathbf{y})$	CIPHER(1.1)	CIPHER(1.2)	CIPHER(1.3)
	187524	187524	116646

Note that *CIPHER(1.1)* and *CIPHER(1.2)* have the same ϕ-value although they result from different monalphabetic substitutions. Monalphabetic substitution renames the letters and hence the vector of letter counts $(N_0(\mathbf{y}), N_1(\mathbf{y}), \ldots, N_{25}(\mathbf{y}))$ of two such substitutions are related by a coordinate permutation and therefore produce the same value for $\phi(\mathbf{y})$. In Tables 4.7.1 and 4.7.2, we show the variation with the period r of the expectation and standard deviation of the random variable $\Phi(\mathbf{Y})$ for the three examples of key selection.

It is reasonable to conclude from Tables 4.7.1 and 4.7.2 that *CIPHER(1.1)* and *CIPHER(1.2)* probably result from monalphabetic substitution, since their (common) measured value $\phi(\mathbf{y})$ of 187524 is closer to the monalphabetic expectation $E\{\Phi(\mathbf{Y})\}$ than to any of the values $E\{\Phi(\mathbf{Y})\}$ for $r > 1$. We also tentatively conclude

TABLE 4.7.1

$E\{\Phi(\mathbf{Y})\}$: Expectation of the Phi-Value for a Key of Period r; n = 1673

r	$E\{\Phi(\mathbf{Y})\}_{KS1}$	$E\{\Phi(\mathbf{Y})\}_{KS2}$	$E\{\Phi(\mathbf{Y})\}_{KS3}$
1	192307.76	192307.76	192307.76
2	149921.94	149921.94	151965.25
3	135793.34	135793.34	138517.74
4	128729.04	128729.04	131793.99
5	124490.47	124490.47	127759.75
6	121664.73	121664.73	125070.24
7	119646.34	119646.34	123149.14
8	118132.58	118132.58	121708.36
9	116955.20	116955.20	120587.74
10	116013.33	116013.33	119691.27
11	115242.64	115242.64	118957.74
12	114600.49	114600.49	118346.54
13	114057.08	114057.08	117829.33
14	113591.32	113591.32	117386.02
15	113187.66	113187.66	117001.82
16	112834.45	112834.45	116665.63
17	112522.79	112522.79	116369.00
18	112245.66	112245.66	116105.23
19	111997.79	111997.79	115869.31
20	111774.82	111774.82	115657.09

TABLE 4.7.2

$\sigma\{\Phi(\mathbf{Y})\}$: Standard Deviation of the Phi-Value for a Key of Period r; n = 1673

r	$\sigma\{\Phi(\mathbf{Y})\}_{KS1}$	$\sigma\{\Phi(\mathbf{Y})\}_{KS2}$	$\sigma\{\Phi(\mathbf{Y})\}_{KS3}$
1	4870.68	4870.68	4870.68
2	9124.26	11012.75	13071.84
3	7079.31	8522.03	10468.57
4	5709.47	6842.85	8665.81
5	4788.80	5712.53	7437.82
6	4136.11	4910.81	6558.99
7	3651.47	4315.46	5901.15
8	3278.15	3856.92	5390.59
9	2982.04	3493.31	4982.72
10	2741.59	3198.16	4649.21
11	2542.50	2953.89	4371.18
12	2375.02	2748.50	4135.73
13	2232.16	2573.42	3933.58
14	2108.91	2422.44	3758.04
15	2001.48	2290.93	3604.08
16	1907.01	2175.38	3467.86
17	1823.31	2073.06	3346.42
18	1748.60	1981.80	3237.38
19	1681.56	1899.97	3138.97
20	1621.07	1826.19	3049.66

that the ciphertext *CIPHER(1.3)* probably results from polyalphabetic substitution, since its measured value $\phi(\mathbf{y})$ of 116646 differs too much from $E\{\Phi(\mathbf{Y})\}$ for $r = 1$.

4.8 USING ϕ TO ESTIMATE THE PERIOD r

The variation of $E\{\Phi(\mathbf{Y})\}$ with r in Table 4.7.1 is too weak to be used to differentiate directly between different values of r. We can use $E\{\Phi(\mathbf{Y})\}$ in another way to estimate the period r. Divide the ciphertext

$$\mathbf{y} = (y_0, y_1, \ldots, y_{n-1})$$

into s subtexts by assigning every s^{th} ciphertext letter to a subtext and calculate the s-dimensional vector

$$\phi_s(\mathbf{y}) = (\phi_{s,0}(\mathbf{y}_0), \phi_{s,1}(\mathbf{y}_1), \ldots, \phi_{s,s-1}(\mathbf{y}_{s-1}))$$

of ϕ-values for each of the subtexts. We use the notation

$$[i_0, i_1, \ldots, i_{n-1}]$$

$$0 \leq i_j < 6 \quad 0 \leq j < n$$

to indicate that in a subtext (of n letters) the rth letter is enciphered by the substitution π_{i_r} $(0 \leq r < n)$. We will call $[i_0, i_i, \ldots, i_{n-1}]$ a *substitution pattern.* For

TABLE 4.8.1
Substitution Patterns

s = 1	**Subtext 0:**	[0, 1, 2, 3, 4, 5, ...]	s = 2	**Subtext 0:**	[0, 2, 4, ...]
				Subtext 1:	[1, 3, 5, ...]
s = 3	**Subtext 0:**	[0, 3, ...]	s = 4	**Subtext 0:**	[0, 4, 2, ...]
	Subtext 1:	[1, 4, ...]		**Subtext 1:**	[1, 5, 3, ...]
	Subtext 2:	[2, 5, ...]		**Subtext 2:**	[2, 0, 4, ...]
				Subtext 3:	[3, 1, 5, ...]
s = 5	**Subtext 0:**	[0, 5, 4, 3, 2, 1, ...]	s = 6	**Subtext 0:**	[0 ...]
	Subtext 1:	[1, 0, 5, 4, 3, 2, ...]		**Subtext 1:**	[1 ...]
	Subtext 2:	[2, 1, 0, 5, 4, 3, ...]		**Subtext 2:**	[2 ...]
	Subtext 3:	[3, 2, 1, 0, 5, 4, ...]		**Subtext 3:**	[3 ...]
	Subtext 4:	[4, 3, 2, 1, 0, 5, ...]		**Subtext 4:**	[4 ...]
				Subtext 5:	[5 ...]

r = 6 and s = 1(1)6, we list the possible substitution patterns in Table 4.8.1.The notation . . . in Table 4.8.1 indicates that the substitution pattern is repeated periodically thereafter. The substitution patterns for the value of s are determined only by the residue of s modulo r. For s = 0 (modulo r) the substitution pattern is that of s monalphabetically enciphered subtexts, while for s $\neq$ 0 (modulo r) the substitution pattern is that of s polyalphabetically enciphered subtexts with a key of period r/gcd{r, s (modulo r)}.

We test a value r as a presumptive period as follows:

- Divide the ciphertext into r subtexts.
- Calculate the vector $\phi_r(\mathbf{y})$ of ϕ-values.

The results of this program for *CIPHER(1.3)* are given in Table 4.8.2. The column with the heading $E\{\Phi(\mathbf{y}_i)\}$ gives the monalphabetic reference value for ciphertext of length n_i.

Table 4.8.2 clearly shows that there is agreement between

$$\phi_r(\mathbf{y}) = (\phi_{r,0}(\mathbf{y}_0), \phi_{r,1}(\mathbf{y}_1), \ldots, \phi_{r,r-1}(\mathbf{y}_{r-1}))$$

and

$$(E\{\Phi(\mathbf{Y}_0)\}, E\{\Phi(\mathbf{Y}_1)\}, \ldots, E\{\Phi(\mathbf{Y}_{r-1})\})$$

only when r = 7 and r = 14 leading us to conjecture that seven is the correct period. We must check this conjecture by dividing the ciphertext into seven cipher subtexts and attempting to recover the key as in Section 4.3. The use of the

TABLE 4.8.2
Observed and Expected Phi-Values for *CIPHER(1.3)*

r = 1

i	n_i	$\varphi(y_i)$	$E\{\Phi(y_i)\}$	$\sigma\{\Phi(Y_i)\}$
0	1673	116646	192307.76	4870.68

r = 2

i	n_i	$\varphi(y_i)$	$E\{\Phi(y_i)\}$	$\sigma\{\Phi(Y_i)\}$
0	837	29372	48105.68	1735.01
1	836	28962	47990.73	1731.93

r = 3

i	n_i	$\varphi(y_i)$	$E\{\Phi(y_i)\}$	$\sigma\{\Phi(Y_i)\}$
0	558	12598	21367.51	950.59
1	558	13352	21367.51	950.59
2	557	12938	21290.93	948.07

r = 4

i	n_i	$\varphi(y_i)$	$E\{\Phi(y_i)\}$	$\sigma\{\Phi(Y_i)\}$
0	419	7366	12040.79	622.50
1	418	7210	11983.31	620.31
2	418	7370	11983.31	620.31
3	418	7122	11983.31	620.31

r = 5

i	n_i	$\varphi(y_i)$	$E\{\Phi(y_i)\}$	$\sigma\{\Phi(Y_i)\}$
0	335	4594	7692.29	447.86
1	335	4640	7692.29	447.86
2	335	4950	7692.29	447.86
3	334	4474	7646.37	445.90
4	334	4572	7646.37	445.90

r = 6

i	n_i	$\varphi(y_i)$	$E\{\Phi(y_i)\}$	$\sigma\{\Phi(Y_i)\}$
0	279	3116	5332.29	342.53
1	279	3352	5332.29	342.53
2	279	3274	5332.29	342.53
3	279	3244	5332.29	342.53
4	279	3432	5332.29	342.53
5	278	3044	5294.06	340.74

r = 7

i	n_i	$\varphi(y_i)$	$E\{\Phi(y_i)\}$	$\sigma\{\Phi(Y_i)\}$
0	239	3772	3910.56	273.26
1	239	3856	3910.56	273.26
2	239	3776	3910.56	273.26
3	239	3642	3910.56	273.26
4	239	4340	3910.56	273.26
5	239	3742	3910.56	273.26
6	239	3786	3910.56	273.26

r = 8

i	n_i	$\varphi(y_i)$	$E\{\Phi(y_i)\}$	$\sigma\{\Phi(Y_i)\}$
0	210	1794	3017.38	226.39
1	209	1738	2988.64	224.83
2	209	1708	2988.64	224.83
3	209	1732	2988.64	224.83
4	209	1882	2988.64	224.83
5	209	1850	2988.64	224.83
6	209	1914	2988.64	224.83
7	209	1740	2988.64	224.83

TABLE 4.8.2 (*Continued*)

r = 9

i	n_i	$\varphi(y_i)$	$E\{\Phi(y_i)\}$	$\sigma\{\Phi(Y_i)\}$
0	186	1444	2365.64	189.88
1	186	1412	2365.64	189.88
2	186	1484	2365.64	189.88
3	186	1502	2365.64	189.88
4	186	1484	2365.64	189.88
5	186	1408	2365.64	189.88
6	186	1314	2365.64	189.88
7	186	1602	2365.64	189.88
8	185	1384	2340.21	188.41

r = 10

i	n_i	$\varphi(y_i)$	$E\{\Phi(y_i)\}$	$\sigma\{\Phi(Y_i)\}$
0	168	1194	1928.81	163.93
1	168	1204	1928.81	163.93
2	168	1240	1928.81	163.93
3	167	1154	1905.85	162.53
4	167	1258	1905.85	162.53
5	167	1164	1905.85	162.53
6	167	1074	1905.85	162.53
7	167	1254	1905.85	162.53
8	167	1186	1905.85	162.53
9	167	1062	1905.85	162.53

r = 11

i	n_i	$\varphi(y_i)$	$E\{\Phi(y_i)\}$	$\sigma\{\Phi(Y_i)\}$
0	153	982	1598.82	143.29
1	152	900	1577.92	141.95
2	152	1012	1577.92	141.95
3	152	1040	1577.92	141.95
4	152	1036	1577.92	141.95
5	152	894	1577.92	141.95
6	152	898	1577.92	141.95
7	152	916	1577.92	141.95
8	152	920	1577.92	141.95
9	152	944	1577.92	141.95
10	152	1006	1577.92	141.95

r = 12

i	n_i	$\varphi(y_i)$	$E\{\Phi(y_i)\}$	$\sigma\{\Phi(Y_i)\}$
0	140	824	1337.85	126.16
1	140	816	1337.85	126.16
2	140	840	1337.85	126.16
3	140	782	1337.85	126.16
4	140	888	1337.85	126.16
5	139	768	1318.74	124.87
6	139	774	1318.74	124.87
7	139	872	1318.74	124.87
8	139	770	1318.74	124.87
9	139	856	1318.74	124.87
10	139	756	1318.74	124.87
11	139	732	1318.74	124.87

r = 13

i	n_i	$\varphi(y_i)$	$E\{\Phi(y_i)\}$	$\sigma\{\Phi(Y_i)\}$
0	29	700	1135.18	112.24
1	129	596	1135.18	112.24
2	129	648	1135.18	112.24
3	129	676	1135.18	112.24
4	129	642	1135.18	112.24
5	129	714	1135.18	112.24
6	129	680	1135.18	112.24
7	129	706	1135.18	112.24
8	129	618	1135.18	112.24
9	128	604	1117.58	111.00
10	128	706	1117.58	111.00
11	128	724	1117.58	111.00
12	128	632	1117.58	111.00

r = 14

i	n_i	$\varphi(y_i)$	$E\{\Phi(y_i)\}$	$\sigma\{\Phi(Y_i)\}$
0	120	924	981.73	101.25
1	120	930	981.73	101.25
2	120	932	981.73	101.25
3	120	856	981.73	101.25
4	120	1124	981.73	101.25
5	120	914	981.73	101.25
6	120	894	981.73	101.25
7	119	924	965.37	100.05
8	119	1002	965.37	100.05
9	119	976	965.37	100.05
10	119	1026	965.37	100.05
11	119	1016	965.37	100.05
12	119	928	965.37	100.05
13	119	960	965.37	100.05

TABLE 4.8.2 (*Continued*)

		r = 15					r = 16		
i	n_i	$\varphi(y_i)$	$E\{\Phi(y_i)\}$	$\sigma\{\Phi(Y_i)\}$	i	n_i	$\varphi(y_i)$	$E\{\Phi(y_i)\}$	$\sigma\{\Phi(Y_i)\}$
0	112	466	854.68	91.80	0	105	400	750.74	83.79
1	112	538	854.68	91.80	1	105	432	750.74	83.79
2	112	560	854.68	91.80	2	105	428	750.74	83.79
3	112	482	854.68	91.80	3	105	428	750.74	83.79
4	112	552	854.68	91.80	4	105	490	750.74	83.79
5	112	530	854.68	91.80	5	105	486	750.74	83.79
6	112	532	854.68	91.80	6	105	508	750.74	83.79
7	112	592	854.68	91.80	7	105	482	750.74	83.79
8	111	510	839.42	90.64	8	105	452	750.74	83.79
9	111	432	839.42	90.64	9	104	418	736.44	82.66
10	111	458	839.42	90.64	10	104	394	736.44	82.66
11	111	450	839.42	90.64	11	104	424	736.44	82.66
12	111	566	839.42	90.64	12	104	498	736.44	82.66
13	111	492	839.42	90.64	13	104	466	736.44	82.66
14	111	526	839.42	90.64	14	104	476	736.44	82.66
					15	104	384	736.44	82.66

ϕ value to estimate the period of the key is another example of a test which dramatically reduces the set of contending values for the key.

4.9 THE INCIDENCE OF COINCIDENCE

This use of the ϕ-value is closely related to the notion of *coincidence* in crypt analysis. Suppose that

$$\mathbf{X}_0 = (X_{0,0}, X_{0,1}, \ldots, X_{0,n-1})$$

$$\mathbf{X}_1 = (X_{1,0}, X_{1,1}, \ldots, X_{1,n-1})$$

are mutually independent sequences of independent and identically distributed random variables,

$$\Pr_{PLAIN}\{X_{j,i} = t\} = p(t) \qquad j = 0,1 \qquad 0 \le i < n \qquad 0 \le t < m$$

Horizontally align the two plaintext sequences

$$\begin{matrix} X_{0,0} & X_{0,1} & X_{0,2} & \ldots & X_{0,n-1} \\ X_{1,0} & X_{1,1} & X_{1,2} & \ldots & X_{1,n-1} \end{matrix}$$

We will say that a *coincidence* occurs at the ith place if $X_{0,i} = X_{1,i}$. How many coincidences should we expect?

Let $\kappa[\mathbf{X}_0,\mathbf{X}_1]$ denote the number of coincidences in $\mathbf{X}_0$ and $\mathbf{X}_1$. $\kappa[\mathbf{X}_0,\mathbf{X}_1]$ may be written as the sum of indicator functions,

$$\kappa[\mathbf{X}_0,\mathbf{X}_1] = \sum_{0\le i<n} \chi_{X_{0,i}}(X_{1,i})$$

$$\chi_{X_{0,i}}(X_{1,i}) = \begin{cases} 1 & \text{if } X_{0,i} = X_{1,i} \\ 0 & \text{if } X_{0,i} \neq X_{1,i} \end{cases}$$

We assert that the event $\{X_{0,i} = X_{1,1}\}$ is of probability

$$\Pr_{PLAIN}\{X_{0,i} = X_{1,i}\} = s_2 \tag{4.9.1}$$

To prove Eq. (4.9.1), we observe that the event $\{X_{0,i} = X_{1,i}\}$ is the union of the m mutually exclusive events

$$\{X_{0,i} = X_{1,i}\} = \bigcup_{0\le t<m} \{X_{0,i} = X_{1,i} = t\}$$

The probability of the event $\{X_{0,i} = X_{1,i} = t\}$ is $p^2(t)$, since the random variables $X_{0,i}$ and $X_{1,i}$ are independent, so that

$$\Pr_{PLAIN}\{X_{0,i} = X_{1,i}\} = \sum_{0\le t<m} \Pr_{PLAIN}\{X_{0,i} = X_{1,i} = t\} = s_2$$

Equation (4.9.1) is also the probability of a coincidence of the ith letters in ciphertexts $\mathbf{Y}_0$ and $\mathbf{Y}_1$, provided that they have been enciphered by the same monalphabetic substitution

$$\pi : \mathbf{X}_0 \to \mathbf{Y}_0$$

$$\pi : \mathbf{X}_1 \to \mathbf{Y}_1$$

This conclusion follows from the observation that the coincidence in the ciphertext $\{Y_{0,i} = Y_{1,i}\}$ occurs if and only if the coincidence in the plaintext $\{X_{0,i} = X_{1,i}\}$ occurs.

If $\mathbf{X}_0$ and $\mathbf{X}_1$ are enciphered by substitutions Π_0 and Π_1 chosen by two independent and identically distributed trials,

$$\Pi_0 : \mathbf{X}_0 \to \mathbf{Y}_0$$

$$\Pi_1 : \mathbf{X}_1 \to \mathbf{Y}_1$$

the event $\{Y_{0,i} = Y_{1,i}\}$ conditioned by the event $\{\Pi_0 = \pi_0, \Pi_1 = \pi_1\}$ occurs if and only if the event $\{\pi_0(X_{0,i}) = \pi_1(X_{1,i})\}$ occurs. The probability of a coincidence of the ith letter conditioned by the event $\{\Pi_0 = \pi_0, \Pi_1 = \pi_1\}$ now is

$$\sum_{0\le t<m} p_{\pi_0}(t)p_{\pi_1}(t)$$

so that the probability of the coincidence $Y_{0,i} = Y_{1,i}$ is

$$p^2[t] = \sum_{\pi_0,\pi_1} q(\pi_0)q(\pi_1) \sum_{0\le t<m} p_{\pi_0}(t)p_{\pi_1}(t)$$

Introduce the two hypotheses

$$H_0\text{: } \mathbf{X}_0 \text{ and } \mathbf{X}_1 \text{ are enciphered by the same substitution } \Pi \in \Xi$$

$$H_1\text{: } \mathbf{X}_0 \text{ and } \mathbf{X}_1 \text{ are enciphered by independently chosen substitutions } \Pi_0, \Pi_1 \in \Xi$$

The probabilities of the event $\{Y_{0,i} = Y_{1,i}\}$ given the hypotheses H_0 and H_1 are

$$\Pr_{CIPHER}\{Y_{0,i} = Y_{1,i}/H_0\} = \sum_{\pi\epsilon\Xi} q(\pi) \sum_{0\leq t<m} p_\pi^2(t) = s_2 \tag{4.9.2}$$

$$\begin{aligned} \Pr_{CIPHER}\{Y_{0,i} = Y_{1,i}/H_1\} &= \sum_{\{\pi_0,\pi_1\epsilon\Xi\}} q(\pi_0)q(\pi_1) \sum_{0\leq t<m} p_{\pi_0}(t)p_{\pi_1}(t) \\ &= \sum_{0\leq t<m} p^2[t] \end{aligned} \tag{4.9.3}$$

From Eqs. (4.9.2) and (4.9.3), we obtain the expected number of coincidences (under each of the two hypotheses):

$$E\{\kappa[\mathbf{Y}_0,\mathbf{Y}_1]/H_0\} = ns_2 \tag{4.9.4}$$

$$E\{\kappa[\mathbf{Y}_0,\mathbf{Y}_1]/H_1\} = n \sum_{0\leq t<m} p^2[t] \tag{4.9.5}$$

Equations (4.9.4) and (4.9.5) provide the following formulae for the expected number of coincidences when key selection is made according to *KS1–3*.

Key Selection	$E\{\kappa[\mathbf{Y}_0,\mathbf{Y}_1]/H_0\}$	$E\{\kappa[\mathbf{Y}_0,\mathbf{Y}_1]/H_1\}$
KS1	0.06875n	0.03846n
KS2	0.06875n	0.03846n
KS3	0.06875n	0.03992n

We expect approximately 14 coincidences when matching 200 letters of *CIPHER* and *CIPHER′* if they have been enciphered by the *same* monalphabetic substitutions, and approximately 8 coincidences if they have been enciphered by

TABLE 4.9.1
Results of Matching First and Second Segments
of 200 Letters of C_7(*PLAIN(1)*)

```
THUFV YNHUP GHAPV UZYLS FVUJV TWBAL YZHUK KHAHJ VTTBU PJHAP
lztvy lwyva ljapv uaohu fvbth fuvdo hclfv bjhuu vdwyv aljap

VUZAV RLLWA OLPYV WLYHA PVUZY BUUPU NZTVV AOSFI FTHRP UNPUM
umvyt hapvu zavyl kvufv bywyl tpzlz ifwoz fpjhs tlhzb ylzao

VYTHA PVUTV YLHJJ LZZPI SLAVT VYLWL VWSLD PAOPU AOLVY NHUPG
haspt pahjj lzzav hbaov ypglk wlvws lzptp shysf pitoh ykdhy

HAPVU IBAHZ PAILJ VTLZT VYLHJ JLZZP ISLPU MVYTH APVUY LXBPY
lhukz vmadh ylwyv kbjaz ohclm lhaby lzaoh ujhui lbzlk avpkl
```

TABLE 4.9.2
Results of Matching the First 200 Letters of C_7(*PLAIN(1)*) and the Following 200 Letters of C_2(*PLAIN(1)*)

THUFV	YNHUP	GHAPV	UZYLS	FVUJV	TWBAL	YZHUK	KHAHJ	VTTBU	PJHAP
guoqt	gstqv	gevkq	pvjcp	aqwoc	apqyj	cxgaq	wecpp	qystq	vgevk
VUZAV	RLLWA	OLPYV	WLYHA	PVUZY	BUUPU	NZTVV	AOSFI	FTHRP	UNPUM
phqto	cvkqp	uvqtg	fqpaq	wtstg	okugu	dasju	akecn	ogcuw	tguvj
VYTHA	PVUTV	YLHJJ	LZZPI	SLAVT	VYLWL	VWSLD	PAOPU	AOLVY	NHUPG
cvnko	kvcee	guuvq	cwvjq	tkbgf	sgqsn	gukok	nctna	kdojc	tfyct
HAPVU	IBAHZ	PAILJ	VTLZT	VYLHJ	JLZZP	ISLPU	MVYTH	APVUY	LXBPY
gcpfu	qhvyc	tgstq	fwevu	jcxgh	gcvwt	guvjc	pecpd	gwugf	vqkfg

independently chosen (and generally *different*) monalphabetic substitutions. In Tables 4.9.1 and 4.9.2 we align the first 200 letters of *CIPHER(1.1)* (enciphered with Caesar C_7) with both the C_7 and C_2 encipherments of the first and second segments of 200 letters in *PLAIN(1)*.

There are 14 coincidences in Table 4.9.1 and 7 in Table 4.9.2 which is consistent with equations (4.9.4 and 4.9.5).

4.10 USING κ TO ESTIMATE THE PERIOD OF A POLYALPHABETIC SUBSTITUTION

The number of coincidences may be used to estimate the period of a polyalphabetic substitution. Let plaintext

$$\mathbf{x} = (x_0, x_1, \ldots, x_{n-1})$$

be enciphered by a polyalphabetic substitution with key $\pi = (\pi_0, \pi_1, \ldots, \pi_{r-1})$:

$$\pi : \mathbf{x} = (x_0, x_1, \ldots, x_{n-1}) \rightarrow \mathbf{y} = (y_0, y_1, \ldots, y_{n-1})$$

$$= (\pi_0(x_0), \pi_1(x_1), \ldots, \pi_{n-1}(x_{n-1}))$$

The period r of π will be estimated from the variation of the number of coincidences $\kappa[\mathbf{y},\mathbf{y}[s]]$ in $\mathbf{y}$ and the cyclic rotation of the ciphertext

$$\mathbf{y}^{(-s)} = (y_s, y_{s+1}, \ldots, y_{n-1}, y_0, \ldots, y_{s-1})$$

What variation in $\kappa[\mathbf{y},\mathbf{y}^{(-s)}]$ with s should we expect? Let

$$(X_0, X_1, \ldots, X_{n-1})$$

be independent and identically distributed $\boldsymbol{Z_m}$-valued random variables

$$\Pr_{PLAIN}\{X_i = t\} = p(t) \qquad 0 \leq i < n, 0 \leq t < m$$

and define

$$(Y_0, Y_1, \ldots, Y_{n-1})$$

by

$$Y_i = \Pi_{(i \text{ modulo } r)}(X_i) \qquad 0 \le i < n$$

where the key

$$\Pi = (\Pi_0, \Pi_1, \ldots, \Pi_{r-1})$$

consists of r independent and identically distributed Ξ-valued random variables

$$Pr_{KEY}\{\Pi = \pi\} = q(\pi)$$

independent of the plaintext.

We denote by $\kappa[\mathbf{Y},\mathbf{Y}^{(-s)}]$ the number of coincidences in $\mathbf{Y}$ and the ciphertext $\mathbf{Y}^{(-s)}$

$$Y_0 \ldots Y_{n-1-s}\, Y_{n-s} \ldots Y_{n-1}$$

$$Y_s \ldots Y_{n-1}\, Y_0 \ldots Y_{s-1}$$

The distribution of Y_i conditioned by the event

$$\{(\Pi_0, \Pi_1, \ldots, \Pi_{r-1}) = (\pi_0, \pi_1, \ldots, \pi_{r-1})\}$$

is

$$Pr_{CIPHER/KEY}\{Y_i = t/(\Pi_0,\Pi_1, \ldots ,\Pi_{r-1}) = (\pi_0,\pi_1, \ldots ,\pi_{r-1})\} = p_{\pi(i \text{ modulo } r)}(t)$$

The number of coincidences $\kappa[\mathbf{Y},\mathbf{Y}^{(-s)}]$ is the sum of indicator functions

(4.10.1) $$\kappa[\mathbf{Y},\mathbf{Y}^{(-s)}] = \sum_{0 \le i < n} \chi_{Y_i}(Y_{((i+s) \text{ modulo } n)})$$

If $0 < s < n$, the probability that $\chi_{Y_i}(Y_{i+s) \text{ modulo } n)}) = 1$ conditioned by the event

$$\{(\Pi_0,\Pi_1, \ldots ,\Pi_{r-1}) = (\pi_0,\pi_1, \ldots , \pi_{r-1})\}$$

is

$$Pr_{CIPHER/KEY}\{\chi_{Y_i}(Y_{((i+s) \text{ modulo } n)}) = 1/(\Pi_0,\Pi_1, \ldots ,\Pi_{r-1}) = (\pi_0,\pi_1, \ldots ,\pi_{r-1})\}$$

(4.10.2) $$= \sum_{0 \le t < m} p_{\pi(i \text{ modulo } r)}(t)p_{\pi(((i+s) \text{ modulo } n) \text{ modulo } r)}(t)$$

The probability that $\chi_{Y_i}(Y_{((i+s) \text{ modulo } n)}) = 1$ is

(4.10.3) $$Pr_{CIPHER}\{\chi_{Y_i}(Y_{((i+s) \text{ modulo } n)}) = 1\}$$

$$= \sum_{\{\pi,\nu\}} q(\pi)q(\nu) \sum_{0 \le t < m} p_\pi(t)p_\nu(t) = \sum_{0 \le t < m} p^2[t]$$

if [i (modulo r)] $\ne$ [((i + s) (modulo n)) (modulo r)] and

(4.10.4)
$$Pr_{CIPHER}\{\chi_{Y_i}(Y_{((i+s) \text{ modulo } n)}) = 1\} = \sum_{\pi} q(\pi) \sum_{0 \leq t < m} p_{\pi}^2(t) = \sum_{0 \leq t < m} p[t,t] = s_2$$

if [i (modulo r)] = [((i + s) (modulo n)) (modulo r)].

We have thus proved the following theorem.

Theorem 4.10.1

(4.10.5)
$$E\{\kappa[\mathbf{Y},\mathbf{Y}^{(-s)}]\} = \begin{cases} n \sum_{0 \leq t < m} p^2[t] & \text{if } s \neq 0 \text{ (modulo r)} \\ ns_2 & \text{if } s = 0 \text{ (modulo r)} \end{cases}$$

Eq. (4.10.5) is the basis of the *κ-test* which is used to estimate the period of a polyalphabetic substitution. By calculating $\kappa[\mathbf{y},\mathbf{y}^{(-s)}]$ and searching for values of s which make the number of coincidences a local maximum, we can distinguish between values of s = 0 (modulo r) and s ≠ 0 (modulo r). The difference

$$s_2 - \sum_{0 \leq t < m} p^2[t]$$

allows us to discriminate between s = 0 (modulo r) and s ≠ 0 (modulo r). Table 4.10.1 lists that the number of coincidences as a function of the shift for *CIPHER(1.3)* with a key of period r = 7. The pronounced local maxima of $\kappa[\mathbf{y},\mathbf{y}^{(-s)}]$ at s = 7, 14 and 21 shown in Table 4.10.1 are a beacon to the period of the Vigenère encipherment.

TABLE 4.10.1

$\kappa[\mathbf{y},\mathbf{y}^{(-s)}]$: *y = CIPHER(1.3)*

s	$\kappa[y, y^{(-s)}]$	s	$\kappa[y, y^{(-s)}]$	s	$\kappa[y, y^{(-s)}]$
1	52	8	55	15	61
2	68	9	66	16	51
3	71	10	67	17	67
4	78	11	49	18	65
5	77	12	67	19	67
6	60	13	46	20	61
7	**103**	14	**95**	21	**96**

4.11 KEY EXPANSION

The success which we have enjoyed in analyzing the Vigenère system is largely due to the low ratio of length of key to text. When the lengths of key and cipher text are comparable, cryptanalysis becomes much more difficult. Indeed, if the number of independently chosen key values is close to the number of plaintext letters, we should obtain an approximation to a one-time system. A recurring theme in cryptographic design is *key expansion;* a *user key* $\pi = (\pi_0, \pi_1, \ldots, \pi_{r-1})$ is expanded to a *working key* $\pi' = (\pi'_0, \pi'_1, \ldots, \pi'_{s-1})$ of length $s \gg r$. Vigenère substitution is an example of key expansion with $\pi'_i = \pi_{(i \text{ modulo } r)}$. The *Hagelin machine* [BA] and *rotor systems* (to be discussed in Chapter 5) provide other types of key expansion. In any key expansion system we must assume that (1) the opponent knows the mechanism of *key expansion,* and (2) the *user key space* is sufficiently large to make key trial impractical. In Secs. 4.12–15 we undertake a cryptanalysis of the *2-loop Vigenère system.* The *s-loop Vigenère system* is defined by s keys of periods $n_0, n_1, \ldots, n_{s-1}$, which are expanded into a composite key whose period is larger than the $\{n_i\}$.

Let

$$\mathbf{k}_j = (k_{j,0}, k_{j,1}, \ldots, k_{j,n_j-1}) \quad 0 \leq j < s$$

be s user keys of lengths $n_0, n_1, \ldots, n_{s-1}$, where $n_0 > n_1 > \ldots > n_{s-1}$ and $k_{i,j} \in \boldsymbol{Z}_{\mathbf{m}}$. Extend the user key $\mathbf{k}_j$ by periodicity:

$$\mathbf{k}_j = (k_{j,0}, k_{j,1}, \ldots, k_{j,n_j-1}, k_{j,n_j}, \ldots)$$

$$k_{j,i} = k_{j,i(\text{modulo } n_j)} \qquad 0 \leq i < \infty \qquad 0 \leq j < s$$

We will assume that the period* of the periodically extended $\mathbf{k}_j$ is n_j.

The *composite key* or *working key* results from the (component-by-component) addition of the periodically extended user keys

$$\mathbf{k} = (k_0, k_1, \ldots) = \mathbf{k}_0 + \mathbf{k}_1 + \ldots + \mathbf{k}_{s-1}$$

$$k_i = \left(\sum_{0 \leq j < s} k_{j,i} \right) (\text{modulo } m)$$

We need the following result from number theory.

Lemma 4.11.1 If the lengths of the user keys are relatively prime, the period of the composite key $(k_0, k_1, \ldots)$ is the product $n_0 n_1 \ldots n_{s-1}$.

Proof. The proof is by induction on s. Let $P = n_0 n_1 \ldots n_{s-1}$. Since $k_{j,i+n_j} = k_{j,i}$ for $0 \leq i < \infty$, it follows that $k_{j,i+P} = k_{j,i}$ for $0 \leq i < \infty$, and hence $k_{i+P} = k_i$ for $0 \leq i < \infty$. Thus P is *a period* of the composite key $\mathbf{k}$. It remains to prove that there is no smaller period.

Suppose Q is *the period* of $\mathbf{k} = (k_0, k_1, \ldots)$. We claim that Q divides P. If not, $P = AQ + B$ for some B with $1 \leq B < Q$. It follows that $k_{i+P} = k_{i+AQ+B} = k_{i+B}$ for all i, $0 \leq i < \infty$, which implies that B is a period of $\mathbf{k}$ smaller than Q, a contradiction. Let us assume that $Q < P$. Since the $\{n_i\}$ are relatively prime, Q must be a multiple of some r of the $\{n_i\}$ and not divisible by the others. Assume

$$Q = Cn_0 n_1 \ldots n_{r-1}$$

---

* A sequence $\boldsymbol{a} = (a_0, a_1, \ldots)$ is *periodic* and P is *a period* if $a_{i+P} = a_i$ for all i. *The period* of $\mathbf{a}$ is the smallest such value P.

and that n_j is not a divisor of Q for all j, $r \le j < s$. It follows that

$$\mathbf{k}' = (k'_0, k'_1, \ldots)$$
$$k'_i = \left(\sum_{0 \le j < r} k_{j,i}\right) \text{(modulo m)}$$

is periodic with period Q′, which must be a divisor of Q (since Q is a period of $\{\mathbf{k}'_i\}$). Thus

$$k''_i = k_i - k'_i = \left(\sum_{r \le j < s} k_{j,i}\right) \text{(modulo m)}$$

is periodic with Q″ as a period; but then Q″ is a divisor of Q. Each n_j with $r \le j < s$ is a divisor of Q″ by the induction hypothesis, and hence of Q, which is a contradiction. Therefore, P = Q. ◀

When the lengths $n_0, n_1, \ldots, n_{s-1}$ are relatively prime, a total of

$$n_0 + n_1 + \ldots + n_{s-1}$$

key values $\{k_{j,i}\}$ have been expanded to form a composite key of period

$$n_0 n_1 \ldots n_{s-1}$$

For example, if s = 5 and

$$n_0 = 29 \quad n_1 = 31 \quad n_2 = 33 \quad n_3 = 35 \quad n_4 = 37$$

we obtain a composite key of period 38,418,765, nearly a 250,000:1 expansion. Does the complexity of cryptanalysis increase like the product? The answer is no; s-loop Vigenère encipherment of plaintext composed of $n_0 n_1 \ldots n_{s-1}$ letters is not equivalent to a one-time system encipherment. We will indicate the general nature of the cryptanalysis for 2-loop Vigenère encipherment, following the argument given in [TU1].

4.12 KEY DIFFERENCING

We assume that plaintext

$$\mathbf{x} = (x_0\ x_1, \ldots, x_{n-1})$$

is enciphered by a 2-loop Vigenère system with user-keys

$$\mathbf{k_0} = (k_{0,0}, k_{0,1}, \ldots, k_{0,n_0-1})$$

$$\mathbf{k_1} = (k_{1,0}, k_{1,1}, \ldots, k_{1,n_1-1})$$

$$k_{j,i} \in \boldsymbol{Z_m} \qquad 0 \le i < n_j \qquad j = 0,1$$

producing ciphertext

$$\mathbf{y} = (y_0, y_1, \ldots, y_{n-1})$$
$$y_i = x_i + k_{0,i} + k_{1,i} \text{ (modulo m)} \qquad 0 \le i < n$$

The relationship between **x** and **y** is multiple or *super-encipherment*

$$(y_0, y_1, \ldots, y_{n-1}) = \mathrm{VIG}_{\mathbf{k}_0}[\mathrm{VIG}_{\mathbf{k}_1}[x_0, x_1, \ldots, x_{n-1}]] \tag{4.12.1}$$

where $\mathrm{VIG}_{\mathbf{k}_j}$ denotes Vigenère encipherment with key $\mathbf{k}_j$. The encipherment defined in Eq. (4.12.1) may also be written as a 1-loop Vigenère encipherment

$$(y_0, y_1, \ldots, y_{n-1}) = \mathrm{VIG}_{\mathbf{k}}[x_0, x_1, \ldots, x_{n-1}]$$

using the composite key

$$\mathbf{k} = (k_0, k_1, \ldots, k_{n-1}) = (k_{0,0} + k_{1,0}, k_{0,1} + k_{1,1}, \ldots, k_{0,n-1} + k_{1,n-1})$$

We encounter equivalent keys in the 2-loop Vigenère system, that is, distinct keys $(\mathbf{k}_0,\mathbf{k}_1) \neq (\mathbf{k}'_0,\mathbf{k}'_1)$ which produce the same substitution

$$\mathrm{VIG}_{\mathbf{k}_0}\mathrm{VIG}_{\mathbf{k}_1} = \mathrm{VIG}_{\mathbf{k}'_0}\,\mathrm{VIG}_{\mathbf{k}'_1}$$

The problem of identifying the user keys

$$\mathbf{k_0} = (k_{0,0}, k_{0,1}, \ldots, k_{0,n_0-1})$$

$$\mathbf{k_1} = (k_{1,0}, k_{1,1}, \ldots, k_{1,n_1-1})$$

does not admit a *unique* solution. The two pairs of user-keys

$$\mathbf{k_0} = (k_{0,0}, k_{0,1}, \ldots, k_{0,n_0-1}) \qquad \mathbf{k_1} = (k_{1,0}, k_{1,1}, \ldots, k_{1,n_1-1})$$

and

$$\mathbf{k}'_0 = (k_{0,0} + h, k_{0,1} + h, \ldots, k_{0,n_0-1} + h)$$

$$\mathbf{k}'_1 = (k_{1,0} - h, k_{1,1} - h, \ldots, k_{1,n_1-1} - h)$$

produce the same composite key. The user-keys may be determined by cryptanalysis only up to an arbitrary additive constant.

To separate the keys in a multi-loop Vigenère encipherment we use key differencing. Given a sequence $\{a_i : 0 \leq i < n\}$ of numbers, define the *difference operator* Δ_s by

$$\Delta_s : a_i \to a_{i+s} - a_i \qquad 0 \leq i < n - s$$

and denote by $a_{i:s}$ the difference $a_{i+s} - a_i$. If s is the period of $\{a_i\}$, then $a_{i:s} = 0$ for all i. Conversely, if s is the smallest positive integer such that $a_{i:s} = \Delta_s a_i = 0$ for all i, then $\{a_i\}$ is periodic with period s.

Applying the difference operator Δ_{n_1} to the ciphertext, we obtain

$$y_{i:n_1} = x_{i:n_1} + k_{0,i:n_1} \tag{4.12.2}$$

since $\mathbf{k}_{i:n_1} = 0$ (for all i). Eq. (4.12.2) is the encipherment equation of a 1-loop Vigenère system for the differenced plaintext

$$\Delta_{n_1}\mathbf{x} = (x_{0:n_1}, x_{1:n_1}, \ldots, x_{n-1:n_1})$$

with the *differenced key*

$$\Delta_{n_1}\mathbf{k}_0 = (k_{0,0:n_1}, k_{0,1:n_1}, \ldots, k_{0,n_0-1:n_1})$$

Differencing thus reduces a 2-loop Vigenère encipherment of plaintext $\mathbf{x}$ to a 1-loop Vigenère encipherment of differenced plaintext $\mathbf{x}_{:n_1}$. The complication in this reduction from 2-loop to 1-loop Vigenère substitution is connected with the nature of the differenced plaintext.

Suppose plaintext $(X_0, X_1, \ldots, X_{n-1})$ consisting of independent and identically distributed random variables

$$\Pr_{\text{PLAIN}}\{X_i = t\} = p(t)$$

is enciphered by a 2-loop Vigenère system with keys

$$\mathbf{K}_0 = (K_{0,0}, K_{0,1}, \ldots, K_{0,n_0-1}) \qquad \mathbf{K}_1 = (K_{1,0}, K_{1,1}, \ldots, K_{1,n_1-1})$$

The differenced random variables

$$\Delta_s\mathbf{X} = (X_s - X_0, X_{s+1} - X_1, \ldots, X_{n-1} - X_{n-1-s})$$

are still identically distributed, but they are no longer independent. Their common distribution is

$$p^*(t) = \Pr\{X_{i+s} - X_i = t\} = \sum_{0 \le u < m} p(u)p(u + t)$$

since the event $\{X_{i,s} - X_i = t\}$ can occur only if both of the events $\{X_i = u\}$ and $\{X_{i+s} = u + t\}$ for some u with $0 \le u < m$.

The distribution $\{p^*(t) : 0 \le t < m\}$ is the *convolution* of $\{p(t) : 0 \le t < m\}$ with itself. In Table 4.12.1, we tabulate the convolution of distribution in Table 2.3.1.

The convoluted probability distribution $\{p^*(t)\}$ is flatter than the probability distribution $\{p(t)\}$ of 2.3.1; the hills and valleys in Fig. 4.12.2 are much less pronounced than in the graph in Fig. 2.3.2. Furthermore while the distribution $\{p(t) : 0 \le t < 26\}$ has a wide range of variability,

TABLE 4.12.1

$\Pr\{X_{i+s} - X_i = t\}$: Probability Distribution of Differenced Plaintext

t	$\Pr\{X_{i+s}-X_i=t\}$	t	$\Pr\{X_{i+s}-X_i=t\}$	t	$\Pr\{X_{i+s}-X_i=t\}$
0	0.0687	1	0.0400	2	0.0327
3	0.0325	4	0.0427	5	0.0335
6	0.0352	7	0.0376	8	0.0314
9	0.0347	10	0.0371	11	0.0454
12	0.0398	13	0.0461	14	0.0398
15	0.0454	16	0.0371	17	0.0347
18	0.0314	19	0.0376	20	0.0352
21	0.0335	22	0.0427	23	0.0325
24	0.0327	25	0.0400		

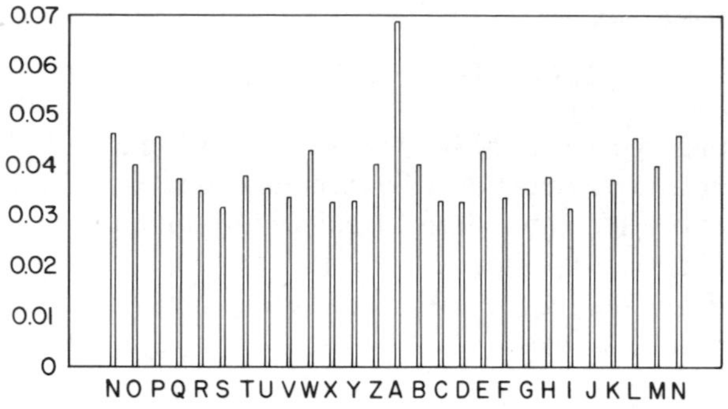

Figure 4.12.2. $\Pr\{X_{i+s} - X_i = t\}$: Graph of the probability distribution of difference plaintext.

$$0.0059 \cong \min_{t,s} p(t)/p(s) < \max_{s,t} p(t)/(s) \cong 169.4$$

the variability of the convolution is far less,

$$0.46 \cong \min_{t,s} p^*(t)/p^*(s) < \max_{s,t} p^*(t)/p^*(s) \cong 2.19$$

Finally, the convolution enjoys the symmetry:

$$p^*(t) = p^*(-t) \qquad 0 \le t < 26$$

We proved in Sec. 2.6 that the condition

$$\star\ p(t + s) = p(t) \quad 0 \le t < m \quad \text{if and only if } s = 0$$

was necessary and sufficient to allow the plaintext to be recovered from the ciphertext enciphered by the Caesar substitution. Suppose $\mathbf{p} = (p(0), p(1), \ldots, p(m-1))$ satisfies condition ★. Does its convolution $\mathbf{p}^* = (p^*(0), p^*(1), \ldots, p^*(m-1))$ satisfy condition ★?

Theorem 4.12.2 If **p** satisfies condition ★, then so does **p***.

Proof. Use Schwarz's inequality* to conclude that

$$(4.12.3) \qquad \sum_{0 \le t < m} p(t)p(t + s) \le \sum_{0 \le t < m} p^2(t)$$

*Schwarz's inequality states that

$$\left| \sum_{0 \le i < n} a_i b_i \right|^2 \le \left(\sum_{0 \le i < n} a_i^2 \right) \left(\sum_{0 \le i < n} b_i^2 \right)$$

with equality if and only if the vectors

$$\mathbf{a} = (a_0, a_1, \ldots, a_{n-1})$$

$$\mathbf{b} = (b_0, b_1, \ldots, b_{n-1})$$

are proportional; that is, $\mathbf{a} = C\mathbf{b}$ for some constant C.

with equality *if and only if* the vector

$$\mathbf{p}^{(s)} = (p(s), p(s+1), \ldots, p(s+m-1))$$

is equal to $\mathbf{Cp}$ for some constant C. But if $\mathbf{p}^{(s)} = \mathbf{Cp}$, then the constant C must equal one since both $\mathbf{p}$ and $\mathbf{p}^{(s)}$ are probability distributions. Equation (4.12.3) shows that

$$p^*(0) > \max_{\{t:t \neq 0\}} p^*(t)$$

so that $\mathbf{p}^*$ satisfies condition ★. ◀

If

$$(Y_0, Y_1, \ldots, Y_{n-1}) = \mathrm{VIG}_{\mathbf{K}_0}[\mathrm{VIG}_{\mathbf{K}_1}[X_0, X_1, \ldots, X_{n-1}]]$$

$$\Delta_{n_1} : (Y_0, Y_1, \ldots, Y_{n-1}) \rightarrow (Y_{0:n_1}, Y_{1:n_1}, \ldots, Y_{n-1:n_1})$$

then

$$(Y_{0:n_1}, Y_{1:n_1}, \ldots, Y_{n-1:n_1}) = \mathrm{VIG}_{\mathbf{K}_{0:n_1}}[X_{0:n_1}, X_{1:n_1}, \ldots, X_{n-1:n_1}]$$

The ciphertext

$$(Y_{0:n_1}, Y_{1:n_1}, \ldots, Y_{n-1:n_1})$$

is polyalphabetically enciphered with a key of period n_0. Divide the ciphertext into ciphersubtexts by placing every n_0^{th} letter in a subtext

$$\mathbf{X}_{j:n_1} = (X_{j:n_1}, X_{j+n_0:n_1}, \ldots) \qquad \mathbf{Y}_{j:n_1} = (Y_{j:n_1}, Y_{j+n_0:n_1}, \ldots)$$

so that each ciphersubtext is the result of a monalphabetic substitution

$$Y_{j+in_0:n_1} = C_{k_{0,j:n_1}}(X_{j+in_0:n_1})$$

Let $N_t(\mathbf{Y}_{j:n_1})$ denote the number of occurrences of the letter t in $\mathbf{Y}_{j:n_1}$ and

$$F_t(\mathbf{Y}_{j:n_1}) = N_{t,j:n_1}(\mathbf{Y}_{j:n_1}) / |\mathbf{Y}_{j:n_1}|$$

where $|\mathbf{Y}_{j:n_1}|$ is the number of (differenced) ciphertext letters in $\mathbf{Y}_{j:n_1}$. We expect that the vector

$$\mathbf{F}(\mathbf{Y}_{j:n_1}) = (F_0(\mathbf{Y}_{j:n_1}), F_1(\mathbf{Y}_{j:n_1}), \ldots, F_{m-1}(\mathbf{Y}_{j:n_1}))$$

will be close to the vector $\mathbf{p}^{*(k_{0,j:n_1})}$ in the Euclidean norm as $n \rightarrow \infty$

$$\|\mathbf{F}(\mathbf{Y}_{j:n_1}) - \mathbf{p}^{*(k_{0,j:n_1})}\|_2 < \|\mathbf{F}(\mathbf{Y}_{j:n_1}) - \mathbf{p}^{*(s)}\|_2 \qquad 0 \leq s < m, s \neq k_{0,j:n_1}$$

by an application of the law of large numbers, which may be invoked for the ciphertext $\mathbf{Y}_{j:n_1} = (Y_{j:n_1}, Y_{j+n_0:n_1}, \ldots)$ since the components in each of these ciphersubtexts are independent and identically distributed. To recover the difference key value $k_{0,j:n_1}$, we compute the correlation coefficient

$$\rho[s : \mathbf{F}(\mathbf{Y}_{j:n_1}), \mathbf{p}^*] = \sum_{0 \le t < m} F_t(\mathbf{Y}_{j:n_1}) p^*(t - s)$$

and search for the value s that maximizes $\rho[s : \mathbf{F}(\mathbf{Y}_{j:n_1}), \mathbf{p}^*]$.

4.13 THE CRYPTANALYSIS OF *CIPHER(1.4)*

In Fig. 4.13.1, we show the 2-loop Vigenère encipherment *CIPHER(1.4)* of *PLAIN(1)*. In Table 4.13.2, we give the values of the $\rho[s : j] = \rho[s : \mathbf{F}(\mathbf{Y}_{j:n_1}), \mathbf{p}^*]$ for $0 \le j < 7$ and $0 \le s < 26$.The flatness of the convoluted probability distri-

```
pvxwm jlxjx xyfoq jhjdc eqdsl lguwz hptfi gvdya grjqc gamzk
kcksf qgufq gviuj fbksy ljxqp mskec eqyuq pwdxs eoqaf mxiqa
eofsy ljxkm jjxyr cqeod htlnd utufb nglhr yqaas wcomp yfkeo
yruup xjlzj ovruz ndevh eoxsh fzcqg tqbec dmdsc pxgmi kskyo
djmrm umkgy hxdgm fyewc wmgsc ucgvy gxuol ttaqi etijt wzmrg
fklnb yruup oigqv jqdol tipuz cflwx etzfq qnzwa kcmyw ntksy
gvbyj hkafx upllt dpdfm jnwas ncavn ahalz rchbv hsmkv hapsw
hvxbq gkqsp pcbxq zjusj ncluc drtxm upmzf qxklz wzpas rmujg
jiaep gptse dtkwc uxnlm rmsxy lnljd dnqur htlqp opwjl friqv
szxkx wjkqw kybip lbuzu ecxni scjyl meozo xbkwn vvgyw ltmkg
rcozk jugqd gvyek dmeqa komzj uorcg trznn nramt wezht ywriv
rkepx qkxpy hinby lfzkc rparc jshqf zgsjf netro xbwsy dxykk
msfyp rgatu ptjlz tcbix mulli apmzf wnzcc vnkbd pkmzk kcxqf
sqdui ntawd ekmgf qjdfc jnqqh cqmyq lwark oeqjb crljj hfmzr
dndpg uypai mddan ahlnv tehom sfrvx hxftq hykry tjckg cgfou
oigqv jqhjo zespd jqxvy rvxmr zjohd ayfoq jpfcu kehom sztzc
ukgwj gzndm juokr cqeop cxldd vneop decut fqbgs wzmfl avrah
rfmte wcjdu aeuyk efrpv jfhfj akyqs jjpsx rfuta kjjbf sokdf
brtlj dpgwy zjbiy kbbha yqbxq rxvdr yaijb lsavz vlklm hyotc
dtmit lralg jrjxg zkedm qfguv cpmzj lwwap quqkv pybnk yhmaj
eujuj hjayz hptln ozdmm dklnr mlfxq haamx gptfo nkefo ykzas
ijbky lnlji fpaai dtfbi erjyl msydx ejuas dosml gkmnd epmso
ecyze judqq dimli qiasw grkpc xjxpj pceov ypfde itofq zedgz
sorhy lipmp efqed lygzq iplht gnbox muwlo xlnln qoopt wsqed
lzkzj aiwqd opqbr rvrrm qmidn fvdgm fzpec eyzgn cdjhk noqda
zbebr xfvzn qystg vzxhx xcezj apdff xkjxj syevp rprky hhola
jdmph ynbrk yplhf tkdvl qdawd ekuwk rmogr axpac rdduo wiwqd
opqbl qtopk kqxjq rxkrg gsxjs clfkt ongti jcjqz ndmxi yztln
riclc lblnz yrfng ntudz bkdwq dimli qihjh rhzsr wwikr yruup
pwwrr sgauv hjuvz tqhvj fminr lmbec dmdsc pxgmr lvuhf scedq
upmzj qzdum jpfjp bbuzk kclnk ngqbd niiwc cqawn ehcsz kdppt
kndux eswrb kawuk diawd ekdwd pvxye wrbji tcdoh erssz upqda
ngeuv jfhff oaoyr mwboi fyfkp dpfbv zjurx rzcfm ommgl uvzfg
uxbyj pgfeq bizdj adiop svm
```

$\underline{\mathbf{k}}_0$ = PICKLES . . . $\underline{\mathbf{k}}_1$ = ONION . . .

$\underline{\mathbf{k}}$ = DVKYYSFXWPYYMGCWPSZRGCQQXZRADVQXTSF . . .

Figure 4.13.1 *CIPHER(1.4)* : 2-Loop Vigenère encipherment of *PLAIN(1)*.

Correlation Between $\mathbf{F}_{j:n_1}$ and $\boldsymbol{p}^*$

s	ρ**[s:0]**	ρ**[s:1]**	ρ**[s:2]**	ρ**[s:3]**	ρ**[s:4]**	ρ**[s:5]**	ρ**[s:6]**
0	0.0393	0.0383	0.0395	0.0384	0.0381	0.0391	0.0380
0	0.0393	0.0388	0.0393	0.0376	0.0386	0.0382	0.0382
0	0.0399	0.0385	0.0390	0.0380	0.0400	0.0384	0.0385
0	0.0386	0.0384	0.0376	0.0380	0.0384	0.0383	0.0397
0	0.0388	0.0384	0.0383	0.0387	0.0384	0.0389	0.0385
0	0.0386	0.0384	0.0381	0.0392	0.0393	0.0383	0.0376
0	0.0385	0.0383	0.0386	0.0379	0.0393	0.0389	0.0390
0	0.0381	0.0380	0.0390	0.0379	0.0385	0.0384	0.0385
0	0.0380	0.0383	0.0388	0.0381	0.0368	0.0386	0.0392
0	0.0382	0.0383	0.0378	0.0396	0.0376	0.0380	0.0382
0	0.0374	0.0394	0.0372	0.0386	0.0381	0.0382	0.0386
0	0.0379	0.0389	0.0384	0.0393	0.0391	0.0383	0.0368
0	0.0378	0.0380	0.0393	0.0382	0.0379	0.0390	0.0385
0	0.0386	0.0375	0.0395	0.0380	0.0393	0.0388	0.0385
0	0.0393	0.0393	0.0384	0.0386	0.0383	0.0380	0.0389
0	0.0402	0.0389	0.0385	0.0387	0.0381	0.0382	0.0388
0	0.0392	0.0384	0.0380	0.0379	0.0382	0.0380	0.0385
0	0.0383	0.0386	0.0388	0.0379	0.0405	0.0392	0.0383
0	0.0379	0.0383	0.0381	0.0391	0.0395	0.0387	0.0382
0	0.0387	0.0376	0.0387	0.0384	0.0379	0.0392	0.0401
0	0.0388	0.0376	0.0380	0.0386	0.0376	0.0380	0.0381
0	0.0380	0.0398	0.0384	0.0387	0.0380	0.0381	0.0384
0	0.0377	0.0388	0.0384	0.0384	0.0381	0.0381	0.0380
0	0.0373	0.0383	0.0381	0.0378	0.0379	0.0384	0.0390
0	0.0381	0.0380	0.0384	0.0395	0.0388	0.0384	0.0372
0	0.0377	0.0390	0.0379	0.0391	0.0377	0.0384	0.0388

bution $\{p^*(t) : 0 \leq t < m\}$ makes it difficult to locate the point (or points) at which $\rho[s : \mathbf{F}(\mathbf{Y}_{j:n_1}), \mathbf{p}^*]$ is a maximum. In Table 4.13.3, we list the values of s corresponding to the five largest values of $\rho[s : \mathbf{F}(\mathbf{Y}_{j:n_1}), \mathbf{p}^*]$ for each j, regarding them as probable values for the keys $\{k_{0,j:n_1} : 0 \leq j < 7\}$.

We could base an analysis on the testing of the values of $\{k_{0,j:n_1} : 0 \leq j < 7\}$

TABLE 4.13.3
Probable Values for $k_{0j:n_1}$ from the Correlation Coefficients in Table 4.13.2

j	**Probable Value For $k_{0,j:n_1}$**				
0	**15**	2	0	1	14
1	21	**10**	14	25	15
2	0	**13**	1	12	7
3	9	**24**	11	5	25
4	**17**	18	5	6	13
5	17	19	0	12	**6**
6	**19**	3	8	23	6

that have the highest correlation, using the ϕ-test to accept or reject values. We prefer to use another approach, combining the information in Table 4.13.3, with certain consistency relationships that the differenced keys must satisfy. Note that we have at least reduced the search for the key of length seven from a set of $26^7 = 8031810176$ possible values to a set of $5^7 = 78125$ probable values, a reduction by a factor of more than 10^5.

4.14 DIFFERENCES OF DIFFERENCED KEYS

Lemma 4.14.1 If n_0 and n_1 are relatively prime, the two sets of index-pairs

$$(n_1,0), (n_1 + 1,1), \ldots, (n_1 + n_0 - 1, n_0 - 1) \text{ (modulo } n_0)$$

$$(n_1,0), (2n_1,n_1), \ldots, (n_0 n_1,(n_0 - 1)n_1) \text{ (modulo } n_0)$$

are permutations of one another.

Proof. The hypothesis $\gcd\{n_0, n_1\} = 1$ implies that the integers

$$\{(i + 1)n_1 \text{ (modulo } n_0) : 0 \leq i < n_0\}$$

are distinct; if

$$n_1(i + 1) = n_1(i' + 1) \text{ (modulo } n_0)$$

then

$$n_1(i - i') = 0 \text{ (modulo } n_0)$$

which is a contradiction unless $i = i'$. ◀

For example, if $n_0 = 7$ and $n_1 = 5$, the first set of index-pairs is

$$(5,0), (6,1), (7,2), (8,3), (9,4), (10,5), (11,6)$$
$$= (5,0), (20,15), (35,30), (15,10), (30,25), (10,5), (25,20) \text{ (modulo 7)}$$

The permutation

$$\pi = (\pi_0, \pi_1, \ldots, \pi_6) = (0, 5, 3, 1, 6, 4, 2)$$

applied to

$$(5,0), (20,15), (35,30), (15,10), (30,25), (10,5), (25,20) \text{ (modulo 7)}$$

yields

$$(5,0), (10,5), (15,10), (20,15), (25,20), (30,25), (35,30)$$

Lemma 4.14.1 implies that the two vectors of key differences

$$(k_{0,n_1} - k_{0,0}, k_{0,1+n_1} - k_{0,1}, \ldots, k_{0,(n_0-1)+n_1} - k_{0,(n_0-1)})$$

$$(k_{0,n_1} - k_{0,0}, k_{0,2n_1} - k_{0,n_1}, \ldots, k_{0,n_0 n_1} - k_{0,(n_0-1)n_1})$$

are related by a coordinate permutation when $\gcd\{n_0, n_1\} = 1$. We may therefore recover the key differences

$$\{k_{0,in_1:n_1} : 0 \le i < n_0\}$$

from the key differences

$$\{k_{0,i:n_1} : 0 \le i < n_0\}$$

Next the partial sums of the key differences $\{k_{0,i:n_1} : 0 \le i < n_0\}$

$$\sum_{0 \le i < j} k_{0,in_1:n_1}$$

give the vector

$$(k_{0,n_1} - k_{0,0}, k_{0,2n_1} - k_{0,0}, \ldots, k_{0,n_0n_1} - k_{0,0})$$

Since $\gcd\{n_0,n_1\} = 1$, the numbers

$$0, n_1, 2n_1, \ldots, (n_0 - 1)n_1 \text{ (modulo } n_0)$$

are a coordinate permutation of $0, 1, \ldots, n_0 - 1$.

We conclude that we can recover $\{k_{0,i} - k_{0,0} : 0 \le i < n_0\}$ from the differences $\{k_{0,i:n_1} : 0 \le i < n_0\}$. Notice that $\mathbf{k}_0$ is only determined up to an arbitrary value for $k_{0,0}$. The process of recovering the key (up to an additive constant) from the key differences is the discrete analog of integration in the same way that differencing is the discrete analog of differentiation.

In Fig. 4.14.1, we show the differenced ciphertext Δ*CIPHER(1.4)*.
Instead of correlating the vectors

$$\mathbf{F}(\mathbf{Y}_{j:n_1}) = (F_0(\mathbf{Y}_{j:n_1}), F_1(\mathbf{Y}_{j:n_1}), \ldots, F_{m-1}(\mathbf{Y}_{j:n_1})) \qquad 0 \le j < r$$

with the probability distribution $\mathbf{p}^* = (p^*(0), p^*(1), \ldots, p^*(m-1))$ of 1-gram differences, we will correlate $\mathbf{F}(\mathbf{Y}_{i:n_1})$ with the cyclic shifts of $\mathbf{F}(\mathbf{Y}_{j:n_1})$, obtaining a *cross-correlation coefficient,*

$$\rho[s : \mathbf{F}(\mathbf{Y}_{i:n_1}), \mathbf{F}(\mathbf{Y}_{j:n_1})] = \sum_{0 \le t < m} F_t(\mathbf{Y}_{i:n_1})F_{t-s}(\mathbf{Y}_{j:n_1})$$

and we will look for the index $s = s(i,j)$ that maximizes $\rho[s : \mathbf{F}(\mathbf{Y}_{i:n_1}), \mathbf{F}(\mathbf{Y}_{j:n_1})]$.

If plaintext

$$(X_0, X_1, \ldots, X_{n-1})$$

consisting of independent and identically distributed random variables

$$\Pr_{PLAIN}\{X_i = t\} = p(t) \qquad 0 \le t < m$$

is enciphered by a 2-loop Vigenère substitution with keys

$$\mathbf{k}_0 = (k_{0,0}, k_{0,1}, \ldots, k_{0,n_0-1})$$

$$\mathbf{k}_1 = (k_{1,0}, k_{1,1}, \ldots, k_{1,n_1-1})$$

$$\gcd\{n_0, n_1\} = 1$$

$$(Y_0, Y_1, \ldots, Y_{n-1}) = \text{VIG}_{\mathbf{k}_0}[\text{VIG}_{\mathbf{k}_1}[X_0, X_1, \ldots, X_{n-1}]]$$

$$\mathbf{Y}_{i:n_1} = (Y_{i:n_1}, Y_{i+n_0:n_1}, \ldots)$$

then the law of large numbers implies that the frequencies of occurrence of letters in $\mathbf{Y}_{i:n_1}$,

$$\mathbf{F}(\mathbf{Y}_{i:n_1}) = (F_0(\mathbf{Y}_{i:n_1}), F_1(\mathbf{Y}_{i:n_1}), \ldots, F_{m-1}(\mathbf{Y}_{i:n_1}))$$

is close to $\mathbf{p}^{*(k_{0,i:n_1})}$ as $n \rightarrow \infty$, where

$$\mathbf{p}^{*(s)} = (p^*(s), p^*(s+1), \ldots, p^*(s+m-1))$$

This means that with probability one

$$\text{limit}_{n\rightarrow\infty} \|\mathbf{F}^{(-s)}(\mathbf{Y}_{i:n_1}) - \mathbf{p}^*\|_2^2 \begin{cases} = 0 & \text{if } s = k_{0,i:n_1} \\ < 0 & \text{if } s \neq k_{0,i:n_1} \end{cases}$$

and

$$\text{limit}_{n\rightarrow\infty} \|\mathbf{F}^{(-t)}(\mathbf{Y}_{j:n_1}) - \mathbf{p}^*\|_2^2 \begin{cases} = 0 & \text{if } t = k_{0,i:n_1} \\ > 0 & \text{if } t \neq k_{0,j:n_1} \end{cases}$$

```
uqanl onift mjepm vjupj hqreo wjzjj zgkts awgsc ajdji ecytv geknl qpopt
zgcyp ginyr bjnon syoqo lgfdc psndn ijsqv srxcy hvsso yaaof thhqm fdhza
najsy tnrcq lkptb ymomx cdwsz amkqb zsrfu rmgvq zinbi rltxa blfyz orzow
kwcoa mldug vvemg trcty rdypm nltao ybbqq rocwa yqadw mvotn nwgcx laitl
sgein jlzwv thjho qrmwg vixyq ksmgo jxwcy coojt muark upncw dryuc tcrgl
bpzho nflgw jasut gytvg epevv nfaqm rvhqw qqfja aidib aviju zptrz jslfb
khtvt otrct qpidk rytct wiymu gcfpt vnfjo swgvj xhtop xerey redpk xpfmm
ubtmf saflo egvwy hwltw rcmhk nipuc ekngz oprst bdtrf tbdoo oamld ucfbd
lxwxz yuwcj qygmk gjcpe sssrt xbsoh xrgmq hcijj kafdx zdilh uabzg jnzva
cssbc tonhc zatab ryqma exmje gkbha sdhzd qolta oybij kxdbk gwcsm jvhof
fovvf ynjsf ejsxy tskdl ovbox wyndx zalzb uxcyh vslrv ioged vdxcv rrmkc
mzrzx tenlf tdwij jgotu diqsr onvai fobqi wirqp rlmlc sfoaf oeini txwbr
zbkhl psoyt abfyi mlsti jxdeo mcbcb vibtt qolgp kmfgv ifart iorvm bprhn
jraoe bpcms ivmlq clnxh mphhd dvbhf twqey ahhpo tqtlm iryge cmzmz rjlzt
ewfvw rkvtx fxxkq eclvq ebxrl faqqo rfrlj jzrcf iwfbd tepif ifbca jdjie
cynlp wuvma lsazc opaqq thugb hdngk nssmy ktkqn mneiq wvypr iyodn yajma
qtvgg rvcrj mkgfo jhkbg fyukg zeldp jjlnz gnxua dpreq agtno hkkbz plibf
jbukz vpvph zpttr hvlaa lavve kzckg dekzk ucpra yefba byexd ibpfm srwxv
zfymt dwubs yfafl anmhq fsfrm uojvs naoho qjkxg rsnah sthzm jnbpj kejcm
rlpbj tkobz tuyfr txbso htqvn xrfid yyqhe ghvxr lrraz tdbeg gecpk phuvg
pjmru ohulo dgbqv zrrmb pjvdz aemyq zzkcl yfkbx llhwq mnoyr yeryw ttxut
fbfor cdhsm dnzgw xvgse vovyg zrnpj qsxbc cwyeh pkpcd ackqv vvsog xtxbs
ohuah ncukh jlbul rgoum fftwp shuli ceyoz uxjug hhniq pvnsm wtibb mcbjp
vpdxr ebdhj lwhof tjjap utjcx nquah pcpqt orjtr cyjps navyz bzsjk fpjsa
cvmky rfcxc dkede pdube mhnak mwbsi gatrl sacoa mldup wyovo hhkwl cniwt
wkrvd tqcpd smpqv jbroa defot acsvz pisal crcwm gwnxu akofe uftxe giadj
tiect bcdaa llucb hwele xlcfz lppes qyylb trorv wzdlk fvhtm ywnqr tcewh
yrarg wupqc sqiop xnkbz gjnzv acctd vjegh mcuzt zvjlg sse
```

Figure 4.14.1. Δ_{n_1} *CIPHER(1.4)* : differenced *CIPHER(1.4)*.

Next we write

$$\|\mathbf{F}^{(-s)}(\mathbf{Y}_{i:n_1}) - \mathbf{F}^{(-t)}(\mathbf{Y}_{j:n_1})\|_2^2 = \|\mathbf{F}^{(-s)}(\mathbf{Y}_{i:n_1}) - \mathbf{p}^* + \mathbf{p}^* - \mathbf{F}^{(-t)}(\mathbf{Y}_{j:n_1})\|_2^2$$

$$= \|\mathbf{F}^{(-s)}(\mathbf{Y}_{i:n_1}) - \mathbf{p}^*\|_2^2 \, \|\mathbf{F}^{(-t)}(\mathbf{Y}_{j:n_1}) - \mathbf{p}^*\|_2^2$$

$$-2(\mathbf{F}^{(-s)}(\mathbf{Y}_{i:n_1}) - \mathbf{p}^*, \mathbf{F}^{(-t)}(\mathbf{Y}_{j:n_1}) - \mathbf{p}^*)$$

$$= T_1^2(s,t) + T_2^2(s,t) - 2T_3(s,t)$$

We use Schwarz's inequality on $T_3(s,t)$:

$$|T_3(s,t)|^2 \leq T_1^2(s,t)\, T_2^2(s,t) \leq \|\mathbf{F}^{(-s)}(\mathbf{Y}_{i;n}) - \mathbf{p}^*\|_2^2 \, \|\mathbf{F}^{(-t)}(\mathbf{Y}_{j:n_1}) - \mathbf{p}^*\|_2^2$$

and conclude that the right-hand side above converges to zero with probability one if and only if $s = k_{0,i:n_1}$ *or* $s = k_{0,j:n_1}$. Thus with probability one,

$$\text{limit}_{n\to\infty}\, T_1^2(s,t) + T_2^2(s,t) - 2T_3(s,t) = 0$$

if and only if $s = k_{0,i:n_1}$ *and* $t = k_{0,j:n_1}$.

The matrices of true key differences and estimated key differences obtained by maximizing the cross-correlation coefficient are

$$\Delta k_{\text{est.},0} = \begin{vmatrix} 0 & 21 & 24 & 9 & 17 & 24 & 10 \\ 5 & 0 & 3 & 10 & 22 & 22 & 24 \\ 2 & 23 & 0 & 11 & 4 & 19 & 21 \\ 17 & 12 & 15 & 0 & 19 & 8 & 8 \\ 9 & 4 & 22 & 7 & 0 & 15 & 12 \\ 2 & 4 & 7 & 18 & 11 & 0 & 17 \\ 12 & 2 & 5 & 18 & 10 & 9 & 0 \end{vmatrix}$$

$$\Delta k_{\text{true}} = \begin{vmatrix} 0 & 21 & 24 & 9 & 2 & 17 & 4 \\ 5 & 0 & 3 & 14 & 7 & 22 & 9 \\ 2 & 23 & 0 & 11 & 4 & 19 & 6 \\ 17 & 12 & 15 & 0 & 19 & 8 & 21 \\ 24 & 19 & 22 & 7 & 0 & 15 & 2 \\ 9 & 4 & 7 & 18 & 11 & 0 & 13 \\ 22 & 17 & 20 & 5 & 24 & 13 & 0 \end{vmatrix}$$

Errors in $\Delta k_{\text{est.},0}$ are due in part to the flatness of the distribution of differenced letters $\{p^*(t) : 0 \leq t < m\}$, which produces a small variation in $\rho[s : \mathbf{F}(\mathbf{Y}_{i:n_1}), \mathbf{F}(\mathbf{Y}_{j:n_1})]$. We attempt to filter out the errors in $\Delta k_{\text{est.},0}$ using the following heuristic device: associate with the r-tuple

$$(i_0, i_1, \ldots, i_{r-1}) \qquad 0 \leq i_j < n_0,\ 0 \leq j < r$$

the *r-cycle* $[i_0, i_1, \ldots, i_{r-1}]$

$$i_0 \to i_1 \to \ldots i_{r-1} \to i_0$$

If $M = (m_{i,j})$ is a n_0-by-n_0 matrix and $\gamma = [i_0, i_1, \ldots, i_{r-1}]$ is a cycle, define the *cycle sum* CYCLE$[\gamma,M]$ by

$$\text{CYCLE}[\gamma, M] = m_{i_0,i_1} + m_{i_1,i_2} + \ldots + m_{i_{r-2},i_{r-1}} + m_{i_{r-1},i_0}$$

Then $\text{CYCLE}[\gamma,\Delta k_{true}] = 0$ for every cycle γ, while in general, $\text{CYCLE}[\gamma, \Delta k_{est.,0}] \neq 0$ because of errors in the matrix $\Delta k_{est.,0}$. In Table 4.14.2, we list the values of $\text{CYCLE}[\gamma, \Delta k_{est.,0}]$ for each 3-cycle, $\gamma = [i,j,k]$.

TABLE 4.14.2
$\text{CYCLE}[\gamma,\Delta k_{est.,0}]$: The Cycle Sum Values for $\Delta K_{est.,0}$

i	j	k	CYCLE[γ,Δk$_{est.,0}$]	i	j	k	CYCLE[γ,Δk$_{est.,0}$]
0	1	2	0	0	1	3	0
0	1	4	0	0	1	5	9
0	1	6	5	0	2	3	0
0	2	4	1	0	2	5	9
0	2	6	5	0	3	4	1
0	3	5	9	0	3	6	4
0	4	5	8	0	4	6	5
0	5	6	1	1	2	3	0
1	2	4	1	1	2	5	0
1	2	6	0	1	3	4	1
1	3	5	0	1	3	6	3
1	4	5	5	1	4	6	0
1	5	6	5	2	3	4	0
2	3	5	0	2	3	6	4
2	4	5	0	2	4	6	1
2	5	6	5	3	4	5	0
3	4	6	3	3	5	6	7
4	5	6	0				

Next we introduce the n_0-by-n_0 matrix $\text{COUNT}_{3,0}$, whose (i,j)-entry is equal to the number of 3-cycles γ containing (i,j), which satisfy $\text{CYCLE}[\gamma,\Delta k_{est.,0}] = 0$.

$$\text{COUNT}_{3,0} = \begin{vmatrix} 0 & 3 & 2 & 2 & 1 & 0 & 0 \\ 3 & 0 & 4 & 3 & 1 & 2 & 1 \\ 2 & 4 & 0 & 4 & 2 & 3 & 1 \\ 2 & 3 & 4 & 0 & 2 & 3 & 0 \\ 1 & 1 & 2 & 2 & 0 & 2 & 0 \\ 0 & 2 & 3 & 3 & 2 & 0 & 0 \\ 0 & 1 & 1 & 0 & 0 & 0 & 0 \end{vmatrix}$$

The relationship between $\Delta k_{est.,0}(i,j)$ and $(k_{0,j:n_1} - k_{0,i:n_1})$ is

$$\Delta k_{est.,0}(i,j) = \epsilon(i,j) + (k_{0,j:n_1} - k_{0,i:n_1})$$

where $\{\epsilon(i,j)\}$ are errors. The errors are complicated functions of the differenced ciphertext and key. A pair of integers i,j with $0 \leq i < j < 7$ appears in five 3-cycles, and hence $0 \leq COUNT_{3,0}(i,j) \leq 5$.

The 3-cycle [i,j,k] contributes to the entry $COUNT_{3,0}(i,j)$ if and only if one of the following four conditions is satisfied:

- $\epsilon(i,j) = \epsilon(j,k) = \epsilon(i,k) = 0$
- $\epsilon(i,j) = 0$ and $\epsilon(j,k) + \epsilon(i,k) = 0$ (modulo 26)
- $\epsilon(j,k) = 0$ and $\epsilon(i,j) + \epsilon(i,k) = 0$ (modulo 26)
- $\epsilon(i,k) = 0$ and $\epsilon(i,j) + \epsilon(j,k) = 0$ (modulo 26)

The heuristic assumes that $\Delta k_{est.,0}(i,j)$ with a large value of $COUNT_{3,0}(i,j)$ is likely to be correct. Thus the entries in $\Delta k_{est.,0}$

$$\Delta k_{est.,0}(1,2) \qquad \Delta k_{est.,0}(2,3)$$

$$\Delta k_{est.,0}(0,1) \qquad \Delta k_{est.,0}(1,3) \qquad \Delta k_{est.,0}(2,5) \qquad \Delta k_{est.,0}(3,5)$$

which have $COUNT_{3,0}$ values of 3 or 4 are likely to be correct.

The key differences with $COUNT_{3,0}$ values of 3 and 4 yield the relations

$$k_{0,1:n_1} = k_{0,0:n_1} + 21$$

$$k_{0,2:n_1} = k_{0,0:n_1} + 24$$

$$k_{0,3:n_1} = k_{0,0:n_1} + 9$$

$$k_{0,5:n_1} = k_{0,0:n_1} + 17$$

An error in $\Delta k_{est.,0}(i,j)$ results from using a value s(i,j), which, while maximizing $\rho[s : \mathbf{F}(\mathbf{Y}_{i:n_1}), \mathbf{F}(\mathbf{Y}_{j:n_1})]$, differs from the true value $k_{0,j:n_1} - k_{0,j:n_1}$. This suggests that we examine values of s which produce the second largest value of $\rho_{i,j}[s : \mathbf{F}(\mathbf{Y}_{i:n_1}), \mathbf{F}(\mathbf{Y}_{j:n_1})]$.

SECOND =

14	7	12	16	2	17	19
19	7	5	16	7	3	18
14	21	21	23	24	5	8
10	10	3	6	2	17	4
24	19	2	24	6	7	2
9	23	21	9	19	9	15
7	8	18	22	24	11	6

We test *perturbations* in $\Delta k_{est.,0}$, replacing the current (i,j) entry by the corresponding entry in SECOND. A perturbation is accepted if the new 3-cycles obtained with $COUNT_{3,1}$ values of 3 and 4 are consistent with the previously established relationships. We begin with the perturbation of the index (i,j) = (0,4) entry, obtaining $\Delta k_{est.,1}$ and $COUNT_{3,1}$.

Perturbation (0,4)

$$\Delta k_{est.,1} = \begin{vmatrix} 0 & 21 & 24 & 9 & 2 & 24 & 14 \\ 5 & 0 & 3 & 14 & 22 & 22 & 24 \\ 2 & 23 & 0 & 11 & 4 & 19 & 21 \\ 17 & 12 & 15 & 0 & 19 & 8 & 8 \\ 24 & 4 & 22 & 7 & 0 & 15 & 12 \\ 2 & 4 & 7 & 18 & 11 & 0 & 17 \\ 12 & 2 & 5 & 18 & 14 & 9 & 0 \end{vmatrix}$$

$$COUNT_{3,1} = \begin{vmatrix} 0 & 2 & 3 & 3 & 3 & 0 & 1 \\ 2 & 0 & 4 & 3 & 0 & 2 & 1 \\ 3 & 4 & 0 & 4 & 3 & 3 & 1 \\ 3 & 3 & 4 & 0 & 3 & 3 & 0 \\ 3 & 0 & 3 & 3 & 0 & 2 & 1 \\ 0 & 2 & 3 & 3 & 2 & 0 & 0 \\ 1 & 1 & 1 & 0 & 1 & 0 & 0 \end{vmatrix}$$

The 3-cycles with $COUNT_{3,1}$ values of 3 and 4 yield the previous three relationships

(4.14.1) $$k_{0,1:n_1} = k_{0,0:n_1} + 21$$

(4.14.2) $$k_{0,2:n_1} = k_{0,0:n_1} + 24$$

(4.14.3) $$k_{0,3:n_1} = k_{0,0:n_1} + 9$$

and two new relationships

(4.14.4) $$k_{0,4:n_1} = k_{0,0:n_1} + 2$$

(4.14.5) $$k_{0,5:n_1} = k_{0,0:n_1} + 17$$

Not all perturbations will yield improvements; for example, the perturbation (2,4) provides fewer relationships than before and is therefore discarded.

The vanishing of the cycle sum CYCLE[[j,0,i],Δk_{true}]

$$(k_{0,j:n_1} - k_{0,i:n_1}) = (k_{0,j:n_1} - k_{0,0:n_1}) + (k_{0,0:n_1} - k_{0,i:n_1})$$

and Eqs. (4.14.1–5) imply that certain of the entries in $\Delta k_{est.,1}$ are incorrect; for example, the entries

$$\Delta k_{est.,2} = \begin{vmatrix} 0 & 21 & 24 & 9 & 17 & 24 & 14 \\ 5 & 0 & 3 & 14 & 22 & 22 & 24 \\ 2 & 23 & 0 & 11 & 24 & 19 & 21 \\ 17 & 12 & 15 & 0 & 19 & 8 & 8 \\ 9 & 4 & 2 & 7 & 0 & 15 & 12 \\ 2 & 4 & 7 & 18 & 11 & 0 & 17 \\ 12 & 2 & 5 & 18 & 14 & 9 & 0 \end{vmatrix}$$

$$\mathrm{COUNT}_{3,2} = \begin{vmatrix} 0 & 3 & 2 & 2 & 1 & 0 & 0 \\ 3 & 0 & 4 & 3 & 1 & 2 & 1 \\ 2 & 4 & 0 & 3 & 0 & 2 & 1 \\ 2 & 3 & 3 & 0 & 1 & 3 & 0 \\ 1 & 1 & 0 & 1 & 0 & 1 & 0 \\ 0 & 2 & 2 & 3 & 1 & 0 & 0 \\ 0 & 1 & 1 & 0 & 0 & 0 & 0 \end{vmatrix}$$

$$\Delta k_{est.,1}(4,1) = 4 \qquad \Delta k_{est.,1}(1,4) = 22$$

$$\Delta k_{est.,1}(0,5) = 24 \qquad \Delta k_{est.,1}(5,0) = 2$$

are inconsistent with Eqs. (4.14.1–5) and should be replaced by

$$\Delta k_{est.,1}(4,1) = 19 \qquad \Delta k_{est.,1}(1,4) = 7$$

$$\Delta k_{est.,1}(0,5) = 17 \qquad \Delta k_{est.,1}(5,0) = 9$$

It remains to obtain information on the key differences involving $k_{0,6:n_1}$. Perturbations involving this key do not yield cycles involving the entry 6 with count of 3 or more. However, the vanishing of the cycle sum CYCLE[[6,0,i],Δk_{true}]

$$(k_{0,6:n_1} - k_{0,i:n_1}) = (k_{0,6:n_1} - k_{0,0:n_1}) + (k_{0,0:n_1} - k_{0,i:n_1})$$

means that if we fix a value for $k_{0,6:n_1} - k_{0,0:n_1}$, then the values of $\{k_{0,6:n_1} - k_{0,i:n_1}: 0 < i < 6\}$ are determined. In Table 4.14.3, we give the differences (modulo 26) of the probable values from Table 4.13.3 of the key differences $\{k_{0,i:n_1} : 0 \leq i < 7\}$

$$\mathrm{PROBABLE}_{0,j:n_1} - \mathrm{PROBABLE}_{0,i:n_1}$$

for each pair of sets of probable values

$$\mathrm{PROBABLE}_{0,i:n_1} \quad \mathrm{PROBABLE}_{0,j:n_1} \quad 0 \leq i,j < 7,\ i \neq j$$

indicating in boldface the differences that are consistent with Eqs. (4.13.9–14).

The location of an entry consistent with Eqs. (4.14.1–5) in Table 4.14.3 pro-

TABLE 4.14.3
Differences of the Probable Key Differences

i = 0 j = 1

True Key Difference : 21

6	19	**21**	20	7
21	8	10	9	22
25	12	14	13	0
10	23	25	24	11
0	13	15	14	1

i = 0 j = 2

True Key Difference : 24

11	**24**	0	25	12
24	11	13	12	25
12	25	1	0	13
23	10	12	11	24
18	5	7	6	19

i = 0 j = 3

True Key Difference : 9

20	7	**9**	8	21
9	22	24	23	10
22	**9**	11	10	23
16	3	5	4	17
10	23	25	24	11

i = 0 j = 4

True Key Difference : 2

2	15	17	16	3
3	16	18	17	4
16	3	5	4	17
17	4	6	5	18
24	11	13	12	25

i = 0 j = 5

True Key Difference : 17

2	15	**17**	16	3
4	**17**	19	18	5
11	24	0	25	12
23	10	12	11	24
17	4	6	5	18

i = 0 j = 6

True Key Difference : 4

4	17	19	18	5
14	1	3	2	15
19	6	8	7	20
8	21	23	22	9
17	4	6	5	18

i = 1 j = 2

True Key Difference : 3

5	16	12	1	11
18	**3**	25	14	24
6	17	13	2	12
17	2	24	13	23
12	23	19	8	18

i = 1 j = 3

True Key Difference : 14

14	25	21	10	20
3	**14**	10	25	9
16	1	23	12	22
10	21	17	6	16
4	15	11	0	10

i = 1 j = 4

True Key Difference : 7

22	**7**	3	18	2
23	8	4	19	3
10	21	17	6	16
11	22	18	7	17
18	3	25	14	24

i = 1 j = 5

True Key Difference : 22

22	7	3	18	2
24	9	5	20	4
5	16	12	1	11
17	2	24	13	23
11	**22**	18	7	17

i = 1 j = 6

True Key Difference : 9

24	**9**	5	20	4
8	19	15	4	14
13	24	20	**9**	19
2	13	9	24	8
11	22	18	7	17

i = 2 j = 3

True Key Difference : 11

9	22	8	23	2
24	**11**	23	12	17
11	24	10	25	4
5	18	4	19	24
25	12	24	13	18

i = 2 j = 4

True Key Difference : 4

17	**4**	16	5	10
18	5	17	6	11
5	18	**4**	19	24
6	19	5	20	25
13	0	12	1	6

i = 2 j = 5

True Key Difference : 19

17	4	16	5	10
19	6	18	7	12
0	13	25	14	**19**
12	25	11	0	5
6	**19**	5	20	25

i = 2 j = 6

True Key Difference : 6

19	**6**	18	7	12
3	16	2	17	22
8	21	7	22	1
23	10	22	11	16
6	19	5	20	25

TABLE 4.14.3 (*Continued*)

i = 3 j = 4

True Key Difference : 19

8	**19**	6	12	18
9	20	7	13	**19**
22	7	20	0	6
23	8	21	1	7
4	15	2	8	14

i = 3 j = 5

True Key Difference : 8

8	19	6	12	18
10	21	**8**	14	20
17	2	15	21	1
3	14	1	7	13
23	**8**	21	1	7

i = 3 j = 6

True Key Difference : 21

10	**21**	8	14	20
20	5	18	24	4
25	10	23	3	9
14	25	12	18	24
23	8	**21**	1	7

i = 4 j = 5

True Key Difference : 15

0	25	12	11	4
2	1	14	13	6
9	8	21	20	13
21	20	7	6	25
15	14	1	0	19

i = 4 j = 6

True Key Difference : 2

2	1	14	13	6
12	11	24	23	16
17	16	3	**2**	21
6	5	18	17	10
15	14	1	0	19

i = 5 j = 6

True Key Difference : 13

2	0	19	7	**13**
12	10	3	17	23
17	15	8	22	2
6	4	23	11	17
15	**13**	6	20	0

vides a clue. For example, when $i = 0$ and $j = 1$, the location of the key difference 21, which is consistent with the relationship

$$k_{0,1:n_1} = k_{0,0:n_1} + 21$$

means that the probable values from Table 4.14.3 for the pair $(k_{0,0:n_1}, k_{0,1:n_1})$ are (0,21) and (15,10). If $i = 0$ and $j = 2$, the location of the key difference 24 in Table 4.14.3, which is consistent with the relationship

$$k_{0,2:n_1} = k_{0,0:n_1} + 24$$

means that the probable values from Table 4.14.3 for the pair $(k_{0,0:n_1}, k_{0,2:n_1})$ are (15,13). Together, these two results suggest that $k_{0,0:n_1}$ is equal to 15. Other consistency checks support the relationships of Eqs. (4.14.1–5).

Still the value for $k_{0,6:n_1}$ alludes us. Note that when we began the cryptanalysis, we were faced with finding two keys of lengths 7 and 5; key search in a key space of size $26^{12} \approx 10^{17}$. We have reduced the search by cryptanalysis to an examination of five possible values for one of the key differences, a reduction by a factor of nearly 2×10^{16}. We will end the cryptanalysis here, leaving the remaining details to the reader.

Having recovered one of the user keys (up to an additive constant), the first encipherment can be peeled off,

$$VIG^{-1}_{k_0+C}[VIG_{k_0}[VIG_{k_1}[PLAIN]]] = VIG_{k_1-C}[PLAIN]$$

and the methods described in Sec. 4.3 for the analysis of a (single-loop) Vigenère cipher can be used.

The cryptanalysis of an s-loop Vigenère with *known* periods uses the same differencing technique. Cryptanalysis becomes harder as s increases; we require a larger sample of ciphertext since the probability distribution $\{p^{(s)*}(t) : 0 \leq t < m\}$ of *s-differenced* plaintext flattens out as s increases.

4.15 THE CRYPTANALYSIS OF MULTILOOP VIGENÈRE WITH UNKNOWN PERIODS

Finally, we address the question of recovery of plaintext from ciphertext when the periods are *unknown* for 2-loop Vigenère substitution. We illustrate only one technique for approaching this problem. We assume that the set of values allowable for the periods is known; n_0 and n_1 are allowed to take values in some set *PERIODS* of size P. We can test all P^2 possible values of (n_0, n_1) but will instead use the ϕ-test as follows: for each pair (n_0, n_1) with $n_0, n_1 \in$ *PERIODS*

- Difference the ciphertext:

$$\Delta CIPHER = \Delta_{n_1}[CIPHER]$$

- Compute the vector of ϕ-values by dividing $\Delta CIPHER$ into n_0 ciphersubtexts

$$\mathbf{y} = (\mathbf{y}_0, \mathbf{y}_1, \ldots, \mathbf{y}_{n_0-1}) \qquad L_i : \text{length of } \mathbf{y}_i$$

$$(\phi_0, \phi_1, \ldots, \phi_{n_0-1})$$

- Calculate

$$\psi[n_0,n_1] = \max_{0\leq i<n_0} \phi_i/L_i(L_i - 1)$$

  and enter into the P by P table *PHI*[*PERIODS*].

What do we expect to see in the array *PHI*[*PERIODS*]? If $n_{true,0}$ and $n_{true,1}$ are the correct periods, the vector

$$(\phi_0, \phi_1, \ldots, \phi_{n_0-1})$$

will consist of the ϕ-values of monalphabetically enciphered ciphertext with plaintext letter distribution $\{p^*(t) : 0 \leq t < m\}$ whenever

- $(n_0,n_1) = (in_{true,0},jn_{true,1})$ or
- $(n_0,n_1) = (in_{true,1},jn_{true,0})$

for any $i,j \geq 1$, and hence $\psi[n_{true,0},n_{true,1}]$ should be relatively large.

If $n_1 \neq n_{true,1}$, then $\Delta_{n_1}[CIPHER]$ is not enciphered by a 1-loop Vigenère substitution, and we expect $\psi[n_0,n_1]$ to be small for all choices of n_0. If $n_1 = n_{true,1}$ but $n_0 \neq n_{true,0}$, then $\Delta_{n_1}[CIPHER]$ is enciphered by a 1-loop Vigenère substitution, but the subtexts $\{\mathbf{y}_i\}$ are not monalphabetically enciphered, so that we also expect $\psi[n_0,n_1]$ to be small.

Note that n_0 and n_1 are not in a symmetric relationship in *PHI*[*PERIODS*] and that the margin is slim for distinguishing between monalphabetic and polyalphabetic encipherment, since

$$\sum_{0 \leq t < 26} (p^*(t))^2$$

is close to1/26 for the differenced ciphertext. In Table 4.15.1 we give the results of this experiment for the ciphertext *CIPHER(1.4)* using *PERIODS* = {4,5, . . . , 15}. We search in the array *PHI*[*PERIODS*] for pairs (i,j) that

- are local maxima

  $$\psi[i,j] > \max\{\psi[i,j+1], \psi[i,j-1], \psi[i+1,j], \psi[i-1,j]\}$$

- and for which the same condition holds when (i,j) is replaced by (ai,bj), with a and b positive integers.

We see that (7,5) meets these conditions; it is then tested by trial decipherment.

TABLE 4.15.1
The Array *PHI*[*PERIODS*]

	4	**5**	**6**	**7**	**8**	**9**	**10**	**11**	**12**	**13**	**14**	**15**
4	0.0385	0.0395	0.0387	0.0394	0.0392	0.0385	0.0398	0.0386	0.0393	0.0401	0.0390	0.0386
5	0.0396	0.0391	0.0397	0.0413	0.0382	0.0390	0.0398	0.0388	0.0400	0.0393	0.0404	0.0401
6	0.0406	0.0403	0.0393	0.0429	0.0389	0.0403	0.0390	0.0402	0.0404	0.0405	0.0407	0.0401
7	0.0400	**0.0447**	0.0413	0.0422	0.0405	0.0407	**0.0439**	0.0400	0.0413	0.0416	0.0412	**0.0412**
8	0.0403	0.0414	0.0395	0.0395	0.0399	0.0388	0.0425	0.0400	0.0409	0.0405	0.0405	0.0408
9	0.0402	0.0421	0.0403	0.0438	0.0436	0.0412	0.0411	0.0432	0.0415	0.0428	0.0421	0.0413
10	0.0419	0.0441	0.0418	0.0414	0.0395	0.0396	0.0407	0.0404	0.0427	0.0424	0.0415	0.0418
11	0.0450	0.0404	0.0400	0.0411	0.0403	0.0401	0.0405	0.0406	0.0420	0.0446	0.0419	0.0428
12	0.0427	0.0404	0.0410	0.0439	0.0425	0.0419	0.0412	0.0407	0.0419	0.0435	0.0448	0.0419
13	0.0414	0.0437	0.0453	0.0431	0.0437	0.0417	0.0420	0.0422	0.0432	0.0422	0.0456	0.0415
14	0.0419	**0.0464**	0.0447	0.0457	0.0440	0.0446	**0.0474**	0.0430	0.0456	0.0459	0.0430	**0.0477**
15	0.0413	0.0414	0.0429	0.0439	0.0410	0.0419	0.0455	0.0450	0.0432	0.0419	0.0442	0.0439

4.16 CODA

Several generalizations of the function $\phi(\mathbf{y})$,

$$\phi(y) = \sum_{0 \leq t < m} N_t(\mathbf{y})(N_t(\mathbf{y}) - 1)$$

are worth noting. Observe that $\phi(\mathbf{y})$ is the difference of two terms

$$\sum_{0 \leq t < m} N_t^2(\mathbf{y}) - \sum_{0 \leq t < m} N_t(\mathbf{y})$$

The second term is equal to the number of letters in the ciphertext and hence is the same for both monalphabetic and polyalphabetic substitution. Thus we are really using

$$\sum_{0 \leq t < m} N_t^2(\mathbf{y})$$

to distinguish between the two hypotheses, monalphabetic or polyalphabetic encipherment. This suggests that we introduce the functions

$$\lambda_k(\mathbf{y}) = \left(\sum_{0 \leq t < m} N_t^k(\mathbf{y}) \right)^{1/k} \qquad 1 \leq k \leq \infty$$

where $k = \infty$ is to be interpreted as the limiting value

$$\lambda_\infty(\mathbf{y}) = \text{limit}_{\lambda \to \infty} \lambda_k(\mathbf{y}) = \max_t N_t(\mathbf{y})$$

We leave to the reader the challenge of exploring this direction.

PROBLEMS

4.1 Let ciphertext

$$\pi_i : \mathbf{x}_i = (x_{i,0}, x_{i,1}, \ldots, x_{i,n_i-1}) \to \mathbf{y}_i = (y_{i,0}, y_{i,1}, \ldots, y_{i,n_i-1})$$

result from monalphabetic substitutions π_i $(i = 0,1)$. Invent the *chi test* χ to decide if the monalphabetic substitutions are the same or different by considering the effect of independently chosen monalphabetic substitutions $\{\Pi_i\}$ on plaintext

$$(X_{i,0}, X_{i,1}, \ldots, X_{i,n_i-1})$$

consisting of independent and identically distributed random variables.

4.2 What modifications are necessary in Eqs. (4.9.4) and (4.9.5) if the plaintext is generated by independent and identical trials which output 2-grams?

4.3 What modifications are necessary in Eqs. (4.9.4) and (4.9.5) if the plaintext is generated by a Markov chain which outputs 1-grams?

4.4 Ciphertext *CIPHER(P4.1–4)*,

$$\textit{CIPHER(P4.j)} : \mathbf{y}_j = (y_{0,j}, y_{1,j}, \ldots, y_{n-1,j}) \qquad 1 \leq j \leq 4$$

each result from a Vigenère substitution. The length of the the ciphertext is 1209. Divide $\mathbf{y}_j$ into i ciphersubtexts,

$$\mathbf{y}_{j,s|i} \qquad 0 \leq s < i$$

In Tables P4.1–4 we list the number of occurrences $N_t(\mathbf{y}_{j,0|i})$ of the letter t in the 0th ciphersubtext of $\mathbf{y}_j$ (when it is divided into i ciphersubtexts). Estimate the period for each of the ciphertexts $\{\mathbf{y}_j\}$.

4.5 Ciphertext *CIPHER(P4.5–9)*,

$$\textit{CIPHER(P4.j)} : \mathbf{y}_j = (y_{0,j}, y_{1,j}, \ldots, y_{n-1,j}) \qquad 5 \leq j \leq 9$$

Table P4.1

$N_t(\mathbf{y}_{1,0|i})$

$j = 1$

i	A	B	C	D	E	F	G	H	I	J	K	L	M	N	O	P	Q	R	S	T	U	V	W	X	Y	Z
1	30	45	37	31	60	52	43	65	77	22	40	39	77	32	10	40	35	38	25	68	48	62	45	98	47	43
2	16	23	24	11	25	27	25	30	40	12	16	19	31	19	7	20	16	22	14	36	24	31	22	49	25	21
3	8	12	8	8	19	20	17	16	24	13	10	10	22	15	4	16	12	11	10	24	17	23	19	40	15	10
4	9	10	11	6	15	10	11	14	20	5	10	6	17	9	4	8	6	14	5	20	11	14	14	28	16	10
5	8	13	3	7	10	8	9	17	21	7	5	5	16	7	1	11	9	5	3	12	9	14	9	13	9	11
6	1	7	5	3	5	12	11	5	12	5	4	6	7	11	2	9	4	5	5	14	12	13	8	19	10	7
7	2	11	1	0	8	8	10	16	5	0	9	11	19	2	3	3	1	4	0	13	1	5	8	23	6	4
8	6	1	6	4	4	6	4	3	11	2	7	4	12	5	2	2	3	5	3	10	6	9	8	17	7	5
9	2	6	3	3	8	6	3	6	10	5	3	4	8	4	1	5	3	2	4	6	5	8	9	12	5	4
10	2	9	2	2	4	3	5	8	10	2	2	2	5	4	1	6	4	1	2	8	6	9	6	7	6	5
11	2	3	1	3	8	9	4	3	4	4	4	6	8	2	2	6	4	6	3	6	3	2	5	6	2	4
12	1	3	3	0	4	5	7	3	5	2	2	1	4	4	1	5	2	2	2	8	4	8	6	10	8	1
13	3	2	1	1	6	3	3	4	8	2	4	2	7	4	2	2	3	2	1	8	2	5	1	8	3	6
14	0	9	0	0	3	2	4	6	4	0	6	6	6	2	1	3	1	3	0	7	0	1	5	15	2	1
15	4	3	1	1	3	2	3	8	4	5	1	1	4	3	0	4	3	2	1	3	6	7	2	4	2	4
16	4	1	3	1	1	2	1	2	5	1	4	3	7	2	1	0	2	4	2	3	2	5	7	8	2	3
17	2	4	1	2	1	5	2	2	5	1	6	1	5	4	0	4	1	4	0	3	3	0	3	8	2	3
18	0	3	2	1	2	3	2	2	6	2	1	2	3	3	1	2	1	0	0	3	4	6	5	7	4	3
19	1	2	0	1	0	0	1	5	1	2	0	0	6	3	0	2	1	2	1	4	6	4	3	11	7	1
20	2	5	1	2	3	2	3	4	6	1	1	0	4	2	0	1	1	1	0	3	1	4	4	5	4	1

Table P4.2

$N_t(\mathbf{y}_{2,0|i})$

$j = 2$

i	A	B	C	D	E	F	G	H	I	J	K	L	M	N	O	P	Q	R	S	T	U	V	W	X	Y	Z
1	38	47	51	9	62	69	100	55	54	23	65	29	36	24	28	36	36	74	52	31	34	80	53	43	36	44
2	7	3	27	5	45	23	52	13	47	20	50	10	12	8	9	23	18	28	24	11	21	65	28	18	13	25
3	15	19	21	2	13	23	65	7	6	4	24	1	0	20	9	17	24	41	7	8	18	25	10	2	14	8
4	5	1	5	2	26	13	30	5	21	11	19	6	6	6	5	16	6	14	11	4	12	39	11	14	5	10
5	8	13	16	3	9	16	17	11	16	2	12	7	11	4	2	4	7	12	12	5	9	15	9	7	7	8
6	2	0	16	2	7	8	43	7	3	2	23	0	0	6	7	11	14	7	0	5	10	16	10	1	2	0
7	8	7	11	0	5	6	12	7	9	5	9	3	8	5	4	4	9	9	5	6	7	8	6	4	5	11
8	1	0	5	0	11	7	20	2	12	5	10	5	5	2	2	8	2	4	4	0	4	25	6	8	1	3
9	4	8	4	0	7	7	23	1	3	2	6	0	0	6	4	6	7	11	3	2	10	6	4	1	7	3
10	1	1	8	2	7	5	7	1	15	2	9	3	4	1	1	1	4	4	4	2	5	14	7	4	4	5
11	4	4	7	1	3	4	9	6	2	0	3	6	6	5	2	6	1	5	7	5	3	5	8	4	1	3
12	2	0	2	0	7	3	26	1	1	2	10	0	0	5	4	8	5	3	0	1	6	10	4	0	1	0
13	3	5	5	1	5	2	4	3	2	1	8	2	6	0	2	3	2	5	6	4	3	8	5	4	3	1
14	3	1	4	0	5	3	6	1	8	5	6	0	2	2	1	4	4	4	2	4	3	8	4	2	0	5
15	2	8	7	0	3	6	10	1	1	0	7	1	0	4	1	3	5	7	2	1	4	3	4	0	0	1
16	0	0	0	0	7	5	9	0	4	4	3	0	4	0	1	6	2	2	0	0	4	14	4	5	0	2
17	0	2	1	0	2	4	2	3	7	2	8	3	4	2	1	2	2	3	0	2	4	5	3	2	6	2
18	1	0	3	0	4	3	16	1	1	1	6	0	0	1	3	4	4	3	0	2	6	2	4	1	2	0
19	2	0	2	0	4	7	5	5	3	1	2	0	3	0	2	2	2	4	3	2	1	8	4	0	1	1
20	1	1	1	1	5	1	6	0	8	2	6	0	1	1	0	1	2	2	2	0	3	7	2	3	2	3

Table P4.3

$N_t(\mathbf{y}_{3,0|i})$

j = 3

i	A	B	C	D	E	F	G	H	I	J	K	L	M	N	O	P	Q	R	S	T	U	V	W	X	Y	Z
1	46	50	43	32	52	80	53	60	37	39	33	19	45	28	42	39	49	57	76	50	30	58	42	72	22	55
2	19	38	22	9	20	39	42	28	11	21	11	9	27	22	29	18	17	26	35	32	12	29	18	43	12	16
3	14	14	18	9	10	23	16	19	17	12	6	5	16	13	16	10	20	22	24	21	10	22	17	29	5	15
4	4	19	1	8	13	24	14	12	4	14	10	8	26	9	12	15	6	2	6	18	10	7	7	42	5	7
5	6	7	9	9	13	18	4	13	6	10	7	5	4	9	11	7	9	9	15	12	6	14	7	18	4	10
6	4	8	9	6	3	14	14	6	5	8	0	2	10	12	9	4	7	9	10	13	4	13	7	20	1	4
7	7	7	11	2	5	12	11	5	5	7	4	2	5	3	8	4	6	10	10	7	2	8	6	16	1	9
8	4	10	0	0	6	2	11	11	0	0	10	8	19	4	1	1	0	2	0	9	0	3	6	38	3	4
9	8	3	6	5	3	8	3	6	6	4	0	2	5	3	3	2	7	6	6	10	3	7	5	14	2	8
10	0	6	4	1	5	9	3	6	3	6	4	2	3	7	8	4	3	4	5	7	3	7	4	10	2	5
11	5	4	6	1	4	6	3	8	4	6	4	3	5	3	7	0	6	5	5	5	2	4	1	6	3	4
12	1	3	0	5	3	9	6	2	1	7	0	2	10	3	3	3	3	0	1	6	3	5	2	20	0	3
13	4	5	3	1	2	5	3	8	2	4	4	1	5	3	2	1	5	2	5	5	4	4	1	7	2	5
14	2	4	6	1	4	4	9	2	1	4	2	1	4	2	5	2	1	4	7	2	0	4	4	9	0	3
15	2	2	4	2	2	3	1	4	2	4	1	0	3	4	4	2	5	3	5	5	1	5	5	6	2	4
16	1	7	0	0	2	1	7	6	0	0	6	6	8	0	1	0	0	1	0	3	0	3	3	16	3	2
17	4	2	3	2	5	2	4	2	2	2	3	0	5	3	0	1	4	5	4	0	3	6	4	4	1	1
18	2	3	3	4	1	4	3	1	3	4	0	0	1	2	1	0	3	3	3	6	1	5	1	11	1	2
19	2	3	2	1	4	7	1	3	1	1	2	0	3	0	1	3	4	3	4	4	1	2	3	4	2	3
20	0	5	0	1	1	5	1	2	1	5	4	2	3	4	1	3	0	0	0	5	3	1	1	10	1	2

Table P4.4

$N_t(\mathbf{y}_{4,0|i})$

j = 4

i	A	B	C	D	E	F	G	H	I	J	K	L	M	N	O	P	Q	R	S	T	U	V	W	X	Y	Z
1	51	38	34	17	52	65	71	36	46	52	65	51	27	43	24	36	29	77	46	43	46	94	47	22	41	56
2	14	5	16	5	24	31	28	16	37	38	45	29	19	25	8	23	12	30	17	23	21	48	27	22	20	22
3	10	15	13	7	11	27	28	14	15	20	27	20	5	14	10	13	8	24	17	14	10	31	7	6	11	26
4	7	3	8	3	14	12	16	7	17	22	20	18	10	12	6	7	8	14	11	10	12	25	10	10	12	9
5	17	1	1	3	2	15	2	9	6	25	6	19	8	16	3	3	4	4	5	16	12	18	14	6	12	15
6	3	2	4	4	7	13	14	8	14	14	19	12	3	9	3	8	3	7	6	7	4	11	5	6	4	12
7	12	8	5	2	8	12	14	6	7	4	9	4	3	8	1	4	5	9	6	8	6	11	6	2	6	7
8	3	1	3	1	9	5	7	4	13	13	12	11	4	6	3	2	3	3	5	2	5	17	5	7	4	4
9	2	6	5	1	3	10	8	6	5	6	7	7	1	3	5	4	1	6	3	5	5	16	4	2	5	9
10	1	1	1	0	0	14	2	2	5	23	2	3	3	15	0	0	3	4	2	8	1	0	11	6	6	8
11	4	5	2	2	4	9	11	3	7	3	5	4	2	3	0	4	5	5	2	4	4	7	3	1	5	6
12	2	1	1	2	4	4	9	2	5	10	9	8	1	5	3	2	2	3	4	4	3	4	2	3	2	6
13	3	2	2	3	7	5	8	0	2	2	3	6	2	7	2	4	2	4	4	3	4	4	4	3	3	4
14	3	2	4	1	3	6	8	0	6	3	7	3	1	4	0	3	2	3	2	4	4	6	4	2	3	3
15	3	0	0	0	0	7	0	5	2	9	3	8	2	7	2	1	1	1	1	4	2	8	2	2	3	8
16	2	0	1	0	6	2	3	2	8	7	5	5	4	1	1	2	1	1	2	1	3	8	3	4	2	2
17	3	1	0	4	2	1	4	2	2	1	7	3	3	4	3	2	2	5	1	2	4	5	3	0	6	2
18	1	1	2	0	2	4	4	4	4	4	4	5	1	2	1	3	0	4	1	2	2	7	2	2	2	4
19	3	1	0	0	4	1	5	4	1	2	5	2	1	4	0	2	3	4	0	4	1	6	2	2	2	5
20	0	1	1	0	0	5	0	2	2	14	0	3	1	8	0	0	1	2	2	4	0	0	4	4	5	2

are the result of a Vigenère substitution with unknown period. The text each are of length 2338. In Table P4.5, we list the the number of coincidences

$$\kappa[\mathbf{y}_j, \mathbf{y}_j^{(-s)}]$$

in $\mathbf{y}_j$ and the shifted ciphertext $\mathbf{y}_j^{(-s)}$.

TABLE P4.5
Number of Coincidences in *CIPHER(P4.5-9)*

s	$\mathbf{y}_5$	$\mathbf{y}_6$	$\mathbf{y}_7$	$\mathbf{y}_8$	$\mathbf{y}_9$
1	97	74	120	115	52
2	98	95	69	83	132
3	94	97	107	87	105
4	106	152	108	85	114
5	93	83	87	90	145
6	78	108	137	88	107
7	80	89	78	86	110
8	100	134	88	91	108
9	78	93	96	96	114
10	150	115	76	150	150
11	92	88	89	94	110
12	96	145	144	74	105
13	114	91	77	90	119
14	86	111	109	86	111
15	102	82	100	87	146
16	78	186	108	75	125
17	94	115	85	82	95
18	87	97	160	77	113
19	91	109	91	100	118
20	152	150	89	151	152
21	81	93	78	87	120
22	98	98	94	98	107
23	75	93	86	96	99
24	92	146	144	76	107
25	112	78	102	108	168

4.6 Let $(X_0, X_1, \ldots, X_{n-1})$ be enciphered by a Vigenère substitution with period r,

$$\mathrm{VIG}_k : (X_0, X_1, \ldots, X_{n-1}) \to (Y_0, Y_1, \ldots, Y_{n-1})$$

$$\mathbf{Y}_j = (Y_j, Y_{j+r}, Y_{j+2r}, \ldots) \quad 0 \le j < r$$

and $N_t(\mathbf{Y})$ be the number of times the letter t appears in $\mathbf{Y}_j$. What is the expectation and variance of the correlation

$$\rho_{i,j}[s] = \sum_{0 \le t < m} N_{t,i}(\mathbf{Y}) N_{i+s,j}(\mathbf{Y})$$

4.7 Find the numerical value for the expectation of $\rho_{i,j}[s]$ when $m = 26$ and the 1-gram probabilities are from Table 2.3.1.

4.8 Find the numerical value of the expectation of $\rho_{i,j}[s]$ when $m = 26$ and the 1-gram probabilities are from Table 4.11.1.

4.9 *CIPHER(P4.10)* is a 2-loop Vigenère encipherment of *PLAIN(P4.10)*; see Fig. P4.6. We assume that ***PERIODS*** $= \{2,3, \ldots, 21\}$; the array

```
vdjmi sddlw hzjeg mghqe owsal nubdi modne jnukz whfrp xmjko xrvxj bduci
gytqa bzovh uhzhe kdorn texmu fhuzh gidmx ihaug ginla qdgas xyogv zthqe
gpmcl goffg qnani awkhg kjlro ndwsz gvohf vetqp gzzpl oqpeh tzmdr tddlr
epymh wzckh dvxsc mkgnn tatdp vopjh mixdk ptugr zljlz nrewd qiyne bwgfr
injcv ozckh dvxsz wcqtq gpfgs xeuzs yjydc ewkeu cbkcj crngr qgkqv xptcg
kksrp vdtaa ggvsz wcvkz gwsbz cnssu qyzlr vskhn okics lnolo uinlf ztfgg
ceqqv osiwc nezbk bwkue gozja bhosz mmbdi vjodr tkkce cdolc dhjqv ltuee
klygv wrush qhzmk apnce iawlb vafjc rdiol bscvn chfpn nqoma nzmnw bgcpf
kpnmu chnwq mgxtc iikqa uptzl nwfus gozcj xakvg kjlsw xetaa ggvsz wcgxr
ppxqp vtmsh ujinm mgjgn fwsbl gsffg ujido btpuv qjtda qdngr qgghe oetqp
goxzb cdwwb uardk znvqf jkwrl wsiwa ayzkc qciru cojzf mdwwz akdmx udfgy
nesea xnmko erzcz lijgb vdjpw xholg mmzkv nicpq yafpl onsus pojez vscpn
eyjna jamwq ahkqz uxugo gpbcl wcflo ugjed wsgnq grjjv ylffh miyrz ujncg
kksrp vdbfr fczpl iakvl qbyfl jmtos dnrdn icvvb iaydy xltaa ggvsz wctgf
whyqu nufjh tzgdj asgvn khjbt xcfdg mmznw btpfr uewck nuffw rxjlg ttzul
upjkz xedga bpodi vtvyb tgxyy nhons eodfr btfub vatpf jmees dozmg zdrqf
gzyfl bhnmz modne wucob faqup cguoc pdaev ztpvy grjjz xeewh mdghe bttgf
vesej xlqgb qiorw wgoka upflj nsiwp aookv vtemf qbyfl bxtls yhvxs mggre
gojla ncjfj qmtez vtfgg ceqfv fdwwf pzozz thvjr pwwgz nzulv qdisv zucer
qbyuv mhgxs dzisc gsgvn khjbt xcfdg uahnu makpf vnzaa rnoko dzjeu quhge
gjybl czjd
```

Figure P4.6. *CIPHER(P4.10)* : 2-Loop Vigenère encipherment of *PLAIN(P4.10)*.

PHI[*PERIODS*] is shown in Table P4.7. What periods are consistent with *PHI*[*PERIODS*]?

4.10 Let $\mathbf{X} = (X_0, X_1, \ldots, X_{n-1})$ be enciphered by a 2-loop Vigenère with keys of lengths n_0 and n_1 with $n_0 > n_1$ and $\gcd\{n_0, n_1\} = 1$:

$$\mathbf{X} = (X_0, X_1, \ldots, X_{n-1}) \rightarrow \mathbf{Y} = (Y_0, Y_1, \ldots, Y_{n-1})$$

$$= \mathrm{VIG}_{\mathbf{K}_0}[\mathrm{VIG}_{\mathbf{K}_1}[(X_0, X_1, \ldots, X_{n-1})]]$$

Are the random variables in $\Delta_{n_1}\mathbf{X}$ independent? Are the random variables in $\Delta_{n_0}\mathbf{X}$ independent?

4.11 If user keys $\mathbf{k}_0, \mathbf{k}_1, \ldots, \mathbf{k}_{s-1}$ in the s-loop Vigenère system have lengths

$$n_0, n_1, \ldots, n_{s-1}$$

what is the length of the composite key? When is the composite key of maximal length?

4.12 For plaintext $(X_0, X_1, \ldots, X_{n-1})$ enciphered by a polyalphabetic substitution $\Pi = (\Pi_0, \Pi_1, \ldots, \Pi_{r-1})$ chosen from Ξ by independent trials with probabilities $\{q(\pi) : \pi \in \Xi\}$,

$$\Pi : (X_0, X_1, \ldots, X_{n-1}) \rightarrow (Y_0, Y_1, \ldots, Y_{n-1})$$
$$= (\Pi_0(X_0), \Pi_1(X_1), \ldots, \Pi_{n-1}(X_{n-1}))$$

calculate $\mathrm{Var}\{\kappa[\mathbf{Y}, \mathbf{Y}^{(-s)}]\}$.

TABLE P4.7
The Array *PHI*[*PERIODS*] for *CIPHER(P4.10)*

	2	**3**	**4**	**5**	**6**	**7**	**8**	**9**	**10**	**11**
2	0.0391	0.0384	0.0395	0.0392	0.0392	0.0389	0.0390	0.0392	0.0387	0.0381
3	0.0388	0.0385	0.0388	0.0392	0.0400	0.0386	0.0387	0.0393	0.0395	0.0384
4	0.0408	0.0400	0.0400	0.0409	0.0393	0.0402	0.0401	0.0400	0.0413	0.0382
5	0.0415	0.0408	0.0419	0.0401	0.0395	0.0403	0.0404	0.0400	0.0396	0.0415
6	0.0395	0.0415	0.0395	0.0414	0.0413	0.0412	0.0386	0.0419	0.0404	0.0396
7	0.0412	0.0398	0.0401	0.0404	0.0398	0.0411	0.0402	0.0391	0.0392	0.0397
8	0.0422	0.0423	0.0406	0.0457	0.0416	0.0422	0.0417	0.0432	0.0430	0.0392
9	0.0400	0.0407	0.0400	0.0430	0.0421	0.0436	0.0419	0.0444	0.0399	0.0395
10	0.0429	0.0444	0.0464	0.0438	0.0434	0.0436	0.0431	0.0419	0.0419	0.0499
11	0.0434	0.0422	0.0419	0.0432	0.0420	0.0416	0.0415	0.0426	0.0452	0.0421
12	0.0426	0.0442	0.0428	0.0440	0.0416	0.0475	0.0444	0.0535	0.0426	0.0416
13	0.0435	0.0425	0.0468	0.0442	0.0439	0.0432	0.0468	0.0468	0.0447	0.0425
14	0.0479	0.0413	0.0438	0.0405	0.0438	0.0427	0.0440	0.0437	0.0424	0.0424
15	0.0475	0.0457	0.0513	0.0446	0.0484	0.0484	0.0449	0.0462	0.0424	0.0451
16	0.0436	0.0512	0.0450	0.0454	0.0429	0.0450	0.0512	0.0508	0.0461	0.0407
17	0.0467	0.0427	0.0467	0.0475	0.0439	0.0451	0.0471	0.0479	0.0459	0.0499
18	0.0457	0.0466	0.0434	0.0466	0.0470	0.0471	0.0443	0.0479	0.0430	0.0466
19	0.0471	0.0522	0.0481	0.0476	0.0511	0.0625	0.0481	0.0471	0.0522	0.0471
20	0.0514	0.0537	0.0585	0.0508	0.0514	0.0497	0.0497	0.0458	0.0503	0.0549
21	0.0484	0.0476	0.0420	0.0445	0.0501	0.0476	0.0484	0.0484	0.0460	0.0482

	12	**13**	**14**	**15**	**16**	**17**	**18**	**19**	**20**	**21**
2	0.0390	0.0385	0.0390	0.0394	0.0395	0.0382	0.0393	0.0389	0.0400	0.0386
3	0.0386	0.0380	0.0395	0.0419	0.0399	0.0382	0.0391	0.0394	0.0421	0.0387
4	0.0393	0.0390	0.0398	0.0427	0.0407	0.0386	0.0404	0.0389	0.0406	0.0398
5	0.0417	0.0392	0.0408	0.0413	0.0494	0.0405	0.0393	0.0393	0.0424	0.0396
6	0.0414	0.0396	0.0396	0.0429	0.0425	0.0388	0.0400	0.0422	0.0445	0.0415
7	0.0402	0.0386	0.0405	0.0407	0.0401	0.0414	0.0394	0.0426	0.0423	0.0387
8	0.0413	0.0403	0.0419	0.0480	0.0425	0.0391	0.0406	0.0395	0.0442	0.0407
9	0.0411	0.0394	0.0439	0.0441	0.0417	0.0389	0.0427	0.0435	0.0490	0.0402
10	0.0466	0.0402	0.0444	0.0427	0.0563	0.0426	0.0416	0.0399	0.0439	0.0422
11	0.0442	0.0418	0.0401	0.0445	0.0426	0.0530	0.0476	0.0474	0.0445	0.0453
12	0.0427	0.0433	0.0428	0.0447	0.0468	0.0410	0.0412	0.0418	0.0437	0.0454
13	0.0475	0.0435	0.0423	0.0459	0.0478	0.0423	0.0437	0.0449	0.0437	0.0452
14	0.0438	0.0448	0.0443	0.0499	0.0420	0.0471	0.0426	0.0443	0.0499	0.0403
15	0.0541	0.0446	0.0465	0.0459	0.0526	0.0443	0.0435	0.0409	0.0516	0.0462
16	0.0450	0.0426	0.0443	0.0490	0.0486	0.0415	0.0448	0.0441	0.0474	0.0429
17	0.0484	0.0443	0.0455	0.0497	0.0455	0.0497	0.0455	0.0447	0.0451	0.0497
18	0.0476	0.0429	0.0452	0.0564	0.0513	0.0424	0.0429	0.0457	0.0555	0.0527
19	0.0466	0.0451	0.0527	0.0466	0.0522	0.0481	0.0492	0.0456	0.0492	0.0555
20	0.0554	0.0446	0.0508	0.0532	0.0599	0.0463	0.0605	0.0456	0.0492	0.0538
21	0.0451	0.0451	0.0455	0.0489	0.0476	0.0495	0.0461	0.0545	0.0597	0.0470

CHAPTER V

Rotor Systems

5.1 ROTORS

A *rotor* or *wired codewheel* is the building block of a variety of polyalphabetic systems. A rotor, as shown in Figure 5.1.1, is an insulating disk (of rubber or bakelite) on which electrical contacts, one for each letter of the alphabet, are placed uniformly around the periphery and on each side. An internal conducting path through the insulating material connects contacts in pairs; one on each side of the disk. An electric current entering on the left-hand side of the rotor travels on an internal path through the rotor cross-section, emerging at one of the con-

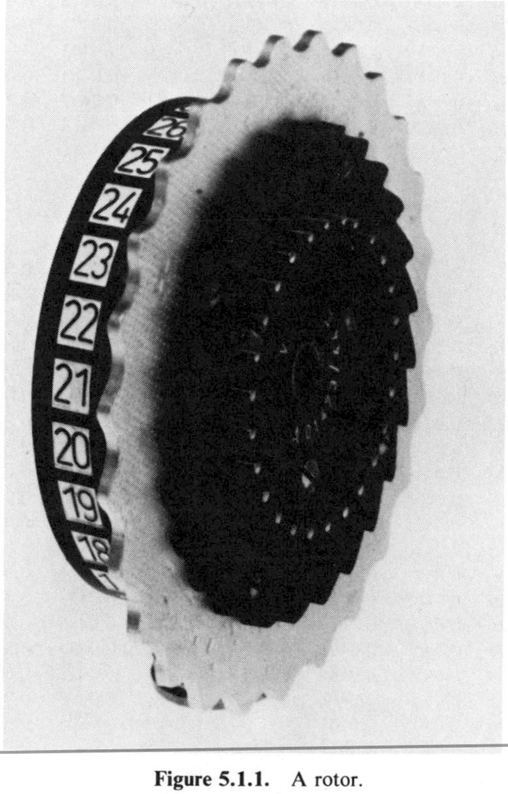

Figure 5.1.1. A rotor.

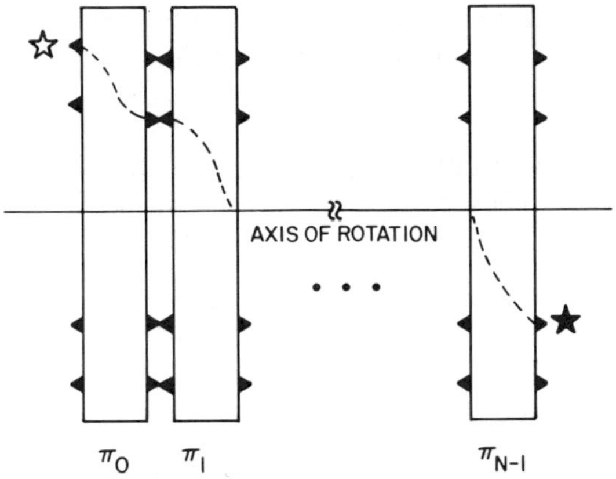

Figure 5.1.2. Side view of a rotor system.

tacts on the right-hand side of the rotor. The rotor implements a monalphabetic substitution electrically. Rotating the rotor counterclockwise k places ($360k/m^{\circ}$ degrees) yields a second (generally different) substitution $T_{k,\pi}$, defined by

$$T_{k,\pi}(x) = \pi(x + k) - k$$

$T_{k,\pi}$ is the composition of π with the Caesar substitutions C_k and C_{-k}:

$$T_{k,\pi} = C_{-k}\, \pi\, C_k$$

Rotor systems are built by concatenating rotors; the German Enigma, the American SIGABA and the Japanese RED and PURPLE machines are examples of World War II vintage rotor systems. A side view of a *straight-through* rotor system is depicted in Fig. 5.1.2. The electric current applied at contact ☆◀ travels along a path passing through each of the N rotors, emerging at the contact ▶★.

The key in a rotor system with N rotors consists of (1) the substitutions $\{\pi_s : 0 \le s < N\}$, and (2) the *initial rotational displacements* $\{k_s : 0 \le s < N\}$ of the rotors. If a rotor system consisted just of the composition of the rotors,

$$C_{-k_{N-1}}\, \pi_{N-1}\, C_{k_{N-1}-k_{N-2}} \cdots C_{k_1-k_0}\, \pi_0\, C_{k_0}$$

little would be achieved cryptographically. What makes a rotor system potentially interesting is the ability to vary the substitution by rotating the individual rotors after the encipherment of each plaintext letter, effectively changing $(k_0, k_1, \ldots, k_{N-1})$.

Definition 5.1.1 A *displacement function for an N-rotor system* is a set of N functions.

$$r_s : Z_\infty = \{0, 1, \ldots\} \to Z_\infty$$

$$r_s : i \to r_s(i) \qquad 0 \le s < N, 0 \le i < \infty$$

$r_s(i)$ is the *rotational displacement* of the sth rotor for the encipherment of the ith plaintext letter. $r_s(0) = k_s$ is the *initial rotational displacement* of the sth rotor.

Remarks
We defined the Caesar substitutions $\boldsymbol{C}_m = \{C_k : 0 \le k < m\}$ for the alphabet $\boldsymbol{Z}_m$ in Chapter 3. It will be convenient to allow the index k in C_k to assume all integer values $-\infty < k < \infty$ by defining

$$C_k = C_{(k \text{ modulo } m)}$$

Here are four *classes* of displacement functions:

(5.1.1) $$r_s(i) = k_s + \lfloor i/m^s \qquad 0 \le s < N$$

(5.1.2) $$r_s(i) = \begin{cases} i + k_0 & \text{if } s = 0 \\ k_s + \lfloor r_{s-1}(i)/m & \text{if } 1 \le s < N \end{cases}$$

(5.1.3) $$r_s(i) = k_i + \alpha_s \lfloor i/m^s \qquad 0 \le s < N$$

(5.1.4) $$r_s(i) = \begin{cases} \alpha_0 i + k_0 & \text{if } s = 0 \\ k_s + \alpha_s \lfloor r_{s-1}(i)/m & \text{if } 1 \le s < N \end{cases}$$

where

- $\lfloor x$ = *the floor of* x is the largest integer $\le x$.
- $(\alpha_0, \alpha_1, \ldots, \alpha_{N-1})$ are each relatively prime to m.

A displacement function is a form of counter, like an automobile odometer; the sth rotational displacement $r_s(i)$ corresponds to the movement of the wheel in the odometer which records the sth decimal digit of mileage. After the encipherment of the ith letter, the sth rotor is displaced counterclockwise $r_s(i+1) - r_s(i)$ places. The displacement function defined in Eq. (5.1.1) defines essentially the *Hebern* polyalphabetic rotor system [HEB].

Definition 5.1.2 The *rotor system with displacement functions* $\{r_s(i)\}$ is the cryptographic transformation

$$(x_0, x_1, \ldots, x_{n-1}, \ldots) \to (y_0, y_1, \ldots, y_{n-1}, \ldots)$$

obtained by the composition of the N rotors

$$C_{-r_s(i)}\pi_s C_{r_s(i)} \qquad 0 \le s < N$$

(5.1.5) $y_i =$

$$\pi_{N-1}(r_{N-1}(i) + \ldots + \pi_1(r_1(i) + \pi_0(r_0(i) + x_i) - r_0(i)) - r_1(i) \ldots) - r_{N-1}(i)$$

The key of a rotor system consists of

- The rotors $(\pi_0, \pi_1, \ldots, \pi_{N-1})$
- The initial rotational displacement $(k_0, k_1, \ldots, k_{N-1})$
- The displacement functions $\{r_s(i) : 0 \le s < N\}$

The rotational displacement functions of War World II rotor systems were achieved by gears and not easily changed. This is not the case if the rotor system is implemented as a microprocessor; a great variety of displacement functions with highly irregular motion are possible, and they may be varied very easily. We will assume that the class of the displacement functions $\{r_s(i) : 0 \le s < N\}$ are known. The rotors $(\pi_0, \pi_1, \ldots, \pi_{N-1})$ and the initial rotational displacement $\mathbf{k} = (k_0, k_1, \ldots, k_{N-1})$ constitute the private key. In typical usuage, the rotors $\pi = (\pi_0, \pi_1, \ldots, \pi_{N-1})$ (the *primary key*) might be changed less frequently than the initial rotational displacement $\mathbf{k} = (k_0, k_1, \ldots, k_{N-1})$ (the *secondary key*). In the analysis that follows, we assume that the rotational displacement is given by one of the four equations (5.1.1–4). We define the transformation $T_{\mathbf{k},\pi}$ by

$$T_{\mathbf{k},\pi}(i) : x_i \to y_i \qquad 0 \le i < \infty$$

where y_i is given by Eq. (5.1.5).

Lemma 5.1.3 The sequence of substitutions on $\boldsymbol{Z}_m$,

$$T_{\mathbf{k},\pi}(0),\ T_{\mathbf{k},\pi}(1),\ \ldots,\ T_{\mathbf{k},\pi}(n-1),\ \ldots$$

is periodic; the period is a divisor of m^N.

Proof. Recall that $\{T_{\mathbf{k},\pi}(i) : 0 \le i < \infty\}$ is *periodic* and P is *a period* if

$$T_{\mathbf{k},\pi}(i) = T_{\mathbf{k},\pi}(i + P) \qquad 0 \le i < \infty \tag{5.1.6}$$

The period of the sequence $\{T_{\mathbf{k},\pi}(i) : 0 \le i < \infty\}$ is the smallest positive integer P that satisfies Eq. (5.1.6). Eqs. (5.1.1–4) show that

$$r_0(i + m^N) = r_0(i) \text{ (modulo } m^N)$$

and by induction

$$r_s(i + m^N) = r_s(i) \text{ (modulo } m^{N-s}) \qquad 0 \le s < N$$

so that

$$r_s(i + m^N) = r_s(i) \text{ (modulo } m) \qquad 0 \le s < N$$

This proves that the sequence of substitutions $\{T_{\mathbf{k},\pi}(i) : 0 \le i < \infty\}$ is periodic and m^N is a period. The rest of the argument is standard; if P is the minimal solution to Eq. (5.1.6) and

$$m^N = MP + L \qquad 0 \le L < P$$

then

$$T_{k,\pi}(i + m^N) = T_{k,\pi}(i + L + MP) = T_{k,\pi}(i + L) \qquad 0 \le i < \infty$$

which is a contradiction unless $L = 0$, implying that P divides m^N. ◀

5.2 ROTATIONAL EQUIVALENCE

In Chapters 3 and 4, we encountered equivalent keys and noted that cryptanalysis could only recover the key up to equivalence. We face the same indeterminancy with rotor systems. First we give the definition of equivalence.

Definition 5.2.1 The keys $(\mathbf{k},\pi)$ and $(\mathbf{j},\nu)$ for rotor systems with displacement functions in the same class are *equivalent* if

$$T_{k,\pi}(i) = T_{j,\tau}(i) \qquad 0 \le i < m^N$$

and we write $T_{k,\pi} \sim T_{j,\nu}$. $\sim$ is an *equivalence* relation,* and the set of all rotor systems with N rotors is divided into *equivalence classes* by the relation $\sim$.

When are two keys equivalent?

Theorem 5.2.2 When the displacement function is given by Eq. (5.1.1), $T_{k,\pi} \sim T_{j,\nu}$, if and only if

$$(5.2.1) \qquad \nu_i = \begin{cases} C_{-d_0}\,\pi_0\,C_{k_0-j_0} & \text{if } i = 0 \\ C_{-d_i}\,\pi_i\,C_{d_{i-1}+k_i-j_i+j_{i-1}-k_{i-1}} & \text{if } 1 \le i < N-1 \\ C_{j_{N-1}-k_{N-1}}\,\pi_{N-1}\,C_{d_{N-2}+k_{N-1}-j_{N-1}+j_{N-2}-k_{N-2}} & \text{if } i = N-1 \end{cases}$$

for some constants $\{d_i : 0 \le i < N - 1\}$ with $0 \le d_i < m$. (When $N = 1$, Eq. (5.2.1) is to be interpreted as $\nu_0 = C_{j_0-k_0}\pi_0 C_{k_0-j_0}$)

Proof. It is simple to verify that if $\nu = (\nu_0, \nu_1, \ldots, \nu_{N-1})$ satisfies Eq. (5.2.1), then $T_{k,\pi} \sim T_{j,\nu}$.

We begin the proof of necessity with the case $N = 2$, assuming

---

*A set S of pairs (s,t) of elements of a set X

$$S \subseteq X \times X$$

is called an *equivalence relation* on X if

- $(x,x) \in S$ for all $x \in X$ *(reflexivity)*.
- $(s,t) \in S$ if and only if $(t,s) \in S$ *(symmetry)*.
- $(s,t) \in S$ and $(t,u) \in S$ imply $(s,u) \in S$ *(transitivity)*.

We say that $(s,t) \in S$ are *equivalent* and write $s \sim t$. The *equivalence relation* $\sim$ on X partitions X into disjoint *equivalence classes* $X = \cup_i X_i$ where $s \sim t$ if and only if s and t belong to the same set X_i for some i.

$$C_{-r_1(i)}\,\pi_1\,C_{r_1(i)-r_0(i)}\,\pi_0\,C_{r_0(i)} = C_{-R_1(i)}\,\nu_1\,C_{R_1(i)-R_0(i)}\,\nu_0\,C_{R_0(i)}$$

with

$$r_s(i) = k_1 + \lfloor i/m^s \qquad R_s(i) = j_1 + \lfloor i/m^s \qquad s = 0,1$$

Then

$$C_{-i}\,\pi_0\,C_{k_0-j_0}\,\nu_0^{-1}\,C_i = C_{k_0-k_1-\lfloor i/m}\,\pi_1^{-1}\,C_{k_1-j_1}\,\nu_1\,C_{j_1-j_0+\lfloor i/m} \tag{5.2.2}$$

The substitution on the right-hand side of Eq. (5.2.2) does not vary with i if $jm \leq i < (j+1)m$. Setting $i = 0$ and $i = 1$ in Eq. (5.2.2), and equating the left-hand sides, we obtain the relationship $C_1\,\lambda\,C_{-1} = \lambda$ or

$$\lambda(t) = \lambda(t-1) + 1 \qquad 0 \leq t < m \tag{5.2.3}$$

where

$$\lambda = \pi_0\,C_{k_0-j_0}\,\nu_0^{-1} \tag{5.2.4}$$

Eq. (5.2.3) implies that

$$\lambda(t) = \lambda(0) + t \qquad 0 \leq t < m$$

so that $\lambda = C_{d_0}$ and $d_0 = \lambda(0)$. This shows that

$$\nu_0 = C_{-d_0}\,\pi_0\,C_{k_0-j_0}$$

$$\nu_1 = C_{j_1-k_1}\,\pi_1\,C_{-d_0+k_1-k_0-j_1+j_0}$$

Suppose next that an N-rotor system satisfies

$$C_{-r_{N-1}(i)}\,\pi_{N-1}\,C_{r_{N-1}(i)-r_{N-2}(i)}\cdots C_{r_1(i)-r_0(i)}\,\pi_0\,C_{r_0(i)} = C_{-R_{N-1}(i)}\,\nu_{N-1}\,C_{R_{N-1}(i)-R_{N-2}(i)}\cdots C_{R_1(i)-R_0(i)}\,\nu_0\,C_{R_0(i)} \tag{5.2.5}$$

with

$$r_s(i) = k_i + \lfloor i/m^s \qquad R_s(i) = j_i + \lfloor i/m^s \qquad 0 \leq s < N$$

Eq. (5.2.5) implies

$$C_{-k_1+k_0-\lfloor i/m}\,\pi_1^{-1}\,C_{r_1(i)-r_2(i)}\cdots\pi_{N-1}^{-1}\,C_{k_{N-1}-j_{N-1}}\,\nu_{N-1}\,C_{R_{N-1}(i)-R_{N-2}(i)}\cdots\nu_1\,C_{j_1-j_0+\lfloor i/m} = C_{-i}\pi_0\,C_{k_0-j_0}\,\nu_0^{-1}\,C_i \tag{5.2.6}$$

The substitution on the left-hand side of Eq. (5.2.6) does not vary with i for $jm \leq i < (j+1)m$. Equating the right-hand member of Eq. (5.2.6) for $i = 0$ and $i = 1$ yields the relationship

$$C_{-1}\,\lambda\,C_1 = \lambda$$

with λ given by Eq. (5.2.4), and we again may conclude that

$$\nu_0 = C_{-d_0}\,\pi_0\,C_{k_0-j_0}$$

and

$C_{d_0} =$

$$C_{-k_1+k_0-\lfloor i/m}\,\pi_1^{-1}\,C_{r_1(i)-r_2(i)}\cdots\pi_{N-1}^{-1}\,C_{k_{N-1}-j_{N-1}}\,\nu_{N-1}\,C_{R_{N-1}(i)-R_{N-1}(i)}\cdots\nu_1\,C_{j_1-j_0+\lfloor i/m}$$

with $d_0 = \lambda(0)$.

We have succeeded in peeling away one of the rotors. The proof proceeds now by induction; assume that we have proved that ν_s satisfies Eq. (5.2.1) for $0 \le s < L < N$. Therefore

(5.2.7) $$\nu_{L-1}\,C_{R_{L-1}(i)-R_{L-2}(i)}\cdots\nu_0\,C_{R_0(i)} = C_{-d_{L-1}}\,\pi_{L-1}\,C_{r_{L-1}(i)-r_{L-2}(i)}\cdots\pi_0\,C_{r_0(i)}$$

which with Eq. (5.2.5) yields

(5.2.8) $$C_{-r_{N-1}(i)}\,\pi_{N-1}\,C_{R_{N-1}(i)-r_{N-2}(i)}\cdots\pi_L\,C_{r_L(i)-r_{L-1}(i)}$$

$$= C_{-R_{N-1}(i)}\,\nu_{N-1}\,C_{R_{N-1}(i)-R_{N-2}(i)}\cdots\nu_L\,C_{-d_{L-1}+R_L(i)-R_{L-1}(i)}$$

Eq. (5.2.8) now yields the relationship

$$C_{k_L-k_{L+1}-\lfloor i/m^{L+1}}\,\pi_{L+1}^{-1}\cdots\pi_{N-1}^{-1}\,C_{k_{N-1}-j_{N-1}}\,\nu_{N-1}\,C_{R_{N-1}(i)-R_{N-1}(i)}\cdots$$

$$\nu_{L+1}\,C_{j_{L+1}-j_L+\lfloor i/m^{L+1}} = C_{-\lfloor i/M^L}\,\pi_L\,C_{d_{L-1}+k_L-k_{L-1}+j_{L-1}-j_L}\,\nu_L^{-1}\,C_{i/m^L}$$

The substitution on the left-hand side of Eq. (5.2.7) does not vary with i for $jm^{L+1} \le i < (j+1)m^{L+1}$. Evaluating the right-hand side of Eq. (5.2.7) for $i = m^L$ and then $i = 2m^L$ yields the relationship

$$C_{-1}\,\pi_L\,C_{d_{L-1}+k_L-k_{L-1}+j_{L-1}-j_L}\,\nu_L^{-1}\,C_1 = \pi_L\,C_{d_{L-1}+k_L-k_{L-1}+j_{L-1}-j_L}\,\nu_L^{-1}$$

from which we conclude

$$\pi_L\,C_{d_{L-1}+k_L-k_{L-1}+j_{L-1}-j_L}\,\nu_L^{-1} = C_{d_L}$$

for some d_L, $0 \le d_L < m$. This implies

$$\nu_L = C_{-d_L}\,\pi_L\,C_{d_{L-1}+k_L-j_L+j_{L-1}-k_{L-1}}$$

Finally, if Eq. (5.2.1) holds for $0 \le i < N-1$, then Eq. (5.2.8) yields the relationship

$$\nu_{N-1} = C_{j_{N-1}-k_{N-1}}\,\pi_{N-1}\,C_{d_{N-2}+k_{N-1}-j_{N-1}+j_{N-2}-k_{N-2}}$$

which completes the proof. ◀

If we examine closely the proof of Theorem 5.2.2, we see that it can be modified to obtain the same conclusion when the displacement function satisfies Eq. (5.1.2). Eq. (5.2.3) becomes

(5.2.9) $$\lambda(t+\alpha_0) - \alpha_0 = \lambda(t) \qquad 0 \le t < m$$

where α_0 is relatively prime to m. Equation (5.2.9) also implies that $\lambda = C_{d_0}$, and the rest of the argument goes through so that we arrive at the following theorem.

Theorem 5.2.3 When the displacement function is given by Eq. (5.1.3), $T_{k,\pi} \sim T_{j,\nu}$ if and only if ν is given by Eq. (5.2.1).

When the displacement function is described by either Eq. (5.1.2) or (5.1.4), the equivalence classes are different.

Theorem 5.2.4 When the displacement function satisfies Eq. (5.1.2), $T_{k,\pi} \sim T_{j,\nu}$ if and only if

(5.2.10)
$$
\nu s = \begin{cases}
C_{-d_0}\,\pi_0\,C_{k_0-j_0} & \text{if } s = 0 \\
C_{-d_s+j_s-k_s}\,\pi_s\,C_{d_{s-1}+k_s-j_s} & \text{if } 1 \le s < N-1 \text{ and } j_t = k_t,\ 0 \le t < s \\
C_{-d_s}\,\pi_s\,C_{d_{s-1}} & \text{if } 1 \le s < N-1,\ j_t \ne k_t, \text{ for some } t,\ 0 \le t < s \text{ and } \pi_s \in \boldsymbol{C}_m \\
C_{j_{N-1}-k_{N-1}}\,\pi_{N-1}\,C_{d_{N-2}+k_{N-1}-j_{N-1}} & \text{if } s = N-1 \text{ and } j_t = k_t,\ 0 \le t < N-1 \\
\pi_{N-1}\,C_{d_{N-2}} & \text{if } s = N-1,\ j_t \ne k_t \text{ for some } t,\ 0 \le t < N-1 \text{ and } \pi_{N-1} \in \boldsymbol{C}_m
\end{cases}
$$

Proof. It is simple to verify that $\nu = (\nu_0, \nu_1, \ldots, \nu_{N-1})$ given by Eq. (5.2.10) is equivalent to $\pi = (\pi_0, \pi_1, \ldots, \pi_{N-1})$, proving sufficiency.

Necessity requires only minor modifications of the proof of Theorem 5.2.2; as before, the proof is by induction on N. When N = 2, we have

(5.2.11)
$$
C_{-i}\pi_0\,C_{k_0-j_0}\,\nu_0^{-1}\,C_i = C_{k_0-k_1-(i+k_0)/m}\,\pi_1^{-1}\,C_{k_1-j_1+(i+k_0)/m-(i+j_0)/m}\,\nu_1\,C_{j_1-j_0+(i+j_0)/m}
$$

For some two consecutive values of i, the same substitution appears on the right-hand side of Eq. (5.2.11), and this allows us to deduce that

$$
\nu_0 = C_{-d_0}\,\pi_0\,C_{k_0-j_0}
$$

and

(5.2.12)
$$
C_{k_0-k_1-(i+k_0)/m}\,\pi_1^{-1}\,C_{k_1-j_1+(i+k_0)/m-(i+j_0)/m}\,\nu_1\,C_{j_1-j_0+(i+j_0)/m} = C_{d_0}
$$

If $j_0 = k_0$, then Eq. (5.2.12) shows that

$$
\nu_1 = C_{j_1-k_1}\,\pi_1\,C_{d_0+k_1-j_1}
$$

If $j_0 \ne k_0$, the function $\lfloor (i + k_0)/m - \lfloor (i + j_0)/m$ generates one of two types of sequences:

$$0\,0\,0\ldots 0\,1\,1\ldots 1 \quad 0\,0\,0\ldots 0\,1\,1\ldots 1 \quad 0\,0\,0\ldots 0\,1\,1\ldots 1 \quad \ldots$$

$$0 \leq j_0 < k_0 < m$$

$$0\,0\,0\ldots 0\,-1\,-1\ldots -1 \quad 0\,0\,0\ldots 0\,-1\,-1\ldots -1$$
$$0\,0\,0\ldots 0\,-1\,-1\ldots -1\ \ldots$$

$$0 \leq k_0 < j_0 < m$$

In either case, Eq. (5.2.12) implies that π_1 and ν_1 are Caesar substitutions. Thus

$$\nu_1 = C_{-d_1}\,\pi_1\,C_{d_0}$$

for some d_1. This completes the analysis of the case $N = 2$.

For general N, we suppose that

$$C_{-r_{N-1}(i)}\,\pi_{N-1}\,C_{r_{N-1}(i)-r_{N-2}(i)}\ldots C_{r_1(i)-r_0(i)}\,\pi_0\,C_{r_0(i)}$$
$$= C_{-R_{N-1}(i)}\,\nu_{N-1}\,C_{R_{N-1}(i)-R_{N-2}(i)}\ldots C_{R_1(i)-R_0(i)}\,\nu_0\,C_{R_0(i)}$$

By induction, we may assume that the relationship in Eq. (5.2.10) between ν_s and π_s has been proved for $0 \leq s < L$. Then if $L < N - 1$

$$C_{-r_{L-1}(i)}\,\pi_{L-1}\,C_{r_{L-1}(i)-r_{L-2}(i)}\ldots C_{r_1(i)-r_0(i)}\,\pi_0\,C_{r_0(i)}$$
$$= C_{d_{L-1}-R_{L-1}(i)}\,\nu_{L-1}\,C_{R_{L-1}(i)-R_{L-2}(i)}\ldots C_{R_1(i)-R_0(i)}\,\nu_0\,C_{R_0(i)}$$

and therefore

$$(5.2.13)\qquad C_{-r_L(i)}\,\pi_L\,C_{d_{L-1}+r_L(i)-R_L(i)}\,\nu_L^{-1}\,C_{R_L(i)}$$
$$= C_{-r_{L+1}(i)}\,\pi_{L+1}^{-1}\ldots\pi_{N-1}^{-1}\,C_{r_{N-1}(i)-R_{N-1}(i)}\,\nu_{N-1}\ldots C_{-R_{L+1}(i)}\,\nu_{L+1}\,C_{R_L(i)}$$

First, suppose $j_s = k_s$ for $0 \leq s < L$. The $r_L(i) - R_L(i)$ is independent of i and there exist values i′, i″ with $i'' > i'$ such that

- $r_L(i'') - r_L(i') = R_L(i'') - R_L(i') = 1$
- $r_s(i'') - r_s(i') = R_s(i'') - R_s(i') = 0 \qquad \text{for } L < s < N$

from which we conclude

$$C_{-k_L}\,\pi_L\,C_{d_{L-1}+k_L-j_L}\,\nu_L^{-1}\,C_{j_L} = C_{d_L}$$

If $j_s \neq k_s$ for some s, $0 \leq s < L$, then we can find i′ and i″ such that

- $r_L(i'') - r_L(i') = 1$
- $R_L(i'') - R_L(i') = 0$
- $r_s(i'') - r_s(i') = R_s(i'') - R_s(i') = 0 \qquad \text{for } L < s < N$

and this implies that both π_L and ν_L are Caesar substitutions, which we may write in the form

$$\nu_L = C_{-d_L}\,\pi_L\,C_{d_{L-1}}$$

completing the induction step. If $L = N - 1$, the right-hand side of Eq. (5.2.13) is the identity element of $\boldsymbol{C}_m$ and hence

$$C_{R_{N-1}(i)-r_{N-1}(i)}\,\pi_{N-1}\,C_{d_{N-2}+r_{N-1}(i)-R_{N-1}(i)} = \nu_{N-1} \quad (5.2.14)$$

If $j_s \neq k_s$ for some s, $0 \leq s < N - 1$, Eq. (5.2.14) requires both π_{N-1} and ν_{N-1} to be Caesar substitutions. This completes the proof. ◀

5.3 CRYPTANALYSIS WITH CORRESPONDING PLAINTEXT AND CIPHERTEXT

We assume the following: (1) that the displacement function is given by Eq. (5.1.1), and (2) that the opponent has corresponding plaintext and ciphertext

$$y_i = \pi_{N-1}(r_{N-1}(i) + \dots$$
$$+ \pi_1(r_1(i) + \pi_0(r_0(i) + x_i) - r_0(i)) - r_1(i) \dots) - r_{N-1}(i)$$

The solution for π_0 is based upon the observation that the rotors $\pi_1, \dots, \pi_{N-1}$ behave like *stators* for i in suitable intervals, since $r_s(i)$ is constant for $1 \leq s < N$ and i in the jth block

$$B_j = \{jm, jm + 1, \dots, (j + 1)m - 1\}$$

Thus $C_{r_{N-1}(i)-r_{N-2}(i)} \dots C_{r_1(i)-r_0(i)}\,\pi_0\,C_{r_0(i)}$ is of the form

$$S_j\,C_{-r_1(i)}\,\pi_0\,C_{r_0(i)}$$

where S_j is a substitution independent of i for $i \in B_j$. We will say that a *hit* occurs at (i_0,i_1) with $i_0 \neq i_1$ if

$$S_j\,C_{-r_1(i_0)}\,\pi_0\,C_{r_0(i_0)} : x_{i_0} \rightarrow y_{i_0}$$

$$S_j\,C_{-r_1(i_1)}\,\pi_0\,C_{r_0(i_1)} : x_{i_1} \rightarrow y_{i_1}$$

$$y_{i_0} = y_{i_1} \qquad i_0,i_1 \in B_j$$

The hit at (i_0,i_1) yields the relationship

$$\pi_0(k_0 + i_1 + x_{i_1}) - k_0 - i_1 = \pi_0(k_0 + i_1 + x_{i_1}) - k_0 - i_1 \quad (5.3.1)$$

Note that since $i_0 \neq i_1$ and $i_0,i_1 \in B_j$, it follows that $k_0 + i_0 + x_{i_0} \neq k_0 + i_1 + x_{i_1}$ (modulo m), and hence Eq. (5.3.1) relates the values of π_0 for two distinct arguments. We can recover π_0 from a sufficient number of such relationships.

We shall assume:

- $k_s = 0$ $(0 \leq i < N)$ by replacing π_s by $C_{-k_s}\,\pi_s\,C_{k_s}$, and
- $\pi_s(0) = 0$, $0 \leq s < N - 1$, replacing the rotors $\{\pi_s\}$ by rotors in the equivalence class of $\{\pi_s\}$:

$$\pi_0 \rightarrow C_{-d_0}\,\pi_0 \qquad d_0 = \pi(0)$$

$$\pi_s \rightarrow C_{-k_s}\,\pi_s\,C_{k_{s-1}}$$

$$d_s = \pi_s(\pi_{s-1} \ldots \pi_0(0) \ldots)) \qquad 1 \le s < N - 1$$

By examining sufficient corresponding plaintext and ciphertext, we will obtain enough relationships to recover π_0.

In Fig. 5.3.1, we give the encipherment of *PLAIN(1)* by a 3-rotor system with rotors shown in Table 5.3.2. The steps in the recovery of π_0 are shown in Table 5.3.3.

Step 1 Examine a sufficient number of consecutive blocks of length 26 of plaintext and corresponding ciphertext to find relationships involving $\pi_0(0)$ and $\pi_0(i)$ for some $i \neq 0$. The first three blocks give two relationships (denoted by ***1*** and ***2*** with $i = 59$ and $i = 76$)

$$\textbf{\textit{1}}\ \pi_0(18) = \pi_0(0) - 7$$

$$\textbf{\textit{2}}\ \pi_0(11) = \pi_0(0) + 6$$

Step 2 *Scan* the first three blocks for any relationships involving $\pi_0(18)$ or $\pi_0(11)$. This yields relationships ***3*** $(i = 16)$, ***4*** $(i = 20)$ ***5*** $(i = 23)$, ***6*** $(i = 66)$, ***7*** $(i = 25)$ and ***8*** $(i = 43)$. Each of these provides additional

```
ropus jvdfx wkhpq yslhq jbusw ucgir dtmfh pswzr lnetq gwkas vfipc pupqi
mwfsg hstav ebhls wewuy cvrcw wteih ttijh ddfcu vgnni lndut wsppe hunyg
xkwqi iabtm tclij jmgpa kqunv snkqr poltq uiumc paair lkvwi dpwus idzpn
mywib imsok idjei inldl joffb ohlqd gnlsk iacxh wzbnz lvckn esino xyjji
ymqxq akvow fpars tjkyr wvsga rwets smvpm cojjx vxhvl cpsut acepr miyzz
nxlny mjwkb fxuxb bnymb jhufm pgrkr dqfer kxcxt kqksu pipma mbunp rjiwz
alhbl eaqwm qwifx bzmsc lujnz goxrh cygsm ymaej tthvr jeuii wpvda frhev
tkcbm qgfrm lxgqw iiywb zolrk ypola bhibd mltma urlln gjrtv sreyo uivsu
zncgn dmqcl niunx monhb wbcgi oczak zjdtc sfpdx sydxm snlkn bkoxg nitey
fdyml dqtlz oevum bfpet vuaru dvqtw ewymg aclgz oxiaf tumnl lvqtz toozw
mbnlg ucibf ymbqx vpmdd afcjo zhoya kzvqf dggsf mhodt rmacy sorvu uhqfo
nwntg ervve ndwkc culxi qiant hkzit ecfav csbch grnve fqcwm dxxkn brqwp
tlyku qmrqc bavgv dnmyl hwmdo kxnjb cfqsq npzxc zhhjj bsgyx klird qrskg
ekecd uivsq peboa elhwx brxyv wgqga lqlup idpvv unvkp aztpm iixyk xxmhy
rypst lpdue dplvt csdug qucsq ksagu oyqce wynto yldjc rhoit zoawn tddpc
orlyi dklqv sxxvh kgfwa zbvpi yxptk cnnaj dizec yftuy xqspk myneo zrnth
npyip tpemu lienn qkhlt jcjqn febcv iyorn vfsvn jyckp dkwte sghmg xvdni
zakmj dvnar lrszh wjiiy bcltu ygxwt higet uqfqc uydvh makdw bpmgw awohp
uanam vqdvl dwtlk jernv uyayj jevdb glmrt duaec lrnqw travx bbswx nhrbt
eoptc prxbh xzufy qwvaf whlsi jctsa pqfad vqmoo gdveq ieijp ajcmg idazo
ulmip exybp rdlpp qbymo anwpo axxdi vmsbl aakbt eehqi rzzmb spmeg lfcfc
ttdky inrua kvrbr rchgv cudmi ysdcc petfg wzfxq qxslo gmioz dfmwe lzbeb
mejyb exanv aijnv llkxo wdqqk aqpjl yzwoe bhxgd vamkv dmqgf tckto gvrrt
fxqxo mfxsi ocvon rxqxe qoqtc kejbg yigvw saess rczim uszvl jdsfc xrmuw
qaumq prizy wiozc wyhxd vwpha ijfyz svmrl bugsl uzdyc atsbv gpzkt dogry
xtphf cnimg gakwe magmq wklik cuxmx xumfj eftqb xqgvb nsduy eddkc yfcwk
rnmtn oczhe knihm rgxpf hhxcv boycn kyvul mhogg ndcif tvswq lvxfg ijegl
vqtby mxhrh joafk ntspt xppun vlskl lnkfr ayxiy apfva uogog nyu
```

Figure 5.3.1 *CIPHER(1.5)* : encipherment of *PLAIN(1)* by a 3-rotor (Hebern) system.

TABLE 5.3.2

π_0, π_1 and π_2 : Rotors Used to Encipher *PLAIN(1)* to *CIPHER(1.5)*

π_0

A	B	C	D	E	F	G	H	I	J	K	L	M	N	O	P	Q	R	S	T	U	V	W	X	Y	Z
0	1	2	3	4	5	6	7	8	9	10	11	12	13	14	15	16	17	18	19	20	21	22	23	24	25
↓	↓	↓	↓	↓	↓	↓	↓	↓	↓	↓	↓	↓	↓	↓	↓	↓	↓	↓	↓	↓	↓	↓	↓	↓	↓
22	6	12	10	17	20	24	19	1	25	7	2	13	23	5	3	9	11	15	4	21	14	0	16	18	8
W	G	M	K	R	U	Y	T	B	Z	H	C	N	X	F	D	J	L	P	E	V	O	A	Q	S	I

π_1

A	B	C	D	E	F	G	H	I	J	K	L	M	N	O	P	Q	R	S	T	U	V	W	X	Y	Z
0	1	2	3	4	5	6	7	8	9	10	11	12	13	14	15	16	17	18	19	20	21	22	23	24	25
↓	↓	↓	↓	↓	↓	↓	↓	↓	↓	↓	↓	↓	↓	↓	↓	↓	↓	↓	↓	↓	↓	↓	↓	↓	↓
8	14	7	2	5	15	19	21	12	6	3	0	25	9	24	20	22	10	23	17	11	13	16	18	1	4
I	O	H	C	F	P	T	V	M	G	D	A	Z	J	Y	U	W	K	X	R	L	N	Q	S	B	E

π_2

A	B	C	D	E	F	G	H	I	J	K	L	M	N	O	P	Q	R	S	T	U	V	W	X	Y	Z
0	1	2	3	4	5	6	7	8	9	10	11	12	13	14	15	16	17	18	19	20	21	22	23	24	25
↓	↓	↓	↓	↓	↓	↓	↓	↓	↓	↓	↓	↓	↓	↓	↓	↓	↓	↓	↓	↓	↓	↓	↓	↓	↓
18	16	20	11	2	1	25	23	8	17	10	0	7	9	15	14	12	4	24	5	22	21	13	6	19	3
S	Q	U	L	C	B	Z	X	I	R	K	A	H	J	P	O	M	E	Y	F	W	V	N	G	T	D

relationships. We continue to rescan (the first three blocks) until no additional relationships are determined. At this point we have found 19 relationships out of a possible total of 25.

Step 3 Adjoin an additional block of 26 plaintext ciphertext and resume scanning until 25 relationships are found.

The relationships in Table 5.3.3 yield

0	1	2	3	4	5	6	7	8	9	10	11	12	13	14	15	16	17	18	19	20	21	22	23	24	25
↓	↓	↓	↓	↓	↓	↓	↓	↓	↓	↓	↓	↓	↓	↓	↓	↓	↓	↓	↓	↓	↓	↓	↓	↓	↓
0	10	16	?	21	24	2	23	5	3	11	6	17	1	9	7	13	15	19	8	25	18	4	20	22	12

The missing value $\pi_0(3)$ is clearly 14.

Having recovered π_0, we may peel it away from the 3-rotor system and repeat the analysis for the residual 2-rotor system;

$$C_{-\lfloor(i/m^2)}\, \pi_2\, C_{\lfloor(i/m^2)-\lfloor i/m}\, \pi_1\, C_{\lfloor i/m}$$

TABLE 5.3.3
Solution for π_0 by Scanning

i	i + x_i	y_i			
0	12	17			
1	1	14			
2	15	15			
3	1	20			
4	18	18			
5	22	9			
6	12	21			
7	7	3			
8	21	5			
9	17	23			
10	9	22			
11	11	10			
12	5	7			
13	21	15	$\pi_0(21) - 13 = \pi_0(15) - 2$		
14	2	16			
15	2	24			
16	8	18	$\pi_0(8) - 16 = \pi_0(18) - 4$	3	$\pi_0(8) = \pi_0(0) + 5$
17	8	11			
18	22	7	$\pi_0(22) - 18 = \pi_0(5) - 12$	9	$\pi_0(5) = \pi_0(0) - 2$
19	4	16	$\pi_0(4) - 19 = \pi_0(2) - 14$		
20	18	9	$\pi_0(18) - 20 = \pi_0(22) - 5$	4	$\pi_0(22) = \pi_0(0) - 22$
21	9	1			
22	9	20	$\pi_0(9) - 22 = \pi_0(1) - 3$	13	$\pi_0(9) = \pi_0(0) + 3$
23	25	18	$\pi_0(25) - 23 = \pi_0(18) - 4$	5	$\pi_0(25) = \pi_0(0) + 12$
24	12	22	$\pi_0(12) - 24 = \pi_0(9) - 10$		
25	11	20	$\pi_0(11) - 25 = \pi_0(1) - 3$	7	$\pi_0(1) = \pi_0(0) - 16$
26	15	2			
27	21	6			
28	21	8			
29	7	17			
30	21	3			
31	23	19			
32	6	12			
33	20	5			
34	11	7			
35	12	15			
36	10	18			
37	4	22			
38	12	25			

TABLE 5.3.3 (*Continued*)

i	$i + x_i$	y_i			
39	15	17	$\pi_0(15) - 13 = \pi_0(7) - 3$	***16***	$\pi_0(15) = \pi_0(0) + 7$
40	2	11			
41	1	13			
42	2	4			
43	11	19	$\pi_0(11) - 17 = \pi_0(23) - 5$	***8***	$\pi_0(23) = \pi_0(0) - 6$
44	5	16			
45	1	6	$\pi_0(1) - 19 = \pi_0(21) - 1$	***14***	$\pi_0(21) = \pi_0(0) - 8$
46	22	22	$\pi_0(22) - 20 = \pi_0(4) - 11$	***10***	$\pi_0(4) = \pi_0(0) - 5$
47	21	10			
48	15	0			
49	5	18	$\pi_0(5) - 23 = \pi_0(10) - 10$	***15***	$\pi_0(10) = \pi_0(0) - 15$
50	12	21			
51	12	5	$\pi_0(12) - 25 = \pi_0(20) - 7$		
52	18	8			
53	20	15			
54	16	2			
55	13	15	$\pi_0(13) - 3 = \pi_0(20) - 1$	***17***	$\pi_0(20) = \pi_0(0) - 1$
56	8	20			
57	9	15	$\pi_0(9) - 5 = \pi_0(20) - 1$		
58	21	16			
59	0	8	$\pi_0(0) - 7 = \pi_0(18) - 0$	***1***	$\pi_0(18) = \pi_0(0) - 7$
60	15	12			
61	13	22			
62	18	5			
63	2	18			
64	0	6			
65	2	7			
66	18	18	$\pi_0(18) - 14 = \pi_0(2) - 11$	***6***	$\pi_0(2) = \pi_0(0) - 10$
67	6	19			
68	16	0			
69	10	21			
70	0	4			
71	7	1			
72	7	7	$\pi_0(7) - 20 = \pi_0(2) - 13$	***11***	$\pi_0(7) = \pi_0(0) - 3$
73	13	11			
74	13	18	$\pi_0(13) - 22 = \pi_0(2) - 11$	***12***	$\pi_0(13) = \pi_0(0) + 1$
75	17	22	$\pi_0(17) - 23 = \pi_0(13) - 9$	***18***	$\pi_0(17) = \pi_0(0) + 15$
76	11	4	$\pi_0(11) - 24 = \pi_0(0) - 18$	***2***	$\pi_0(11) = \pi_0(0) + 6$
77	12	22	$\pi_0(12) - 25 = \pi_0(13) - 9$	***19***	$\pi_0(12) = \pi_0(0) + 17$
78	8	20			
79	14	24			
80	8	2			
81	21	21			
82	16	17			

TABLE 5.3.3 (*Continued*)

i	$i + x_i$	y_i			
83	19	2	$\pi_0(19) - 5 = \pi_0(8) - 2$	***20***	$\pi_0(19) = \pi_0(0) + 8$
84	20	22			
85	0	22	$\pi_0(0) - 7 = \pi_0(20) - 6$		
86	15	19			
87	20	4			
88	8	8			
89	12	7			
90	10	19	$\pi_0(10) - 12 = \pi_0(15) - 8$		
91	25	19	$\pi_0(25) - 13 = \pi_0(15) - 8$		
92	14	8	$\pi_0(14) - 14 = \pi_0(8) - 10$	***21***	$\pi_0(14) = \pi_0(0) + 9$
93	25	9			
94	24	7	$\pi_0(24) - 16 = \pi_0(12) - 11$	***22***	$\pi_0(24) = \pi_0(0) + 18$
95	4	3			
96	24	3	$\pi_0(24) - 18 = \pi_0(4) - 17$		
97	1	5			
98	7	2	$\pi_0(7) - 20 = \pi_0(8) - 2$		
99	0	20	$\pi_0(0) - 21 = \pi_0(8) - 0$		
100	10	21	$\pi_0(10) - 22 = \pi_0(21) - 3$		
101	14	6			
102	10	13			
103	25	13	$\pi_0(25) - 25 = \pi_0(10) - 24$		
104	19	8			
105	9	11			
106	16	13			
107	16	3			
108	16	20			
109	19	19			
110	23	22			
111	11	18			
112	8	15			
113	11	15	$\pi_0(11) - 9 = \pi_0(8) - 8$		
114	12	4			
115	15	7			
116	4	20	$\pi_0(4) - 12 = \pi_0(16) - 4$	***23***	$\pi_0(16) = \pi_0(0) - 13$
117	5	13	$\pi_0(5) - 13 = \pi_0(16) - 2$		
118	22	24			
119	16	6			
120	1	23			
121	21	10			
122	11	22	$\pi_0(11) - 18 = \pi_0(23) - 6$		
123	7	16			
124	6	8	$\pi_0(6) - 20 = \pi_0(19) - 0$	***24***	$\pi_0(6) = \pi_0(0) + 2$

TABLE 5.3.3 (*Continued*)

i	$i + x_i$	y_i	
125	9	8	$\pi_0(9) - 21 = \pi_0(19) - 0$
126	13	0	
127	1	1	
128	13	19	$\pi_0(13) - 24 = \pi_0(19) - 5$
129	3	12	

which enciphers the plaintext $x_i' = \pi_0(k_0 + i + x_i) - i - k_0$ into ciphertext y_i

$$C_{-\lfloor(i/m^2)} \pi_2 C_{\lfloor(i/m^2)} : x_i' \rightarrow y_i$$

observing that the substitution $C_{-\lfloor(i/m^2)} \pi_2 C_{\lfloor(i/m^2)}$ is constant on blocks of length m^2.

5.4 CRYPTANALYSIS WITH CIPHERTEXT ONLY: N = 1

We now make the following assumptions:

- X_i is enciphered into $Y_i = \Pi(X_i + i) - i$
- The substitution Π is a random variable with values in and uniformly distributed over the symmetric group $SYM(\boldsymbol{Z_m})$.
- The $\{X_i : 0 \leq i < n\}$ are independent and identically distributed random variables with probability distribution

$$Pr_{PLAIN}\{X_i = t\} = p(t) \qquad 0 \leq i < n, 0 \leq t < m$$

- Π and $(X_0, X_1, \ldots, X_{n-1})$ are independent.

We observe ciphertext $\{Y_i : 0 \leq i < n\}$ and attempt to estimate plaintext $\{X_i : 0 \leq i < n\}$. Cryptanalysis is based upon the observation that

$$Y_i + i = Y_j + j \quad \textit{if and only if} \quad X_i + i = X_j + j$$

We intend to estimate the plaintext $\{X_i\}$ letter by letter; the procedure is a modification of Bayesian estimation, described in Chapter 2. The Bayesian estimate for X_0 *given* the ciphertext $(Y_0, Y_1, \ldots, Y_{n-1}) = (y_0, y_1, \ldots, y_{n-1})$ is the value of x_0 that makes the conditional probability

(5.4.1) $$Pr_{PLAIN/CIPHER}\{X_0 = x_0/(Y_0, Y_1, \ldots, Y_{n-1}) = (y_0, y_1, \ldots, y_{n-1})\}$$

$$= \frac{Pr_{PLAIN,CIPHER}\{X_0 = x_0 \text{ and } (Y_0, Y_1, \ldots Y_{n-1}) = (y_0, y_1, \ldots y_{n-1})\}}{\sum_{0 \leq t < m} Pr_{PLAIN,CIPHER}\{X_0 = t \text{ and } (Y_0, Y_1, \ldots, Y_{n-1}) = (y_0, y_1, \ldots y_{n-1})\}}$$

a maximum. The denominator in Eq. (5.4.1) does not depend on the value of x_0, so that maximizing the conditional probability

$$\Pr_{PLAIN/CIPHER}\{X_0 = x_0/(Y_0, Y_1, \ldots, Y_{n-1}) = (y_0, y_1, \ldots, y_{n-1})\}$$

with respect to x_0 is equivalent to maximizing the joint probability,

$$\Pr_{PLAIN,CIPHER}\{X_0 = x_0 \text{ and } (Y_0, Y_1, \ldots, Y_{n-1}) = (y_0, y_1 \ldots, y_{n-1})\}$$

In Sec. 2.6, we carried out a similar maximization; there the relationship between plaintext and ciphertext was addition modulo m, the key space was $\boldsymbol{K} = \boldsymbol{C}_m$, and we obtained a simple explicit formula for the joint probability. Here, the relationship between plaintext and ciphertext is more complicated: $\boldsymbol{K}$ = SYM($\boldsymbol{Z}_m$) contains m! substitutions, and a simple formula for the joint probability does not exist. To show the nature of the difficulty, consider the following Bayesian estimation problem; suppose the following:

- Plaintext $(X_0, X_1, \ldots, X_{n-1})$ is enciphered to ciphertext $(Y_0, Y_1, \ldots, Y_{n-1})$ by the monalphabetic substitution Π,

$$Y_i = \Pi(X_i) \qquad 0 \le i < n$$

- Π is a random variable with values in and uniformly distributed over the symmetric group SYM($\boldsymbol{Z}_m$),

$$\Pr_{KEY}\{\Pi = \pi\} = 1/m! \qquad \pi \in \text{SYM}(\boldsymbol{Z}_m)$$

- Π is independent of the plaintext $(X_0, X_1, \ldots, X_{n-1})$.

Let $N_t(\mathbf{y})$ denote the number of times the letter t appears in the sample of ciphertext $\mathbf{y} = (y_0, y_1, \ldots, y_{n-1})$. We may assume that n is sufficiently large so that $N_t(\mathbf{y}) > 0$ for $0 \le t < m$. Define the sequence $y_{i_0}, y_{i_1}, \ldots, y_{i_{m-1}}$ by

$$i_0 = 0$$

$$i_1 = \min\{j : y_j \ne y_{i_0}\}$$

$$i_2 = \min\{j : y_j \ne y_{i_0}, y_j \ne y_{i_1}\}$$

$$\cdots$$

$$\cdots$$

$$\cdots$$

$$i_{m-1} = \min\{j : y_j \ne y_{i_0}, y_j \ne y_{i_1}, \ldots, y_j \ne y_{i_{m-2}}\}$$

Thus

- i_1 is the first index at which a letter different from $y_{i_0} = y_0$ occurs
- i_2 is the first index at which a letter different from y_{i_0} or y_{i_1} occurs

and so forth.

The joint probability is a summation over substitutions π which satisfy $\pi(x_0) = y_0$

(5.4.2) $$\Pr_{\text{PLAIN,CIPHER}}\{X_0 = x_0 \text{ and } (Y_0, Y_1, \ldots, Y_{n-1}) = (y_0, y_1, \ldots, y_{n-1})\} = (1/m!) \sum_{\{\pi:\pi(x_0)=y_0\}} \prod_{0\le s<m} (p(\pi^{-1}(s)))^{N_s(y)}$$

To evaluate the right-hand side in Eq. (5.4.2), we describe the substitutions π satisfying $\pi(x_0) = y_0$ by the system of equations

$$\pi(t_s) = y_{i_s} \qquad 0 \le s < m$$

where $t_0 = x_0$, and we sum over $(t_1, t_2, \ldots, t_{m-1})$. Equation (5.4.2) becomes

(5.4.3) $$\Pr_{\text{PLAIN,CIPHER}}\{X_0 = x_0 \text{ and } (Y_0, Y_1, \ldots, Y_{n-1}) = (y_0, y_1, \ldots, y_{n-1})\} = \frac{1}{(m-1)!} \sum_{\{0\le t_1<m, t_1\ne t_0\}} \cdots \sum_{\{0\le t_{m-1}<m, t_{m-1}\ne t_0, t_1, \ldots, t_{m-2}\}} \prod_{0\le s<m} (p(t_s))^{N_{y_{i_s}}(y)}$$

The right-hand side in Eq. (5.4.3) may be expressed in terms of the numbers

$$s_k = \sum_{0\le t<m} p^k(t) \qquad 0 \le k < \infty$$

introduced in Chapter 4. For example,

$$\sum_{\{0\le t_{m-1}<m, t_{m-1}\ne t_0, \ldots, t_{m-2}\}} \prod_{0\le s<m} (p(t_s))^{N_{y_{i_s}}(y)} = \prod_{0\le s<m-1} (p(t_s))^{N_{y_{i_s}}(y)} [s_{N_{y_{i_{m-1}}}(y)} - \sum_{0\le i<m-1} (p(t_i))^{N_{y_{i_{m-1}}}(y)}]$$

$$\sum_{\{0\le t_{m-2}<m, t_{m-2}\ne t_0, \ldots, t_{m-3}\}} \sum_{\{0\le t_{m-1}<m, t_{m-1}\ne t_0, t_1, \ldots, t_{m-2}\}} \prod_{0\le s<m} (p(t_s))^{N_{y_{i_s}}(y)}$$

$$= \prod_{0\le s<m-2} (p(t_s))^{N_{y_{i_s}}(y)} s_{N_{y_{i_{m-1}}}(y)} [s_{N_{y_{i_{m-2}}}(y)} - \sum_{0\le i<m-2} (p(t_i))^{N_{y_{i_{m-2}}}(y)}]$$
$$+ \sum_{0\le i<m-2} (p(t_i))^{N_{y_{i_{m-1}}}(y)} \prod_{0\le s<m-2} (p(t_s))^{N_{y_{i_s}}(y)} [s_{N_{y_{i_{m-2}}}(y)} - \sum_{0\le i<m-2} (p(t_i))^{N_{y_{i_{m-1}}}(y)}]$$
$$+ \prod_{0\le s<m-2} (p(t_s))^{N_{y_{i_s}}(y)} [s_{N_{y_{i_{m-1}}}(y)+N_{y_{i_{m-2}}}(y)} - \sum_{0\le i<m-2} (p(t_i))^{N_{y_{i_{m-1}}}(y)+N_{y_{i_{m-2}}}(y)}]$$

The source of the complication is now evident; the summation in Eq. (5.4.3) is a multivariate polynomial in the variables $\{s_k\}$,

$$\sum_{\{r,(k_0,k_1,\ldots,k_{r-1})\}} \alpha_{k_0,k_1,\ldots,k_{r-1}} s_{k_0} s_{k_1} \cdots s_{k_{r-1}}$$

whose degree is an exponential function of m. One way around this difficulty is to reduce the general case to $m = 2$, where we have the simple formula

$$\Pr_{\text{PLAIN,CIPHER}}\{X_0 = x_0 \text{ and } (Y_0, Y_1, \ldots, Y_{n-1}) = (y_0, y_1, \ldots, y_{n-1})\}$$
$$= (p(y_{i_0}))^{N_{y_{i_0}}(y)} [1 - p(y_{i_0})]^{n-N_{y_{i_0}}(y)}$$

The reduction of $m = 2$ is achieved by recognizing only one letter in the ciphertext. Introduce the random variables

$$Z_j = \begin{cases} 1 & \text{if } Y_j = Y_0 \\ 0 & \text{if } Y_j \neq Y_0 \end{cases}$$

and consider the estimation problem with $(Z_0, Z_1, \ldots, Z_{n-1})$ instead of $(Y_0, Y_1, \ldots, Y_{n-1})$. We throw away information by failing to recognize all ciphertext values, but this reduction yields manageable formulae for the joint and conditional probabilities. It remains to see if the loss of information is critical in the cryptanalysis process.

We replace the problem of finding the value of x_0, which maximizes

$$\Pr_{\text{PLAIN/CIPHER}}\{X_0 = x_0/(Y_0, Y_1, \ldots, Y_{n-1}) = (y_0, y_1, \ldots, y_{n-1})\}$$

by the problem of finding the value of x_0, which maximizes

$$\Pr_{\text{PLAIN/Z-CIPHER}}\{X_0 = x_0/(Z_0, Z_1, \ldots, Z_{n-1}) = (z_0, z_1, \ldots, z_{n-1})\}$$

using the notations $\Pr_{\text{PLAIN,Z-CIPHER}}$ and $\Pr_{\text{PLAIN/Z-CIPHER}}$ to denote the joint and conditional distributions of plaintext and Z-valued ciphertext induced by the probability distribution $\Pr_{\text{PLAIN,CIPHER}}$. We have

$$\Pr_{\text{PLAIN,Z-CIPHER}}\{X_{i_0} = x_0 \text{ and } (Z_0, \ldots, Z_{n-1}) = (z_0, \ldots, z_{n-1})\}$$
$$= (p(x))^{N_{y_{i_0}}(y)} [1 - p(x)]^{n-N_{y_{i_0}}(y)}$$

Will the Bayesian estimate x^*

$$\Pr_{\text{PLAIN/Z-CIPHER}}\{X_0 = x^*/(Z_0, Z_1, \ldots, Z_{n-1}) = (z_0, z_1, \ldots, z_{n-1})\}$$
$$= \max_t \Pr_{\text{PLAIN/Z-CIPHER}}\{X_0 = t/(Z_0, Z_1, \ldots, Z_{n-1}) = (z_0, z_1, \ldots, z_{n-1})\}$$

yield the correct plaintext? If

$$\Pr_{\text{PLAIN,Z-CIPHER}}\{X_0 = x_0 \text{ and } (Z_0, Z_1, \ldots, Z_{n-1}) = (z_0, z_1, \ldots, z_{n-1})\}$$
$$= (p(x))^{N_{Z_0}(\mathbf{Z})} (1 - p(x))^{n-N_{Z_0}(\mathbf{Z})}$$

is maximized by $x_0 = x^*$, then

$$-(1/n)\Pr_{\text{PLAIN,Z-CIPHER}}\{X_0 = x_0 \text{ and } (Z_0, Z_1, \ldots, Z_{n-1}) = (z_0, z_1, \ldots, z_{n-1})\}$$

(5.4.4) $$= -(N_{z_0}(\mathbf{Z})/n) \log p(x_0) - [1 - (N_{z_0}(\mathbf{Z})/n)] \log (1 - p(x_0))$$
$$= -(N_{y_0}(\mathbf{Y})/n) \log p(x_0) - [1 - (N_{y_0}(\mathbf{Y}/n)] \log (1 - p(x_0))$$

is minimized by $x_0 = x^*$. As $n \to \infty$, the right-hand side of Eq. (5.4.4) converges with probability one to

(5.4.5) $$-p(\pi^{-1}(y_{i_0}))) \log p(x_0) - [1 - p(\pi^{-1}(y_{i_0}))] \log (1 - p(x_0))$$

If the probability distribution

$$(p(0),\ p(1),\ \ldots,\ p(m-1))$$

satisfies condition ★,

$$\star\ p(t) = p(s) \quad \textit{if and only if } s = t$$

then by Theorem 2.8.3 the expression in Eq. (5.4.5) is minimized only when $x_0 = \pi^{-1}(y_{i_0})$. Even if the condition ★ fails to hold, this only means that there are several letters which we cannot distinguish between after the reduction.

Now we apply this idea to cryptanalyze a 1-rotor system with ciphertext only. To find the value of x_0 that maximizes the conditional probability

$$\Pr_{\text{PLAIN/CIPHER}}\{X_0 = x_0/(Y_0, Y_1, \ldots, Y_{n-1}) = (y_0, y_1, \ldots, y_{n-1})\}$$

we introduce the random variables $\{Z_j\}$ defined by

$$Z_j = \begin{cases} 1 & \text{if } Y_j + j = Y_0 \text{ (modulo m)} \\ 0 & \text{if } Y_j + j \neq Y_0 \text{ (modulo m)} \end{cases}$$

We will estimate X_0 by maximizing

$$\Pr_{\text{PLAIN,Z-CIPHER}}\{X_0 = x_0 \text{ and } (Z_0, Z_m, \ldots) = (z_0, z_m, \ldots)\}$$

with respect to x_0. Let

$N_{j,t}(\mathbf{Y})$ = the number of occurrences of t in the shifted ciphertext

$$(Y_j,\ Y_{j+m} + j,\ Y_{j+2m} + j, \ldots)$$

L_j = the number of indices $0 \leq i < n$ that are congruent to j modulo m

$N_{j,t}(\mathbf{Z})$ = the number of occurrences of t in the ciphertext

$$(Z_j,\ Z_{j+m},\ Z_{j+2m}, \ldots)$$

Then

$$(5.4.6)\quad \Pr_{\text{PLAIN,Z-CIPHER}}\{X_0 = x_0 \text{ and } (Z_0, Z_1, \ldots) = (z_0, z_m, \ldots)\} = \prod_{0 \leq j < m} (p(x_0 - j))^{N_{j,y_0}(\mathbf{y})} (1 - p(x_0 - j))^{L_{j,y_0}(\mathbf{y})}$$

Maximizing the right-hand side of Eq. (5.4.6) with respect to x_0 is the same as minimizing

$$(5.4.7)\quad -(1/n) \log \Pr_{\text{PLAIN,Z-CIPHER}}\{X_0 = x_0 \text{ and } (Z_0, Z_1, \ldots) = (z_0, z_m, \ldots)\}$$
$$= -\sum_{0 \leq j < m} (N_{j,y_0}(\mathbf{y})/n) \log p(x_0 - j) - ((L_j - N_{j,y_0}(\mathbf{y})/n) \log (1 - p(x_0 - j))$$

As $n \to \infty$, the right-hand side of Eq. (5.4.7) converges with probability one to

$$-\sum_{0 \leq j < m} p(\pi^{-1}(y_0) - j) \log p(x_0 - j) + (1 - p(\pi^{-1}(y_0) - j) \log (1 - p(x_0 - j))$$

TABLE 5.4.1

$\tau(i)$ i = 0(1)25

i	$\tau(i)$	i	$\tau(i)$	i	$\tau(i)$
0	5.5206	9	7.4018	18	7.4320
1	7.0454	10	7.3921	19	6.8976
2	7.0212	11	6.5789	20	7.5859
3	7.6531	12	6.6847	21	7.4901
4	7.0151	13	6.5693	22	6.9350
5	7.5938	14	7.3046	23	7.1737
6	6.8489	15	6.8379	24	7.3392
7	7.1345	16	7.0103	25	6.8263
8	7.4144	17	7.3127		

TABLE 5.4.2

CIPHER(2.3) : Encipherment of *PLAIN(2)* by a 1-Rotor (Hebern) System

```
eawzw lqvsw ysycy jwucv ynptb fwufi hpyai nvujq fbbaq ltvlk yllew volbl
odbbk ghlbl kumno xlqfo uivop xibas yylvq lknhg gjfuf qfgvp vpzhq fbkkb
uucsh kojfq rjxgl epqbt xpryl pqdbb yghlp dnfme xsmbe ofzgt kmtnv uyqoj
eqttm quiyh whzoj hzvra aumng jfmbd mqhni zaxht itqcd dwegk jhaqt ydmkz
avuti ziizc axciy skffd wepqu isltt asybk mcnpu mndlp opukg melif qnzit
xplra ftqvm wfxuc zxwso ubgmx efoca yxbkn iomdt czlww lsfae xbsbj rxyge
dloge yhglc sbqxa sghrj zbeuy vhofj cqwlj xypsc azrkm hpdbx ithxp owxmq
ksyby qepbl mvuhi osemx eqttw hkelt wqghj jhcau pxhbe kopmc dmonb lokcg
xvwjb evvdv lcjje awank qgtta jyygr riket ieebr nflqm bppqj vzkcw jfeev
dplkz llyhv mibgb ncgip wpcik aoebj yjpum exksp envxz kwcqr dldpl kljxq
mexeb ffmcx zhzej xzkhs cepjk dhymi bbfqy lebvo jrgft maiay kawsx nrvyo
wfptg tqdxh enekl hfwdh jkwha fxpep vvwtx umnec pfxuh ywukf btvbx xnbdx
zxzkj qbjmt sihnr vokcg xvwpd rghpn juuic tvhqz kmyoq xyyyx xdhra eezyz
wokrm ukwlq atkjm xlxdu sedfe ldcfg mcpza jvbjt xmaxp xgedz nrdth yavba
btatk jmezd cvysd jipbu xxyuv yscds lyfnf xcliv oxnlm uysne tvocz hbffp
daxus oagyy nwkon lbasr brywt odxxf wclpn pwowx xoros miajy kmauk ksdxv
ojoff cntfv braex wbsfv giend mzlly hvlcc yfjer wjbal mpuyy gjfuf qxqku
cyftw tiygb bagzt nxjyq bcbzw brmyl vmbfu wbikd vmoje grori kgsoz oabbw
bvyjb xiplz nzrfp rovss qhtzm qacdx wngkv fekrd mlmzs ssrct rygov vixrk
aknyx cysup imrce tipyg wubis gqmwl dtcyl vjmgt vmskg ozqio schxy mfxme
xllby oqmkv wvuxc utpdm pqtth pxvsi wxrzi yilph qxzda soidt cylvj mgtvm
skgoz qiosc hxymd tczlw mzzaa bbjkh tqeaz mbfyl kncqw pkvrk gxgyr xliko
bpqun sfoqh kwplj oepxh fovve jmnmq okbcs ihobp voxbt immfn keitx zohbd
fihlr mcoss xjioo xxfwk ojlrp uwapu mwxrx hrbic qxzxz kemay xdmhk nbazh
qfbla plngi yekqo kucca nkvvi nvujq fbbax fwnpt bfwuf ihtbs sfvzg tgplh
ivsbv lzlly hvsis pbxae xsbej nqasv afmdw jxzhu plxqg tqkfb bajey chxpo
aakxj lcyfh ysykf buzps tkacn ypnjm lvcmg eoebl rjfqq xoidl nufet zmlrh
emnly tlbox jeych xpoea wzhnb lttat kjkow dcpdr afzll fmzhx mnodv fttic
baifd corzz rekcd zkwya qzztg dbypv mnmob uxspi fgsta hdsfh yjlnq xwixx
evmcd anpya odibb rbrta xpyya knzsi xqhgq byyvj wwbjl qgawv lcjjw esxyu
zlfwt stlkv uqqxf nbppk nfbrx gqbyy vlyyx bzqih fnbxp neawx xorob zhsfg
kpojg ofnbp pknfb rxuam wbxgj tsoue boyxv lnufe snksy qyavu xhmzu uchsy
geodr emhms poiax zxhgo uzizi efgad dmwen ktstm djekf bbaka nivmo lcfii
kpcvo cqjek fbbab xiplz yynik sjkhp voybx wmwjx wiysk ffdwe pqssc yyavr
tlnoq uddsn pjigr orikg sozoi yiysj fwila cftvy lqwyx ocbbr aexwb eczca
inbip kpybx yumno dvfue yzduz bsgqq okbcs zmsmo slxij wbhpu dvymh jixrm
fqvnr mydbs uyggb kzlzv aqflk ypxjz ymgev nbfno jrgff sllom pdxio etufq
gtwlb zdusi bshfm qttsq eufhi fvhiy qgbkk jdrbf rvtcy xaukw se
```

Condition ★ is replaced by

$$☆\ \tau(0) < \min_{0<i<m} \tau(i)$$

$$\tau(i) = -\sum_{0 \le j < m} p(i-j)\log p(-j) + (1 - p(i-j))\log(1 - p(-j))$$

In Table 5.4.1 we show that condition ☆ is satisfied for the probability distribution from Table 2.3.1. *CIPHER(2.3)* shown in Fig. 5.4.2, is the encipherment of *PLAIN(2)* by a 1-rotor system.

In Table 5.4.3, we show the effect of estimating $(X_0, X_1, \ldots, X_{N-1})$ from $(Y_0, Y_1, \ldots, Y_{N-1})$ with increasing amounts of ciphertext.

TABLE 5.4.3
Effect on the Accuracy of Bayesian Estimation of Increasing Amounts of *CIPHER(2.3)*

N	% of Ciphertext	Number Correctly Estimated	% Correct
113	5	59	52.2
227	10	189	83.2
341	15	325	95.3
454	20	454	100

5.5 CRYPTANALYSIS WITH CIPHERTEXT ONLY: N = 2

We assume first that the polyalphabetic substitution

$$C_{-r_1(i)}\ \pi_1\ C_{r_1(i)-r_0(i)}\ \pi_0\ C_{r_0(i)} \qquad r_0(i) = i \qquad r_1(i) = \lfloor i/m$$

enciphers the plaintext $(X_0, X_1, \ldots, X_{n-1})$ into the ciphertext $(Y_0, Y_1, \ldots, Y_{n-1})$, and second, that the $\{X_i : 0 \le i < n\}$ are independent and identical distribution random variables with probability distribution

$$\Pr_{PLAIN}\{X_i = t\} = p(t) \qquad 0 \le i < n,\ 0 \le t < m$$

Thus

$$Y_i = \pi_1(\lfloor i/m + (\pi_0(i + X_i) - i)) - \lfloor i/m \qquad 0 \le i < n \tag{5.5.1}$$

We will reduce the cryptanalysis with N = 2 rotors to the case of N = 1 rotor. Fix j and consider values of i for which

$$\lfloor i/m - i = j \text{ (modulo m)}$$

For these values of i, the substitution $C_{-r_i(i)}\ \pi_1\ C_{r_1(i)-r_0(i)}\ \pi_0\ C_{r_0(i)}$ is of the form $C_{-j-i}\ \pi_1\ C_j\ \pi_0\ C_i$, and Eq. (5.5.1) becomes

$$Y_i + j + i = \pi_1(j + \pi_0(i + X_i)) \tag{5.5.2}$$

We divide the ciphertext into m ciphersubtexts corresponding to the values of $\lfloor i/m - i = j$ (modulo m). On each of these ciphersubtexts we apply the Bayesian estimation for 1-rotor encipherment. We need to have considerably more ciphertext than in the previous section, since we are applying the Bayesian estimate to $(1/m)^{th}$ of the original ciphertext. In Table 5.5.1, we show the effect of Bayesian estimating for the first ten letters of the plaintext if we encipher c copies of *PLAIN(2)* with $1 \leq c \leq 8$. We tabulate for each of the first ten plaintext letters the five letters with the largest conditional probability.

TABLE 5.5.1
Bayesian Estimates of the Plaintext with Increasing Amounts of Ciphertext

Length of Ciphertext : 2272

T	H	E	I	S	S	U	E	O	F
T	G	E	E	E	S	G	E	T	F
O	A	D	I	I	I	T	T	O	T
E	E	H	A	S	O	U	I	N	U
S	T	O	S	H	H	N	H	E	E
N	F	I	R	T	V	C	D	R	O

Length of Ciphertext 4544

T	H	E	I	S	S	U	E	O	F
T	H	E	I	E	S	G	E	U	F
S	T	D	H	S	O	U	I	T	E
H	W	H	S	I	F	K	O	I	U
O	G	S	O	H	E	V	B	O	T
U	V	O	A	W	I	O	D	A	S

Length of Ciphertext : 6816

T	H	E	I	S	S	U	E	O	F
S	H	E	I	S	S	G	E	O	F
T	W	D	H	H	D	U	T	Y	T
H	T	H	O	W	F	N	F	M	E
O	I	U	S	I	O	H	R	C	S
F	A	S	A	T	E	O	I	V	D

Length of Ciphertext : 9088

T	H	E	I	S	S	U	E	O	F
T	H	E	I	S	S	G	E	O	F
H	W	H	O	H	D	U	T	I	E
S	S	D	H	T	O	N	F	T	D
O	I	T	A	W	E	H	O	D	T
F	L	U	S	I	F	O	R	M	U

Length of Ciphertext : 11360

T	H	E	I	S	S	U	E	O	F
T	H	E	I	S	S	G	E	O	F
H	W	H	H	H	D	U	T	D	E
O	S	D	A	T	O	N	A	C	S
S	I	U	W	C	H	V	I	M	T
G	L	T	G	E	F	K	R	B	L

Length of Ciphertext 13631

T	H	E	I	S	S	U	E	O	F
T	H	E	I	S	S	U	E	O	F
H	W	H	H	H	D	G	T	D	E
S	S	U	W	T	H	Y	I	B	S
G	L	T	G	C	O	H	R	V	T
R	G	D	A	I	F	J	A	X	B

5.6 THE ENIGMA MACHINE

The principal encipherment system used by the German military forces in the Second World War was the *Enigma machine* shown in Fig. 5.6.1. U.S. Patent 1,657,411, filed on February 6, 1923, and assigned to Arthur Scherbius for the German firm of Chiffriermaschinen Aktiengesellschaft of Berlin is the basic

Figure 5.6.1. An Enigma machine.

Enigma machine, which consists of (1) a *plugboard,* (2) three rotors whose rotational positions change with encipherment, and (3) a *reflecting rotor.* The Enigma substitution is

$$E_i : x_i \to y_i$$

$$E_i = IP^{-1}\, T_i\, IP$$

$$T_i = C_{-r_0(i)}\pi_0^{-1}C_{r_0(i)}C_{-r_1(i)}\pi_1^{-1}C_{r_1(i)}C_{-r_2(i)}\pi_2^{-1}C_{r_2(i)}\pi_R C_{-r_2(i)} \times \pi_2 C_{r_2(i)}C_{-r_1(i)}\pi_1 C_{r_1(i)}C_{-r_0(i)}\pi_0 C_{r_0(i)}$$

The reflecting rotor π_R is an *involution* on $\boldsymbol{Z_m}$

$$\pi_R^2 = I$$

which is realized by a rotor with contacts on one side only that are connected in pairs.

The steps in Enigma encipherment are:

Step 1 The plaintext is subjected to the initial permutation IP;

Step 2 The ciphertext resulting from *Step 1* is enciphered by the three rotor substitution;

$$C_{-r_2(i)}\ \pi_2\ C_{r_2(i)-r_1(i)}\ \pi_1\ C_{r_1(i)-r_0(i)}\ \pi_0\ C_{r_0(i)}$$

Step 3 The ciphertext resulting from *Step 3* is enciphered by the reflecting rotor π_R;

Step 4 The ciphertext resulting from *Step 3* is enciphered by passing it back through the three rotors in the reverse direction;

$$C_{-r_0(i)}\ \pi_0^{-1}\ C_{r_0(i)}\ C_{-r_1(i)}\ \pi_1^{-1}\ C_{r_1(i)}\ C_{-r_2(i)}\ \pi_2^{-1}\ C_{r_2(i)}$$

Step 5 The ciphertext resulting from *Step 4* is subjected to the inverse IP^{-1} of the initial permutation IP.

The Enigma key consists of (1) the rotors π_0, π_1, π_2, π_R; (2) the plugboard IP; and (3) the initial rotational displacements of π_0, π_1, π_2. The rotors $\{\pi_i\}$ were changed infrequently and were selected from a set of nine possible rotors in the naval model and four in the Wehrmacht model.

The analysis of the Enigma machine is one of the triumphs of the Allied cryptographers during the Second World War [WI]. Although the details of their solutions have not been published, it is clear that they resulted from the newly emerging technology of digital computation. While the Enigma is certainly secure against pen and pencil attacks, high speed computation provided the margin of success. We will present an analysis and discussion of Enigma-like machines in the concluding sections of this chapter.

5.7 PROPERTIES OF ENIGMA ENCIPHERMENT

Let

(5.7.1) $$T_i = C_{-r_0(i)}\pi_0^{-1}C_{r_0(i)}C_{-r_1(i)}\pi_1^{-1}C_{r_1(i)}C_{-r_2(i)}\pi_2^{-1}C_{r_2(i)}\ \pi_R \times C_{-r_2(i)}\ \pi_2 C_{r_2(i)}\ C_{-r_1(i)}\pi_1 C_{r_1(i)}\ C_{-r_0(i)}\pi_0 C_{r_0(i)}$$

with $r_s(i)$ given by Eq. (5.1.1).

Theorem 5.7.1 T_i is an involution; if $T_i(x) = y$, then $T_i(y) = x$.

Proof. Suppose $T_i(x) = y$; then

(5.7.2) $$\pi_R\ C_{-r_2(i)}\ \pi_2\ C_{r_2(i)-r_1(i)}\ \pi_1\ C_{r_1(i)-r_0(i)}\ \pi_0\ C_{r_0(i)}\ (x) = C_{-r_2(i)}\ \pi_2\ C_{r_2(i)-r_1(i)}\ \pi_1\ C_{r_1(i)-r_0(i)}\ \pi_0\ C_{r_0(i)}\ (y)$$

Since π_R is an involution, Eq. (5.7.2) shows that

$$(5.7.3) \quad \pi_R\, C_{-r_2(i)}\, \pi_2\, C_{r_2(i)-r_1(i)}\, \pi_1\, C_{r_1(i)-r_0(i)}\, \pi_0\, C_{r_0(i)}\, (y) = C_{-r_2(i)}\, \pi_2\, C_{r_2(i)-r_1(i)}\, \pi_1\, C_{r_1(i)-r_0(i)}\, \pi_0\, C_{r_0(i)}\, (x) \quad \blacktriangleleft$$

Thus if the ith letter of plaintext is `A`, and it is enciphered by T_i into `E`, we know that T_i enciphers `E` into `A`.

If two Enigma machines

$$E : \{\pi_0, \pi_1, \pi_2, \pi_R\} \qquad E' : \{\nu_0, \nu_1, \nu_2, \nu_R\}$$

are related by

$$\nu_0 = C_{-A}\, \pi_0 \qquad \nu_1 = C_{-B}\, \pi_1\, C_A$$

$$\nu_2 = C_{-C}\, \pi_2\, C_B \qquad \nu_R = C_{-C}\, \pi_R\, C_C$$

then E and E′ are equivalent Enigma machines producing the same ciphertext. This allows us to assign arbitrary values for $\pi_i(t_i)$ for any choice of t_0, t_1, t_2.

5.8 CRYPTANALYSIS OF THE ENIGMA WITH CORRESPONDING PLAINTEXT AND CIPHERTEXT

The solution for the rotors with corresponding plaintext and ciphertext is a variant on the method used in Sec. 5.3 for the Hebern system. In Fig. 5.8.1, we show rotors for a 3-rotor Enigma machine. Figure 5.8.2 is the encipherment of *PLAIN(1)* by this Enigma machine.

We shall assume that

- Plaintext $(x_0, x_1, \ldots, x_{n-1})$ was enciphered to ciphertext $(y_0, y_1, \ldots, y_{n-1})$.
- The initial rotational displacements are all zero.

Let i take values in the jth block

$$B_j = \{jm, jm + 1, \ldots, (j + 1)m - 1\}$$

Equation (5.7.2) then is of the form

$$(5.8.1) \qquad \pi_R(S_j(\pi_0(x_i + i) - i)) = S_j(\pi_0(y_i + i) - i)$$

where S_j is the substitution

$$S_j = C_{-r_2(i)}\, \pi_2\, C_{r_2(i)-r_1(i)}\, \pi_1\, C_{r_1(i)}$$

which is independent of i on B_j.

We recover π_0 starting from the following observation: if $i_0 \neq i_1$ are in B_j, then

$$(5.8.2) \qquad \pi_R(S_j(\pi_0(x_{i_0} + i_0) - i_0)) = \pi_R(S_j(\pi_0(x_{i_1} + i_1) - i_1))$$

$$\textit{if and only if} \quad S_j(\pi_0(y_{i_0} + i_0) - i_0) = S_j(\pi_0(y_{i_1} + i_1) - i_1)$$

π_0

A	B	C	D	E	F	G	H	I	J	K	L	M	N	O	P	Q	R	S	T	U	V	W	X	Y	Z
0	1	2	3	4	5	6	7	8	9	10	11	12	13	14	15	16	17	18	19	20	21	22	23	24	25
↓	↓	↓	↓	↓	↓	↓	↓	↓	↓	↓	↓	↓	↓	↓	↓	↓	↓	↓	↓	↓	↓	↓	↓	↓	↓
22	5	1	19	8	25	13	20	21	2	16	4	9	15	14	10	18	7	23	6	12	0	3	24	17	11
W	F	B	T	I	Z	N	U	V	C	Q	E	J	P	O	K	S	H	X	G	M	A	D	Y	R	L

π_1

A	B	C	D	E	F	G	H	I	J	K	L	M	N	O	P	Q	R	S	T	U	V	W	X	Y	Z
0	1	2	3	4	5	6	7	8	9	10	11	12	13	14	15	16	17	18	19	20	21	22	23	24	25
↓	↓	↓	↓	↓	↓	↓	↓	↓	↓	↓	↓	↓	↓	↓	↓	↓	↓	↓	↓	↓	↓	↓	↓	↓	↓
7	12	17	6	13	16	15	10	9	2	0	8	21	22	11	20	4	1	5	25	18	24	23	19	3	14
H	M	R	G	N	Q	P	K	J	C	A	I	V	W	L	U	E	B	F	Z	S	Y	X	T	D	O

π_2

A	B	C	D	E	F	G	H	I	J	K	L	M	N	O	P	Q	R	S	T	U	V	W	X	Y	Z
0	1	2	3	4	5	6	7	8	9	10	11	12	13	14	15	16	17	18	19	20	21	22	23	24	25
↓	↓	↓	↓	↓	↓	↓	↓	↓	↓	↓	↓	↓	↓	↓	↓	↓	↓	↓	↓	↓	↓	↓	↓	↓	↓
3	17	20	0	7	11	1	5	25	21	6	12	22	2	10	23	15	8	16	24	18	14	13	19	9	4
D	R	U	A	H	L	B	F	Z	V	G	M	W	C	K	X	P	I	Q	Y	S	O	N	T	J	E

π_R

A	B	C	D	E	F	G	H	I	J	K	L	M	N	O	P	Q	R	S	T	U	V	W	X	Y	Z
0	1	2	3	4	5	6	7	8	9	10	11	12	13	14	15	16	17	18	19	20	21	22	23	24	25
↓	↓	↓	↓	↓	↓	↓	↓	↓	↓	↓	↓	↓	↓	↓	↓	↓	↓	↓	↓	↓	↓	↓	↓	↓	↓
14	22	19	21	18	10	24	15	9	8	5	12	11	20	0	7	17	16	4	2	13	3	1	25	6	23
O	W	T	V	S	K	Y	P	J	I	F	M	L	U	A	H	R	Q	E	C	N	D	B	Z	G	X

Figure 5.8.1. π_0, π_1, π_2 and π_R : A set of enigma substitutions.

Moreover, since π_R is an involution,

(5.8.3) $$\pi_R(S_j(\pi_0(x_{i_0} + i_0) - i_0)) = S_j(\pi_0(y_{i_1} + i_1) - i_1)$$

if and only if $$S_j(\pi_0(x_{i_1} + i_1) - i_1) = \pi_R(S_j(\pi_0(x_{i_0} + i_0) - i_0))$$

The analogous set of Eqs. (5.8.2) and (5.8.3) for the Hebern rotor is

```
grsuz tldsz nkwne rdpfb ovvqn obkyi qnjrc qlifr vtpki lhgqv tmmjy majuj
lljqn gljyl uglet deyxo cpgiz lffsi nrfdf siyag hhzhf ksccz wolta nqtbv
ekyhe yhmsl zeyzr goijr himzv huwzl qbcyy flvlt nhwkd namvn sihlz onukh
uzmpx bfslv paveq ioxbf bywul whtsz qnnhu uszlr obntu uugle kissv tojyp
uogsz dxxxs qyrhz qexui gcmdo tfbsd ahkxj ncvxg wloqv xtmme wrdik wwwxs
jawmj xbfnq lfdes dsqie yyemg emcha sfqjc hkbjq lkumi zjhxw olalt grqaw
cozih fvimv tscqw xxxha ionks clgxo wngjj amgmm vvfga yhhtj gbnvd acnkg
ypbkj ncnte qfika hmvhx eftgh wxruz jhpez jtics rkkbg hyflj hbnfi fpplu
cfxsz klcic phzer irjun ifyim qsmzo qhmsj kwmsh jyaiy ggyav fjllc gabsw
ikkpu cwyhj dznlk iirnf fbxnw xcwvl mtbgt hcipg gkunb ebfzw dytrg pufxf
eydmp fnqqd auzsm ympge mzfxe hhdkz oasfi qooeu gxfyt pgsph izbwy wzygs
ctziz xggzz vdbjr aprdc ixupi dpybn nhmfb dzzxi poywo sfocr jlcrt myeuo
essof ddwwz bjumk ikhmw ahyeb yumrm cqyfy vpnge yldpa besru ijpgr jzezm
kglaa tnfib maicw bderm fojhn mrldn lbqkf srfps rnpfj dobqj sdvym kgxit
apyqg chfft cvffj vvxme moygr chywd gkrvr noikr jwnan nfscx fzqod prdmb
sfmte lebtc gwyat csdhr szqkk qfsoh mpuhb seecg ampae ugymo vrezq gmnum
gnubz dnnel ymygc qqrmk oaxaq miccb lbwlv recye tcibz skzla efzfp iznib
iyivi ktwkt udfra tzsqm xfmuv jgzqb wdhpk dwbcg ziawt tttny ssfbk zqgnh
rqefh ssaio bdgvm qprti ainob ykmeq vsnsa wfsuf jgfhn efcbd unmxe vjqgg
rzbzg lrboc qnixz efdtg yyuwu rjmmr slecy vdigc vratp wahrd xpqbl lbxai
wuqnt psupt pkqdk tgmqw dmsvh mecyz bkebx qvwhx mqepe yspzq zikxr zxtkl
bvrnt vrfpj rmtvt xneaw eersi deqmp mnlwl ipdse ujvju sznoc iqnhs lhvyj
sjilg hbpvq uojyc gftrj udfxk buqqx yxvoz wqrok axzdh lfjzf piddh wpwlf
yzwez cyahs hacsl lrecx xqgei ygzhp topgu tkjzv tuapp vdoaq hvcfw gxvih
onjnu gvpeu hejrg bbdjl qywud vveyq gorzv vgphc qivxl menam wgjur utslz
tiuva etnuu lqhrd mftcj xhqun jzzne neoze tunrz sovlg qeack vnqfn fqbvn
qebxy zitru afphr jdytj ystrh prhlq jwikg diepk vzzae zpbxr qdfog ngitc
wiesv vwkir wnrmw rfhej sdkbk vnguy exaup yhxza ervnp vcdkb rrs
```

Figure 5.8.2. *CIPHER(1.6)* : enigma encipherment of *PLAIN(1)* using substitutions from Fig. 5.8.1.

$$\pi_0(x_{i_0} + i_0) - i_0 = \pi_0(x_{i_1} + i_1) - i_1$$

$$\textit{if and only if} \quad \pi_0(y_{i_0} + i_0) - i_0 = \pi_0(y_{i_1} + i_1) - i_1$$

Here we have an additional complication; in order to check that the left-hand relationship in Eq. (5.8.2) is an equality, we need to determine if

$$\pi_0(x_{i_0} + i_0) - i_0 = \pi_0(x_{i_1} + i_1) - i_1$$

and this generally requires information about the very rotor π_0 we are attempting to recover. We will answer the opposite question; when are the relationships in Eqs. (5.8.2) and (5.8.3) *not* satisfied? If i_0 and i_1 in B_j are distinct, Eq. (5.8.2) is not satisfied if

$$x_{i_0} + i_0 = x_{i_1} + i_1$$

We will call this a *miss,* and from this deduce that

$$\pi_0(y_{i_0} + i_0) - i_0 \neq \pi_0(y_{i_1} + i_1) - i_1$$

which provides one constraint upon π_0. We will keep track of the constraints for each pair (i,j) in the vector

$$\Gamma_{i,j} = (\gamma_{i,j}(0), \gamma_{i,j}(1), \ldots, \gamma_{i,j}(25))$$

where $\gamma_{i,j}(t)$ represents the status of the constraint on $\pi_0(i) - \pi_0(j)$:

$$\gamma_{i,j}(t) = \begin{cases} 0 & \text{if we have ruled out the possibility that } \pi_0(i) - \pi_0(j) \neq t \\ 1 & \text{if we have not ruled out the possibility that } \pi_0(i) - \pi_0(j) \neq t \end{cases}$$

We start the cryptanalysis with $\{\Gamma_{i,j} : 0 \leq i,j < m\}$ given by

$$\Gamma_{i,j} = (0, 1, 1, \ldots, 1) \qquad 0 \leq i,j < m \; i \neq j$$

$$\Gamma_{i,i} = (1, 0, 0, \ldots, 0) \qquad 0 \leq i < m$$

If after *scanning* the set of plaintext-ciphertext pairs, $\Gamma_{i,j}$ becomes a unit vector

$$\Gamma_{i,j} = (\underbrace{0, 0, \ldots, 0}_{\text{k-1 zeros}}, 1, \underbrace{0, 0, \ldots, 0}_{\text{26-k zeros}})$$

we can conclude $\pi_0(i) - \pi_0(j) = k$ (modulo m). The analysis will be successful if a sufficient number of the $\{\Gamma_{i,j}\}$ ultimately become unit vectors. We begin by scanning the entries in block B_0 updating $\{\Gamma_{i,j}\}$ with the discovery of each miss. We scan by choosing a value $k \in \boldsymbol{Z}_m$ and searching for pairs (i_0, i_1) $(i_0 \neq i_1)$ in the 0th block, for which one of the following three conditions is satisfied:

$$x_{i_0} + i_0 = x_{i_1} + i_1 = k \qquad y_{i_0} + i_0 = y_{i_1} + i_1 = k \qquad x_{i_0} + i_0 = y_{i_1} + i_1 = k$$

We repeatedly scan B_0 until no new misses are found; then we proceed to scan B_1, and so forth. In Table 5.8.3 we show the 0th block of shifted plaintext-ciphertext pairs.

The pairs of corresponding entries in Table 5.8.3,

$$\pi_0(1) - 1 \qquad \pi_0(18) - 1$$

$$\pi_0(18) - 4 \qquad \pi_0(3) - 4$$

TABLE 5.8.3
Zeroth Block of Corresponding Shifted Plaintext and Ciphertext

Shifted Plaintext	Shifted Ciphertext	Shifted Plaintext	Shifted Ciphertext
$\pi_0(12) - 0$	$\pi_0(6) - 0$	$\pi_0(1) - 1$	$\pi_0(18) - 1$
$\pi_0(15) - 2$	$\pi_0(20) - 2$	$\pi_0(1) - 3$	$\pi_0(23) - 3$
$\pi_0(18) - 4$	$\pi_0(3) - 4$	$\pi_0(22) - 5$	$\pi_0(24) - 5$
$\pi_0(12) - 6$	$\pi_0(17) - 6$	$\pi_0(7) - 7$	$\pi_0(10) - 7$
$\pi_0(21) - 8$	$\pi_0(0) - 8$	$\pi_0(17) - 9$	$\pi_0(8) - 9$
$\pi_0(9) - 10$	$\pi_0(23) - 10$	$\pi_0(11) - 11$	$\pi_0(21) - 11$
$\pi_0(5) - 12$	$\pi_0(8) - 12$	$\pi_0(21) - 13$	$\pi_0(0) - 13$
$\pi_0(2) - 14$	$\pi_0(18) - 14$	$\pi_0(2) - 15$	$\pi_0(6) - 15$
$\pi_0(8) - 16$	$\pi_0(19) - 16$	$\pi_0(8) - 17$	$\pi_0(6) - 17$
$\pi_0(22) - 18$	$\pi_0(23) - 18$	$\pi_0(4) - 19$	$\pi_0(20) - 19$
$\pi_0(18) - 20$	$\pi_0(8) - 20$	$\pi_0(9) - 21$	$\pi_0(16) - 21$
$\pi_0(9) - 22$	$\pi_0(17) - 22$	$\pi_0(25) - 23$	$\pi_0(13) - 23$
$\pi_0(12) - 24$	$\pi_0(11) - 24$	$\pi_0(11) - 25$	$\pi_0(13) - 25$

imply that

$$\pi_0(3) - 4 \neq \pi_0(1) - 1$$

and hence we can set $\gamma_{1,3}(23) = 0$.

We repeat the scan of B_0 and update the vectors $\{\Gamma_{i,j}\}$. The value of $\Gamma_{0,j}$ for $0 \leq j < 26$ after repeated scanning of B_0 is shown in Table 5.8.4 (replacing the unit entries by blank spaces).

We can now repeat the scan using the information acquired in the previous

TABLE 5.8.4
$\Gamma_{0,j}$ After Repeated Scanning of B_0

t	0	1	2	3	4	5	6	7	8	9	10	11	12	13	14	15	16	17	18	19	20	21	22	23	24	25
$\Gamma_{0,0}$		0	0	0	0	0	0	0	0	0	0	0	0	0	0	0	0	0	0	0	0	0	0	0	0	0
$\Gamma_{0,1}$	0					0		0			0	0		0			0				0	0	0	0		0
$\Gamma_{0,2}$	0		0	0													0							0		
$\Gamma_{0,3}$	0		0						0	0					0	0						0	0	0	0	0
$\Gamma_{0,4}$	0				0	0		0				0				0	0				0					
$\Gamma_{0,5}$	0			0	0			0	0	0	0					0				0		0				0
$\Gamma_{0,6}$	0	0	0	0			0	0	0					0		0		0		0		0			0	
$\Gamma_{0,7}$	0			0			0					0		0			0			0			0		0	
$\Gamma_{0,8}$	0			0	0						0						0	0	0	0	0			0		
$\Gamma_{0,9}$	0				0					0	0		0						0			0		0	0	
$\Gamma_{0,10}$	0							0		0		0		0			0		0			0			0	
$\Gamma_{0,11}$	0	0	0	0	0			0				0				0								0		
$\Gamma_{0,12}$	0				0						0	0			0						0	0			0	
$\Gamma_{0,13}$	0	0	0				0		0	0		0	0		0			0		0	0				0	
$\Gamma_{0,14}$	0	0	0										0		0			0				0				
$\Gamma_{0,15}$	0		0				0					0								0	0					
$\Gamma_{0,16}$	0	0		0							0				0	0							0			
$\Gamma_{0,17}$	0		0				0						0					0							0	
$\Gamma_{0,18}$	0	0					0		0			0		0		0	0		0	0		0	0		0	
$\Gamma_{0,19}$	0		0		0	0		0	0				0	0				0	0		0					0
$\Gamma_{0,20}$	0	0		0	0	0	0					0	0	0		0			0	0		0	0	0	0	0
$\Gamma_{0,21}$	0		0	0	0	0												0			0	0			0	
$\Gamma_{0,22}$	0			0		0							0	0		0		0			0					
$\Gamma_{0,23}$	0					0		0			0									0	0	0	0			
$\Gamma_{0,24}$	0			0			0		0					0								0				
$\Gamma_{0,25}$	0	0			0		0				0			0		0	0		0	0				0		

scan; for example, since $\gamma_{0,1}(5) = 1$, any pair (i_0, i_1) in the same block for which one of the following four sets of conditions holds,

$$x_{i_0} + i_0 = 0 \qquad x_{i_1} + i_1 = 1 \qquad i_0 - i_1 = 5$$

$$y_{i_0} + i_0 = 0 \qquad y_{i_1} + i_1 = 1 \qquad i_0 - i_1 = 5$$

$$y_{i_0} + i_0 = 0 \qquad x_{i_1} + i_1 = 1 \qquad i_0 - i_1 = 5$$

$$x_{i_0} + i_0 = 0 \qquad y_{i_1} + i_1 = 1 \qquad i_0 - i_1 = 5$$

TABLE 5.8.5

$\Gamma_{0,j}$ After Repeated Scanning of B_0–B_9

t	0	1	2	3	4	5	6	7	8	9	10	11	12	13	14	15	16	17	18	19	20	21	22	23	24	25
$\Gamma_{0,0}$		0	0	0	0	0	0	0	0	0	0	0	0	0	0	0	0	0	0	0	0	0	0	0	0	0
$\Gamma_{0,1}$	0	0	0	0	0	0		0	0	0	0	0	0	0	0	0	0		0	0	0	0	0	0	0	0
$\Gamma_{0,2}$	0	0	0	0	0	0	0	0	0		0	0	0		0	0	0	0	0		0		0	0		0
$\Gamma_{0,3}$	0		0				0		0	0			0		0	0			0	0		0	0	0	0	0
$\Gamma_{0,4}$	0		0	0	0	0	0	0	0	0	0	0		0		0	0	0			0	0	0			0
$\Gamma_{0,5}$	0	0		0	0	0		0	0	0	0	0	0		0	0	0	0	0	0	0	0	0		0	0
$\Gamma_{0,6}$	0	0	0	0	0		0	0	0		0			0		0	0	0		0		0		0	0	0
$\Gamma_{0,7}$	0	0	10	0	0	0	0	0	0	0	0	0	0	0	0	0	0	0	0	0	0	0	0	0	0	
$\Gamma_{0,8}$	0		0	0	0						0	0	0	0			0	0	0	0	0	0		0	0	0
$\Gamma_{0,9}$	0	0			0			0		0	0	0	0		0			0	0			0	0	0	0	
$\Gamma_{0,10}$	0	0	0	0	0	0		0	0	0	0	0		0		0	0	0	0	0	0	0	0		0	0
$\Gamma_{0,10}$	0	0	0	0	0	0	0	0	0	0	0	0		0	0	0		0			0	0		0	0	0
$\Gamma_{0,12}$	0		0	0	0	0	0	0	0	0	0	0			0		0	0	0		0	0	0		0	
$\Gamma_{0,13}$	0	0	0	0	0		0		0	0	0	0	0	0	0		0	0	0	0	0	0	0	0	0	0
$\Gamma_{0,14}$	0	0	0		0		0	0		0	0	0	0		0			0	0	0	0	0	0	0	0	0
$\Gamma_{0,15}$	0		0		0	0	0			0	0	0		0		0	0		0	0	0		0	0	0	0
$\Gamma_{0,16}$	0	0	0	0		0		0			0	0	0		0	0	0	0	0		0	0	0	0		
$\Gamma_{0,17}$	0		0		0	0	0	0	0	0	0		0				0	0	0		0	0	0	0	0	
$\Gamma_{0,18}$	0	0	0	0	0	0	0	0	0	0		0	0	0	0	0	0	0	0	0		0	0		0	
$\Gamma_{0,19}$	0		0		0	0		0	0		0		0	0	0	0		0	0	0	0		0	0	0	0
$\Gamma_{0,20}$	0	0	0	0	0	0	0	0	0	0	1	0	0	0	0	0	0	0	0	0	0	0	0	0	0	
$\Gamma_{0,21}$	0		0	0	0	0	0		0		0	0	0		0	0	0	0	0	0	0	0		0	0	
$\Gamma_{0,22}$	0	0	0	0	0	0		0	0	0	0	0	0	0	0	0	0	0	0		0	0				
$\Gamma_{0,23}$	0		0	0	0	0		0	0	0	0	0		0	0				0	0	0	0	0	0		
$\Gamma_{0,24}$	0	0		0			0		0			0	0	0	0	0	0	0	0	0		0		0		0
$\Gamma_{0,25}$	0	0		0	0	0	0		0	0	0		0	0	0	0	0	0	0	0		0	0	0	0	0

will yield a constraint on π_0. We have carried out this program of repeated scanning of the blocks of corresponding shifted plaintext and ciphertext. The values of $\Gamma_{0,j}$ for $0 \leq j < 26$ after repeated scanning of blocks B_0 to B_9 are shown in Table 5.8.5 (replacing the unit entries by blank spaces).

We note from Table 5.8.5 that $\Gamma_{0,7}$ and $\Gamma_{0,20}$ contain a single unit entry and provide the relationships

$$\pi_0(0) - \pi_0(7) = 2$$

$$\pi_0(0) - \pi_0(20) = 10$$

TABLE 5.8.6

Relationships Obtained After Repeated Scanning of B_0–B_{19}

B_9	$\pi_0(0) - \pi_0(7) = 2$	$\pi_0(0) - \pi_0(20) = 10$
B_{10}	$\pi_0(10) - \pi_0(18) = 19$	
B_{12}	$\pi_0(18) - \pi_0(16) = 5$	
B_{13}	$\pi_0(13) - \pi_0(18) = 18$	
B_{14}	$\pi_0(0) - \pi_0(5) = 23$	$\pi_0(12) - \pi_0(21) = 9$
	$\pi_0(20) - \pi_0(23) = 14$	$\pi_0(21) - \pi_0(12) = 17$
B_{15}	$\pi_0(0) - \pi_0(13) = 7$	$\pi_0(0) - \pi_0(25) = 11$
	$\pi_0(1) - \pi_0(16) = 13$	$\pi_0(4) - \pi_0(11) = 4$
	$\pi_0(5) - \pi_0(13) = 10$	$\pi_0(13) - \pi_0(20) = 3$
	$\pi_0(16) - \pi_0(18) = 21$	
B_{16}	$\pi_0(0) - \pi_0(1) = 17$	$\pi_0(1) - \pi_0(2) = 4$
	$\pi_0(2) - \pi_0(9) = 25$	$\pi_0(4) - \pi_0(24) = 17$
	$\pi_0(13) - \pi_0(9) = 13$	$\pi_0(14) - \pi_0(20) = 2$
	$\pi_0(18) - \pi_0(13) = 8$	$\pi_0(18) - \pi_0(20) = 11$
	$\pi_0(20) - \pi_0(24) = 21$	
B_{17}	$\pi_0(15) - \pi_0(23) = 12$	$\pi_0(22) - \pi_0(4) = 21$
	$\pi_0(17) - \pi_0(18) = 10$	$\pi_0(3) - \pi_0(9) = 17$
	$\pi_0(19) - \pi_0(11) = 2$	$\pi_0(21) - \pi_0(11) = 22$
B_{19}	$\pi_0(6) - \pi_0(1) = 8$	

We continue the scanning process until we obtain a sufficient number of relationships to recover π_0. For the rotors of Fig. 5.8.1, this process terminates after scanning of B_0 to B_{19}. (There are 63 complete blocks and one partial block.) In Table 5.8.6, we summarize the relationships obtained by scanning.

5.9 THE PLUGBOARD

What is the effect of the plugboard IP on the analysis given in Sec. 5.8? Equation (5.8.1) changes to

$$\pi_R(S_j(\pi_0(IP(x_i) + i) - i)) = S_j(\pi_0(IP(y_i) + i) - i) \tag{5.9.1}$$

for i in the jth block B_j. To search for misses, we have to determine if one of the following three relationships holds:

$$\pi_R(S_j(\pi_0(IP(x_{i_0}) + i_0) - i_0)) \neq \pi_R(S_j(\pi_0(IP(x_{i_1}) + i_1) - i_1))$$

$$S_j(\pi_0(IP(y_{i_0}) + i_0) - i_0)) \neq S_j(\pi_0(IP(y_{i_1}) + i_1) - i_1)$$

$$\pi_R(S_j(\pi_0(IP(x_{i_0}) + i_0) - i_0)) \neq s_j(\pi_0(IP(y_{i_1}) + i_1) - i_1)$$

We cannot directly verify any of these relationships since IP is unknown. One way to circumvent this difficulty is a variant on the idea used in Sec. 5.8; we shall make a guess as to the relationship between IP(t) and IP(s) for $t \neq s$

$$IP(t) = IP(s) + u \tag{5.9.2}$$

We then scan the plaintext and ciphertext pairs $(IP(x_i), IP(y_i))$ and record the consequences of the assumption made in Eq. (8.9.2). We introduce the vectors

$$\Gamma_{i,j} = (\gamma_{i,j}(0), \gamma_{i,j}(1), \ldots, \gamma_{i,j}(25))$$

where

$$\gamma_{i,j}(t) = \begin{cases} 0 & \text{if we have ruled out the possibility that } IP(i) - IP(j) \neq v \\ 1 & \text{if we have ruled out the possibility that } IP(i) - IP(j) \neq v \end{cases}$$

Initially,

$$\Gamma_{i,j} = (0, 1, 1, \ldots, 1) \qquad 0 \leq i,j < 26 \quad i \neq j \qquad (i,j) \notin \{s,t\}$$

$$\Gamma_{s,t} = (\underbrace{0, 0, \ldots, 0}_{\text{u-1 zeros}}, 1, \underbrace{0, 0, \ldots, 0}_{\text{26-u zeros}})$$

$$\Gamma_{i,i} = (1, 0, 0, \ldots 0)$$

We continue scanning and updating the set of vectors $\{\Gamma_{i,j}\}$ until an inconsistency is found, i.e., until for some pair (i,j) with $i \neq j$,

$$\Gamma_{i,j} = (0, 0, \ldots, 0)$$

An inconsistency implies that the relationship in Eq. (5.9.2) is incorrect. We repeat the analysis for another choice of u until scanning yields a determination of some relationship involving the substitution IP.

We have performed scanning on ciphertext enciphered by the Enigma, including an initial permutation. Starting with u = 1, an inconsistency occurs after the scan of the first 20 blocks; with u = 2, an inconsistency occurs after the scan of the first 21 blocks.

PROBLEMS

5.1 What is the decipherment equation for the *straight-through* rotor?

5.2 What is the decipherment equation for the *Enigma system?*

5.3 We shall say that $\pi, \nu \in \mathrm{SYM}(\boldsymbol{Z}_m)$ are $\boldsymbol{C}_m$*-conjugate* if $\nu = C_{-t}\, \pi\, C_t$ for some $t \in \boldsymbol{C}_m$ and write $\nu \sim \pi$. Let $[\pi]$ denote the set of $\boldsymbol{C}_m$-conjugates of $\pi \in \mathrm{SYM}(\boldsymbol{Z}_m)$. Prove $\sim$ is an equivalence relation on $\mathrm{SYM}(\boldsymbol{Z}_m)$.

5.4 Let $\pi \in \mathrm{SYM}(\boldsymbol{Z}_m)$. An *r-cycle* of π is a sequence of distinct indices $t_0, t_1, \ldots, t_{r-1}$ such that $\pi(t_i) = t_{i+1}$ for $0 \leq i < r$ with $t_r = t_0$. Prove that π decomposes $\boldsymbol{Z}_m$ into disjoint cycles, called the *cycle decomposition* of π.

5.5 Find the cycle decomposition of the substitutions in $\mathrm{SYM}(\boldsymbol{Z}_m)$

$$\pi(t) = t \qquad \pi(t) = t + 1 \qquad \pi(t) = t + k$$

5.6 What are the possible lengths for the cycles of $\pi \in \mathrm{SYM}(\boldsymbol{Z}_m)$?

5.7 Find the cycle decomposition of the rotors in Table 5.3.2.

5.8 Find the cycle decomposition of the rotors in Table 5.8.1.

5.9 What is the relationship between the cycle decompositions of π and ν when $\nu = C_{-t}\, \pi\, C_t$ with $\pi \in \mathrm{SYM}(\boldsymbol{Z}_m)$?

5.10 When does the equation $\pi = C_{-t}\, \pi\, C_t$ ($\pi \in \mathrm{SYM}(\boldsymbol{Z}_m)$) have a solution?

5.11 How many substitutions are there in the equivalence class $[\pi]$ of π under $\sim$?

5.12 We shall say that $\pi, \nu \in \mathrm{SYM}(\boldsymbol{Z}_m)$ are **-conjugate* if $\nu = C_s\, \pi\, C_t$ for some $s,t \in \boldsymbol{Z}_m$ and write $\nu < \pi$. Let $[\pi]$ denote the set of *-conjugates of π. Prove that $<$ is an equivalence relation on $\mathrm{SYM}(\boldsymbol{Z}_m)$.

5.13 When does the equation $\pi = C_{-a}\, \pi\, C_b$ ($\pi \in \mathrm{SYM}(\boldsymbol{Z}_m)$) have a solution?

5.14 How many elements are there in the equivalence class $[\pi]$ of π under $<$?

5.15 In the analysis of the *straight-through* rotor

$$C_{r_{N-1}(i)}\, \pi_{N-1}\, C_{r_N(i)-r_{n-2}(i)} \cdots C_{r_1(i)-r_0(i)}\, \pi_0\, C_{r_0(i)}$$

with $\{r_s(i);\ 0 \leq s < N\}$ given by Eq. (5.1.1), we have assumed that $k_s = r_s(0) = 0$ for $0 \leq s < N$, replacing π_s by $C_{-k_s}\, \pi_s\, C_{k_s}$. How can we analyze the straight-through rotor if $\{r_s(i) : 0 \leq s < N\}$ is given by Eq. (5.1.2)?

5.16 *(CIPHER(P5.1)* (see Fig. P5.1) results from the encipherment by a 2-rotor system.

In Table P5.2, we list the corresponding triples ($i, x_i + i, y_i$) for the first twelve blocks. Recover π_0.

```
eaegh jufio wrmkf cefgw xrpvi yqzth wzgfz rnorh hblni cyshw zbfbd wbmbl
sqsrr ibjcy iglyg uqqna ohycf ggkse cpsjn exqst utaaq excvl gxzfg waont
icmrj tgroq fumoo ifsai ofepb sggdl cigcu uvzyt jekfv tzapr ufbtd bdpba
cwnor wgjrc ffyns krppo fcjft merol xkhug gubdh sjslb rdlus cmdrt gscpm
vlhjj jyonu rsqld ahysb onzkt swsfg kviae nlalc svmuq axkbr sjzfj xzjew
mymil pbhlz jajbe fktra qpkyb qtsug vozcv xjukd hxmjk kiroq twwzy flqeg
tjaun rujjt cmprl sxyfk hfoih mtcwr zqkov vdxrx ikrlp truja giuix zdsas
ngatx tpfvx iveiz cvads izqkr vbrvb bymgv qygot dvalj pbkli xpwxw pgkwp
czhvf plpfw lyoor jrrdh chnrh nytdf gpxya fqpxo ldkno rjbhn ogsio zuvqv
xwwyh mgxtf wtdow bdtyn wlepq lgenm gxjdb rgtvk zzosa colav saepp yauct
ljesz jsgzp yglom inwrt zkwxu razja xxqxa xevbn rcfvn bmfhk rlnyy wvzce
maett qhhdo ujgch qtind vywzn cfbzj ijeab zwrwr qyjzu jitip nxnfz lcbyf
ortbk kqypk mpgrz tsnbl fdkav mjbay aizxi bhrml lboio kcpks enbeq mdmgd
doniu xiaam jgozv joocg akltv tyouo agfcl balxu lpslh xlhjh zomqm izyfo
qanbo kcbdw fmdeg ahqyx tpebc mhbgf vvirn evucv cwydg qfejv aiajo lnfgc
bfbhn jotqq zvgrb eqsvd ikupk ggsgi oxdwm xopgw oizfo xghhn enxbo qwyhf
veiiw owsdr snavk llsof wrzlk zcebs nipyy zzqce qljkw cumtv azwwn rroac
npppr szxcz hdcil auptn ejlme sqgii gtcgo dxxzx qziny vhlty ehfqv zilfe
efsaj agyyd bcfvp etavy anchq qyjfr kkrpn pitwg dzkul vmcyp myhwj gxvgf
upuzy ihafc lhund bdjix zidij ztmzd qepbo jrear elavd azils gelhs jenhc
adlky cyesg odfsk yjwil berwt kqenf hxlmy dtsql cbskc ahiqo efsbn ounoa
uckup madvo atdbh dkzpf bfbnr inbxp oumgw envav umlom kmgpm bglxk oylbk
qdtbm ehwuu jadgo evdsr adgpp agjyr johfj xzmgq hsfnh tugvs imzyd aroid
thwob nupdj zmuyt fypcb wxcvb fdddj emwpt wislw qrmoj zloef ecmre apaqe
ohjor yaizk hmsye pbcbr xjgcl huahw wtbun yqfuz djeju cvapx emair uusls
gyttk chdgu mhemz rquns gyibh tsczf slerh btvcb ajzvh coeid gojzi ouwbq
lxbnd nrvvw mwlug sojxv bsowo qqmvc lnoxg upmef watmm zwzwd msynv njwzc
hxhni qkzqp siujy kqajc jxtmx qdjat mobbj gxchv veceb rufml lkvyg thxni
egyve gmiun lxlvu qqfsf spncc qhsgk kaifi esuqh lrcsw sxsjy jkwbe vtvvl
yoytl kxodl zuklf qeagw hdyzb gbcok gsxfi txumg snngr eoizt qnffm yllsh
ajriz bupwl uuuvu blzhy mjska oewbp hwqwx dlkuw kyjsn arjrg xyune wwbox
acdfd sibgs dtldn fabao rppvl bcjfv miwyr wfskd nphie lvnwn gllkc uddna
iphsu jbzow uwdvs ndxku mkagy bljik hysjw rjqtg ktoif vkdeg cqcqc vvcvd
zkpgv fewey dsljs ieddt kkuxd yxfzt begws jrxpw xzamf vwtig lycct ezjpo
hztbt ffojr pemdy fvhjy oampx gbspa mqccm ndmsz fxdyi wqbkp unfyy ghjba
gymjj bpfsj azqxi nbhys knfkj ajtmy epica mueze dgclh ffcdc cpwdq rsffg
ubsld avgwk spulr ntgup zsldc ulzks yquhq jzqwu hzrts eddiy vztiv mqamv
hcwcf ualxl mtudt udfnk ajzhq zflst suyde gyons pltlx eebme vu
```

Figure P5.1. *CIPHER(P5.1)* : encipherment of *PLAIN(P5.1)* by 2-rotor (Herbern) system.

TABLE P5.2
Results of Matching in *CIPHER(P5.1)*

	i	x_i+i	y_i
Block 0	0	19	4
	1	8	0
	2	6	4
	3	11	6
	4	22	7
	5	23	9
	6	0	20
	7	11	5
	8	22	8
	9	14	14
	10	25	22
	11	15	17
	12	3	12
	13	18	10
	14	2	5
	15	6	2
	16	2	4
	17	17	5
	18	5	6
	19	21	22
	20	24	23
	21	25	17
	22	17	15
	23	23	21
	24	9	8
	25	19	24
Block 1	26	0	16
	27	20	25
	28	10	19
	29	17	7
	30	17	22
	31	5	25
	32	19	6
	33	10	5
	34	23	25
	35	0	17
	36	14	13
	37	14	14
	38	20	17
	39	15	7
	40	7	7
	41	23	1
	42	4	11
	43	4	13
	44	25	8
	45	19	2
	46	12	24
	47	23	18
	48	10	7
	49	10	22
	50	0	25
	51	3	1
Block 2	52	17	5
	53	14	1
	54	6	3
	55	6	22
	56	24	1
	57	23	12
	58	10	1
	59	24	11
	60	0	18
	61	2	16
	62	17	18
	63	2	17
	64	0	17
	65	7	8
	66	20	1
	67	22	9
	68	4	2
	69	11	24
	70	11	8
	71	12	6
	72	1	11
	73	25	24
	74	3	6
	75	5	20
	76	16	16
	77	18	16
Block 3	78	14	13
	79	18	0
	80	0	14
	81	17	7
	82	9	24
	83	7	2
	84	20	5
	85	19	6
	86	23	6
	87	3	10
	88	3	18
	89	15	4
	90	3	2
	91	17	15
	92	9	18
	93	3	9
	94	1	13
	95	11	4
	96	11	23
	97	1	16
	98	8	18
	99	8	19
	100	11	20
	101	1	19
	102	15	0
	103	7	0

TABLE P5.2 (*Continued*)

	i	x_i+i	y_i		i	x_i+i	y_i
Block 4	104	14	16	Block 5	130	4	5
	105	4	4		131	3	20
	106	10	23		132	9	12
	107	16	2		133	16	14
	108	9	21		134	18	14
	109	5	11		135	16	8
	110	8	6		136	20	5
	111	0	23		137	13	18
	112	10	25		138	16	0
	113	23	5		139	11	8
	114	22	6		140	10	14
	115	23	22		141	22	5
	116	12	0		142	15	4
	117	13	14		143	17	15
	118	6	13		144	9	1
	119	23	19		145	19	18
	120	3	8		146	1	6
	121	17	2		147	5	6
	122	5	12		148	7	3
	123	17	17		149	5	11
	124	8	9		150	24	2
	125	14	19		151	8	8
	126	3	6		152	15	6
	127	1	17		153	25	2
	128	15	14		154	12	20
	129	18	16		155	11	20
Block 6	156	12	21	Block 7	182	7	13
	157	1	25		183	5	14
	158	21	24		184	21	17
	159	10	19		185	7	22
	160	8	9		186	6	6
	161	13	4		187	12	9
	162	24	10		188	19	17
	163	25	5		189	21	2
	164	2	21		190	19	5
	165	13	19		191	23	5
	166	18	25		192	16	24
	167	3	0		193	9	13
	168	24	15		194	20	18
	169	1	17		195	5	10
	170	6	20		196	12	17
	171	8	5		197	3	15
	172	16	1		198	10	15
	173	19	19		199	4	14
	174	12	3		200	24	5
	175	12	1		201	12	2
	176	24	3		202	1	9
	177	17	15		203	25	5
	178	3	1		204	11	19
	179	1	0		205	1	12
	180	11	2		206	15	4
	181	18	22		207	17	17

TABLE P5.2 (*Continued*)

	i	x_i+i	y_i		i	x_i+i	y_i
Block 8	208	8	14	Block 9	234	7	19
	209	19	11		235	9	6
	210	21	23		236	14	18
	211	7	10		237	18	2
	212	17	7		238	21	15
	213	24	20		239	19	12
	214	21	6		240	1	21
	215	1	6		241	11	11
	216	25	20		242	11	7
	217	1	1		243	11	9
	218	4	3		244	24	9
	219	19	7		245	3	9
	220	5	18		246	5	24
	221	1	9		247	20	14
	222	19	18		248	12	13
	223	4	11		249	4	20
	224	7	1		250	23	17
	225	5	17		251	21	18
	226	21	3		252	5	16
	227	13	11		253	8	11
	228	22	20		254	24	3
	229	14	18		255	12	0
	230	14	2		256	1	7
	231	19	12		257	11	24
	232	6	3		258	15	18
	233	18	17		259	11	1

	i	x_i+i	y_i		i	x_i+i	y_i
Block 10	260	0	14	Block 11	286	18	23
	261	14	13		287	20	10
	262	4	25		288	2	1
	263	7	10		289	16	17
	264	6	19		290	23	18
	265	12	18		291	16	9
	266	6	22		292	4	25
	267	24	18		293	18	5
	268	8	5		294	12	9
	269	11	6		295	9	23
	270	3	10		296	13	25
	271	15	21		297	3	9
	272	3	8		298	5	4
	273	21	0		299	1	22
	274	6	4		300	17	12
	275	8	13		301	19	24
	276	24	11		302	8	12
	277	19	0		303	25	8
	278	10	11		304	24	11
	279	12	2		305	6	15
	280	1	18		306	12	1
	281	25	21		307	17	7
	282	9	12		308	4	11
	283	25	20		309	16	25
	284	12	16		310	5	9
	285	12	0		311	19	0

CHAPTER VI

Block Ciphers and the Data Encryption Standard

6.1 BLOCK CIPHERS

By an *N-block* we mean a sequence of 0s and 1s of length N:

$$\mathbf{x} = (x_0, x_1, \ldots, x_{N-1}) \in \boldsymbol{Z}_{2,N}$$

It will be useful to interpret $\mathbf{x}$ in $\boldsymbol{Z}_{2,N}$ both as a vector and as the binary representation of the integer

$$\|\mathbf{x}\| = \sum_{0 \leq i < N} x_i 2^{N-i-1}$$

in $\boldsymbol{Z}_{2^N}$. For example, when N = 4

$$\begin{array}{lll} (0,0,0,0) \longleftrightarrow 0 & & (0,0,0,1) \longleftrightarrow 1 \\ (0,0,1,0) \longleftrightarrow 2 & & (0,0,1,1) \longleftrightarrow 3 \\ (0,1,0,0) \longleftrightarrow 4 & & (0,1,0,1) \longleftrightarrow 5 \\ (0,1,1,0) \longleftrightarrow 6 & & (0,1,1,1) \longleftrightarrow 7 \\ (1,0,0,0) \longleftrightarrow 8 & & (1,0,0,1) \longleftrightarrow 9 \\ (1,0,1,0) \longleftrightarrow 10 & & (1,0,1,1) \longleftrightarrow 11 \\ (1,1,0,0) \longleftrightarrow 12 & & (1,1,0,1) \longleftrightarrow 13 \\ (1,1,1,0) \longleftrightarrow 14 & & (1,1,1,1) \longleftrightarrow 15 \end{array}$$

An element π of SYM($\boldsymbol{Z}_{2,N}$)

$$\pi : \mathbf{x} \to \mathbf{y} = \pi(\mathbf{x})$$

$$\mathbf{x} = (x_0, x_1, \ldots, x_{N-1}) \quad \mathbf{y} = (y_0, y_1, \ldots, y_{N-1})$$

corresponds also to an element of SYM($\boldsymbol{Z}_{2^N}$). We will call π a *block cipher*. Although block ciphers are just special cases of substitutions considered in Chapters 3–5, they are singled out for special treatment in this chapter for two reasons. First, information stored in and transmitted between information processing systems is represented as n-grams in the alphabet $\boldsymbol{Z}_{2,8}$. Second, the Data Encryption Standard (DES) is most naturally studied as a block cipher.

6.2 BUILDING BLOCKS OF BLOCK CIPHERS

Each of the substitution systems discussed in Chapters 3–5 can be defined for the alphabet $Z_{2,N}$. Rather than considering the form they take as block ciphers, we begin this chapter by considering several *primitives,* from which general block ciphers may be constructed.

- λ *Shift left circular*

$$\lambda : (x_0, x_1, \ldots, x_{N-1}) \rightarrow (x_1, \ldots, x_{N-1}, x_0)$$

- ρ *Shift right circular*

$$\rho : (x_0, x_1, \ldots, x_{N-1}) \rightarrow (x_{N-1}, x_0, \ldots, x_{N-2})$$

- σ *Addition with carry*

$$\sigma : \mathbf{x} \rightarrow \mathbf{y} \quad \|\mathbf{y}\| = (\|\mathbf{x}\| + 1) \text{ (modulo } 2^N)$$

- *Linear transformation*

L is a nonsingular N by N matrix of 0's and 1's:

$$L = \begin{vmatrix} \alpha_{0,0} & \alpha_{0,1} & \ldots & \alpha_{0,N-1} \\ \alpha_{1,0} & \alpha_{1,1} & \ldots & \alpha_{1,N-1} \\ \cdot & \cdot & \ldots & \cdot \\ \cdot & \cdot & \ldots & \cdot \\ \cdot & \cdot & \ldots & \cdot \\ \alpha_{N-1,0} & \alpha_{N-1,1} & \ldots & \alpha_{N-1,N-1} \end{vmatrix}$$

L determines a transformation on $Z_{2,N}$ enciphering the plaintext N-block

$$\mathbf{x} = (x_0, x_1, \ldots, x_{N-1})$$

into the ciphertext N-block,

$$\mathbf{y} = (y_0, y_1, \ldots, y_{N-1})$$

where

$$y_i = \alpha_{i,0}x_0 + \alpha_{i,1}x_1 + \ldots + \alpha_{i,N-1}x_{N-1} \text{ (modulo 2)} \qquad 0 \le i < N$$

Recall that *nonsingular* means that $\mathbf{x} = \mathbf{0} = (0,0, \ldots, 0)$ is the *only* solution of the equation

$$L\mathbf{x} = \mathbf{0}$$

- γ *Transposition*

$$\gamma_j(\mathbf{x}) = \begin{cases} \mathbf{y} & \text{if } \|\mathbf{x}\| = j \text{ and } \|\mathbf{y}\| = j + 1 \\ \mathbf{y} & \text{if } \|\mathbf{x}\| = j + 1 \text{ and } \|\mathbf{y}\| = j \\ \mathbf{x} & \text{if } \|\mathbf{x}\| \neq j, j + 1 \end{cases}$$

- *Wire crossing (coordinate permutation)*

$$\tau : \text{a permutation of the integers } \{0, 1, \ldots, N-1\}$$

$$\pi_\tau : (x_0, x_1, \ldots, x_{N-1}) \rightarrow (x_{\tau(0)}, x_{\tau(1)}, \ldots, x_{\tau(N-1)})$$

Wire crossing is a special case of a nonsingular linear transformation; the ith row of the matrix L_τ corresponding to π_τ has a 1 in column j, where $j = \tau(i)$. For example, when $N = 4$ and τ is the coordinate permutation,

$$\tau(0) = 2 \qquad \tau(1) = 3 \qquad \tau(2) = 0 \qquad \tau(3) = 1$$

$$L_\tau = \begin{vmatrix} 0 & 0 & 1 & 0 \\ 0 & 0 & 0 & 1 \\ 1 & 0 & 0 & 0 \\ 0 & 1 & 0 & 0 \end{vmatrix}$$

- *Affine transformation*

$$L : \text{a nonsingular linear transformation } \mathbf{a} \in \boldsymbol{Z}_{2,N}$$

$$\pi : \mathbf{x} \rightarrow L\mathbf{x} + \mathbf{a}$$

6.3 WHAT DOES CORRESPONDING PLAINTEXT AND CIPHERTEXT REVEAL ABOUT π?

Suppose

$$\pi(\mathbf{x}_i) = \mathbf{y}_i \qquad 0 \leq i < m$$

for some $\pi \in \text{SYM}(\boldsymbol{Z}_{2,N})$, plaintext $\{\mathbf{x}_i\}$, and ciphertext $\{\mathbf{y}_i\}$. What can we say about $\pi(\mathbf{x})$ if $\mathbf{x} \notin \{\mathbf{x}_i\}$? Since π is a permutation on $\boldsymbol{Z}_{2,N}$, we know that the $\{\mathbf{y}_i\}$ are distinct and $\pi(\mathbf{x}) \notin \{\mathbf{y}_i\}$ when $\mathbf{x} \notin \{\mathbf{x}_i\}$. Can we say more about π? $(2^N - m)!$ of the $(2^N)!$ permutations in $\text{SYM}(\boldsymbol{Z}_{2,N})$ satisfy the equations

$$\pi(\mathbf{x}_i) = \mathbf{y}_i \qquad 0 \leq i < m$$

and in absence of *additional information,* we have no way to further specify $\pi(\mathbf{x})$. This assertion depends crucially upon the assumption that π could have been *any* element of $\text{SYM}(\boldsymbol{Z}_{2,N})$. If instead, we knew that π was a member of a small subset Ξ of $\text{SYM}(\boldsymbol{Z}_{2,N})$, then we might be able to make a stronger assertion. For example, if $\Xi = \{\pi_j : 0 \leq j < 2^N\}$

$$\pi_j(i) = (i + j) \text{ (modulo } 2^N) \qquad 0 \leq i < 2^N$$

then the value of $\pi(\mathbf{x})$ for just *one* $\mathbf{x}$ uniquely determines π. In this case, Ξ is the subset of *Caesar substitutions* on $\boldsymbol{Z}_{2,N} = \boldsymbol{Z}_{2^N}$.

The cryptographic significance of this property should be obvious; if plaintext is enciphered by the permuation π chosen from the full symmetric group, then an opponent who learns the correspondence between some subset of plaintext and ciphertext

$$\mathbf{x}_i \leftarrow\rightarrow \mathbf{y}_i \qquad 0 \leq i < m$$

cannot on the basis of this information alone find the plaintext corresponding to $\mathbf{y} \notin \{\mathbf{y}_i\}$.

6.4 BLOCK CIPHER SYSTEMS

When we use a permutation π from $\Xi \subseteq \mathrm{SYM}(\boldsymbol{Z}_{2,N})$ to encipher plaintext, we call the resulting substitution system Ξ a *block cipher system* or *block substitution system.* A block cipher is the special case of a monalphabetic substitution with alphabet $\boldsymbol{Z}_{2^N} = \boldsymbol{Z}_{2,N}$. If the plaintext data are not represented by N-blocks, as is the case with standard alpha-numeric plaintext, the first step is to code the plaintext in this format. The coding can be effected in several ways, and it will not matter which particular coding we use. Two standard mappings of alpha-numeric characters into binary strings are:

- EBCDIC—*Extended Binary Coded Decimal Interchange Code.*
- USASCII—*USA Standard Code for Information Interchange.*

EBCDIC (Table P6.1) codes each element of a large character set, including

- Upper and lower case alphabetic characters.
- Numerals.
- Punctuation, space, special symbols.
- Carriage controls.

into an N = 8-byte block (1 *byte* = 8 *bits*).

In an information processing environment, a block cipher system will be used by many participants. A *keyed block cipher system* is a subset $\Xi[\boldsymbol{K}]$ of the symmetric group $\mathrm{SYM}(\boldsymbol{Z}_{2,N})$

$$\Xi[\boldsymbol{K}] = \{\pi\{k,.\} : k \in \boldsymbol{K}\}$$

indexed by a parameter k belonging to a set $\boldsymbol{K}$; k is the *key* and $\boldsymbol{K}$ the *key space.* We do not require that distinct keys correspond to distinct permutations of $\boldsymbol{Z}_{2,N}$.

Example 6.4.1: Ceasar Substitution Use EBCIDIC or USACII to code alpha-numeric plaintext into a sequence of 0s and 1s. Divide the resulting EBCIDIC (or USACII) plaintext into N-blocks

$$\mathbf{x}_0, \mathbf{x}_1, \ldots, \mathbf{x}_{m-1}$$

where the length of the *partial* block $\mathbf{x}_{m-1}$ (if present) is L, $0 \leq L < N$. The key space $\boldsymbol{K}$ is the set $\boldsymbol{Z}_{2,N}$; a key $\mathbf{k}$ is an N-block

$$\mathbf{k} = (k_0, k_1, \ldots, k_{N-1}) \qquad k_i = 0 \text{ or } 1 \qquad (0 \leq i < N)$$

Encipher the ith block of plaintext $\mathbf{x}_i$ $(0 \leq i < m - 1)$ by *exclusive or* of $\mathbf{x}_i$ with the key $\mathbf{k}$

$$\textit{plaintext} \quad \mathbf{x}_i \rightarrow \mathbf{y}_i = (\mathbf{x}_i + \mathbf{k}) \text{ (modulo 2)} \quad \textit{ciphertext}$$

A final partial block $\mathbf{x}_{m-1}$, if present, is enciphered by exclusive *or* with the key formed by the first L bits of $\mathbf{k}$,

$$(k_0, k_1, \ldots, k_{L-1})$$

The key space contains 2^N keys; each key corresponds to a distinct element of $SYM(\boldsymbol{Z}_{2,N})$. As in Chapter 2, we might use some key word or phrase

`NOW IS THE TIME FOR ...`

to provide a key.

A keyed block cipher system $\Xi[\boldsymbol{K}]$ is used as follows: *User i* and *User j* agree in some manner upon a key k in $\boldsymbol{K}$, thereby choosing an element of $\Xi[\boldsymbol{K}]$, and transmit plaintext $\mathbf{x}$ enciphered by the permutation chosen. We use the notion

$$\mathbf{y} = \pi\{k,\mathbf{x}\}$$

to denote the ciphertext N-block $\mathbf{y}$ that results from the encipherment of the plaintext N-block $\mathbf{x}$ by the substitution $\pi\{k,.\}$, corresponding to the key k. We assume that the opponent

- Knows the key space $\boldsymbol{K}$.
- Knows the algorithm by which k corresponds to the substitution $\pi\{k,.\}$.
- *Does not know* which key k the users have selected.

What strategies are available to the opponent? The opponent might

- Find the key if *User i* or *User j* carelessly leaves a recorded copy of the key accessible.
- Intercept (by wiretapping) ciphertext $\mathbf{y}$ from *User i* to *User j* and test *all* keys in $\boldsymbol{K}$ until decipherment of $\mathbf{y}$ produces a readable plaintext message.
- Obtain corresponding plaintext and ciphertext ($\mathbf{x} \leftarrow\rightarrow \mathbf{y}$) and use *key trial.*
- Obtain corresponding plaintext and ciphertext and search for relationships involving key k, plaintext $\mathbf{x}$ and ciphertext $\mathbf{y}$ in order to recover key from plaintext and ciphertext.
- Build a catalogue of N-blocks and record the frequency of occurrence of plaintext (ciphertext) N-blocks. A catalogue might permit the opponent to search for probable words; for example,
  - A memorandum might always begin with `To`:.
  - An assembly language listing has a very structured format.
  - Digital representation of photographs might have limited character sets.

Suppose that N = 64 and every element of SYM($\mathbf{Z}_{2,N}$) can be used as a substitution, so that $\mathbf{K}$ = SYM($\mathbf{Z}_{2,N}$). Then

- There are 2^{64} 64-blocks; an opponent cannot maintain a catalogue with $2^{64} \approx 1.8 \times 10^{19}$ entries.
- Key trial with $(2^{64})!$ different keys is impractical.
- The correspondence between plaintext and ciphertext for some m N-blocks

$$\pi\{k,\mathbf{x}_i\} = \mathbf{y}_i \qquad 0 \le i < m$$

does not provide an opponent with any information about the value of $\pi\{k,\mathbf{x}\}$ for $\mathbf{x} \notin \{\mathbf{x}_i\}$.

A keyed block cipher system with alphabet $\mathbf{Z}_{2,64}$ and key space $\mathbf{K}$ = SYM($\mathbf{Z}_{2,64}$) is effectively unbreakable. This "unbreakability" statement is different from the same assertion made for the one-time system in Section 4.1. Here it is a reflection of the computational requirements of cryptanalysis. Maintaining a catalogue of the frequency of occurrence of letters (64 blocks) or testing the $2^{64}!$ possible keys is beyond the resources of any opponent. This should be compared with the problem faced by an opponent attempting to analyze Caesar-enciphered ciphertext with the alphabet $\mathbf{A}$ = {`A B . . . Z`}; in which only $\log_2 26 \approx 4.7$ bits are required to specify a Caesar substitution key compared to $2^{65} \approx \log_2(2^{64})!$ bits for the key space $\mathbf{K}$ = SYM($\mathbf{Z}_{2,64}$). Alas, the designer and the opponent find themselves in the same position; the designer cannot build a system which can implement all of the $2^{64}!$ substitutions in SYM($\mathbf{Z}_{2,64}$) for the same reason that the opponent cannot test this number of keys. One remedy is not to insist that every element of SYM($\mathbf{Z}_{2,N}$) be able to serve as a substitution. We formulate the desiderata of a good block cipher as follows:

- a large block size N to foil cataloguing.
- a key space large enough to prevent key trial.
- a complicated relationship

$$\pi\{k,.\} : \mathbf{x} \to \mathbf{y} = \pi\{k,\mathbf{x}\}$$

between plaintext and ciphertext so that analytical and/or statistical methods to recover the plaintext and/or key from corresponding plaintext and ciphertext are not likely to succeed.*

6.5 GENERATING SYM($Z_{2,N}$)

There are many ways to construct a block cipher system starting with cryptographic primitives by iteration. We begin our study with the three substitutions of $\mathbf{Z}_{2,N}$:

*We cannot *prove* that relationships involving k, $\mathbf{x}$, and $\mathbf{y}$ do not exist which enable the recovery of k from $\mathbf{x}$ and $\mathbf{y}$.

$$\lambda : (x_0, x_1, \ldots, x_{N-1}) \to (x_1, \ldots, x_{N-1}, x_0) \qquad \textit{(shift left circular)}$$

$$\rho : (x_0, x_1, \ldots, x_{N-1}) \to (x_{N-1}, x_0, \ldots, x_{N-2}) \qquad \textit{(shift right circular)}$$

$$\sigma : \mathbf{x} \to \mathbf{y} \qquad \|\mathbf{y}\| = (\|\mathbf{x}\| + 1) \text{ (modulo } 2^N) \quad \textit{(addition with carry)}$$

Note that ρ and λ are inverse operations:

$$\rho(\lambda(\mathbf{x})) = \lambda(\rho(\mathbf{x})) = \mathbf{x}$$

Denote by σ^{-1} the inverse operation of σ *(subtraction with carry)*

$$\sigma^{-1} : \mathbf{x} \to \mathbf{y} \qquad \|\mathbf{y}\| = (\|\mathbf{x}\| - 1) \text{ (modulo } 2^N)$$

By a *word* in ρ, λ, σ, and σ^{-1} we mean a finite sequence of these permutations:

$$(\pi_1, \pi_2, \ldots, \pi_m) \qquad \pi_i \in \{\rho,\lambda,\sigma,\sigma^{-1}\}$$

The word

$$(\pi_1, \pi_2, \ldots, \pi_m)$$

corresponds to the product of permutations

$$\pi_1\pi_2 \ldots \pi_m$$

For example, with $N = 4$, the word $\sigma\lambda\sigma\lambda$ maps (0,0,0,1) into (0,1,1,1)

$$(0,0,0,1) \xrightarrow{\lambda} (0,0,1,0) \xrightarrow{\sigma} (0,0,1,1) \xrightarrow{\lambda} (0,1,1,0) \xrightarrow{\sigma} (0,1,1,1)$$

Each word is a permutation of $Z_{2,N}$. We may represent a word by means of the coding

$$\lambda \leftarrow\rightarrow (0,0) \qquad \rho \leftarrow\rightarrow (0,1) \qquad \sigma \leftarrow\rightarrow (1,0) \qquad \sigma^{-1} \leftarrow\rightarrow (1,1)$$

so that (1,0,0,0,1,0,0,0) corresponds to the word $\sigma\lambda\sigma\lambda$.

Let $G = G[\rho,\lambda,\sigma,\sigma^{-1}]$ denote the set of all words in $\{\rho,\lambda,\sigma,\sigma^{-1}\}$. The properties (1) that the product of two words is a word, and (2) that the set $\{\rho,\lambda,\sigma,\sigma^{-1}\}$ contains with each permutation its inverse,

$$\rho^{-1} = \lambda \qquad (\sigma^{-1})^{-1} = \sigma$$

implies that G is a group under multiplication. Let G_m denote the subset of G consisting of words of length m or less. G_m is not a group under multiplication; the product of two words of length $\leq$ m may not always be representable as a word of length $\leq$ m. G_m will serve as the key space. Note that the 2^{2m} keys in G_m do not correspond to distinct substitutions. In some sense

$$G = \text{limit}_{m\to\infty} G_m$$

and thus G_m should be "close" to G for m large.

Theorem 6.5.1 $G = \text{SYM}(Z_{2,N})$

Proof. The proof consists of showing that the transpositions $\{\gamma_j : 0 \leq j < 2^N\}$ are in G. We will then conclude that the transpositions $\{\gamma_{i,j} : 0 \leq i,j < 2^N\}$

$$\gamma_{i,j}(k) = \begin{cases} j & \text{if } k = i \\ i & \text{if } k = j \\ k & \text{if } k \neq i,j \end{cases}$$

are in G. From this it will follow that every π in SYM($\boldsymbol{Z}_{2,N}$) is an element of G since every π may be written as a product of the transpositions $\{\gamma_{i,j} : 0 \leq i,j < 2^N\}$. For example, if N = 4 and

$$\pi : (0,1,2,3) \rightarrow (0,3,1,2)$$

then π is the product of two transpositions $\pi = \gamma_{2,3}\gamma_{1,2}$

$$\gamma_{1,2} : (0,1,2,3) \rightarrow (0,2,1,3)$$

$$\gamma_{2,3} : (0,2,1,3) \rightarrow (0,3,1,2)$$

$$\gamma_{2,3}\gamma_{1,2} : (0,1,2,3) \rightarrow (0,3,1,2)$$

Consider the word

$$\beta = \sigma^2\lambda\sigma^{-1}\rho$$

By applying the substitutions ρ, σ^{-1}, λ, and σ^2, we obtain

$$(x_0, x_1, \ldots, x_{N-1}) \xrightarrow{\rho} (x_{N-1}, x_0, \ldots, x_{N-2}) \xrightarrow{\sigma^{-1}} (y_{N-1}, y_0, \ldots, y_{N-2})$$
$$\xrightarrow{\lambda} (y_0, y_1, \ldots, y_{N-1}) \xrightarrow{\sigma^2} (z_0, z_1, \ldots, z_{N-1})$$

Thus

$$(0, 0, \ldots, 0) \xrightarrow{\rho} (0, 0, \ldots, 0) \xrightarrow{\sigma^{-1}} (1, 1, \ldots, 1)$$
$$\xrightarrow{\lambda} (1, 1, \ldots, 1) \xrightarrow{\sigma^2} (0, 0, \ldots, 0, 1)$$

$$(0, 0, \ldots, 0, 1) \xrightarrow{\rho} (1, 0, 0, \ldots, 0) \xrightarrow{\sigma^{-1}} (0, 1, 1, \ldots, 1, 1)$$
$$\xrightarrow{\lambda} (1, 1, \ldots, 1, 0) \xrightarrow{\sigma^2} (0, 0, \ldots, 0)$$

The word β transposes the elements 0 and 1 in $\boldsymbol{Z}_{2N}$. We claim that β is actually equal to the transposition $\gamma_0 = \gamma_{0,1}$. This follows from the observation that $y_{N-1} = x_{N-1}$, if $x_k = 1$ for *some* k, $0 \leq k < N - 1$.

Next let $\beta_j = \sigma^j\beta\sigma^{-j}$ and note that if $\mathbf{x} \in \boldsymbol{Z}_{2,N}$ and $\|\mathbf{x}\| \notin \{j, j + 1\}$, then $\|\sigma^{-j}\mathbf{x}\| \notin \{0, 1\}$. It follows that β_j is the transposition $\gamma_j = \gamma_{j,j+1}$.

Finally every transposition $\gamma_{i,j}$ may be written as a product of the transposition

$$\{\gamma_j : 0 \leq j < 2^N\}$$

$$\gamma_{i,j} = \gamma_i\gamma_{i+1} \cdots \gamma_{j-1}\gamma_j\gamma_{j-1} \cdots \gamma_i$$ ◀

Theorem 6.5.1 provides a method for constructing a keyed block cipher system. The key space is the set $\boldsymbol{K} = \{0,1\}^{2m}$, and each 2m-block $(k_0, k_1, \ldots, k_{2m-1})$

corresponds to some word ω in the substitutions $\{\rho, \lambda, \sigma\,\sigma^{-1}\}$. Encipherment of an N-block $\mathbf{x} = (x_0, x_1, \ldots, x_{N-1})$ is by the action of the word ω on $\mathbf{x}$.

Theorem 6.5.1 is an example of a class of theorems that describe the group generated by some set of primitives. We state without proof a second theorem of this type.

Theorem 6.5.2 [GR1] The substitutions σ *(addition with carry)* and

$$\alpha_i : (x_0, x_1, \ldots, x_{n-1})$$

$$\rightarrow (x_0, x_1, \ldots, x_{i-1}, x_i + 1, x_{i+1}, \ldots, x_{n-1}) \qquad 0 \leq i < n - 1$$

generate (under composition) a subgroup of SYM($Z_{2,N}$) of order $2^{2^{n-1}+n-1}$.

6.6 INVOLUTIONS

If a cryptographic system is to be implemented in an information processing system, we must provide for both the encipherment and decipherment of text. It would be nice if the "box" that enciphers plaintext could serve (with minor modifications) as the "box" to decipher ciphertext. For one class of block ciphers, there is a particularly simple relationship between the operations of decipherment and encipherment.

Definition 6.6.1 A mapping π on $Z_{2,N}$ into $Z_{2,N}$ is called an *involution* if $\pi^2 = I$, the *identity* transformation.

Theorem 6.6.2 An involution π on $Z_{2,N}$ is an element of SYM($Z_{2,N}$).

Proof. If

$$\pi(\mathbf{x}) = \pi(\mathbf{x}')$$

then

$$\pi^2(\mathbf{x}) = \mathbf{x} = \mathbf{x}' = \pi^2(\mathbf{x}') \qquad ◀$$

Suppose T is any mapping on $Z_{2,N}$, *not* necessarily a permutation. Define the mapping π_T on Z_{2N} by

$$\pi_T : (\mathbf{x},\mathbf{x}') \rightarrow (\mathbf{x} + T(\mathbf{x}'),\mathbf{x}') \qquad (6.6.1)$$

π_T consists of the following steps:

- Transformation of the right-half N-block $\mathbf{x}'$ of $(\mathbf{x},\mathbf{x}')$ by T

$$T : \mathbf{x}' \rightarrow T(\mathbf{x}')$$

- Component-by-component addition (modulo 2) of this result to the left-half N-block $\mathbf{x}$ of $(\mathbf{x},\mathbf{x}')$

$$T(\mathbf{x}') + \mathbf{x}$$

- Concatenation of $T(\mathbf{x}') + \mathbf{x}$ to the right-half N-block $\mathbf{x}'$

$$(T(\mathbf{x}') + \mathbf{x}, \mathbf{x}')$$

Computing π_T^2, we find

$$\pi_T^2(\mathbf{x}, \mathbf{x}') = \pi_T(\mathbf{x} + T(\mathbf{x}'), \mathbf{x}') = (\mathbf{x} + T(\mathbf{x}') + T(\mathbf{x}'), \mathbf{x}') = (\mathbf{x}, \mathbf{x}')$$

since $T(\mathbf{x}') + T(\mathbf{x}') = \mathbf{0}$. Thus π_T is an involution and therefore an element of $SYM(\boldsymbol{Z}_{2,2N})$.

Let $\mathbf{T} = \{T_i : 1 \leq i \leq m\}$ be a family of mappings on $\boldsymbol{Z}_{2,N}$ and ϑ the interchange mapping

$$\vartheta : (\mathbf{x},\mathbf{x}') \rightarrow (\mathbf{x}',\mathbf{x})$$

Define the mapping π_T by

(6.6.2) $$\pi_T = \vartheta \times \pi_{T_m} \times \ldots \times \vartheta \times \pi_{T_1}$$

Since $(\pi_{T_i}^2) = \vartheta^2 = I$ (the identity substitution) we have

(6.6.3) $$\pi_T^{-1} = \pi_{T_1} \times \vartheta \times \ldots \times \pi_{T_m} \times \vartheta$$

The block cipher π_T (on $\boldsymbol{Z}_{2,2N}$) is the product of 2m involutions. Figure 6.6.1 shows $\vartheta \times \pi_{T_i}$, which is the ith *round* of π_T.

What elements of $SYM(\boldsymbol{Z}_{2,2N})$ are realizable in this form?

Definition 6.6.3 A function π on $\boldsymbol{Z}_{2,N}$,

$$\pi : (x_0, x_1, \ldots, x_{N-1}) \rightarrow (y_0, y_1, \ldots, y_{N-1})$$

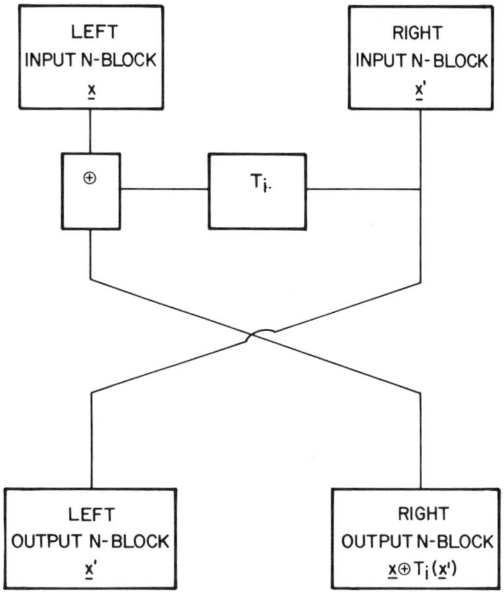

Figure 6.6.1. $\vartheta\pi_{T_i}$: Product of two involutions.

is a *k-function* if

- There is a (0,1)-valued function F whose domain is $\boldsymbol{Z}_{2,k}$
- There is a subset of k indices $\{i_0, i_1, \ldots, i_{k-1}\}$ of $\{0, 1, \ldots, N-1\}$ and an integer $j \in \{i_0, i_1, \ldots, i_{k-1}\}$

such that the $\{y_j\}$ and $\{x_j\}$ are related by

$$y_m = \begin{cases} x_m & \text{if } m \neq j \\ x_j + F(x_{i_0}, x_{i_1}, \ldots, x_{i_{k-1}}) & \text{if } m = j \end{cases}$$

The k-function π leaves all but one component of its input N-block $(x_0, x_1, \ldots, x_{N-1})$ unchanged; x_j is replaced by $x_j + F(x_{i_0}, x_{i_1}, \ldots, x_{i_{k-1}})$.

Example The function $\pi = (x_0 + x_1 + x_2, x_1, x_2)$

$$\pi(0,0,0) = (0,0,0) \quad \pi(0,0,1) = (1,0,1) \quad \pi(0,1,0) = (1,1,0)$$

$$\pi(0,1,1) = (0,1,1) \quad \pi(1,0,0) = (1,0,0) \quad \pi(1,0,1) = (0,0,1)$$

$$\pi(1,1,0) = (0,1,0) \quad \pi(1,1,1) = (1,1,1)$$

is a 2-function with

$$F(0,0) = F(1,1) = 0 \qquad F(0,1) = F(1,0) = 1$$

$$\{i_0, i_1\} = \{1,2\} \qquad j = 0$$

Theorem 6.6.4 A k-function on $\boldsymbol{Z}_{2,N}$ belongs to SYM($\boldsymbol{Z}_{2,N}$).

Proof. If

$$\pi(\mathbf{x}) = \pi(\mathbf{x}')$$

then $x_m = x'_m$ for all $m \neq j$, and hence

$$F(x_{i_0}, x_{i_1}, \ldots, x_{i_{k-1}}) = F(x'_{i_0}, x'_{i_1}, \ldots, x'_{i_{k-1}})$$

since $j \notin \{i_0, i_1, \ldots, i_{k-1}\}$. This implies $x_j = x'_j$. ◀

Theorem 6.6.5 A k-function π is an involution.

Theorem 6.6.6 The involutory block cipher shown in Fig. 6.6.1 is the product of 2-functions on $\boldsymbol{Z}_{2,2N}$.

Proof. We only need to prove that the interchange ϑ

$$\vartheta : (x_0, x_1, \ldots, x_{N-1}, x_N, x_{N+1}, \ldots, x_{2N-1})$$

$$\rightarrow (x_N, x_{N+1}, \ldots, x_{2N-1}, x_0, x_1, \ldots, x_{N-1})$$

is a 2-function. Let $\pi_{s,t}$ denote the 2-function with $i_0 = t$, $j = s$, and $F(x) = x$

$$(x_0, \ldots, x_{s-1}, x_s, x_{s+1}, \ldots, x_N, \ldots, x_{t-1}, x_t, x_{t+1}, \ldots, x_{2N-1})$$

$$\downarrow \pi_{s,t}$$

$$(x_0, \ldots, x_{s-1}, x_s + x_t, x_{s+1}, \ldots, x_{N-1}, \ldots, x_{t-1}, x_t, x_{t+1}, \ldots, x_{N-1})$$

$$\downarrow \pi_{t,s}$$

$$(x_0, \ldots, x_{s-1}, x_s + x_t, x_{s+1}, \ldots, x_{N-1}, \ldots, x_{t-1}, x_s, x_{t+1}, \ldots, x_{N-1})$$

$$\downarrow \pi_{s,t}$$

$$(x_0, \ldots, x_{s-1}, x_t, x_{s+1}, \ldots, x_{N-1}, \ldots, x_{t-1}, x_s, x_{t+1}, \ldots, x_{N-1})$$

so that we have interchanged the sth and t^{th} components by applying the product of three 2-functions. ◀

Let $\Xi_k(\boldsymbol{Z}_{2,N})$ denote the set of k-functions on $\boldsymbol{Z}_{2,N}$. $\Xi_k(\boldsymbol{Z}_{2,N})$ is not a group, since the product of k-functions is generally *not* a k-function. However, the set of all *words* $\Xi_k^*(\boldsymbol{Z}_{2,N})$ formed by the elements in $\Xi_k(\boldsymbol{Z}_{2,N})$

$$\pi_1 \times \pi_2 \times \ldots \times \pi_m \qquad \pi_i \in \Xi_k(\boldsymbol{Z}_{2,N}) \qquad (1 \le i \le m)$$

is a group. Don Coppersmith and Edna Grossman have proved the following result.

Theorem 6.6.7 [CO]

- If $N \ge 4$ and $2 \le k \le N - 2$,

  $\Xi_k^*(\boldsymbol{Z}_{2,N})$ is the *alternating group*, a subgroup of $SYM(\boldsymbol{Z}_{2,N})$

- If $N > 1$ and $k = N - 1$,

  $$\Xi_{N-1}^*(\boldsymbol{Z}_{2,N}) = SYM(\boldsymbol{Z}_{2,N})$$

- If $N = 1$ and $k = 1$,

  $\Xi_1^*(\boldsymbol{Z}_{2,N})$ is a group of affine transformations of $\boldsymbol{Z}_{2,N}$

Remarks

Every permutation may be written as a product of the transpositions $\{\gamma_{i,j}\}$ of Theorem 6.5.1. While the representation of a permutation as such a product is not unique, the number of transpositions in any representation is always either even or odd. Thus the permutations in $SYM(\boldsymbol{Z}_{2,N})$ can be divided into the two subsets $SYM_{odd}(\boldsymbol{Z}_{2,N})$ and $SYM_{even}(\boldsymbol{Z}_{2,N})$ consisting of permutations requiring an odd and even number of transpositions in their representation. Call a permutation *odd (even)* if it requires an odd (even) number of transpositions in its representation. It is simple to show that the product of

- An *odd* permutation with an *odd* permutation is an *even* permutation.
- An *odd* permutation with an *even* permutation is an *odd* permutation.
- An *even* permutation with an *even* permutation is an *even* permutation.

Thus $SYM_{even}(\boldsymbol{Z}_{2,N})$ is a subgroup of $SYM(\boldsymbol{Z}_{2,N})$ called the *alternating group.** The number of elements in $SYM_{even}(\boldsymbol{Z}_{2,N})$—the *order of* the alternating group—is $(2^N)!/2$. We shall not give the proof of Theorem 6.6.7; the interested reader is directed to [CO]. Theorem 6.6.7 asserts that every element of the alternating group is realizable by a sufficiently long product of involutions $\{\pi_{T_i}\}$.

6.7 DES

The Data Encryption Standard (DES) is a product of 33 mappings:

(6.7.1) $$DES = IP^{-1} \times \pi_{T_{16}} \times \ldots \times \vartheta \times \pi_{T_1} \times IP$$

- IP (the *initial permutation*) is a wire crossing with inverse IP^{-1}.
- $\{\pi_{T_i} : 1 \leq i \leq 16\}$ are described by Eq. (6.6.1).
- ϑ is the interchange involution.

The inverse to DES (providing the decipherment of DES-enciphered data) is

(6.7.2) $$DES^{-1} = (IP)^{-1} \times \pi_{T_1} \times \vartheta \times \ldots \times \vartheta \times \pi_{T_{16}} \times IP$$

The advantage of a block cipher having this form is apparent from Eqs. (6.7.1) and (6.7.2); the decipherment of DES-enciphered text is achieved by essentially running DES backwards.

The block of length $N = 64$ is broken into a right and left half and operated upon as shown. In Fig. 6.7.1, we illustrate a DES of smaller dimension ($N = 32$).

The encipherment of the plaintext 64-block $\mathbf{x} = (x_0, x_1, \ldots, x_{63})$ involves the following operations.

Step 1 The input plaintext block $\mathbf{x}$ is subject to an *initial permutation* IP as given in Table 6.7.2. Thus the permutated plaintext 64-block is

$$(x_{57}, x_{49}, \ldots, x_1, x_{59}, \ldots, x_6)$$

*The alternating group arises in the evaluation of the determinant of an n by n matrix $M = (m_{i,j})$. The determinant of M is the sum of the terms

$$\pm\, m_{0,\pi_0} m_{1,\pi_1} \cdots m_{n-1,\pi_{n-1}}$$

over all permutations $\pi = (\pi_0, \pi_1, \ldots, \pi_{n-1})$ of $(0, 1, \ldots, n-1)$. The "sign" $\pm$ is the parity of number of transpositions in π; $+1$ if π is an even permutation and -1 if π is an odd permutation.

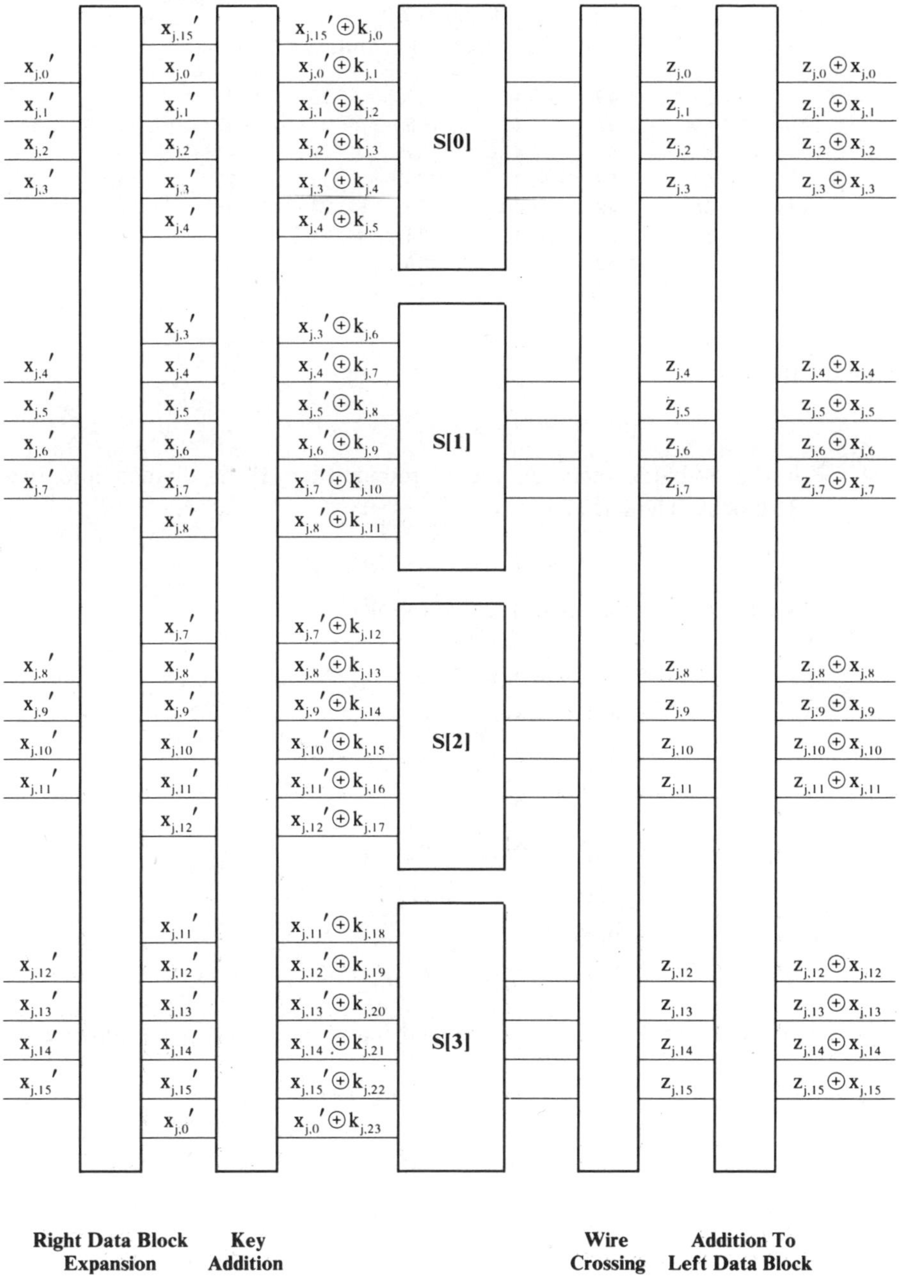

Figure 6.7.1. 32-bit wide DES.

TABLE 6.7.2
IP : DES Initial Permutation

IP :

57	49	41	33	25	17	9	1
59	51	43	35	27	19	11	3
61	53	45	37	29	21	13	5
63	55	47	39	31	23	15	7
56	48	40	32	24	16	8	0
58	50	42	34	26	18	10	2
60	52	44	36	28	20	12	4
62	54	46	38	30	22	14	6

Step 2 If

$$\mathbf{x}^{(i)} = (x_{i,0}, x_{i,1}, \ldots, x_{i,63})$$

is the 64-block input on the ith round, then $\mathbf{x}^{(i)}$ is divided into two 32-blocks. The left 32-block

$$(x_{i,0}, x_{i,1}, \ldots, x_{i,31})$$

is viewed as consisting of the eight 4-blocks:

$x_{i,0}$	$x_{i,1}$	$x_{i,2}$	$x_{i,3}$
$x_{i,4}$	$x_{i,5}$	$x_{i,6}$	$x_{i,7}$
$x_{i,8}$	$x_{i,9}$	$x_{i,10}$	$x_{i,11}$
$x_{i,12}$	$x_{i,13}$	$x_{i,14}$	$x_{i,15}$
$x_{i,16}$	$x_{i,17}$	$x_{i,18}$	$x_{i,19}$
$x_{i,20}$	$x_{i,21}$	$x_{i,22}$	$x_{i,23}$
$x_{i,24}$	$x_{i,25}$	$x_{i,26}$	$x_{i,27}$
$x_{i,28}$	$x_{i,29}$	$x_{i,30}$	$x_{i,31}$

These eight 4-blocks are expanded into eight 6-blocks by copying the outer bit positions:

$x_{i,31}$	$x_{i,0}$	$x_{i,1}$	$x_{i,2}$	$x_{i,3}$	$x_{i,4}$
$x_{i,3}$	$x_{i,4}$	$x_{i,5}$	$x_{i,6}$	$x_{i,7}$	$x_{i,8}$
$x_{i,7}$	$x_{i,8}$	$x_{i,9}$	$x_{i,10}$	$x_{i,11}$	$x_{i,12}$
$x_{i,11}$	$x_{i,12}$	$x_{i,13}$	$x_{i,14}$	$x_{i,15}$	$x_{i,16}$
$x_{i,15}$	$x_{i,16}$	$x_{i,17}$	$x_{i,18}$	$x_{i,19}$	$x_{i,20}$
$x_{i,19}$	$x_{i,20}$	$x_{i,21}$	$x_{i,22}$	$x_{i,23}$	$x_{i,24}$
$x_{i,23}$	$x_{i,24}$	$x_{i,25}$	$x_{i,26}$	$x_{i,27}$	$x_{i,28}$
$x_{i,27}$	$x_{i,28}$	$x_{i,29}$	$x_{i,30}$	$x_{i,31}$	$x_{i,0}$

Step 3 On the ith round, 48 bits of key

$$(k_{i,0}, k_{i,1}, \ldots, k_{i,47})$$

are added (modulo 2) to the plaintext:

$x_{i,31}+k_{i,0}$	$x_{i,0}+k_{i,1}$	$x_{i,1}+k_{i,2}$	$x_{i,2}+k_{i,3}$	$x_{i,3}+k_{i,4}$	$x_{i,4}+k_{i,5}$
$x_{i,3}+k_{i,6}$	$x_{i,4}+k_{i,7}$	$x_{i,5}+k_{i,8}$	$x_{i,6}+k_{i,9}$	$x_{i,7}+k_{i,10}$	$x_{i,8}+k_{i,11}$
$x_{i,7}+k_{i,12}$	$x_{i,8}+k_{i,13}$	$x_{i,9}+k_{i,14}$	$x_{i,10}+k_{i,15}$	$x_{i,11}+k_{i,16}$	$x_{i,12}+k_{i,17}$
$x_{i,11}+k_{i,18}$	$x_{i,12}+k_{i,19}$	$x_{i,13}+k_{i,20}$	$x_{i,14}+k_{i,21}$	$x_{i,15}+k_{i,22}$	$x_{i,16}+k_{i,23}$
$x_{i,15}+k_{i,24}$	$x_{i,16}+k_{i,25}$	$x_{i,17}+k_{i,26}$	$x_{i,18}+k_{i,27}$	$x_{i,19}+k_{i,28}$	$x_{i,20}+k_{i,29}$
$x_{i,19}+k_{i,30}$	$x_{i,20}+k_{i,31}$	$x_{i,21}+k_{i,32}$	$x_{i,22}+k_{i,33}$	$x_{i,23}+k_{i,34}$	$x_{i,24}+k_{i,35}$
$x_{i,23}+k_{i,36}$	$x_{i,24}+k_{i,37}$	$x_{i,25}+k_{i,38}$	$x_{i,26}+k_{i,39}$	$x_{i,27}+k_{i,40}$	$x_{i,28}+k_{i,41}$
$x_{i,27}+k_{i,42}$	$x_{i,28}+k_{i,43}$	$x_{i,29}+k_{i,44}$	$x_{i,30}+k_{i,45}$	$x_{i,31}+k_{i,46}$	$x_{i,0}+k_{i,47}$

Step 4 The ith 6-block $(0 \leq i < 8)$ forms the input to the *substitution box (S-box)* S[i]. S[i] has a 6-bit input and a 4-bit output and represents four transformations from $\boldsymbol{Z}_{2,4}$ to $\boldsymbol{Z}_{2,4}$; the outer two bit positions in the 6-block select one of the four mappings. Each of the eight substitutions S[0], S[1], . . . , S[7] is represented as a 4-row, 16-column matrix with entries {0, 1, . . . , 15}. They are given in Table 6.7.3. Each 4-by-16 array defines a substitution on $\boldsymbol{Z}_{2,4}$ as follows. If the input is the 6-block

$$(z_0, z_1, z_2, z_3, z_4, z_5)$$

the outer two positions (z_0, z_5) are interpreted as the binary representation of an integer in the set {0,1,2,3}. This integer specifies the row number (labeling the rows from 0 to 3). The remaining four bits (z_1, z_2, z_3, z_4) are interpreted as the binary representation of an integer in the set {0, 1, . . . , 15}, which specifies the column of the array (labeling columns from 0 to 15). Thus the input 6-block

$$(0,0,1,0,1,1)$$

refers to row = 1, column = 5, and hence yields

n	Output of S[n]
0	(0,0,1,0) = 2
1	(0,0,1,0) = 2
2	(0,1,0,0) = 4
3	(1,1,1,1) = 15
4	(0,1,1,1) = 7
5	(1,1,0,0) = 12
6	(1,0,0,1) = 9
7	(0,0,1,1) = 3

TABLE 6.7.3

S[i]i = 0(1)7 : DES S-boxes

S[0]	14	4	13	1	2	15	11	8	3	10	6	12	5	9	0	7
	0	15	7	4	14	2	13	1	10	6	12	11	9	5	3	8
	4	1	14	8	13	6	2	11	15	12	9	7	3	10	5	0
	15	12	8	2	4	9	1	7	5	11	3	14	10	0	6	13
S[1]	15	1	8	14	6	11	3	4	9	7	2	13	12	0	5	10
	3	13	4	7	15	2	8	14	12	0	1	10	6	9	11	5
	0	14	7	11	10	4	13	1	5	8	12	6	9	3	12	15
	13	8	10	1	3	15	4	2	11	6	7	12	0	5	14	9
S[2]	10	0	9	14	6	3	15	5	1	13	12	7	11	4	2	8
	13	7	0	9	3	4	6	10	2	8	5	14	12	11	15	1
	13	6	4	9	8	15	3	0	11	1	2	12	5	10	14	7
	1	10	13	0	6	9	8	7	4	15	14	3	11	5	2	12
S[3]	7	13	14	3	0	6	9	10	1	2	8	5	11	12	4	15
	13	8	11	5	6	15	0	3	4	7	2	12	1	10	14	9
	10	6	9	0	12	11	7	13	15	1	3	14	5	2	8	4
	3	15	0	6	10	1	13	8	9	4	5	11	12	7	2	14
S[4]	2	12	4	1	7	10	11	6	8	5	3	15	13	0	14	9
	14	11	2	12	4	7	13	1	5	0	15	10	3	9	8	6
	4	2	1	11	10	13	7	8	15	9	12	5	6	3	0	14
	11	8	12	7	1	14	2	13	6	15	0	9	10	4	5	3
S[5]	12	1	10	15	9	2	6	8	0	13	3	4	14	7	5	11
	10	15	4	2	7	12	9	5	6	1	13	14	0	11	3	8
	9	14	15	5	2	8	12	3	7	0	4	10	1	13	11	6
	4	3	2	12	9	5	15	10	11	14	1	7	6	0	8	13
S[6]	4	11	2	14	15	0	8	13	3	12	9	7	5	10	6	1
	13	0	11	7	4	9	1	10	14	3	5	12	2	15	8	6
	1	4	11	13	12	3	7	14	10	15	6	8	0	5	9	2
	6	11	13	8	1	4	10	7	9	5	0	15	14	2	3	12
S[7]	13	2	8	4	6	15	11	1	10	9	3	14	5	0	12	7
	1	15	13	8	10	3	7	4	12	5	6	11	0	14	9	2
	7	11	4	1	9	12	14	2	0	6	10	13	15	3	5	8
	2	1	14	7	4	10	8	13	15	12	9	0	3	5	6	11

Step 5 The 32 bits that constitute the output of the eight S-boxes are subject to a wire crossing *(P-box)* as shown in Table 6.7.4. Thus if the output of the *S-box layer* is

$$(y_{i,0}, y_{i,1}, \ldots, y_{i,31})$$

then the output of the *P-box layer* is

$$(y_{i,15}, y_{i,6}, \ldots, y_{i,24})$$

TABLE 6.7.4
P : DES Wire-Crossing

P :	15	6	19	20
	28	11	27	16
	0	14	22	25
	4	17	30	9
	1	7	23	13
	31	26	2	8
	18	12	29	5
	21	10	3	24

Step 6 The right input N-block $\mathbf{x}'$ ($N = 32$), now transformed to $T_i(\mathbf{x}')$, is added (component-wise modulo 2) to the left input N-block $\mathbf{x}$. Next, the interchange ϑ is applied to the two halves:

- The left output N-block is now $\mathbf{x}'$.
- The right output N-block is now $\mathbf{x} + T(\mathbf{x}')$.

Steps 2–6 constitute one *round* of the DES block cipher. There are 16 rounds in a DES encipherment. On the final round, the interchange ϑ of messages halves is omitted and the output 64-block is operated on by the inverse of the initial permutation IP.

On each round, 48 bits of key $(k_{i,0}, k_{i1,}, \ldots, k_{i,47})$ are required. Since the DES *input key* is a 56-block $\mathbf{k} = (k_0, k_1, \ldots, k_{55})$, each component of $\mathbf{k}$ is used many times. The key used on the ith round is specified by a *key schedule.* To describe the key schedule, we need to introduce several auxilliary quantities, as given in Tables 6.7.5–8.

We now define the key schedule. Start with a *user supplied key* of 56 bits:

$$\mathbf{k} = (k_0, k_1, \ldots, k_{55})$$

- $\mathbf{k}$ is initially permuted by PC-1. The resulting 56-bit vector is regarded as being composed of a left-half block of 28 bits, C_0, and a right-half block of 28 bits, D_0.

TABLE 6.7.5
DES Key Schedule

	k_{49}	k_{42}	k_{35}	k_{28}	k_{21}	k_{14}	k_{7}
C_0:	k_{0}	k_{50}	k_{43}	k_{36}	k_{29}	k_{22}	k_{15}
	k_{8}	k_{1}	k_{51}	k_{44}	k_{37}	k_{30}	k_{23}
	k_{16}	k_{9}	k_{2}	k_{52}	k_{45}	k_{38}	k_{31}
	k_{55}	k_{48}	k_{41}	k_{34}	k_{27}	k_{20}	k_{13}
D_0:	k_{6}	k_{54}	k_{47}	k_{40}	k_{33}	k_{26}	k_{19}
	k_{12}	k_{5}	k_{53}	k_{46}	k_{39}	k_{32}	k_{25}
	k_{18}	k_{11}	k_{4}	k_{24}	k_{17}	k_{10}	k_{3}

TABLE 6.7.6
Table of DES Key Schedule Shifts

Round i:	1	2	3	4	5	6	7	8	9	10	11	12	13	14	15	16
Number of Left Shifts $\sigma[i]$:	1	1	2	2	2	2	2	2	1	2	2	2	2	2	2	1

TABLE 6.7.7
PC-1 : DES Permuted Choice 1

	49	42	35	28	21	14	7
	0	50	43	36	29	22	15
	8	1	51	44	37	30	23
PC-1 :	16	9	2	52	45	38	31
	55	48	41	34	27	20	13
	6	54	47	40	33	26	19
	12	5	53	46	39	32	25
	18	11	4	24	17	10	3

TABLE 6.7.8
PC-2 : DES Permuted Choice 2

	13	16	10	23	0	4
	2	27	14	5	20	9
	22	18	11	3	25	7
PC-2 :	15	6	26	19	12	1
	40	51	30	36	46	54
	29	39	50	44	32	47
	43	48	38	55	33	52
	45	41	49	35	28	31

- The blocks C_0 and D_0 are shifted left-circular $\sigma[1]$ times to obtain the blocks C_1 and D_1

$$C_1 = \lambda^{\sigma[1]}C_0 \qquad D_1 = \lambda^{\sigma[1]}D_0$$

- The subset function PC-2 selects 48 bits from the concatenated blocks (C_1, D_1). These are the key bits used on the first round.

- The key bits used on round i are defined inductively. Given the blocks C_{i-1} and D_{i-1}, we apply a shift-left circular $\sigma[i]$ times to obtain the blocks C_i and D_i:

$$C_i = \lambda^{\sigma[i]}C_{i-1} \qquad D_i = \lambda^{\sigma[i]}D_{i-1} \qquad 1 \le i \le 16$$

  These blocks are concatenated, and the subset function PC-2 selects the 48 bits to be used on round i.

Thus on *rounds* one and two, the key used is

Round 1

k_8	k_{44}	k_{29}	k_{52}	k_{42}	k_{14}
k_{28}	k_{49}	k_1	k_7	k_{16}	k_{36}
k_2	k_{30}	k_{22}	k_{21}	k_{38}	k_{50}
k_{51}	k_0	k_{31}	k_{23}	k_{15}	k_{35}
k_{19}	k_{24}	k_{34}	k_{47}	k_{32}	k_3
k_{41}	k_{26}	k_4	k_{46}	k_{20}	k_{25}
k_{53}	k_{18}	k_{33}	k_{55}	k_{13}	k_{17}
k_{39}	k_{12}	k_{11}	k_{54}	k_{48}	k_{27}

Round 2

k_1	k_{37}	k_{22}	k_{45}	k_{35}	k_7
k_{21}	k_{42}	k_{51}	k_0	k_9	k_{29}
k_{52}	k_{23}	k_{15}	k_{14}	k_{31}	k_{43}
k_{44}	k_{50}	k_{49}	k_{16}	k_8	k_{28}
k_{12}	k_{17}	k_{27}	k_{40}	k_{25}	k_{55}
k_{34}	k_{19}	k_{24}	k_{39}	k_{13}	k_{18}
k_{46}	k_{11}	k_{26}	k_{48}	k_6	k_{10}
k_{32}	k_5	k_4	k_{47}	k_{41}	k_{20}

6.8 PRELIMINARY ASSESSMENT OF DES

What can we say about the strength of DES? First, since the plaintext blocks are of length 64, the maintenance of a catalogue of frequency of usage of blocks is beyond the capability of an opponent. Second, key trial is unfeasible: the key space contains 2^{56} keys. DES exhibits the following symmetry with respect to the complementation ($\sim$).

Theorem 6.8.1 $\text{DES}\{\sim\mathbf{k},\sim\mathbf{x}\} = \sim\text{DES}\{\mathbf{k},\mathbf{x}\}$

Proof. It suffices to show that

$$\pi_{T_i}\{\sim\mathbf{k},\sim\mathbf{x}\} = \sim\pi_{T_i}\{\mathbf{k},\mathbf{x}\}$$

for each round of DES. The essential point is that certain bits in the key, say $\mathbf{k}^*$, are added (modulo 2) to certain bits in $\mathbf{x}^*$ ($\mathbf{x}$ suitably expanded) to form the input to the layer of S-boxes. But under complementation, we have

$$\sim\mathbf{k}^* + \sim\mathbf{x}^* = \mathbf{k}^* + \mathbf{x}^*$$

and this implies the symmetry property on each round. ◀

6.9 THE CRITICISM OF DES

Three major technical issues were raised by critics of the Data Encryption Standard:

- The criteria for the design of the substitutions *(S-boxes),* fixed permutation *(P-box),* and key schedule were not published by the designers.
- A 16-round DES might not be adequate.
- A 56-bit DES key might not be adequate.

6.10 THE S- AND P-BOX DESIGN CRITERIA

The design of DES and its predecessor LUCIFER by Horst Feistel is based on the iteration or composition of transformations, as suggested in Shannon's 1949 secrecy paper [SHA]. DES iterates the two transformations:

- Substitution: a nonlinear transformation realizable for small block size.
- Coordinate permutation (wire crossing): a linear transformation realizable for arbitrary block size.

Shannon referred to substitution and coordinate permutation as *confusion* and *diffusion.* The substitution makes the output a nonlinear function of the input, certainly necessary for a good block cipher since we have already shown for the Hill system that linearity is to be avoided. A coordinate permutation is a linear transformation (on $Z_{2,N}$), but its function in DES is to spread the dependence of the output from a small number of input bit positions to a larger number. Even if we accept the idea of iterating or layering involutions, as in Fig. 6.6.1, the design of DES requires the specification of (1) the substitutions *(S-boxes),* (2) the permutation *(P-box),* and (3) the key schedule.

The National Security Agency advised the designers that certain of the design criteria were considered by the agency to be "sensitive." IBM was requested not to publish the selection criteria. Critics have suggested that special properties might have been incorporated in the design of the substitutions and permutation *(trap doors)* which would give a cryptanalytic advantage to a knowledgeable party. No proof can be offered to refute the existence of trap doors. Even if IBM, the National Bureau of Standards, or the National Security Agency were to reveal the criteria, there would undoubtably be critics who would suggest that not *all* were revealed. The bottom line is that after nearly five years of scrutiny, no viable method of cryptanalyzing DES has been discovered and published. Bell Telephone Laboratories [MO1] and the Lexar Corporation [LEX, HE4] examined the properties of the substitutions and permutations. While the Lexar reported some "peculiar" properties of the S-boxes, to date, *no feasible cryptanalytic technique for DES has been found.* In response to questions raised at the second workshop on DES, the National Security Agency revealed several of the design criteria [BR2]:

- No S-box is a linear or affine function of its input.
- Changing one bit in the input of an S-box results in changing at least two output bits.
- The S-boxes were chosen to minimize the difference between the number of 1s and 0s when any single input bit is held constant.

6.11 THE NUMBER OF ITERATIONS

The number of iterations controls the *mixing* of input bit values, that is, the amount of diffusion introduced by the coordinate permutation. If DES consisted of only one round,

$$IP^{-1} \times \pi_{T_1} \times IP : (x_0, x_1, \ldots, x_{63}) \rightarrow (y_0, y_1, \ldots, y_{63})$$

y_i would be strongly correlated with a small number of values $x_{i_0}, x_{i_1}, \ldots$ Experimentation with DES and LUCIFER revealed that dependence, as measured by the χ^2-test (see Sec. 6.16), disappears after eight rounds.

6.12 THE KEY LENGTH

By far the greatest source of controversy has been the choice of 56 bits as a key length. The length of the DES key determines the feasibility of key trial. If DES keys were tested at the rate of one per 60 μs on a general purpose computer, key trial would require in excess of 68,000 years, since $2^{56} \approx 7.206 \times 10^{16}$. Critics were quick to correctly point out that this calculation is misleading; a special purpose machine built just to carry out key trial could make substantial improvements. By parallelism and pipelining, the time to recover a key can be reduced to any value. In [HE2], a tradeoff between time and memory is proposed (see Sec. 6.23). By properly combining precomputation, a machine can be constructed that would recover the key with high probability in one day. The estimates are:

cost: four million dollars

precomputation: two years

Even if these estimates are accepted, the way that DES would normally be used, with *chaining* and an *initial chaining value* (see Sec. 6.24), would negate the advantage gained in the time-memory tradeoff. Multiple encipherment (with different keys) also defeats the tradeoff. It is certainly questionable if any organization would risk an investment of four million dollars and two years of precomputation under these circumstances.

6.13 CRYPTANALYSIS OF DES: THE GROUND RULES

It remains to look for relationships existing between plaintext and ciphertext that would enable the recovery of plaintext and/or key from known corresponding plaintext and ciphertext. We might uncover a functional relationship and construct a feasible analytic technique based on it to recover plaintext and/or key. We would then need to reconsider the viability of the DES algorithm. Thus we must answer these questions:

- Is it reasonable to assume that an opponent can obtain the required information to use the technique?
- What is the computational cost of the attack?
- How much time does it require?

If we do not find any relationship or procedure to recover plaintext and/or key, this does not *prove* the nonexistence of a relationship, nor does it prove that the algorithm is strong. The evaluation of DES by IBM consisted of the application of various cryptanalytic techniques to determine whether or not the algorithm exhibited any weakness. We will describe several of these cryptanalytic attacks on DES.

6.14 CYCLE LENGTH

DES is a mapping on $\boldsymbol{Z}_{2,64}$ onto itself. The iterates $\{\mathrm{DES}^{(n)} : 1 \leq n < \infty\}$, defined by

$$\mathrm{DES}^{(n)}\{\mathbf{k},\mathbf{x}\} = \mathrm{DES}\{\mathbf{k},\mathrm{DES}^{(n-1)}\{\mathbf{k},\mathbf{x}\}\}$$

are likewise one-to-one mappings on $\boldsymbol{Z}_{2,64}$. If

$$\text{DES}^{(N)}\{\mathbf{k},\mathbf{x}\} = \mathbf{x}$$

for a small value of N (depending on **x** and **k**) called the *period* of **x** and **k**, then recovery of plaintext might be possible. If DES behaves like a random permutation, then the average cycle length is approximately $2^{64} \div \log_e 64 \approx 4.44 \times 10^{18}$, making such an approach impractical. Tests were made which indicate that the period is consistent with the hypothesis that DES behaves like a random permutation.

6.15 CORRELATION BETWEEN OUTPUT AND INPUT SUBBLOCKS

Even though the ciphertext N-block **y** is uniquely determined by the plaintext N-block

$$\mathbf{y} = \text{DES}\{\mathbf{k},\mathbf{x}\} \leftarrow \rightarrow \mathbf{x}$$

there may be dependence between an *output subblock*

$$(y_{j_0}, y_{j_1}, \ldots, y_{j_{N_0-1}})$$

and an *input subblock*

$$(x_{i_0}, x_{i_1}, \ldots, x_{i_{N_1-1}})$$

Dependence might enable one to deduce values of the input based upon a frequency analysis of the output. The existence of this type of dependence can be checked using the χ^2-*test*.

6.16 THE χ^2-TEST

Let

$$\mathbf{X} = (X_0, X_1, \ldots, X_{n-1})$$

be independent and identically distributed random variables taking values in the set $\{a_0, a_1, \ldots, a_{m-1}\}$ with *unknown* probability distribution. The χ^2-test is used to decide if an observation $X_0, X_1, \ldots, X_{n-1}$ is consistent with the hypothesis

(6.16.1) $$\Pr\{X = a_j\} = p(j) \quad 0 \leq j < m$$

where $\{p(j)\}$ is a probability distribution on $\boldsymbol{Z}_{\mathbf{m}}$.

The χ^2-*statistic* is the random variable defined by

(6.16.2) $$\chi^2 = \sum_{0 \leq j < n} (N_{a_j}(\mathbf{X}) - np(j))^2/np(j)$$

The term

$$(N_{a_j}(\mathbf{X}) - np(j))^2/np(j)$$

in Eq. (6.16.2) is the product of two factors; the first

$$n/p(j)$$

tends to ∞ with n while the second

$$(N_{a_j}(\mathbf{X}) - np(j))^2/n^2$$

converges to 0 as $n \to \infty$ by the law of large numbers. Theorem 6.16.1, due to K. Pearson [PE, CR, KN], shows that the sum of these products has a limiting distribution and is the basis of the χ^2-test.

Theorem 6.16.1 If $\{p(j) : 0 \leq j < m\}$ is the common distribution of $X_0, X_1, \ldots, X_{n-1}$, the random variable of χ^2 converges in distribution as $n \to \infty$; its limiting distribution is

$$\Pr\{\chi^2 \leq x\} = \int_0^x \frac{2^{-(m-1)}y^{(m-3)/2}e^{-y/2}}{\Gamma((m-1)/2)}\, dy$$

where

$$\Gamma(a) = \int_0^\infty x^{a-1}e^{-x}\, dx \qquad 0 < a < \infty$$

is the *gamma function.* $\Gamma(a)$ satisfies the functional equation

$$\Gamma(a) = a\Gamma(a-1)$$

and extends the definition of the *factorial* n! from nonnegative integer values to all real numbers, excluding the negative integers; $\Gamma(a) = (a-1)!$ whenever a is a positive integer.

Theorem 6.16.1 is a *limit theorem;* if the $\{p(j) : 0 \leq j < m\}$ is the probability distribution of $X_0, X_1, \ldots, X_{n-1}$, the *sample distribution function*

$$\Pr\{\chi^2 \leq x\} = \Pr\left\{\sum_{0 \leq j < m} (N_{a_j}(\mathbf{X}) - np(j))^2/np(j) \leq x\right\}$$

converges to the integral

$$\int_0^x k_{m-1}(y)\, dy$$

with

$$k_{m-1}(y) = \frac{2^{-(m-1)}y^{(m-3)/2}e^{-y/2}}{\Gamma((m-1)/2)}$$

The limiting distribution of χ^2 does not depend on the numbers $\{p(i) : 0 \leq i <$

m}. $k_{m-1}(y)$ is the *probability density of the* χ^2 *distribution** with $m - 1$ *degrees of freedom,* and satisfies

- $0 \leq k_{m-1}(y) < \infty$
- $1 = \int_0^\infty k_{m-1}(y)\, dy$

The parameter $d = m - 1$ is the number of degrees of freedom of the χ^2-distribution.

For $0 \leq p \leq 100$, define $\chi_{p,m-1}$ by

$$p/100 = \int_{\chi_{p,m-1}}^\infty k_{n-1}(y)\, dy$$

$\chi_{p,m-1}$ is the pth *percentage value of* χ^2 with $m - 1$ degrees of freedom. A random variable having the χ^2 distribution (with $m - 1$ degrees of freedom) will exceed $\chi_{p,m-1}$ with probability 0.01p. By the law of large numbers, the statistic

$$\chi^2 = \sum_{0 \leq j < m} (N_{a_j}(X) - np(j))^2/np(j)$$

will exceed $\chi_{p,m-1}$ with probability approximately 0.01p as the sample size $n \to \infty$. For $m > 31$, $\chi_{p,m-1}$ is given by the formula [AB]

$$\chi_{p,m-1} \approx (m - 1)\{1 - 2/9(m - 1) + x_p[2/9(m - 1)]^{1/2}\}^{1/3}$$

The values of x_p for $p = 1$ and $p = 99$ are [KN]

$$x_1 \approx -2.33 \qquad x_{99} \approx 2.33$$

*Our use of probability theory up to this point has required only the *discrete theory* which deals with random variables that assume only a finite or countably-infinite number of values (discrete-valued random variables). The random variable χ^2 takes all values in the interval $[0, \infty)$ and the study of its properties belongs to the *continuous theory*. In the discrete theory, we associate a probability distribution $p_X(i)$ to a random variable X with values in $\{0, 1, \ldots, n - 1\}$ satisfying:

$$0 \leq p_X(i) \leq 1 \qquad 0 \leq i < n$$

$$1 = \sum_{0 \leq i < n} p_X(i)$$

In the continuous theory, the random variable, with values in $[0, \infty)$, is described by a probability density $p_X(x)$ which satisfies the properties analogous to those above:

$$p_X(x) \geq 0 \qquad 0 \leq x < \infty$$

$$1 = \int_0^\infty p_X(x)\, dx$$

The probability of the event $\{a \leq X \leq b\}$, which was the sum

$$\Pr\{a \leq X \leq b\} = \sum_{a \leq i \leq b} p_X(i)$$

when X was discretely valued, is replaced by the integral

$$\int_a^b p_X(x)\, dx$$

The χ^2-*test* is used to decide between the *null hypothesis,*

H_0 : $\{p(j) : 0 \leq j < m\}$ *is* the probability distribution of $X_0, X_1, \ldots, X_{n-1}$

and the *alternate hypothesis,*

H_1 : $\{p(j) : 0 \leq j < m\}$ *is not* the probability distribution of $X_0, X_1, \ldots, X_{n-1}$

There are two versions of the χ^2-test.

The One-Tailed χ^2-Test

First, compute χ^2 from $(X_0, X_1, \ldots, X_{n-1})$:

$$\chi^2 = \sum_{0 \leq j < n} (N_{a_j}(\mathbf{X}) - np(j))^2/np(j)$$

Then compare χ^2 with $\chi_{p,m-1}$, accepting H_0 if $\chi^2 \leq \chi_{p,m-1}$.

The Two-Tailed χ^2-Test

First, compute χ^2 from $(X_0, X_1, \ldots, X_{n-1})$:

$$\chi^2 = \sum_{0 \leq j < n} (N_{a_j}(\mathbf{X}) - np(j))^2/np(j)$$

Second, choose p_U and p_L with $p_L < p_U$; define $\chi_{p_U,m-1}$ and $\chi_{p_L,m-1}$ by

$$p_L/100 = \int_0^{\chi_{p_L,m-1}} k_{m-1}(y)\, dy$$

$$p_U/100 = \int_0^{\chi_{p_U,m-1}} k_{m-1}(y)\, dy$$

Third, check if χ^2 is in the interval $[\chi_{p_L,m-1}, \chi_{p_U,m-1}]$, and accept H_0 if

$$\chi_{p_U,m-1} \leq \chi^2 \leq \chi_{p_L,m-1}$$

In practice, the acceptance or rejection of the null hypothesis is based upon the results of several independent χ^2-tests. The evaluation of multiple χ^2-tests is often made using the Kolmogorov-Smirnov test.

6.17 THE KOLMOGOROV-SMIRNOV TEST

Suppose $X_0, X_1, \ldots, X_{n-1}$ are nonnegative real-valued independent and identically distributed random variables with a continuous distribution function

$$F(x) = \Pr\{X_i \leq x\} \qquad 0 \leq x < \infty \qquad 0 \leq i < n$$

Form the *sample distribution function* of $X_0, X_1, \ldots, X_{n-1}$

$$F_n(x \mid \mathbf{X}) = F_n(x \mid X_0, X_1, \ldots, X_{n-1}) = (1/n) \sum_{0 \leq i < n} \chi_{(-\infty,x]}(X_i)$$

where

$$\chi_{(-\infty,x]}(X_i) = \begin{cases} 1 & \text{if } -\infty < X_i \leq x \\ 0 & \text{otherwise} \end{cases}$$

The law of large numbers implies that

$$\text{limit}_{n\to\infty} F_n(x \mid X_0, X_1, \ldots, X_{n-1}) = F(x) \tag{6.17.1}$$

for each fixed value of x. The convergence in Eq. (6.17.1) is *convergence in distribution.* The law of large numbers and the continuity and monotonicity of F imply that the convergence is uniform in x; given $\epsilon > 0$ and $\delta > 0$, there is an $N = N(\epsilon,\delta)$ such that

$$\Pr\{|F_n(x \mid X_0,X_1, \ldots ,X_{n-1}) - F(x)| \leq \epsilon\} > 1 - \delta \qquad n \geq N$$

Definition 6.17.1 Let $X_0, X_1, \ldots, X_{n-1}$ be independent and identically distributed random variables with continuous distribution function F(x). Assume that observations $X_0, X_1, \ldots, X_{n-1}$ are sorted

$$X_0 \leq X_1 \leq \ldots \leq X_{n-1}$$

The *Kolmogorov-Smirnov statistics* are defined by

$$K_{n,+} = n^{1/2} \max_{0 \leq i < n} ((i + 1)/n - F(X_i \mid X_0,X_1, \ldots, X_{n-1})) \tag{6.17.2}$$

$$K_{n,-} = n^{1/2} \max_{0 \leq i < n} (F(X_i \mid X_0,X_1, \ldots, X_{n-1}) - i/n) \tag{6.17.3}$$

The value of the sample distribution function of $X_0, X_1, \ldots, X_{n-1}$ at $x = (i + 1)/n$ is equal to $(i + 1)/n$, and thus

$$(i + 1)/n - F(X_i \mid \mathbf{X})$$

measures the positive deviation of the sample distribution function F_n from the actual distribution function F at the points $X_0, X_1, \ldots, X_{n-1}$. Similarly,

$$F(X_i \mid \mathbf{X}) - i/n$$

measures the negative deviation of the sample distribution function F_n from the actual distribution function at the points $X_0, X_1, \ldots, X_{n-1}$.

Theorem 6.17.2 [DA] If $X_0, X_1, \ldots, X_{n-1}$ are independent and identically distributed random variables with a continuous distribution function F, then

$$\text{limit}_{n\to\infty} \Pr\{K_{n,+} \leq s\} = 1 - e^{2s^2} \qquad \text{if } s \geq 0 \tag{6.17.4}$$

$$\text{limit}_{n\to\infty} \Pr\{K_{n,-} \leq s\} = 1 - e^{2s^2} \qquad \text{if } s \geq 0 \tag{6.17.5}$$

The Kolmogorov-Smirnov test is used to decide between the null hypothesis,

$$H_0 : F \text{ is the common distribution of } X_0, X_1, \ldots, X_{n-1}$$

and the *alternate hypothesis,*

$$H_1 : \text{F is not the common distribution of } X_0, X_1, \ldots, X_{n-1}$$

at selected confidence levels $p_L/100$ and $p_U/100$:

- Choose confidence levels p_L and p_U.
- Compute $K_{n,+}$ and $K_{n,-}$ defined in Eqs. (6.17.2) and (6.17.3).
- Accept H_0 if both $K_{n,+}$ and K_{n-1} belong to the interval $[x_{p_L}, x_{p_U}]$.

The numbers x_{p_L} and x_{p_U} are [KN]

$$x_{p_L} \approx 0.03807 \quad \text{for } p_L = 99 \qquad x_{p_U} \approx 1.4698 \quad \text{for } p_U = 1$$

6.18 APPLYING THE χ^2-TEST TO DETECT DEPENDENCE BETWEEN OUTPUT AND INPUT

Let plaintext $\mathbf{x} = (x_0, x_1, \ldots, x_{63})$ be enciphered by DES with key $\mathbf{k} = (k_0, k_1, \ldots, k_{55})$ into ciphertext $\mathbf{y} = (y_0, y_1, \ldots, y_{63})$:

$$\mathbf{y} = \text{DES}\{\mathbf{k},\mathbf{x}\}$$

Each *output bit coordinate* y_i $(0 \le i < 64)$ is a function of the 64 *input bit coordinates* x_i $(0 \le i < 64)$ and 56 *key coordinates* k_i $(0 \le i < 56)$. We want to test if one of the following conditions holds

- Some set of output bits coordinates CO_{out} are dependent on some set of input bit coordinates CO_{in} for a fixed key $\mathbf{k}'$ or sequence of keys $\{\mathbf{k}_2\}$.
- Some set of output bit coordinates CO_{out} are dependent on some set of key coordinates CO_{key} for a fixed input $\mathbf{x}$.

Dependence might be used to estimate the key or plaintext; for example, if k_i is dependent on some set of output or input bit positions, we could make this the basis of the recovery of k_i from corresponding plaintext and ciphertext.

There is dependence, of course, if CO_{in} or CO_{out} is the set $\{0, 1, \ldots, 63\}$ of all input/output bit positions. What we intend to check is dependence for small subsets CO_{in}, CO_{out}, and CO_{key}. We use the χ^2-test as follows:

- Choose small subsets CO_{in} and CO_{out} of sizes N_{in} and N_{out}:

$$CO_{\text{in}} = \{i_0, i_1, \ldots, i_{N_{\text{in}}-1}\} \qquad CO_{\text{out}} = \{j_0, j_1, \ldots, j_{N_{\text{out}}-1}\}$$

- Choose a key $\mathbf{k} = (k_0, k_1, \ldots, k_{55})$.
- Take a sample of random variables $(X_0, X_1, \ldots, X_{63})$ that are independent and uniformly distributed on $\mathbf{Z_2}$:

$$\Pr\{(X_0, X_1, \ldots, X_{63}) = (x_0, x_1, \ldots, x_{63})\} = 2^{-64}$$

$$\mathbf{x}_i = (x_{i,0}, x_{i,1}, \ldots, x_{i,63}) \rightarrow \mathbf{y}_i = (y_{i,0}, y_{i,1}, \ldots, y_{i,63}) = \mathrm{DES}\{\mathbf{k},\mathbf{x}_i\}$$

$$0 \leq i < N_{samples}$$

- Form the $2^{N_{in}}$ by $2^{N_{out}}$ *contingency table;* the (s,t)-entry is the number of times

$$(x_{i,i_0}, x_{i,i_1}, \ldots, x_{i,i_{N_{in}}}) = (s_0, s_1, \ldots, s_{N_{in}-1})$$

$$(y_{i,j_0}, y_{i,j_1}, \ldots, y_{i,j_{N_{out}}}) = (t_0, t_1, \ldots, t_{N_{out}-1})$$

where

$$(s_0, s_1, \ldots, s_{N_{in}-1}) \qquad (t_0, t_1, \ldots, t_{N_{out}-1})$$

are the base 2 representations of s and t. We decide between the *null hypothesis,*

H_0 : the output bit positions in CO_{out} are independent of the input bit positions in CO_{in} with the key **k**

and the *alternate hypothesis,*

H_1 : the output bit positions in CO_{out} are dependent on the input bit positions in CO_{in} with the key **k**

by computing the χ^2-statistic with $2^{N_{in}+N_{out}-1}$ degrees of freedom:

$$\chi^2 = \sum_{0 \leq s < 2^{N_{in}}\, 0 \leq t < 2^{N_{out}}} (N_{s,t}(\mathbf{X}) - N_{samples} 2^{-(N_{out}+N_{sin})})^2 / 2^{-(N_{out}+N_{in})} N_{samples}$$

using the two-tailed χ^2-test at the 1 and 99% confidence levels. Tables 6.18.1–3 are the contingency tables and computed χ^2-values with $N_{samples} = 500$ for three independently chosen keys.

We will apply the Kolmogorov-Smirnov test with one randomly chosen key. In Table 6.18.4, we give the results of 20 χ^2-tests (each with $N_{samples} = 500$).

To apply the Kolmogorov-Smirnov test, we need the values

$$\chi^{2*} = [\chi^2 - 63]/126^{1/2}$$

and $F_{63}(\chi^2)$, where

$$F_{63}(x) = \int_0^x k_{63}(y)\, dy$$

A useful approximation in evaluating the distribution function $F_r(x)$ of χ^2 with r degrees of freedom is

$$F_r(x) \sim \mathrm{ERF}[(x - r)/(2r)^{1/2}]$$

TABLE 6.18.1
Contingency Table for a Two-Tailed χ^2-Test at 1% And 99% Confidence Levels

	000	**001**	**010**	**011**	**100**	**101**	**110**	**111**
	9	10	12	13	3	0	8	9
000	9	6	7	7	14	10	10	10
	10	7	9	7	11	7	8	9
	2	8	8	9	10	7	9	12
001	6	6	9	4	11	6	7	9
	6	7	6	8	8	10	13	9
	9	6	8	14	7	6	7	5
010	12	5	6	4	10	8	12	7
	7	16	9	10	8	5	8	7
	7	7	8	5	6	10	8	8
011	8	10	6	3	8	4	4	6
	9	4	2	4	11	8	4	9
	8	4	9	8	8	10	9	3
100	12	8	8	10	6	6	4	3
	5	7	8	9	8	8	6	5
	15	10	9	6	8	12	5	8
101	8	6	9	6	13	7	6	8
	3	6	6	11	13	7	5	9
	6	4	8	10	2	7	9	12
110	6	10	7	8	6	11	7	11
	10	6	13	7	3	5	6	7
	6	5	5	7	9	9	11	8
111	11	9	7	4	10	12	8	9
	11	7	16	6	12	7	6	6

key_1 : 1100100 0011101 1011110 0010010 0101101 0111010 0001010 0010101
key_2 : 1001111 1010101 1011010 1000110 1110101 1101010 0100111 0011001
key_3 : 1011010 1111001 0100010 1010000 0010111 1111011 1111110 0110101

$$\chi^2_{\text{run 1}} = 65.248 \qquad \chi^2_{\text{run 2}} = 53.216 \qquad \chi^2_{\text{run 3}} = 64.992$$

$$\chi_{\text{lower}} = 39.8052 \qquad \chi_{\text{upper}} = 92.0791$$

$$\boldsymbol{CO}_{\mathbf{in}} = \boldsymbol{CO}_{\mathbf{out}} = \{0,1,2\} \qquad N_{\text{samples}} = 500$$

TABLE 6.18.2
Contingency Table for a Two-Tailed χ^2-Test at 1% And 99% Confidence Levels

	000	**001**	**010**	**011**	**100**	**101**	**110**	**111**
	8	8	8	8	7	7	4	5
000	15	7	7	6	11	5	5	13
	11	10	10	14	8	5	11	12
	5	12	6	10	8	5	8	9
001	10	6	11	10	6	8	10	6
	8	9	10	6	12	4	5	8
	9	14	8	6	8	9	6	4
010	13	5	12	12	15	4	3	9
	8	11	6	5	2	6	9	9
	9	9	7	6	12	7	10	6
011	6	11	4	5	4	6	2	4
	9	7	5	9	5	7	13	5
	9	5	3	8	9	9	4	8
100	8	10	6	12	9	8	8	7
	12	8	9	7	5	5	7	5
	9	6	8	9	6	8	9	9
101	14	4	4	7	7	12	5	7
	9	10	8	10	15	12	6	8
	4	11	6	6	8	16	7	7
110	9	6	8	10	8	5	5	3
	5	7	4	9	6	6	6	7
	12	6	6	5	14	7	9	9
111	8	13	10	8	11	4	4	9
	5	8	2	8	4	10	8	10

key_1 : 0111101 0100101 0010101 1100001 1001011 0000101 1100110 0110001

key_2 : 0101010 0110111 1001010 0100010 0000101 0110110 1011001 0110001

key_3 : 1010100 1001010 1101000 0110100 1000000 1000100 1001001 0101101

$$\chi^2_{\text{run 1}} = 50.912 \qquad \chi^2_{\text{run 2}} = 83.168 \qquad \chi^2_{\text{run 3}} = 62.432$$

$$\chi^2_{\text{lower}} = 39.8052 \qquad \chi^2_{\text{upper}} = 92.0791 \qquad N_{\text{samples}} = 500$$

$$\boldsymbol{CO}_{\textbf{in}} = \{0,1,2\} \qquad \boldsymbol{CO}_{\textbf{out}} = \{61,62,63\}$$

TABLE 6.18.3

Contingency Table for a Two-Tailed χ^2-Test at 1% And 99% Confidence Levels

	000	001	010	011	100	101	110	111
	8	8	10	12	9	3	6	5
000	6	7	7	5	10	10	6	9
	4	12	15	4	15	7	10	9
	8	10	14	3	6	9	11	6
001	7	7	8	8	8	9	9	5
	9	8	5	8	8	3	9	6
	4	10	13	8	8	5	9	8
010	11	8	10	13	11	8	3	10
	13	8	9	10	6	5	6	9
	5	11	7	8	8	10	7	12
011	4	7	7	9	8	8	10	7
	8	3	7	6	6	3	5	8
	6	10	5	3	6	5	8	6
100	8	8	7	12	6	8	6	5
	8	6	8	8	3	8	12	8
	7	1	9	7	6	6	6	6
101	6	8	6	15	1	10	5	4
	6	10	8	11	8	7	13	4
	10	14	10	4	13	14	9	6
110	9	10	8	5	10	11	3	11
	7	9	10	6	11	8	8	6
	10	5	4	8	9	8	7	11
111	9	6	8	7	12	8	5	8
	5	9	8	7	12	7	11	4

key_1 : 1101001 0111011 0111111 1101111 0101011 0001110 1110011 0001100

key_2 : 0001001 1111001 0100111 0111010 0110010 1000101 0111111 1010110

key_3 : 0001111 0010001 1110101 0100011 0000100 0111001 0100010 1010000

$$\chi^2_{\text{run 1}} = 67.552 \qquad \chi^2_{\text{run 2}} = 51.168 \qquad \chi^2_{\text{run 1}} = 62.176$$

$$\chi^2_{\text{lower}} = 39.8052 \qquad \chi^2_{\text{upper}} = 92.0791 \qquad N_{\text{samples}} = 500$$

$$\boldsymbol{CO}_{\mathbf{in}} = \boldsymbol{CO}_{\mathbf{out}} = \{61,62,63\}$$

TABLE 6.18.4
Results of 20 χ^2-Tests

χ^2	χ^{2*}	$F_{63}(\chi^2)$	χ^2	χ^{2*}	$F_{63}(\chi^2)$
64.22	0.1090	0.5434	55.7760	0.6436	0.2599
61.41	−0.1418	0.4436	64.4800	0.1318	0.5524
58.59	−0.3927	0.3473	61.1520	0.1646	0.4346
83.42	1.8195	0.9656	66.5280	0.3143	0.6234
47.84	−1.3506	0.0884	77.0240	1.2494	0.8942
52.19	−0.9629	0.1678	58.0800	0.4383	0.3306
83.94	1.8651	0.9689	49.3760	1.2137	0.1124
65.50	0.2231	0.5883	48.8640	1.2593	0.1040
51.68	−1.0085	0.1566	65.7600	0.2459	0.5971
47.33	−1.3962	0.0813	53.2160	0.8716	0.1917

$$N_{\text{samples}} = 500$$

$$\boldsymbol{CO}_{\text{in}} = \boldsymbol{CO}_{\text{out}} = \{1, 2, 3\}$$

key : 1100000 1011111 0000101 1100100 1011000 0010100 0000001 1011011

where ERF(x) is the *error function*

$$\text{ERF}(x) = (1/\sqrt{2\pi}) \int_0^x e^{-y^2/2}\, dy$$

The data in Table 6.18.3 yields the values

$$K_{20,-} = 0.3637 \qquad K_{20,+} = 1.1036$$

resulting in the acceptance of H_0.

What does one test with one key prove? Very little and a great deal at the same time. We have not shown that the output

$$(y_{j_0}, y_{j_1}, \ldots, y_{j_{N_{out}-1}})$$

is independent of the input

$$(x_{i_0}, x_{i_1}, \ldots, x_{i_{N_{in}-1}})$$

for every CO_{in}, CO_{out}; nor have we tested dependence between key and output or key and input. On the other hand, for correlation to be of value in cryptanalyzing DES, either (1) the correlation is present for only a limited number of pairs

$$(i, CO_{in}, CO_{out})$$

and we have some way of predetermining which pairs, or (2) correlation is present in a relatively large number of pairs so that random sampling uncovers them. We cannot exhaustively test all pairs (CO_{in}, CO_{out}).

This application of the χ^2-test was carried out both by IBM Research as part of its internal *validation* of DES and by the National Bureau of Standards and the National Security Agency.

6.19 THE AVALANCHE EFFECT

If a small change in the key or plaintext were to produce a corresponding small change in the ciphertext, this might be used to effectively reduce the size of the plaintext (or key) space to be searched. DES exhibits what Horst Feistel referred to as the *avalanche effect;* a "small" change in the plaintext or key gives rise to a "large" change in the ciphertext.

In Table 6.19.1, we show the effect of the change of a single input bit value in the plaintext. We encipher

$$\mathbf{x} = (00000000\ 00000000\ 00000000\ 00000000\ 00000000\ 00000000\ 00000000\ 00000000)$$

$$\mathbf{x}' = (10000000\ 00000000\ 00000000\ 00000000\ 00000000\ 00000000\ 00000000\ 00000000)$$

with a randomly chosen key and show the effect of changing a single bit as a function of the number of rounds. δ denotes the *Hamming distance:* the number of bit positions in which the 64-blocks differ. In Table 6.19.2 we repeat the calculation, now fixing the plaintext and changing a single bit in the key.

6.20 DEPENDENCE OF OUTPUT ON INPUT

The reason for iterating the substitutions $\{\pi_{T_i}\vartheta\}$ in DES is to make each of the output coordinates $(y_0, y_1, \ldots, y_{63})$ complicated functions of the input. After one round, the output value y_i with

$$\mathbf{y} = \pi_{T_1}\vartheta\mathbf{x}$$

depends on only a small number of values $\{x_j\}$. This functional dependence increases with the number of rounds. In Table 6.20.1 we show the functional dependence of each output coordinate y_i for $0 \leq i < 64$ as a function of the number of rounds r for $1 \leq r \leq 16$.

After five rounds, each output coordinate y_i is a function of each input coordinate x_j. These results are perhaps misleading; even if y_i depends upon all of the components of $(x_0, x_1, \ldots, x_{63})$, we do not know if the relationship is complicated enough to preclude inverting the function

$$\mathbf{y} = \mathrm{DES}\{\mathbf{k},\mathbf{x}\}$$

TABLE 6.19.1
Avalanche Effect in DES : Change in Plaintext

Rnd									δ
0	00000000	00000000	00000000	00000000	00000000	00000000	00000000	00000000	
	10000000	00000000	00000000	00000000	00000000	00000000	00000000	00000000	1
1	00000000	00000000	00000000	00000000	10000101	01111110	00101010	01000011	
	00000001	00000000	00000000	00000000	11000001	01111111	00101011	01010011	6
2	10000101	01111110	00101010	01000011	11010111	00101111	00001101	01111011	
	11000001	01111111	00101011	01010011	00011111	11010001	00100001	11011001	21
3	11010111	00101111	00001101	01111011	11000111	01101110	01101100	10110001	
	00011111	11010001	00100001	11011001	01001010	10010100	11010111	11101001	35
4	11000111	01101110	01101100	10110001	01001100	10110000	01110111	10001010	
	01001010	10010100	11010111	11101001	10100000	00011101	10101010	00101111	39
5	01001100	10110000	01110111	10001010	01110010	00101011	10111100	10000001	
	10100000	00011101	10101010	00101111	11111100	01100010	01111110	10010110	34
6	01110010	00101011	10111100	10000001	01011001	10000101	01110010	01111011	
	11111100	01100010	01111110	10010110	11000010	00011100	10001110	01010001	32
7	01011001	10000101	01110010	01111011	10000010	01100111	10101110	10011100	
	11000010	00011100	10001110	01010001	10110100	01011101	10011110	10110000	31
8	10000010	01100111	10101110	10011100	11100111	11011101	11011011	10010100	
	10110100	01011101	10011110	10110000	00100110	10010010	00101000	00010101	29
9	11100111	11011101	11011011	10010100	01110001	10010000	00001111	00010001	
	00100110	10010010	00101000	00010101	00001111	01101011	10110010	10101110	42
10	01110001	10010000	00001111	00010001	00001010	10101101	00110011	11100100	
	00001111	01101011	10110010	10101110	11001100	10000110	00001001	10011111	44
11	00001010	10101101	00110011	11100100	01010001	01100001	10110010	10000001	
	11001100	10000110	00001001	10011111	11110000	00000110	01110111	10010000	32
12	01010001	01100001	10110010	10000001	01111101	11011101	01001010	10011110	
	11110000	00000110	01110111	10010000	00101000	11111110	01110101	11111010	30
13	01111101	11011101	01001010	10011110	01110101	00010111	00111001	00101000	
	00101000	11111110	01110101	11111010	11011001	00000010	10111010	11100100	30
14	01110101	00010111	00111001	00101000	10011101	10100000	00011110	01001110	
	11011001	00000010	10111010	11100100	00111111	00100110	11010111	00001111	26
15	10011101	10100000	00011110	01001110	10111011	00010100	11111100	11110010	
	00111111	00100110	11010111	00001111	01010010	00011101	01000001	00011010	29
16	11000100	11010111	00101100	10011101	11101110	11011110	01011110	10001011	
	00101100	10010111	01100000	01110110	10100111	00000101	10001101	01000100	34
key :	00000011	10010110	01001001	11000101	00111001	00110001	00111001	01100101	

6.21 BOOLEAN REPRESENTATION OF DES

DES is a one-to-one mapping of $Z_{2,64}$ onto itself and thus corresponds to a system of 64 Boolean truth functions

$$\text{DES} : (x_0, x_1, \ldots, x_{63}) \rightarrow (y_0, y_1, \ldots, y_{63})$$

$$y_i = F_i(x_0, x_1, \ldots, x_{63}) \qquad 0 \leq i < 64$$

Table 6.19.2
Avalanche Effect in DES : Change in Key

Rnd									δ
0	01101000	10000101	00101111	01111010	00010011	01110110	11101011	10100100	
	01101000	10000101	00101111	01111010	00010011	01110110	11101011	10100100	0
1	11000010	11101101	01001101	01111100	00111101	01001000	10110010	00101000	
	11000010	11101101	01001101	01111100	00111101	00001000	10100010	00101000	2
2	00111101	01001000	10110010	00101000	00110111	01011110	01101101	11111000	
	00111101	00001000	10100010	00101000	01100010	01110111	00001100	01111100	14
3	00110111	01011110	01101101	11111000	11111000	01000100	11111010	00010100	
	01100010	01110111	00001100	01111100	10100011	01110111	00110010	01100110	28
4	11111000	01000100	11111010	00010100	01011110	01010101	00000000	01101110	
	10100011	01110111	00110010	01100110	11001011	11011001	01011001	00011101	32
5	01011110	01010101	00000000	01101110	11010111	10111111	11010111	00010110	
	11001011	11011001	01011001	00011101	10101101	11111111	00011011	01011000	30
6	11010111	10111111	11010111	00010110	11111001	11101000	10010011	01000111	
	10101101	11111111	00011011	01011000	00100101	10000110	01010110	00100010	32
7	11111001	11101000	10010011	01000111	00100001	00110100	01110110	10110110	
	00100101	10000110	01010110	00100010	11101011	11011101	00010111	10011001	35
8	00100001	00110100	01110110	10110110	10010000	10110010	01011001	11101110	
	11101011	11011101	00010111	10011001	01100010	10100100	11110100	11010010	34
9	10010000	10110010	01011001	11101110	10011011	01011010	10110110	01000101	
	01100010	10100100	11110100	11010010	01110100	11101100	11101000	10101011	40
10	10011011	01011010	10110110	01000101	10001010	11111110	10010001	10000010	
	01110100	11101100	11101000	10101011	10010101	01001011	11110001	00100000	38
11	10001010	11111110	10010001	10000010	10111110	01000110	10011011	00011111	
	10010101	01001011	11110001	00100000	01000010	01101111	00110001	10001110	31
12	10111110	01000110	10011011	00011111	11111011	10010110	00100100	01110010	
	01000010	01101111	00110001	10001110	11001111	01001011	11010010	00110011	33
13	11111011	10010110	00100100	01110010	01011111	11110111	11010011	00110000	
	11001111	01001011	11010010	00110011	00011011	10110011	01010110	10010110	28
14	01011111	11110111	11010011	00110000	10110001	00010100	01101011	01010101	
	00011011	10110011	01010110	10010110	01111111	10010110	11100000	10011100	26
15	10110001	00010100	01101011	01010101	10011101	01110010	00010011	00010010	
	01111111	10010110	11100000	10011100	00100110	00111111	01000100	00100111	34
16	11001000	01101011	10010000	10010001	10101011	01110001	01100101	10000001	
	00100011	11100010	11101011	00100100	00110101	10110010	01011100	00010001	35
key_1 :	11100100	11110111	11011110	00110001	00111011	00001000	01100011	11011100	
key_2 :	01100100	11110111	11011110	00110001	00111011	00001000	01100011	11011100	

Any Boolean function of 64 variables may be written in one of several standard forms:

- *Disjunctive normal form:*

$$F(\mathbf{x}) = (x_0 \wedge x_1) \vee (\sim x_1 \wedge x_3) \ldots$$

- *Conjunctive normal form:*

$$F(\mathbf{x}) = (x_0 \vee x_1) \wedge (\sim x_1 \vee x_3) \ldots$$

TABLE 6.20.1

DES Dependence of Output Coordinates on Input Coordinates

Rounds r

Coordinate	1	2	3	4	5	6	7	8	9	10	11	12	13	14	15	16
0	1	7	34	60	64	64	64	64	64	64	64	64	64	64	64	64
1	1	7	28	54	64	64	64	64	64	64	64	64	64	64	64	64
2	1	7	28	54	64	64	64	64	64	64	64	64	64	64	64	64
3	1	7	30	56	64	64	64	64	64	64	64	64	64	64	64	64
4	1	7	32	58	64	64	64	64	64	64	64	64	64	64	64	64
5	1	7	32	58	64	64	64	64	64	64	64	64	64	64	64	64
6	1	7	31	57	64	64	64	64	64	64	64	64	64	64	64	64
7	1	7	28	54	64	64	64	64	64	64	64	64	64	64	64	64
8	1	7	28	54	64	64	64	64	64	64	64	64	64	64	64	64
9	1	7	32	58	64	64	64	64	64	64	64	64	64	64	64	64
10	1	7	30	56	64	64	64	64	64	64	64	64	64	64	64	64
11	1	7	32	58	64	64	64	64	64	64	64	64	64	64	64	64
12	1	7	32	58	64	64	64	64	64	64	64	64	64	64	64	64
13	1	7	28	54	64	64	64	64	64	64	64	64	64	64	64	64
14	1	7	34	60	64	64	64	64	64	64	64	64	64	64	64	64
15	1	7	30	56	64	64	64	64	64	64	64	64	64	64	64	64
16	1	7	32	58	64	64	64	64	64	64	64	64	64	64	64	64
17	1	7	32	58	64	64	64	64	64	64	64	64	64	64	64	64
18	1	7	32	58	64	64	64	64	64	64	64	64	64	64	64	64
19	1	7	30	56	64	64	64	64	64	64	64	64	64	64	64	64
20	1	7	30	56	64	64	64	64	64	64	64	64	64	64	64	64
21	1	7	30	56	64	64	64	64	64	64	64	64	64	64	64	64
22	1	7	34	60	64	64	64	64	64	64	64	64	64	64	64	64
23	1	7	28	54	64	64	64	64	64	64	64	64	64	64	64	64
24	1	7	30	56	64	64	64	64	64	64	64	64	64	64	64	64
25	1	7	34	60	64	64	64	64	64	64	64	64	64	64	64	64
26	1	7	29	55	64	64	64	64	64	64	64	64	64	64	64	64
27	1	7	32	58	64	64	64	64	64	64	64	64	64	64	64	64
28	1	7	32	58	64	64	64	64	64	64	64	64	64	64	64	64
29	1	7	32	58	64	64	64	64	64	64	64	64	64	64	64	64
30	1	7	33	59	64	64	64	64	64	64	64	64	64	64	64	64
31	1	7	28	54	64	64	64	64	64	64	64	64	64	64	64	64
32	7	34	60	64	64	64	64	64	64	64	64	64	64	64	64	64
33	7	28	54	64	64	64	64	64	64	64	64	64	64	64	64	64
34	7	28	54	64	64	64	64	64	64	64	64	64	64	64	64	64
35	7	30	56	64	64	64	64	64	64	64	64	64	64	64	64	64
36	7	32	58	64	64	64	64	64	64	64	64	64	64	64	64	64
37	7	32	58	64	64	64	64	64	64	64	64	64	64	64	64	64
38	7	31	57	64	64	64	64	64	64	64	64	64	64	64	64	64
39	7	28	54	64	64	64	64	64	64	64	64	64	64	64	64	64
40	7	28	54	64	64	64	64	64	64	64	64	64	64	64	64	64
41	7	32	58	64	64	64	64	64	64	64	64	64	64	64	64	64
42	7	30	56	64	64	64	64	64	64	64	64	64	64	64	64	64
43	7	32	58	64	64	64	64	64	64	64	64	64	64	64	64	64
44	7	32	58	64	64	64	64	64	64	64	64	64	64	64	64	64
45	7	28	54	64	64	64	64	64	64	64	64	64	64	64	64	64
46	7	34	60	64	64	64	64	64	64	64	64	64	64	64	64	64
47	7	30	56	64	64	64	64	64	64	64	64	64	64	64	64	64
48	7	32	58	64	64	64	64	64	64	64	64	64	64	64	64	64
49	7	32	58	64	64	64	64	64	64	64	64	64	64	64	64	64
50	7	32	58	64	64	64	64	64	64	64	64	64	64	64	64	64
51	7	30	56	64	64	64	64	64	64	64	64	64	64	64	64	64
52	7	30	56	64	64	64	64	64	64	64	64	64	64	64	64	64
53	7	30	56	64	64	64	64	64	64	64	64	64	64	64	64	64
54	7	34	60	64	64	64	64	64	64	64	64	64	64	64	64	64
55	7	28	54	64	64	64	64	64	64	64	64	64	64	64	64	64
56	7	30	56	64	64	64	64	64	64	64	64	64	64	64	64	64
57	7	34	60	64	64	64	64	64	64	64	64	64	64	64	64	64
58	7	29	55	64	64	64	64	64	64	64	64	64	64	64	64	64
59	7	32	58	64	64	64	64	64	64	64	64	64	64	64	64	64
60	7	32	58	64	64	64	64	64	64	64	64	64	64	64	64	64
61	7	32	58	64	64	64	64	64	64	64	64	64	64	64	64	64
62	7	33	59	64	64	64	64	64	64	64	64	64	64	64	64	64
63	7	28	54	64	64	64	64	64	64	64	64	64	64	64	64	64

- *Canonical form* (disjunctive or conjunctive), in which each variable x_i or its complement x_i appears in each word; for example, the word

$$x_0 \vee \sim x_1 \vee \dots \vee x_{63}$$

The operations $\vee$ and $\wedge$ are *or* and *and* and satisfy the relationships

$$0 \vee 0 = 0 \qquad 0 \vee 1 = 1 \vee 0 = 1 \vee 1 = 1$$

$$1 \wedge 1 = 1 \qquad 1 \wedge 0 = 0 \wedge 1 = 0 \wedge 0 = 0$$

A Boolean representation with key-dependent coefficients will be useful for cryptanalysis only if the number of coefficients is small. On the contrary, experiments with DES show that the number of coefficients (as a function of the number of rounds) grows too rapidly for the Boolean representation to be of any use.

6.22 POWER SYSTEMS

DES is the product

$$IP^{-1} \times \vartheta \times \pi \times IP$$

where IP is a known coordinate permutation and

$$\pi = \vartheta \times \pi_{T_{16}} \times \dots x\, \vartheta\, x\, \pi_{T_1}$$

$$\pi : (\mathbf{x}_0,\mathbf{x}_1) \rightarrow (\mathbf{x}_{16},\mathbf{x}_{17})$$

$$\vartheta \times \pi_{T_i} : (\mathbf{x}_{i-1},\mathbf{x}_i) \rightarrow (\mathbf{x}_i,\mathbf{x}_{i+1}) = (\mathbf{x}_i,\mathbf{x}_{i-1} + T(\mathbf{x}_i))$$

DES uses a *rotating key;* on each round the basic DES transformation π_{T_i} uses a different vector of 48 key bits. What would happen if the same fixed set of key values were used on each round; that is, if

$$\pi = \vartheta \times \pi_T \times \dots \times \vartheta \times \pi_T \qquad (n = 16 \text{ copies})$$

This is an example of a *power system*; π is the nth power of the transformation $\vartheta \times \pi_T$

$$\pi = (\vartheta \times \pi_T)^n$$

Let

$$\mathbf{x}_i = (x_{i,0}, x_{i,1}, \dots, x_{i,m-1})$$

$$\pi : (\mathbf{x}_0,\mathbf{x}_1) \rightarrow (\mathbf{x}_n,\mathbf{x}_{n+1})$$

$$\vartheta\pi_T : (\mathbf{x}_{i-1},\mathbf{x}_i) \rightarrow (\mathbf{x}_i,\mathbf{x}_{i+1}) = (\mathbf{x}_i,\mathbf{x}_{i-1} + T(\mathbf{x}_i)) \qquad 1 \leq i \leq n$$

Observe that if $\mathbf{u} = T(\mathbf{x}_1)$, $\mathbf{y}_0 = \mathbf{x}_1$ and $\mathbf{y}_1 = \mathbf{x}_0 + \mathbf{u}$, then

$$\pi : (\mathbf{y}_0,\mathbf{y}_1) \rightarrow (\mathbf{y}_n,\mathbf{y}_{n+1})$$

$$\vartheta\pi_T : (\mathbf{y}_{i-1},\mathbf{y}_i) \rightarrow (\mathbf{y}_i,\mathbf{y}_{i+1}) = (\mathbf{y}_i,\mathbf{y}_{i-1} + T(\mathbf{y}_i)) \qquad 1 \leq i \leq n$$

and $\mathbf{x}_{n+1} = \mathbf{y}_n$.

A correct guess for $T(\mathbf{x}_1)$ may thus be verified by the equality $\mathbf{x}_{n+1} = \mathbf{y}_n$. It may be that an incorrect guess $\mathbf{u} \neq T(\mathbf{x}_1)$ will also yield $\mathbf{x}_{n+1} = \mathbf{y}_n$, but we will *assume* that the complexity of T makes this unlikely. A power system block cipher operating on 64-blocks can be analyzed by making guesses for $T(\mathbf{x})$, where $\mathbf{x}$ is a 32-block and verifying the condition $\mathbf{x}_{n+1} = \mathbf{y}_n$. This approach will be of value only in some power systems. It is shown in [GR2] that a Feistel-like system without a rotating key succumbs easily to cryptanalysis even with a key space containing 2^{2048} keys. The analysis also measures the amount of computation required to recover the key. The analysis in [GR2] *does not* apply to DES.

6.23 TIME-MEMORY TRADE-OFF

Let $\pi\{\mathbf{k},.\}$ be a keyed-block cipher transforming N-blocks

$$\pi\{\mathbf{k},.\} : \mathbf{x} = (x_0, x_1, \ldots, x_{N-1}) \rightarrow \mathbf{y} = (y_0, y_1, \ldots, y_{N-1})$$

$$\mathbf{k} = (k_0, k_1, \ldots, k_{m-1})$$

with $m \leq N$. We will call any mapping from $\boldsymbol{Z}_{2,N}$ to $\boldsymbol{Z}_{2,m}$ a *projection:*

$$\rho : (y_0, y_1, \ldots, y_{N-1}) \rightarrow \rho(\mathbf{y}) = \mathbf{z} = (z_0, z_1, \ldots, z_{m-1})$$

Examples of projections include:

- Dropping some set of $N - m$ bits of $\mathbf{y}$
- Linear transformation:

$$z_i = \left(\sum_{0 \leq j < N} a_{i,j} y_j \right) \text{(modulo 2)} \qquad 0 \leq i < m$$

We denote by $\sigma(\mathbf{k}, \mathbf{x})$ the composition of π followed by ρ:

$$\sigma(\mathbf{k},\mathbf{x}) = \rho(\pi\{\mathbf{k},\mathbf{x}\})$$

If we fix the plaintext N-block $\mathbf{x}^{(0)}$ (known plaintext), σ is a mapping from the key space $\boldsymbol{Z}_{2,m}$ into itself. The iterates of σ are defined by

$$\text{(6.23.1)} \qquad \sigma^{(j)}(\mathbf{k}, \mathbf{x}^{(0)}) = \begin{cases} \mathbf{k} & \text{if } j = 0 \\ \sigma(\sigma^{(j-1)}(\mathbf{k}, \mathbf{x}^{(0)}), \mathbf{x}^{(0)}) & \text{if } 1 \leq j < \infty \end{cases}$$

Equation (6.23.1) gives a recursive procedure to generate keys $\mathbf{k}_{(1)}, \mathbf{k}_{(2)}, \ldots$ starting with a key $\mathbf{k}_{(0)} = \mathbf{k} \in \boldsymbol{Z}_{2,m}$ and plaintext $\mathbf{x}^{(0)} \in \boldsymbol{Z}_{2,N}$.

The time-memory tradeoff analysis assumes that an opponent is given the encipherment of some known plaintext $\mathbf{x}^{(0)}$. This assumption is not as restrictive as it may appear; the plaintext an opponent is attempting to cryptanalyze may begin with some standard message, for example, `Dear Sir`:, as in a letter. The first step in the attack is precomputation.

Precomputation

Let $\mathbf{k}_0, \mathbf{k}_1, \ldots, \mathbf{k}_{n-1}$ be n m-blocks chosen as the result of independent and identical and uniformly distributed trials. Define

$$\mathbf{k}_{(i,j)} = \begin{cases} \sigma^{(j)}(\mathbf{k}_i, \mathbf{x}^{(0)}) & \text{if } 0 \leq j < t \\ \pi\{\sigma^{(t-1)}(\mathbf{k}_i,\mathbf{x}^{(0)}),(\mathbf{x}^{(0)}\} & \text{if } j = t \end{cases}$$

$$\mathbf{K} = \begin{vmatrix} \mathbf{k}_{(0,0)} & \mathbf{k}_{(0,1)} & \cdots & \mathbf{k}_{(0,t-1)} & \mathbf{k}_{(0,t)} \\ \mathbf{k}_{(1,0)} & \mathbf{k}_{(1,1)} & \cdots & \mathbf{k}_{(1,t-1)} & \mathbf{k}_{(1,t)} \\ \cdot & \cdot & \cdots & \cdot & \cdot \\ \cdot & \cdot & \cdots & \cdot & \cdot \\ \cdot & \cdot & \cdots & \cdot & \cdot \\ \mathbf{k}_{(n-1,0)} & \mathbf{k}_{(n-1,1)} & \cdots & \mathbf{k}_{(n-1,t-1)} & \mathbf{k}_{(n-1,t)} \end{vmatrix}$$

The pairs $\{(\mathbf{k}_{(i,0)}, \mathbf{k}_{(i,t)}) : 0 \leq i < n\}$ are stored sorted on the value $\{\mathbf{k}_{(i,t)}\}$.The precomputation of an *(n,t)-array* requires nt π-evaluations. To sort the array requires t log t operations. To store the initial and endpoints, we require a memory of size 2t.

Identification of an Unknown Key

Suppose the opponent wants to find the key **k**, which has enciphered plaintext **x** into ciphertext **y**. The opponent is assumed to know $\mathbf{y}^{(0)} = \pi\{\mathbf{k},\mathbf{x}^{(0)}\}$.

Step 1 Search **K** for an entry $\{\mathbf{k}_{(i,t)}\}$ equal to $\mathbf{y}^{(0)}$. There are two possibilities.

Case 1 There is at least one entry $\{\mathbf{k}_{(i,t)}\}$ equal to $\mathbf{y}^{(0)}$.

Case 2 There is no entry $\{\mathbf{k}_{(i,t)}\}$ equal to $\mathbf{y}^{(0)}$.

In the first case

$$\pi\ \{\mathbf{k}_{(i,t-1)},\mathbf{x}^{(0)}\} = \mathbf{y}^{(0)}$$

for any index i for which $\mathbf{k}_{(i,t)} = \mathbf{y}^{(0)}$. If more than one index exists, there are several possible keys; each must be examined separately. It is conjectured, but *not proved,* that any reasonable amount of corresponding plaintext and DES-enciphered ciphertext uniquely determines the key. The opponent is assumed to have sufficient corresponding plaintext and ciphertext.

In *Case 2* we proceed to *Step 2.*

Step 2 Encipher $\mathbf{x}^{(0)}$ with the key $\rho(\mathbf{y}^{(0)})$ and return to *Step 1.*
A match means that there is a pair of indices (i,j) with

$$\mathbf{y}^{(0)} = \pi\{\mathbf{k}_{(i,j-1)}, \mathbf{x}^{(0)}\}$$

We assume that the possibility that two distinct keys will match is negligible. The following lower bound for the probability of success is given in [HE2].

Theorem 6.23.1

$$\Pr\{\text{Success}\} \geq (t/2^{56})e^{-t^2/2^{56}}\ [1 - e^{-nt^2/2^{56}}]/[1 - e^{-t^2/2^{56}}]$$

When $n = t = O(2^{56/3}) \approx 10^6$, the probability of success is bounded below by $1/2^{56/3}$. Thus if $O(2^{56/3})$ independently chosen projections $\rho_1, \rho_2, \ldots$ are used, the probability of success can be arbitrary close to unity. Of course, the use of multiple arrays means that we must exhaustively precompute $\pi\{\mathbf{k}, \mathbf{x}^{(0)}\}$ for essentially every key $\mathbf{k}$.

6.24 CHAINING

DES has been defined as a substitution on the alphabet $Z_{2,64}$. To encipher plaintext of arbitrary length (in bytes), we must extend the definition of DES. Of the many possible extensions of DES, we will describe three in this section.

We use the notation

$$<\mathbf{x}> = (\mathbf{x}_0, \mathbf{x}_1, \ldots, \mathbf{x}_{m-1})$$

to denote plaintext consisting of the m 64-blocks $\{\mathbf{x}_i : 0 \leq i < m\}$. If the length of plaintext (in bytes) is not a multiple of eight, we may *pad* the plaintext on the right with a suitable number of standard bytes; for example, with blank spaces if the alpha-numeric plaintext is first coded into EBCIDIC characters.

The Standard Extension of DES

The DES encipherment of

$$<\mathbf{x}> = (\mathbf{x}_0, \mathbf{x}_1, \ldots, \mathbf{x}_{m-1})$$

with key **k** is defined by

$$\text{(6.24.1)} \qquad \mathbf{y}_i = \text{DESST}\{\mathbf{k}, \mathbf{x}_i\} \qquad 0 \leq i < m$$

Since DES is a one-to-one transformation on $Z_{2,64}$, DESST defined by Eq. (6.24.1) is a one-to-one transformation on $Z_{2,64N}$ for every $N \geq 1$.

This "standard" extension of DES suffers from one minor defect; plaintext that contains properly aligned repetitive blocks of data will yield ciphertext in which these repetitions are reflected. For example, an assembly language program usually has a very structured format; statement numbers occupy designated positions in each line of the program, the instructions appear in specified positions, and there are many blank spaces. These characteristics of the plaintext are mirrored in the ciphertext. In Fig. 6.24.1, we show an assembly language program *PLAIN(4)*, and we show its DESST encipherment in Fig. 6.24.2. The use of DESST to encipher plaintext with repetitive blocks may not present an exposure. Starting from the ciphertext in Fig. 6.24.2, there does not appear to be any

```
***********************************************************************
*                                                                     *
* FINAL PROCESSING                                                    *
*                                                                     *
*   Free the SYSPRINT ddname, and if allocated by INDATASET and       *
*   OUTDATASET the input (SYSUT1) and output (SYSUT2) ddnames also.   *
*   Ddnames provided by INDD and OUTDD are left alone: since they     *
*   were allocated by the user, they should be freed by the user.     *
*                                                                     *
*   If any deallocation fails, DAIRFAIL will write a message, and     *
*   this routine will set return code 12.                             *
*                                                                     *
*   Following the deallocations, control is returned to the TSO       *
*   Supervisor.                                                       *
*                                                                     *
***********************************************************************
FINAL00  SR    R3,R3                   ZERO TEMPORARY RETURN CODE
         TM    FREESYSP,X'80'          IS "FREE SYSPRINT" ON?
         BZ    FINAL01                  NO, SKIP IT
         LA    R2,DDNSYSP              ADDRESS THE SYSPRINT DDNAME
         BAL   R10,FREEDDN0            FREE THE DDNAME
         LTR   R15,R15                 TEST FREEDD0 RETURN CODE
         BZ    FINAL01                 NORMAL RETURN FROM FREE
         LA    R3,12                   ERROR: SET RETURN CODE 12
         SPACE
FINAL01  TM    FREEUT1,X'80'           IS "FREE INPUT DDNAME" ON?
         BZ    FINAL02                  NO, SKIP IT
         LA    R2,DDNUT1               ADDRESS THE INPUT DDNAME
         BAL   R10,FREEDDN0            FREE THE DDNAME
         LTR   R15,R15                 TEST FREEDD0 RETURN CODE
         BZ    FINAL02                 NORMAL RETURN FROM FREE
         LA    R3,12                   ERROR: SET RETURN CODE 12
         SPACE
FINAL02  TM    FREEUT2,X'80'           IS "FREE OUTPUT DDNAME" ON?
         BZ    FINAL03                  NO, SKIP IT
         LA    R2,DDNUT2               ADDRESS THE OUTPUT DDNAME
         BAL   R10,FREEDDN0            FREE THE DDNAME
         LTR   R15,R15                 TEST FREEDD0 RETURN CODE
         BZ    FINAL03                 NORMAL RETURN FROM FREE
         LA    R3,12                   ERROR: SET RETURN CODE 12
FINAL03  LR    R0,R3                   COPY "FREE DD" RETURN CODE
         BAL   R10,RCSET               INCREASE RETURN CODE IF HIGHER
         SPACE
         L     R1,RC                   LOAD RETURN CODE
         CVD   R1,DOUBLE               RETURN CODE TO DECIMAL
         LA    R1,AM29                 "END OF PROGRAM - RC NNN"
         BAL   R10,PREPRNT0            MOVE MESSAGE TEXT TO 'OUTLINE'
         ED    OUTLINE+M29B-M29A(L'M29B),DOUBLE+6  EDIT TO MSG
         BAL   R10,PRINT00             PRINT THE MESSAGE
         SPACE
         L     R2,RC                   LOAD RETURN CODE FROM DSAVE
         LA    R0,DSAVEL               SET R0 TO LENGTH OF DSAVE
         LR    R1,R13                   AND R1 TO ITS ADDRESS
         L     R13,4(0,R13)            RESTORE CALLER'S SAVEAREA ADDRESS
         FREEMAIN R,LV=(0),A=(1)       FREE DSAVE WORKAREA
         LR    R15,R2                  SET RETURN CODE IN REGISTER 15
         RETURN (14,12),T,RC=(15)      RETURN TO TSO
```

Figure 6.24.1. *PLAIN(4)* : an assembly language program.

method for using the repetitions in the ciphertext to reverse the process and obtain the key or plaintext. Nevertheless, this repetition in ciphertext is discomforting. Fortunately, it may be circumvented by the technique of chaining proposed by Bryant Tuckerman. Chaining means that the ith block of ciphertext

$$\langle \mathbf{y} \rangle = (\mathbf{y}_0, \mathbf{y}_1, \ldots, \mathbf{y}_{m-1})$$

$\mathbf{y}_i$ depends upon the first i − 1 blocks of plaintext. Chaining also provides an

```
-> T   -> T   -> T   -> T   -> T   -> T   -> T   -> T    )n"0    Joz :
g;   . # Joz :   Joz :   Joz :   Joz :   Joz :   Joz :   Joz :     m R    Joz :
 r a   &dD5   N  @  *   Joz :   Joz :   Joz :   Joz :   Joz :     m R    Joz :
g;   . # Joz :   Joz :   Joz :   Joz :   Joz :   Joz :   Joz :     m R    Joz :
       E     D X a     @    zL        '   3       > Y9 a qy!,    m R    Joz :
@ q t X       T  d .  3 j<  AnE   T 5  ; D  V     i7       VO E  E  pn Joz :
 *k  e    @Y      m aP taJ uF  ;4  N x  'zM      > s  @    F   &   K : h¬ Joz :
 T    P ¢(  ? w       ,  sk&A E1xF       m *  @ ;   !      Z  v U @ s f  Joz :
g;   . # Joz :   Joz :   Joz :   Joz :   Joz :   Joz :   Joz :     m R    Joz :
  (   Z    C |  *i     a     6        E   3N b  I ;  E o ,       ? se;    Joz :
m     z   PV  nU    75       /         +       /  Joz :   Joz :     m R    Joz :
g;   . # Joz :   Joz :   Joz :   Joz :   Joz :   Joz :   Joz :     m R    Joz :
 6  ' U 4    i H s  N;   ;o   ( tW 8   9 B        0   b j  3      m R    Joz :
   Z a1  f   @  Joz :   Joz :   Joz :   Joz :   Joz :   Joz :     m R    Joz :
g;   . # Joz :   Joz :   Joz :   Joz :   Joz :   Joz :   Joz :     m R    Joz :
-> T   -> T   -> T   -> T   -> T   -> T   -> T   -> T    )n"0    Joz :
  4   0+    5 H 'I      Joz :   ! t      x  g  IHUT# _ J c  H   Joz :   Joz :
 Joz :   8 q  0F  o?   A      *  >¢ =.    <  f P      + k x   2K Joz :   Joz :
 Joz :  p1g   ) y  g ,    Joz :  sj  r l 8 /l     Joz :   Joz :   Joz :   Joz :
 Joz :    r s   @*           "     .      ¢K   F B  (  W   xm   ZO Joz :   Joz :
 Joz :    tw      v s     _  E      D       X*      d    Joz :   Joz :   Joz :
 Joz :   t<   F  _       Joz :  y  '       c yW    O|   N $        Joz :   Joz :
 Joz :  p1g   ) y  g ,    Joz :      a 5  ( c8      9V   W >       Joz :   Joz :
 Joz :    r s    rt    d Joz :     U RdX E ' k  (;y$- E9  $  ¬T+ Joz :   Joz :
 Joz :  U      L  Joz :   Joz :   Joz :   Joz :   Joz :   Joz :   Joz :   Joz :
 OJa"   8 q  0F      z    I(   u>¢ =.     9 m  L    p      0#* D Joz :   Joz :
 Joz :  p1g   ) H ,Jf  N Joz :  sj  r l 8 /l     Joz :   Joz :   Joz :   Joz :
 Joz :    r s  E   tl   Joz :    .      ¢   J    D  k. 3    :      Joz :   Joz :
 Joz :    tw      v s     _  E      D       X*      d    Joz :   Joz :   Joz :
 Joz :   t<   F  _       Joz :  y  '       c yW    O|   N $        Joz :   Joz :
 Joz :  p1g   ) H ,Jf  N Joz :      a 5  ( c8      9V   W >       Joz :   Joz :
 Joz :    r s    rt    d Joz :     U RdX E ' k  (;y$- E9  $  ¬T+ Joz :   Joz :
 Joz :  U      L  Joz :   Joz :   Joz :   Joz :   Joz :   Joz :   Joz :   Joz :
   k  o 8 q  0F      B    I(   u>¢ =.    1& 3 #     ¢s    s   k gz Joz :   Joz :
 Joz :  p1g   )      4  + Joz :  sj  r l 8 /l     Joz :   Joz :   Joz :   Joz :
 Joz :    r s      T<  Y Joz :    .            W)   K    i   H E   Joz :   Joz :
 Joz :    tw      v s     _  E      D       X*      d    Joz :   Joz :   Joz :
 Joz :   t<   F  _       Joz :  y  '       c yW    O|   N $        Joz :   Joz :
 Joz :  p1g   )      4  + Joz :      a 5  ( c8      9V   W >       Joz :   Joz :
 Joz :    r s    rt    d Joz :     U RdX E ' k  (;y$- E9  $  ¬T+ Joz :   Joz :
 G 'a    uG 0Qk kv?C   V Joz :  ;x  ;        r72X      | aJ c  H   Joz :   Joz :
 Joz :    tw      >      Joz :  z? l     a4,Uu  Mu         7             Joz :
 Joz :  U      L  Joz :   Joz :   Joz :   Joz :   Joz :   Joz :   Joz :   Joz :
 Joz :  |&J M   J X7 5a  Joz :  Wqj  2    O|   N $        Joz :   Joz :   Joz :
 Joz :    (      J Ti <j  Joz :    T  ,   d       ¬ Xj X  2 s O   Joz :   Joz :
 Joz :    r s      7W¢   Joz :                @&?4W< l        W   Joz :   Joz :
 Joz :    tw      W| D        z  M  . DB   -     -    _:'d 6t 5    t   y u  Joz :
 Joz :  Yt d  !      V    UP6 7           $       P 85|!      v 5 : " Joz :   Joz :
 Joz :    tw      D .     d   Y    3<  K  U    fR  Vt      Joz :   Joz :   Joz :
 Joz :  U      L  Joz :   Joz :   Joz :   Joz :   Joz :   Joz :   Joz :   Joz :
 Joz :  |&J M       1#< R Joz :  Wqj  2    O|   N z     m  z  _    Joz :   Joz :
 Joz :    r s     &  5 p Joz :   #fR   n n   DL   x I@          LI Joz :   Joz :
 Joz :   uG 0Qk       ;   Joz :      8@    1d:C#  > Uw        +    Joz :   Joz :
 Joz :  |&J M      n ¢  !q   k S 2 9     RX u=    K   p¬3 L    Q ( _     *  Joz :
 Joz :  8V  Nn      fe)U ¢i         D      I       v    q   Joz :   Joz :   Joz :
 Joz :   uG 0Qk  X M   .  Joz :   #fR   n 1 <A >$    "    h      i      ¢JK   Joz :
 Joz :    K t ' , ?qa    ;h   I         n  VC .fG @ Joz :   Joz :   Joz :   Joz :
```

Figure 6.24.2. DESST encipherment of *PLAIN(4)*.

extension of DES that enciphers plaintext of arbitrary length in bytes. Let us begin by assuming that the length N of the plaintext is a multiple of eight bytes.

Let plaintext

$$<\mathbf{x}> = (\mathbf{x}_0, \mathbf{x}_1, \ldots, \mathbf{x}_{m-1})$$

consist of m blocks each of length eight (bytes). Define DESCH (DES *with chaining*) by

$$\text{DESCH} : <\mathbf{x}> \rightarrow <\mathbf{y}> = \text{DESCH}\{\mathbf{k}, <\mathbf{x}>\}$$

$$\mathbf{y}_{-1} = \mathbf{ICV}$$

$$\mathbf{y}_j = \text{DES}\{\mathbf{k},\mathbf{x}_j + \mathbf{y}_{j-1}\} \qquad 0 \leq j < m$$

where **ICV** is the eight-byte initial chaining value. Thus the first plaintext block $\mathbf{x}_1$ is added to the initial chaining value **ICV** and enciphered by the DES to yield $\mathbf{y}_1$, and the jth plaintext block $\mathbf{x}_j$ is added to the $(j - 1)^{st}$ eight-byte block of ciphertext $\mathbf{y}_{j-1}$ and enciphered by the DES to yield $\mathbf{y}_j$. If we want to show the dependence of DESCH{**k**, <**x**>} on the initial chaining value, we will write DESCH{**k**, <**x**>|**ICV**}.

DESCH as defined above is a one-to-one transformation; that is, a block of 8m bytes of ciphertext can arise from only one 8m-byte block of plaintext. Indeed, if <**y**> is an 8m-byte block of ciphertext, $<\mathbf{y}> = (\mathbf{y}_0, \mathbf{y}_1, \ldots, \mathbf{y}_{m-1})$, the rules for decipherment $\text{DESCH}^{-1}\{\mathbf{k}, <\mathbf{y}>\} = \text{DESCH}^{-1}\{\mathbf{k}, \mathbf{y}|\mathbf{ICV}\}$ are

$$\mathbf{y}_{-1} = \mathbf{ICV} : \text{initial chaining value}$$

$$\mathbf{x}_j = \text{DES}^{-1}\{\mathbf{k},\mathbf{y}_j\} + \mathbf{y}_{j-1} \qquad 0 \leq j < m$$

Both encipherment and decipherment proceed from left to right. Note that we can decipher the fragment $(\mathbf{y}_j, \mathbf{y}_{j+1}, \ldots, \mathbf{y}_{m-1})$ from the key **k** and the previous ciphertext eight-byte block $\mathbf{y}_{j-1}$.

It remains to extend this notion of chaining to plaintext blocks whose length either is greater than eight bytes but not a multiple of eight bytes, or is less than eight bytes. Let <**x**> be a block of 8m + s bytes with $0 < s < 8$, $m \geq 1$. Then

$$<\mathbf{x}> = (\mathbf{x}_0, \ldots, \mathbf{x}_{m-1}, \mathbf{x}_m)$$

where $\mathbf{x}_m$ is a *short block* of s bytes.

The chained encipherment <**y**> = DESCH{**k**,<**x**>} is defined by

$$<\mathbf{y}> = (\mathbf{y}_0, \ldots, \mathbf{y}_{m-1}, \mathbf{y}_m)$$

$$\mathbf{y}_{-1} = \mathbf{ICV}_1 : \text{initial chaining value}$$

$$\mathbf{y}_j = \text{DES}\{\mathbf{k},\mathbf{x}_j + \mathbf{y}_{j-1}\} \qquad 0 \leq j < m$$

$$\mathbf{y}_m = \mathbf{x}_m + \text{LEFT}_s[\text{DES}\{\mathbf{k},\mathbf{y}_{m-1}\}]$$

where $\text{LEFT}_s[\cdot]$ means the leftmost s bytes of $[\cdot]$. That is, the first m *full* blocks are enciphered with chaining as just described, and the $(m + 1)^{st}$ (short) block of ciphertext is the sum of the short block of plaintext (of length s) with the left s bytes of the encipherment of $\mathbf{y}_{m-1}$ by the DES. It is easy to verify that the DES so extended is one-to-one; that is, the ciphertext uniquely determines the plaintext. Decipherment proceeds from left to right and includes an *encipherment* step to determine $x_m = \text{LEFT}_s[\text{DES}\{\mathbf{k},\mathbf{y}_{m-1}\}]$.

Finally, we must define the encipherment of a *short record;* that is, an s-byte block, where s is less than 8. We define the *chaining* encipherment of the short record **x**,

$$\mathbf{x} = (x_0, x_1, \ldots, x_{8s-1}) \qquad 1 \leq s < 8$$

by

$$\mathbf{y} = \mathbf{x} + \text{LEFT}_s[\text{DES}\{\mathbf{k},\mathbf{ICV}\}]$$

That is, we add the encipherment of the initial chaining value **ICV**, to the leftmost s bytes of the plaintext **x**.

A *file F* in an information processing system is a collection of *records.*

$$F: <\mathbf{x}^{(0)}>, <\mathbf{x}^{(1)}>, \ldots, <\mathbf{x}^{(r-1)}>$$

The ith-record in F is the concatenation of plaintext blocks

$$<\mathbf{x}^{(i)}> = (\mathbf{x}_{i,0}, x_{i,1}, \ldots, x_{i,m-1})$$

We can encipher a file without padding with chaining, and we call this *block chaining.* Block chaining has a limitation: with respect to short records it constitutes an *interrupted Vernam system.* This means that the plaintext and a sufficient length of key are added to produce the ciphertext (Vernam), and that the use of the key is interrupted; that is, it starts over at the beginning at irregular intervals—at the beginning of each short record. The actual Vernam key (of which at most seven bytes are ever used) is the encipherment of the initial chaining value. This system is easily cryptanalyzed on the basis of a moderate amount of ciphertext. Its use is not recommended; from enough such enciphered short blocks, a cryptanalyst could recover the Vernam key and thus decipher the short blocks. Even a more elaborate cryptographic function, which depended, however, only on the given plaintext short block, the key, and the starting initial chaining value, would at best be a simple substitution on the set of possible short blocks (and under our assumptions would be length-preserving) and thus might be subject to cryptanalysis. With the availability of record chaining, to be described next, such an elaborate encipherment of short blocks is not warranted.

In addition, if a file contains two or more records that begin with identical fragments, including the first t blocks, then independent DESCH encipherments of those records begins with identical ciphertext fragments, through the first t blocks. This too presents an exposure, although a much lesser one. We remedy these possible defects by extending the DESCH still further by introducing the notion of record chaining.

Let **ICV** be the initial chaining value. The encipherment of F

$$<\mathbf{y}^{(0)}>, <\mathbf{y}^{(1)}>, \ldots, <\mathbf{y}^{(r-1)}>$$

under *record chaining* is defined according to the principle that *the input chaining value for the record* $\mathbf{y}^{(i)}$ *is the most recent eight bytes of ciphertext (where the ciphertext is considered to be prefixed by the starting initial chaining value).* More precisely, if we introduce the notations

$$\text{i}^{\text{th}} \text{ record input chaining value} : \mathbf{ICV}^{(i)} \qquad 0 \le i < r$$

$$\text{i}^{\text{th}} \text{ record output chaining value} : \mathbf{OCV}^{(i)} \qquad 0 \le i < r$$

then the encipherment of *F* is defined by

$$\mathbf{ICV}^{(0)} = \mathbf{ICV} \text{ (initial chaining value)} \qquad \mathbf{ICV}^{(i)} = \mathbf{OCV}^{(i-1)} \qquad 1 \le i < r$$

$$<\mathbf{y}^{(i)}> = \text{DESCH}\{\mathbf{k},<\mathbf{x}^{(i)}>|\mathbf{ICV}^{(i)}\} \qquad 0 \le i < r$$

$$\mathbf{OCV}^{(i)} = \text{RIGHT8}[\mathbf{ICV}^{(i)} \| <\mathbf{y}^{(i)}>] \qquad 0 \le i < r$$

where RIGHT8 means the rightmost eight bytes and $\|$ denotes concatenation. Thus the first record $<\mathbf{x}^{(0)}>$ is enciphered by the DES into $<\mathbf{y}^{(0)}>$, using the initial chaining value **ICV**, and the ith record $<\mathbf{x}^{(i)}>$ is enciphered by the DES into $<\mathbf{y}^{(i)}>$, using the initial chaining value

$$\mathbf{ICV}^{(i)} = \mathbf{OCV}^{(i-1)} \ (1 \le i < r)$$

It is simple to verify that we can recover the ith plaintext record $<\mathbf{x}^{(i)}>$ from the ith ciphertext record $<\mathbf{y}^{(i)}>$, the key, and the $(i - 1)^{\text{st}}$ output chaining value $\mathbf{OCV}^{(i-1)}$ (the immediately preceding eight bytes of ciphertext).

Record chaining does for records, including short records, what chaining accomplishes for repeated eight-byte blocks and trailing short blocks. Thus even if a file contains identical records, or short records, the ciphertext records are all distinct. In Figures 6.24.3 and 6.24.4 we show the effect of encipherment of *PLAIN(4)* with block and record chaining.

Block and *record chaining* possesses an important *self-healing property*. Suppose that $<\mathbf{x}> = (\mathbf{x}_0, \mathbf{x}, \ldots, \mathbf{x}_{m-1})$ (8m bytes of plaintext) has been enciphered with chaining into ciphertext $<\mathbf{y}> = (\mathbf{y}_0, \mathbf{y}_1, \ldots, \mathbf{y}_{m-1})$, and that an error has been made (in storage, say) in the jth ciphertext block $\mathbf{y}_j$, replacing it with $\mathbf{y}'_j$. Thus when decipherment is attempted, the ciphertext is $<\mathbf{y}'> = (\mathbf{y}'_0, \mathbf{y}'_1, \ldots, \mathbf{y}'_{m-1})$, with

$$\mathbf{y}'_i = \begin{cases} \mathbf{y}_i & \text{if } i \ne j \\ \mathbf{y}_j + \mathbf{e} \ne \mathbf{y}_j & \text{if } i = j \end{cases}$$

Decipherment of $\mathbf{y}'$ with *initial chaining value* $\mathbf{ICV} = \mathbf{y}_1$ results in $<\mathbf{x}'> = (\mathbf{x}'_0, \ldots, \mathbf{x}'_{m-1})$, where

- The first $(j - 1)$ plaintext blocks are correctly obtained:

  $$\mathbf{x}'_i = \text{DES}^{-1}\{\mathbf{k},\mathbf{y}'_i\} + \mathbf{y}'_{i-1} = \text{DES}^{-1}\{\mathbf{k},\mathbf{y}_i\} + \mathbf{y}_{i-1} = \mathbf{x}_i \qquad 0 \le i < j$$

- The jth and $(j + 1)^{\text{st}}$ deciphered plaintext blocks contain errors:*

*Note: The jth plaintext block is entirely incorrect because an incorrect block was subjected to DES decipherment; the $(j + 1)^{\text{st}}$ plaintext block is in error only in the bit positions corresponding to the errors in $\mathbf{y}'_j$.

```
lFnJ U ¢  O E  $               c   S   A96  $             U.1  9;    )  =    3 9 K D
      S4Y¢D z    p          e  )  L8X    _F J    U  _   g  E  xc  d1& X  a E  -   ¬
    C ¢$6 p t  @7X    7  L    I        o L@U      x   Rc       uTJ 1 8     V    o 5  H
      S4Y¢D z    p          e  )  L8X    _F J    U  _   g  E  xc  d1& X  a E  -   ¬
?s      C  YK        @O   =      f y _z        T0,6          >F d        v   w      X vK  ;
     @ b ! A  u  A  g f lEosg t      L    d & SC        2Ri       s j&m    #8+
  Z  1      H      M6     /  3 UP  t!       m    v Q x        be !  T E  0 $  T '
t  T      4   ME 2          G t  Om       bm(  C      S!  P!t 7     B. Sc       K    k    >
      S4Y¢D z    p          e  )  L8X    _F J    U  _   g  E  xc  d1& X  a E  -   ¬
E q     M ?    J u           =          K  p   d  v     b c            P         w         ;
  j¬    j  G   e H +c)    v   8    X     G          1     L  :  =   y  r      D     U     F
      S4Y¢D z    p          e  )  L8X    _F J    U  _   g  E  xc  d1& X  a E  -   ¬
 >  N   n     ¬pn=  Cv     3   y  =>  $n B 8  s y       PL   g       5FU          3 i 1
   7       k *Y8  m¬           =  v  X ¬9M  1A     h       L ¢S    .   29  dIN4+         5
      S4Y¢D z    p          e  )  L8X    _F J    U  _   g  E  xc  d1& X  a E  -   ¬
lFnJ U ¢  O E  $              c   S    A96  $             U.1  9;    )  =    3 9 K D
     K    x O          s _  ,  s 3 M      HG     of     q  $  K i)     Lq- k    l
J 1x@ = (         ?/      x            U D        * xO)          +   Z       q        P   F_8
J 1x@ = 1"         Eob H       2 j  C      jq ?  Y       * A 2yy7D        ' Lv ¢      N r Z8io
J 1x@ = 6 =    W   Mv       .  n      ?  1  o  4    * /  T  W  u  1_ES           5        ¬
J 1x@ = <"o1 RE   r Vt4    Jg           +<uHRS, !X         h )          1X) WlJ     1  p
J 1x@ =  A B  /    !+S    $  k:y    um !F  !       (      NB v G        B         o     ! 0     ¬
J 1x@ = 1"         Eob H       2 j  C + :a      @l    R9  -XN      " .: E  m-          R   l+ r
J 1x@ = 6 =     W     i  P   "eF     +        EW S9      A¢       L g     b           c  H      ¢f$
J 1x@ =  $ ;  d  A            O qC O@ ? k'!*    .V  ND     M +@I       E. w            7    7t
eq         5m     9       BH 5 b  Tv7                d  6d "+)        s K B s        3 n  x     7n
J 1x@ = 1"         D      Sg9 G>:J      "|        E   r          f':  0   |6. cv          7  K
J 1x@ = 6 =     W |   1  U     X$  C   : ( v +    n5>       s¬ (      ¢      n a    CR 5  1          ¬
J 1x@ = <"o1 RE   r Vt4    Jg           +<uHRS, !X         h )          1X) WlJ     1  p
J 1x@ =  A B  /    !+S     $  k:y    um !F  !       (      NB v G        B         o     ! 0     ¬
J 1x@ = 1"         D      Sg9 G>:J     "  x. u e 9 f K   s     P         Y  >      >  r.  >1    E
J 1x@ = 6 =     W     i  P   "eF     +        EW S9      A¢       L g     b           c  H      ¢f$
J 1x@ =  $ ;  d  A            O qC O@ ? k'!*    .V  ND     M +@I       E. w            7    7t
 E a     ( w          - |o FI c U S     | ¢  aT kx         x o       >           3 ;t up        @
J 1x@ = 1"          lu M ?s    |       j       v0 J  ?'>jab @  4   N Y           #hBq*n   # Q3
J 1x@ = 6 =     W EL a        _      wN  Y                G  )Ze   V       c    A     S     a     EY   1
J 1x@ = <"o1 RE   r Vt4    Jg           +<uHRS, !X         h )          1X) WlJ     1  p
J 1x@ =  A B  /    !+S     $  k:y    um !F  !       (      NB v G        B         o     ! 0     ¬
J 1x@ = 1"          lu M ?s    |       j          T          '  P   4< R jS      _ Q    h    R t     0
J 1x@ = 6 =     W     i  P   "eF     +        EW S9      A¢       L g     b           c  H      ¢f$
 O X( z   F8     Qr   va+f0L     5+             L V   fI   7     2 xMu$$"      6  ) w _          h#
J 1x@ = <"o1 RE     Z y=o         '  *    1m'  IY7 3       Y s9  I o     2  p   fk  6 *
J 1x@ =  $ ;  d  A            O qC O@ ? k'!*    .V  ND     M +@I       E. w            7    7t
J 1x@ = sg CDrU0 Q16         y    b E I¢    Y  # s,v v Q   Ys      T d &          @ /" H Z Y
J 1x@ = _    o         j4 *               -" >     s  Z m   5      y (     +z !       N    ?b h0 F
J 1x@ = 6 =     W qy     H          / c!L&  X     +m-Li       |          E=        n  w    1  ¬  W  6 W
J 1x@ = <"o1 RE K   e     y       jI -R                 .U:   Z )      |      K.          YS-Iq > )
J 1x@ =     -2 E@" @_ JF       ) rU               r l          x      D                c        #  #|   wE
J 1x@ = <"o1 RE     S          !y   ? j     (   @O K|      X          .     : k k X       d   d     R
J 1x@ =  $ ;  d  A            O qC O@ ? k'!*    .V  ND     M +@I       E. w            7    7t
J 1x@ = sg CDrU0 6      2     *u      R W yv       Jp     O h Bxr +H S         o=   6.r ET    S 8
J 1x@ = 6 =     W   l      y G KI                   5'    @     2b       :fT         x G        /       z8          "
J 1x@ =       h V M     R                  -    * '   +|q      >b         aAQ  BN    o hW   y4 (b         Ok
J 1x@ = sg CDrU0        a Hz i |X          .    . s Z B     >  Jo<ycqfy           = N   o q          _
J 1x@ =    1               6 ( G @   , d   7U              l |Iv   zaC @                d        5/ z
J 1x@ =       h V Mf '          p7k_     sp H      ¬    fy u                       * ,        J   ¬ " l lx
J 1x@ = c         ou 5      p2v' 2 N          7 :Z      fP             g    I   v6G!     n E     ;
```

Figure 6.24.3. Block chaining encipherment of *PLAIN(4)*.

$$\mathbf{x}_j' = \text{DES}^{-1}\{\mathbf{k},\mathbf{y}_j'\} + \mathbf{y}_{j-1}' = \text{DES}^{-1}\{\mathbf{k},\mathbf{y}_j + \mathbf{e}\} + \mathbf{y}_{j-1}$$

$$\neq \text{DES}^{-1}\{\mathbf{k},\mathbf{y}_j\} + \mathbf{y}_{j-1} = \mathbf{x}_j\mathbf{x}_j$$

$$= \text{DES}^{-1}\{\mathbf{k},\mathbf{y}_{j+1}'\} + \mathbf{y}_j' = \text{DES}^{-1}\{\mathbf{k},\mathbf{y}_{j+1}\} + \mathbf{y}_j + \mathbf{e}$$

$$\neq \text{DES}^{-1}\{\mathbf{k},\mathbf{y}_{j+1}\} + \mathbf{y}_j = \mathbf{x}_{j+1}$$

- The self-healing property yields the $(j + 2)^{\text{nd}}$ through m^{th} plaintext blocks correctly:

$$\mathbf{x}_i' = \text{DES}^{-1}\{\mathbf{k},\mathbf{y}_i'\} + \mathbf{y}_{i-1}' = \text{DES}^{-1}\{\mathbf{k},\mathbf{y}_i\} + \mathbf{y}_{i-1} = \mathbf{x}_i \qquad j + 1 < i < m$$

```
      7R 5e)1 1 mF C 7i +   O H  q ?N    C    yr     W¬ G>  D      X       & _t 9 $ '    P )
 "  JGY 5      &ə       E(ns$qY c?  W¬ Z7           lh  :ry,p  U   C3    x -       B           i
s8 v $   * i  !  L         .7 A o  R;b;a    =      *  ,    y    , *  ¢m     z  x F
  G    NX   ) P      Q# s  J  P ə h      y  6(? $    M41U  U       h      /     9
 /   /     D        85z   <  U4 c    )    Xwa 7 /  V       K;       JEYOC    s  B S zA
In O  49 |u9n Dd   e        'n   D  (;8 7m W  /  H RL   4      ( B='
     /     6        v4 3 P|    B  9 ?u   M M=    3   ; n   h   7   Q4:  *            F
,2Y *2U K T    T        7 P  Y  q GM   uX sk  KO    qx   f D5       e        > P
C= ? ' =    4  ) 87   ¢     <   H !57    1 s    1$    o   rn b&        .W5T  bo|
   O_   W  42oeA_  j-  6_8T _  G Ij   B  J B q  Pxa¬ə y f+  K   |  (g zCW,7    ə
VGJ us    <      ;       kl I    $ V:_6sə            K =   j    I) P 9vC$    0  =
i   #  z Q   Iy   m f#   WU .    w= Y ; &   97   .  D      q V 1> 1v|   6  K
    9      bM   g  w j db N     ə          k V  >' H   LV .,    V    G ə
q v   NcpV   *   yt' Jk O<HW      y      &R    B p    >          d1T_ N  L #
? 'Cb'¢S    ¬QJ      l  y/ Yk  f c     Z    /8Tu f  ¢e   .N      s D   ¬<         8
j    #EEx   :D0      5 q    G    N Z  y i n t!L 7! 1    1"-Puc x  d   Xqt.
  Q  M (L  y ¬s!o>R P (    7           ig:    pS W(  y        9 L   kR V    s.
; k O P       I .      /        8K   Sq  sYFwIh D 7  Cu        T r      6 G   47G
QW  5,+ Db M 8 k  Fət            rv    / (RP  >Q       6     mJP  vnS H t    8
     BK  < 1  v       ¢ 4(  gQ     Y  A & D     #O om   g       f > L        3q
M   W      3 ,      j  #D       =  y  7 O M X  4    XY  8f   "9  '  R
 YF       < W>  " Q>  &N       e  s    7_ _       T) g C    H9     5    a> W t 2
e$ a   6     r     "     ¬U ¢ )RT    v C      a  f       B >_   W     Z g  ')         4
 0C 8JC T y- ZE wI O.     L  K dv|           G  q       d        Jk / 3
T    * C xa     C g '   b  o 2o  ia   .f g¢RL  c-   O  >       &u2    8c  8=
 dg =    41'  zJD  *z    E 4& O   VC #-' F ' 8|       n S   5A      ə  P
  G     o  4? OlRV   s o  U d    | U     Z &         Q u>.,  ioə)   X  CyR I
Sh   M   (       Lx   41 k 5  vd  Wa$    D6 )    )A+  b( o +>        tK  8  k
   k  F  U       lzI  (   ə  u  k4      (H P />&  q 3p ,(8K ə w P?    =    T
     O           f   5Y  z 8z   P  =5  H6#    N  *  ə  / j : M$
d N   *       $L p   m  t    n.9 MY|:    L      W  f    Xc    X |      Ki ,
 v P      _ z  heə d   ə   j  XD   J  m  f  7f  AN    j K    X       k XA
   b   /  7 p"C  egI u c $*   N    u     z  g d  t w   M  <+     E
U 7    u   B ə  X    >  WEO¬        io       c           ,x   qi* n   MG
   M  MT  p2   c   t   v $ g6D    io    '  z ! _v vK         c ;  U< L  iP
   y     )  E  ¢ c Pə $  E   gh 8V   T     )O* a*     ijGZ¢        e yN
t  9M     ə ə V   #2 " U &L      #t *  | u  p :8     kR   v  8   F 9 br  y8
 : *  i  A W  4 y   z+ F   icv.v   & <    3        E q     ə    cjN "
7b ?   z> a   H    M   >=8E 4 t        s          l ə   t        s)       1
+4        1   ex     ;A  8  )    E  0 :1     N$  5   G:   6_Yq   ;j     l  A
 O U    YZ +  = B0   /     Q   FM J *d F  E    (ə fnz    I.h pLU   z P)
  aQ  5 v   +    D      c   ;?   9H  _M  ( w t   f u /     , H X  6 Zr 7
>   e#G 3  aU 6_FN.d  L  j     Nj,  9h q h    t  ' z            y  1
 $u Y U $  5 CK    ?Jh    T         RU   jc  x  67T  k  qX     B
D   7 3 A   r   &M   L m ¢h n   c   d ( | ¬¢ /,hk  0   $ R    m 2    u +
  i# x  u   ¢  =p  A     , w     iXR W    <     5 w  w   Q     1'3f  s
F   _1YHd   qCF(  w   (iB       # !   I D      cT      ,  M  ¬rR# F
      f        B  e  s ; X ;Y  x =2    P c     ¬l= :      m       KJH
?p  l     ?+ y   Fu   r P  m  cZ1V  q m    2L_6      2I  1 H  G 1 W  J 3h I
 *    x C D  3YbM;K   h  u    *) WNH<Xr q    # E     0 VU     y d a a
_GeEqe  k    K  E    <v0  :wf ə2    ) :       G(   "g  d? jR I N    9
 * ¬ ə vc  *    16 ?L  X o P H     r : ə 9  #dc  |    t  i  (          M6
 K  L1 s Q i   b   ,   R   Q       9      V6      $  E o    3  8 CQ
U    f $  O      W .    lzf5  h    MDZ      & 9  #7K    8_E         Y  s
WO < E     c   _ y uY      "    gb*   Nm   ME    k wP  h ;    1  ¢&jaN = +)   E :R
   ə   x   +  < 2    '      H: 'H08  -  " !    Z hr  3ə  &   pp          T *  c
Z  - c x V      QX  V          zvl Ei#    :    x  ¬n         g     b/D      ?i ?
```

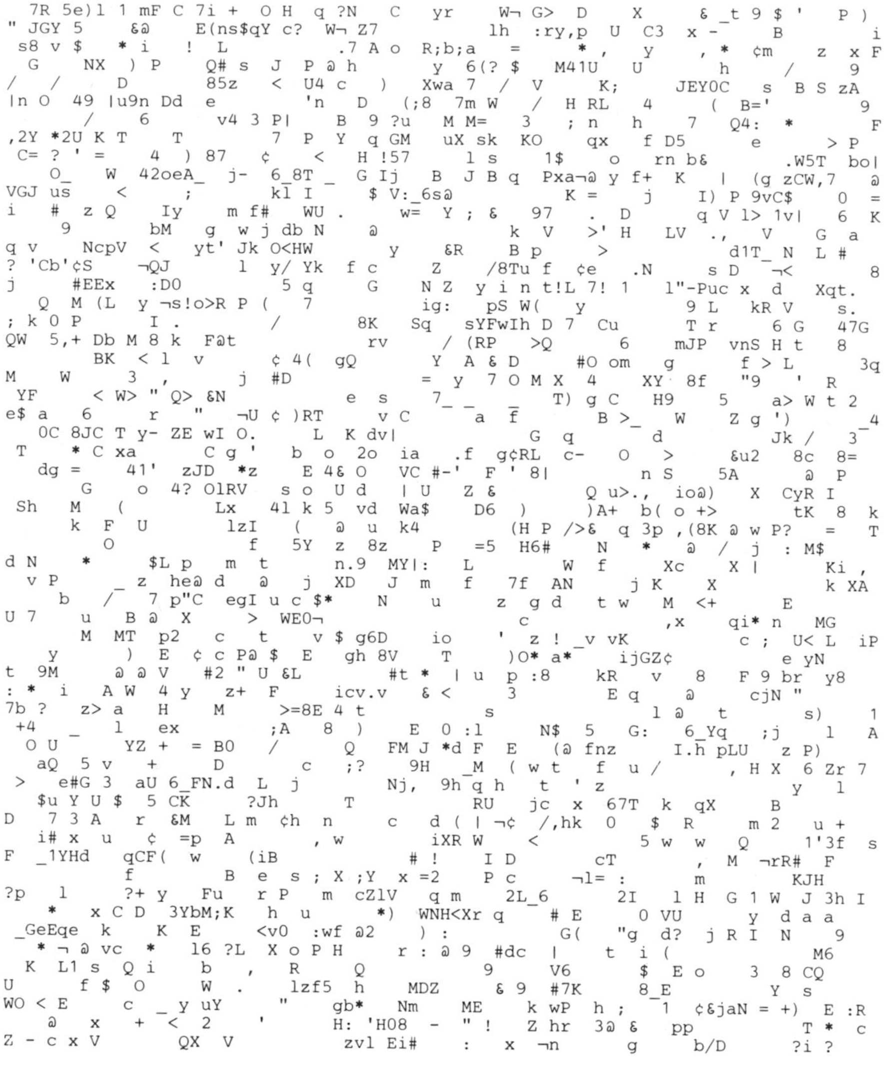

Figure 6.24.4. Record chaining encipherment of *PLAIN(4)*.

Thus an error in the jth eight-byte block of ciphertext results (upon decipherment) in errors in the jth and $(j + 1)^{st}$ eight-byte blocks of plaintext. The error does not propagate further. In Fig. 6.24.5, we show the effect of an error in the record-chained encipherment of *PLAIN(4)* after decipherment.

6.25 STEP ENCIPHERMENT

In some applications, the self-healing property is not wanted; we want an error in the ciphertext to propagate throughout the decipherment so that no portion of the plaintext is obtained after decipherment. We may accomplish this by *step enci-*

```
    q O *****************************************************************
xn  H  t                                                                *
  !  FX PR CESSING                                                      *
T    |'                                                                 *
   n  p the'SYSPRINT ddname, and if allocated by INDATASET and          *
a  ztj"OATASE  the input (SYSUT1) and output (SYSUT2) ddnames also.     *
   W   mes prNvided by INDD and OUTDD are left alone: since they        *
 e7 B    alloca ed by the user, they should be freed by the user.       *
*              E                                                        *
*   If a7  1    o ation fails, DAIRFAIL will write a message, and       *
*   this   o  I  wrll set return code 12.                               *
*              Q  Z   >                                                 *
*   Foll      U    e de llocations, control is returned to the TSO      *
*   Supe      > F       &                                               *
*          1   yE                                                       *
********(4          ******O*********************************************
FINAL00  SR     R ;   j&                  ZERO TEMPORARY RETURN CODE
         TM     F      O    X 80'         IS "FREE SYSPRINT" ON?
         BZ     FmS    K                   NO, SKIP IT
         LA     R    |(   XP              ADDRESS THE SYSPRINT DDNAME
         BAL    R f      O DNO J          FREE THE DDNAME
         LTR    R    6   K                TEST FREEDDO RETURN CODE
         BZ     F   r     1         8     NORMAL RETURN FROM FREE
         LA     R        ?                ERROR: SET RETURN CODE 12
         SPACE              uR   E?b
FINAL01  TM     FREEUT1,X p        ?      IS "FREE INPUT DDNAME" ON?
         BZ     FINAL02    =       T       NO, SKIP IT
         LA     R2,DDNUT1 tR               DDRESS THE INPUT DDNAME
         BAL    R10,FREED          |      F|EE THE DDNAME
         LTR    R15,R15   ! p       X     TE T FREEDDO RETURN CODE
         BZ     FINAL02   d 9X 0a         NOR AL RETURN FROM FREE
         LA     R3,12      y   ,    :     ERRO : SET RETURN CODE 12
         SPACE                           S    H
FINAL02  TM     FREEUT2,X'80'                  R E OUTPUT DDNAME" ON?
         BZ     FINAL03              zc "     SK P IT
         LA     R2,DDNUT2             n5x    ISS !HE OUTPUT DDNAME
         BAL    R10,FREEDDNO         N       -THE  DNAME
         LTR    R15,R15              Q  ) u FREED 0 RETURN CODE
         BZ     FINAL03              P  S2  RL RETU N FROM FREE
         LA     R3,12                     A?   : SET R TURN CODE 12
FINAL03  LR     R0,R3                     COPY "FREE DD" RETURN CODE
         BAL    R10,RCSET                 INCRE&  |    aR  CODE IF HIGHER
         SPACE                                   Mp tX  m
         L      R1,RC                     LOAD     J:B :ODEE
         CVD    R1,DOUBLE                 RETUR     P(  O DEjIMAL
         LA     R1,AM29                   "END        G DAM -  C NNN"
         BAL    R10,PREPRNTO              MOVE 6   e  aTEXT T+ 'OUTLINE'
         ED     OUTLINE+M29B-M29A(L'M29B)  o    e 6  EDIT$TO MSG
         BAL    R10,PRINTOO               PRINT THE MES|W
         SPACE                                         k    ) g
         L      R2,RC                     LOAD RETURN C 5     +R D AVE
         LA     R0,DSAVEL                 SET R0 TO LEN PFT    !SAV
         LR     R1,R13                     AND R1 TO IT   & . | S
         L      R13,4(0,R13)              RESTORE CALLE'  S     AREA  DDRESS
         FREEMAIN R,LV=(0),A=(1)          FREE DSAVE WO U  da/        m
         LR     R15,R2                    SET RETURN CO    f D  GISTER J5
         RETURN (14,12),T,RC=(15)         RETURN TO TSO            m ¬ S
```

Figure 6.24.5. The self-healing property of chaining.

pherment. If $\mathbf{x}$ is a plaintext N-block, we denote by $\mathbf{x}[i,j)$ the segment of $\mathbf{x}$ formed by deleting components $x_0, x_1, \ldots, x_{i-1}$ and $x_j, x_{j+1}, \ldots, x_{N-1}$:

$$\mathbf{x}[i,j) = (x_i, x_{i+1}, \ldots, x_{j-1})$$

Suppose $N \geq 64$, $\{m_i : 0 \leq i < s\}$ are nonnegative integers ($m_i \leq N - 64$) and $\{\mathbf{k}_i : 0 \leq i < s\} \subseteq Z_{2,56}$ are s keys. The step encipherment of plaintext

$$\mathbf{x} = (x_0, x_1, \ldots, x_{N-1})$$

$$\mathbf{y} = \mathrm{DESSTEP}(\{\mathbf{k}_i\},\{m_i\},\mathbf{x})$$

$$\mathbf{y} = (y_0, y_1, \ldots, y_{N-1})$$

is defined by the rules

$$\mathbf{z}^{(i)} = \begin{cases} \mathbf{x}[0,m_0)\|\mathrm{DES}\{\mathbf{k}_i,\mathbf{x}[m_0,m_0+64)\}\|\mathbf{x}[m_0+64,N) & \text{if } i = 0 \\ \mathbf{z}^{(i-1)}\|\mathrm{DES}\{\mathbf{k}_i,\mathbf{z}^{(i-1)}[m_i,m_i+64)\}\|\mathbf{z}^{(i-1)}[m_i+64,N) & \text{if } 0 < i < s \end{cases}$$

$$\mathbf{y} = \mathbf{z}^{(s-1)} = \mathrm{DESSTEP}(\{\mathbf{k}_i\},\{m_i\},\mathbf{x})$$

where $\|$ denotes the concatenation of blocks. In Fig. 6.25.1, we illustrate step coding for $s = 3$ and $N = 78$. When the $\{m_i\}$ are properly chosen, each component of $\mathbf{y}$ is dependent upon each component of $\mathbf{x}$.

6.26 STREAM ENCIPHERMENT

DES can be used for the *stream* or *letter-by-letter* encipherment of plaintext,

$$(x_0, x_1, \ldots, x_{n-1}) \rightarrow (y_0, y_1, \ldots, y_{n-1})$$

where the alphabet is now Z_2. There are several possible stream cipher versions of DES.

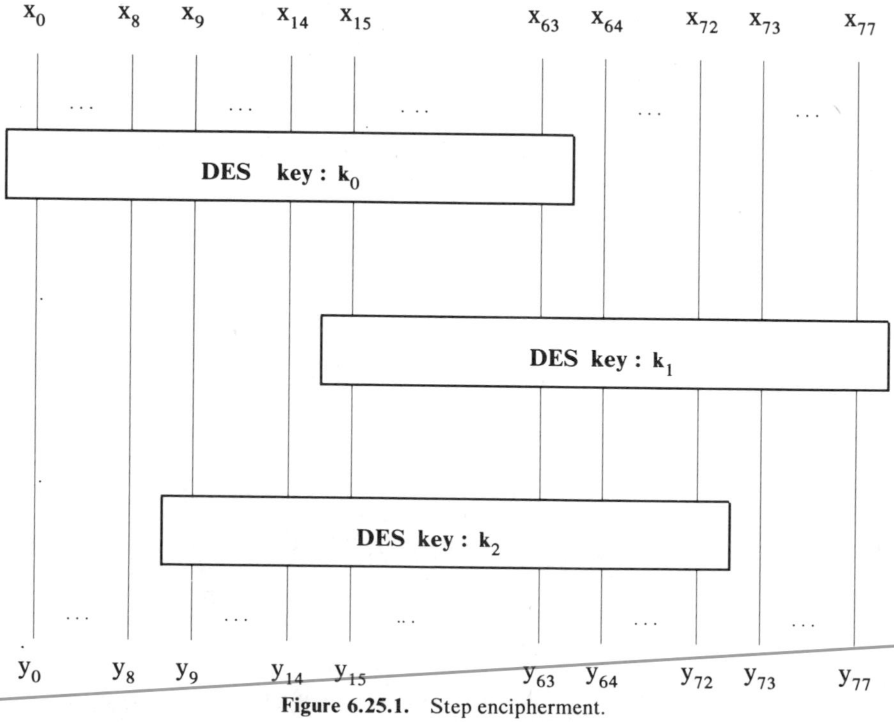

Figure 6.25.1. Step encipherment.

Let

$$\mathbf{x} = (x_0, x_1, \ldots, x_{n-1}) \qquad (\textit{plaintext})$$

$$\mathbf{k} = (k_0, k_1, \ldots, k_{55}) \qquad (\textit{key})$$

$$\mathbf{z} = (z_0, z_1, \ldots, z_{63}) \qquad (\textit{initial seed})$$

and define

$$\mathbf{y} = (y_0, y_1, \ldots, y_{n-1}) \quad (\textit{ciphertext})$$

$$\mathbf{z}^{(0)}, \mathbf{z}^{(1)}, \ldots$$

$$\mathbf{z}^{(j)} = (z_{j,0}, z_{j,1}, \ldots, z_{j,63}) \qquad -1 \leq j < n$$

$$\mathbf{z}^{(-1)} = \mathbf{z}$$

$$\mathbf{z}^{(j)} = \mathrm{DES}\{\mathbf{k}, \mathbf{z}^{(j-1)}\} \qquad 0 \leq j < n$$

$$y_j = x_j + z_{j,0} \qquad 0 \leq j < n$$

The initial seed need not be kept a secret. It may be transmitted as an initiator from one user to the other in plaintext. Stream encipherment is preferred over block encipherment when the transmission channel is noisy. Unlike the block cipher version of DES, a single error in transmission results in only a single error upon decipherment.

PROBLEMS

6.1 Write

$$\mathrm{DES} = \mathrm{IP}^{-1} \times \pi_{T_{16}} \times \ldots \times \vartheta \times \pi_{T_1} \times \mathrm{IP}$$

$$\mathrm{DES} : (\mathbf{x}_0, \mathbf{x}_1) \rightarrow (\mathbf{x}_{16}, \mathbf{x}_{17})$$

$$\vartheta \times \pi_{T_i} : (\mathbf{x}_{i-1}, \mathbf{x}_i) \rightarrow (\mathbf{x}_i, \mathbf{x}_{i+1}) = (\mathbf{x}_i, \mathbf{x}_{i-1} + T_i(\mathbf{x}_i))$$

Are the $\{T_i : 1 \leq i \leq 16\}$ invertible?

6.2 What is the expected length of a cycle if π is chosen from SYM $(Z_{2,N})$ according to the uniform distribution?

6.3 Write a program for DES encipherment; check your program using the two sets of test data,

$\mathbf{k}_1$: 00010011 00110100 01010111 01111001
10011011 10111100 11011111 11110001

$\mathbf{x}_1$: 00000001 00100011 01000101 01100111
10001001 10101011 11001101 11101111

$\mathbf{y}_1$: 10000101 11101000 00010011 01010100
00001111 00001010 10110100 00000101

$\mathbf{k}_1$:	133457799BBCDFF1	(hex)*
$\mathbf{x}_1$:	0123456789ABCDEF	(hex)
$\mathbf{y}_1$:	85E813540F0AB405	(hex)

and

$\mathbf{k}_2$:	00010011 00110100 01010111 01111001 10011011 10111100 11011111 11110001
$\mathbf{x}_2$:	01010101 01010101 01010101 01010101 01010101 01010101 01010101 01010101
$\mathbf{y}_2$:	01101111 00010101 10011011 10011010 10110111 10000100 00010101 1001100

$\mathbf{k}_2$:	133457799BBCDFF1	(hex)
$\mathbf{x}_2$:	5555555555555555	(hex)
$\mathbf{y}_2$:	6F159B9AB784158C	(hex)

6.4 Define $\text{DES}_{[r]}$, that is, *DES of r rounds* by

$$\text{DES}_{[r]} = \text{IP}^{-1} \times \pi_{T_r} \times \ldots \times \vartheta \times \pi_{T_1} \times \text{IP}$$

Attempt cryptanalysis of $\text{DES}_{[r]}$ for $r = 1, 2, 3$?

6.5 Run χ^2-tests on $\text{DES}_{[r]}$; test dependence between x_i with $i \in \boldsymbol{CO}_{\text{in}}$ and y_j with $j \in CO_{\text{out}}$.

6.6 Each of the components of $\mathbf{k} = (k_0, k_1, \ldots, k_{55})$ is used in a DES-encipherment in several ways; we will say that k_j is *used in position i (in an S-box)* $(0 \leq t < 6)$ on round r if the key schedule uses k_j on round r on the ith input wire to an S-box. For example, from Sec. 6.7,

- k_8 is used in position 0 on round 1.
- k_{41} is used in position 0 on round 1.
- k_{41} is used in position 4 on round 2.

Determine the usage of each key value $\{k_j\}$.

---

* *Hex* or *hexidecimal* is the representation to base 16.

Binary	Hex	Binary	Hex
0000	0	1000	8
0001	1	1001	9
0010	2	1010	A
0011	3	1011	B
0100	4	1100	C
0101	5	1101	D
0110	6	1110	E
0111	7	1111	F

6.7 Call two keys $\mathbf{k}_1$ and $\mathbf{k}_2$ *inverse reciprocal* if

$$\mathbf{y} = \text{DES}\{\mathbf{k}_1,\mathbf{x}\} \qquad \mathbf{x} = \text{DES}^{-1}\{\mathbf{k}_2,\mathbf{y}\}$$

Do inverse reciprocal keys exist?

6.8 **Research Problem:** What criteria should the S-boxes in DES satisfy?

6.9 **Research Problem:** What criteria should the P-box (wirecrossing) in DES satisfy?

6.10 **Research Problem:** What criteria should the key schedule DES satisfy?

6.11 **Research Problem:** What relationships should exist between the key schedule and the P-box?

6.12 **Research Problem:** Does the initial permutation IP in DES have a cryptographic function?

6.13 If plaintext $\mathbf{x} = (x_0, x_1, \ldots, x_{64N-1})$ is enciphered with chaining by DES with key $\mathbf{k}$,

$$\mathbf{y} = \text{DESCH}\{\mathbf{k},\mathbf{x}\}$$

$$\mathbf{y} = (y_0, y_1, \ldots, y_{64N-1})$$

then y_i with $0 \le i < 64j$ is a Boolean function of $(x_0, x_1, \ldots, x_{64j-1})$ but *not* functionally dependent on $(x_{64j}, x_{64j+1}, \ldots, x_{64N-1})$. Invent a form of chaining in which each output ciphertext variable is a Boolean function of all plaintext coordinates. What are its error propagation properties?

6.14 The chaining described in Sec. 6.24 *chains on the plaintext-ciphertext.* Invent a form of chaining on the key and investigate its error propagation properties.

6.15 Suppose DES users choose a key of seven alpha-numeric characters and code into an element of $Z_{2,56}$ by the EBCIDIC mapping (Table P6.1); for example

TABLE P6.1
Partial EBCIDIC Coding

	hex	0	1	2	3	4	5	6	7	8	9	A	B	C	D	E	F
	binary	**0000**	**0001**	**0010**	**0011**	**0100**	**0101**	**0110**	**0111**	**1000**	**1001**	**1010**	**1011**	**1100**	**1101**	**1110**	**1111**
4	**0100**	*bs*										¢	.	<	(	+	|
5	**0101**																
6	**0110**	-	/										,	%	_	>	?
7	**0111**											:	#	@	'	=	"
8	**1000**		a	b	c	d	e	f	g	h	i						
9	**1001**		j	k	l	m	n	o	p	q	r						
A	**1010**			s	t	u	v	w	x	y	z						
B	**1011**																
C	**1100**	{	A	B	C	D	E	F	G	H	I						
D	**1101**	}	J	K	L	M	N	O	P	Q	R						
E	**1110**	\		S	T	U	V	W	X	Y	Z						
F	**1111**	0	1	2	3	4	5	6	7	8	9	|					

KONHEIM → D2D6D5C8C5C9D4

Discuss the implications of this type of key selection.

6.16 What effect does chaining and the use of a random initial chaining value have on the time-memory tradeoff?

6.17 Start with the primitive building blocks:

P : wirecrossing

S : substitution ($Z_{2,4} \rightarrow Z_{2,4}$)

and construct a block cipher system. Start your own controversy!

PART TWO

APPLICATIONS OF CRYPTOGRAPHY

CHAPTER VII

Key Management

7.1 COMMUNICATIONS SECURITY/FILE SECURITY

The application of cryptographic methods to protect information processing systems typifies the way cryptography has responded to technological change. This chapter begins an examination of the two principal applications of cryptographic methods in information processing:

- Protection of communications between *terminals* and *host processor.*
- Protection of on-line files.

The use of cryptographic methods in an information processing environment differs from the classical employment in military and diplomatic applications in one crucial aspect; in the latter, the key required by both parties is distributed by an alternate secure path. For example, the key used to secure communications between the State Department in Washington and the United States Embassy in Moscow might be sent to Moscow by diplomatic courier; in battlefield situations, the key for the day may be distributed at the start of the engagement. If cryptography is to be used to protect communications between a terminal and the host processor, the key, or a quantity equivalent to the key, must reside within the operating system. In most computing systems, some class of users are given *privileged status,* allowing them access to all tables and data within the system including any set of key variables. Even if we do not suspect these users to be untrustworthy, present day operating systems can be penetrated. In [AT], a study of VM/370 revealed various methods for the penetration of virtual systems. Any way of protecting data that stores a key within the system and is predicated on the system protecting the keys must be evaluated with this fact in mind.

7.2 CURRENT APPLICATIONS OF CRYPTOGRAPHY

We begin by describing some current applications of cryptography in information processing systems.

Banking Terminals

Some banks provide a round-the-clock capability to execute a variety of banking functions—payment of loans, transfers between checking and savings accounts, cash dispensing—at unattended stand-alone banking terminals. *"Citibank Never Sleeps!"* ® The bank provides each customer with (1) a banking card on which a primary key or *account number* (ACCT) is magnetically recorded, and (2) a secondary key or *personal identification number* (PIN). In a transaction,

- ACCT is read from the card inserted in the terminal's card reader.
- The PIN is entered at the terminal keyboard.
- A *transaction request* is made:

  transfer $50 from savings account ACCT to checking account ACCT, or

  dispense $50 and debit ACCT.

The system checks if

- ACCT is a valid account number.
- The user-supplied PIN is the correct personal identification number corresponding to ACCT.

The PIN is a *secondary key* whose function is to deny part of the private information to someone in possession of a stolen credit card. The PIN plays much the same role as a signature in a conventional credit card transaction. Customers are advised by the bank to memorize the PIN and *not* to write it on the card. The PIN must therefore consist of only a small number of alpha-numeric characters, usually four to six. Here we meet one of the compromises needed in the commercial application of cryptography; if the PIN length is short enough to facilitate easy memorization, then key trial in the PIN key space might be a viable method of attack. On the other hand, if the PIN is long enough to protect against key trial, users will write the PIN on their card, negating the purpose of the second separate key.

Any transaction system is vulnerable to attack if the communications are in plaintext. An opponent

- Records the message *Response,* which authorizes the terminal to dispense cash.
- Disables the communication line from host-to-terminal, connecting a "fake" host to the terminal.
- Replays the message *Response* from the processor to the terminal, instructing it to dispense cash—Play It Again Sam!

Encipherment alone will not defend against this attack. If the ciphertext message $\pi\{Response\}$ authorizes the terminal to dispense cash, the opponent needs only replace the third item above with:

- Replays the message $\pi\{Response\}$ from the processor to the terminal, instructing it to dispense cash.

The above attack can be defeated only if the opponent is unable to construct a proper response. The message authorizing the terminal to issue cash must contain some variable and unpredictable information precluding the reuse of a *stale* message. One solution is to incorporate some combination of *the transaction number* (TN) or *current bill counter* (BC) in the plaintext, which changes with each transaction and causes an unpredictable change in the ciphertext. In this case, recording the ciphertext messages

$$\begin{gathered}\mathrm{E}\{\text{Request, BC, TN}\}\\ \text{terminal} \rightarrow \text{host}\end{gathered}$$

$$\begin{gathered}\mathrm{E}\{\text{Response, BC, TN}\}\\ \text{host} \rightarrow \text{terminal}\end{gathered}$$

of a previous transaction may not provide enough information to construct the message

$$\begin{gathered}\mathrm{E}\{\text{Response, BC}', \text{TN}'\}\\ \text{host} \rightarrow \text{terminal}\end{gathered}$$

which will authorize the terminal to dispense cash, where BC′ and TN′ are the updated bill counter and transaction number.

Personal Key Cards

A standard method of restricting access to a building is based on identical *key cards* containing magnetically coded information which are issued to each employee. The loss of a *single* key card compromises the "lock." Personal key cards, equivalent to a separate (key, lock) pair for each employee can be implemented cryptographically as follows; a *facility number* FACNUM is assigned to each facility or building. A randomly chosen (n decimal digit) number RAN is selected for each employee. The encipherment of the concatenation of RAN_i and $\mathrm{FACNUM}—\mathrm{RAN}_i$

$$\pi\{\mathrm{RAN}_i \| \mathrm{FACNUM} - \mathrm{RAN}_i\}$$

is recorded on the *key card* of the ith employee E_i. To gain entry, the ith employee inserts the key card into a reader, the host deciphers $\mathrm{CIPHER} = \pi\{X\|Y\}$ and obtains the pair of numbers (X,Y), presumptively equal to (RAN_i, $\mathrm{FACNUM} - \mathrm{RAN}_i$). The sum $X + Y$ is compared with FACNUM to check if E_i is authorized to enter FACNUM and a *lost* or *stolen list* is searched for X. If E_i's card is lost, a new RAN_i' is assigned to E_i and RAN_i joins the stolen/lost list.

Log-On Passwords

The conventional log-on procedure is based on passwords. The processor stores a table of passwords (in a protected area), which is referenced during a log-on. A region in memory containing several hundred entries cannot really be protected against reading, deleting, and/or alteration. An alternate solution is to store the encipherment $\pi\{K,PASS\}$ of the password PASS; only a single key K has to be protected. The system checks the validity of the offered plaintext password by encipherment and comparison. Encipherment does not completely resolve the problem; an opponent who wiretaps terminal-to-host communications *during* a log-on and records the plaintext password can masquerade as the user [PU].

Encipherment of On-Line Files

Applications include

- APL workspaces stored as CMS files.
- Data bases that contain valuable information; for example, design data of electronic circuit chips.
- Files containing cryptographic keys generated by the repeated modification and encipherment of a random data string.

Hash Values

This application generates hash table values from long character strings, the hash value being the rightmost bytes of the block-chained encipherment of the character string.

7.3 KEY MANAGEMENT IN AN INFORMATION PROCESSING SYSTEM

When a keyed cryptographic system is to be used in a data processing environment, some provision must be made for the distribution of keys. A keyed cryptograhic system protecting *terminal-to-host* communications requires either that

- Keys be loaded into the system whenever encipherment/decipherment is required, or
- *The key or some means of constructing the key must be present in the host.*

If only *terminal-to-terminal* communications, routed through but not deciphered at the host *(end-to-end encryption)* are to be protected, no key needs be stored at the host. No operating system today can protect a long list of user keys, and it is questionable as to what is gained by using a cryptographic system whose ultimate effectiveness depends on keeping such a list secret. Several proposals for key management have been made.

7.4 SESSION KEYS

In 1977, IBM announced several cryptographic products [IBM1,2] for end-to-end encryption using the DES algorithm. A description of the design principles is given in [EH,LEN,MA]. An independent and similar proposal was made in [EVER]. The IBM Crytographic Subsystem is based upon the concept of a *session key* KS, a key shared by host and terminal and used only for the duration of a session.

The basic features of the IBM Cryptographic Subsystem are:

- Two classes of keys: *operational keys* (*session* and *device*), which perform encipherment and *system keys,* used to encipher operational keys that are stored in the host.
- No operational key is stored in plaintext in the host.
- A single *host master key,* KMH, stored at the host in a secure device capable of executing a small set of instructions. Two variants of the master key, KMH0 and KMH1, are obtained by complementing certain bits in KMH.
- *Device* (or *terminal*) *master keys,* KMT_1, KMT_2, . . . , KMT_N, stored in a secure manner at the devices (terminals). A host table containing {DES{KMH1, KMT_i} : i = 1, 2, . . . }.
- A session key KS is an operational key used to encipher transmissions between the host and a device (terminal). The session key is generated by the host at the initiation of the session.
- Four nonprivileged instructions for enciphering/deciphering data.

(*i*) **ECPH** : *Encipher Data (Fig. 7.4.1)*

ECPH[DES{KMH0,KS},PLAIN] = DES{KS,PLAIN}

The arguments of **ECPH** are (1) the encipherment of the session key KS under KMH0,

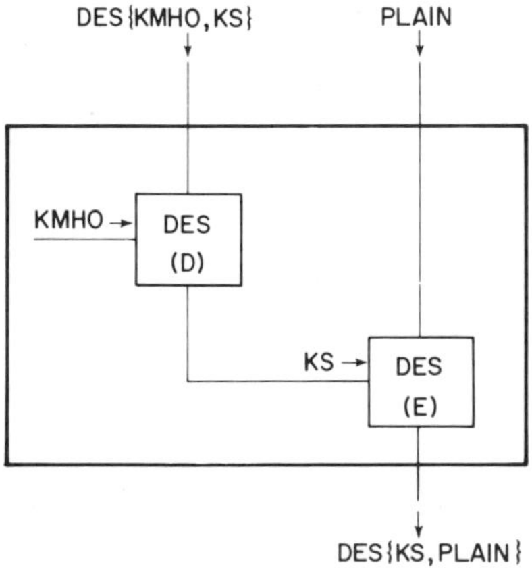

Figure 7.4.1. ECPH : *encipher data.*

$$\text{DES}\{\text{KMH0,KS}\}$$

and (2) plaintext PLAIN.
ECPH returns the encipherment of PLAIN under KS,

$$\text{CIPHER} = \text{DES}\{\text{KS,PLAIN}\}$$

(*ii*) **DCPH** : *Decipher Data (Fig. 7.4.2)*

$$\mathbf{DCPH}[\text{DES}\{\text{KMH0,KS}\},\text{DES}\{\text{KS,PLAIN}\}] = \text{PLAIN}$$

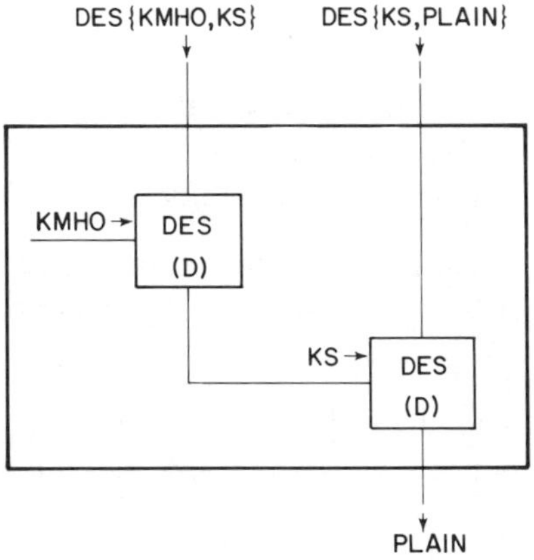

Figure 7.4.2. DCPH : *decipher data.*

The arguments of **DCPH** are (1) the encipherment of the session key KS under KMH0,

$$\text{DES}\{\text{KMH0,KS}\}$$

and (2) ciphertext CIPHER = DES{KS,PLAIN}.
DCPH returns the plaintext PLAIN:

$$\text{PLAIN} = \text{DES}^{-1}\{\text{KS,CIPHER}\}$$

(*iii*) An Instruction Executed at a Terminal (Device) (Fig. 7.4.3)
DMK : *decipher under terminal (device) key*

$$\mathbf{DMK}[\text{KMT}_i,\text{DES}\{\text{KMT}_i,\text{KS}\}] = \text{KS}$$

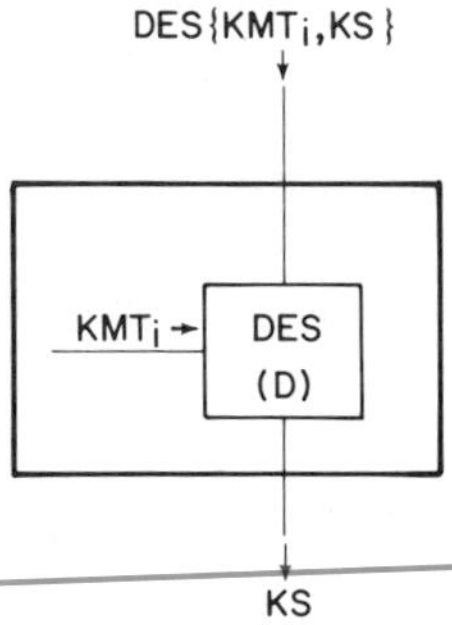

Figure 7.4.3. DMK : *decipher under terminal (device) key.*

The arguments of **DMK** are (1) the key KMT_i of the ith-device, and (2) the encipherment DES{KMT_i,KS} of the session key under KMT_i.
DMK returns the session key KS,

$$KS = DES^{-1}\{KMT_i, DES\{KMT_i, KS\}\}$$

(*iv*) A Translation Facility ***RFMK*** *: Reencipher from Master Key (Fig. 7.4.4)*

$$\mathbf{RFMK}[DES\{KMH1,KMT_i\},DES\{KMH0,KS\}] = DES\{KMT_i,KS\}$$

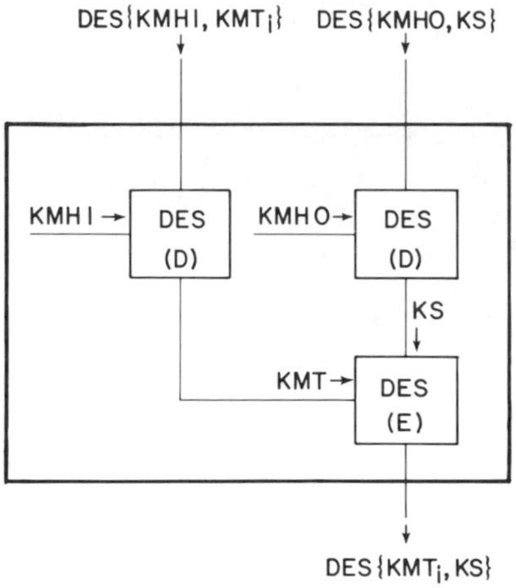

Figure 7.4.4. RFMK : *reencipher from master key.*

The arguments of **RFMK** are (1) the encipherment DES{KMH1,KMT_i} of the key KMT_i of the ith device under KMH1, and (2) the encipherment DES{KMH0,KS} of the session key KS under KMH0.
RMFK returns the encipherment DES{KMT_i,KS} of the session key under KMT_i.

A *session* linking the ith device (terminal) to the host processor involves the following steps.

Step 1 A "random" number RN is generated at the host by repeated DES encipherment of the time-of-day clock. RN is interpreted as the encipherment of the session key KS under KMH0

$$RN = DES\{KMH0,KS\}$$

RN is stored at the host in a table associated with the ith device for the duration of the session.

Step 2 The session key must be made available to the ith device. The translation facility is used for this purpose; **RFMK** with input arguments (1) the DES encipherment of KMT_i under KMH1 (from the host table),

$$\text{DES}\{\text{KMH1},\text{KMT}_i\}$$

and (2) RN yields

$$\text{DES}\{\text{KMT}_i,\text{KS}\} = \textbf{RFMK}[\text{DES}\{\text{KMH1},\text{KMT}_i\},\text{DES}\{\text{KMH0},\text{KS}\}]$$

which is transmitted by the host to the ith device (terminal).

Step 3 The ith device (terminal), having KMT_i, uses **DMK** to obtain

$$\text{KS} = \textbf{DMK}[\text{KMT}_i,\text{DES}\{\text{KMT}_i,\text{KS}\}]$$

Both parties to the communication, the host and the terminal, have now established and exchanged a common key KS.

Plaintext PLAIN can be DES-enciphered with key KS at the host with **ECPH**,

$$\textbf{ECPH}[\text{DES}\{\text{KMH0},\text{KS}\}, \text{PLAIN}] \rightarrow \text{CIPHER} = \text{DES}\{\text{KS},\text{PLAIN}\}$$

while PLAIN can be recovered from CIPHER at the host with **DCPH**,

$$\textbf{DCPH}[\text{DES}\{\text{KMH0},\text{KS}\}, \text{CIPHER}] \rightarrow \text{PLAIN} = \text{DES}^{-1}\{\text{KS},\text{CIPHER}\}$$

7.5 DISCUSSION AND CRITIQUE

Variants of the host master key KMH (three are defined in [EH]) are introduced to prevent a combination of instructions resulting in the recovery of a session key. If KMH0 = KMH1 = KMH, the combination of

- A wire-tap of a host → terminal communication recording

$$\text{DES}\{\text{KMT}_i,\text{KS}\}$$

- **DCPH**[DES{KMH1,KMT_i}, DES{KMT_i,KS}] recovers KS.

What are the exposures in this key management system? The keys stored at the host:

- The host master keys KMH, KMH0, KMH1.
- The terminal master keys $\{KMT_i : 1 \leq i \leq N\}$.
- The enciphered session key RN = DES{KMH0,KS} *during* the session

must be protected. The random number RN is functionally equivalent to the key; PLAIN can be recovered with RN and CIPHER = DES{KS,PLAIN} with **DCPH**. If a session lasts many hours, the exposure of RN may pose a risk.

KMH and its variants KMH0, KMH1 are protected by storing them in a device that is not addressable [IBM3,4]. RN is not capable of such protection since there are too many sessions in progress to store all session keys. Moreover, if we were to store a table of all session keys in main memory in a "secure" area or in the IBM 3848 (which is attached to an IO channel), we still have the problem of preventing the opponent from masquerading as *User i* and thereby obtaining *User i*'s RN. On the other hand, RN is transient, and so the exposure may be tolerable. In addition, an opponent who obtains RN must use the host to obtain the plaintext unless some way is found to recover KS from DES{KMH0,KS}. Note that the IBM approach to key management assigns keys to *devices* and not to *users*.

7.6 THE MIDNIGHT ATTACK

The term *midnight attack* refers to the recording of the transmissions between a terminal and host that are to be replayed later for decipherment (at midnight). Variability must be introduced in the transmissions from the host to the terminal, as in the banking application, when the session is established, to preclude the reuse of a previous transmission. The variable information in the IBM Cryptographic Subsystem is derived from the terminal—the contents of some registers—and is believed to be beyond the control of an opponent.

PROBLEMS

7.1 What is the effect of adding the instruction **EMKi**

$$\textbf{EMKi} : \mathrm{X} \rightarrow \mathrm{DES\{KMHi,X\}} \qquad \mathrm{i} = 0,1$$

to the set of instructions in the IBM Cryptographic Subsystem?

7.2 What is the effect of adding the instruction **DMKi**

$$\textbf{DMKi} : \mathrm{X} \rightarrow \mathrm{DES}^{-1}\mathrm{\{KMHi,X\}} \qquad \mathrm{i} = 0,1$$

to the set of instructions in the IBM Cryptographic Subsystem?

7.3 Suppose several processing systems use the IBM Cryptographic Subsystem with host master keys $\mathrm{KMH}^{(i)}$ (i = 1, 2, . . . , N). Devise a method for communicating between systems without requiring the system to either share a common host master key or to divulge their individual host master keys.

7.4 The principal objective of the IBM Cryptographic Subsystem is to protect transmissions between a terminal and the processing system. Devise a procedure, perhaps adding instructions, which will allow the processor to generate a session key KS distribute it to *Terminal i* and *Terminal j* without having to store a key-equivalent variable at the host.

7.5 To counter the *midnight attack* devise a *handshaking protocol,* in which the terminal and host sequentially interchange data. What is the principal characteristic required of the handshaking to counter the midnight attack?

CHAPTER VIII

Public Key Systems

8.1 WHY PUBLIC KEY SYSTEMS?

The *key management* solution described in Chapter 7 is limited by the necessity to store in the operating system a variable equivalent to the key. This would not be required if the processing system acted only as a switch, routing traffic between users but not deciphering at the host. We are then operating in the environment of classical cryptography, and the key can be distributed to each of the users by an alternate secure path. Distributing a key to users in an information processing system by an alternate path is a formidable problem. An elegant solution is provided by the use of public key systems, a method of key management in which the key is split up: part of the key is public information and part is private information. In this chapter, we review the recent work on public key systems.

8.2 COMPLEXITY THEORY

There are some computational problems that we feel are more complicated than others; for example, division is "harder" than addition. Complexity theory is a collection of results in computer science that attempts to quantify the statement

Problem A is harder than Problem B

Suppose $\{X^{(n)}\}$ is a sequence of sets

$$X^{(1)} \subset X^{(2)} \subset \ldots \subset X^{(n)} \subset \ldots$$

and f is a function defined on each $X^{(n)}$

$$f : X^{(n)} \rightarrow Y^{(n)}$$

Suppose we have an algorithm (program) ALG(f) for evaluating f(x) for each x in $\cup_{1 \leq n < \infty} X^{(n)}$. By the *running time ALF(f,x) of the algorithm at x,* we mean roughly the number of instructions or primitive operations required by ALG(f) to evaluate f(x). Which operations are primitive depends on the processor and programming language. For example, to sort a sequence of numbers

$$x_0, x_1, \ldots, x_{n-1}$$

means to find the permutation π of $(0, 1, \ldots, n-1)$ for which

$$x_{\pi(0)} \leq x_{\pi(1)} \leq \ldots \leq x_{\pi(n-1)}$$

Sorting uses the comparison operation

$$\text{COMPARE}\{x,y\} = \begin{cases} x & \text{if } x \leq y \\ y & \text{if } y < x \end{cases}$$

and so it is natural to treat comparison as one of the primitive operations when evaluating an algorithm to sort numbers. The complexity of ALG(f) on $\mathcal{X}^{(n)}$ is the maximum running time over all points in $\mathcal{X}^{(n)}$:

$$\text{ALG}(f, \mathcal{X}^{(n)}) = \max_{x \in \mathcal{X}^{(n)}} \text{ALG}(f,x)$$

The *complexity of f on* $\mathcal{X}^{(n)}$ is

$$\text{RT}(f, \mathcal{X}^{(n)}) = \min_{\text{ALG}} \text{ALG}(f, \mathcal{X}^{(n)})$$

We say that the algorithm ALG computes f in *polynomial time* if

$$\text{ALG}(f, \mathcal{X}^{(i)}) \leq P(i) \qquad \text{as } i \rightarrow \infty$$

where P is some polynomial, and we write ALG(f) = O(P).* **P** is the class of all polynomial time algorithms. An algorithm belongs to the class **EXP** if its running time is $O(e^{|P(i)|})$ for some polynomial P. We have

$$\mathbf{P} \subseteq \mathbf{EXP}$$

Two additional classes of problems are defined [AH]. Suppose F is a statement in the predicate calculus which is either true or false (1 or 0).

$$F : \mathcal{X}^{(n)} \rightarrow \{0,1\}$$

The problem of deciding whether F is true or false belongs to the class **NP** if there is an algorithm G in **P** that can check the truth of F given a possible solution. For example, let $F(L : x_0, x_1, \ldots, x_{n-1})$ be the problem of determining if the equation

$$L = \sum_{0 \leq i < n} x_i y_i$$

has a solution $(y_0, y_1, \ldots, y_{n-1}) \in \mathbf{Z}_{2,n}$. F is in **NP**, since a guess $(y_0, y_1, \ldots, y_{n-1}) \in \mathbf{Z}_{2,n}$ can be checked in polynomial time (proportional to n) by evaluating the sum. We have the containing relationship

---

*O(P) is the notation of G. F. Hardy; if h and g are functions of some parameter n, which takes values 1, 2, . . . , we write h = O(g) as $n \rightarrow \infty$, which is read: "h is big-O of g at ∞" if for some constant C

$$|h(n)| \leq C|g(n)|$$

for all n.

We write h = o(g) as $n \rightarrow \infty$, which is read: "h is little-o of g at ∞" if for every $\epsilon > 0$, there is a value $N = N(\epsilon)$ such that

$$|h(n)| \leq \epsilon|g(n)| \qquad \text{for } n \geq N$$

$$\mathbf{P} \subseteq \mathbf{NP}$$

It is *not* known if **NP** is strictly bigger than **P**.

There is a distinguished subclass of **NP**, the class of **NP-complete** problems, which in a sense are the "hardest" **NP** problems. A problem F in **NP-complete** is characterized by the fact that any problem G in **NP** is reducible to F; an algorithm ALG(G) of running time T_G to solve G can be transformed to an algorithm ALG(F) of running time $P(T_G)$ to solve F, where P is a polynomial.

The class **NP-complete** is thought to be a source of problems that can be adapted to cryptographic applications, and will, by virtue of their computational complexity, produce strong cryptographic systems. We shall consider examples that both support and run counter to this conjecture.

8.3 TRAP DOOR AND ONE-WAY FUNCTIONS

Suppose that

$$\boldsymbol{X}^{(1)} \subset \boldsymbol{X}^{(2)} \subset \ldots \subset \boldsymbol{X}^{(n)} \subset \ldots$$

and f is a function defined on each $\boldsymbol{X}^{(n)}$.

Definition 8.3.1 The function f is *easy to compute* if there exists an algorithm ALG(f) to compute f in **P**. The function f is *hard to compute* if no algorithm ALG(f) to compute f belongs to **P** *or* if an algorithm that computes f is not *known* to belong to **P**.

Now let us further assume that f is a one-to-one mapping from its domain $\boldsymbol{X}^{(n)}$ to its range $\boldsymbol{Y}^{(n)}$,

$$f : \boldsymbol{X}^{(n)} \to \boldsymbol{Y}^{(n)}$$

so that f^{-1} exists,

$$f^{-1} : \boldsymbol{Y}^{(n)} \to \boldsymbol{X}^{(n)}$$

Definition 8.3.2 A function f is a *one-way function* if f is easy to compute but f^{-1} is hard to compute.

Definition 8.3.3 A function f is a *trap door function* if (1) f is easy to compute, and (2) there exists some side information (or key) without which f is a one-way function; given the side information, f^{-1} is easy to compute. A few examples will illustrate the meaning of "hard" and "easy."

Example 8.3.1 A *primitive* root of a prime number p is an integer q, $1 < q \leq p - 1$, with the property that the sequence of residues

$$q^i \text{ (modulo p)} \qquad 0 \leq i < p$$

is a permutation of $\boldsymbol{Z}_p - \{0\} = \{1, 2, \ldots, p-1\}$. For example, with $p = 7$,

k	**1**	**2**	**3**	**4**	**5**	**6**
2^k (modulo 7)	2	4	1	2	4	1
3^k (modulo 7)	3	2	6	4	5	1
4^k (modulo 7)	4	2	1	4	2	1
5^k (modulo 7)	5	4	6	2	3	1
6^k (modulo 7)	6	1	6	1	6	1

Thus 3 and 5 are primitive roots modulo 7. In general, there are $\varphi(p-1)$ primitive roots modulo p [WA], where $\varphi(k)$ (the *Euler totient* function) is the number of integers less than k that are relatively prime to k.

Enumerate the prime numbers

$$p_1, p_2, \ldots$$

choose a primitive q_n for each prime p_n and set

$$f : X^{(n)} = Z_{p_n} \rightarrow Y^{(n)} = Z_{p_n}$$

$$f(j) = q_n^j \text{ (modulo p)} \qquad 1 \leq n < \infty$$

f is easy to compute; it requires approximately $\log_2 p_n$ multiplications [KN]. For example, to compute q^{74}, we write the base 2 representation of 74

$$74 \rightarrow (1,0,0,1,0,1,0) = 2^6 + 2^3 + 2^1$$

We then evaluate by successive squaring the products

q^2	1 multiplication	$q \times q$
q^4	1 multiplication	$q^2 \times q^2$
q^8	1 multiplication	$q^4 \times q^4$
q^{16}	1 multiplication	$q^8 \times q^8$
q^{32}	1 multiplication	$q^{16} \times q^{16}$
q^{64}	1 multiplication	$q^{32} \times q^{32}$

and finally multiply $q^{64} \times q^8 \times q^2$ (2 multiplications) to obtain q^{74}.

The inverse problem

given : q^k (modulo p) *find* : k

is *conjectured* to be more difficult. Because of the analogy with exponentiation and logarithms, the problem of finding k given q^k (modulo p) is called the *logarithm problem.* The only bounds on the number of computational steps required to solve the logarithm problem are upper bounds. For example, it is known that the logarithm problem can be solved in $O(p^{1/2})$ steps [KN]. Under an additional hypothesis on the factors of $p-1$, one can sharpen this upper bound to $O(\log^2 p)$ [PO2]. The best known upper bound is [AD2]:

$$O(e^{O((\log p \log\log p)^{1/2})})$$

What is really wanted is a *lower bound* L(p); a statement that the number of steps is at least L(p). No lower bound is known.

Example 8.3.2 Let $\mathbf{a} = (a_0, a_1, \ldots, a_{n-1})$ be a vector of positive integers,

$$X = Z_{2,n} \qquad Y = Z_A \qquad A = 1 + \sum_{0 \le i < n} a_i$$

and let f be defined by

$$f : \mathbf{x} = (x_0, x_1, \ldots, x_{n-1}) = \sum_{0 \le i < n} x_i a_i$$

The function f is easy to compute; it requires $n - 1$ additions. The inverse problem,

$$\textit{given} : \mathbf{a} = (a_0, a_1, \ldots, a_{n-1}) \text{ and } L = \sum_{0 \le i < n} a_i x_i$$

$$\textit{find} : \mathbf{x} = (x_0, x_1, \ldots, x_{n-1}) \in Z_{2,n}$$

called the *knapsack problem,* is believed to be much harder. The knapsack problem is **NP-complete.**

If we have an algorithm for the knapsack problem $ALG(L : a_0, a_1, \ldots, a_{n-1})$, which answers *yes* or *no* to the question of whether or not a solution exists, it can be modified to find a solution in polynomial time as follows:

Step 1 Set $j = 0$

Step 2 Evaluate $ALG(L : a_{j+1}, \ldots, a_{n-1})$

Step 3 If *yes,* replace j by $j + 1$ and return to *Step 2* if $j < n$; otherwise END. If *no,* replace L by $L - a_j$, j by $j + 1$, and return to *Step 2* if $j < n$; otherwise END.

8.4 A PUBLIC KEY SYSTEM BASED ON THE LOGARITHM PROBLEM

Assume that for suitably large p, the logarithm problem is computationally intractable; given q^k (modulo p), q, and p, the number of operations required to recover k is too large for practical computation. Starting with this assumption, we can construct a strong *public key interchange system* [DI].

The *public key directory* shown in Fig. 8.4.1 is prepared with entries for each user of the system. The ith user selects a *secret key* k_i and computes the *directory entry* q^{k_i} (modulo p). When *User i* and *User j* wish to communicate, the following steps are followed:

- *User i* uses k_i and the directory entry q^{k_j} of *User j* to calculate

$$k_{i,j} = (q^{k_j})^{k_i} \text{ (modulo p)} = q^{k_j k_i} \text{ (modulo p)}.$$

- *User j* uses k_j and the entry q^{k_i} of *User i* to calculate

$$k_{j,i} = (q^{k_i})^{k_j} \text{ (modulo p)} = q^{k_i k_j} \text{ (modulo p)}.$$

User Name	Directory Entry
User 1	q^{k_1}
User 2	q^{k_2}
.	.
.	.
.	.
User N	q^{k_N}

Figure 8.4.1. Public Key Directory.

Since $k_{i,j} = k_{j,i}$, the two parties have established a common key. If there is concern that the repeated use by *User i* and *User j* of the same key might compromise the key, the encipherment protocol can be modified; $k_{i,j} = k_{j,i}$ will serve as an *intermediate key* used to encipher some known but variable information—say the time and date concatenated with the users' names—to derive a common *working key.*

(User i, User j) can communicate with a special shared key without revealing their private keys to the system. The problem of user-to-user key distribution has not been completely solved, since the directory must be accessible by the users of the system and might be altered in some attack. For example, the *User m* might take the following steps to masquerade as *User j* to *User i:*

- *User m* replaces the entry (j,q^{k_j}) by (j,q^{k_m}) in order to masquerade as *User j* to *User i*
- *User i* computes the common key $k'_{i,j} = (q^{k_m})^{k_i}$ (modulo p), believing it to be $k_{i,j}$
- At the conclusion of the communication, *User m* restores the entry (j,q^{k_m}) to (j,q^{k_j})

We cannot truly protect a directory with 1000 entries; many users will have privileged status, allowing unlimited access to the directory. There are several possible remedies for this exposure. For example, we could provide each user with a directory enciphered in his private key or publish a "telephone" directory with each user's entry. It is characteristic of this and other public key exchange systems that the public information, in this case the pairs $\{(i,q^{k_i} \text{ (modulo p)})\}$ must be protected against alteration.

8.5 ADELMAN'S ANALYSIS OF THE LOGARITHM PROBLEM

The Logarithm Problem

Given α, β, and p (a prime), find x satisfying

$$\alpha^x = \beta \text{ (modulo p)}$$

In this section we sketch a recent solution to the logarithm problem announced in [AD2]. The results are based on unpublished work of R. Schroepel.

Definition 8.5.1 A number γ is *smooth* with respect to a bound BD, if the factorization of γ into primes,

$$\gamma = p_1^{e_1} p_2^{e_2} \ldots p_k^{e_k}$$

involves only prime numbers $\{p_k\}$ that satisfy $p_k \leq BD$.

The following algorithm solves the logarithm problem.

Step 1 Find by random sampling (and checking) an integer R such that (1) $B = \beta^R$ (modulo n) is smooth with respect to the bound

$$BD(p) = e^{(\log p \ \log\log p)^{0.5}}$$

and (2)

$$(R, p - 1) = 1$$

Step 2 Let $p_1, p_2, \ldots, p_m$ be the primes $\leq BD(p)$. Find by random sampling (and checking) integers $\{R_i : 1 \leq i \leq m\}$ such that (1) $A_i = \alpha^{R_i}$ (modulo p) is smooth with respect to the bound BD(p), and (2) the vectors $\mathbf{A}_i$,

$$\mathbf{A}_i = (e_{i,1}, e_{i,2}, \ldots, e_{i,m})$$

$$A_i = \prod_{1 \leq j \leq m} p_j^{e_{i,j}}$$

span the m-dimensional vector space over the field $\boldsymbol{Z}_p$.

Step 3 By Gaussian elimination express

$$\mathbf{B} = (f_1, f_2, \ldots, f_m)$$

$$B = \prod_{1 \leq j \leq m} p_j^{f_j}$$

as a linear combination of the $\{\mathbf{A}_i\}$,

$$\mathbf{B} = \eta_1 \mathbf{A}_1 + \eta_2 \mathbf{A}_2 + \ldots + \eta_m \mathbf{A}_m \text{ (modulo p } - 1)$$

We claim

$$B = \prod_{1 \le i \le m} \alpha^{\eta_i R_i}$$

To prove this, write

$$\log B = \sum_{1 \le j \le m} f_j \log p_j$$

Then

$$\log B = \sum_{1 \le j \le m} \left(\sum_{1 \le i \le m} \eta_i e_{i,j} + K_j(p-1) \right) \log p_j,$$

which when exponentiated, yields

$$B = \prod_{1 \le i \le m} \left(\prod_{1 \le j \le m} p_j^{e_{i,j}} \right)^{\eta_i} \text{(modulo p)}$$

or

$$B = \prod_{1 \le i \le m} A_i^{\eta_i}$$

Replacing A_i by α^{R_i} completes the proof.

Step 4 Calculate R^{-1} (modulo $p - 1$). Then

$$\beta = \prod_{1 \le i \le m} \alpha^{\eta_i R_i R^{-1}}$$

It remains to estimate how much computation is required by this algorithm. Let

$$\Psi(x,y)/x = \Pr\{Z \text{ is smooth with respect to } y/z \le x\}$$

We will use the following result of P. Erdos.

Theorem 8.5.2 [VE,HAL]

(8.5.1) $$\log \Psi(x,y) \approx \log C(\pi(y) + [u],[u])$$

where $C(n,m)$ is the binomial coefficient, $\pi(y)$ is the number of primes less than or equal to y, [u] is the integer part of u and $u \approx \log x/\log y$. Equation (8.5.1) holds uniformly in y,

$$2 \le y \le x^{\epsilon(x)}$$

where $\epsilon(x) \to 0$ as $x \to \infty$.

We shall prove the weaker result:

$$\Psi(x,y) \geq C(\pi(y) + [u],[u])$$

Proof. $C(n + m,m)$ is the number of partitions of the integer n into $m + 1$ parts. If the integer v has the prime factorization

$$v = \prod_{1 \leq i \leq s} p_i^{e_i}$$

and is smooth with respect to y, then

$$v \leq y^{e_1 + \ldots + e_s}$$

If $\{e_i : 0 \leq i \leq s\}$ is a partition of $[u]$ into $s + 1 = \pi(y) + 1$ parts, then

$$v \leq y^{e_0 + e_1 + \ldots + e_s} \leq y^{e_1 + \ldots + e_s} = y^{[u]} = y^{[\log x/\log y]} \leq x$$

so that each of the $C(\pi(y) + [u],[u])$ partitions of $[u]$ into $\pi(y) + 1$ parts yields a distinct an integer $\leq x$. ◀

Now let $y = e^{(\log x \ \mathrm{loglog}\ x)^{0.5}}$; then

$$u = \log x/\{\log x \ \mathrm{loglog}\ x\}^{0.5} < \log x < \pi(y)$$

so that

$$C(\pi(y) + [u],[u]) \approx (\pi(y))^{[u]}/[u]!$$

Apply Stirling's estimate for the factorial [FEL],

$$\log \Psi(x,y) \approx [u](\log \pi(y) - \log[u] + 1)$$

substitute $u = \log x/\log y$ and use the estimate from the prime number theorem [LEV],

$$\pi(y) \approx y/\log y$$

We obtain

$$\log \Psi(x,y) \approx (\log x/\log y)[\log y - \mathrm{loglog}\ y - \mathrm{loglog}\ x + \mathrm{loglog}\ y + 1]$$

or

$$\log \Psi(x,y) \approx \log x - [\log x \ \mathrm{loglog}\ x/\log y] + [\log x/\log y]$$

$$\Psi(x,y)/x \approx e^{-(\log x/\log y)(\mathrm{loglog}\ x - 1)}$$

Thus the expected number of tries need to obtain a smooth number is approximately

$$T(x,y) \approx e^{(\log x/\log y)(\mathrm{loglog}\ x - 1)}$$

This search must be carried out $\pi(y) \approx y/\log y = e^{\log y - \mathrm{loglog}\ y}$ times, so that the computational effort is

$$T(x,y)\pi(y) \approx e^{(\log x/\log y)(\log\log x - 1) + \log y)}$$

But $e^{a/b+b}$ $(a > 0)$ is maximized when $b = a^{0.5}$, and this gives a computational effort of the order

$$\text{(8.5.2)} \qquad RT(p) = e^{2(\log x \ \log\log x)^{0.5}}$$

A sharper analysis can be made that gets rid of the factor 2 in the exponent in Eq. (8.5.2) and yields the following theorem.

Theorem 8.5.3 An upper bound for the logarithm problem is

$$\text{(8.5.3)} \qquad RT(p) = e^{(\log p \ \log\log p)^{0.5}}$$

RT(p) grows very rapidly with p. If we assume that each operation requires 1 μs, the bound in Eq. (8.5.3) yields the following running times for the logarithm problem [RI1]:

D(p)	Number of Operations	Time
50	1.4×10^{10}	3.9 hours
75	9.0×10^{12}	104 days
100	2.3×10^{15}	73 years
200	1.2×10^{23}	3.8×10^{9} years
300	1.5×10^{29}	4.8×10^{15} years
500	1.3×10^{39}	4.2×10^{25} years

8.6 A PUBLIC KEY SYSTEM BASED ON THE KNAPSACK PROBLEM

Given an integer N and the vector

$$\mathbf{a} = (a_0, a_1, \ldots, a_{n-1})$$

the *knapsack problem* is to find a solution

$$\mathbf{x} = (x_0, x_1, \ldots, x_{n-1}) \qquad x_i = 0 \text{ or } 1,\ 0 \le i < n$$

of the equation

$$N = \sum_{0 \le i < n} a_i x_i$$

We refer to **x** as the $\{a_i\}$-*representation* of N and $\{a_i\}$ as the *knapsack lengths.* As **x** ranges over the set $\boldsymbol{Z}_{2,n}$ of n-grams, the sum

$$\sum_{0 \le i < n} a_i x_i$$

takes values in a set denoted by $KNAPV[\{a_i\}]$. $KNAPV[\{a_i\}]$ contains *at most* 2^n entries. For example, for $n = 3$,

$$KNAPV[\{1,2,3\}] = \{0,1,2,3,4,5,6\}$$
$$KNAPV[\{1,2,4\}] = \{0,1,2,3,4,5,6,7\}$$

When $\mathbf{a} = (1,2,3)$, the integer $N = 3$ admits two representations, while for $\mathbf{a} = (1,2,4)$, each integer in $\{0,1,2,3,4,5,6,7\}$ has a unique representation.

A *polynomial time algorithm* for the knapsack problem $ALG(\{a_i\},N)$ is an algorithm which:

given : knapsack lengths $\mathbf{a} = (a_0, a_1, \ldots, a_{n-1})$ and N

finds : a solution $\mathbf{x} = (x_0, x_1, \ldots, x_{n-1})$

$$N = \sum \mathbf{a}_i \mathbf{x}_i$$

or shows that there is no solution in polynomial time. The knapsack problem belongs to **NP-complete** and is hard in the sense that no polynomial-time algorithm to solve the general knapsack problem is known.

The assertion that the knapsack problem is **NP-complete** means that there exists *at least one* hard knapsack problem $\{a_i\}$. For special knapsack lengths, finding a solution to the knapsack problem poses no difficulty. For example, if

$$\mathbf{a} = (1,2, \ldots, 2^{n-1})$$

the (unique) knapsack representation of each integer N, $0 \leq N < 2^n$, requires finding the base 2 representation of N and presents no difficulties. More generally, if the numbers $\{a_i : 0 \leq i < n\}$ increase fast enough,

$$a_i > \sum_{0 \leq j < i} a_j \qquad 0 \leq i < n \tag{8.6.1}$$

the determination of the (unique) $\{a_i\}$-representation for each N in $KNAPV[\{a_i\}]$ involves at most n computational steps. For example, with

$$\mathbf{a} = (1,3,9,15)$$

we determine the representation of $N = 16$ as follows. Since

$$a_0 + a_1 + a_2 = 13 < N < 28 = a_0 + a_1 + a_2 + a_3$$

we must require $x_3 = 1$. Replacing N by $N - a_3 = 1$, we have to solve the reduced knapsack problem

$$1 = a_0x_0 + a_1x_1 + a_2x_2$$

Since $\min\{a_1,a_2\} > 1$, it follows that $x_1 = x_2 = 0$, and we finally conclude that $x_0 = 1$. Equation (8.o.1) implies both that (1) the representation of N, when possible, is unique and that (2) the representation may be found in at most n computational steps. It is believed that "most" knapsack problems are hard, and thus finding the solution to a randomly chosen knapsack problem will be hard.

Let m be a large positive integer. The *knapsack problem modulo m* is

$$\textit{given}: \mathrm{N} \in \boldsymbol{Z}_{\mathbf{m}} \text{ and } \mathbf{a} = (a_0, a_1, \ldots, a_{n-1})$$

$$\textit{find}: \mathbf{x} = (x_0, x_1, \ldots, x_{n-1}) \in \boldsymbol{Z}_{\mathbf{2,n}}$$

satisfying

$$N = \left(\sum_{0 \le i < n} a_i x_i\right) \text{ (modulo m)}$$

Deciding if the *knapsack problem modulo m* has a solution is also an **NP-complete** problem and has been made the basis of a public key system.

Randomly select an easy knapsack problem $\mathbf{a}'$ from some class *EASY*[n,m] of easy knapsack problems modulo m and an integer w in $\boldsymbol{Z}_{\mathbf{m}}$ relatively prime to m, so that the equation

$$ww' = 1 \text{ (modulo m)}$$

has a solution w′. Replace the easy knapsack problem $\{a_i'\}$ by the knapsack problem $\{a_i\}$, using the transformation

$$a_i' \rightarrow a_i = T_w a_i' = (w a_i') \text{ (modulo m)}$$

It is hoped that the transformation T_w replaces an easy knapsack problem $\{a_i'\}$ with a hard knapsack problem $\{a_i\}$. Why is $\{a_i\}$ believed to be a hard problem? It is primarily an act of faith based upon the supposition that (1) almost all knapsack problems are hard, and that (2) the transformation T_w maps *EASY*[n,m] in a uniform manner into the class of all knapsack problems modulo m. If *EASY*[n,m] contains a large number of easy problems, an opponent who has access to **a** but not w is confronted either with

- The task of trying all possible values of w relatively prime to m and $\mathbf{a}' \in$ *EASY*, or
- Solving the knapsack problem **a** directly.

If *EASY*[n,m] contains a large number of knapsack lengths and m is large, the first option is not feasible, while the second option depends upon finding a good algorithm for a seemingly general knapsack problem. These assertions are conjectural, since there is no proof that the transformation

$$\mathbf{a}' \rightarrow T_w \mathbf{a}' = \mathbf{a}$$

replaces most easy knapsack problems by hard knapsack problems.

To use the knapsack problem as a public key system, *User i*

- Chooses an easy knapsack problem,

$$\{a_{i,j}' : 0 \le j < n\} \subseteq EASY[n,m]$$

- A secret w (relatively prime to m), and
- Publishes the vector $\mathbf{a} = (a_{i,0}, a_{i,1}, \ldots, a_{i,n-1})$ with $a_{i,j} = wa'_{i,j}$ (modulo m).

If *User j* wishes to transmit the plaintext $\mathbf{x} = (x_0, x_1, \ldots, x_{n-1})$ to *User i,* the public table of knapsack entries is referenced to find

$$\mathbf{a} = (a_{i,0}, a_{i,1}, \ldots, a_{i,n-1})$$

and the integer N

$$N = \left(\sum_{0 \le j < n} a_{i,j} x_j \right) \text{ (modulo m)}$$

is transmitted to *User i. User i* then may calculate

$$N' = w'N \text{ (modulo m)}$$

since w is known by *User i.* But the equation

$$N' = \left(\sum_{0 \le j < n} w' a_{i,j} x_j \right) \text{ (modulo m)}$$

is the same as the equation

$$N' = \left(\sum_{0 \le j < n} a'_{i,j} x_j \right) \text{ (modulo m)}$$

User i can solve this easy knapsack problem and thus recover the plaintext $\mathbf{x}$.

We can generate easy knapsack problems as follows; take $n = 100$ and choose $\{a'_i : 0 \le i < n\}$ by n independent chance experiments; the value of a'_i is the result of a chance experiment with values uniformly distributed over an interval I_i:

$$I_i = \begin{cases} [1, 2^{100}] & \text{if } i = 0 \\ [1 + (2^{i-1} - 1)2^{100}, 2^{100+i-1}] & \text{if } 0 < i < n \end{cases}$$

The knapsack lengths $\{a'_i\}$ that result then satisfy Eq. (8.6.1). There are 2^{100} possible values for a'_i. The $\{a'_i\}$ satisfy

$$a'_i > \sum_{0 \le j < i} a'_j \qquad 0 \le i < n$$

Next, w is derived from of a chance experiment. Select an integer v as the result of a chance experiment with values in and uniformly distributed on $\boldsymbol{Z}_\mathbf{m} - \{0\}$ and define w by $w = v/\gcd(v,m)$. *User i* publishes the knapsack vector

$$\mathbf{a}_i = (a_{i,0}, a_{i,1}, \ldots, a_{i,n-1})$$

with

$$a_{i,j} = wa'_{i,j} \text{ (modulo m)}$$

If m is a prime number, then each a_i is uniformly distributed on $\boldsymbol{Z}_\mathbf{m} - \{0\}$. Each

$$N = \left(\sum_{0 \le i < n} a_i x_i \right) \text{ (modulo m)}$$

requires (at most) 202 bits in its binary representation,

$$N = (N_0, N_1, \ldots, N_{201})$$

so that encipherment maps a plaintext block of 100 bits,

$$\mathbf{x} = (x_0, x_1, \ldots, x_{99})$$

into a ciphertext block of 202 blocks, a 2.02:1 data expansion. Only 2^{100} of the approximately 2^{202}-blocks in $\boldsymbol{Z}_{2,101}$ correspond to ciphertext N

$$N = \left(\sum_{0 \leq i < n} a_i x_i \right) (\text{modulo } m)$$

If there is some doubt about the difficulty of solving the knapsack problem,

$$\mathbf{a} = (a_0, a_1, \ldots, a_{n-1})$$

iterate the transformation T_w; choose a sequence of numbers $\{m_k : 0 \leq k \leq K\}$ and randomly select integers $\{w_k : 0 \leq k \leq K\}$ with w_k relatively prime to m_k. Starting with an easy knapsack problem,

$$\mathbf{a}' = (a'_0, a'_1, \ldots, a'_{n-1})$$

we define the sequence of knapsack lengths

$$\mathbf{a}_k = (a_{k,0}, a_{k,1}, \ldots, a_{k,n-1}) \qquad 1 \leq k \leq K$$

by

$$\mathbf{a}_k = w_k \mathbf{a}_{k-1} (\text{modulo } m_k) \qquad 1 \leq k \leq K, \quad \mathbf{a}_0 = \mathbf{a}'$$

The *public key* of *User i* is the vector of knapsack lengths $\mathbf{a}_K$.

8.7 CRITIQUE OF THE KNAPSACK PROBLEM AS THE BASIS FOR A PUBLIC KEY SYSTEM

The private information in the knapsack problem consists of both the modulus m and the multiplier w. What happens if m is known? In [SH4], an analysis of the knapsack problem is given to recover the knapsack lengths

$$\mathbf{a}' = (a'_0, a'_1, \ldots, a'_{n-1})$$

$$a_i = w a'_i (\text{modulo } m) \qquad 0 \leq i \leq n$$

$$a'_i \in I_i = [1 + (2^i - 1)2^{100}, 2^{100+i}] \qquad 0 \leq i < n$$

$$a'_i > \sum_{0 \leq j < i} a'_j \qquad 0 < i < n$$

if m is known.

The analysis starts by determining the ratio

$$\rho = a_0/a_1 \text{ (modulo m)*}$$

Since $a_i = wa_i'$ (modulo m), it follows that

$$\rho = a_0'/a_1' \text{ (modulo m)}$$

Next, consider the set of residues modulo m

$$\Delta = \{\rho \text{ (modulo m)}, 2\rho \text{ (modulo m)}, \ldots, 2^{101}\rho \text{ (modulo m)}\}$$

Since $a_1' \in I_1 = [1 + 2^{100}, 2^{101}]$, the knapsack length $a_0' = \rho a_1'$ is an element of Δ. A sequence of integers from $\boldsymbol{Z}_{\mathbf{m}}$

$$\mathbf{c} = (c_0, c_1, \ldots, c_{N-1}, \ldots)$$

is said to be *uniformly distributed* (on $\boldsymbol{Z}_{\mathbf{m}}$) if the ratio

$$(1/N)\,|\{j : 0 \leq j < N \textit{ and } \alpha \leq c_j < \beta\}|$$

has the limiting value $(\beta - \alpha)/m$ as $N \rightarrow \infty$ for every α, and β, $0 \leq \alpha \leq \beta < m$. For example, the sequence of residues

$$j\rho \text{ (modulo m)} \qquad 0 \leq j < \infty$$

is known to be uniformly distributed on $\boldsymbol{Z}_{\mathbf{m}}$ [CA,LEV].

The residues in Δ are "approximately" uniformly distributed. Thus we will argue that the smallest element of Δ is likely to be of the order

$$m/2^{101} \approx 2^{202}/2^{101} = 2^{101}.$$

Since $a_0' \in I_0 = [1,2^{100}]$, it is reasonable to expect that a_0' will be the minimal element of Δ. Once a_0' is found, w and

$$\mathbf{a}' = (a_0', a_1', \ldots, a_{n-1}')$$

can be recovered. It remains to show that the minimal element in Δ can be determined by a computationally feasible procedure.

8.8 BEST RATIONAL APPROXIMATIONS TO ϑ

If ϑ is a real number, let

$$[\vartheta] : \text{integer part of } \vartheta \qquad \{\vartheta\} : \text{fractional part of } \vartheta$$

$$\|\vartheta\| : \text{distance from } \vartheta \text{ to the nearest integer}$$

We have

$$0 \leq \|\vartheta\| = \min(\{\vartheta, 1 - \{\vartheta\}) \leq 1/2$$

*We assume that m is a prime so that a_1^{-1} exists.

Fix an integer q and consider the minimum value of $|(p/q) - \vartheta|$ over all choices of integers p. Since $|(p/q) - \vartheta| = q^{-1}|q\vartheta - p|$, we have

$$\min_p |(p/q) - \vartheta| = q^{-1}\|q\vartheta\|$$

Lemma 8.8.1 For each $Q > 1$, there exists an integer q satisfying

$$\|q\vartheta\| \leq Q^{-1} \qquad 0 < q < Q \tag{8.8.1}$$

Proof. Assume without loss of generality that Q is an integer. By the *pigeon-hole principle,* at least two of the $Q + 1$ numbers,

$$0, \{\vartheta\}, \{2\vartheta\}, \ldots, \{(Q-1)\vartheta\}, 1$$

belong to a common subinterval $\{J_j : 0 \leq j < Q\}$

$$J_0 = [0, 1/Q)$$
$$J_1 = [1/Q, 2/Q)$$
$$\ldots$$
$$\ldots$$
$$\ldots$$
$$J_{Q-2} = [(Q-2)/Q, (Q-1)/Q)$$
$$J_{Q-1} = [(Q-1)/Q, 1]$$

This implies that $|(r_1\vartheta - s_1) - (r_2\vartheta - s_2)| < Q^{-1}$ and $r_1 \geq r_2$, which proves the lemma by setting $q = r_1 - r_2$. ◀

Remark Lemma 8.8.1 implies that there are infinitely many integer solutions to the inequality

$$q\|q\vartheta\| < 1$$

Definition 8.8.2 A fraction p/q is a *best rational approximation to* ϑ if

$$\|q\vartheta\| = |q\vartheta - p|$$
$$\|q'\vartheta\| > \|q\vartheta\| \quad \text{for } q' < q$$

both hold.

Define the sequences $\{q_i : i \geq 1\}$ and $\{p_i : i \geq 1\}$ by

$$\|q_n\vartheta\| = |q_n\vartheta - p_n| \tag{8.8.2}$$

$$\|q_{n+1}\vartheta\| < \|q_n\vartheta\| \tag{8.8.3}$$

$$\|q\vartheta\| \geq \|q_n\vartheta\| \qquad 0 < q < q_{n+1} \tag{8.8.4}$$

$$1 = q_1 < q_2 < \ldots \tag{8.8.5}$$

Remarks

1. The rational numbers $\{p_n/q_n\}$ are *all* of the best rational approximations to ϑ arranged in ascending order of q_n.
2. If ϑ is a rational number, then $\vartheta = p_N/q_N$ for some N.

In the next group of lemmata, we prove several important properties of the best rational approximation.

Lemma 8.8.3

$$(q_{n+1}\vartheta - p_{n+1})(q_n\vartheta - p_n) \leq 0 \tag{8.8.6}$$

Proof. Suppose that, on the contrary,

$$(q_{n+1}\vartheta - p_{n+1})(q_n\vartheta - p_n) > 0$$

Then either

$$q_n\vartheta - p_n > q_{n+1}\vartheta - p_{n+1} > 0 \tag{8.8.7}$$

or

$$p_n - q_n\vartheta > p_{n+1} - q_{n+1}\vartheta > 0$$

If Eq. (8.8.7) holds, then by setting $q' = q_{n+1} - q_n$, we obtain

$$\|q'\vartheta\| < \|q_n\vartheta\| \qquad 0 < q' < q_{n+1}$$

which is contradicted by Eq. (8.8.4). ◀

Lemma 8.8.4

$$q_{n+1}p_n - q_np_{n+1} = \pm 1$$

Proof. First,

$$|q_{n+1}p_n - q_np_{n+1}| = |q_n(q_{n+1}\vartheta - p_{n+1}) - q_{n+1}(q_n\vartheta - p_n)| \tag{8.8.8}$$

$$\leq q_n\|q_{n+1}\vartheta\| + q_{n+1}\|q_n\vartheta\|$$

We assert that

$$q_{n+1}\|q_n\vartheta\| \leq 1 \tag{8.8.9}$$

To prove the inequality (8.8.9), apply Lemma 8.8.1 with $Q = q_{n+1}$; accordingly, there is an integer q, $0 < q < q_{n+1}$ such that

$$q_{n+1}\|q\vartheta\| \leq 1$$

If the inequality (8.8.9) does not hold,

$$q_{n+1}\|q_n\vartheta\| > 1$$

then

$$\|q\vartheta\| < \|q_n\vartheta\| \qquad \text{for some q, } 0 < q < q_{n+1}$$

which contradicts Eq. (8.8.4). Finally,

$$q_n\|q_{n+1}\| < q_{n+1}\|q_n\| \leq 1$$

by Eqs. (8.8.3) and (8.8.5). Thus

$$|q_{n+1}p_n - q_np_{n+1}| < 2$$

which implies that the integer $q_{n+1}p_n - q_np_{n+1}$ takes the value 1 or -1. ◀

Lemma 8.8.5

$$\text{sign}(q_{n+1}p_n - q_np_{n+1}) \times \text{sign}(q_n\vartheta - p_n) = -1$$

Proof. Equations (8.8.6) and (8.8.8). ◀

Lemma 8.8.6

$$q_{n+1}p_n - q_np_{n+1} = -[q_np_{n-1} - q_{n-1}p_n] \tag{8.8.10}$$

Proof. Lemmata 8.8.2 and 8.8.4. ◀

Lemma 8.8.7

$$q_n\|q_{n+1}\vartheta\| + q_{n+1}\|q_n\vartheta\| = 1$$

Proof. Equation (8.8.8) and Lemmata 8.8.2 and 8.8.4. ◀

Lemma 8.8.8 $\gcd\{p_n, q_n\} = 1$

Proof. Since

$$p_nq_{n+1} - q_np_{n+1} = \pm 1$$

p_n and q_n cannot have a nontrivial common factor. ◀

Lemma 8.8.9 For $n \geq 2$, there exists an integer a_n such that

$$p_{n+1} = a_np_n + p_{n-1} \tag{8.8.11}$$

$$q_{n+1} = a_nq_n + q_{n-1} \tag{8.8.12}$$

Proof. Using Eq. (8.8.10) and Lemma 8.8.8, we have

$$p_n(q_{n+1} - q_{n-1}) = q_n(p_{n+1} - p_{n-1})$$

which implies that both of the ratios

$$(q_{n+1} - q_{n-1})/q_n \qquad (p_{n+1} - p_{n-1})/p_n$$

must be integers and equal. ◀

Lemma 8.8.10 For $n \geq 2$,

$$|q_{n-1}\vartheta - p_{n-1}| = a_n|q_n\vartheta - p_n| + |q_{n+1}\vartheta - p_{n+1}|$$

Proof. Multiply Eq. (8.8.12) by ϑ, subtract Eq. (8.8.11), and use Lemma 8.8.3. ◀

Lemma 8.8.11

$$a_n = \left[\frac{|q_{n-1}\vartheta - p_{n-1}|}{|q_n\vartheta - p_n|} \right]$$

Proof. By Lemma 8.8.10, the integer a_n is the ratio

$$a_n = (\|q_{n-1}\vartheta\| - \|q_{n+1}\vartheta\|)/\|q_n\vartheta\|$$ ◀

Remark

The sequences $\{p_n\}$ and $\{q_n\}$ admit an alternate interpretation which merits a short digression. Let $x = x_0 = s/t$ be a rational number and define the sequence z_i, $i = 0, 1, 2, \ldots$ by

$$\begin{array}{ll} x_0 = z_0 + 1/x_1 & x_1 > 1 \\ x_1 = z_1 + 1/x_2 & x_2 > 1 \\ x_2 = z_2 + 1/x_3 & x_3 > 1 \\ \cdots & \\ \cdots & \\ \cdots & \end{array} \tag{8.18.13}$$

Equation (8.18.13) is the *continued fraction* expansion of x denoted either by

$$x = z_0 + \cfrac{1}{z_1 + \cfrac{1}{z_2 + \ddots + \cfrac{1}{z_{k-1} + 1/x_k}}} \tag{8.8.14}$$

or in the more compact notation,

$$x = \{z_0; z_1, z_2, \ldots, z_k\} \qquad (z_k = x_k)$$

The *convergents* of Eq. (8.8.14) are the continued fractions

$$\{z_0;\}$$
$$\{z_0;z_1\}$$
$$\{z_0;z_1,z_2\}$$
$$\cdots$$
$$\cdots$$
$$\cdots$$
$$\{z_0;z_1,\ldots,z_k\}$$

If we write

$$\{z_0;\} = \frac{z_0}{1} = \frac{p_0}{q_0}$$

$$\{z_0;z_1\} = \frac{z_0 z_1 + 1}{z_1} = \frac{p_1}{q_1}$$

$$\{z_0;z_1,z_2\} = \frac{z_0 z_1 z_2 + z_0 + z_2}{z_1 z_2 + 1} = \frac{p_2}{q_2} \tag{8.8.15}$$

$$\cdots$$
$$\cdots$$
$$\cdots$$

the sequences of integers $\{p_n\}$ and $\{q_n\}$ appearing in the convergents [Eq. (8.8.15)] are identical to those defined by Eqs. (8.8.2–4) with $z_n = a_{n-1}$.

From this point on, we assume that ϑ was ρ/m, so that $0 < \vartheta < 1$.

Lemma 8.8.12

1. If $0 < \vartheta < 1/2$,
   $\min_{\{j:1 \le j \le q_{2n-1}\}} j\rho \text{ (modulo m)} = q_{2n-1}\rho \text{ (modulo m)}$
   $\max_{\{j:1 \le j \le q_{2n}\}} j\rho \text{ (modulo m)} = q_{2n}\rho \text{ (modulo m)}$

2. If $1/2 < \vartheta < 1$
   $\min_{\{j:1 \le j \le q_{2n}\}} \text{(modulo m)} = q_{2n}\rho \text{ (modulo m)}$
   $\max_{\{j:1 \le j \le q_{2n-1}\}} j\rho \text{ (modulo m)} = q_{2n-1}\rho \text{ (modulo m)}$

Proof. Introduce the notation

$$r_j = \begin{cases} j\rho \text{ (modulo m)} & \text{if } 0 \le j\rho \text{ (modulo m)} \le m/2 \\ m - j\rho \text{ (modulo m)} & \text{if } m/2 < j\rho \text{ (modulo m)} < m \end{cases}$$

Equation (8.8.1) implies that

$$r_{q_1} > r_{q_2} > \dots \tag{8.8.16}$$

$$r_{q_n} = \begin{cases} q_n\rho - p_n m & \text{if } q_n\vartheta - p_n > 0 \\ m + [q_n\rho - p_n m] & \text{if } q_n\vartheta - p_n < 0 \end{cases}$$

It is obvious that

$$r_j = m\|j\vartheta\|$$

From Lemma 8.8.3, it follows that

$0 < \vartheta < 1/2$	$1/2 < \vartheta < 1$
$r_{q_{2n+1}} = q_{2n+1}\rho$ (modulo m)	$r_{q_{2n}} = q_{2n}\rho$ (modulo m)
$r_{q_{2n}} = m - q_{2n}\rho$ (modulo m)	$r_{q_{2n+1}} = m - q_{2n+1}\rho$ (modulo m)
$j\rho$ (modulo m) $< r_{q_{2n}}$	$j\rho$ (modulo m) $< r_{q_{2n-1}}$
if $1 \leq j < q_{2n}$	if $1 \leq j < q_{2n-1}$
$j\rho$ (modulo m) $> r_{q_{2n-1}}$	$j\rho$ (modulo m) $> r_{q_{2n}}$
if $1 \leq j < q_{2n-1}$	if $1 \leq j < q_{2n}$

which completes the proof. ◀

Theorem 8.8.13

1. If $0 < \vartheta < 1/2$ and $q_{2n-1} \leq J < q_{2n} + q_{2n-1}$,
$$\min_{\{j:1\leq j\leq J\}} j\rho \text{ (modulo m)} = q_{2n-1}\rho \text{ (modulo m)}$$
2. If $0 < \vartheta < 1/2$
$$\min_{\{j:1\leq j\leq q_{2n-1}+tq_{2n}\}} j\rho \text{ (modulo m)} = [q_{2n-1} + tq_{2n}]\rho \text{ (modulo m)}$$
$$1 \leq t < a_{2n}$$
3. If $1/2 < \vartheta < 1$ and $q_{2n} \leq J < q_{2n+1} + q_{2n}$
$$\min_{\{j:1\leq j\leq J\}} j\rho \text{ (modulo m)} = q_{2n}\rho \text{ (modulo m)}$$
4. If $1/2 < \vartheta < 1$
$$\min_{\{j:1\leq j\leq q_{2n-2}+tq_{2n-1}\}} j\rho \text{ (modulo m)} = (q_{2n-2} + tq_{2n-1})\rho \text{ (modulo m)}$$
$$1 \leq t < a_{2n-1}$$

Proof. We give the proof only in *Case 4* above.

$$1/2 < \vartheta < 1 \qquad q_{2n-1} < J < q_{2n}$$

We have

$$r_{q_{2n-2}} = q_{2n-2}\rho \text{ (modulo m)} \tag{8.8.17}$$
$$r_{q_{2n-1}} = m - q_{2n-1}\rho \text{ (modulo m)}$$

Observe that Eqs. (8.8.16) and (8.8.17) imply

$$(q_{2n-2} + sq_{2n-1})\rho \text{ (modulo m)} < q_{2n-2}\rho \text{ (modulo m)}$$

and moreover that the left-hand side is strictly decreasing in s. If

$$j\rho \text{ (modulo m)} = \min\{s\rho \text{ (modulo m)} : 1 \le s \le q_{2n-2} + tq_{2n-1}\}$$

then $r_{j-q_{2n-2}} < r_{q_{2n-2}}$ which implies by Eq. (8.8.4) that $j \ge q_{2n-2} + q_{2n-1}$. If we set $j = q_{2n-2} + Lq_{2n-1} + b$ for $0 \le b < q_{2n-1}$, $1 \le L \le t$, we may conclude

$$r_b < r_{q_{2n-2}} = q_{2n-2}\rho \text{ (modulo m)}$$

which is a contradiction unless $b = 0$. ◀

Remark
The computation of the sequences $\{p_n\}$ and $\{q_n\}$ by the Euclidean algorithm has complexity that is logarithmic in m [KN].

Example Let $\vartheta = 500/719$. Tables 8.8.1–2 contain the values of $\{p_n\}$, $\{q_n\}$, $\|q_n\vartheta\|$, and $(500q_n - 719p_n)$ (modulo 719) for $n = 1(1)7$, and 500n (modulo 719) for $n = 1(1)174$.

TABLE 8.8.1
$\{p_n\}$, $\{q_n\}$, $\|q_n\vartheta\|$ and $(500q_n - 719p_n)$ (modulo 719)

n	z_n	p_n	q_n	$\|q_n\vartheta\|$	$(500q_n-719p_n)$(modulo 719)
1	1	1	1	0.3046	500
2	2	2	3	0.0862	62
3	3	7	10	0.0459	686
4	1	9	13	0.0403	29
5	1	16	23	0.0056	715
6	7	121	174	0.0014	1
7	4	500	719	0.0000	0

The value of j that minimizes 500j (modulo 719) with $1 \le j \le 72$ is $j = 13 + 2 \times 23 = 59$.

8.9 REVIEW OF SOME NUMBER THEORY

Theorem 8.9.1 (Fermat) [WA] If p is a prime, then

$$x^{p-1} = 1 \text{ (modulo p)} \tag{8.9.1}$$

TABLE 8.8.2
500n (modulo 719)

	n	500n (modulo 719)	n	500n (modulo 719)		n	500n (modulo 719)
q_1	**1**	**500**	59	21		117	261
	2	281	60	521		118	42
q_2	**3**	**62**	61	302		119	542
	4	562	62	83		120	323
	5	343	63	583		121	104
	6	124	64	364		122	604
	7	624	65	145		123	385
	8	405	66	645		124	166
	9	186	67	426		125	666
q_3	**10**	**686**	68	207		126	447
	11	467	69	707		127	228
	12	248	70	488		128	9
q_4	**13**	**29**	71	269		129	509
	14	529	72	50		130	290
	15	310	73	550		131	71
	16	91	74	331		132	571
	17	591	75	112		133	352
	18	372	76	612		134	133
	19	153	77	393		135	633
	20	653	78	174		136	414
	21	434	79	674		137	195
	22	215	80	455		138	695
q_5	**23**	**715**	81	236		139	476
	24	496	82	17		140	257
	25	277	83	517		141	38
	26	58	84	298		142	538
	27	558	85	79		143	319
	28	339	86	579		144	100
	29	120	87	360		145	600
	30	620	88	141		146	381
	31	401	89	641		147	162
	32	182	90	422		148	662
	33	682	91	203		149	443
	34	463	92	703		150	224
	35	244	93	484		151	5
	36	25	94	265		152	505
	37	525	95	46		153	286
	38	306	96	546		154	67
	39	87	97	327		155	567
	40	587	98	108		156	348
	41	368	99	608		157	129
	42	149	100	389		158	629
	43	649	101	170		159	410
	44	430	102	670		160	191
	45	211	103	451		161	691
	46	711	104	232		162	472
	47	492	105	13		163	253
	48	273	106	513		164	34
	49	54	107	294		165	534
	50	554	108	75		166	315
	51	335	109	575		167	96
	52	116	110	356		168	596
	53	616	111	137		169	377
	54	397	112	637		170	158
	55	178	113	418		171	658
	56	678	114	199		172	439
	57	459	115	699		173	220
	58	240	116	480	q_6	**174**	**1**

for every x relatively prime to p and

(8.9.2) $$x^p = x \text{ (modulo p)}$$

for every x.

Proof. It suffices to prove Eq. (8.9.1) or (8.9.2) for x in $\boldsymbol{Z}_p$. The proof is by induction; Eq. (8.9.2) clearly holds for x = 0 and 1. Next,

$$x^p = (x - 1 + 1)^p = \sum_{0 \le j \le p} C(p,j)(x - 1)^j = (x - 1)^p + 1 \text{ (modulo p)}$$

since C(p,j) = 0 (modulo p) for $0 < j < p$. This equality together with the induction hypothesis completes the proof. ◀

Definition 8.9.2 The *Euler totient function* $\varphi(n)$ is the number of positive integers less than n that are relatively prime to n.

The first few values of $\varphi(n)$ are

n :	2	3	4	5	6	7	8	9	10	11	12	13
$\varphi(n)$:	1	2	2	4	2	6	4	6	4	10	4	12

Theorem 8.9.3 If n = pq (p and q distinct primes), then

$$\varphi(n) = (p - 1)(q - 1)$$

Proof. We use the principle of inclusion-exclusion [FEL]. Let E and F denote the subsets of the integers $\{1, 2, \ldots, n - 1\}$, which are divisible by p and q, respectively. $\varphi(n)$ is the number of integers in

$$F^c \cap E^c$$

where E^c and F^c are the complements (in $\{1, 2, \ldots, n - 1\}$) of E and F, respectively. By DeMorgan's law,

$$|F^c \cap E^c| = (n - 1) - |F \cup E|$$

We apply the principle of inclusion-exclusion to

$$|F \cup E|$$

Thus

$$|E| = [(n - 1)/p]$$

$$|F| = [(n - 1)/q]$$

$$|E \cap F| = [(n - 1)/q] = 0$$

where [.] denotes the *integer part of*. From the principle of inclusion-exclusion, we conclude

$$\begin{aligned}|F \cup E| &= [(n-1)/p] + [(n-1)/pq] - [(n-1)/pq] \\ &= (p-1) + (q-1) \\ &= n - 1 - (p-1)(q-1)\end{aligned}$$

which completes the proof. ◀

If the integer n has the prime factorization

$$p_1^{e_1} p_2^{e_2} \ldots p_k^{e_k}$$

then $\varphi(n)$ is given by

$$\varphi(n) = \prod_{1 \le i \le k} p_i^{e_i - 1}(p_i - 1)$$

Theorem 8.9.4 If n = pq (p and q distinct primes), and x is relatively prime to p and q, then

$$x^{\varphi(n)} = 1 \text{ (modulo n)}$$

Proof. If x is relatively prime to both p and q, then

$$x^{p-1} = 1 \text{ (modulo p)}$$

$$x^{q-1} = 1 \text{ (modulo q)}$$

so that $y = x^{\varphi(n)} = x^{(p-1)(q-1)}$ is equal to one both modulo p *and* modulo q. Thus y − 1 is divisible by both p and q and hence is equal to zero modulo n = pq. ◀

Corollary 8.9.5 If n = pq (p and q distinct primes) and e is relatively prime to $\varphi(n)$, the mapping

$$E_{e,n} : x \to x^e \text{ (modulo n)}$$

is a one-to-one mapping on Z_n.

Proof. If e is relatively prime to $\varphi(n)$, there exists an integer d such that

(8.9.3) $$ed = 1 \text{ (modulo } \varphi(n))$$

and hence

$$(x^e)^d = x^{ed} = x^{1+C\varphi(n)} = x \text{ (modulo n)}$$

whenever x is relatively prime to n.

If x = py with y relatively prime to q, then

$$x^{1+K\varphi(n)} - x$$

is clearly divisible by p. Since x is not divisible by q,

$$x^{1+K\varphi(n)} - x = x[(x^{q-1})^{K(p-1)} - 1]$$

The expression with the square brackets is equal to 0 modulo q by Fermat's Theorem (Theorem 8.9.1), and thus

$$x^{ed} - x = 0 \text{ (modulo n)}$$ ◀

Remark
The mapping $E_{e,n}$ has been defined on $\boldsymbol{Z}_n$. We can extend its definition to $\boldsymbol{Z}_\infty = \{0, 1, \ldots\}$ as follows: for an integer N, write the base n representation

$$N = c_0 + c_1 n + \ldots + c_k n^k + \ldots \qquad c_k \in \boldsymbol{Z}_n \qquad 0 \leq k < \infty$$

and define $E_{e,n}$ on $\boldsymbol{Z}_\infty$ by

$$E_{e,n} : N \rightarrow E_{e,n}N = (E_{e,n}c_0) + (E_{e,n}e_1)n + \ldots + (E_{e,n}c_k)n^k + \ldots$$

$E_{e,n}$ so extended is a one-to-one mapping on $\boldsymbol{Z}_\infty$ with inverse $E_{d,n}$, where e and d are related as in Eq. (8.9.3).

8.10 THE RIVEST-SHAMIR-ADELMAN ENCIPHERMENT SYSTEM [RI1]

Let $n = pq$ with p and q distinct primes. If e and d satisfy Eq. (8.9.3), then the mappings $E_{e,n}$ and $E_{d,n}$ are inverses on the set $\boldsymbol{Z}_n$. Both $E_{e,n}$ and $E_{d,n}$ are easy to compute when e, d, p, and q are known. If e and n are known, but p and q are secret, it is believed that $E_{e,n}$ is a one-way function; to find $E_{d,n}$ from n is equivalent to the factorization of n. When p and q are large enough primes, the factorization of n appears to be impractical. This is the basis of the Rivest-Shamir-Adelman encipherment system.

User i chooses a pair of distinct primes p_i, q_i and computes a pair (e_i, d_i) of integers that are relatively prime to $\varphi(n_i)$ with $n_i = p_i q_i$. A directory (Table 8.10.1) lists the public keys $\{(e_i, n_i)\}$.

We assume that plaintext

$$\mathbf{x} = (x_0, x_1, \ldots, x_{n-1}) \qquad x_i \in \boldsymbol{Z}_m \qquad 0 \leq i < n$$

is first represented in the base n_i:

$$N = c_0 + c_1 n_i + \ldots$$

User i enciphers plaintext for transmission to *User j* by applying E_{d_i,n_i} to N.

$$N \rightarrow E_{d_i,n_i}N = N'$$

User j deciphers N′ by applying E_{e_i,n_i} (found in Table 8.10.1):

$$N' \rightarrow E_{e_i,n_i}N' = E_{e_i,n_i}E_{d_i,n_i}N = N$$

It appears that to find the inverse E_{d_i,n_i} of E_{e_i,n_i}, we require the factors of $n_i = p_i q_i$. The running time of the best known factorization algorithm is given in Theorem 8.5.3.

TABLE 8.10.1
Public Directory of Encipherment Functions for the RSA System

Public Key Directory	
USER	***Public Key***
1	$E_{e_1,n_1} \leftrightarrow (e_1,n_1)$
2	$E_{e_2,n_2} \leftrightarrow (e_2,n_2)$
.	.
.	.
.	.
N	$E_{e_N,n_N} \leftrightarrow (e_N,n_N)$

8.11 CRITIQUE AND DISCUSSION OF THE RIVEST-SHAMIR-ADELMAN PUBLIC KEY SYSTEM

The strength of the Rivest-Shamir-Adelman proposal is dependent upon the complexity of finding the factors of the integer n, which is the product of two large primes. Techniques for factorization have been studied for centuries, although not in the cryptographic context. It is difficult to predict if the interest in factorization brought about by cryptography will lead to significant advances. It is also an open question if "hard" computational problems translate into "hard" cryptanalytic problems; is a cryptanalytic solution of the Rivest-Shamir-Adelman encipherment equivalent to a factorization? Michael Rabin [RA2] has considered a closely related problem and proved the equivalence.

Definition 8.11.1 An element x of $\boldsymbol{Z}_n$ is called a *quadratic residue* of n if

$$y^2 = x \text{ (modulo n)} \tag{8.11.1}$$

has a solution.

Lemma 8.11.2 If $n = p$, an odd prime, then Eq. (8.11.1) has either zero or two solutions.

Proof. Suppose $y^2 = (y')^2 = x$ (modulo p) with $0 \leq y \leq y' < p$. Then

$$(y - y')(y + y') = y^2 - (y')^2 = 0 \text{ (modulo p)}$$

Since p is a prime, it must divide either $(y - y')$ or $(y + y')$. If $y \neq y'$, then $y + y' = p$ and $y' = p - y$. ◀

Lemma 8.11.3 The set of quadratic residues modulo p (an odd prime), denoted by *QUAD*[p], contains $(p - 1)/2$ elements congruent modulo p to the numbers

$$1^2, 2^2, \ldots, ((p - 1)/2)^2$$

Proof. If $i^2 = j^2$ (modulo p) with $0 \leq i < j < p$, then $(j - i)(j + i) = 0$ (modulo p) which implies $j + i = p$. Thus the elements of *QUAD*[p] are the $(p - 1)/2$ distinct residues in the set $\{i^2 : 0 \leq i \leq (p-1)/2\}$. ◀

Lemma 8.11.4 $y \in$ QUAD[p] (p an odd prime) if and only if

$$y^{(p-1)/2} = 1 \text{ (modulo p)}$$

$y \notin$ *QUAD*[p] if and only if

$$y^{(p-1)/2} = -1 \text{ (modulo p)}$$

Proof. By Fermat's theorem (Theorem 8.9.1),

$$y^{p-1} = 1 \text{ (modulo p)} \quad 0 \neq y \in \boldsymbol{Z}_p$$

so that$(y^{(p-1)/2} - 1)(y^{(p-1)/2} + 1) = 0$(modulo p) for every y, $0 \neq y \in \boldsymbol{Z}_p$. This implies either

$$\text{(8.11.2)} \qquad y^{(p-1)/2} - 1 = 0 \text{ (modulo p)}$$

or

$$\text{(8.11.3)} \qquad y^{(p-1)/2} + 1 = 0 \text{ (modulo p)}$$

Equations (8.11.2) and (8.11.3) cannot simultaneously hold, for otherwise, $1 = -1$ (modulo p). If $y = x^2$ (modulo p), then $y^{(p-1)/2} = 1$ (modulo p), so that the solutions of $y^{(p-1)/2} = 1$ (modulo p) are all of the quadratic residues.

The polynomial equation

$$y^{p-1} = 1 \text{ (modulo p)}$$

has $p - 1$ solutions. The solutions of the polynomial equation

$$y^{(p-1)/2} = 1 \text{ (modulo p)}$$

account for $(p - 1)/2$ of them. The remaining $(p - 1)/2$ solutions must be the quadratic nonresidues and hence the solutions of ◀

$$y^{(p-1)/2} = -1 \text{ (modulo p)}$$

8.12 BERLEKAMP'S SOLUTION OF $y^2 = \alpha$ (MODULO p)

If α is a quadratic residue modulo p, the polynomial $F(y) = y^2 - \alpha$ factors (over the field $\mathbf{Z}_p$):

$$F(y) = (y - \beta)(y + \beta) \qquad \beta, -\beta \in \mathbf{Z}_p$$

If $z \in \mathbf{Z}_p$, denote by $F_z(y)$ the shifted polynomial $F(y - z)$. We have

$$F_z(y) = (y - z - \beta)(y - z + \beta)$$

Let $G_z(y)$ be the greatest common divisor of $F_z(y)$ and $y^{(p-1)/2} - 1$:

$$G_z(y) = \gcd\{F_z(y), y^{(p-1)/2} - 1\}$$

The greatest common divisor $\gcd\{R(y), S(y)\}$ of two polynomials R(y) and S(y) is found by the Euclidean algorithm as follows:

Step 1 Divide R(y) by S(y) and let Q(y) denote the remainder,

$$R(y) = A(y)S(y) + Q(y)$$

Step 2 if $Q(y) = 0$, the algorithm terminates and

$$\gcd\{R(y), S(y)\} = S(y)$$

if $Q(y) \neq 0$, replace R(y) and S(y) by S(y) and Q(y), respectively, and return to *Step 1*.

For example, if $p = 23$ and

$$R(y) = y^3 + 2y^2 + 3y + 2$$

$$S(y) = y^4 + y^3 + y + 1$$

then

R(y)	**S(y)**	**A(y)**	**Q(y)**
$y^3 + 2y^2 + 3y + 2$	$y^4 + y^3 + y + 1$	0	$y^3 + 2y^2 + 3y + 2$
$y^4 + y^3 + y + 1$	$y^3 + 2y^2 + 3y + 2$	$y - 1$	$-y^2 + 2y + 3$
$y^3 + 2y^2 + 3y + 2$	$-y^2 + 2y + 3$	$-y - 4$	$14y + 14$
$-y^2 + 2y + 3$	$14y + 14$	$5(-y + 3)$	0

Thus

$$\gcd\{y^3 + 2y^2 + 3y + 2, y^4 + y^3 + y + 1\} = y + 1$$

There are four cases to be examined:

Case			$G_z(y)$
1	$(z + \beta) \in QUAD[p]$	$(z - \beta) \in QUAD[p]$	$F_z(y)$
2	$(z + \beta) \notin QUAD[p]$	$(z - \beta) \notin QUAD[p]$	1
3	$(z + \beta) \in QUAD[p]$	$(z - \beta) \notin QUAD[p]$	$(y - z + \beta)$
4	$(z + \beta) \notin QUAD[p]$	$(z - \beta) \in QUAD[p]$	$(y - z - \beta)$

We determine a root of $F(y) = 0$ by *shifting* in *Cases 3* and *4*. If we detect (by the Euclidean algorithm) that we are in *Case 1* or *Case 2*, the experiment is repeated with a new value for z.

How often are we successful? Let Z be a random variable that is uniformly distributed on $\boldsymbol{Z}_p$; evaluate $F_Z(y)$:

1. If $F_Z(0) = 0$ (modulo p), then $Z = \beta$, and good fortune has indeed smiled on us
2. If $F_Z(0) \neq 0$ (modulo p), calculate $G_Z(y)$

When will we be successful in factoring $F_z(y)$ in (2) above? Define the mapping $w = w(z)$ on $\boldsymbol{Z}_p - \{\beta\}$ by

$$w : \boldsymbol{Z}_p - \{\beta\} \rightarrow \boldsymbol{Z}_p - \{1\}$$

$$w : z \rightarrow w(z) = (z + \beta)/(z - \beta)$$

The mapping w is one-to-one; if

$$(z + \beta)/(z - \beta) = (z' + \beta)/(z' - \beta)$$

then

$$\beta(z - z') = -\beta(z - z')$$

which implies that $z = z'$. Thus the image of $\boldsymbol{Z}_p - \{\beta\}$ under w contains all but one of the quadratic residues of p, and hence

$$\Pr\{(Z + \beta)/(Z - \beta) \notin QUAD[p]\} \simeq 1/2$$

Finally, we use the important observation, which follows from Lemma 8.11.4, that

$(z + \beta)/(z - \beta)$ is a quadratic residue modulo p if and only if both or neither $z + \beta$ and $z - \beta$ are quadratic residues modulo p

to conclude with the following theorem.

Theorem 8.12.1 If α is a quadratic residue modulo p, *shifting* finds it with probability approximately 1/2. The expected number of shifts to be tested before success is approximately two.

There are other methods of finding quadratic residues; the classical method uses the *Jacobi symbol,* which we will describe in Sec. 8.18; a third method is described in [AD1].

8.13 SOLUTION OF $y^2 - \alpha = 0$ (MODULO m), WHERE m = pq WITH p,q KNOWN PRIMES

Suppose

(8.13.1) $$y^2 - \alpha = 0 \text{ (modulo pq)}$$

has a solution. Then, there is a solution to the pair of congruences

(8.13.2) $$y_1^2 - \alpha = 0 \text{ (modulo p)}$$

(8.13.3) $$y_2^2 - \alpha = 0 \text{ (modulo q)}$$

Conversely, by the Chinese Remainder Theorem, a solution (y_1, y_2) to Eqs. (8.13.2) and (8.13.3) can be transformed to a solution of Eq. (8.13.1).

Theorem 8.13.1 *The Chinese Remainder Theorem.* If p and q are distinct primes, there is precisely one integer n, $0 \leq n < pq$, which satisfies

$$n = a_1 \text{ (modulo p)}$$

$$n = a_2 \text{ (modulo q)}$$

Proof. If there were two intergers, say n amd m $(0 \leq n \leq m < pq)$, then

$$m - n = 0 \text{ (modulo p)}$$

$$m - n = 0 \text{ (modulo q)}$$

which implies n = m. To prove that there exists a solution, we observe that as n takes on the pq values 0, 1, . . . , pq − 1, the vector (n (modulo p), n (modulo q)) takes on pq distinct values by the argument given above for uniqueness. This proves that there is a solution. ◀

8.14 RABIN'S EQUIVALENCE THEOREM

The strength of the Rivest-Shamir-Adelman encipherment system depends on the supposed intractability of factoring n = pq, where p and q are large primes. First, a word about what a "large" prime is.

In cryptography, the term "large prime" is a synonym for large *probable* prime. By this we mean a number n that satisfies a sufficient number of tests of the probabilistic algorithm of Solovay and Strassen [SO]; to test if n is a prime number, choose α in $\{1, 2, \ldots, n-1\}$ with the uniform distribution and check if

$$\star \ \gcd\{\alpha,n\} = 1 \quad \text{and} \quad J(\alpha,n) = \alpha^{(n-1)/2} \text{ (modulo n)}$$

where $J(\alpha,n)$ is the Jacobi symbol defined by

$$J(\alpha,n) = \begin{cases} 1 & \text{if } \alpha = 1 \\ J(\alpha/2,n)(-1)^{(n^2-1)/3} & \text{if } \alpha \text{ is even} \\ J(n(\text{modulo } \alpha),n)(-1)^{(\alpha-1)(n-1)/4} & \text{if } \alpha > 1 \text{ and odd} \end{cases}$$

If n is a prime, then ★ will hold; if α is composite, then ★ will hold with probability 1/2. If we repeat the test N times, and ★ is satisfied each time, then we are confident with probability 2^{-N} that n is a prime.

The equivalence of factoring and breaking the system has been resolved for the special case e = 2 in [RA2].

Theorem 8.14.1 The problem of solving

$$y^2 - \alpha = 0 \text{ (modulo pq)} \tag{8.14.1}$$

is equivalent to the factorization of n = pq.

Proof. If we have a factorization of n = pq, Berlekamp's method and the Chinese Remainder Theorem enable us to solve Eq. (8.14.1). To prove the reverse implication, begin by observing that in general there are four solutions to the quadratic equation

$$y^2 - \alpha = 0 \text{ (modulo n)}$$

which we may denote by

$$\gamma,\ \beta,\ n - \gamma,\ n - \beta$$

with $\beta \notin \{\gamma, n - \gamma\}$. Since

$$\gamma^2 - \alpha = 0 \text{ (modulo n)} \qquad \beta^2 - \alpha = 0 \text{ (modulo n)}$$

it follows that

$$\gamma^2 - \beta^2 = (\gamma + \beta)(\gamma - \beta) = 0 \text{ (modulo n)}$$

The primes p and q cannot both divide $(\gamma + \beta)$ or $(\gamma - \beta)$, so that either

- p is a factor of $(\gamma - \beta)$ and q is a factor of $(\gamma + \beta)$, or
- q is a factor of $(\gamma - \beta)$ and p is a factor of $(\gamma + \beta)$.

In both cases, the greatest common divisor of n and $(\gamma - \beta)$ provides a factor of n, so that two independent solutions of $y^2 - \alpha = 0$ (modulo n) provide a factorization of n.

Suppose ALG is some algorithm, which

given: n and α a quadratic residue of n

returns: a solution $y = \text{ALG}(n,\alpha)$ of $y^2 = \alpha$ (modulo n)

Choose β with $1 < \beta < n$ and $\gcd\{\beta,n\} = 1$. Then $\alpha = \beta^2$ (modulo n) is a quadratic residue, so that ALG(n,α) is a solution of $y^2 = \alpha$ (modulo n). With probability 1/2, ALG(n,α) $\notin \{\beta, n - \beta\}$, so that the factors of n are obtained. If ALG(n,α) $\in \{\beta, n - \beta\}$, the experiment is repeated with a new value of β. The expected number of trials until success is 2. ◀

8.15 THE PITFALLS OF COMPLEXITY THEORY IN CRYPTOGRAPHY

The strength of many of the proposed cryptographic systems for public key exchange and electronic signature rests upon the supposed intractibility of some associated computational problems, such as factorization, taking logarithms in a finite field, and solving the knapsack problem. It may well be that the cryptographic systems derived from **NP-complete** problems are strong. None of these proposed cryptographic systems have been subjected to the same scrutiny as DES.

In [EV1,2], two examples of private key systems that are based upon "hard" problems are shown to lead to cryptographically weak encipherment systems.

Example 8.15.1 A Knapsack-Like Private Key System Let

$$\mathbf{a} = (a_0, a_1, \ldots, a_{m-1}) \qquad \text{(knapsack lengths)}$$

$$\mathbf{k} = (k_0, k_1, \ldots, k_{m-1}) \in \boldsymbol{Z}_{\mathbf{2,m}} \quad \text{(key)}$$

$$N = [\log_2 (1 + a_0 + \ldots + a_{n-1})] \qquad \text{(message block length)}$$

where [.] does *integer-part-of.*

To encipher the plaintext block

$$\mathbf{x} = (x_0, x_1, \ldots, x_{N-1}) \in \boldsymbol{Z}_{\mathbf{2,N}}$$

randomly generate

$$\mathbf{z} = (z_0, z_1, \ldots, z_{m-1}) \in \boldsymbol{Z}_{\mathbf{2,m}}$$

add to **k**

$$\mathbf{z}' = (z_0', z_1', \ldots, z_{m-1}') = \mathbf{k} + \mathbf{z}$$

and evaluate

$$S = \sum_{0 \le i < m} a_i z_i'$$

$$S = \mathbf{a}(\mathbf{k} + \mathbf{z})$$

The ciphertext **y** is the concatentation of **z** and **x** + **s**

$$\mathbf{s} = (s_0, s_1, \ldots, s_{m-1})$$

$$S = \|\mathbf{s}\| = \sum_{0 \le i < m} 2^{n-1-i} S_i$$

Given **a** and **k**, **s** can be calculated recovering the plaintext from the ciphertext.

Given corresponding plaintext and ciphertext, an opponent is faced with the task of determining the key **k** given **s**, **a**, and **r** where

$$\mathrm{S} = \sum_{0 \le i < m} a_i z_i'$$

This is equivalent to solving a general knapsack problem.

Suppose however, that many pairs of corresponding plaintext and ciphertext are obtained by the opponent with different values of **z**:

$$\mathbf{x}^{(i)}\ \mathbf{y}^{(i)}\ \mathbf{z}^{(i)}\ \mathbf{s}^{(i)}\ \mathrm{S}^{(i)} \quad 0 \le i < t$$

If there are m linearly independent vectors in

$$\mathbf{u}^{(i)} = (1, 1, \ldots, 1) - 2\mathbf{z}^{(i)} \quad 1 \le i \le t$$

a cryptanalytic solution is possible; assume that $t = m$ and the vectors $\{\mathbf{u}^{(i)}\}$ are linearly independent. Write

$$\mathbf{k} + \mathbf{z}^{(i)} = \mathbf{k} + \mathbf{z}^{(i)} - 2\mathbf{k}{*}\mathbf{z}^{(i)}$$

where * denotes the component-by-component multiplication. Then

$$\begin{aligned}(8.15.1)\qquad \mathrm{S}^{(i)} &= \mathbf{a}(\mathbf{k} + \mathbf{z}^{(i)}) = \mathbf{a}(\mathbf{z}^{(i)} + \mathbf{k}{*}\mathbf{u}^{(i)}) = \mathbf{a}\mathbf{z}^{(i)} + \mathbf{a}(\mathbf{k}{*}\mathbf{u}^{(i)}) \\ &= \mathbf{a}\mathbf{z}^{(i)} + \mathbf{k}(\mathbf{a}{*}\mathbf{u}^{(i)})\end{aligned}$$

Let $\mathbf{t}^{(i)} = \mathrm{S}^{(i)} - \mathbf{a}\mathbf{z}^{(i)}$ and write the N equations in (8.15.1) in matrix notation:

$$(8.15.2)\qquad \begin{vmatrix} \mathbf{t}^{(0)} \\ \mathbf{t}^{(1)} \\ \cdot \\ \cdot \\ \cdot \\ \mathbf{t}^{(N-1)} \end{vmatrix} = \begin{vmatrix} \mathbf{u}^{(0)} \\ \mathbf{u}^{(1)} \\ \cdot \\ \cdot \\ \cdot \\ \mathbf{u}^{(N-1)} \end{vmatrix} \begin{vmatrix} a_0 & 0 & \ldots & 0 \\ 0 & a_1 & \ldots & 0 \\ \cdot & \cdot & \ldots & \cdot \\ \cdot & \cdot & \ldots & \cdot \\ \cdot & \cdot & \ldots & \cdot \\ 0 & 0 & \ldots & a_{N-1} \end{vmatrix} \begin{vmatrix} x_0 \\ x_1 \\ \cdot \\ \cdot \\ \cdot \\ x_{N-1} \end{vmatrix}$$

If the $\{\mathbf{u}^{(i)}\}$ are independent and the $\{a_i\}$ are all positive, the matrix in Eq. (8.15.2) may be inverted to obtain the plaintext **x.** It is shown in [EV1,2] that the probability that $\{\mathbf{u}^{(i)} : 0 \le i < t\}$ will contain N linearly independent vectors rapidly approaches unity as t increases.

Example 8.15.2 A Factorization Private Key System Let $n = pq$ (p and q distinct primes). The block length of messages is $N = [\log_2 \varphi(n)]$ where [.] denotes *integer-part-of*. To encipher the plaintext $\mathbf{x} = (x_0, x_1, \ldots, x_{N-1})$

- Choose e by a chance experiment relatively prime to $\varphi(n)$ and $1 \le e < \varphi(n)$.
- Compute the $\varphi(n)$-multiplicative inverse d to e

$$de = 1 \ (\text{modulo } \varphi(n))$$

- by the Euclidean algorithm

The ciphertext

$$\mathbf{y} = (y_0, y_1, \ldots, y_{N-1})$$

is the concatenation of $\mathbf{x} + \mathbf{d}$ and $\mathbf{e}$, where

$$\mathbf{e} = (e_0, e_1, \ldots, e_{N-1})$$

$$\mathbf{d} = (d_0, d_1, \ldots, d_{N-1})$$

$$e = \sum_{0 \le j < N} 2^{N-1-j} e_j$$

$$d = \sum_{0 \le j < N} 2^{N-1-j} d_j$$

The key is the integer $k = (p - 1)(q - 1)$; given k, we can recover $\mathbf{x}$ from $\mathbf{y}$. If only ciphertext is available to the opponent, the cryptanalytic task is certainly as great as that faced in the Rivest-Shamir-Adelman signature system.

If corresponding pairs of plaintext and ciphertext are available to the opponent,

$$\mathbf{x}^{(i)}\ \mathbf{y}^{(i)}\ \mathbf{e}^{(i)}\ \mathbf{d}^{(i)} \qquad 0 \le i < i$$

the opponent (1) computes the t products $f_i = e_i d_i$ $(0 \le i < t)$, and (2) uses the Euclidean algorithm to obtain the greatest common divisor of the numbers $\{f_i - 1\}$:

$$f = \gcd\{f_0 - 1, f_1 - 1, \ldots, f_{t-1} - 1\}$$

Note that

$$e_i d_i = 1 + h_i(p - 1)(q - 1)$$

and hence f is a multiple of $(p - 1)(q - 1)$. Also,

$$\gcd\{f_0 - 1, f_1 - 1, \ldots, f_{t-1} - 1\} = (p - 1)(q - 1)$$

if and only if

$$\gcd\{h_0, h_1, \ldots, h_{t-1}\} = 1$$

It is proved in [EV1,2] that if the $\{e_i\}$ are chosen independently with the uniform distribution on the subset of $\boldsymbol{Z}_{(p-1)(q-1)}$ of integers that are relatively prime to $(p - 1)(q - 1)$, the probability that

$$\gcd\{h_0, h_1, \ldots, h_{t-1}\} = 1$$

is bounded from below by $1/\zeta(n)$, where $\zeta(n)$ is the Riemann Zeta function,* and hence approaches unity rapidly.

---

*The *Riemann zeta function* is defined by the series

$$\zeta(n) = \sum_{1 \le i < \infty} i^{-n} \qquad n > 1$$

Conclusion? Merely starting with a computationally "hard" problem is not enough.

PROBLEMS

8.1 In the public key system of Sec. 8.4, the system stores pairs

$$(\textit{User Name},\ q^{k_{\textit{User Name}}}\ (\text{modulo } p))$$

To prevent *User O* from replacing the entry

$$(\textit{User } i,\ q^{k_{\textit{User } i}}\ (\text{modulo } p))$$

by

$$(\textit{User } O,\ q^{k_{\textit{User } O}}\ (\text{modulo } p))$$

and masquerading at *User i,* we propose to store the triples

$$(\textit{User Name},\ X_{\textit{User Name}, k_{\textit{User Name}}},\ q^{k_{\textit{User Name}}}\ (\text{modulo } p))$$

Can we prevent or at least inhibit masquerading by the use of an additional entry in the table? What characteristics should $X_{\textit{User Name}, k_{\textit{User Name}}}$ have?

8.2 Let

$$n = 8 \qquad m = 2^{11} - 1 = 2047$$

$$\mathbf{a}' = (2,4,9,17,38,75,180,529)$$

$$\mathbf{a} = (633,1266,1825,263,1792,197,1701,598)$$

Find w such that

$$w\mathbf{a}' = \mathbf{a}\ (\text{modulo } p)$$

8.3 **Continuation.** Let **a**, w, and m define the mapping

$$\pi : Z_{2,8} \rightarrow Z_{2,11}$$

$$\pi : (x_0, x_1, \ldots, x_7) \rightarrow (y_0, y_1, \ldots, y_{10})$$

$$N = \sum_{0 \le i < 8} a_i x_i\ (\text{modulo } m) = \sum_{0 \le i < 11} y_i 2^{10-i}$$

Use Table P6.1 and encipher the message `Send More Money`. Decipher the message

10111110110 00101111001 00010011010 10011010011

8.4 **Continuation.** Use the χ^2 and Kolmogorov-Smirnov tests to check independence of x_i with $i \in CO_{in}$ and y_j with $j \in CO_{out}$.

8.5 Use the χ^2 and Kolmogorov-Smirnov tests to check independence of x_i with $i \in CO_{in}$ and y_j with $j \in CO_{out}$ for the Rivest-Shamir-Adelman encipherment system with $n = pq$, $p = 23$, $q = 29$, and

$$\mathbf{x} = (x_0, x_1, \ldots, x_{n-1}) \rightarrow \mathbf{y} = (y_0, y_1, \ldots, y_{N-1})$$

$$\|\mathbf{x}\| = \sum_{0 \le i < n} x_i 2^{n-1-i} \qquad \|\mathbf{y}\| = \sum_{0 \le i < N} y_i 2^{N-1-i}$$

$$\|\mathbf{y}\| = \|\mathbf{x}\|^e \text{ (modulo n)}$$

8.6 Conferencing. Construct a variant of the public key system described in Sec. 8.4, allowing N users to generate a common shared key. Assume that the public key directory (Fig. 8.4.1) is available.

8.7 File Access. Design a file access system to allow certain users to read and write access to a file, depending upon authorization set up by the system. The instructions should be of the format

`READ` (F, User A) : attempt by *User A* to read the file *F*
`WRITE` (F, User A) : attempt by *User A* to store a possibly modified copy of the file *F*

Each file has a *header record,* which contains authorization priveleges; that is, a list of users who can read and write. The file is to be enciphered by a key which is *not* shared by the users.

8.8 Suppose $p(x) = x^3$ (modulo n), where $n = pq$ (p and q primes). Is the problem of finding the factors of n equivalent to the decomposition of $p(x) - \alpha = 0$ (modulo n) into linear factors over the ring $\boldsymbol{Z}_n$ when α is a *cubic residue modulo n?*

8.9 Suppose $p(x) = x^2$ (modulo n), where $n = prq$ (p, q, r primes). Is the problem of finding the factors of n equivalent to the decomposition of $p(x) - \alpha = 0$ (modulo n) into a linear factors over the ring $\boldsymbol{Z}_n$, when α is a quadratic residue modulo n?

CHAPTER IX

Digital Signatures and Authentications

9.1 THE PROBLEM

We consider *transactions* between pairs of *users* of the form

Customer A to *Broker B* : Purchase for my account . . . shares of XYZ Corporation at a price not exceeding $ . . .

Bank A to *Bank B* : Credit account 853134 the sum of $1,000

In normal commercial transactions *protocols* are introduced to protect each party against harmful acts by the other or by a third party; arbitration procedures are agreed upon to resolve disputes if they should arise. We are rapidly moving toward an era of electronic digital communication in which transactions for goods and services may be managed by a data processing system linking users by teleprocessing lines, as shown in Fig. 9.1.1. The usual element of personal contact, physical, visual, or voice, may be absent. Electronic messages are easily forged or altered. For example, the sequence of 0s and 1s in a message that represents the transaction

Bank A to *Bank B* : Credit account 853134 the sum of $1,000

can easily be changed so that $1,000 becomes $1,000,000 or account number 853134 is replaced by 765541. The protocols in commercial transactions, which either prevent or discourage misuse by making detection and apprehension likely, need to be defined for transactions managed by a data processing system. We formulate the requirements of *transaction verification systems* and survey some proposed solutions in this chapter.

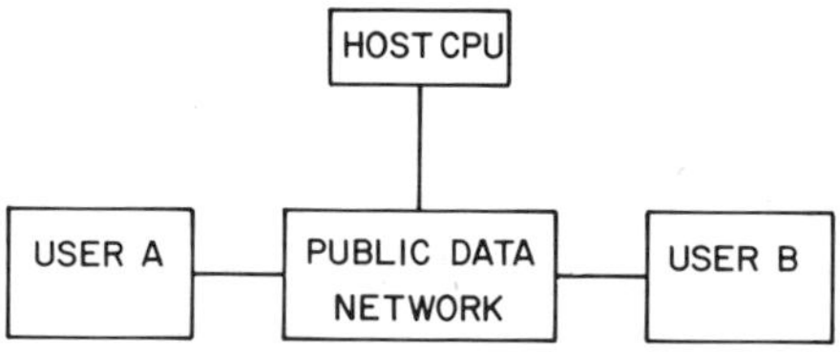

Figure 9.1.1. Electronic transaction network.

9.2 THE THREATS

A transaction from the *originator (User A)* to the *recipient (User B)* involves the transmission of DATA, committing the users to some course of action. DATA may represent an interbank funds transfer, the sale of stock or bonds in an automated market, or electronic mail containing sensitive material. The participants require protection against a variety of harmful acts, including:

reneging	the *originator* subsequently disowns a transaction
forgery	the *recipient* fabricates a transaction
alteration	the *recipient* alters a previous valid transaction
masquerading	a user attempts to masquerade as another

9.3 WHAT DOES TRANSACTION VERIFICATION REQUIRE?

To verify DATA from *User A* to *User B* the protocol should involve the following elements:

- The *originator (User A)* must incorporate with DATA a *signature;* additional information that depends on the DATA, the *recipient* of the transaction, and the secret information k_A, known only to the *originator*. SIG{k_A,DATA,*User B*} denotes the signature of DATA to *User B* by *User A*.
- A correct signature SIG{k_A,DATA,*User B*} of DATA to *User B* must be *effectively* impossible to construct without k_A.
- *User B* must be capable of verifying that SIG{k_A,DATA,*User B*} is a correct signature of DATA by *User A*.
- The verification process must involve "time" dependence to prevent the reuse of *stale* messages.

Discussion

1. A *signed transaction* is some type of encipherment of DATA by a cryptographic transformation. The secret element k_A in the transformation,

$$\textit{User B}, \text{DATA} \rightarrow \text{SIG}\{k_A, \text{DATA}, \textit{User B}\}$$

is the *key*. In any practical cryptogaphic system, k_A belongs to a finite set ***K***. *Exhaustive testing of all keys, given corresponding pairs,*

$$\text{DATA}_i, \textit{User } B_i \leftarrow\rightarrow \text{SIG}\{k_A, \text{DATA}_i, \textit{User } B_{i,}\}$$

generally leads to a determination of k_A by an opponent. If the cardinality of ***K*** is sufficiently large, and if k_A is chosen randomly, exhaustive testing of keys is impractical. To say that it is *effectively* impossible to construct a valid signature without the key means the determination of SIG{k_A,DATA,*User B*} without k_A is computationally equivalent to key search.

2. Access to facilties, programs, and files in an information processing system is usually controlled by *passwords*. A signature is a type of password functionally dependent upon the *originator*, *recipient*, and the content of the transaction.

3. The signature must vary from transaction to transaction, in order to prevent the reuse of a previous signature to verify a new transaction. A digital signature differs from a hand-written signature, which is normally both time and data independent. The digital and hand-written signatures are similar in that both are derived from characteristics peculiar to the owner.

4. Even though the *recipient* cannot construct a valid signature, the *recipient* must be capable of verifying that a signature is proper. In many current commercial transactions, for example, the sale of real property in New York State, a trusted independent third party (a notary) plays this role.

9.4 AUTHENTICATION

Authentication, according to Webster's dictionary, is a process by which each party to a communication verifies the identity of the other. Implicit in an authentication process is some element of secrecy; information by which a participant in the communication identifies him or herself to the other party. In many day-to-day activities, we authenticate ourselves, using, for example, a signature or driver's license when cashing a check, or a photograph on a passport when crossing national boundaries. In order for the *originator* to be authenticated to the *recipient* in a data processing system,

- The *originator (User A)* must provide the *recipient (User B)* authenticating information AUTH{k_A, *User B*} depending on the secret information k_A known only to *User A*.
- A valid authentication AUTH{k_A, *User B*} by *User A* to *User B* must be effectively impossible to construct without k_A.
- *User B* must have a procedure for checking that AUTH{k_A, *User B*} properly authenticates *User A*.
- The authentication process must have some "time" dependence to prevent the use of previous authenticating information.

We note that *authentication* and *transaction verification* involve similar elements; a digital signature is authentication information with the added requirement that it is dependent upon the content of the transaction.

9.5 EXAMPLES OF SIGNATURES

Example 9.5.1 Signature by Chaining Let (DATA, *User Name*) be the concatention of N 8-byte blocks,

$$\text{(DATA, } \textit{User Name}\text{)} = (\mathbf{x}^{(0)}, \mathbf{x}^{(1)}, \ldots, \mathbf{x}^{(N-1)})$$

Encipher (DATA, *User Name*) by DES with chaining,

$$\text{DES}\{\text{k,(DATA, } \textit{User Name}\text{)}\} = (\mathbf{y}^{(0)}, \mathbf{y}^{(1)}, \ldots, \mathbf{y}^{(N-1)})$$

$$\mathbf{y}^{(i)} = \text{DES}\{\mathbf{k}, \mathbf{x}^{(i)} + \mathbf{y}^{(i-1)}\}\ 0 \leq \mathbf{i} < \text{N} \qquad \mathbf{y}^{(0)} = \text{DES}\{\mathbf{k}, \mathbf{x}^{(0)} + \mathbf{ICV}\}$$

and define SIG{**k**,DATA,*User Name*} $= \mathbf{y}^{(N-1)}$. The mapping S{**k**,.} from $\boldsymbol{Z}_{2,64N}$ to $\boldsymbol{Z}_{64}$ is $2^{64(N-1)}$ to 1.

Example 9.5.2 Signature by Compressed Encoding. With (DATA, *User Name*) as above, define $(\mathbf{y}^{(0)}, \mathbf{y}^{(1)}, \ldots, \mathbf{y}^{(N-1)})$ by

$$\mathbf{y}^{(i)} = \text{DES}\{\mathbf{y}^{(i-1)}, \mathbf{x}^{(i)}\} \qquad 0 \leq \text{i} < \text{N} \qquad \mathbf{y}^{(-1)} = \mathbf{k}$$

and define the signature of DATA with the key **k** to be

$$\text{SIG}\{\mathbf{k}, \text{DATA, } \textit{User Name}\} = \mathbf{y}^{(N-1)}$$

Compressed encoding is chaining on the key.

9.6 HANDSHAKING

Signing a transaction requires the transmission of information from the *originator* to the *recipient*, followed by the validation of this information by the *recipient*. One method of signing a transaction uses a sequential interchange of information and is sometimes referred to as *handshaking*. The first example of a digital signature used handshaking and is described in [RA1]. A *contract*, shown in Fig. 9.6.1, is constructed for each pair of users who participate in the transaction system. The contract records 2T signatures of a *standard message* (SM) by T keys selected by each of the two participants. The *(User A-User B)-Contract* is signed (in the usual way) and notarized by the *arbiter*, a trusted third party. The *signature* of DATA to *User B* by *User A* with the key k_A is some encipherment of (DATA, *User B*) by a cryptographic system with the key k_A. In [RA1], compressed encoding (as in *Example 9.5.2*) is proposed as the means to derive the signature, but chaining the ciphertext (as in *Example 9.5.1*) (or a variant of it) seems to have more desirable properties.

9.7 THE TRANSACTION

A *transaction* from *User A* to *User B* involves these steps.

Step 1 On the ith transaction, the *originator (User A)* sends DATA to the *recipient (User B)* appended by 21 signatures.

SM : Standard Message	
User A	*User B*
$SIG\{k_{A,0}, SM, \textit{User B}\}$	$SIG\{k_{B,0}, SM, \textit{User A}\}$
$SIG\{k_{A,1}, SM, \textit{User B}\}$	$SIG\{k_{B,1}, SM, \textit{User A}\}$
.	.
.	.
.	.
$SIG\{k_{A,T-1}, SM, \textit{User B}\}$	$SIG\{k_{B,T-1}, SM, \textit{User A}\}$
Alan G. Konheim	Carol L. Konheim

Figure 9.6.1. *User A-User B* contract.

$$DATA, SIG\{k_{A,21i}, DATA, \textit{User B}\}, \ldots, SIG\{k_{A,21i+20}, DATA, \textit{User B}\}$$

constructed from the ith block of keys:

$$k_{A,21i}, k_{A,21i+1}, \ldots, k_{A,21i+20}$$

Step 2 *User A* is now required by *User B* to reveal 10 of the 21 keys:

$$k_{A,21i+r_0}, k_{A,21i+r_1}, \ldots, k_{A,21i+r_9}$$

$$0 \le r_0 < r_1 < \ldots < r_9 < 21$$

The choice of $r_0, r_1, \ldots, r_9$ is made by *User B.*

Step 3 *User B* is now able to check if the keys

$$k_{A,21i+r_0}, \ldots, k_{A,21i+r_9}$$

(1) are consistent with the entries in the ith block in the contract, and
(2) are consistent with the 10 signatures:

$$SIG\{k_{A,21i+r_s}, DATA, \textit{User B}\} \qquad 0 \le s < 9$$

Step 4 The protocol requires an acknowledgment from *User B* to *User A*,

ACKDATA : *I acknowledge receipt of DATA on date . . .*

which is signed as in *Steps 1–3*, using *User B's* i^{th} block of keys.

A key is used in only one transaction. When the keys in the contract are nearly depleted, the transaction system is used to sign a supplement to the contract containing T newly generated keys.

9.8 ASSUMPTIONS

If the signature is defined as in *Example 9.6.1* or *9.6.2*, any solution to either of the following problems is equivalent to key trial:

Problem 1 *Given*

$$(\mathrm{DATA}_i, \mathit{User}\ B_i) \quad \text{and } \mathrm{SIG}\{k_A, \mathrm{DATA}_i, \mathit{User}\ B_i\} = \mathbf{y}_i$$

find k_A

Problem 2 *Given*

$$(\mathrm{DATA}_i, \mathit{User}\ B_i) \quad \text{and } \mathrm{SIG}\{k_A, \mathrm{DATA}_i, \mathit{User}\ B_i\} = \mathbf{y}_i \quad i = 0, 1, \ldots$$

find $\mathrm{SIG}\{k_A, \mathrm{DATA}, \mathit{User}\ B\}$ for $\mathrm{DATA} \notin \{\mathrm{DATA}_i\}$

9.9 DISPUTES

A variety of disputes can arise;

R a claim by the *recipient* that the *originator* has failed to honor a contract.
O a claim by the *originator* that the *recipient* has failed to honor a contract.

Dispute *R* can arise if there has been

- *Reneging by the originator.*
- *Forgery by either the originator or recipient.*
- *Masquerading by a third party.*

Dispute *O* can arise if there has been

- *Reneging by the recipient.*
- *Forgery by either the originator or recipient.*
- *Masquerading by a third party.*

The resolution of a dispute in Rabin's proposed solution as in others is made by *the arbiter*. The participants in any signature system must agree to abide by the rules of the system and accept the decision of the arbiter. We indicate how one type of dispute is resolved.

9.10 SETTLING A DISPUTE

Dispute R

The *recipient (User B)* provides the arbiter DATA, the 21 signatures,

$$\mathrm{SIG}\{k_{A,21i}, \mathrm{DATA}, \textit{User } B\}, \ldots, \mathrm{SIG}\{k_{Ai,21i+20}, \mathrm{DATA}, \textit{User } B\}$$

and the 10 keys,

$$k_{A,21i+r_0}, k_{A,21i+r_1}, \ldots, k_{A,21i+r_9}$$

The arbiter requires the *originator (User A)* to supply the ith block of keys,

$$k_{A,21i}, k_{A,21i+1}, \ldots, k_{A,21i+20}$$

and checks if

- *User A*'s i^{th} block of keys is consistent with the contract entries

$$\mathrm{SIG}\{k_{A,21i+t}, \mathrm{SM}, \textit{User } B\} \qquad 0 \leq t < 21$$

- If the 21 signatures sent by *User A* to *User B*

$$\mathrm{SIG}\{k_{A,21i+t}, \mathrm{DATA}, \textit{User } B\} \qquad 0 \leq t < 21$$

are correct.

The arbiter decides for *User B* if *either*

- There is any inconsistency between the keys $\{k_{A,21i+t}\}$ supplied by *User A* and the contract entries, or
- Eleven or more of the signatures $\mathrm{SIG}\{k_{A,21i+t}, \mathrm{DATA}, \textit{User } B\}$ are proper.

Dispute *O* is dual to Dispute *R* and is resolved by interchanging the roles of *User A* and *User B* and DATA and ACKDATA.

Discussion

Can the *originator* successfully renege? If reneging is to be successful, no more than 10 of the 21 signatures can be correct. Since the choice (in *Step 1*) of which 10 keys are required for verification is made by the *recipient*, reneging by the *originator* will escape detection by the *recipient* (in *Step 2*) with probability

$$1/C(21,s) = 11!10!/21! \cong 5 \times 10^{-6}$$

If the probability 10^{-6} is thought to be too large, the number 21 (in *Step 2*) may be increased to $2s + 1$ with $s > 10$; s signatures are requested by the *recipient* (in *Step 3*) and a dispute is resolved in the favor of the *recipient* if $s + 1$ or more are correct.

Can alteration or forgery be successful? To alter or forge a properly signed transaction requires the capability of finding the proper signature to DATA′ from SIG{k_A,DATA,*User B*}, which is assumed to be intractable.

9.11 THE RIVEST-SHAMIR-ADELMAN SIGNATURE SYSTEM [RI1]

The Rivest-Shamir-Adelman cryptographic system can be used to produce a signature system. We assume

$$d,p,q \text{ secret}$$

$$e,n = pq \text{ public}$$

Remarks

1. Factorization of n yields $\varphi(n) = (p - 1)(q - 1)$; $\varphi(n)$ and e yield d.
2. e and d yield a multiple of $\varphi(n)$; a multiple of $\varphi(n)$ gives a factorization of n [MI].

User A signs DATA for *User B* by transmitting

$$E_{e_B,n_B}\{E_{d_A,n_A}\{\text{DATA}\}\}$$

using

User A's secret E_{d_A,n_A}

User B's public E_{e_B,n_B}

User B can read this signed transaction, first using *User B*'s secret E_{d_B,n_B} to obtain

$$E_{d_A,n_A}\{\text{DATA}\} = E_{d_B,n_B}\{E_{e_B,n_B}\{E_{d_A,n_A}\{\text{DATA}\}\}\}$$

and then using *User A*'s public E_{e_A,n_A} to obtain

$$\text{DATA} = E_{e_A,n_A}\{E_{d_A,n_A}\{\text{DATA}\}\}$$

9.12 THE QUADRATIC RESIDUE SIGNATURE SCHEME

Theorem 8.14.1 can be made the basis for a signature scheme. Let p and q be large primes and $n = pq$. Let DATA be represented in the form

$$\text{DATA} : (x_0,x_1, \ldots ,x_{N-1}) \in \boldsymbol{Z}_{2,N}$$

To sign DATA, first randomly generate a sequence

$$R : (r_0,r_1, \ldots ,r_{M-1}) \in \boldsymbol{Z}_{2,M}$$

Next, map the concatenation

$$(x_0,x_1, \ldots ,x_{N-1}, r_0,r_1, \ldots ,r_{M-1}) \in \boldsymbol{Z}_{2,N+M}$$

into an integer in $\boldsymbol{Z}_n$ $(n = pq)$

$$(x_0,x_1, \ldots ,x_{N-1}, r_0,r_1, \ldots ,r_{M-1}) \rightarrow \alpha \qquad 0 \leq \alpha < n$$

For example, compress encode

$$(x_0,x_1, \ldots ,x_{N-1}, r_0,r_1, \ldots ,r_{M-1})$$

and reduce the result modulo n.

There are two possibilities; if α is a quadratic residue (modulo n)

$$\beta^2 = \alpha \text{ (modulo n)}$$

the signature of DATA is the pair

$$(r_0,r_1, \ldots ,r_{M-1}) \quad \beta$$

If α is not a quadratic residue (modulo n), which may be checked by raising α to the powers $(p - 1)/2$ and $(q - 1)/2$ (or by computing the Jacobi symbol), the process is repeated; a new value of R is generated and a new α is computed.

Discussion

If the mapping

$$\text{DATA,R} \rightarrow \alpha$$

is a nice mapping, the probability of selecting an R for which the associated α is a quadratic residue (modulo n) is approximately $\frac{1}{4}$.

9.13 THE TRUSTED AUTHORITY

The final method of transaction verification to be discussed uses the DES algorithm in conjunction with special hardware. The idea is to use VERIFY (a microprocessor), which will respond to a very limited set of commands. The internal operations and intermediate results of VERIFY cannot be examined from the system. We make the following assumptions.

Assumption 1 Any method to recover the key from corresponding pairs of plaintext and DES-enciphered ciphertext is equivalent to key trial.

Assumption 2 Any method to properly sign DATA with key $\mathbf{k_A}$, using corresponding pairs

$$\text{DATA}_i \qquad \text{SIG}\{\mathbf{k_A},\text{DATA}_i\}$$

with

$$\text{DATA} \notin \{\text{DATA}_i\}$$

without $\mathbf{k}_A$ is equivalent to key trial.

The system has a *host master verification key* $\mathbf{k}_{HV}$, and each user has a private *verification key,*

$$A \longleftrightarrow \mathbf{k}_A$$

$$B \longleftrightarrow \mathbf{k}_B$$

$$C \longleftrightarrow \mathbf{k}_C$$

...

...

...

Assumption 3 No user has access to the key $\mathbf{k}_{HV}$. *User A* reveals $\mathbf{k}_A$ only to the arbiter.

The transaction verification system makes use of two tables; the *-table stored at the processor and a second (off-line) table held by the arbiter (see Table 9.13.1):

*-TABLE — $\mathbf{k}_A^* = \text{DES}\{\mathbf{k}_{HV}, (\textit{User A}, \mathbf{k}_A)\}$
$A \longleftrightarrow \mathbf{k}_A^*$
$B \longleftrightarrow \mathbf{k}_B^*$
$C \longleftrightarrow \mathbf{k}_C^*$
...
...

TABLE 9.13.1
Arbiter's Table

$A \longleftrightarrow \mathbf{k}_A \longleftrightarrow \mathbf{k}_A^*$
$B \longleftrightarrow \mathbf{k}_B \longleftrightarrow \mathbf{k}_B^*$
$C \longleftrightarrow \mathbf{k}_C \longleftrightarrow \mathbf{k}_C^*$
...
...

$$\text{DATA} = (\mathbf{x}^{(0)}, \mathbf{x}^{(1)}, \ldots, \mathbf{x}^{(N-1)}) \qquad \mathbf{x}^{(i)} : i^{\text{th}} \text{ block of 8-bytes}$$

$$\text{DES}\{\mathbf{k}_A, \text{DATA}\} = (\mathbf{y}^{(0)}, \mathbf{y}^{(1)}, \ldots, \mathbf{y}^{(N-1)}) \qquad \textit{(chained encipherment of DATA)}$$

$$\mathbf{y}^{(N-1)} : \textit{signature of DATA by User A}$$

The mapping

$$\text{DATA} \rightarrow \text{SIG}\{\mathbf{k}_A,\text{DATA}\}$$

on $Z_{2,64N}$ is $2^{64(N-1)}$ to 1.

9.14 HARDWARE ASSUMPTIONS

- Each terminal is fitted with a DES encipherment box.
- Each terminal has clock or counter.
- VERIFY is under physical security at the CPU. It contains the master verification key $\mathbf{k}_{HV}$. System dumps do not provide the results of intermediate calculations of the verify unit.

9.15 THE TRANSACTION

A transaction from the *originator (User A)* to the *recipient (User B)* consists of the following steps.

Step 1 *User A* and *User B* establish a link. *User B* sends *User A* a counter (or time) value CT_{rec}.

Step 2 *User A* constructs the signature SIG{$\mathbf{k}_A$,DATA} of DATA and sends the pair

$$\text{DATA SIG}\{\mathbf{k}_A,\text{DATA}\}$$

to *User B*. We assume that the DATA is *prefixed* by

- The date of the transaction
- The current counter value CT_{ori} at *User A's* terminal and the received counter value CT_{rec} from *User B's* terminal.

DATA : 1/11/80, CT_{ori}, Ct_{rec}—buy 100 shares of . . .

Step 3 *User B* receives the pair (X,Y) where X and Y are *presumptively equal* to

$$X = \text{DATA} \quad Y = \text{SIG}\{\mathbf{k}_A,\text{DATA}\}$$

The verification process continues if and only if

- The date information is current
- The counter value in the prefix is CT_{rec}

User B is not capable of checking the relationship

$$Y = \mathrm{SIG}\{\mathbf{k}_A, X\}$$

since $\mathbf{k}_A$ is not known by *User B*. The verification of the proper relationship between X and Y will be made by VERIFY. *User B* enciphers the concatenation (n,X,Y, *User A*, *User B*) with key $\mathbf{k}_B$,

$$n = \text{length of X (in bytes)}$$

$$U = \mathrm{DES}\{\mathbf{k}_B, (n, X, Y, \textit{User A}, \textit{User B})\}$$

transmits U to VERIFY, and requests that VERIFY check if Y is a proper signature for X by *User A*. *User B* also sends VERIFY the names of the *originator (User A)* and *the recipient (User B)* in plaintext.

Step 4 VERIFY obtains

- $\mathbf{k}_A^* = \mathrm{DES}\{\mathbf{k}_{HV}, \mathbf{k}_A\}$
- $\mathbf{k}_B^* = \mathrm{DES}\{\mathbf{k}_{HV}, \mathbf{k}_B\}$

from the *-table and calculates $\mathbf{k}_A$ and $\mathbf{k}_B$,

$$(\textit{User A}, \mathbf{k}_A) = \mathrm{DES}^{-1}\{\mathbf{k}_{HV}, \mathbf{k}_A^*\} \quad (\textit{User B}, \mathbf{k}_B) = \mathrm{DES}^{-1}\{\mathbf{k}_{HV}, \mathbf{k}_B^*\}$$

deciphers U under the key k_B,

$$\underline{U} = \mathrm{DES}^{-1}\{\mathbf{k}_B, U\}$$

setting

- $\underline{U}_1 = \underline{U}[1,m]$ (bytes 1 to m of $\underline{U}$)
- $\underline{U}_2 = \underline{U}[m+1, m+n]$ (bytes m + 1 to m + n of $\underline{U}$)
- $\underline{U}_3 = \underline{U}[n+m+1, n+m+8]$ (bytes n + m + 1 to n + m + 8 of $\underline{U}$)
- $\underline{U}_4 = \underline{U}[n+m+9, n+m+16]$ (bytes n +m + 9 to n + m + 16 of $\underline{U}$)
- $\underline{U}_5 = \underline{U}[n+m+17, n+m+24]$ (bytes n + m + 9 to n + m + 16 of $\underline{U}$)

In a valid verification sequence,

$$\underline{U}_1 = \underline{U}[1,m] = n(\text{length of DATA})$$

$$\underline{U}_2 = \underline{U}[m+1, m+n] = \text{DATA}$$

$$\underline{U}_3 = \underline{U}[m+n+1, m+n+8] = \mathrm{SIG}\{k_A, \text{DATA}\}$$

$$\underline{U}_4 = \underline{U}[n+m+9, n+m+16] = \textit{User A}$$

$$\underline{U}_5 = \underline{U}[n+m+17, n+m+24] = \textit{User B}$$

The verification process will not continue (with an indication of this sent to *User B*) if any of the following conditions holds:

- The name of the originator and $\underline{U}_4$ are not equal.
- The name of the recipient and $\underline{U}_5$ are not equal.
- The prefix in $DES^{-1}\{\mathbf{k}_{HV},\mathbf{k}_A^*\}$ and $\underline{U}_4$ are not equal.
- The prefix in $DES^{-1}\{\mathbf{k}_{HV},\mathbf{k}_B^*\}$ and $\underline{U}_5$ are not equal.

VERIFY then calculates the signature of $\underline{U}_2$ with key $\mathbf{k}_A$

$$SIG\{\mathbf{k}_A, \underline{U}_2\}$$

and compares this VERIFY-derived signature with $\underline{U}_3$

- $C = 1$ if there is agreement
- $C = 0$ otherwise
- If $C = 1$, VERIFY will derive the signature of $\sim\underline{U}$ with DES using key $\mathbf{k}_B$ and returns $V = SIG\{\mathbf{k}_B, \sim\underline{U}\}$ to *User B*.
- If $C = 0$, VERIFY will derive the signature of $\underline{U}$

$$V = SIG\{\mathbf{k}_B, \underline{U}\}$$

and return V to *User B*.

Step 5 *User B* calculates

$$SIG\{\mathbf{k}_B, \sim(n,X,Y,\mathit{User\ A},\mathit{User\ B})\}$$

and compares it with the response V received from VERIFY.

Step 6 *User B* accepts the transaction if and only if

- The date information in X is current
- The counter value in X agrees with the stored counter value, and
- The verify is valid

$$V = SIG\{\mathbf{k}_B, \sim(n,X,Y,\mathit{User\ A},\mathit{User\ B})\}$$

The flow of data in this transaction verification system is

Message	From	To
CT_{rec}	*User A*	*User B*
n X Y	*User A*	*User B*
$DES\{\mathbf{k}_B,(n,X,Y,\mathit{User\ A},\mathit{User\ B})\}$, *User A*, *User B*	*User B*	VERIFY
V	VERIFY	*User B*

9.16 THREAT ANALYSIS

In Dispute *R,* a claim by *User B* that *User A* has failed to honor a signed transaction,

$$X = \text{DATA} \qquad Y = \text{SIG}\{\mathbf{k}_A,\text{DATA}\}$$

the arbiter will check if Y is the signature of X with k_A and decide for *User B* in this case. Can a transaction (X,Y) with

$$X = \text{DATA} \qquad Y \neq \text{SIG}\{\mathbf{k}_A,\text{DATA}\}$$

be verified to *User B?*

Suppose *User B* has received (X,Y), believing *User A* to have been the source of the communication. In reality, (X,Y) has been sent by *User C* (or so *User A* might claim in attempting to renege), so that

$$Y \neq \text{SIG}\{\mathbf{k}_A,\text{DATA}\}$$

By Assumptions 1 and 2, *User C* cannot effectively sign DATA, that is, derive SIG{$\mathbf{k}_A$,DATA} without $\mathbf{k}_A$. The possible strategies for *User C* include:

- To replace the message

  $$U, \textit{User A}, \textit{User B}$$

  $$U = \text{DES}\{\mathbf{k}_B,(n,X,Y,\textit{User A},\textit{User B})\}$$

  from *User B* to VERIFY by a message

  $$U', \textit{User A}', \textit{User B}'$$

  which will cause VERIFY to return the proper response to *User B*

  $$V = \text{SIG}\{\mathbf{k}_B,\sim\underline{U}\}$$

  verifying the transaction of *User B.*

or

- To replace the message V from VERIFY to *User B,*

  $$V = \text{SIG}\{\mathbf{k}_B,\underline{U}\}$$

  alerting *User B* that Y is not a proper signature of X by *User A* by

  $$V = \text{SIG}\{\mathbf{k}_B,\sim\underline{U}\}$$

  causing *User B* to accept the transaction.

The reuse of previously verified transactions is prevented by the use of counter values which "time-stamp" transactions. We assume that the period of the counter is sufficiently large.

Assumptions 1 and 2 imply that without $\mathbf{k}_B$, *User C* cannot effectively compute

$$U' = \text{DES}\{\mathbf{k}_B,(n,X,Y,\textit{User }A',\textit{User }B')\}$$

for the attack • with $Y = \text{SIG}\{\mathbf{k}_{A'},\text{DATA}\}$ without $\mathbf{k}_{A'}$ and $\mathbf{k}_B$ *or* $\text{SIG}\{\mathbf{k}_B,\sim U\}$ for the attack •• without $\mathbf{k}_B$.

User C can change the plaintext *User A* in the message

$$U, \textit{User A}, \textit{User B}$$

to *User C* so that $Y = \text{SIG}\{\mathbf{k}_C,\text{DATA}\}$ is a proper signature by *User C* to X. When VERIFY receives

$$U, \textit{User C}, \textit{User B}$$

$$U = \text{DES}\{\mathbf{k}_B,(n,X,Y,\textit{User }A,\textit{User }B)\}$$

the transaction will not be verified by VERIFY, since the plaintext name *User C* will not match $\underline{U}_4$.

Guessing the correct message U from *User B* to VERIFY or the proper verification response $\text{SIG}\{\mathbf{k}_B,\sim U\}$ from VERIFY to *User B* is always possible. We claim that properties of the chaining transformation imply that the probability of success by random sampling is of the order 2^{-63}.

Finally, the on-line *-Table might be altered by *User C* in an attempt at deception; for example, by replacing the entry $\mathbf{k}_A^*$ by $\mathbf{k}_C^*$. Again VERIFY will detect such an attack after deciphering the presumptive $\mathbf{k}_A^*$ and comparing the prefixes of $\text{DES}^{-1}\{\mathbf{k}_{HV},\mathbf{k}_A^*\}$ $\text{DES}^{-1}\{\mathbf{k}_{HV},\mathbf{k}_B^*\}$ with the decipherment of

$$\text{DES}\{\mathbf{k}_B,(n,X,Y,\textit{User }A,\textit{User }B)\}$$

9.17 CRYPTOGRAPHY WITHOUT SECRECY

Throughout our discussion of encipherment, we have assumed that in order for users to hide their communications, they must share a common key—derived in some fashion by the system, or by using a public key system. Shamir in unpublished work has observed that user-to-user encipherment can be implemented without this sharing of a key.

Let p be a prime known to both *User i* and *User j*. We assume that each user has a secret key that is revealed to no other user; k_i is the key of *User i*. The following steps are taken by *User i* and *User j* to exchange a key during a session.

1. *User i* selects a *session key* k_0,

$$k_0 \in \boldsymbol{Z}_p - \{0\}$$

and transmits $k_1 = k_0^{k_i}$ (modulo p) to *User j*.

2. *User j* evaluates

$$k_2 = k_1^{k_j} = (k_0^{k_i})^{k_j} \text{ (modulo p)}$$

and returns k_2 to *User i*.

3. *User i* evaluates

$$k_3 = k_2^{k_i^{-1}} = ((k_0^{k_i})^{k_j})^{k_i^{-1}} \text{(modulo p)}$$

where k_i^{-1} is the multiplicative inverse modulo p − 1 of k_i:

$$k_i k_i^{-1} = 1 \text{ (modulo p − 1)}$$

(Fermat's) Theorem 8.9.1 and the commutativity of multiplication imply

$$k_3 = ((k_0^{k_i})^{k_j})^{k_i^{-1}} \text{(modulo p)} = k_0^{k_j} \text{ (modulo p)} = k_4$$

k_4 is returned to *User j*.

4. *User j* evaluates

$$k_5 = k_4^{k_j^{-1}} \text{(modulo p)} = (k_0^{k_j})^{k_j^{-1}} \text{(modulo p)}$$

where k_j^{-1} is the multiplicative inverse modulo p − 1 of k_j:

$$k_j k_j^{-1} = 1 \text{ (modulo p − 1)}$$

(Fermat's) Theorem 8.9.1 and the commutativity of multiplication imply

$$k_5 = k_0$$

User i and *User j* have now exchanged a common key.

Is there anything wrong? No, except that *User j* and *User i* are not certain that they are communicating with each other. *User O* might masquerade as *User j*, and *User i* (in the absence of other information) cannot be certain that *User j* is the party at the other end of the transmission. This example shows that secrecy is not enough; for two users to securely communicate, they must be certain of the authenticity of the party at the other end.

PROBLEMS

9.1 Credit card transactions are currently "protected" by comparing the signature at the time of purchase with a *reference signature* on the card. Most people are not sufficiently trained to detect clever forgeries. Design a new type of credit card system to protect the seller *and* the card-holder against forgery.

Assume that each point-of-sale station has a card reader and associated microprocessor. Consider two cases:

- The store is linked by teleprocessing lines to a central processor.
- The store is not linked by teleprocessing lines to a central processor.

The solution must not require storing any secret information *at the point of sale* station.

9.2 How can the Rivest-Shamir-Adelman encipherment system be used for authentication?

9.3 Why are the counter values CT_{rec} and CT_{ori} exchanged in the verification protocol in Sec. 9.13?

9.4 Prove that the *multiplicity* of the mapping

$$\sigma_N(\mathbf{k}) : \boldsymbol{Z}_{2,64N} \rightarrow \boldsymbol{Z}_{2,64}$$

$$\sigma_N(\mathbf{k}) : \mathbf{x} = (\mathbf{x}^{(0)}, \mathbf{x}^{(1)}, \ldots, \mathbf{x}^{(N-1)}) \rightarrow \mathrm{SIG}\{\mathbf{k}, \mathbf{x}\}$$

$\mathrm{SIG}\{\mathbf{k},\mathbf{x}\}$: final 8 bytes of chained encipherment of $\mathbf{x}$ by DES with key $\mathbf{k}$

is $2^{64(N-1)}$ to 1; that is, if $\mathbf{y} \in \boldsymbol{Z}_{2,64}$, then

$$\text{multiplicity of } \mathbf{y} = |\{\mathbf{x} \in \boldsymbol{Z}_{2,64N} : \sigma_N(\mathbf{k}) : \mathbf{x} \rightarrow \mathbf{y}\}| = 2^{64(N-1)}$$

9.5 If

$$\sigma_N(\mathbf{k}) : \boldsymbol{Z}_{2,64N} \rightarrow \boldsymbol{Z}_{2,64}$$

$$\sigma_N(\mathbf{k}) : \mathbf{x} = (\mathbf{x}^{(0)}, \mathbf{x}^{(1)}, \ldots, \mathbf{x}^{(N-1)}) \rightarrow \mathbf{y}^{(N-1)}$$

$$\mathbf{y}^{(i)} = \mathrm{DES}\{\mathbf{y}^{(i-1)}, \mathbf{x}^{(i)}\} \qquad 0 \le i < N \quad \mathbf{y}^{(-1)} = \mathbf{k}$$

what is the multiplicity of $\sigma_N(\mathbf{k})$,

$$|\{\mathbf{x} = (\mathbf{x}^{(0)}, \mathbf{x}^{(1)}, \ldots, \mathbf{x}^{(N-1)}) : \sigma_N(\mathbf{k}) : \mathbf{x} \rightarrow \mathbf{y}\}|?$$

CHAPTER X

File Security

10.1 THE PROBLEM

In the third quarter of 1974, IBM's Research Division began an investigation of ways to improve computing-center security at the Thomas J. Watson Research Center in Yorktown Heights, New York. Several steps were taken to improve physical security. Transparent protective walls were constructed to make access difficult for unauthorized persons. Procedures for changing combinations on push-button-code locks were tightened, and other measures of a similar nature were adopted.

Nevertheless, a serious problem remained; behind the locked doors and protective walls were computing systems with security exposures not related to their physical surroundings. For example, except for the most highly classified data, any tape could be mounted by knowledgeable users of our computing systems, which share a common operations staff and tape library. In OS/MVT, any on-line data set could be read by any job. It is shown in [AT] that VM/370 could be penetrated by a determined attacker.

Several alternatives were considered for improving the security of on-line and off-line data at Yorktown. The OS/MVT *password* facility was considered for data sets, but was rejected because of its operational inconvenience and because the demonstrated weakness in VM/370 made it difficult to justify serious inconvenience in OS/MVT. If a "protected" OS/MVT volume could easily be mounted by a VM/370 user, no real protection existed. A manual record-keeping system to prevent unauthorized mounts in VM/370 was also rejected as awkward and error-prone. Further, it was concluded that confidential data could not be considered really safe if it could be accessed by operators, system programmers, and other users with privileged access to the system.

To meet the needs of users who held confidential data in this environment, a cryptographic system based on DES and called the *Information Protection System (IPS)* was developed. By using IPS programs to apply a cryptographic transformation to their data, users have been able to protect confidential information against unauthorized release. While encipherment does not protect a file against accidental or malicious destruction, the owner can be confident that the information in an IPS-enciphered file will almost certainly never be read in plaintext by an opponent, nor will an attempt to modify the data in secret be successful.

IPS-enciphered data is now used in our computing systems in substantial quantity, and its owners still enjoy convenient access to their files. Although IPS does not provide an absolute answer to the problems of computing-center security, it has been in use at Yorktown and has been delivered to many IBM locations over the course of more than four years. The real usefulness of IPS goes beyond the basic cryptographic function provided; it is the protection offered in the users' natural programming environment.

10.2 THE DESIGN PHILOSOPHY OF IPS

The goal of IPS is to offer an implementation of the Data Encryption Standard that is easy to use while providing the Standard's full cryptographic strength, as well as several additional features. The design principles of IPS are as follows:

Key Management

No key or variable equivalent to a key resides permanently in the computing system. Keys are the responsibility of each user; they are entered into the system at the time of encipherment or decipherment. Keys are thus exposed in the system only during residence of the job or command that uses IPS, not on a permanent basis.

A cryptographic system that links two users must provide a mechanism for establishing a common operational key. If one of the users is a host operating system, some provision must be made either for storing keys in the host or for the host to construct the operational key. If keys are permanently resident in the system, then users with privileged status may be able to obtain them. While such users might possibly place traps in an operating system to recover keys during an IPS session, this exposure is smaller, and the attack is probably more dangerous to the attacker than inspection of a permanently resident file of keys.

Key Formats

A variety of key formats is offered to users.

The DES algorithm specifies a 64-bit key, but makes use of only 56 bits, with eight bits serving as parity check bits. IPS allows the direct entry of eight-byte DES deys expressed in hexadecimal notation. For maximum safety, the 56 active key bits should be chosen randomly, but randomness is not always easy to achieve, even by experienced users. Therefore, in addition to direct DES key input, IPS allows a user to specify the key as a long character string to be converted internally to a form suitable for DES. It is believed that a key expressed as a character string is easier for a user to invent and remember, and if chosen with reasonable care, it can be the equivalent of a random DES key. (Users should avoid familiar names, numbers, and phrases, and they should use long keys when the individual key characters are not selected randomly. These matters are discussed under *Key selection and key crunching,* below.

Record Size Preservation

Although DES requires eight-byte inputs, IPS is so designed that data records whose lengths are eigher less than eight bytes, or not a multiple of eight bytes, are accepted and do not increase in size under encipherment.

Users are not required to pad their data to conform with DES, nor do the IPS programs lengthen data in this way. Altered data lengths would unnecessarily complicate the computing environment by requiring changes in data set attributes and in application-program array sizes and string lengths.

Repetitive Plaintext Patterns and Chaining

Repetitive patterns in plaintext are not to be mirrored in the ciphertext.

DES is a block cipher that enciphers identical eight-byte plaintext blocks into identical eight-byte ciphertext blocks (under the same key—an assumption made throughout). By employing *chaining* in IPS, it is possivle to use DES in such a manner that identical eight-byte plaintext blocks virtually always yield different ciphertext blocks, without altering the security of the existing algorithm. (The interpretation of *virtually always* is discussed below, under *Block chaining* and *Record chaining.*)

IPS Facilities

Utilities and commands are provided for handling OS/VS data sets, and VM/370 CMS files and data can be enciphered and deciphered from within user programs in FORTRAN, PL/I, and Assembler. Ciphertext files produced by the utilities and by user programs are compatible, provided that users follow IPS conventions when creating files to be deciphered by the utilities, or deciphering files created by the utilities. For nonsequential access methods not supported by the utilities, for example, VSAM and BDAM, encipherment from within user programs still permits the creation of ciphertext files. When needed, the use of IPS within user programs permits the designing of applications that read and write data sets entirely in ciphertext, without ever having to expose files of plaintext.

It is important to provide a service that is sufficiently flexible to keep users satisfied, that is, pleased at the way IPS fits into their environment and content with the investment of time and effort required to introduce cryptography into their applications. Therefore, IPS supports both batch and interactive use, and it makes both utilities and subroutines available. In designing IPS, it was not feasible that the utilities be made to handle all conceivable types of data sets (at least with the development time available to us). Thus the subroutines provide an important mechanism for enciphering files of all types, because the user programs themselves will handle I/O. And if user programs read and write in ciphertext, plaintext files need never exist.

Header Record

IPS-enciphered files ordinarily contain a header record to identify and describe them as IPS ciphertext. The record is inserted and removed automatically by the utilities, and is passed back to those who use IPS from within their own code.

The header record includes (1) information about the type of encipherment used, (2) a time-date stamp, (3) the version of IPS employed, (4) cryptographic chaining information, (5) a verification field to warn a user at time of decipherment when an incorrect key has been supplied, without providing information that enables the correct key to be recovered, and (6) an optional user comment field.

File Exhange

To the extent that plaintext files can be exchanged between OS/VS and VM/370 CMS systems, the corresponding IPS-enciphered files are also exchangeable, with encipherment in one system and decipherment in the other, as needed.

Programming And Documentation

Programs must be designed and coded with great care, since incorrect output is not easily detected in ciphertext. Similarly, because misuse of the programs can cause loss of user data, and worried users may not submit their data to cryptographic transformation, the documentation has been made as clear and helpul as possible.

10.3 AUGMENTATION OF DES BY CHAINING/KEY CRUNCHING

Certain plaintext files exhibit great regularity, with many identical eight-byte blocks (for example, blocks of eight blanks to fill out lines of computer source programs to a fixed length). Normally, under DES encipherment, such identical blocks of plaintext yield identical blocks of ciphertext (under the same key). Thus the eight-byte blocks of blanks may be identifiable, and a rough geometric outline of regions of nonblank characters among blank characters in the plaintext may be discernible in the ciphertext. Repetitions of some other blocks may also be visible; for example, identical records in the plaintext, or identical parts of records when aligned with the eight-byte DES blocks, can be recognized as identical in the ciphertext. It is doubtful whether this phenomenon is a serious weakness: to date no technique has been found that uses it to determine the key or to obtain usable plaintext of alphabetic or numeric files (although some of the structure of digitized line drawings could be visible). However, if the existence of identical blocks can be concealed, a cryptographic system is strengthened at least intuitively, because the amount of information available to an opponent is reduced. Because of the possibility that under some circumstances, with some ciphertexts, an opponent might be able to make use of repetitions, an augmentation of the DES algorithm was deemed advisable in IPS.

After all the eight-byte blocks of a record have been enciphered using DES, there frequently remains a *short block,* a block of fewer than eight bytes. A short block cannot be enciphered directly by DES, since DES requires eight-byte inputs. It could be padded on the right with zeros or blanks and then enciphered, but all eight bytes of the resulting ciphertext, and preferably information as to the length of the padding, would have to be preserved for future decipherment, and the ciphertext would be longer than the original plaintext. This condition is undesirable because, for example, the ciphertext might have to replace the plaintext in some previously allocated space, or be written according to some previously defined record length. Alternatively, some key-dependent "simple substitution" encipherment could be designed for short blocks; but if it depended only on that block (and the key), it could be subject to cryptanalysis, especially when the length of identical blocks, is potentially more serious, because some nonblank short-block plaintext could be discovered. To handle both types of programs, *chaining,* described in Sec. 6.23, is used. Chaining is a process by which each block of ciphertext is made to depend not only on the corresponding plaintext and key, but also on the preceding ciphertext. If the dependence starts anew with each record, the process is termed *block chaining;* if it continues across record boundaries, it is termed *record chaining.* Augmentation of DES by chaining eliminates repetitiveness in ciphertext arising from repetitive plaintext, it provides for the encipherment and decipherment of data of arbitrary length (not necessarily multiples of eight bytes); and it allows the user to enter keys as long character strings.

10.4 KEY SELECTION AND KEY CRUNCHING

In the past there has been a tendency among users of cryptographic systems to use a *word* or a *name* as a key. Today this procedure is unsafe. There are fewer than a million words in an unabridged dictionary, and fewer than a million names in a large telephone directory. That number of potential keys could be tested in a few minutes on a System/370 Model 168. Even the use of eight randomly chosen EBCDIC characters is unsafe, because only about a third of the 256 EBCDIC characters can be printed at a terminal, which reduces the available keys by a factor of about 1.5×10^{-4}. Instead, if a DES key is introduced *directly,* it should consist of *16 hexadecimal digits, chosen randomly or essentially so* (except for parity).

IPS provides for an additional way of defining a key. It permits the user to enter a *user key* of more than eight bytes, say 16 bytes or more (usually, but not necessarily, printable characters and blanks). With this freedom, the user might, for example, enter several words (say five or more) chosen *randomly* and *independently* from an unabridged dictionary. Or the user might enter some phrase. It is essential that these choices be made in such a way that the key cannot practically be found by an opponent, either by guesswork or by enumerating some plausible set of keys.

To produce a suitable DES key from such a longer user key, some good *hashing* function is needed. It should be sufficiently complicated to produce essentially unbiased and statistically independent bits in the DES key. It would not be desirable, for example, merely to XOR various bytes together to form the DES key. The EBCDIC representations of decimal digits and capital letters all commence with binary 11, hence the XOR of any number of these commences with 11 or 00, so that the leading two bits of such an XOR are perfectly correlated, thereby limiting the set of possible keys. More generally, any linear combination of biased or correlated bits will have a nonuniform distribution, which might be useful to an opponent by allowing him to search only over the more likely keys.

This problem is solved by the use of chaining. IPS enciphers the long user key under a selected key, with chaining, and it uses the rightmost 56 bits of the resulting ciphertext as the DES key; this procedure is called *key crunching.* It is believed that correlations in the user key are adequately smoothed out by crunching. The DES key can be returned to the user so that either it or the long key can be used for future decipherments.

10.5 COMPONENTS OF IPS

The OS/VS version of IPS has two components: a utility program called IEBCODE for enciphering (or deciphering) sequential data sets, and a set of cryptographic subroutines intended for calling from Assembler, FORTRAN, and PL/I Optimizing Compiler progams. In addition, an interactive CIPHER command is provided for TSO (the Time Sharing Option) runnning under MVS (Miltiple Virtual Storage). The VM/370 CMS version of IPS has two components: an interactive CIPHER command used to process CMS files and the same set of subroutines used in OS/VS.

The IEBCODE Utility Program

IEBCODE is a cryptographic utility for sequential data sets. That is, it produces an enciphered copy of a sequential plaintext file, or a deciphered copy of a sequential ciphertext file. Individual members of a partitioned data set can also be processed, provided that it is not necessary to preserve the user data fields, if any, in the partitioned-data-set directory entry. If other types of data sets are to be protected, then either the data must be unloaded (by one of the normal utilities) and the resulting sequential data set enciphered by IEBCODE, or, better, the data sets can be processed by user programs that read and write the data sets themselves and call IPS subroutines for cryptographic services.

IEBCODE can process any data set accessible by the Queued Sequential Access Method (QSAM). All valid fixed-length, variable-length, variable-spanned, and undefined-length data sets can be processed. IEBCODE does not allow a change of record format, but it permits the reblocking of data as requested by the user in the Job Control Language DD statement DCB parameter.

Logical Record Encipherment

IEBCODE enciphers logical records individually, rather than in any larger or different unit, for compatibility with user application programs that make use of

IPS subroutines. Because both the subroutines and IEBCODE were to be used as part of the same package, it is important that the exchange of data between them be relatively easy. Further, for applications that must be as secure as possible, it is intended that the IPS subroutines be used in preference to IEBCODE, or used after IEBCODE had converted all the old plaintext secret files to ciphertext. It is believed that many of the most important applications of IPS would use subroutines almost exclusively, because under the subroutines, plaintext external files need never exist: instead, the data is left in ciphertext until the moment that each data item is to be used in main storage by a running program. It is important that the two parts of IPS be compatible in order to support this type of application, in which IEBCODE is used for the initial bulk conversion of data files from plaintext to ciphertext, or used occasionally to create ciphertext files from newly arrived data, while the subroutines would be used for updating. IEBCODE, therefore, had to be designed to produce ciphertext that could easily be read and processed by user programs.

Data to be deciphered by a subroutine call are handled most easily if ciphertext records are processed one at a time, in the same manner as the processing of ordinary records by an application that does not use cryptography. This natural processing of data set records by an application program is possible only if the unit of encipherment, the data enciphered in one logical operation, is exactly one logical record. It cannot, for example, be a group of records, because such a technique would force the application program to read and process records in groups. For most applications, substantial program changes would be required to adopt such a scheme. Therefore, under IEBCODE, each record in the data set is enciphered separately, so that ciphertext produced by IEBCODE can easily be read and processed by user programs.

For fixed-length records, the unit of encipherment is the logical record. For variable-length records, the unit of encipherment is the data portion of the logical record; the record descriptor word remains in plaintext, to be accessible to data management routines. For undefined-length records, the unit of encipherment is the physical data block, because user programs must also treat each such a block as an individual record. For spanned variable-length records, the unit of encipherment is the data portion of the entire spanned record, no matter how many segments or physical blocks it may occupy. By making the unit of encipherment for spanned records the entire record rather than a record segment, IEBCODE ensures that the ciphertext produced is independent of block size and record segmentation.

For users of IEBCODE who employ it only for the bulk encipherment and decipherment of data, logical record encipherment is of no particular importance. But that technique makes it possible for users to exchange data between IEBCODE and their own cryptographic application programs with minimal difficulty. This design also permits the exchange of files between OS/VS systems and IPS CIPHER command running under VM/370 CMS.

Logical record encipherment can be set aside if the benefits of incompatibility exceed the costs. For instance, it is possible to imagine a scheme in which incoming plaintext records are processed by a data compaction routine to save space and the CPU time needed to encipher them, then are placed in successive portions of a standardized fixed buffer, enciphered, and transmitted to an output data set. Such a compressed and enciphered file theoretically could be processed by a user program, but that is not likely to happen for practical reasons. For most purposes, and in the absence of special reasons as in the above example, the logical record encipherment technique is preferred.

The Encode ID Record

Enciphered files are identified as such by IEBCODE. A header record, the *encode ID record,* is written at the front of each file of ciphertext. This ID *(identification)* record contains the date and time of the run, the version of IPS used, a security classification text chosen by the user, initializing information concerning the cryptographic chaining (block or record) used in the file, an optional user comment field, and a cryptographic *key test* field. The key test field is based on the user key, but does not contain it. During subsequent decipherment, IEBCODE can determine almost certainly, from the key test field, whether or not the key supplied at that time is the same as the key used in the original encipherment, thus providing early warning if the user has inadvertently supplied the wrong key. (The key test field consists of the XOR of the left and right halves of the encipherment of the ID record time-and-date field under the user key. Because of the XORing, the time-and-date and key test fields do not exhibit matching plaintext and ciphertest.)

When IEBCODE is used to *encipher* a file, it begins by initializing for encipherment under the user key and writing the *encode ID record* into the output file. Then each logical record in the input file is read and enciphered separately, and its ciphertext is transmitted to the output file.

When IEBCODE is used to *decipher* a file, it begins by searching for an *encode ID record* at the beginning of the file to determine the chaining mode and test the key. If a recognizable *encode ID record* is not found, all the data in the file are treated as ciphertext, and the ID record processing is bypassed. The ciphertext logical records are then read from the file one at a time and deciphered, and the plaintext equivalents are transmitted to the output file.

A cryptographic "round trip" using IEBCODE, from a plaintext file to a ciphertext file and, in a separate run, from ciphertext to plaintext again, naturally yields the original plaintext logical records. However, the data set blocking can be changed if requested by the user. And, as mentioned above, the method of encipherment is compatible with record-by-record cryptographic processing by user application programs.

IEBCODE Control Statement

A control statement is required for the user to specify the function to be performed and to supply required and optional parameters. At the user's option, the text of the control statement may be printed, or the printing may be bypassed for security reasons. The control statement options are:

1. Function: either ENCODE or DECODE must be specified.

2. Cryptographic key: a key must be specified, but a wide variety of key formats is permitted, such as direct DES keys (expressed in hexadecimal) or long-character-string keys (expressed in either character or hexadecimal form). When hexadecimal notation is used, commas and blanks can be inserted to improve readability without affecting the active key characters. If a DES key is supplied, it is used "as is" in the encipherment process. Longer keys are converted to DES keys by the chained encipherment method described in a previous section.

3. Security classification: a parameter can be specified to place a classification text (in the clear) in the ID record.

4. Cryptographic chaining: either the block chaining or record chaining option can be chosen. If the option is not specified with ENCODE, record chaining is assumed.

5. ID record comment: a comment of up to 40 bytes of text can be included in the ID record, if supplied on the control statement. This comment is not enciphered, but remains as a single line of plaintext user documentation (of ownership, for example, or for file identification) in what otherwise (except for the security classification) is a file of unrecognizable ciphertext.

Error Conditions and Messages

When an error occurs, IEBCODE attempts to continue execution, if it is reasonable to do so, but with an appropriate error message. For many conditions, execution must terminate; but the text of the message produced, and an expanded explanation in IPS user documentation, are intended to get the user past the difficulty in as short a time as possible.

IEBCODE can produce 49 separate informational, warning, or error messages. One reason for so many messages and conditions is that enciphered data sets are fundamentally different from other data sets in that they look like "garbage." When a conventional program produces incorrect output, it may be recognizable as such. With cryptographic programs, great care is needed to avoid producing files that look like garbage and really *are* garbage! (It is not unlikely that an installation will eventually use IEBCODE without testing each file of ciphertext to be certain it can be deciphered, in which case it is important that any errors be properly detected and reported.)

IEBCODE Summary

IEBCODE processes a variety of sequential data sets and individual partitioned-data-set members. Because of this flexibility, users generally do not need to alter their data to use the IPS cryptographic system. IEBCODE's control statement is easily coded and provides a method for the simple entry of a cryptographic key in different formats, including character strings with meaning to individual users. The large number of error messages that can be produced under different circumstances, and their explanatory texts, help users solve difficulties quickly and easily.

IEBCODE is used to encipher files to be sent between computing centers and also to protect on-line data. For application programs that do not call IPS subroutines for encipherment and decipherment (see below), IEBCODE performs these services, typically with ciphertext in permanent data sets and plaintext in temporary ones.

IPS Subroutines

Users are encouraged to call IPS subroutines from their own FORTRAN, PL/I Optimizing and Checkout Compiler, or Assembler programs. When calling IPS from an application program, the user passes data in main storage and receives data from IPS the same way. I/O is the user's responsibility and is handled in the usual way according to the programming language chosen. Since the subroutines depend on the chosen programming language for almost all operating system services (the major exception is the OS/VS TIME macro), experience has shown that they work equally well in any OS/VS system and in VM/370 CMS, and that ciphertext produced in any of these systems can be deciphered in any other.

One advantage of encipherment by a subroutine call, mentioned above under *The IEBCODE Utility Program,* is that no plaintext need ever exist on external files. Instead, the user program reads enciphered data from a file and deciphers it only at the time of use, and likewise enciphers data before writing it to a file. Therefore, no plaintext data need ever exist outside of main storage (except for transient residence in paging data sets).

IPS subroutines can also be used for enciphering and deciphering nonsequential files, which cannot be processed by IEBCODE. Of particular interest are nonsequential files from which only selected records are read at any one time. The use of IPS subroutines avoids the cost of deciphering an entire file in order to access only a few records. In such applications, block chaining generally is more appropriate than record chaining.

Encipherment by a subroutine call also allows users to select the data that is to be enciphered in a file. If only certain fields of each record are to be concealed, for example, customer name and address, those fields can be enciphered by a subroutine call, and the remainder of the record left in plaintext. This procedure can save a significant amount of CPU time if large files are being processed. If necessary, the various confidential parts of records can be enciphered under different keys, making it possible to grant selective access to the enciphered material, according to the distribution of keys. In these cases also, block chaining is more appropriate than record chaining.

In general, the subroutines for different languages work in similar ways. Each set has four entry points: two for encipherment and two for decipherment. One of each pair is an initializer, to which the cryptographic key and the processing options are given. Initialization normally is performed once for each run. The other routine in each pair performs the actual encipherments or decipherments, one call for each record. The initialization function is separated from the encipherment or decipherment function to save the time that otherwise would be required to initialize IPS working storage before processing each piece of data.

When the *encode* initializer is called, it is given the key, the security classification, and the cryptographic chaining option. The encode initializer prepares a table to speed the encipherments under the specified key, prepares for chaining, and passes back the *encode ID record,* which the user may optionally write into the output file to identify the data. The *encode ID record* is identical to that produced by IEBCODE. When the *decode* initializer is called, it is given the key and the optional *encode ID record* if saved at the time of encipherment, or the chaining information if needed because the ID record is missing. The decode initializer prepares the table for decipherment under the specified key and prepares for chaining according to the ID record or the user argument.

When the *encoder* is called, it is passed the plaintext and the area where it is to place the corresponding ciphertext. This area can be the plaintext area itself, since the routine can process data "in place." When the *decoder* is called, it is passed ciphertext and the area where it is to place the corresponding plaintext, which similarly can be the ciphertext area itself for "in place" decipherment.

The required attributes of the data to be enciphered are natural to the programming language the user has chosen, to the extent that it is possible to do this. That is, in Assembler language, a user is expected to pass the addresses of the input and output data areas and their length. In FORTRAN, a user is expected to pass FORTRAN variables (usually arrays) for the data areas, and an integer variable containing their length (in bytes). In PL/I, a user is asked to pass either fixed or varying character strings, or a mixture. If PL/I data of other types is to be processed, the user is instructed to either pass BASED fixed-length character strings (whose pointers address the data to be processed), or define and initialize structures that imitate PL/I's character string descriptors, and call IPS through alternate entry points declared with OPTIONS(ASSEMBLER).

Error Handling

In the IPS subroutines, difficulties are divided into two classes, *warnings* and *errors*. And, like many other programs, the IPS subroutines take corrective action and continue, perhaps after a warning message, when a minor difficulty arises. But because there is a danger of transmitting wrong data in the belief that it is valid ciphertext, IPS terminates a user program in the presence of a serious error. Because termination is implemented with FORTRAN and PL/I language features, not the system ABEND macro, users can easily override the termination if they choose. Termination occurs if all of the following three conditions hold:

- A difficulty defined as an IPS *error* has occurred. For example, the user has supplied a cryptographic key shorter than the DES minimum, or has requested that a negative number of data bytes be enciphered. (IPS *warnings,* resulting, for example, from a request to encipher a zero-byte record, do not cause termination.)
- The user has called IPS from one of the languages for which the protection is defined; that is, PL/I in all cases, or FORTRAN, if the installation's system programmers have prepared FORTRAN's extended error handling facility for use by IPS.

- The user has not prepared for the possibility of such errors; that is, he has not called the FORTRAN ERRSET routine, or has not supplied a suitable PL/I ON-unit.

In other words, if a user is willing to handle errors, and signals that fact by establishing the correct FORTRAN or PL/I error environment, IPS will not terminate the program in the presence of an error. But if the user permits an error to occur and has not prepared for it, IPS will terminate the program to prevent destruction of the user's data.

A great deal of thought was given to this problem before deciding to provide for the termination of user programs, but it was implemented because it is important that users should be protected from serious errors. It would be possible for a user who supplies erroneous arguments to write either nonsense data or actual plaintext under the impression that it is valid ciphertext. If indicative return codes were ignored in such situations, the result could be a serious loss, which is guarded against to the extent possible. To be sure, the protection is not perfect. It is not present in an Assembler language environment, and it is lost if the user takes the bypass actions offered in user documentation. But these risks have to be taken if careful users are to be allowed to continue in execution.

Warning and error messages have as much variety and detail as those for the IEBCODE utility, but they are modified to report in terms of the programming language chosen. Assembler language users may choose from two versions of the IPS subroutines: one that presents only a return code, or one that presents both the return code and formatted error messages. FORTRAN and PL/I users will find messages in the standard output print file unless suppressed by standard language features (ERRSET in FORTRAN, ON-units in PL/I).

A limitation of the subroutines in their vulnerability to any user error in which the IPS tables are overlaid by user data. For example, except in PL/I with SUBSCRIPTRANGE enabled, it is possible to store data outside the boundaries of arrays. If such an operation should alter the IPS tables, the encipherment process would give incorrect results while appearing to be correct.

Interactive IPS Commands

Any programmer can encipher information interactively by including calls to IPS subroutines in his own interactive programs. In this sense, IPS has always been available to TSO and VM/370 application programmers. But for secretarial use, and for programmers who want a convenient way to encipher entire files, IPS includes a CIPHER command for VM/370 CMS files and another for TSO sequential data sets.

The VM/370 CMS CIPHER command is a *copy* utility combined with encipherment. With the *encode* option, CIPHER creates an enciphered copy of a CMS disk file. With the *decode* option, it creates a plaintext copy of a previously enciphered file. This command provides the easiest way to use IPS in the CMS environment. CIPHER is invoked either from a terminal or from a CMS EXEC file (one that contains a sequence of CMS commands to be executed). It is commonly used to encipher confidential documents that otherwise could not be stored on line, and to encipher confidential material to be sent from one location to another over the IBM VM/370 network. The command itself initiates all terminal interaction and I/O, and it calls the IPS cryptographic subroutines for encipherments and decipherments. The ciphertext produced by CIPHER is IPS standard ciphertext. That is, each file of ciphertext contains an identifying record (the *encode ID record*) at the beginning, and each record in the CMS file is enciphered separately for convenient use by application programs. This format is the same as that used by the IEBCODE utility in OS/VS systems, and experience has shown that the OS/VS and CMS systems can exchange ciphertext without difficulty.

The TSO CIPHER command can be used in MVS to encipher sequential data sets and individual partitioned-data-set members during a TSO session. CIPHER itself initiates all terminal interaction, then invokes IEBCODE for data set I/O and cryptographic services. Thus it ensures compatibility of ciphertexts between batch and interactive uses.

10.6 IPS AND THE IBM CRYPTOGRAPHIC PRODUCTS

Programmed Cryptographic Facility

The IPS cryptographic programs and the IBM cryptographic program products were developed separately for different purposes, and they have interesting similarities and differences. The IBM OS/VS1 and OS/VS2 MVS Programmed Cryptographic Facility [IBM1] is a software implementation of DES, together with key management and handling services. Assembler language programmers can call on the Facility for the encipherment and decipherment of data in main storage. The Facility is used also by other IBM program products that require cryptographic services, such as the ACF/VTAM Encrypt/Decrypt Feature for enciphered telecommunications and the Access Method Services (AMS) Cryptographic Option [IBM5] for enciphered VSAM and non-VSAM data sets. Unlike IPS, the Programmed Cryptographic Facility will not run in VM/370, except as a component of an OS/VS1 or OS/VS2 virtual machine. The Facility uses the storage protection feature of IBM System/370 hardware, so its cryptographic tables cannot be damaged by the *store* error discussed above in the discussion of the IPS subroutines.

The IPS method of block chaining is also included in the IBM cryptographic products. Accordingly, Programmed Cryptographic Facility encipherments follow the IPS block chaining technique, with the initial chaining value supplied as a parameter at each call to the CIPHER macro. Record chaining is not now explicitly available, but it can be obtained by generating an output chaining value from each encipherment to be used as the input chaining value for the next encipherment, in the manner described earlier in this paper. With the correct setting of the initial chaining value, IPS and the Programmed Cryptographic Facility encipher and decipher data in an identical manner.

Key Management

It is believed that requiring users to enter keys only at the time of their use for encipherment or decipherment and *not* storing them permanently in the system is an asset of IPS. But for many applications, cryptography would not be practical in computer systems if manual key entry were required. For instance, if a terminal can communicate with the host computer in ciphertext, the host must have the cryptographic key needed to start communications. There would be confusion and delay if each such key had to be entered manually by a system operator. Moreover, to prevent different sessions at a given terminal from using the same key, provision is made in the ACF/VTAM Encrypt/Decrypt Feature, in concert with the Programmed Cryptographic Facility, to generate cryptographic *session keys* by the system itself, rather than by a user. (The newly generated session key is transmitted to the terminal shortly after the user logs on, and it is enciphered under the terminal's own key. The terminal then switches keys for the rest of the session.)

For these and similar reasons, the Programmed Cryptographic Facility offers a key generation and management service that was not contemplated in the design of IPS. For file protection, users of the Facility can elect to supply their own private DES keys (IPS-like long-character-string keys are not accepted); they can request that the Facility generate keys as needed, and then treat these keys as private keys; or they can request key generation, then store enciphered versions of the keys with the associated data to permit automatic decipherment (that is, without the user having to supply the key) under various circumstances. This latter choice carries a risk that privileged users of the system might make unauthorized decipherments.

The greater the importance of keeping a particular file of data secure against a wide variety of threats, the more important it becomes to use private keys; but for many files, the protection of encipherment is justified, while the inconvenience of private keys is not. IPS was designed in the belief that keys should not be stored in the system *in any form,* and at a time when the protective features offered by MVS and used by the Programmed Cryptographic Facility were not available. Arguments can be advanced in favor of either the IPS or the Programmed Cryptographic Facility approach to key management, depending on different operating environments and attack scenarios. Under IPS, only private keys are allowed; the Programmed Cryptographic Facility gives the user a choice, which depends on the importance of the data, the relative safety of private keys, and the convenience of system-managed keys.

AMS Cryptographic Option

Another product, the Access Method Services (AMS) Cryptographic Option [IBM5], is roughly equivalent to the IPS IEBCODE utility, as invoked through the TSO CIPHER command. Both are intended for the encipherment and decipherment of data files as a whole. The Cryptographic Option is an extension of the AMS REPRO command. As such, it can make enciphered copies of non-

VSAM sequential data sets (as IEBCODE does) and process most VSAM files, which are inaccessible to IEBCODE. AMS does not perform encipherments directly, but calls on the Programmed Cryptographic Facility for the encipherment and decipherment of data, and for certain key handling services.

AMS-enciphered files by default use logical record encipherment with block chaining. To improve performance and short-record security, AMS can (at user option) read logical records in groups and encipher each group in one operation. This mode of processing resembles IPS record chaining, because the chaining operation continues across record boundaries within the groups; but the method is not equivalent, because DES eight-byte encipherment blocks are not necessarily aligned with logical record boundaries (as in IPS), and because the chaining operations are reset at the beginning of each group instead of continuing throughout the file. As a consequence, record grouping is probably not a good idea when user programs (not AMS itself) might be used to decipher such files.

Key Handling

AMS offers the key generation and key management services of the Programmed Cryptographic Facility. Therefore, unless the user enters a key for the encipherment of a file, one will be generated automatically. The generated key can be returned to the user in the clear, or it can be enciphered under another key, a *secondary file key,* and its encipherment returned to the user. Thus access to both the enciphered text of the data key and to the secondary file key (by its identifying key name) is required to decipher the data file. At user option, the enciphered data key and the name of the secondary key can be placed in a file header to permit automatic decipherment under selected conditions.

The IBM 3848 Cryptographic Unit

The IBM 3848 Cryptographic Unit and the OS/VS2 MVS Cryptographic Unit Support Program [IBM3,4] provide a hardware replacement for the software encipherments performed in the Programmed Cryptographic Facility. The 3848 attaches to an I/O channel and performs encipherments and decipherments of the data transmitted to it. The Cryptographic Unit Support Program replaces the Programmed Cryptographic Facility and transforms invocations of the CIPHER macro into the I/O operations required to drive the 3848. The preceding discussion of the IPS cryptographic design and the Programmed Crytographic Facility applies equally to the 3848 and its Support Program.

Where large amounts of data are to be enciphered or deciphered, the 3848 Cryptographic Unit should be considered, for by replacing the software encipherment routines in the Programmed Cryptographic Facility with hardware, significant savings of CPU time can be achieved.

10.7 SUMMARY

The IPS programs have succeeded in bringing cryptography to a large community of users, both programmers and nonprogrammers, at IBM computing centers. IPS has contributed significant augmentations to the Data Encryption Standard: techniques of cryptographic chaining, which help to conceal the underlying structure of plaintext; a consistent definition of the encipherment of data of any length (not just multiples of eight bytes); and an increased number of ways in which cryptographic keys can be defined by users. Some of these implementation options are also included in the IBM cryptographic products.

References

AB Abramowitz, Milton, *Handbook of Mathematical Functions with Formulas, Graphs And Mathematical Tables,* National Bureau of Standards, Applied Mathematics Series, **55,** June 1964.

AD1 Adelman, L., K. Manders, and G. Miller, "On Taking Roots in Finite Fields," in Proceedings of IEEE Conference on Switching and Automata Theory, 1976.

AD2 Adelman, L., "A Subexponential Algorithm for the Discrete Logarithm Problem with Applications to Cryptography," working abstract, Department of Mathematics and Laboratory for Computer Science, Massachusetts Institute of Technology.

AH Aho, Alfred V., John E. Hopcroft, and Jeffrey D. Ullman, *The Design and Analysis of Computer Algorithms,* Addison-Wesley, Reading, Mass., 1975.

AN Andelman, Dov, "Maximum Likelihood Estimation Applied To Cryptanalysis," Information Systems Laboratory, Stanford University, Department of Electrical Engineering, December 1979.

AT Attansio, C. R., P. W. Markstein, and R. J. Phillips, "Penetrating An Operating System: A Study of VM/370 Integrity," *IBM Systems Journal,* **15,** No. 1, pp. 102–116, 1976.

BA Barker, Wayne G., *Cryptanalysis of the Haegelin Cryptograph,* Aegean Park Press, Laguna Hills, CA, 1977.

BE Berlekamp, E. R., "Factoring Polynomials over Large Finite Fields," *Mathematics of Computation,* **24,** No. 111, pp. 713–735, July 1970.

BL1 Blakely, G. R. and I. Borosh, "Rivest-Shamir-Adelman Public Key Cryptosystems Do Not Always Conceal Messages," *Computers and Mathematics with Applications,* **5,** 1979.

BL2 Blakely, Bob and G. R. Blakely, "Security of Number Theoretic Public Key Cryptosystems Against Random Attack," I, *Cryptologia,* **2,** No. 4, pp. 305–321, October 1978.

BL3 ———, "Security of Number Theoretic Public Key Cryptosystems against Random Attack," II, *Cryptologia,* **3,** No. 1, pp. 29–42, January 1979.

BL4 ———, "Security of Number Theoretic Public Key Cryptosystems against Random Attack," *Cryptologia,* **3,** No. 2, pp. 105–118, April 1979.

BL5 Blakely, G. R., "Safeguarding Cryptographic Keys," *AFIPS Conference Proceedings,* **48,** pp. 313–317, 1979.

BO1 Bowers, William Maxwell, *Practical Cryptanalysis—Volume I, Digraphic Substitution,* The American Cryptogram Association, 1960.

BO2 ———, *Practical Cryptanalysis—Volume II, The BIFID Cipher,* The American Cryptogram Association, 1960.

BO3 ———, *Practical Cryptanalysis—Volume III, The TRIFID Cipher,* The American Cryptogram Association, 1961.

BR1 Branstead, Dennis K., "Security Aspects of Computer Networks," AIAA Computer Network Systems Conference, Paper **73-427,** April 1973.

BR2 Branstead, Dennis K., Jason Gait, and Stuart Katzke, "Report of the Workshop on Cryptography in Support of Computer Security," National Bureau of Standards, September 21–22, 1976, **NBSIR 77-1291,** September 1977.

BRO Brown, Anothony Cave, *Bodyguard of Lies,* Bantam, Toronto, 1976.

BRY1 Bryan, William G., *Cryptographic ABC's, Volume I, Substitution and Transposition Ciphers,* The American Cryptogram Association, 1967.

BRY2 ———, *Cryptographic ABC's, Volume II, Periodic Ciphers,* The American Cryptogram Association, 1967.

CA Cassels, J. W. S., *An Introduction to Diophantine Approximation,* Cambridge University Press, Cambridge, U.K., 1957.

CO Coppersmith, Don and Edna Grossman, "Generators for Certain Alternating Groups with Applications to Cryptography," *SIAM Journal on Applied Mathematics,* **29,** No. 4, pp. 624–627, December 1975.

CR Cramer, Harold, *Mathematical Methods of Statistics,* Princeton University Press, Princeton, N.J., 1957.

DA Darling, D. A., *Annals of Mathematical Statistics,* **28,** pp. 823–838, 1957.

DE Deavours, C. A. and J. Reeds, "The Enigma, Part I, Historical Perspectives," *Cryptologia,* **1,** pp. 381–391, October 1977.

DES *Data Encryption Standard,* Federal Information Processing Standard (FIPS), Publication **46,** National Bureau Of Standards, U.S. Department of Commerce, January 1977.

DI1 Diffie, Whit and Martin Hellman, "New Directions in Cryptography," *IEEE Transactions on Information Theory,* **IT-22,** pp. 644–654, November 1976.

DI2 ———, "Exhaustive Cryptanalysis of the NBS Data Encryption Standard," *Computer,* **10,** No. 6, pp. 74–84, June 1977.

DI3 ———, "Privacy and Authentication—An Introduction to Cryptography," *Proceedings of the IEEE,* **67,** No. 3, pp. 397–427, March 1979.

DI4 ———, "Multiuser Cryptographic Techniques," presented at the 1976 National Computer Conference, New York City, June 7–10, 1976.

EH Ehrsam, W. F., S. M. Matyas, C. H. Meyer, and W. L. Tuchman, "A Cryptographic Key Management Scheme for Implementing the Data Encryption Standard," *IBM Systems Journal,* **17,** No. 2, pp. 106–125, 1978.

EV Evans, A., W. Kantrowitz, and E. Weiss, "A User Authentication Scheme Not Requiring Secrecy in the Computer," *Communications of the ACM,* **17,** pp. 437–442, August 1974.

EVE1 Even, S. and Y. Yacobi, "On The Cryptocomplexity Of A Public-Key System," Computer Science Department, The Technion, Haifa, Israel, July 1979.

EVE2 ———, "Cryptosystems Which Are NP-Hard To Break," Computer Science Department, The Technion, Haifa, Israel, July 1979.

EVER Everton, Joseph K., "A Hierarchical Basis for Encryption Key Management in a Computer Communications Network," *Proceedings ICC'78,* Toronto, 1978.

FA Farago, Ladislas, *The Broken Seal,* Random House, New York, 1967.

FE1 Horst Feistel, "Cryptography and Computer Privacy," *Scientific American,* **228,** pp. 15–23, May 1973.

FE2 ———, "Cryptographic Coding For Data-Bank Privacy," IBM Research Report, **RC 2827,** March 18, 1970.

FE3 Feistel, Horst, William A. Notz, and J. Lynn Smith, "Some Cryptographic Techniques For Machine-To-Machine Data Communications," *Proceedings of the IEEE,* **63,** No. 11, pp. 1545–1554, November 1975.

FEL Feller, William, *An Introduction to Probability Theory and Its Applications, Volumes I and II,* Wiley, New York, 1957, 1966.

FL Flicke, Wilhem F., *War Secrets In The Ether, Volumes I and II,* Aegean Park Press, Laguna Hills, CA, 1967.

FR1 Friedman, William F., *The Classic Elements of Cryptanalysis,* Aegean Park Press, Laguna Hills, CA, 1976.

FR2 ———, "A Method of Reconstructing the Primary Alphabet from a Single One of the Series of Secondary Alphabets," Riverbank Laboratories, Publication **15**, 1917.

FR3 ———, "Methods for the Solution of Running-Key Ciphers," Riverbank Laboratories, Publication **16**, 1918.

FR4 ———, "Formula for the Solution of Geometrical Transposition Ciphers," Riverbank Laboratories, Publication **19**, 1918.

FR5 ———, "Several Machine Ciphers and Methods for Their Solution," Riverbank Laboratories, Publication **20**, 1918.

FR6 ———, "Methods for the Reconstruction of Primary Alphabets," Riverbank Laboratories, Publication **21**, 1918.

FR7 ———, "The Index of Coincidence and Its Applications in Cryptography," Riverbank Laboratories, Publication **22**, 1922.

GA Gaines, Helen Fouche, *Cryptanalysis, A Study of Ciphers and Their Solution,* Dover Publications, 1944.

GR1 Grossman, Edna, "Group Theoretic Remarks on Cryptographic Systems Based on Two Types of Addition," IBM Research Report, **RC 4742**, February 26, 1974.

GR2 Grossman, Edna and Bryant Tuckerman, "Analysis of a Feistel-like Cipher Weakened by Having No Rotating Key," IBM Research Report, **RC 6375**, January 31, 1977; also, *Proceedings ICC'78.*

HA Harris, Frances A., *Solving Simple Substitution Ciphers,* The American Cryptrogram Association, 1959.

HAL Halberstam, H., "On Integers All of Whose Prime Factors are Small," *Proceedings of the London Mathematical Society,* **3**, No. 21, pp. 102–107, 1970.

HE1 Hellman, M. E., "An Extension of the Shannon Theory Approach to Cryptography," *IEEE Transactions on Information Theory,* **IT-23**, pp. 289–294, May 1977.

HE2 ———, "A Cryptanalytic Time-Memory Tradeoff," to appear in *Transactions of the Professional Group on Information Theory.*

HE3 ———, "The Mathematics of Public-Key Cryptography," *Scientific American,* pp. 130–139, August 1979.

HE4 Hellman, M., R. Merkle, R. Schroeppel, L. Washington, W. Diffie, S. Pohlig, and P. Schweitzer, "Results of an Initial Attempt to Cryptanalyze the NBS Encryption Standard," Standford University Systems Laboratory Report, September 9, 1976.

HI Higenbottam, Frank, *Codes and Ciphers,* St. Paul's House, London, 1973.

HIL1 Lester S. Hill, "Cryptography In An Algebraic Alphabet," *American Mathematical Monthly,* **36**, 306–312, June–July 1929.

HIL2 ———, "Concerning Certain Linear Transformation Apparatus of Cryptography," *American Mathematical Monthly,* **38**, pp. 135–154, March 1931.

IBM1 "Programmed Cryptographic Facility Program Product—General Information Manual," IBM Systems Library, order number GC28-0942.

IBM3 "IBM 3848 Cryptographic Unit Product Description And Operating Procedures," IBM Systems Library, order number GA22-7073-0.

IBM4 "OS/VS2 MVS Cryptographic Unit Support: General Information Manual," IBM Systems Library, order number GC28-1015-1.

IBM5 "OS/VS1 And OS/VS2 MVS Access Method Services Cryptographic Option," IBM Systems Library, order number SC26-3916.

IN Ingemarsson, Ingemar, Rolf Blom, and Robert Forchheimer, "A System For Data Security Based on Data Encryption," Linoeping University, Department of Electrical Engineering, 1974.

KA1 Kahn, David, *The Codebreakers,* MacMillan, New York, 1972.

KA2 ———, "Cryptology Goes Public," *Foreign Affairs,* Fall 1979, pp. 141–59.

KE Kent, Stephen T., "Network Security: A Top-Down View Shows Problem," *Data Communications,* pp. 57–75, June 1978.

KN Knuth, Donald E., *The Art of Computer Programming, Volumes I, II,* Addison-Wesley, Reading, Mass., 1969, 1973.

KU Kullback, Solomon, "Statistical Methods in Cryptanalysis," War Department, Office of Chief Signal Officer, United States Government Printing Office, 1938.

LE1 Levine, Jack, "Variable Matrix Substitution in Algebraic Cryptography," *American Mathematical Monthly,* **65,** pp. 170–179, 1958.

LE2 ———, "Some Further Methods in Algebraic Cryptography," *Journal Elisha Mitchell Science Society,* **74,** pp. 110–113, 1958.

LE3 ———, "Some Elementary Cryptanalysis of Algebraic Cryptography," *American Mathematical Monthly,* **68,** pp. 411–418, 1961.

LE4 ———, "Analysis of the Case N = 3 in Algebraic Cryptography with Involutory Key-Matrix and Known Alphabet, *Journal Reine und Agenwandte Mathematik,* **213,** pp. 1–30, 1963/4.

LE5 ———, "Some Applications of High-Speed Computers to the Case N = 2 of Algebraic Cryptography," *Mathematics of Computation,* **15,** pp. 254–260, 1961.

LE6 Levine, Jack and Joel V. Brawley, Jr., "Involutory Commutants with Some Applications to Algebraic Cryptography I," *Journal Reine und Angewandte Mathematik,* **224,** pp. 20–43, 1966.

LE7 ———, "Involutory Commutants with Some Applications to Algebraic Cryptography II," *Journal Reine und Angewandte Mathematik,* **227,** pp. 1–24, 1967.

LE8 Levine, Jack and H. M. Nahikian, "On the Construction of Involutory Matrices," *American Mathematical Monthly,* **69,** pp. 267–272, 1962.

LEM Lempel, Abraham, "Cryptography in Transition: a Survey," *ACM Computing Surveys,* to appear.

LEN Lennon, R. E., "Cryptography Architecture for Information Security," *IBM Systems Journal,* **17,** No. 2, pp. 138–150, 1978.

LEX Lexar Corporation, "An Evaluation of the NBS Data Encryption Standard," September 1976.

LEV LeVeque, William J., *Elementary Theory of Numbers,* Addison-Wesley, Reading, Mass., 1962.

LO Lord, Walter, *Incredible Victory,* Harper and Row, New York, 1967.

LY Lynch, Frederick D., "An Approach To Cryptarithms."

MA Matyas, S. M. and C. H. Meyer, "Generating, Distribution, and Installation of Cryptographic Keys," *IBM Systems Journal,* **17,** No. 2, pp. 126–137, 1978.

MC McEliece, R. J., A Public-Key Cryptosystem Based on Algebraic Coding Theory," DSN Progress Report **42-44,** pp. 114–116, January-February 1978.

MCN McNeill, Robert K., and Bryant Tuckerman, "User's Guide to the IPS Cryptographic Programs for the OS and OS/VS/TSO Systems," IBM Research Report, **RC 5942,** April 13, 1976.

ME Merkle, Ralph C., and Martin E. Hellman, "Hiding Information and Receipts in Trap Door Knapsacks," Stanford University Report; also *1977 IEEE International Symposium On Information Theory,* Ithaca, New York, October 1977; also *IEEE Transactions on Information Theory,* **24,** No. 5, pp. 525–530, September 1978.

MEY1 Meyer, Carl H., and Walter L. Tuchman, "Breaking a Cryptographic Scheme Employing a Linear Shift Register with Feedback I," IBM Systems Product Division, **TR 21.506,** November 1972.

MEY2 ———, "Breaking a Cryptographic Scheme Employing a Linear Shift Register With Feedback II," IBM Systems Product Division, **TR 27.101,** May 1973.

MI Miller, Gary L., "Riemann's Hypothesis and Tests for Primality," *Proceeding of Seventh Annual ACM Symposium on Theory of Computing,* Albuquerque, New Mexico, pp. 234–239, May 5–7, 1975.

MO1 Morris, Robert, N. J. Sloane, and A. D. Wyner, "Assessment of the National Bureau of Standards Proposed Federal Data Encryption Standard," *Cryptologia* **1,** No. 3, pp. 281–291, July 1977.

MO2 Morris, Robert, "The Data Encryption Standard—Retrospective and Prospects," *IEEE Communications,* **16,** No. 6, pp. 11–14, November 1978.

NBS "Report of the Workshop on Cryptography in Support of Computer Security," National Bureau Of Standards, September 21–22, 1976, NBSIR77–1291, September 1977.

NI Niven, Ivan, and Herbert Zuckerman, *An Introduction to the Theory of Numbers,* Wiley, New York, 1972.

PE Pearson, Karl, "On the Criteria That a Given System of Deviations From The Probable in the Case of S Correlated System of Variables Is Such that It Can Be Reasonably Supposed to Have Arisen from Random Sampling," *Philosophical Magazine, Series 5,* **50,** 157–172, 1900.

PO1 Pohlig, Stephen, "Algebraic and Combinatorial Aspects of Cryptography," PhD Thesis, Stanford University; Technical Report 6602-1, October 1977.

PO2 Pohlig, Stephen, and Martin E. Hellman, "An Improved Algorithm for Computing Logarithms Over GF[p] and Its Cryptographic Significance," *IEEE Transactions On Information Theory,* to appear. Vol. **24,** No. 1 pp. 106–110, January 1978.

PU Purdy, G. B., "A High Security Log-In-Procedure," *Communications of the ACM,* **17,** pp. 442–445, August 1974.

RA1 Rabin, Michael, Signature and Certification by Coding," *IBM Technical Disclosure Bulletin,* **20,** No. 8, pp. 3337–8, January 1978.

RA2 ———, "Digitalized Signatures and Public Key Functions as Intractable as Factorization," Laboratory For Computer Science, Massachusetts Institute of Technology, **MIT/LCS/TR-212,** January 1979.

RA3 ———, "Digitalized Signatures," in *Foundations of Secure Computation,* Richard A. DeMillo, Ed., Academic, pp. 155–167, 1978.

RI1 Rivest, Ronald, Adi Shamir, and Len Adelman, "A Method For Obtaining Digital Signatures and Public-Key Cryptosystems," Laboratory for Computer Science, Massachusetts Institute of Technology, **MIT/LCS/TM-82,** April 1977.

RI2 Rivest, Ronald, "The Impact of Technology on Cryptography," *Proceedings ICC '78.*

RO Rohrbach, H., "Mathematical and Mechanical Mehods in Cryptography," *FIAT Review Of German Science, Applied Mathematics, Part I* (translated by Bradford Hardie, El Paso, 1963), Wiesbaden, pp. 233–257, 1948.

SA Sacco, Luigi, *Manual Of Cryptography,* Aegean Park Press, Laguna Hills, CA. (translation of "Manuale di Cripttografia," Roma, 1936).

SH1 Shamir, Adi, "A Fast Signature Scheme," Laboratory for Computer Science, Massachusetts Institute Of Technology, **MIT/LCS/TM-107,** July 1978.

SH2 ———, "How to Share a Secret," Technical Report, Department Of Mathematics, Massachusetts Institute Of Technology, April 1979.

SH3 ———, "On the Cryptocomplexity of Knapsack Systems," Laboratory for Computer Science, Massachusetts Institute Of Technology, **MIT/LCS/TM-129,** April 1979.

SH4 Shamir, Adi, and Richard E. Zippel, "On the Security of the Merkle-Hellman Cryptographic Scheme," submitted to *IEEE Transactions on Information Theory.*

SH5 Shamir, Adi, and Richard Schroeppel, "A $TS^2 = 0(2^n)$ Time/Space Tradeoff for Certain NP-Complete Problems."

SHA Shannon, Claude E., "Communication Theory of Secrecy Systems," *Bell System Technical Journal,* **28,** pp. 656–715, 1949.

SI1 Simmons, Gustave J., "Computational Complexity and Secure Communications," The Sandia Corporation: Internal Report.

SI2 ———, "Cryptology, the Mathematics of Secure Communication," *The Mathematical Intelligencer,* **1,** No. 4, pp. 233–46, 1979.

SIN Sinkov, Abraham, *Elementary Cryptanalysis—a Mathematical Approach,* Random House, New York, 1968.

SM Smith, Laurence Dwight, *Cryptography—the Science of Secret Writing,* Dover Publications, New York, 1955.

SO Solovay, Robert, and V. Strassen, "A Fast Monte-Carlo Test for Primality," *SIAM Journal On Computing,* pp. 84–85, March 1977.

STE Stevenson, William, *A Man Called Intrepid,* Ballantine, New York, 1976.

TU1 Tuckerman, Bryant, "A Study of the Vigenère-Vernam Single and Multiple Enciphering Loop Systems," IBM Research Report, **2879,** May 14, 1970.

TU2 ———, "Solution of a Fractionation-Transposition Cipher," IBM Research Report, **RC 4537,** September 21, 1973.

VE Veikko, Ennola, "On Numbers with Small Prime Divisors," *Ann. Acad. Sci. Fenn. Series A I,* **440,** 1969.

WA Van der Waerden, B. L., *Modern Algebra—Volumes I, II,* Frederick Ungar, New York, 1953.

WI Winterbotham, F. W., *The Ultra Secret,* Dell, New York, 1974.

WO Wohlstetter, Roberta, *Pearl Harbor: Warning And Decision,* Stanford University Press, Stanford, CA, 1962.

WOL Wolfe, James Raymond, *Secret Writing—The Craft of the Cryptographer,* McGraw-Hill, New York, 1970.

APPENDIX P

Probability Theory

This appendix reviews the notation and basic concepts in probability that we will use in this book.

Probability theory studies *chance experiments;* for example, tossing a coin, rolling a pair of dice or generating text from some language. While God may not roll dice, as Einstein cautioned, probability theory is nevertheless used to describe such experiments in order to obtain effective computational procedures to "predict" their outcomes. Two examples will indicate what we mean by "effective." A Newtonian would suggest that the outcome—heads or tails— of the chance experiment

$$E : \textit{toss a coin}$$

could be obtained by (1) applying the laws of mechanics to the falling coin and (2) solving the resulting system of differential equations. One might criticize this "solution" claiming that either (1) the laws of mechanics describe the falling coin only approximately or that (2) the Heisenberg uncertainty principle precludes measuring the initial conditions of the mechanical system accurately enough to predict the outcome. Aside from these limitations, the computational task of obtaining a "deterministic solution" in this manner is certainly Herculean. In other "experiments," we may not be able to collect the data which effect the outcome. For example, the time until a program P is completed in a data processing system is dependent on (1) other programs which compete with P for the system resources, and (2) the scheduling algorithm of the processing system. Although we can calculate a posteriori the effects of sharing the system resources given a complete description of the programs competing for the system resources, it is normally impossible to find the completion time of *P in advance* of program execution since we have no way of knowing what programs will compete with P for the resources of the system.

To circumvent these limitations in the description of real phenomena, probability theory (1) constructs a model for the experiment and (2) describes the factors that effect the outcome in statistical terms. We will use probabilistic models in cryptography; its role here will be to describe the generation of text. The models we introduce will provide us with the operational capability of studying the effect of encipherment.

P.1 CHANCE EXPERIMENTS AND THEIR SAMPLE SPACES

We use probability theory in cryptanalysis mainly to develop models for the generation of text to be enciphered. In any application of statistical modeling, there is the question of the relevance of the model: Do we deviate too much from the actual phenomena in order to achieve analytical tractability? In cryptanalysis, we can answer this question or at least verify that our models are not entirely without merit, since we can apply the theory to actual examples.

Our starting point is the notion of a chance experiment $\boldsymbol{E}$ whose outcomes correspond to the possible results of the experiment. We use the symbol ω (with or without subscripts) to denote a generic outcome of $\boldsymbol{E}$; ω is called a *sample point* of $\boldsymbol{E}$. The *sample space* Ω of $\boldsymbol{E}$ is the set of all outcomes of $\boldsymbol{E}$.

Example P.1.1 E : *toss a coin* : the outcomes of the experiment are H (for heads) and T (for tails) with sample space

$$\Omega = \{H,T\}$$

It is preferable for computational purposes to replace the symbols H and T by numerical values, 0 for heads and 1 for tails: $\Omega = \{0,1\}$

Example P.1.2 E : *toss a coin n times* : an outcome may be represented by an n-tuple (or *vector of dimension n*),

$$\omega = (\omega_0, \omega_1, \ldots, \omega_{n-1})$$

ω_i is the outcome of the ith toss; $\omega_i = 0$ if a head results on the ith toss, and $\omega_i = 1$ if a tail results on the ith toss. The sample space

$$\Omega = \{\omega = (\omega_0, \omega_1, \ldots, \omega_{n-1}) : \omega_i = 0 \text{ or } 1, 0 \leq i < n\}^*$$

contains 2^n outcomes.

Example P.1.3 E : *roll a pair of dice* : an outcome is a pair (i,j)† with $1 \leq i,j \leq 6$ representing the face values of each die. The sample space

$$\Omega = \{(i,j) : 1 \leq i,j \leq 6\}$$

contains 36 outcomes.

Example P.1.4 E : *generate a "word" of 6 letters from the alphabet* {`A B . . . Z`}:

`PICKLE` and `RTUWQN` are outcomes of $\boldsymbol{E}$

*The notation $E = \{x : \text{some condition} \bigstar\}$ is read

"E is the set of all points x which satisfy the condition ★"

†We normally do not distinguish the dice (by coloring them) so that the outcomes (i,j) and (j,i) are indistinguishable; the sample space Ω here contains only 30 outcomes. Indistinguishability requires only minor modifications in discussing *Example P.1.3*.

P.2 PROBABILITY DISTRIBUTIONS

A *probability distribution* on Ω is a sequence of numbers

$$\{p(\omega) : \omega \in \Omega\}^*$$

that satisfy the conditions

$$0 \leq p(\omega) \leq 1 \qquad \omega \in \Omega$$
$$1 = \sum_{\omega \in \Omega} p(\omega)$$

We say that $p(\omega)$ is the probability of the *elementary event* or *outcome* ω. The following are examples of probability distributions.

Example P.2.1 $p = p(0) \quad q = 1 - p(0) \quad 0 \leq p \leq 1$
If $p = 1/2$, the coin is *fair;* if $p \neq 1/2$, the coin is *biased*

Example P.2.2 The outcome of the n tosses of a coin

$$\omega = (\omega_0, \omega_1, \ldots, \omega_{n-1})$$

is assigned probability $p(\omega)$ by the expression

$$p(\omega) = \prod_{1 \leq i \leq n} p^{(1-\omega_i)} q^{\omega_i} = p^{\text{number of heads}} q^{\text{number of tails}}$$

$$(0,0, \ldots ,0) : \text{all heads} \quad p(0,0, \ldots ,0) = p^n$$
$$(1,1, \ldots ,1) : \text{all tails} \quad p(1,1, \ldots ,1) = q^n$$

Example P.2.3 The die are not loaded; assign probability 1/36 to each outcome (i,j).

Example P.2.4 Assign probabilities to all words of length n (the concatenation of n letters from {A B . . . Z}),

$$\omega = (\omega_0, \omega_1, \ldots, \omega_{n-1})$$

by multipling the letter probabilities in Table P.2.1 to obtain the probability

$$p(\omega) = p(\omega_0)p(\omega_1) \ldots p(\omega_{n-1})$$

In the sample space Ω of words of length 7, PICKLES is assigned the probability

$$p(\text{PICKLES}) = p(\text{P})p(\text{I})p(\text{C})p(\text{K})p(\text{L})p(\text{E})p(\text{S})$$
$$= 0.0199 \times 0.0627 \times 0.0279 \times 0.0042 \times 0.0339$$
$$\times 0.1304 \times 0.0607 \approx 0.3905 \times 10^{-10}$$

*The symbol $\in$ stands for "element of". The notation $\omega \in \Omega$ is read:
"ω is an element of (the set) Ω"

TABLE P.2.1
Probability Distribution of Letters

Letter	p	Letter	p	Letter	p
A	0.08563	J	0.00129	S	0.06073
B	0.01394	K	0.00418	T	0.10454
C	0.02788	L	0.03385	U	0.02489
D	0.03783	M	0.02489	V	0.00916
E	0.13043	N	0.07069	W	0.01493
F	0.02887	O	0.07965	X	0.00169
G	0.01991	P	0.01991	Y	0.01991
H	0.05277	Q	0.00119	Z	0.00077
I	0.06273	R	0.06770		

Since

$$1 = p(\mathtt{A}) + p(\mathtt{B}) + \ldots + p(\mathtt{Z})$$

the sum of $p(\omega) = p(\omega_0,\omega_1, \ldots ,\omega_{n-1})$ over all words $\omega = (\omega_0,\omega_1, \ldots ,\omega_{n-1})$ of *fixed* length n is equal to one.

P.3 EVENTS

An *event* E in a chance experiment with sample space Ω is a *subset* of Ω. Examples of events are given as follows.

Example P.3.1 E : *head resulted in one toss,*

$$E = \{0\}$$

Example P.3.2 E : *one head resulted in five tosses of a coin,*

$$E = \{(1,0,0,0,0,), (0,1,0,0,0), (0,0,1,0,0), (0,0,0,1,0), (0,0,0,0,1)\}$$

Example P.3.3 E : *the sum of the faces of the die is equal to 4,*

$$E = \{\omega = (i,j) : i + j = 4\} = \{(1,3), (2,2), (3,1)\}$$

Example P.3.4 E : *words of length 4 begining with* QU,

$$E = \{\mathtt{QUAA}, \mathtt{QUAB}, \ldots, \mathtt{QUZZ}\}$$

The *probability of an event* E is the sum of $p(\omega)$ over the points ω belonging to the event E:

$$\Pr\{E\} = \sum_{\omega \in E} p(\omega)$$

Example P.3.5 E : *one head resulted in five tosses of a fair coin,*

$$\Pr\{E\} = p(1,0,0,0,0) + p(0,1,0,0,0) + p(0,0,1,0,0) + p(0,0,0,1,0) + p(0,0,0,0,1) = 5/32$$

Example P.3.6 E : *the sum of the faces of an unloaded die is equal to 4,*

$$\Pr\{E\} = p(1,3) + p(2,2) + p(3,1) = 3/36$$

Example P.3.7 E : *words of length 4 beginning with* QU,

$$\Pr\{E\} = p(\text{QUAA}) + p(\text{QUAB}) + \ldots + p(\text{QUZZ}) \approx 2.974 \times 10^{-5}$$

A *probability space* is a pair (Ω, p) consisting of the sample space Ω and a probability distribution p on Ω.

P.4 RANDOM VARIABLES

A *random variable* on a probability space (Ω,p) is a function X defined for each outcome ω of the chance experiment *E*:

$$X : \omega \rightarrow X(\omega)^*$$

The *range* of X is the set of values X(ω) that X assumes as ω varies over the sample space Ω.

Example P.4.1 $X(\omega) = \sum_{0 \le i < n} (1 - \omega_i)$: the number of heads that result in n tosses.
$Y(\omega) = \sum_{0 \le i < n} \omega_i$: the number of tails that result in n tosses.
The ranges of X and Y are {0, 1, . . . , n}.

Example P.4.2 X(ω) = X(i,j) = i + j : the sum of faces of the dice.
The range of X is {2, 3, . . . , 12}.

Example P.4.3 V(ω) = the number of vowels in a word of length n.
C(ω) = the number of consonants in a word of length n.
$N_A(\omega)$ = the number of times A appears in a word of length n.
The ranges of V, C, and N_A are {0, 1, . . . , n}.

We denote random variables by upper case letters (with or without subscripts), X, Y, Z_1, Z_2,. . . . If the range of the random variable X is the set of integers

*We use the notation

$$f : x \rightarrow f(x)$$

to denote the function f whose value at the point x in X is f(x). If X is the set of points on which f is defined and f(x) is an element of the set Y, we also write

$$f : X \rightarrow Y$$

$$\text{Range of } X = \{0, 1, \ldots, n-1\}$$

The *probability distribution of X* is defined by

$$p_X(i) = \Pr\{X = i\} = \sum_{\{\omega \in \Omega; X(\omega) = i\}} p(\omega)$$

$p_X(i)$ is the probability of the event consisting of the points ω in Ω for which $X(\omega) = i$; we denote this event by either $\{X = i\}$ or $\{\omega : X(\omega) = i\}$.

The probability distribution of a random variable with range $\{0, 1, \ldots, n-1\}$ satisfies the conditions

$$0 \leq p_X(i) \leq 1 \qquad 0 \leq i < n$$

$$1 = \sum_{0 \leq i < n} p_X(i)$$

Example P.4.4 *E* : toss a biased coin 4 times
$p = 1/3, q = 2/3 \qquad X(\omega) = \text{the number of tails}$

i	**{X = i}**	**$p_X(i)$**
0	(0,0,0,0)	1/81
1	(1,0,0,0) (0,1,0,0) (0,0,1,0) (0,0,0,1)	4 × 2/81
2	(1,1,0,0) (1,0,1,0) (1,0,0,1) (0,1,1,0) (0,1,0,1) (0,0,1,1)	6 × 4/81
3	(1,1,1,0) (1,1,0,1) (1,0,1,1) (0,1,1,1)	4 × 8/81
4	(1,1,1,1)	1 × 16/81

Example P.4.5 *E* : a roll of a pair of unloaded dice
$X(\omega)$ = number of dice with the face 3 appearing

i	**{X = i}**	**$p_X(i)$**
0	(1,1) (1,2) (1,4) (1,5) (1,6) (2,1) (2,2) (2,4) (2,5) (2,6) (4,1) (4,2) (4,4) (4,5) (4,6) (5,1) (5,2) (5,4) (5,5) (5,6) (6,1) (6,2) (6,4) (6,5) (6,6)	25 × 1/36
1	(3,1) (3,2) (3,4) (3,5) (3,6) (1,3) (2,3) (4,3) (5,3) (6,3)	10 × 1/36
2	(3,3)	1 × 1/36

P.5 DISTRIBUTION FUNCTIONS

The *distribution function* of a random variable X is the function

$$F_X(x) = \Pr\{X \leq x\}$$

is defined for all real numbers x. It enjoys the properties:

- $0 \leq F_X(x) \leq 1$ for $-\infty < x < \infty$
- $\text{limit}_{x \to -\infty} F_X(x) = 0 \quad \text{limit}_{x \to \infty} F_X(x) = 1$
- $F_X(x)$ is *monotone nondecreasing* in x: $F_X(x_1) \leq F_X(x_2)$ if $x_1 \leq x_2$
- $F_X(x)$ is *continuous from the right:* $F_X(x) = \text{limit}_{y \downarrow x} F_X(y)$

If X and Y are random variables, their *joint probability distribution* and *joint distribution function* are defined by

$$p_{X,Y}(i,j) = \Pr\{X = i, Y = j\} = \sum_{\{\omega \in \Omega : X(\omega) = i,\ Y(\omega) = j\}} p(\omega)$$

$$F_{X,Y}(x,y) = \Pr\{X \leq x \text{ and } Y \leq y\}$$

P.6 MOMENTS

If the range of a random variable X has a large number of values, the probability distribution may be unwieldy to manipulate. Moments often provide a concise enough description of the random variable.

The *expectation* of a random variable X is the number denoted by E{X} and defined by

$$E\{X\} = \sum_{0 \leq i < n} i p_X(i)$$

The jth moment of X is the expectation of X^j:

$$E\{X^j\} = \sum_{0 \leq i < n} i^j p_X(i)$$

More generally, if f is a function whose domain contains the range {0, 1, . . . , n − 1} of the random variable X, so that f(X) is defined, then f(X) is also a random variable. The *expectation of f(X)* is

$$E\{f(X)\} = \sum_{0 \leq i < n} f(i) p_X(i)$$

The *j^{th}-moment about a* of a random variable X is the expectation of the function f(X) with $f(x) = (x - a)^j$:

$$E\{(X - a)^j\} = \sum_{0 \leq i < n} (i - a)^j p_X(i)$$

The *variance of X* is the second moment of X about the expectation of X:

$$\text{Var}\{X\} = E\{(X - E\{X\})^2\} = E\{X^2\} - E^2\{X\}*$$

The *standard deviation of X* is the square root of Var{X}

*The two expressions for the variance follow from the fact that expectation $E\{\cdot\}$ is a *linear operator*:

$$E\{aX + bY\} = aE\{X\} + bE\{Y\}$$

$$\sigma^2\{X\} = \mathrm{Var}\{X\}$$

If X and Y are random variables with values in $\{0, 1, \ldots, n-1\}$ and joint probability distribution $p_{X,Y}$, the *mixed moment of order (j,k)* is

$$E\{X^jY^k\} = \sum_{0 \le r,s < n} r^j s^k p_{X,Y}(r,s)$$

The *covariance* of X and Y is

$$\mathrm{Cov}\{X,Y\} = E\{XY\} - E\{X\}E\{Y\}$$

The *correlation coefficient* of X and Y is $\rho\{X,Y\} = \mathrm{Cov}\{X,Y\}/\sigma\{X\}\sigma\{Y\}$

Except for pathological cases, the sequence of moments $\{E\{X^n\} : 1 \le n < \infty\}$ uniquely determines the probability distribution $\{p_X(i)\}$.

P.7 EXAMPLES OF PROBABILITY DISTRIBUTIONS

A random variable X with range $\{0,1, \ldots, n-1\}$ is *uniformly distributed* if

$$\Pr\{X = i\} = 1/n \quad 0 \le i < n$$

The expectation and variance of X are

$$E\{X\} = \sum_{0 \le i < n} i/n = (n-2)/2$$

$$\mathrm{Var}\{X\} = (n^2 - 1)/12$$

A random variable X has the *binomial distribution* B(n,p) with parameters n and p,

$$n : \text{nonnegative integer, } 0 \le p \le 1$$

if

$$\Pr\{X = k\} = C(n,k)\, p^k(1-p)^{n-k} \qquad 0 \le k \le n$$

where C(n,k) is the *binomial coefficient*

$$C(n,k) = n!/k!(n-k)! \qquad 0 \le k \le n$$

The expectation and variance of X are

$$E\{X\} = np \quad \mathrm{Var}\{X\} = np(1-p)$$

A sequence of M random variables $X_0, X_1, \ldots, X_{M-1}$ has the *multinomial distribution* with parameters n (a nonnegative integer) and $p(0), p(1), \ldots, p(M-1)$

$$0 \le p(s) < 1, \quad 0 \le s < M \qquad 1 = p(0) + (1) + \ldots + p(M-1)$$

if

$$\Pr\{X_0 = k_0, X_1 = k_1, \ldots, X_{M-1} = k_{M-1}\} = n! \prod_{0 \le s < M} p^{k_s}(s)/K_s!$$

where$(k_0, k_1, \ldots, k_{M-1})$ satisfies the conditions

$$0 \leq k_i < n \quad 0 \leq i < M$$

$$n = k_0 + k_1 + \ldots + k_{M-1}$$

The expectation of X_i and covariance between X_i and X_j $(i \neq j)$ are

$$E\{X(i)\} = np(i)$$

$$\mathrm{Cov}\{X_i, X_j\} = -np(i)p(j)$$

A random variable has the *Poisson distribution* $P(\lambda)$ with $0 \leq \lambda < \infty$ if

$$p_X(i) = (\lambda^i/i!)e^{-\lambda} \quad 0 \leq i < \infty$$

The expectation and variance of X are

$$E\{X\} = \lambda \quad \mathrm{Var}\{X\} = \lambda$$

P.8 INDEPENDENCE

In 1933, A. N. Kolmogorov provided the axiomatic setting for probability theory within the framework of the theory of measure and integration. What makes probability theory a rich and distinctive subject are the concepts of *independence, conditioning,* and *dependence.*

Let (Ω,p) be a probability space, Events E_1 and E_2 are *independent* in (Ω,p) if

$$\Pr\{E_1 \cap E_2\} = \Pr\{E_1\}\Pr\{E_2\}$$

A sequence of events

$$E_0, E_1, \ldots, E_{n-1}$$

is independent in (Ω,p) if for every integer $m \geq 1$ and set of m indices $0 \leq j_0 < j_1 < \ldots < j_{m-1} < n$

$$\Pr\{E_{j_0} \cap E_{j_1} \cap \ldots \cap E_{j_{m-1}}\} = \prod_{0 \leq s < m} \Pr\{E_{j_s}\}$$

The notion of independence may be extended to random variables; random variables X and Y are independent in (Ω,p) if

$$\Pr\{X = i, Y = j\} = \Pr\{X = i\}\Pr\{Y = j\}$$

for all values of i and j. The random variables X and Y are independent in (Ω,p) if and only if the events $\{X = i\}$ and $\{Y = y\}$ are independent for all i and j.

The random variables $X_0, X_1, \ldots, X_{n-1}$ are independent in (Ω,p) if

$$\Pr\{X_0 = i_0, X_1 = i_1, \ldots, X_{n-1} = i_{n-1}\}$$

$$= \Pr\{X_0 = i_0\}\Pr\{X_1 = i_1\} \ldots \Pr\{X_{n-1} = i_{n-1}\}$$

for all $(i_0, i_1, \ldots, i_{n-1})$.

Independence is the basic concept in formulating the notion of *repeated independent trials of an experiment* $\boldsymbol{E}$. Let $\{\boldsymbol{E}_i\}$ be experiments with probability spaces $(\Omega^{(i)},p^{(i)})$ $(0 \le i < n)$. The experiment $\boldsymbol{E}_{(0,1,\ldots,n-1)}$ consists of performing the n experiments $\boldsymbol{E}_0, \boldsymbol{E}_1, \ldots, \boldsymbol{E}_{n-1}$. Its sample space is $\Omega^{(0,1,\ldots,n)}$ with sample points

$$\omega = (\omega_0, \omega_1, \ldots, \omega_{n-1}) \qquad \omega_i \in \Omega^{(i)} \qquad 0 \le i < n$$

The sample space $\Omega^{(0,1,\ldots,n-1)}$ is called the *Cartesian product* of the sample spaces of the experiments $\{\boldsymbol{E}_i\}$.

$$\Omega^{(0,1,\ldots,n-1)} = \Omega^{(0)} \times \Omega^{(1)} \times \ldots \times \Omega^{(n-1)}$$

The probability distribution $p^{(0,1,\ldots,n-1)}$ on $\Omega^{(0,1,\ldots,n-1)}$ defined by

$$p^{(0,1,\ldots,n-1)}(\omega) = \prod_{0 \le i < n} p^{(i)}(\omega_i)$$

is called the *product probability distribution* on $\Omega^{(0,1,\ldots,n-1)}$. In this case, we say that $\boldsymbol{E}_0, \boldsymbol{E}_1, \ldots, \boldsymbol{E}_{n-1}$ are performed independently of one another.

An event E_i in $\Omega^{(0,1,\ldots,n-1)}$ depends *on the outcome of the ith trial* if

$$\omega = (\omega_0, \omega_1, \ldots, \omega_{n-1}) \in E_i$$

depends only on the ith component ω_i of ω. *E_i is then called a *cylinder event* in the Cartesian product sample space $\Omega^{(0,1,\ldots,n-1)}$.

The special case of independent experiments in which all of the experiments $\boldsymbol{E}_0, \boldsymbol{E}_1, \ldots, \boldsymbol{E}_{n-1}$ are identical, meaning $\Omega^{(i)} = \Omega$ and $p^{(i)} = p$ (independent of i), is referred to as *repeated independent trials of the experiment* $\boldsymbol{E}$. In this case, the product probability distribution $p^{(0,1,\ldots,n-1)}$ is given by

$$p^{(0,1,\ldots,n-1)}(\omega) = \prod_{0 \le i < n} p(\omega_i)$$

A random variable X_i on $\Omega^{(0,1,\ldots,n-1)}$ depends only on the ith trial if

$$X_i(\omega) = X_i(\omega_i)$$

If the experiment $\boldsymbol{E}_{(0,1,\ldots,n-1)}$ consists of repeated independent trials, the cylinder events $\{E_i : 1 \le i \le n\}$ and the random variables $\{X_i : 1 \le i \le n\}$, in which X_i depends on the ith trial, are independent.

A sequence of independent and identically distribution random variables $X_1, X_2, \ldots$, which take the values 0 and 1,

$$\Pr\{X_i = 1\} = p \qquad \Pr\{X_i = 0\} = 1 - p$$

is called a *Bernoulli sequence*. The random variable $S_n = X_1 + X_2 + \ldots + X_n$ has the binomial distribution B(n,p).

*To say that $\omega = (\omega_0, \omega_1, \ldots, \omega_{n-1})$ depends on the ith trial means that if $\omega \in E_i$ and if $\omega' = (\omega_0', \omega_1', \ldots, \omega_{n-1}')$ with $\omega_i' = \omega_i$, then $\omega' \in E_i$.

P.9 CONDITIONAL PROBABILITY AND DEPENDENCE

Dependence is the opposite of independence: events E and F are dependent if

$$\Pr\{E \cap F\} < \Pr\{E\}\Pr\{F\} \qquad \text{or} \qquad \Pr\{E \cap F\} > \Pr\{E\}\Pr\{F\}$$

The *conditional probability* of the event E *given* or *conditioned by* the event F is defined only when $\Pr\{F\} > 0$; it is the ratio

$$\Pr\{E/F\} = \Pr\{E \cap F\}/\Pr\{F\}$$

If E and F are independent events,

$$\Pr\{E/F\} = \Pr\{E\}$$

Conversely, $\Pr\{E/F\} = \Pr\{E\}$ implies that E and F are independent. Roughly speaking, if E and F are independent, the occurrence of the event F does not give us information about the occurrence of the event E. A precise statement is

the *a posteriori* probability of the event E *after*

the occurence of the event F $\quad \Pr\{E/F\}$

is the same as

the *a priori* probability of the event E *before*

the event F has occurred $\quad \Pr\{E\}$

If X and Y are random variables, the distribution of X *conditioned by* or *given* Y is the function

$$P_{X/Y}(i/j) = \Pr\{X = i/Y = j\}$$

The function $p_{X/Y}(i/j)$ satisfies the two conditions:

$$0 \leq p_{X/Y}(i/j) \leq 1$$

$$1 = \sum_i p_{X/Y}(i/j)$$

Conditioning X by the event $\{Y = j\}$ effectively replaces the sample space Ω by $\Omega' = \{\omega : Y(\omega) = j\}$ and the probability distribution p on Ω by p′ on Ω':

$$p'(\omega) = p(\omega)/\Pr\{Y = j\}$$

We have the inportant relationship

$$p_X(i) = \sum_j p_{X/Y}(i/j)p_Y(j)$$

The random variables X and Y are independent if and only if

$$p_{X/Y}(i/j) = p_X(i)$$

for *all* i and j.

The *conditional expectation* of X (with range of values {0, 1, . . . , n − 1}) *given* Y is the *function* (of j)

$$E\{X/Y = j\} = \sum_{0 \le i < N} i p_{X/Y}(i/j)$$

P.10 CHEBYSHEV'S INEQUALITY

A frequent problem is the approximation of probabilities of events. We will discuss limit theorems in the next three sections, which provide one type of approximation. Here we state the crude but often useful Chebyshev's inequality.

Let X be a random variable with expectation and variance

$$E\{X\} = \mu \qquad Var\{X\} = \sigma^2$$

X is close to its expectation μ in the following sense; given $\epsilon > 0$, the probability that X differs from μ by more than ϵ in absolute value is bounded from above:

$$Pr\{\omega : |X(\omega) - \mu| > \epsilon\} \le \sigma^2/\epsilon^2$$

Chebyshev's inequality is only of value when ϵ is small compared to the standard deviation σ, so that the number σ^2/ϵ^2 is smaller than one.

P.11 LIMIT THEOREMS: THE LAWS OF LARGE NUMBERS

Limit theorems in probability theory describe the limiting behavior of probabilities as some parameter, usually the number of trials $n \to \infty$. The most famous limit theorem is the *law of large numbers;* it provides the link between our intuition about averages and the axiomatic development.

Suppose

$$\{X_i : 0 \le i < \infty\}$$

are independent and identically distributed random variables with expected value $\mu = E\{X\}$. The law of large numbers asserts that the *sample average,*

$$S_n/n = (X_0 + X_1 + \ldots + X_{n-1})/n$$

is close to the expectation μ with probability approaching one as $n \to \infty$. The law of large numbers comes in two flavors, whose subtle difference will not be elaborated on.

- *The weak law of large numbers:* for every $\epsilon > 0$ and $\delta > 0$, there is an integer $N(\epsilon,\delta)$ depending on ϵ and δ such that

  $$Pr\{|S_n/n - \mu| > \epsilon\} < \delta \qquad \text{for } n \ge N(\epsilon,\delta)$$

  The probability that the sample mean S_n/n differs from μ by more than ϵ is smaller than δ for all n sufficiently large.

- *The strong law of large numbers:*

$$\Pr\{\text{limit}_{N\to\infty} S_N/N = \mu\} = 1$$

P.12 LIMIT THEOREMS: THE POISSON APPROXIMATION TO THE BINOMIAL DISTRIBUTION

Suppose Y has the binomial distribution

$$p_Y(i) = C(n,i)p^i(1 - p)^{n-i} \qquad 0 \le i \le n$$

If n is large and p is small, but np is of moderate magnitude, say near unity, then $p_Y(i)$ may be approximated by the Poisson distribution P(np) for values of i in the "middle" of the interval [0,n]. In Fig. P.12.1, we graph B(50,0.024) and P(1.2).

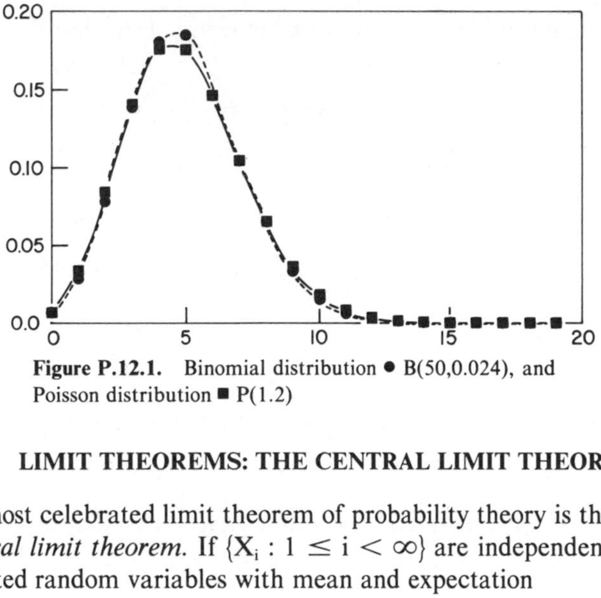

Figure P.12.1. Binomial distribution ● B(50,0.024), and Poisson distribution ■ P(1.2)

P.13 LIMIT THEOREMS: THE CENTRAL LIMIT THEOREM

The second most celebrated limit theorem of probability theory is the DeMoivre-Laplace *central limit theorem.* If $\{X_i : 1 \le i < \infty\}$ are independent and identically distributed random variables with mean and expectation

$$\mu = E\{X_i\} \qquad \sigma^2 = \text{Var}\{X_i\}$$

then

$$\text{limit}_{n\to\infty} \Pr\{y \le (S_n - n\mu)/\sigma\sqrt{n} \le x\} = 1/\sqrt{2\pi} \int_x^y e^{-t^2/2}\, dt$$

P.14 GENERATING FUNCTIONS

Generating functions are computational tools; if a random variable X has range $\{0, 1, \ldots, n - 1\}$, its generating function (or more precisely, the generating function of its probability distribution) is the polynomial

$$G_X(z) = \sum_{0 \le i < n} p_X(i) z^i$$

The generating function $G_X(z)$ is the expectation of the random variable z^X,

$$G_X(z) = E\{z^X\}$$

since z^X takes the values $z^0, z^1, \ldots, z^{n-1}$, with probabilities

$$p_X(0), p_X(1), \ldots, p_X(n-1)$$

Two special properties of the generating function will be used:

- If X and Y are independent random variables with generating functions $G_X(z)$ and $G_Y(z)$, then the random variable $X + Y$ has generating function

$$G_{X+Y}(z) = G_X(z) G_Y(z)$$

- The moments of X may be expressed in terms of the derivatives of $G_X(z)$ at $z = 1$:

$$(d/dz)\, G_X(z)_{|z=1} = E\{X\}$$

$$(d^2/d^2z)\, G_X(z)_{|z=1} = E\{X(X-1)\}$$

$$(d^n/d^nz)\, G_X(z)_{|z=1} = E\{X(X-1)\ldots(X-(n-1))\}$$

The generating function of the pair X,Y of random variables with values in $\{0, 1, \ldots, n-1\}$ is the function

$$G_{X,Y}(z,w) = E\{z^X w^Y\} = \sum_{\{i,j:0 \le i,j < n\}} p_{X,Y}(i,j) z^i w^j$$

The random variables X and Y are independent if and only if

$$G_{X,Y}(z,w) = G_X(z) G_Y(w)$$

We also define the *conditional generating function* of the random variable X conditioned by $\{Y = j\}$ by

$$G_{X/\{Y=j\}}(z) = \sum_{0 \le i < n} p_{X/Y}(i/j) z^i$$

The conditional and joint generating functions are related by

$$G_{X,Y}(z,w) = \sum_{0 \le j < n} p_Y(j) w^j G_{X/\{Y=j\}}(z)$$

APPENDIX V

The Variance of Φ

Let Ξ be a subset of SYM($\boldsymbol{Z}_m$) and $\{q(\pi) : \pi \in \Xi\}$ a probability distribution of Ξ. An *r-polyalphabetic substitution key* is a sequence

$$(\pi_0, \pi_1, \ldots, \pi_{r-1})$$

with $\pi_1 \in \Xi$ for each i, $0 \leq i < r$.

(KS1)	$\Xi = \text{SYM}(\boldsymbol{Z}_m)$	$q(\pi) = 1/m!$
(KS2)	$\Xi = \boldsymbol{C}_m$: Caesar substitutions	$q(\pi) = 1/m$
(KS3)	$\Xi = \boldsymbol{C}_m$: Caesar substitutions	$\{q(\pi)\}$ from Table 2.3.1

Let

$$\mathbf{Y}_0 = (Y_0, Y_r, \ldots, Y_{r(n_0-1)})$$

$$\mathbf{Y}_1 = (Y_1, Y_{r+1}, \ldots, Y_{1+r(n_1-1)})$$

$$\ldots$$

$$\ldots$$

$$\ldots$$

$$\mathbf{Y}_{r-1} = (Y_{r-1}, Y_{2r-1}, \ldots, Y_{r-1+r(n_{r-1}-1)})$$

$$n = n_0 + n_1 + \ldots + n_{r-1} \qquad n_{r-1} \leq \ldots \leq n_1 \leq n_0 \qquad n_0 - n_{r-1} \leq 1$$

by random variables with values in $\boldsymbol{Z}_m$ and assume

- $\{Y_i : 0 \leq i < n\}$ are independent and identically distributed, taking values in $\boldsymbol{Z}_m$
- For each j with $0 \leq j < r$, the distribution of Y_{j+ri} conditioned by $\{\Pi_0 = \pi_0, \Pi_1 = \pi_1, \ldots, \Pi_{r-1} = \pi_{r-1}\}$ is

  $$\Pr_{\text{CIPHER/KEY}}\{Y_{j+ri} = t/\Pi_0 = \pi_0, \Pi_1 = \pi_1, \ldots, \Pi_{r-1} = \pi_{r-1}\} = p_{\pi_j}(t)$$
- The random variables $\{Y_i : 0 \leq i < n\}$ and $\{\Pi_j : 0 \leq j < r\}$ are independent

It follows that the unconditional distribution of Y_{j+ri} is

$$\Pr_{\text{CIPHER}}\{Y_{j+ri} = t\} = \sum_{\pi \in \Xi} p[\pi]_t q(\pi)$$

We interpret

$$(Y_0, Y_1, \ldots, Y_{n-1})$$

as the polyalphabetic encipherment of plaintext

$$(X_0, X_1, \ldots, X_{n-1})$$

obtained by

- Dividing the plaintext into r plainsubtexts; the ith plainsubtext consists of

$$(X_i, X_{i+r}, \ldots, X_{i+r(n_i-1)})$$

- Choosing the r substitutions

$$(\Pi_0, \Pi_1, \ldots, \Pi_{r-1})$$

  from Ξ by r independent experiments, according to the distribution $\{q(\pi) : \pi \in \Xi\}$

- Enciphering the ith plainsubtext $\mathbf{X}_i$ by the substitution Π_i

Let

$$N_t(\mathbf{Y}) = \text{number of occurrences of the integer t in } \mathbf{Y}:$$

$$N_t(\mathbf{Y}) = \sum_{0 \le j < r} N_t(\mathbf{Y}_j)$$

$$\Phi(\mathbf{Y}) = \sum_{0 \le t < m} N_t(\mathbf{Y})(N_t(\mathbf{Y}) - 1)$$

Simple algebraic manipulation expresses $\Phi(\mathbf{Y})$ as the sum of $r + 1$ terms,

$$\Phi(\mathbf{Y}) = \chi(\mathbf{Y}) + \sum_{0 \le j < r} \Phi(\mathbf{Y}_j) \tag{V.1}$$

where

$$\Phi(\mathbf{Y}_j) = \sum_{0 \le t < m} N_t(\mathbf{Y}_j)(N_t(\mathbf{Y}_j) - 1) \qquad 0 \le j < r$$

and

$$\chi(\mathbf{Y}) = \sum_{\{0 \le t < m\}} \sum_{\{0 \le i,j < r, i \ne j\}} N_t(\mathbf{Y}_i) N_t(\mathbf{Y}_j)$$

The random variables $\{\Phi(\mathbf{Y}_j) : 0 \leq j < r\}$ are independent; their expectation and variance from Theorem 4.6.1 are

$$E\{\Phi(\mathbf{Y}_j)\} = s_2[n_j^2 - n_j]$$

$$\text{(V.2)} \qquad \text{Var}\{\Phi(\mathbf{Y}_j)\} = 4n_j^3[s_3 - s_2^2] + 2n_j^2[5s_2^2 + s_2 - 6s_3] + 2n_j[4s_3 - s_2 - 3s_2^2]$$

Next

$$\text{Var}\{\Phi(\mathbf{Y})\} = \sum_{0\leq j<r} \text{Var}\{\Phi(\mathbf{Y}_j)\} + \text{Var}\{\chi(\mathbf{Y})\} + 2 \sum_{0\leq j<r} \text{Cov}\{\Phi(\mathbf{Y}_j),\chi(\mathbf{Y})\}$$

where the *covariance* is

$$\text{Cov}\{\Phi(\mathbf{Y}_j),\chi(\mathbf{Y})\} = E\{\Phi(\mathbf{Y}_j)\chi(\mathbf{Y})\} - E\{\Phi(\mathbf{Y}_j)\}E\{\chi(\mathbf{Y})\}$$

Thus from Eq. (V.2), we have

$$\sum_{0\leq j<r} \text{Var}\{\Phi(\mathbf{Y}_j)\} = 4n^{(3)}[s_3 - s_2^2] + 2n^{(2)}[5s_2^2 + s_2 - 6s_3] + 2n^{(1)}[4s_3 - s_2 - 3s_2^2]$$

where

$$n^{(k)} = \sum_{0\leq i<r} n_i^k \qquad 1 \leq k < \infty$$

It remains to compute $\text{Var}\{\chi(\mathbf{Y})\}$ and $\text{Cov}\{\Phi(\mathbf{Y}_j),\chi(\mathbf{Y})\}$; we begin with $\text{Var}\{\chi(\mathbf{Y})\}$.

To compute $E\{\chi(\mathbf{Y})\}$, we use Eq. (V.1) and the conditional generating function

$$\text{(V.3)} \qquad E\{z^{N_t(\mathbf{Y}_j)}/\Pi_j = \pi_j\} = (p_{\pi_j}(t)z + 1 - p_{\pi_j}(t))^{n_j}$$

Differentiating the conditional generating function in Eq. (V.3) with respect to z and evaluating at $z = 1$ yields

$$\text{(V.4)} \qquad E\{N_t(\mathbf{Y}_j)/\Pi_j = \pi_j\} = n_j p_{\pi_j}(t)$$

The unconditional expectation is obtained from Eq. (V.4) by averaging π_j over Ξ with respect to the probability distribution $\{q(\pi) : \pi \in \Xi\}$, obtaining

$$E\{N_t(\mathbf{Y}_j)\} = n_j p[t]$$

Finally if $i \neq j$, $N_t(\mathbf{Y}_i)$ and $N_t(\mathbf{Y}_j)$ are independent variables and

$$E\{N_t(\mathbf{Y}_i)N_t(\mathbf{Y}_j)\} = n_i n_j p^2[t]$$

which yields the formula

$$\text{(V.5)} \qquad E\{\chi(\mathbf{Y})\} = \left(\sum_{0\leq t<m} p^2[t]\right)[(n^{(1)})^2 - n^{(2)}]$$

To obtain $E\{\chi^2\}$, we write

$$(\text{V.6})\quad (\chi(\mathbf{Y}))^2 = \sum_{\{(i,j,u,v,s,t):0\le i,j,u,v<r,i\ne j,u\ne v,0\le s,t<m\}} N_t(\mathbf{Y}_i)N_t(\mathbf{Y}_j)N_s(\mathbf{Y}_u)N_s(\mathbf{Y}_v)$$

The terms appearing in the summation in Eq. (V.6) are of three types:

- i,j,u,v distinct indices.
- Three of the indices i,j,u,v distinct ($i \ne j$, $u \ne v$).
- Two of the indices i,j,u,v distinct ($i \ne j$, $u \ne v$).

The evaluation of $E\{\chi^2(\mathbf{Y})\}$ requires consideration of each of these cases.

The generating function of the pair of random variables $N_t(\mathbf{Y}_i)$, $N_s(\mathbf{Y}_j)$ conditioned by $\{\Pi_i = \pi_i, \Pi_j = \pi_j\}$ is

$$E\{z^{N_t(Y_i)}w^{N_s(Y_j)}/\Pi_i = \pi_i, \Pi_j = \pi_j\}$$

$$(\text{V.7})\quad = [p_{\pi_i}(t)z + (1 - p_{\pi_i}(t))]^{n_i}[p_{\pi_j}(s)w + (1 - p_{\pi_j}(s))]^{n_j}$$

$$0 \le i,j < r \qquad i \ne j \qquad 0 \le s,t < m$$

and

$$E\{z^{N_t(Y_j)}w^{N_s(Y_j)}/\Pi_j = \pi_j\} = [p_{\pi_j}(t)z + p_{\pi_i}(s)w + (1 - p_{\pi_i}(t) - p_{\pi_j}(s))]^{n_j}$$

$$(\text{V.8})\quad 0 \le j < r \qquad 0 \le s,t < m \qquad s \ne t$$

In the following three cases, the conditional expectations are obtained from Eqs. (V.7) and (V.8) by differentiation and evaluation at $z = 1$ and/or $w = 1$.

Case 1 Four i,j,u,v distinct indices

$$E\{N_t(\mathbf{Y}_i)N_t(\mathbf{Y}_j)N_s(\mathbf{Y}_u)N_s(\mathbf{Y}_v)/\Pi_i = \pi_i, \Pi_j = \pi_j, \Pi_u = \pi_u, \Pi_v = \pi_v\}$$

$$= n_i n_j n_u n_v p_{\pi_i}(t)p_{\pi_j}(t)p_{\pi_u}(s)p_{\pi_v}(s)$$

$$0 \le i,j,u,v < r \qquad i,j,u,v \text{ distinct} \qquad 0 \le s,t < m$$

$$(\text{V.9})\quad \sum_{\{(i,j,u,v,s,t):0\le i,j,u,v<r,(i,j,u,v)\text{-distinct},0\le s,t<m\}} E\{N_t(\mathbf{Y}_i)N_t(\mathbf{Y}_j)N_s(\mathbf{Y}_u)N_s(\mathbf{Y}_v)\}$$

$$= \left(\sum_{0\le t<m} p^2[t]\right)^2 [(n^{(1)})^4 - 6(n^{(1)})^2 n^{(2)} + 8n^{(1)}n^{(3)} - 6n^{(4)} + 3(n^{(2)})^2]$$

Case 2 Three distinct indices

i,j,v distinct indices : $u = i$

i,j,u distinct indices : $v = i$

$$\text{i,j,v distinct indices} : u = j$$

$$\text{i,j,u distinct indices} : v = j$$

The expectation $E\{N_t(\mathbf{Y}_i)N_t(\mathbf{Y}_j)N_s(\mathbf{Y}_u)N_s(\mathbf{Y}_v)\}$ in *Case 2* also depends on whether or not t and s are distinct. There are two possible expressions:

$$E\{N_t(\mathbf{Y}_i)N_s(\mathbf{Y}_i)N_t(\mathbf{Y}_j)N_s(\mathbf{Y}_v)\} = n_i(n_i - 1)n_j n_v p[t,s]p[t]p[s]$$

$$0 \le i,jv < r \qquad i,j,v \text{ distinct} \qquad 0 \le s,t < m \qquad s \ne t$$

$$E\{N_t^2(\mathbf{Y}_i)N_t(\mathbf{Y}_j)N_t(\mathbf{Y}_v)\} = n_i(n_i - 1)n_j n_v p[t,t]p^2[t] + n_i n_j n_v p^3[t]$$

$$0 \le i,j,v < r \qquad i,j,v \text{ distinct} \qquad 0 \le t < m$$

yielding

$$\text{(V.10)} \qquad \sum_{\{(i,j,v,s,t):0\le i,j,v<r,(i,j,v\text{-distinct}),0<s,t<m\}} E\{N_t(\mathbf{Y}_i)N_t(\mathbf{Y}_j)N_s(\mathbf{Y}_i)N_s(\mathbf{Y}_v)\}$$

$$= \sum_{\{(i,j,u,s,t):0\le i,j,u<r,(i,j,u\text{-distinct}),0\le s,t<m\}} E\{N_t(\mathbf{Y}_i)N_t(\mathbf{Y}_j)N_s(\mathbf{Y}_u)N_s(\mathbf{Y}_i)\}$$

$$= \sum_{\{(i,j,v,s,t):0\le i,j,v<r,(i,j,v\text{-distinct}),0\le s,t<m\}} E\{N_t(\mathbf{Y}_i)N_t(\mathbf{Y}_j)N_s(\mathbf{Y}_j)N_s(\mathbf{Y}_v)\}$$

$$= \sum_{\{(i,j,u,s,t):0\le i,j,u<r,(i,j,u\text{-distinct}),0\le s,t<m\}} E\{N_t(\mathbf{Y}_i)N_t(\mathbf{Y}_j)N_s(\mathbf{Y}_u)N_s(\mathbf{Y}_j)\}$$

$$= \left(\sum_{0\le s,t<m} p[t,s]p[t]p[s] \right)$$

$$\times [2n^{(4)} + (n^{(1)})^2 n^{(2)} - (n^{(2)})^2 - 2n^{(1)}n^{(3)} + 3n^{(1)}n^{(2)} - (n^{(1)})^3 - 2n^{(3)}]$$

$$+ \left(\sum_{0\le t<m} p^3[t] \right) [(n^{(1)})^3 + 2n^{(3)} - 3n^{(1)} n^{(2)}]$$

Case 3 Two distinct indices

$$i \ne j, u \ne v \quad u = i, v = j$$

$$i \ne j, u \ne v \quad v = i, u = j$$

The expectation $E\{N_t(\mathbf{Y}_i)N_t(\mathbf{Y}_j)N_s(\mathbf{Y}_u)N_s(\mathbf{Y}_v)\}$ in *Case 3* also depends upon whether or not t and s are distinct. There are two types of expressions:

$$E\{N_t(\mathbf{Y}_i)N_t(\mathbf{Y}_j)N_s(\mathbf{Y}_i)N_s(\mathbf{Y}_j)\} = n_i(n_i - 1)n_j(n_j - 1)p^2[t,s]$$

$$0 \le i,j < r \qquad i \ne j \qquad 0 \le s,t < m \qquad s \ne t$$

$$E\{[N_t(\mathbf{Y}_i)N_t(\mathbf{Y}_j)]^2\} = n_i(n_i - 1)n_j(n_j - 1)p^2[t,t])$$

$$+ [n_i n_j(n_j - 1) + n_j n_i(n_i - 1)]p[t,t]p[t] + n_i n_j p^2[t]$$

$$0 \le i,j < r \qquad i \ne j \qquad 0 \le t < m$$

$$\text{(V.11)} \quad \sum_{\{(i,j,s,t):0\le i,j<r,i\ne j,0\le s,t<m\}} E\{N_t(\mathbf{Y}_i)N_t(\mathbf{Y}_j)N_s(\mathbf{Y}_i)N_s(\mathbf{Y}_j)\}$$

$$= \left(\sum_{0\le s,t<m} p^2[t,s]\right)[(n^{(2)})^2 - n^{(4)} - 2n^{(1)}n^{(2)} + 2n^{(3)} - n^{(2)} + (n^{(1)})^2]$$

$$+ \left(\sum_{0\le t<m} p[t,t]p[t]\right) 2[n^{(1)}n^{(2)} - n^{(3)} - (n^{(1)})^2 + n^{(2)}]$$

$$+ \left(\sum_{0\le t<m} p^2[t]\right)[(n^{(1)})^2 - n^{(2)}]$$

Adding the right-hand side of Eq. (V.9), four times the right-hand side of Eq. (V.10), and two times the right-hand side of Eq. (V.11), we obtain

$$\text{(V.12)} \quad E\{\chi^2(\mathbf{Y})\} =$$

$$\left(\sum_{0\le t<m} p^2[t]\right)^2 [(n^{(1)})^4 - 6(n^{(1)})^2n^{(2)} + 8n^{(1)}n^{(3)} - 6n^{(4)} + 3(n^{(2)})^2]$$

$$+ \left(\sum_{0\le s,t<m} p[t,s]p[t]p[s]\right)$$

$$\times 4[2n^{(4)} + (n^{(1)})^2n^{(2)} - (n^{(2)})^2 - 2n^{(1)}n^{(3)} + 3n^{(1)}n^{(2)} - (n^{(1)})^3 - 2n^{(3)}]$$

$$+ \left(\sum_{0\le t<m} p^3[t]\right) 4[(n^{(1)})^3 + 2n^{(3)} - 3n^{(1)}n^{(2)}]$$

$$+ \left(\sum_{0\le t<m} p^2[t]\right) 2[(n^{(1)})^2 - n^{(2)}]$$

$$+ \left(\sum_{0\le s,t<m} p^2[t,s]\right) 2[(n^{(2)})^2 - n^{(4)} - 2n^{(1)}n^{(2)} + 2n^{(3)} - n^{(2)} + (n^{(1)})^2]$$

$$+ \left(\sum_{0\le t<m} p[t,t]p[t]\right) 4[n^{(1)}n^{(2)} - n^{(3)} - (n^{(1)})^2 + n^{(2)}]$$

Eqs. (V.5) and (V.12) provide the formula for $\mathrm{Var}\{\chi(\mathbf{Y})\}$:

$$\mathrm{Var}\{\chi(\mathbf{Y})\} =$$

$$\left(\sum_{0\le t<m} p^2[t]\right)^2 [-4(n^{(1)})^2n^{(2)} + 8n^{(1)}n^{(3)} - 6n^{(4)} + 2(n^{(2)})^2]$$

$$+ \left(\sum_{0\le s,t<m} p[t,s]p[t]p[s]\right)$$

$$\times 4[2n^{(4)} + (n^{(1)})^2n^{(2)} - (n^{(2)})^2 - 2n^{(1)}n^{(3)} + 3n^{(1)}n^{(2)} - (n^{(1)})^3 - 2n^{(3)}]$$

$$+ \left(\sum_{0\le t<m} p^3[t]\right) 4[(n^{(1)})^3 + 2n^{(3)} - 3n^{(1)}n^{(2)}]$$

$$+ \left(\sum_{0\le s,t<m} p^2[t,s]\right) 2[(n^{(2)})^2 - n^{(4)} - 2n^{(1)}n^{(2)} + 2n^{(3)} - n^{(2)} + (n^{(1)})^2]$$

$$+\left(\sum_{0\le t<m} p[t,t]p[t]\right)4[n^{(1)}n^{(2)} - n^{(3)} - (n^{(1)})^2 + n^{(2)}]$$
$$+\left(\sum_{0\le t<m} p^2[t]\right)2[(n^{(1)})^2 - n^{(2)}]$$

Next we must compute

$$\mathrm{Cov}\{\Phi(\mathbf{Y}_j),\chi(\mathbf{Y})\} = E\{\Phi(\mathbf{Y}_j)\chi(\mathbf{Y})\} - E\{\Phi(\mathbf{Y}_j)\}E\{\chi(\mathbf{Y})\}$$

First

(V.13) $\mathrm{Cov}\{\Phi(\mathbf{Y}_j,\chi(\mathbf{Y})\}$

$$= E\{\sum_{0\le t<m} N_{t,j}(N_{t,j} - 1) \sum_{\{(s,u,v):0\le u,v<r,u\ne v,0\le s<m\}} N_s(\mathbf{Y}_u)N_s(\mathbf{Y}_v)\}$$
$$- E\{\sum_{0\le t<m} N_t(\mathbf{Y}_j)(N_t(\mathbf{Y}_j) - 1)\}\, E\{\sum_{\{(u,v,s):0\le u,v<r,u\ne v,0\le s<m\}} N_s(\mathbf{Y}_u)N_s(\mathbf{Y}_v)\}$$
$$= 2 \sum_{\{(u,s,t):0\le u<r,i\ne u,0\le s,t<m\}} E\{N_{t,i}(N_{t,i} - 1)\, N_{s,i}N_{s,u}\}$$
$$- 2\sum_{0\le t<m} E\{N_{t,i} - 1)\} \sum_{\{0\le u<r,u\ne i,0\le s<m\}} E\{N_{s,i}N_{s,u}\}$$
$$= 2 \sum_{\{(u,s):0\le u<r,i\ne u,0\le s,t<m\}} E\{N_{s,u}\}\mathrm{Cov}\{N_{t,i}(N_{t,i} - 1),N_{s,i}\}$$

$$E\{N_t(\mathbf{Y}_j)(N_t(\mathbf{Y}_j) - 1)N_s(\mathbf{Y}_j)\} = \begin{cases} n_j(n_j - 1)(n_j - 2)p[t,t,s] & \text{if } t \ne s \\ n_j(n_j - 1)(n_j - 2)p[s,s,s] \\ \quad + 2n_j(n_j - 1)p[s,s] & \text{if } t = s \end{cases}$$

But

$$E\{N_t(\mathbf{Y}_j)(N_t(\mathbf{Y}_j) - 1)\} = n_j(n_j - 1)p[t,t]$$

and

$$E\{N_s(\mathbf{Y}_j)\} = n_j p[s]$$

so that

$$\text{(V.14)}\quad \mathrm{Cov}\{n_t(\mathbf{Y}_j)(N_t(\mathbf{Y}_j) - 1)N_s(\mathbf{Y}_j)\} = \begin{cases} n_j(n_j - 1)(n_j - 2)p[t,t,s] \\ \quad - n_j^2(n_j - 1)p[t,t]p[s] & \text{if } t \ne s \\ n_j(n_j - 1)(n_j - 2)p[s,s,s] \\ \quad + 2n_j(n_j - 1)p[s,s] \\ \quad - n_j^2(n_j - 1)p[s,s]p[s] & \text{if } t = s \end{cases}$$

Combining Eqs. (V.13) and (V.14), we have

$$\mathrm{Cov}\{\Phi(\mathbf{Y}_j)\chi(\mathbf{Y})\} = \left(\sum_{0\le s,t<m} p[s]p[t,t,s]\right) 2[n_j(n_j-1)(n_j-2)(n^{(1)}-n_j)]$$
$$-\left(\sum_{0\le s,t<m} p[s]p[t,t]\right) 2[n_j^2(n_j-1)(n^{(1)}-n_j)]$$
$$+\left(\sum_{0\le s<m} p[s]p[s,s]\right) 4[n_j(n_j-1)(n^{(1)}-n_j)]$$

and hence $\mathrm{Cov}\{\Phi(\mathbf{Y}),\chi(\mathbf{Y})\} = \sum_{0\le j<r} \mathrm{Cov}\{\Phi(\mathbf{Y}_j)\chi(\mathbf{Y})\}$ is given by

$$\text{(V.15)}\quad \mathrm{Cov}\{\Phi(\mathbf{Y}),\chi(\mathbf{Y})\} =$$
$$\left(\sum_{0<s,t<m} p[s]p[t,t,s]\right)$$
$$\times\, 2[n^{(1)}n^{(3)} - n^{(4)} - 3n^{(1)}n^{(2)} + 3n^{(3)} + 2(n^{(1)})^2 - 2n^{(2)}]$$
$$-\left(\sum_{0\le s,t<m} p^2[t,t]p[s]\right) 2[n^{(1)}n^{(3)} - n^{(4)} - n^{(1)}n^{(2)} + n^{(3)}]$$
$$+\left(\sum_{0\le s<m} p[s,s]p[s]\right) 4[n^{(1)}n^{(2)} - n^{(3)} - (n^{(1)})^2 + n^{(2)}]$$

We simplify (V.15) by recognizing that

$$\sum_{0\le t<m} p[t,t,s] = s_2p[s] \qquad \sum_{0\le t<m} p[t,t] = s_2$$

so that the covariance may be written as

$$\mathrm{Cov}\{\Phi(\mathbf{Y}),\chi(\mathbf{Y})\} = \left(s_2 \sum_{0\le t<m} (p[t])^2 - \sum_{0\le t<m} p[t,t]p^2[t]\right)$$
$$\times\, 4[-n^{(1)}n^{(2)} + n^{(3)} + (n^{(1)})^2 - n^{(2)}]$$

We have thus obtained the formula given earlier in this book.

Theorem 4.3

$$\mathrm{Var}\{\Phi(\mathbf{Y})\} =$$

$$4n^{(3)}[s_3 - s_2^2] + 2n^{(2)}[5s_2^2 + s_2 - 6s_3] + 2n^{(1)}[4s_3 - s_2 - 3s_2^2]$$

$$+\left(\sum_{0\le t<m} p^2[t])\right)^2 [-4(n^{(1)})^2n^{(2)} + 8n^{(1)}n^{(3)} - 6n^{(4)} + 2(n^{(2)})^2]$$

$$+\left(\sum_{0\le s,t<m} p[t,s]p[t]p[s]\right)$$

$$\times\, 4[2n^{(4)} + (n^{(1)})^2n^{(2)} - (n^{(2)})^2 - 2n^{(1)}n^{(3)} + 3n^{(1)}n^{(2)} - (n^{(1)})^3 - 2n^{(3)}]$$

$$+\left(\sum_{0\le t<m} p^3[t]\right) 4[(n^{(1)})^3 + 2n^{(3)} - 3n^{(1)}n^{(2)}]$$

$$+ \left(\sum_{0 \le s,t < m} p^2[t,s] \right) 2[(n^{(2)})^2 - n^{(4)} - 2n^{(1)}n^{(2)} + 2n^{(3)} - n^{(2)} + (n^{(1)})^2]$$

$$+ \left(\sum_{0 \le t < m} p^2[t] \right) 2[(n^{(1)})^2 - n^{(2)}]$$

$$+ \left(8s_2 \sum_{0 \le t < m} p^2[t] - 12 \sum_{0 \le t < m} p[t,t]p^2[t] \right) [-n^{(1)}n^{(2)} + n^{(3)} + (n^{(1)})^2 - n^{(2)}]$$

Solutions to Selected Problems

CHAPTER 2

2.1 The source entropy and redundancy are

$$H(S) = -\sum_{0 \le t,s < m} p(t,s) \log_2 p(t,s) \approx 7.4298$$

$$D(S) = \log_2 26^2 - H(S) \approx 1.9710 \text{ (bits/letter)}$$

2.2 Suppose plaintext $\mathbf{x}$ is generated by the source described in Example 2.3.3 with transition matrix $P = (p(s/t))$ and stationary distribution π, and is enciphered into $\mathbf{Y} = \mathbf{X} + k$ (modulo m). Then

$$\Pr_{\text{PLAIN/CIPHER}}\{\mathbf{x} + k - j/\mathbf{x} + k\}$$

$$= \pi(x_0 + k - j) \frac{\prod_{0 \le s < n-1} p(x_{s+1} + k - j/x_s + k - j)}{\sum_{0 \le i < m} \pi(x_0 + i) \prod_{0 \le s < m} p(x_{s+1} + i/x_s + i)}$$

$$= \pi(x_0 + k - j) \frac{\prod_{0 \le t,s < m} (p(s + k - j/t + k - j))^{N_{t,s}}}{\sum_{0 \le i < m} \pi(x_0 + i) \prod_{0 \le t,s < m} (p(s + i/t + i))^{N_{t,s}}}$$

where $N_{t,s}$ is the number of times the 2-gram (t,s) occurs in $\mathbf{x}$. This conditional probability is maximized by a value of j that minimizes

$$-\sum_{0 \le t,s < m} N_{t,s} \log p(t + k - j, s + k - j) - \log \pi(x_0 + k - j)$$

The law of large numbers implies

$$\pi(t)p(s/t) = \text{limit}_{n \to \infty} N_{t,s}/n$$

with probability one, so that

$$-\text{limit}_{n \to \infty} (1/n)\left(\sum_{0 \le t,s < m} N_{t,s} \log p(s + k - j/t + k - j) - \log \pi(x_0 + k - j) \right)$$

$$= -\sum_{0 \le t < m} \pi(t) \sum_{0 \le s < m} p(s/t) \log p(s + k - j/t + k - j)$$

Now we use Theorem 2.8.3 to conclude that

$$-\sum_{0 \le t,s < m} \pi(t)p(s/t) \log p(s + k - j/t + k - j)$$

is minimized only by k = j, provided

$$\blacklozenge \text{ for some t with } \pi(t) > 0$$

$$(p(0/t), p(1/t), \ldots, p(m-1/t)) = (p(j/t+j), p(j+1/t+j), \ldots, p(j-1/t+j)) \quad \textit{if and only if } j = 0$$

is satisfied.

2.5 By an induction argument,

$$\sigma^{(n)}(s) = \sum_{0 \le u < m} \sigma^{(n-1)}(u)p(u/s)$$

where

$$\sigma^{(n)}(s) = \sum_{0 \le t < m} p^{(n)}(t/s)$$

Since $\sigma^{(1)}(u) = 1$ for $0 \le u < m$, it follows that $\sigma^{(n)}(u) = 1$ for $0 \le u < m$ and all $n \ge 1$.

Assume plaintext is generated by a Markov chain with transition matrix $P = (p(s/t))$ and stationary distribution π

$$Pr_{PLAIN}\{x_0, x_1, \ldots, x_{n-1}\} = \pi(x_0)p(x_1/x_0)p(x_2/x_1) \cdot p(x_{n-1}/x_{n-2})$$

It follows that

$$Pr_{PLAIN}\{X_j = t, X_{j+n-1} = s\} = \sum_{\{x_0,\ldots,x_{j+n-1}: x_j = t, x_{j+n-1} = s\}} Pr_{PLAIN}\{x_0, \ldots, x_{j+n-1}\} = \pi(s)p^{(n)}(t/s)$$

2.6 Assume

- the source generates plaintext by a Markov chain with transition matrix $P = (p(t/s))$ and stationary distribution λ
- $\mathbf{y} = T_\pi(\mathbf{x})$

$$y_{i+rs} = x_{\pi(i)+sr} \quad 0 \le i < t, 0 \le s < n$$

The Bayesian strategy estimates π by a value of ν that maximizes

$$Pr_{PLAIN/CIPHER}\{T_\nu^{-1}(\mathbf{y})/\mathbf{y}\} = Pr_{PLAIN/CIPHER}\{T_\nu^{-1}(T_\pi(\mathbf{x}))/T_\pi(\mathbf{x})\}$$

We argue as before that ν makes this conditional probability a maximum if it makes

$$-\log Pr_{PLAIN,CIPHER}\{T_\nu^{-1}(\mathbf{y}), \mathbf{y}\}$$

a minimum. Let $N_{s,t,i}(\mathbf{y})$ denote the number of solutions of

$$y_{i+kr} = s \quad y_{i+1+kr} = t \quad 0 \le i < r$$

in **y** with k taking values in $\{0, 1, \ldots, n-1\}$. Then

$$\begin{aligned}
-(1/n) \log \Pr_{\text{PLAIN,CIPHER}}\{T_\nu^{-1}(\mathbf{y}),\mathbf{y}\} \\
&= -(1/n) \log \pi_{\nu^{-1}}(0) \\
&\quad -(1/n) \sum_{0 \le k < n} \left(\sum_{0 \le i < r-1} \log p(y_{\nu^{-1}(i+1)+kr}/y_{\nu^{-1}(i)+kr}) \right) \\
&\quad -(1/n) \sum_{0 \le k < n-1} \log p(y_{\nu^{-1}(0)+(k+1)r}/y_{\nu^{-1}(r-1)+kr}) \\
&= -\sum_{0 \le i < r} \sum_{0 \le s,t < m} (N_{s,t,i}(\mathbf{y})/n) \log \eta_{i,\nu}(s,t) + o(1)
\end{aligned}$$

where o(1) denotes a quantity tending to zero as $n \to \infty$, and $\eta_{i,\nu}(s,t)$ is defined by

$$\eta_{i,\nu}(s,t) = \begin{cases} \lambda(s)p^{(a_i)}(t/s) & \text{if } \nu^{-1}(i+1) - \nu^{-1}(i) = a_i > 0 \\ \lambda(t)p^{(b_i)}(s/t)/\lambda(s) & \text{if } \nu^{-1}(i) - \nu^{-1}(i+1) = b_i > 0 \end{cases}$$

If $\mathbf{Y} = T_\pi(\mathbf{X})$, the law of large numbers implies $\text{limit}_{n\to\infty} N_{s,t,i,\nu}(\mathbf{Y})/nr = \eta_{i,\pi}(s,t)$, so that

$$\begin{aligned}
\text{limit}_{n\to\infty} &- (1/n) \log \Pr_{\text{PLAIN,CIPHER}}\{T_\nu^{-1}(\mathbf{Y}),\mathbf{Y}\} \\
&= -\sum_{0 \le i < r} \sum_{0 \le s,t < m} \eta_{i,\pi}(s,t) \log \eta_{i,\nu}(s,t) \\
&\ge -\sum_{0 \le i < r} \sum_{0 \le s,t < m} \eta_{i,\pi}(s,t) \log \eta_{i,\pi}(s,t)
\end{aligned}$$

If for at least one i, $\eta_{i,\pi}(s,t) \neq \eta_{i,\nu}(s,t)$,

$$\text{limit}_{n\to\infty} - (1/n) \log \Pr_{\text{PLAIN,CIPHER}}\{T_\nu^{-1}(\mathbf{Y}),\mathbf{Y}\}$$

is minimized only when $\nu = \pi$.

2.7 By Theorem 2.8.2, $H(Y_0,Y_1, \ldots ,Y_{n-1}) \le m \log n$. Next,

$$\begin{aligned}
H(Y_0, Y_1, \ldots ,Y_{n-1},\boldsymbol{K}) &= H(X_0, X_1, \ldots ,X_{n-1},\boldsymbol{K}) \\
&= H(X_0,X_1, \ldots ,X_{n-1}) + H(\boldsymbol{K})
\end{aligned}$$

But

$$\begin{aligned}
H(Y_0, Y_1, \ldots ,Y_{n-1},\boldsymbol{K}) \\
&= H(Y_0,Y_1, \ldots ,Y_{n-1}) + H(\boldsymbol{K}/Y_0,Y_1, \ldots ,Y_{n-1})
\end{aligned}$$

which proves the assertion.

CHAPTER 3

3.1 *PLAIN(P3.1)* = *PLAIN(2)* and k = 11.

3.2 Caesar encipherment of n-grams $C_k : \mathbf{x} \rightarrow \mathbf{y}$

$$\mathbf{k} = (k_0, k_1, \ldots, k_{n-1}) \qquad \mathbf{x} = (x_0, x_1, \ldots) \qquad \mathbf{y} = (y_0, y_1, \ldots)$$

is defined by

$$y_{i+tn} = (x_{i+tn} + k_i + \epsilon_{i+tn}) \text{ (modulo 26)}$$

where $\epsilon_{(n-1)+tn} = 0$ and

$$\epsilon_{(n-i-1)+tn} = \begin{cases} 1 & \text{if } x_{(n-1)+tn} + k_{n-i} + \epsilon_{(n-i)t+tn} > 26 \\ 0 & \text{otherwise} \end{cases}$$

for i = 1, 2, . . . , n − 1. Thus the n key coordinates can be determined by analyzing the n subtexts in the reverse order,

$$\mathbf{y}^{(n-1)} = (y_{n-1}, y_{2n-1}, \ldots)$$

$$\ldots$$

$$\ldots$$

$$\mathbf{y}^{(1)} = (y_1, y_{n+1}, \ldots)$$

$$\mathbf{y}^{(0)} = (y_0, y_n, \ldots)$$

noting that the letters in the ith subtext $\mathbf{y}^{(i)}$ are enciphered by either k_i or $k_i + 1$.

3.3 a = 7 b = 4 *PLAIN(3.2)* = *PLAIN(1)*

3.4 The mapping

$$T(x) = ax^2 + bx \text{ (modulo 26)}$$

$$T : \mathbf{Z_{26}} \rightarrow \mathbf{Z_{26}}$$

is in SYM($\mathbf{Z_{26}}$) if and only if

$$T(x) = T(y) \text{ (modulo 26)} \qquad x,y \in \mathbf{Z_{26}}$$

implies x = y. Since T(x) − T(y) = (x − y)(a(x + y) + b), T ∈ SYM($\mathbf{Z_{26}}$) if and only if x = y is the only solution to

$$(x - y)(a(x + y) + b) = 0 \text{ (modulo 2)}$$

$$(x - y)(a(x + y) + b) = 0 \text{ (modulo 13)}$$

Theorem P3.1 The only polynomials in SYM($\mathbf{Z_{26}}$) of degree two are

$$T(x) = 2x + 13x^2 \qquad T(x) = 4x + 13x^2 \qquad T(x) = 6x + 13x^2$$

$$T(x) = 8x + 13x^2 \qquad T(x) = 10x + 13x^2 \qquad T(x) = 12x + 13x^2$$

$T(x) = 14x + 13x^2$ $T(x) = 16x + 13x^2$ $T(x) = 18x + 13x^2$

$T(x) = 20x + 13x^2$ $T(x) = 22x + 13x^2$ $T(x) = 24x + 13x^2$

Proof.

Case 1 $a \neq 0, 13$. If $x = y + 2$, then $T(x) - T(y) = 2(a(2 + 2y) + b)$ so that

$$T(y + 2) - T(y) = 0 \text{ (modulo 26)}$$

has a solution if $2a(1 + y) + b = 0$ (modulo 13). This is clearly the case if $a \neq 0, 13$, or if $a = 0$ and $b = 13$.

Case 2 $a = 13$. If $x = y + 13$, $T(x) - T(y) = 13[13(2y + 13) + b]$, so that

$$T(x) - T(y) = 0 \text{ (modulo 26)}$$

if $13^2 + b = 0$ (modulo 2). which holds only if b is odd.

Finally, if $a = 12$ and b is even, the statement

$$T(x) - T(y) = (x - y)[13(x + y) + b] = 0 \text{ (modulo 26)}$$

implies $x = y$, since

if $x - y$ is even, *then* $13(x + y) + b = 0$ (modulo 13) *so* $b = 0$

if $x - y$ is odd, *then* $13(x + y) + b = 0$ (modulo 2) *and* b is odd

3.5 $T(x) = 11x$

3.6 *PLAIN(P3.4)* is

```
In the previous chapters we have dealt with the opera-
tional aspects of a business—the analysis of results
and the projection of operating conditions. In both
cases we had to assume that the decisions to invest
and to finance these operations had been made in an
appropriate fashion to permit profitable operation
to take place. In this chapter, we shall concentrate
on the analytical techniques which are used to sup-
port business investment decisions. We shall assume
that there exists in a company the capability to oper-
ate new facilities and other investments, and that
the necessary capital can be provided to finance the
investments under review.

 The process of investment in land, productive
equipment, buildings, working capital, raw material
deposits, and other assets for future economic gain
is particularly difficult and a cause for careful
```

analysis. Decisions in this area usually commit a business enterprise for a considerable time period to an activity, line of business, or geographic region. As one of the three basic areas of decision making—investment, operations and financing—the investment process has the longest time horizon and rests most heavily on careful forecasts and detailed assumptions about the likely future conditions which will provide the economic gain to justify the contemplated outlay of funds.

Before we turn to specific concepts and the framework for analysis, it should be emphasized that in this book we are viewing the capital investment problem (a part of capital budgeting) in a narrow sense. The critical task of management is to establish the general objectives and specific goals of the enterprise. On the basis of these and the known strengths and limitations in administrative talent, manpower, technical know-how, market standing, financial possibilities, and so on, management must formulate appropriate strategies.*

The substitution π : *PLAIN(P3.4)* → *CIPHER(P3.4)* is

A	B	C	D	E	F	G	H	I	J	K	L	M	N	O	P	Q	R	S	T	U	V	W	X	Y	Z
↓	↓	↓	↓	↓	↓	↓	↓	↓	↓	↓	↓	↓	↓	↓	↓	↓	↓	↓	↓	↓	↓	↓	↓	↓	↓
w	g	m	k	r	u	y	t	b	z	h	c	n	x	f	d	j	l	p	e	v	o	a	q	s	i

3.7 We begin by using the partial correspondence between the ciphertext letters of highest frequency of occurrence in *CIPHER(P3.5)* and E T A O N I R S H

★r f e b x w l c ←→E T A O N I R S H

from Table P3.11. Now we search for the probable words tennis, soccer and football in *CIPHER(P3.5)*.

Case 1 TENNIS. The only ciphertext 6-grams in *CIPHER(P3.5)* of the form $(y_0,y_1,y_2,y_2,y_3,y_4)$ with distinct $\{y_i\}$ are

mwxxfe wuffeg

The two possible plaintext-to-ciphertext correspondences,

TENNIS →mwxxfe TENNIS →wuffeg

imply T → m or E → u, both of which are inconsistent with ★.

*From Erich A. Helfert, *Techniques of Financial Analysis,* third edition, (Homewood, Illinois, Richard D. Irwin, 1972), pp. 107–8. © 1972 by Richard D. Irwin, Inc.

Case 2 SOCCER. The only ciphertext 6-grams in *CIPHER(P3.5)* that can correspond to SOCCER are those in *Case 1;* these imply the plaintext-ciphertext correspondences C → x or C → f, both of which are inconsistent with ★.

Case 3 FOOTBALL. The only ciphertext 8-gram in *CIPHER(P3.5)* $(y_0, y_1, y_1, y_2, y_3, y_4, y_5, y_5)$ with distinct $\{y_i\}$ is

FOOTBALL → uffegwcc

which is consistent with ★, yielding the partial ciphertext alphabet

```
A B C D E F G H I J K L M N O P Q R S T U V W X Y Z
↓ ↓ ↓ ↓ ↓ ↓ ↓ ↓ ↓ ↓ ↓ ↓ ↓ ↓ ↓ ↓ ↓ ↓ ↓ ↓ ↓ ↓ ↓ ↓ ↓ ↓
w g       u           c     f         e
```

It is likely therefore that E → r, which we add to our list of ciphertext-to-plaintext correspondences,

```
A B C D E F G H I J K L M N O P Q R S T U V W X Y Z
↓ ↓ ↓ ↓ ↓ ↓ ↓ ↓ ↓ ↓ ↓ ↓ ↓ ↓ ↓ ↓ ↓ ↓ ↓ ↓ ↓ ↓ ↓ ↓ ↓ ↓
w g     r u           c     f         e
```

It is reasonable to conjecture that {I, N} ← → {b, x}. When we make the plaintext-to-ciphertext correspondences

I → b N → x

and decipher a segment of *CIPHER(P3.5)*, we obtain

```
aEmAL LOvly AnEFO OTBAL LANkI
FsOvm ANNOT hImhs OvmAN NOTBE
mOnEA FOOTB ALLEl IFsOv LEAlN
TOhIm haITt EITtE lFOOT sOvaI
LLBEA NINFI NITEL snOlE oALvA
BLEdL AsElT tANIF sOvhI mhaIT
tONEA NkvpE TtEOT tElnE lELsT
OpTAN kONTt ElEAl EOFmO vlpEk
IFFEl ENTpT sLEpO FhImh INyAB
ALLAN kApLI ytTlE Akzvp TnENT
OFTEm tNIjv EIpNE EkEkF OlABA
LLlvN NINyA aAsFl OnTtE hImhE
lOlmO nINyF lOnTt ELEFT OllIy
tTIFs OvAlE INsOv lTEEN psOvm
ANNOT sETEq dEmTT OEqEl Tnvmt
dOaEl BvTTt ElEAl EmElT AINFv
NkAnE NTALd lINmI dLEpI NhImh
INyhE EdsOv lEsEO NTtEB ALLEN
```

Now we can recognize the word Mannot as cannot and therefore the partial decipherment, which begins AeMall is Aecall, which is likely wecall.

We make the changes w → A and c → M, obtaining

```
WECAL LOvly AnEFO OTBAL LANkI
FsOvC ANNOT hIChs OvCAN NOTBE
COnEA FOOTB ALLEl IFsOv LEAlN
TohIC hWITt EITtE lFOOT sOvWI
LLBEA NINFI NITEL snOlE oALvA
BLEdL AsElT tANIF sOvhI ChWIT
tONEA NkvpE TtEOT tElnE lELsT
OpTAN kONTt ElEAl EOFCO vlpEk
IFFEl ENTpT sLEpO FhICh INyAB
ALLAN kApLI ytTlE Akzvp TnENT
OFTEC tNIjv EIpNE EkEkF OlABA
LLlvN NINyA WAsFl OnTtE hIChE
lOlCO nINyF lOnTt ELEFT OllIy
tTIFs OvAlE INsOv lTEEN psOvC
ANNOT sETEq dECTT OEqEl TnvCt
dOWEl BvTTt ElEAl ECElT AINFv
NkAnE NTALd lINCI dLEpI NhICh
INyhE EdsOv lEsEO NTtEB ALLEN
```

The rest of the argument is clear. The plaintext deals with the sport of SOCCER, almost universally referred to as football. The actual text and the substitution π are

We call our game football and if you cannot kick you cannot become a footballer. If you learn to kick with either foot you will be an infinitely more valuable player than if you kick with one and use the other merely to stand on. There are of course different styles of kicking a ball and a slight readjustment of technique is needed for a ball running away from the kicker or coming from the left or right. If you are in your teens you cannot yet expect to exert much power but there are certain fundamental principles in kicking. Keep your eye on the ball. Ensure that you are balanced. Position the non kicking foot correctly. follow through with the kicking leg. Aim for accuracy rather than power. Let us look more closely at the various methods of kicking a football and we shall discover the importance of these five principles. Kicking with the instep. This is probably the most common way of kicking and is valuable when passing and shooting whether short long low or high. *

A	B	C	D	E	F	G	H	I	J	K	L	M	N	O	P	Q	R	S	T	U	V	W	X	Y	Z
↓	↓	↓	↓	↓	↓	↓	↓	↓	↓	↓	↓	↓	↓	↓	↓	↓	↓	↓	↓	↓	↓	↓	↓	↓	↓
w	g	m	k	r	u	y	t	b	z	h	c	n	x	f	d	j	l	p	e	v	o	a	q	s	i

*From *Your Book Of Soccer*, by Robin Trimby. Reprinted with permission of the publisher Faber and Faber Ltd., London, England. © 1970.

3.8 The cryptanalysis of the Playfair ciphertext *CIPHER(P3.6)* is carried out in the following sequence of steps:

Step 1 If TH $\rightarrow$ hy, then T H and Y must be adjacent in a row or column of the Playfair square.

$$\text{T} \rightarrow \text{H} \rightarrow \text{Y} \qquad \text{T} \downarrow \text{H} \downarrow \text{Y}$$

Step 2 The right contact letters of (ciphertext) hy suggest that

$$\{\text{L, F, K, I}\} \subseteq E_{\text{E}}$$

We make this hypothesis. *Claim:* $\text{Y} \notin E_{\text{E}}$

Case 2.1 E $\downarrow$ Y

$$\begin{array}{lllll} & & \text{E L F K I} \\ \text{T} \rightarrow \text{H} \rightarrow \text{Y} & & \end{array}$$

In *Case 2.1,* TE $\rightarrow$ ky, which means that K $\downarrow$ T, so that TI $\rightarrow$ *K, which is inconsistent with Table P3.16.

Case 2.2 E and Y are in the same row.

$$\begin{array}{c} \text{T} \\ \downarrow \\ \text{H} \\ \downarrow \\ \text{E} \rightarrow \text{Y} \quad \text{3 of the letters } \{\text{L K F I}\} \end{array}$$

Case 2.2 and Table P3.16 imply TE $\rightarrow$ ky, which contradicts the hypothesis of *Step 2.*

Step 3 Since the right contact letters of plaintext H are E, A and I in the ratio 4.5 : 1.5 : 1, it is reasonable to assume $\text{Y} \in E_{\text{A}}$.

Step 4 From Table P3.16 and the hypothesis in *Step 2,*

$$\{\text{L, K, F, I}\} \subseteq E_{\text{E}}$$

we may further conclude that the ciphertext of EN and ES appears in the set

{lm lp ky ih lh}

Step 5 Looking at the results of the search for the ciphertext of *I NV ES TM EN T*, we see that the candidates are

Case	Word *investment*	Count
5.1	nkuwlmhtihvm	1
5.2	pluwlmhtihzy	1

Case	Word	Count
	investment	
5.3	ikuwlmhtihwe	1
5.4	lmhtihzykylp	1
5.5	pspqlhyvihit	1
5.6	yvhyihkylmod	1
5.7	mlhwlhsnlpfi	1

Case 5.6 Contradicts TH → hy.

Case 5.4 lmhtihzykylp, implies ES → ih, EN → kv, and NV → ht Since T → H → Y or T ↓H ↓Y, the correspondence NV → ht is impossible.

Case 5.5 pspqlhyvihit, implies ES → lh and EN → ih, so that H $\in E_S \cap E_N$. By Theorem 3.12.2 (viii), this implies either

```
        S
        ↓
    T → H → Y   N
        ↓       ↓
        E       I
        ↓
        L
```

from which we conclude that tI → n*, which is inconsistent with Table P3.16, *or*

```
        I
        ↓
        E      L
        ↓
        N
        ↓
    T → H → Y S
```

which contradicts I $\in E_E$, *or*

```
        E     L i
    T → H → Y S N
```

which implies that TI → *n, which is inconsistent with Table P3.16.

Case 5.7 mlhwlhsnlpfi, implies ES → lh and EN → lp. If S and E are in the same row, then L, H and E are in the same row, a contradiction. Can S and E be in the same column? If so,

```
        E
        ↓
        L
        S
        ↓
    T → H → Y
```

which means that N, P and E are in the same column, a contradiction.

Conclusion nkuwlmhtihvm, pluwlmhtihzy and ikuwlmhtihwe are encipherments of *I NV ES TM EN T*.

ES → lm   EN → ih   NV → uw   TM → ht

$\{V, Z, H, W\} \subseteq E_T$ $\{K, L\} \subseteq E_I$

and we may conclude that

T   V   W   Z
↓
H
↓
Y

E and I are in the same row (Theorem 3.12.2 (vi)) and $\{L, K, I, F\} \subseteq E_E$.

Step 6 Look for the ciphertext of *B US IN ES S*. The only possibilities are

Case	Word *BUSINESS*
6.1	bkekwelmbu
6.2	hyihkylmod
6.3	iaropblmmp
6.4	ipekwelmbu

Case 6.1 Implies B $\in E_S$ and US → ek, IN → we, so that E $\in E_U \cap E_N$, which implies by Theorem 3.2 (viii) that E, U and N appear in the Playfair square in one of the following three arrangements:

U   N
↓   ↓
E N   E U   E U N

But EN → ih, which shows that all of these configurations are impossible.

Case 6.2 Is inconsistent with TH → hy.

Case 6.4 Implies P $\in E_B$ and US → ek, IN → we, which is inconsistent with TH → hy.

Conclusion *BUSINESS* → iaropblmmp implies

A $\in E_B$ US → ro   IN → pb

Step 7 Look for the ciphertext of *F IN AN CE ** and *F IN AN CI AL. The only possibilities are

Case	Word *FINANCE**/*FINANCIAL
7.1	vopbbuykhy
7.2	ylpbbubosn
7.3	ucpblpobhz
7.4	grpbbuduus
7.5	yspblpzhyv
7.6	ukpbbubkgr

The appearance of the pair of 2-grams pbbu three times suggests that IN → pb and AN → bu, but we may argue more directly as follows: if ucpblpobhz is the ciphertext of *FINANC***, then P $\in E_I \cap E_N$, so that by Theorem 3.2 (viii), I, P, and N appear in the Playfair square in one of the following three arrangements:

```
I     N
↓     ↓
P N   P I   I P N
```

The first and second arrangements contradict EN → ih, while the third contradicts the hypothesis in *Step 2.*

Conclusion vopbbuykhy, ylpbbubosn, grpbbuduus, and ukpbbubkgr are encipherments of *FINANCE** or *FINANCIAL.

IN → pb AN → bu

Step 8 E and H are in the same column, and N and H are in the same row.

Proof. EN → ih and I is in the row of E *(Step 5).* ◀

```
T
↓
H  N
↓
Y
E  I
```

Partial Determination of Playfair Square:—*Steps 1–8*

Step 9 L and E are in the same row.

Proof. L $\in E_I \cap E_E$, since ES → lm *(Step 5)* and hypothesis of *Step 2.* But I is in the row of E, so that *Step 10* follows from Theorem 3.2 (viii). ◀

```
T
↓
H  N
↓
Y
E  I  L
```

Partial Determination of Playfair Square: *Steps 1–9*

Step 10 E ↓ M and L ↓ S.

Proof. ES → lm *(Step 5),* so that E and M are in the same column. Either E ↓ T or E ↓ M. The first possibility implies that ET → th, which is inconsistent with Table P3.16. ◀

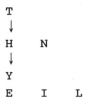

```
T
↓
H   N
↓
Y
E   I   L
↓       ↓
M       S
```

Partial Determination of Playfair Square: ***Steps 1–10***

Step 11 N ↓ B and I ↓ P.

Proof. IN → pb and *Step 9.* ◀

```
T
↓
H   N
↓   ↓
Y   B
E   I   L
↓   ↓   ↓
M   P   S
```

Partial Determination of Playfair Square: ***Steps 1–11***

Step 12 W ↓ N and V ↓ U.

Proof. NV → uw *(Step 5),* W, V and T are in the row above that which contains H. ◀

```
T   V   W
↓   ↓   ↓
H   U   N
↓       ↓
Y       B
E       I   L
↓       ↓   ↓
M       P   S
```

Partial Determination of Playfair Square: ***Steps 1–12***

Step 13 O and S in the same row; O and U in the same column; U and R in the same row; R and S in the same column.

Proof. US → ro *(Step 6).* ◀

```
T   V   W
↓   ↓   ↓
H   U   N   R
↓       ↓
Y       B
E       I   L
↓       ↓   ↓
M   O   P   S
```

Partial determination of Playfair Square: ***Steps 1-13***

Step 14. U ↓A and N ↓B.

Proof: AN → bu. ◀

```
T   V   W
↓   ↓   ↓
H   U   N   R
↓   ↓   ↓
Y   A   B
E       I   L
↓       ↓   ↓
M   O   P   S
```

Partial Determination of Playfair Square: ***Steps 1–14***

Step 15 Search for OP ER AT IO N*. Since ER → lh, AT → yv, and IO → *p, we have

OP ER AT IO N* → pq lh yv fp

which proves O → P → Q and F ↓O.

```
T    V  W
↓    ↓  ↓
H    U  N        R
↓    ↓  ↓
Y    A  B
E    F  I        L
↓    ↓  ↓        ↓
M    O→ P → Q    S
```

Partial Determination of Playfair Square: ***Steps 1–15***

Step 16 K ↓ Q.

Proof. K has been identified as a ciphertext equivalent of E. ◀

```
T    V  W
↓    ↓  ↓
H    U  N       R
↓    ↓  ↓
Y    A  B

E    F  I  K    L
↓    ↓  ↓  ↓    ↓
M    O→ P →Q    S
```

Partial Determination of Playfair Square: ***Steps 1–16***

Step 17 Using the present partial determination of the Playfair Square, we make a partial decipherment of *CIPHER(P3.6);* we replace all known 2-gram plaintext-to-ciphertext correspondences, *and* those ciphertext 2-grams whose first or second entry is known, leaving the remaining entry in ciphertext. We obtain

```
IN TH EP RE VI vU qd HA PT ER pz EH fV ly fy
ez WI TH TH EO PE ud TI ON df do PE yx mO Ff
BU SI NE ms mz ym AN df dm IS vF RE US ez od
Nb TH EP OR If yx IO NO Fv PE ud TI gr aO Nb
IT IO NS IN BO TH db ES pz EH by TO do US tE
```

Partial Decipherment of a Fragment of ***CIPHER(P3.6)***

A search for words or word fragments completes the determination of the Playfair Square. The Playfair enciphering matrix is based on the key HUNGRY.

```
H U N G R
Y A B C D
E F I K L
M O P Q S
T V W X Z
```

```
IN TH EP RE VI OU SC HA PT ER SW EH AV ED EA
LT WI TH TH EO PE RA TI ON AL AS PE CT SO FA
BU SI NE SS TH EA NA LY SI SO FR ES UL TS AN
DT HE PR OJ EC TI ON OF OP ER AT IN GC ON DI
TI ON SI NB OT HC AS ES WE HA DT OA SS UM ET
HA TT HE DE CI SI ON ST OI NV ES TA ND TO FI
NA NC ET HE SE OP ER AT IO NS HA DB EE NM AD
EI NA NA PP RO PR IA TE FA SH IO NT OP ER MI
TP RO FI TA BL EO PE RA TI ON TO TA KE PL AC
EI NT HI SC HA PT ER WE SH AL LC ON CE NT RA
TE ON TH EA NA LY TI CA LT EC HN IQ UE SW HI
CH AR EU SE DT OS UP PO RT BU SI NE SS IN VE
```

```
ST ME NT DE CI SI ON SW ES HA LL AS SU ME TH
AT TH ER EE XI ST SI NA CO MP AN YT HE CA PA
BI LI TY TO OP ER AT EN EW FA CI LI TI ES AN
DO TH ER IN VE ST ME NT SA ND TH AT TH EN EC
ES SA RY CA PI TA LC AN BE PR OV ID ED TO FI
NA NC ET HE IN VE ST ME NT SU ND ER RE VI EW
TH EP RO CE SS OF IN VE ST ME NT IN LA ND PR
OD UC TI VE EQ UI PM EN TB UI LD IN GS WO RK
IN GC AP IT AL RA WM AT ER IA LD EP OS IT SA
ND OT HE RA SS ET SF OR FU TU RE EC ON OM IC
GA IN IS PA RT IC UL AR LY DI FF IC UL TA ND
AC AU SE FO RC AR EF UL AN AL YS IS DE CI SI
ON SI NT HI SA RE AU SU AL LY CO MM IT AB US
IN ES SE NT ER PR IS EF OR AC ON SI DE RA BL
ET IM EP ER IO DT OA NA CT IV IT YL IN EO FB
US IN ES SO RG EO GR AP HI CR EG IO NA SO NE
OF TH ET HR EE BA SI CA RE AS OF DE CI SI ON
MA KI NG IN VE ST ME NT OP ER AT IO NS AN DF
IN AN CI NG TH EI NV ES TM EN TP RO CE SS HA
ST HE LO NG ES TT IM EH OR IZ ON AN DR ES TS
MO ST HE AV IL YO NC AR EF UL FO RC AS TS AN
DD ET AI LE DA SS UM PT IO NS AB OU TT HE LI
KE LY FU TU RE CO ND IT IO NS WH IC HW IL LP
RO VI DE TH EE CO NO MI CG AI NT OJ US TI FY
TH EC ON TE MP LA TE DO UT LA YO FF UN DS BE
FO RE WE TR UN TO SP EC IF IC CO NC EP TS AN
DT HE FR AM EW OR KF OR AN AL YS IS IT SH OU
LD BE EM PH AS IZ ED TH AT IN TH IS BO OK WE
AR ER EV IE WI NG TH EC AP IT AL IN VE ST ME
NT PR OB LE MA PA RT OF CA PI TA LB UD GE TI
NG IN AN AR RO WS EN SE TH EC RI TI CA LT AS
KO FM AN AG EM EN TI ST OE ST AB LI SH TH EG
EN ER AL OB JE CT IV ES AN DS PE CI FI CG OA
LS OF TH EE NT ER PR IS EO NT HE BA SI SO FT
HE SE AN DT HE KN OW NS TR EN GT HS AN DL IM
IT AT IO NS IN AD MI NI ST RA TI VE TA LE NT
MA NP OW ER TE CH NI CA LK NO WH OW MA RK ET
ST AN DI NG FI NA NC IN GP OS SI BI LI TI ES
AN DS OO NM AN AG EM EN TM US TF OR MU LA TE
AP PR OP RI AT ES TA TE GI ES
```

PLAIN(P3.6)

3.9 A Mixed Caesar substitution.

3.11 The enciphering matrix Γ is

$$\Gamma = \begin{vmatrix} 17 & 17 & 5 \\ 21 & 18 & 21 \\ 2 & 2 & 19 \end{vmatrix}$$

3.16 Use the φ-test to show that a monalphabetic substitution has been used and the κ-test to discover the period of the transposition.

CHAPTER 4

4.1 Let $N_t(\mathbf{X}_j)$: the number of times the letter t occurs in $\mathbf{X}_j$ (j = 0,1) and

$$\chi = \chi\{\mathbf{X}_0,\mathbf{X}_1\} = \sum_{0 \le t < m} N_t(\mathbf{X}_0)N_t(\mathbf{X}_1)$$

By Schwarz's inequality,

$$E\{\chi\} = n_0 n_1 \sum_{0 \le t < m} p_{\pi_0}(t)p_{\pi_1}(t) \le n_0 n_1 s_2$$

with equality if and only if

$$\bigstar\ (p_{\pi_0}(0), \ldots, p_{\pi_0}(m-1)) = (p_{\pi_1}(0), \ldots, p_{\pi_1}(m-1))$$

implies $\pi_0 = \pi_1$. Assuming that the probability distribution of 1-grams satisfies ★,

$$s_2 > \max_{\{\pi_0,\pi_1:\pi_0 \ne \pi_1\}} \sum_{0 \le t < m} p_{\pi_0}(t)p_{\pi_1}(t)$$

4.2 None, provided we interpret p(t) as the probability of the 2-gram $t = (t_1,t_2)$, replacing s_2 by

$$s_2 = \sum_{0 \le t_1,t_2 < m} p^2(t_1,t_2)$$

4.3 None, provided p(t) is interpreted as the stationary distribution of the Markov chain.

4.4 The periods (and user keys) of the Vigenère encipherment are

j	r	User Key
0	7	TRUMPET
1	6	CORNET
2	8	TROMBONE
3	10	FRENCHHORN

4.5 The periods (and user keys) of the Vigenère encipherments are

j	r	User Key
5	10	CANTELOUPE
6	4	PEAR

j	r	User Key
7	6	ORANGE
8	10	WATERMELON
9	5	APPLE

4.6 Differentiating the product of the generating functions with $i \neq j$,

$$E\{z^{N_{t,i}}\} = (zp(t) + 1 - p(t))^{n_i}$$

$$E\{z^{N_{t+s,j}}\} = (zp(t+s) + 1 - p(t+s))^{n_j}$$

$$(d/dz)\, E\{z^{N_{t,i}}\}E\{z^{N_{t+s,j}}\} = (d/dz)\, E\{z^{N_{t,i}+N_{t+s,j}}\}$$

$$= n_i n_j p(t)p(t+s)(zp(t) + 1 - p(t))^{n_i - 1}(zp(t+s) + 1 - p(t+s))^{n_j - 1}$$

yields

$$E\{\rho_{i,j}[s]\} = n_i n_j \sum_{0 \le t < m} p(t)p(t+s)$$

The computation of the variance uses the multivariate generating function,

$$E\{z^{N_{t,i}}w^{N_{u,i}}\} = (p(t)z + p(u)w + 1 - p(t) - p(u))^{n_i} \qquad (u \neq t)$$

and yields

$$\mathrm{Var}\{\rho_{i,j}[s]\} = n_i(n_i - 1)n_j \left[\sum_{0 \le t < m} p^2(t)p(t+s) - \left(\sum_{0 \le t < m} p(t)p(t+s) \right)^2 \right]$$

$$+ n_j(n_j - 1)n_i \left[\sum_{0 \le t < m} p^2(t+s)p(t) - \left(\sum_{0 \le t < m} p(t)p(t+s) \right)^2 \right]$$

$$+ n_i n_j \left[\sum_{0 \le t < m} p(t)p(t+s) - \left(\sum_{0 \le t < m} p(t)p(t+s) \right)^2 \right]$$

Using the 1-gram distribution (Table 2.3.1), we obtain the values

s	$S_{1,1}$	$S_{2,1}$	s	$S_{1,1}$	$S_{2,1}$
0	0.0687	0.0060	13	0.0461	0.0034
1	0.0400	0.0026	14	0.0398	0.0030
2	0.0327	0.0018	15	0.0454	0.0037
3	0.0325	0.0023	16	0.0371	0.0023
4	0.0427	0.0033	17	0.0347	0.0021
5	0.0335	0.0021	18	0.0314	0.0019
6	0.0352	0.0018	19	0.0376	0.0023
7	0.0376	0.0027	20	0.0352	0.0025
8	0.0314	0.0019	21	0.0335	0.0021
9	0.0347	0.0026	22	0.0427	0.0032
10	0.0371	0.0028	23	0.0325	0.0017
11	0.0454	0.0033	24	0.0327	0.0022
12	0.0398	0.0023	25	0.0400	0.0027

$$S_{1,1} = \sum_{0 \le t < m} p(t)p(t+s) \quad S_{2,1} = \sum_{0 \le t < m} p^2(t)p(t+s)$$

4.9

```
THEOB JECTI VEOFP ERFOR MANCE EVALU
ATION BYSIM ULATI ONISA LWAYS TOSAV
ECOST SANDT IMEIN COMPA RISON WITHT
UNING ASYST EMINT HEFIE LDTHE REFOR
ETHEE XPENS ESFOR SHIFT INGTH EEVAL
UATIO NPROC EDURE FROMT HEREA LOBJE
CTTOA NABST RACTL EVELA REOFI MPORT
ANCET HESEE XPENS ESDEP ENDON THEDE
GREEO FABST RACTI ONORD ETAIL OFTHE
MODEL WHICH AFFEC TSMOD ELPRE PARAT
IONTI MESIM ULATI ONTIM EANDS TORAG
EDEMA NDIFA MODEL CONTA INSMO REDET
AILSO FTHEO BJECT THISR ESULT SINAL
ARGER NUMBE ROFEX TENTO RMORE DESCR
IPTIO NSTAT EMENT SALAR GERNU MBERO
FINPU TDATA ALARG ERNUM BEROF TRANS
ITION TIMEC ALCUL ATION STOBE EXECE
UTEDS PLITT INGUP OFSIM ULATI ONEVE
NTSSI MULAT IONOV ERHEA DANDE XTENS
IONEX TENSI ONOFT HEMOD ELLIN GPROC
ESSBU TEVEN IFWET RYTOS HORTE NTHEM
ODELL INGPH ASEBY DEVEL OPING MODEL
LINGT OOLSA SWEDI DTHEO THERP OINTS
ARELE FTAND WEARE FORCE DTOFI NDANA
CCEPT ABLEC OMPRI MISEB ETWEE NDETA
ILOFM ODELD EVELO PMENT ANDSI MULAT
IONTI MEAND THEQU ALITY OFTHE ANSWE
RSWEW ANTTO GETFR OMSIM ULATI ONRES
ULTSN EVERT HELES SDETA ILEDM ODELS
AREOF TENDE SIRED EVENI FCOMP LEXSY
STEMS OFCOM PUTER NETWO RKSAR EINVE
STIGA TEDSO TEORY ANDME RTENP ROPOS
EDTHE SIMUL ATION OFAMO DELWI THTWO
DIFFE RENTL EVELS OFDET AILIN TERES
TINGC OMPON ENTSF ORMIN STANC ETHEB
OTTLE NECKS OFTHE SYSTE MMAYB EREPR
ESENT EDINV ERYFI NEDET AILHO WEVER
DETAI LSTHE NARIS EATTH EINTE RFACE
OFTWO DIFFE RENTL YDETA ILEDM ODELS
IFMOD ELINS TRUCT IONSA REOFD IFFER
ENTDE TAIL
```

PLAIN(P4.10)

$$CIPHER(P4.10) = \mathrm{VIG}_{\mathrm{VIOLA}}\mathrm{VIG}_{\mathrm{HORN}}(PLAIN(P4.10))$$

4.11 The least common multiple of $n_0, n_1, \ldots, n_{s-1}$. The key is of maximal length if and only if the $\{n_i : 0 \leq i < s\}$ are relatively prime.

4.12 We begin with the formulae

$$\kappa_s = \sum_{0 \leq i < n} \chi_{Y_i}(Y_{i+s})$$

$$\kappa_s^2 = \sum_{0 \leq i < n} \chi_{Y_i}(Y_{i+s}) + 2 \sum_{0 \leq i < j < n} \chi_{Y_i}(Y_{i+s})\chi_{Y_j}(Y_{j+s})$$

$$E\{\chi_{Y_i}(Y_{i+s})\} = \begin{cases} \sum_{0 \leq t < m} p^2(t) = s_2 & \text{if } s = 0 \text{ (molulo r)} \\ \sum_{0 \leq t < m} p^2[t] & \text{if } s \neq 0 \text{ (modulo r)} \end{cases}$$

To evaluate $E\{\chi_{Y_i}(Y_{i+s})\chi_{Y_j}(Y_{j+s})\}$, we need to consider several cases.

Case 1.1. $s = 0$ (modulo r) and i, $i + s$, j, and $j + s$ are distinct indices (modulo n)

$$E\{\chi_{Y_i}(Y_{i+s})\chi_{Y_j}(Y_{j+s})\} = \left(\sum_{0 \leq t < m} p[t,t] \right)^2 = s_s^2$$

Case 1.2 $s \neq 0$ (modulo r) and i, $i + s$, j, and $j + s$ are distinct indices (modulo n)

$$E\{\chi_{Y_i}(Y_{i+s})\chi_{Y_j}(Y_{j+s})\} = \sum_{0 \leq t < m} p^2[t]$$

Case 2.1 $s = 0$ (modulo r) and $i + s = j$, i, and $j + s$ are distinct indices (modulo n)

$$E\{\chi_{Y_i}(Y_{i+s})\chi_{Y_j}(Y_{j+s})\} = \sum_{0 \leq t < m} p[t,t,t] = s_3$$

Case 2.2 $s \neq 0$ (modulo r) and $i + s = j$, i, and $j + s$ are distinct indices (modulo n)

$$E\{\chi_{Y_i}(Y_{i+s})\chi_{Y_j}(Y_{j+s})\} = \sum_{0 \leq t < m} p^3[t]$$

Case 3.1 $s = 0$ (modulo r) and $i = j + s$, $i + s$, and j are distinct indices (modulo n)

$$E\{\chi_{Y_i}(Y_{i+s})\chi_{Y_j}(Y_{j+s})\} = \sum_{0 \leq t < m} p[t,t,t] = s_3$$

Case 3.2 $s \neq 0$ (modulo r) and $i = j + s$, $i + s$, and j are distinct indices (modulo n)

$$E\{\chi_{Y_i}(Y_{i+s})\chi_{Y_j}(Y_{j+s})\} = \sum_{0 \leq t < m} p^3[t]$$

This yields

$$E\{\kappa_s^2\} = ns_2 + [n^2 - 3n]s_2^2 + 2ns_3$$

if s = 0 (modulo r) and

$$E\{\kappa_s^2\} = n \sum_{0\le t<m} p^2[t] + (n^2 - 3n) \sum_{0\le t<m} p^2[t] + 2n \sum_{0\le t<m} p^3[t]$$

if s ≠ 0 (modulo r). Thus

$$\mathrm{Var}\{\kappa_s\} = \begin{cases} ns_2 - 3ns_2^2 + 2ns_3 & \text{if } s = 0 \text{ (modulo r)} \\ n \sum_{0\le t<m} p^2[t] - 3n \sum_{0\le t<m} p^2[t] + 2n \sum_{0\le t<m} p^3[t] & \text{if } s \neq 0 \text{ (modulo r)} \end{cases}$$

If $p[t] = \frac{1}{26}$, then

$$\mathrm{Var}\{\kappa_s\} = \begin{cases} 0.06652n & \text{if } s = 0 \text{ (modulo r)} \\ 0.03698n & \text{if } s \neq 0 \text{ (modulo r)} \end{cases}$$

CHAPTER 5

5.1 Decipherment is given by

$$C_{-r_0(i)}\ \pi_0^{-1}\ C_{r_0(i)-r_1(i)} \ldots C_{r_{N-2}(i)-r_{N-1}(i)}\ \pi_{N-1}^{-1}\ C_{r_{N-1}(i)}$$

5.2 Decipherment is given by

$$C_{-r_0(i)}\pi_0^{-1}C_{r_0(i)-r_1(i)}\pi_1^{-1}C_{r_1(i)-r_2(i)}\pi_2^{-1}C_{r_2(i)}\ \pi_R\ C_{-r_2(i)} \times \pi_2 C_{r_2(i)} C_{-r_1(i)}\pi_1 C_{r_1(i)-r_0(i)}\pi_0 C_{r_0(i)}$$

since the Enigma substitution is an involution.

5.3 If $\nu \sim \pi$ and $\pi \sim \sigma$,

$$\nu = C_{-t}\ \pi\ C_t \qquad \pi = C_{-s}\ \sigma\ C_s$$

then $\pi = C_t\ \nu\ C_{-t}$, so that ~ is reflexive. Also $\nu = C_{-(t+s)}\ \sigma\ C_{t+s}$, so that ~ is transitive. The symmetry of ~ is obvious.

5.4 Consider the images of $t \in \boldsymbol{Z}_m$ under $\pi \in \mathrm{SYM}(\boldsymbol{Z}_m)$:

$$t_0, t_1, \ldots$$

$$t_{i+1} = \pi(t_i) \qquad i = 0, 1, \ldots \qquad t_0 = t$$

Since $\boldsymbol{Z}_m$ is a finite set, there must be a first index r such that $t_r \in \{t_0, t_1, \ldots, t_{r-1}\}$. If $t_i = t_r$ with $i \neq 0$, then $t_{i-1} = t_{r-1}$, contradicting the minimality of r. Thus $t_0 = t_4$. Denote the *orbit* of t by $ORB_\pi = \{t_0, t_1, \ldots, t_{r-1}\}$. If $s \in ORB_\pi[t]$, then $ORB_\pi[s] = ORB_\pi[t]$, while if $s \notin ORB_\pi[t]$, $ORB_\pi[s] \cap ORB_\pi[t] = \phi$. The equivalence relation ~ partitions $\boldsymbol{Z}_m$ into disjoint sets of orbits.

5.5 The cycle decomposition of $\pi(t) = t$ consists of m 1-cycles:

$$\pi : (0)\ (1) \dots (m - 1)$$

The cycle decomposition of $\pi(t) = t + 1$ consists of one m-cycle:

$$\pi : (0, 1, \dots, m - 1)$$

The cycle decomposition of $\pi(t) = t + k$ depends on the greatest common divisor of k and m; if $\gcd\{k,m\} = 1$, the cycle decomposition of π consists of one m-cycle. If $\gcd\{k,m\} = j$, the cycle decomposition of π consists of j (m/j)-cycles.

5.6 The divisors of m.

5.7 From Table 5.3.2,

π_0 : (1, 6, 24, 18, 15, 3, 10, 7, 19, 4, 17, 11, 2, 12, 13, 23, 16, 9, 25, 8)
(5, 20, 21, 14) (0,22)

π_1 : (0, 8, 12, 25, 4, 5, 15, 20, 11) (1, 14,24)
(2, 7, 21, 13, 9, 6, 19, 17, 10, 3) (16, 22) (18,23)

π_2 : (0, 18, 24, 19, 5, 1, 16, 12, 7, 23, 6, 25, 3, 11) (2, 20, 22, 13, 9, 17, 4)
(8) (10) (21) (14, 15)

5.8 From Table 5.8.1,

π_0 : (0, 22, 3, 19, 6, 13, 15, 10, 16, 18, 23, 24, 17, 7, 20, 12, 9, 2, 1, 5, 25, 11, 4, 8, 21)
(14)

π_1 : (1, 12, 21, 24, 3, 6, 15, 20, 18, 5, 16, 4, 13, 22, 23, 19, 25, 14, 11, 8, 9, 2, 17)
(0, 7, 10)

π_2 : (1, 17, 8, 25, 4, 7, 5, 11, 12, 22, 13, 2, 20, 18, 16, 15, 23, 19, 24, 9, 21, 14, 10, 6)
(0, 3)

π_R : (0, 14) (1, 22) (2, 19) (3, 21) (4, 18) (5, 10) (6, 24)
(7, 15) (8, 9) (11, 12) (13, 20) (16, 17) (23, 25)

5.9 If $\nu = C_{-t}\, \pi\, C_t$ and

$$\pi(u_i) = u_{i+1} \text{ for } 0 \le i < r \qquad u_0 = u_r$$

then

$$u_0 - t, u_1 - t, \dots, u_{r-1} - t$$

5.10 If $\pi = C_{-a}\, \pi\, C_a$, then

$$\pi(t + a) = \pi(t) + a$$

In particular, $\pi(sa) = \pi(0) + sa$ for $s = 0, 1, \dots$. If $\gcd\{a,m\} = 1$, this implies that $\pi(t) = \pi(0) + t$ for all $t \in \boldsymbol{Z}_m$, so that $\pi = C_d$ (with $d = \pi(0)$). If $\gcd\{a,m\} = j$, then

$$\{0, a, 2a, \dots\} = \{0, j, 2j, \dots, ((m/j) - 1)j\}$$

and thus π is the one-to-one mapping of $\Gamma_{r,j,m}$ onto $\Gamma_{\pi(r),j,m}$

$$\pi : r + sj \to \pi(r) + sj$$

$$\Gamma_{r,j,m} = \{r, r + j, r + 2j, \dots, r + ((m/j) - 1)j\} \qquad 0 \le r < j$$

5.11 The equivalence class $[\pi]$ of π generally contains m substitutions; if π is the one-to-one mapping of $\Gamma_{r,j,m}$ into $\gamma_{\pi(r),j,m}$,

$$\pi : r + sj \to \pi(r) + sj$$

then $[\pi]$ contains m/j elements.

5.12 If $\pi \prec \nu$ and $\nu \prec \sigma$,

$$\pi = C_a \, \nu \, C_b \qquad \sigma = C_c \, \pi \, C_d$$

then $\nu = C_{-b} \, \pi \, C_{-a}$, so that $\prec$ is reflexive and $\sigma = C_{a+c} \, \nu \, C_{b+d}$, so that $\prec$ is transitive. The symmetry of $\prec$ is obvious.

5.13 Suppose $C_{-a} \, \pi \, C_b = \pi$; then

$$\pi(t + b) = \pi(t) + a \qquad t \in \boldsymbol{Z_m}$$

which implies $\pi(sb) = \pi(0) + sa$ for $s = 0, 1, \ldots$. If $\gcd\{a,m\} = \gcd\{b,m\} = 1$, then

$$\pi(t) = \gamma(t + \tau) \qquad \gamma = ab^{-1} \qquad \tau = \pi(0)\gamma^{-1}$$

If $j = \gcd\{a,m\}$,

$$\pi(jb) = \pi(0) + ja = \pi(0)$$

so that $jb = 0$ (modulo m). If $k = \gcd\{b,m\}$,

$$\pi(0) = \pi(kb) = \pi(0) + ka$$

so that $ka = 0$ (modulo m). Thus the only possibility is $\gcd\{a,m\} = \gcd\{b,m\} = j$. In this case, π is the one-to-one mapping of $\Gamma_{r,j,m}$ onto $\Gamma_{\pi(r),j,m}$ for each r:

$$\pi : r + sj \rightarrow \pi(r) + s\gamma j$$

with $\gamma = (a/j)(b/j)^{-1}$.

5.14 The *-conjugate class of π generally contains m^2 substitutions; if π is the one-to-one mapping of $\Gamma_{r,j,m}$ onto $\Gamma_{\pi(r),j,m}$ (for each r, $0 \leq r < m$),

$$\pi : r + sj \rightarrow \pi(r) + s\gamma j$$

with $\gamma = (a/j)(b/j)^{-1}$, then $[\pi]$ contains $(m/j)^2$ substitutions.

5.15 If $r_s(i)$ is given by Eq. (5.1.2), we cannot absorb the unknown initial rotational displacements $(k_0, k_1, \ldots, k_{N-1})$ in the rotors by replacing π_s by $C_{-k_s} \, \pi_s \, C_{k_s}$. One method of recovery of the rotor π_0 with corresponding plaintext and ciphertext is to make guesses as to the value of k_0. We check the validity of a guess by attempting an analysis as in Sec. 5.3. An inconsistency will be detected if an incorrect guess is made provided there is sufficient corresponding plaintext and ciphertext.

5.16 Matching yields the following relationships:

Block 0

$$\pi_0(19) - 0 = \pi_0(6) - 2 = \pi_0(2) - 16$$
$$\pi_0(11) - 3 = \pi_0(5) - 18$$
$$\pi_0(15) - 11 = \pi_0(25) - 21$$
$$\pi_0(11) - 7 = \pi_0(2) - 14 = \pi_0(17) - 17$$
$$\pi_0(22) - 8 = \pi_0(9) - 24$$
$$\pi_0(25) - 10 = \pi_0(21) - 19$$

Block 1

$$\pi_0(23) - 15 = \pi_0(3) - 25$$
$$\pi_0(14) - 10 = \pi_0(4) - 17$$
$$\pi_0(17) - 4 = \pi_0(10) - 23$$
$$\pi_0(17) - 3 = \pi_0(15) - 13 = \pi_0(7) - 14 = \pi_0(10) - 22$$
$$\pi_0(0) - 9 = \pi_0(20) - 12$$
$$\pi_0(20) - 1 = \pi_0(5) - 5 = \pi_0(23) - 8 = \pi_0(0) - 24$$

Block 2

$\pi_0(14) - 1 = \pi_0(24) - 4 = \pi_0(10) - 6 = \pi_0(20) - 14$
$\pi_0(7) - 13 = \pi_0(11) - 18$
$\pi_0(2) - 9 = \pi_0(16) - 24 = \pi_0(18) - 25$
$\pi_0(0) - 8 = \pi_0(17) - 10$
$\pi_0(12) - 19 = \pi_0(3) - 22$
$\pi_0(24) - 7 = \pi_0(1) - 20$
$\pi_0(2) - 11 = \pi_0(0) - 12$
$\pi_0(11) - 17 = \pi_0(25) - 21$

Block 3$

$\pi_0(18) - 1 = \pi_0(15) - 24 = \pi_0(7) - 25$
$\pi_0(15) - 11 = \pi_0(11) - 17$
$\pi_0(14) - 0 = \pi_0(1) - 16$
$\pi_0(8) - 21 = \pi_0(1) - 23$
$\pi_0(7) - 5 = \pi_0(3) - 12$
$\pi_0(19) - 7 = \pi_0(23) - 8$
$\pi_0(3) - 10 = \pi_0(9) - 14 = \pi_0(8) - 20$
$\pi_0(3) - 10 = \pi_0(9) - 14 = \pi_0(8) - 20$

Block 4

$\pi_0(16) - 3 = \pi_0(17) - 17$
$\pi_0(13) - 13 = \pi_0(15) - 24$
$\pi_0(17) - 19 = \pi_0(1) - 23$
$\pi_0(10) - 2 = \pi_0(0) - 7$
$\pi_0(8) - 6 = \pi_0(22) - 10 = \pi_0(3) - 22$
$\pi_0(14) - 0 = \pi_0(18) - 25$
$\pi_0(23) - 15 = \pi_0(14) - 21$

Block 5

$\pi_0(24) - 20 = \pi_0(25) - 23$
$\pi_0(1) - 16 = \pi_0(5) - 17 = \pi_0(15) - 22$
$\pi_0(16) - 3 = \pi_0(18) - 4 = \pi_0(10) - 10$
$\pi_0(3) - 1 = \pi_0(12) - 24 = \pi_0(11) - 25$
$\pi_0(4) - 0 = \pi_0(20) - 6 = \pi_0(22) - 11$
$\pi_0(16) - 5 = \pi_0(11) - 9 = \pi_0(8) - 21$
$\pi_0(13) - 7 = \pi_0(19) - 15$

Block 6

$\pi_0(3) - 11 = \pi_0(1) - 23$
$\pi_0(12) - 18 = \pi_0(24) - 20$
$\pi_0(24) - 12 = \pi_0(17) - 21$
$\pi_0(12) - 0 = \pi_0(2) - 8$
$\pi_0(16) - 16 = \pi_0(12) - 19 = \pi_0(3) - 22$
$\pi_0(25) - 7 = \pi_0(8) - 15$
$\pi_0(10) - 3 = \pi_0(13) - 9 = \pi_0(19) - 17$
$\pi_0(1) - 1 = \pi_0(18) - 10$

Block 7

$\pi_0(21) - 7 = \pi_0(12) - 19$
$\pi_0(12) - 5 = \pi_0(1) - 20$
$\pi_0(5) - 1 = \pi_0(4) - 17$
$\pi_0(21) - 2 = \pi_0(19) - 6 = \pi_0(12) - 14 = \pi_0(17) - 25$
$\pi_0(19) - 8 = \pi_0(23) - 9 = \pi_0(24) - 18 = \pi_0(25) - 21$
$\pi_0(7) - 0 = \pi_0(9) - 11$
$\pi_0(3) - 15 = \pi_0(10) - 16$

Block 8

$\pi_0(1) - 9 = \pi_0(7) - 16$
$\pi_0(21) - 6 = \pi_0(1) - 7$
$\pi_0(19) - 1 = \pi_0(4) - 15 = \pi_0(13) - 19$
$\pi_0(5) - 12 = \pi_0(19) - 14 = \pi_0(14) - 21$
$\pi_0(4) - 10 = \pi_0(21) - 18 = \pi_0(6) - 24$
$\pi_0(17) - 4 = \pi_0(19) - 11$
$\pi_0(5) - 17 = \pi_0(18) - 25$
$\pi_0(24) - 5 = \pi_0(25) - 8 = \pi_0(22) - 20$

Block 9

$\pi_0(11) - 8 = \pi_0(1) - 22$
$\pi_0(11) - 7 = \pi_0(8) - 19$
$\pi_0(5) - 12 = \pi_0(11) - 23$
$\pi_0(11) - 9 = \pi_0(24) - 10 = \pi_0(3) - 11$
$\pi_0(14) - 2 = \pi_0(21) - 17 = \pi_0(15) - 24$

The substitution π is

π_0

A	B	C	D	E	F	G	H	I	J	K	L	M	N	O	P	Q	R	S	T	U	V	W	X	Y	Z
0	1	2	3	4	5	6	7	8	9	10	11	12	13	14	15	16	17	18	19	20	21	22	23	24	25
↓	↓	↓	↓	↓	↓	↓	↓	↓	↓	↓	↓	↓	↓	↓	↓	↓	↓	↓	↓	↓	↓	↓	↓	↓	↓
8	14	7	2	5	15	19	21	12	6	3	0	25	9	24	20	22	10	23	17	11	13	16	18	1	4
I	O	H	C	F	P	T	V	M	G	D	A	Z	J	Y	U	W	K	X	R	L	N	Q	S	B	E

CHAPTER 6

6.1 T_i is the composition of the S-box and the P-box mappings. Let

$$S[j](u_{i,4j-1}, u_{i,4j}, u_{i,4j+1}, u_{i,4j+2}, u_{i,4j+3}, u_{i,4j+4})$$

denote the mapping by S[j] on the ith round, where $(u_{i,0}, u_{i,1} \ldots, u_{i,31}) = (x_{i,0}, x_{i,1} \ldots, x_{i,31}) + (k_{i,0}, k_{i,1} \ldots, k_{i,31})$ is the sum of thc expanded plaintext and key on the ith round. T_i is a one-to-one mapping if and only if the only solution to

$$S[j](u_{4j-1}, u_{4j}, u_{4j+1}, u_{4j+2}, u_{4j+3}, u_{4j+4}) = S[j](v_{4j-1}, v_{4j}, v_{4j+1}, v_{4j+2}, v_{4j+3}, v_{4j+4})$$

is $(u_0, u_1 \ldots, u_{31}) = (v_0, v_1 \ldots, v_{31})$. Table 6.7.3 shows that when

$$(u_{23}, u_{24}, u_{25}, u_{26}, u_{27}, u_{28}) = (0, 0, 1, 1, 1, 0)$$

$$(v_{23}, v_{24}, v_{25}, v_{26}, v_{27}, v_{28}) = (0, 0, 0, 0, 0, 1)$$

$$(u_{27}, u_{28}, u_{29}, u_{30}, u_{31}, u_0) = (1, 0, 0, 0, 0, 1)$$

$$(v_{27}, v_{28}, v_{29}, v_{30}, v_{31}, v_0) = (0, 1, 1, 1, 1, 1)$$

$$(u_{31}, u_0, u_1, u_2, u_3, u_4) = (0, 1, 0, 1, 1, 0)$$

$$(v_{31}, v_0, v_1, v_2, v_3, v_4) = (1, 1, 0, 0, 1, 0)$$

we have

$$S[6](0, 0, 1, 1, 1, 0) = (1, 1, 0, 1) \qquad S[6](0, 0, 0, 0, 0, 1) = (1, 1, 0, 1)$$

$$S[7](1, 0, 0, 0, 0, 1) = (0, 0, 1, 0) \qquad S[7](0, 1, 1, 1, 1, 1) = (0, 0, 1, 0)$$

$$S[0](0, 1, 0, 1, 1, 0) = (1, 1, 0, 0) \qquad S[0](1, 1, 0, 0, 1, 0) = (1, 1, 0, 0)$$

If u_i and z_i are as above for $i \in \{0, 1, 2, 3, 4, 23, 24, \ldots, 31\}$, and $u_i = v_i$ for $i \in \mathbf{Z}_{32} - \{0, 1, 2, 3, 4, 23, 24, \ldots, 31\}$, then

$$\star\ S[j](u_{4j-1}, u_{4j}, u_{4j+1}, u_{4j+2}, u_{4j+3}, u_{4j+4})$$
$$= S[j](v_{4j-1}, v_{4j}, v_{4j+1}, v_{4j+2}, v_{4j+3}, v_{4j+4}) \quad 0 \leq j < 8$$

Any solution $\mathbf{u} \neq \mathbf{v}$ of ☆ requires $(u_{4j-1}, u_{4j}, u_{4j+1}, u_{4j+2}, u_{4j+3}, u_{4j+4}) \neq (v_{4j-1}, v_{4j}, v_{4j+1}, v_{4j+2}, v_{4j+3}, v_{4j+4})$ for any least three values of j.

6.6 The usage of key components by position is shown in Table S6.1.
The key usage by round for each S-box is shown in Table S6.2.

6.7 The key components used on the ith round of a DES encipherment may be written in the form

$$\text{SELECT}_{PC-2}(\lambda^{\tau(i)}\text{SELECT}_{PC-1,L}(\mathbf{k}), \lambda^{\tau(i)}\text{SELECT}_{PC-1,R}(\mathbf{k}))$$

$\text{SELECT}_{PC-1,L}$: the left 28 bits selected by PC-1

TABLE S6.1
Key Usage by Position

	Position							Position					
Key	0	1	2	3	4	5	Key	0	1	2	3	4	5
0	0	4	2	3	3	2	1	3	2	3	2	2	3
2	4	1	2	2	1	2	3	3	2	3	2	2	2
4	2	3	3	1	2	3	5	2	3	1	2	3	3
6	2	2	2	4	2	1	7	4	1	2	2	2	3
8	3	2	2	2	3	1	9	1	3	2	3	3	2
10	2	2	1	3	2	3	11	2	2	3	4	2	1
12	3	2	3	2	2	1	13	2	3	2	1	3	3
14	0	4	2	4	2	2	15	2	3	3	2	2	3
16	4	1	2	1	2	3	17	2	3	3	1	2	3
18	2	3	3	1	2	3	19	2	3	1	3	2	3
20	2	1	2	3	3	2	21	4	1	2	2	2	3
22	3	1	3	2	3	1	23	0	4	2	4	3	1
24	2	2	2	3	2	2	25	2	2	2	3	2	2
26	3	3	3	1	2	2	27	2	3	2	1	4	3
28	1	3	2	3	2	2	29	1	3	3	2	3	3
30	4	1	2	2	2	3	31	3	2	2	2	3	1
32	2	3	2	1	4	3	33	2	2	2	3	2	2
34	3	1	3	3	1	2	35	4	2	2	2	2	3
36	3	1	3	2	1	2	37	0	4	2	3	2	2
38	1	3	3	2	3	3	39	3	1	2	3	2	2
40	2	3	3	1	2	3	41	2	3	2	2	3	3
42	2	2	2	2	3	2	43	1	3	2	3	3	3
44	4	2	2	2	2	2	45	3	1	3	2	2	1
46	2	3	2	2	3	3	47	2	2	2	4	2	1
48	4	1	3	2	2	1	49	2	3	3	2	2	3
50	4	1	2	1	1	3	51	2	3	2	2	2	2
52	1	3	2	3	3	3	53	4	1	3	3	1	1
54	2	2	3	2	2	3	55	1	3	1	3	3	3

$\text{SELECT}_{\text{PC}-1,\text{R}}$: the right 28 bits selected by PC-1

$\text{SELECT}_{\text{PC}-2}$: the 48 bits selected by PC-2

$$\tau(\mathrm{i}) = \sum_{1 \le \mathrm{j} \le \mathrm{i}} \sigma(\mathrm{i}) \text{ : the cumulative number of left shifts}$$

λ : shift left-circular

The key components for DES decipherment are described by the function

$$\text{SELECT}_{\text{PC}-2}(\lambda^{\tau(29-\mathrm{i})}\text{SELECT}_{\text{PC}-1,\text{L}}(\mathbf{k}), \lambda^{\tau(29-\mathrm{i})}\text{SELECT}_{\text{PC}-1,\text{R}}(\mathbf{k}))$$

Thus $\mathbf{k}_1$ and $\mathbf{k}_2$ are inverse reciprocal if and only if

Table S6.2
Key Usage in Each Round

		Round															
S[0]	—	8	1	44	30	16	2	45	31	49	35	21	7	50	36	22	15
	—	44	37	23	9	52	38	49	35	28	14	0	43	29	15	1	51
	—	29	22	8	51	37	23	9	52	45	31	42	28	14	0	43	36
	—	52	45	31	42	28	14	0	43	36	22	8	51	37	23	9	2
	—	42	35	21	7	50	36	22	8	1	44	30	16	2	45	31	49
	—	14	7	50	36	22	8	51	37	30	16	2	45	31	42	28	21
S[1]	—	28	21	7	50	36	22	8	51	44	30	16	2	45	31	42	35
	—	49	42	28	14	0	43	29	15	8	51	37	23	9	52	38	31
	—	1	51	37	23	9	52	38	49	42	28	14	0	43	29	15	8
	—	7	0	43	29	15	1	44	30	23	9	52	38	49	35	21	14
	—	16	9	52	38	49	35	21	7	0	43	29	15	1	44	30	23
	—	36	29	15	1	44	30	16	2	52	38	49	35	21	7	50	43
S[2]	—	2	52	38	49	35	21	7	50	43	29	15	1	44	30	16	9
	—	30	23	9	52	38	49	35	21	14	0	43	29	15	1	44	37
	—	22	15	1	44	30	16	2	45	38	49	35	21	7	50	36	29
	—	21	14	0	43	29	15	1	44	37	23	9	52	38	49	35	28
	—	38	31	42	28	14	0	43	29	22	8	51	37	23	9	52	45
	—	50	43	29	15	1	44	30	16	9	52	38	49	35	21	7	0
S[3]	—	51	44	30	16	2	45	31	42	35	21	7	50	36	22	8	1
	—	0	50	36	22	8	51	37	23	16	2	45	31	42	28	14	7
	—	31	49	35	21	7	50	36	22	15	1	44	30	16	2	45	38
	—	23	16	2	45	31	42	28	14	7	50	36	22	8	51	37	30
	—	15	8	51	37	23	9	52	38	31	42	28	14	0	43	29	22
	—	35	28	14	0	43	29	15	1	51	37	23	9	52	38	49	42
S[4]	—	19	12	53	39	25	11	24	10	3	48	34	20	6	47	33	26
	—	24	17	3	48	34	20	6	47	40	26	12	53	39	25	11	4
	—	34	27	13	54	40	26	12	53	46	32	18	4	17	3	48	41
	—	47	40	26	12	53	39	25	11	4	17	3	48	34	20	6	54
	—	32	25	11	24	10	55	41	27	20	6	47	33	19	5	46	39
	—	3	55	41	27	13	54	40	26	19	5	46	32	18	4	17	10
S[5]	—	41	34	20	6	47	33	19	5	53	39	25	11	24	10	55	48
	—	26	19	5	46	32	18	4	17	10	55	41	27	13	54	40	33
	—	4	24	10	55	41	27	13	54	47	33	19	5	46	32	18	11
	—	46	39	25	11	24	10	55	41	34	20	6	47	33	19	5	53
	—	20	13	54	40	26	12	53	39	32	18	4	17	3	48	34	27
	—	25	18	4	17	3	48	34	20	13	54	40	26	12	53	39	32
S[6]	—	53	46	32	18	4	17	3	48	41	27	13	54	40	26	12	5
	—	18	11	24	10	55	41	27	13	6	47	33	19	5	46	32	25
	—	33	26	12	53	39	25	11	24	17	3	48	34	20	6	47	40

TABLE S6.2 (*Continued*)

		Round															
	—	55	48	34	20	6	47	33	19	12	53	39	25	11	24	10	3
	—	13	6	47	33	19	5	46	32	25	11	24	10	55	41	27	20
	—	17	10	55	41	27	13	54	40	33	19	5	46	32	18	4	24
S[7]	—	39	32	18	4	17	3	48	34	27	13	54	40	26	12	53	46
	—	12	5	46	32	18	4	17	3	55	41	27	13	54	40	26	19
	—	11	4	17	3	48	34	20	6	54	40	26	12	53	39	25	18
	—	54	47	33	19	5	46	32	18	11	24	10	55	41	27	13	6
	—	48	41	27	13	54	40	26	12	5	46	32	18	4	17	3	55
	—	27	20	6	47	33	19	5	46	39	25	11	24	10	55	41	34

$$\lambda_{\tau(29-i)}\mathrm{SELECT}_{PC-1,L}(\mathbf{k}_1) = \lambda_{\tau(i)}\mathrm{SELECT}_{PC-1,L}(\mathbf{k}_2)$$

$$\lambda_{\tau(29-i)}\mathrm{SELECT}_{PC-1,R}(\mathbf{k}_1) = \lambda_{\tau(i)}\mathrm{SELECT}_{PC-1,R}(\mathbf{k}_2)$$

Table S6.2 shows that this requires k_i to be constant for i in each of the complementary sets; these conditions hold if and only if k_i is constant for i in each of the sets

{0, 1, 2, 7, 8, 9, 14, 15, 16, 21, 22, 23, 28, 29, 30, 31, 35, 36, 37, 38, 42, 43, 44, 45, 49, 50, 51, 52}

{3, 4, 5, 6, 10, 11, 12, 17, 18, 19, 20, 24, 25, 26, 27, 32, 33, 34, 39, 40, 41, 46, 47, 48, 53, 54, 55}

There are four inverse reciprocal pairs.

6.13 Multiple encipherment by chaining first in the forward direction and then in the reverse direction will produce the desired dependence. Define DESCHR{**k**,$<\mathbf{x}>$|**ICV**} by

$$<\mathbf{x}> = (\mathbf{x}_0, \mathbf{x}_1, \ldots, \mathbf{x}_{m-1}) \qquad \mathbf{x}_i \in \mathbf{Z}_{2,64} \qquad (0 \le i < m)$$

$$\mathrm{DESCHR}\{\mathbf{k}, <\mathbf{x}> | \mathbf{ICV}\} = <\mathbf{z}>$$

$$<\mathbf{z}> = (\mathbf{z}_0, \mathbf{z}_1, \ldots, \mathbf{z}_{m-1})$$

$$\mathrm{DESCH}\{\mathbf{k}, <\mathbf{x}> | \mathbf{ICV}\} = <\mathbf{y}>$$

$$<\mathbf{y}> = (\mathbf{y}_0, \mathbf{y}_1, \ldots, \mathbf{y}_{m-1})$$

$$\mathbf{y}_i = \mathrm{DES}\{\mathbf{k}, \mathbf{x}_i + \mathbf{y}_{i-1}\} \qquad 0 \le i < m$$

$$\mathbf{ICV} = \mathbf{y}_{-1}$$

$$\mathrm{DESCH}\{\mathbf{k}, \phi<\mathbf{y}> | \mathbf{ICV}\} = <\mathbf{z}>$$

$$\phi<\mathbf{y}> = (\mathbf{y}_{m-1}, \mathbf{y}_{m-2}, \ldots, \mathbf{y}_0)$$

An error in the ith block of $<\mathbf{z}>$ yields after decipherment errors in blocks (m − i) and (m − i − 1) of <**y**> and thus errors in blocks (m − i), (m − i − 1), and (m − i − 2) of <**x**>.

6.14 One form of *chaining on the key* is *compressed encoding,* defined by

$$\text{DESCOM}\{\mathbf{k},\mathbf{x}\} = <\mathbf{y}>$$

$$<\mathbf{x}> = (\mathbf{x}_0, \mathbf{x}_1, \ldots, \mathbf{x}_{m-1})$$

$$<\mathbf{y}> = (\mathbf{y}_0, \mathbf{y}_1, \ldots, \mathbf{y}_{m-1})$$

$$\mathbf{y}_i = \text{DES}\{\mathbf{k}_i,\mathbf{x}_i\}$$

$$\mathbf{k}_i = \mathbf{x}_{i-1} \qquad 0 \leq i < m, \mathbf{x}_{-1} = \mathbf{k}$$

In general an error in the ith block of the ciphertext <**y**> will produce errors upon decipherment in all plaintext blocks $\mathbf{x}_j$ with $i \leq j < m$.

6.15 This is an unsuitable method of key selection for two reasons; the use of names (addresses, social security numbers, etc.) and the translation of seven alpha-numeric characters into 56-blocks by the EBCIDIC coding. Only about one-third of the elements of $Z_{2,56}$ obtained from an EBCIDIC translation correspond to printable terminal characters, which reduces the key space by a factor of about 1.5×10^{-4}. Key trial thus becomes a viable method of cryptanalysis.

6.16 The use of chaining and a randomly chosen initial chaining value means that plaintext $\mathbf{x}_0$ and $\mathbf{x}_1$, each beginning with `Dear Sir`: and enciphered with the same key, will almost always produce ciphertext that begins differently. Assuming that the ciphertext of chosen plaintext is known for every key is no longer a reasonable hypothesis in the time memory tradeoff.

CHAPTER 7

7.1 Adding **EMKO** would allow users to generate personal session keys, which could be exchanged, avoiding the necessity of storing a key variable in a terminal-to-terminal session.

7.3 *Host i* has master key KMH_i with variants $\text{KMH}_{i,j}$, j = 0, 1, 2

$\text{KMH}_{i,0}$: used to encipher session keys KS

$\text{KMH}_{i,1}$: used to encider terminal master keys (at *Host i*)

$\text{KMH}_{i,2}$: used to encipher *cross domain key* KMH(i,j) = KMH(j,i) (*Host i* to *Host j*)

Host i stores DES{$\text{KMH}_{i,2}$, KMH(i,j)} and uses a translation instruction **RFMK′** :

DES{$\text{KMH}_{i,2}$, KMH(i,j)} RN = DES{$\text{KMH}_{i,0}$, KS} → DES{KMH(i,j), K

A second translation instruction **RTMK** (at *Host j*)

$$\text{DES}\{\text{KMH}_{j,2}, \text{KMH}(j,i)\}\ \text{DES}\{\text{KMH}(i,j),\text{KS}\} \rightarrow \text{DES}\{\text{KMH}_{j,0}, \text{KS}\}$$

which may be deciphered by a terminal attached to *Host j.*

7.4 One solution is to add an instruction similar to **RFMK** of the form

KEYGEN[RN, KMT_i, KMT_j]

which will interpret RN as DES{KMH0,KS} and return both DES{KMT_i,KS} and DES{KMT_j,KS}, which are sent to the terminals i and j, respectively. RN need not be maintained at the host.

7.5 An effective handshaking protocol requires the inclusion of variables which

- Are determined by the host, and
- Are unpredictable by the terminal.

CHAPTER 8

8.1 The required features are:

- *User i* can verify if the elements of the triple

  $$(\textit{User Name}, X_{\textit{User Name},k_{\textit{User Name}}}, q^{k_{\textit{User Name}}} \text{ (modulo p)})$$

  are properly related.
- It is effectively impossible for any user to derive $X_{\textit{User Name},k_{\textit{User Name}}}$.

One solution is to have a trusted authority derive a square root molulo rs of the concatenation *User Name,* $q^{k_{\textit{User Name}}}$ (modulo p)
$(X_{\textit{User Name},k_{\textit{User Name}}})^2 = (\textit{User Name}, q^{k_{\textit{User Name}}} \text{ (modulo p)}) \text{ (modulo rs)}$
where r and s are large (secret primes). If *User Name,* $q^{k_{\textit{User Name}}}$ (modulo p) is not a quadratic residue modulo rs, we pad the base 2 representation of *User Name,* $q^{k_{\textit{User Name}}}$ (modulo p) on the right by a sufficient number of binary digits.

8.2 $w = 1340 \quad w^{-1} = 1798$

8.3 `Send More Money` is enciphered by **a**′ into

195	606	623	77	4
98	274	586	606	4
98	274	623	606	49

and by **a** into

5424	1428	1691	830	1266
2359	2794	3286	1428	1266
2359	2794	1691	1428	4250

10 100 1 1000 1	10 1 100 10 100	1 10 100 1 10 1 1
0 1 100 1 1 1 1 10	100 1 1 1 100 10	00 100 1 10 1 1 1
0 10 1 1 10 10 10	100 1 10 10 1 10	10 1 100 10 100
100 1 1 1 100 10	00 100 1 10 1 1 1	0 10 1 1 10 10 10
1 10 100 1 10 1 1	10 1 100 10 100	000 100 1 10 10

8.6 Assume that *User i* has selected key k_i, and q^{k_i} (modulo p) is stored in the public key directory. *User 1, User 2, . . . , User M* establish a common key *(conferencing)* with the following steps:

- *User i* computes $L(i{:}1,M) = q^{k_i K(1,M)}$ (modulo p) by raising the product

$$q^{K(1,M)} = \prod_{1 \le j \le M} q^{k_j} \text{ (modulo p)}$$

to the k_i^{th} power (modulo p).

- *User i* enciphers L(i:1,M) with DES (say) using the *User i-User j* shared key $q^{k_i k_j}$ and transmits

$$DES\{q^{k_i k_k}, L(i{:}1,M)\}$$

to *User j.*

The common conference key is

$$\prod_{1 \le i \le M} L(i{:}1,M) \text{ (modulo p)} = q^{(k_1 + \cdots + k_M)^2} \text{ (modulo p)}$$

8.7 The system enciphers files with a system key KMH, which is stored in a secure channel attachment as in the IBM Cryptographic Subsystem. The header record contains a list of users and their read/write privileges. When *User i* attempts to read a file *F*, the header is deciphered, *User i*'s read privilege is checked, the file is deciphered by KMH, and then reenciphered in *User i*'s key (in the channel attachment) for transmission to *User i.* `WRITE` is handled in a similar manner.

8.8 α is a cubic residue modulo p with p = 1 (modulo 3) if and only if $\alpha^{(p-1)/3} = 1$ (modulo p). Solving

$$y^2 - \alpha = 0 \text{ (modulo n)}$$

$$n = pq \text{ (p, q primes) } p = q = 1 \text{ (modulo 3)}$$

is equivalent to factoring n.

8.9 In general, there are eight solutions to

$$x^2 - \alpha = 0 \text{ (modulo n)} \qquad n = pqr$$

when α is a quadratic residue modulo n. If we find "independent" solutions

$$u^2 - \alpha = 0 \text{ (modulo n)} \qquad v^2 - \alpha = 0 \text{ (modulo n)} \qquad n = pqr$$

then

$$(u - v)(u + v) = u^2 - v^2 = 0 \text{ (modulo n)}$$

and one of the factors p, q, or r must divide either (u − v) or (u + v).

CHAPTER 9

9.1 One solution is to use a one-way function E_e with inverse E_d. We record on the credit card the encipherment of some personal characteristic of the user under E_e:

User name
E_e\{*User Characteristics*\}

The point-of-sale station has E_d (which need *not* be protected). In a credit card transaction, the characteristics of the individual presenting the card for a transaction are compared with

$$E_d\{E_e\{\textit{User Characteristics}\}\}$$

9.3 To prevent the reuse of stale messages.

Index